INDIANA DAILY STUDENT

CITY EDITOR

INDIANA DAILY STUDENT

150 YEARS

of Headlines, Deadlines and Bylines

Edited by
RACHEL KIPP, AMY WIMMER SCHWARB
and **CHARLES SCUDDER**

With contributions from generations of Indiana Daily Student staff

WELL HOUSE
BOOKS

AN IMPRINT OF INDIANA UNIVERSITY PRESS

This book is a publication of

WELL HOUSE BOOKS
an imprint of
Indiana University Press
Office of Scholarly Publishing
Herman B Wells Library 350
1320 East 10th Street
Bloomington, Indiana 47405 USA

iupress.indiana.edu

Proceeds from this book support the Indiana Daily Student Legacy Fund, which ensures IDS journalists will continue producing the first draft of IU history for years to come.

This book is printed on acid-free paper.

Manufactured in China

Cataloging information is available
from the Library of Congress.

ISBN 978-0-253-04612-3 (cloth)
ISBN 978-0-253-04615-4 (ebook)

1 2 3 4 5 24 23 22 21 20 19

Dedicated to the staff of the Indiana Daily Student
—past, present and future.

Contents

5 | 1970–1981

6 | 1982–1996

7 | 1997–2008

8 | 2009–Present

| Postscript

Foreword

THE IDS, HELD UP TO LIGHT

More than four dozen color slides live in a shoebox on a top shelf of my laundry room. They were shot by Jay Hagenow, the IDS photo editor during my stint as editor in chief. In a chaotic college newsroom, he was a friendly, unflappable force, even in my haggard final days as its leader.

I was tired by then, resigned to the idea that I was a lame duck whose lofty goals for the semester would not be realized. Jay's slides contain clues that my tenure was limping toward its end: The Salvador Dali poster I hung carefully in my office before classes started dangles from a single thumbtack. The sports staff plays trash-can basketball; midway through the semester, I had confiscated a football after their antics perturbed the campus desk.

In one shot, I edit a story from a computer positioned not on Ernie Pyle's rolltop throne—the workspace of honor awarded to every IDS editor in chief of my era—but atop a standard metal office desk. The caption for this photo should read: "Ready to relinquish."

In Jay's slides we consult over stories, hash out budget lines, pore over copy, hug, steal one another's fries, laugh, nap on the couch, proof pages, select photos, call sources, eat too many Pizza Express breadsticks, put out a paper. Yet they document more than the everyday goings-on of a college newsroom. In these images, our tasks appear elevated. The scenes are lush with color and depth. Even the dingy, earth-toned textured wallpaper—remember the olive and brown vertical stripes, 1970s, '80s and '90s IDSers?—appears warm and multidimensional.

Perhaps the preserved vibrance of slide film manages this feat. Or maybe the vitality is released by holding the frames up to light to reveal their magic.

When my co-editors and I launched this book project, we didn't know which version of the IDS story would emerge. Would the stories told from memory be Kodachrome, with colors more rich than real? Would our tendency to romanticize the IDS soften its edges like Vaseline on a lens? Could a bunch of nostalgic alumni—not just the editors, but the more than two dozen other former IDSers who contributed to this project—be trusted to get their own story right?

We found our answer at the IU Archives. Beyond the original editions of the newspaper itself—nearly 20,000 published since the first in 1867—the preserved documents from IDS history are sparse, made up of just three bankers' boxes of materials. Packed within them, though, is the raw and honest story the IDS has told about itself from the beginning.

Among the treasures found in this repository are page after page of daily critiques of the paper, such as Department of Journalism chair John Stempel's assessment of a September 1938 issue. "The band story on page one smacks of propaganda," he wrote. "It might have been handled

Top, Editor-in-Chief Amy Wimmer consults with Campus Editor Jake Goshert, fall 1995. *Photo courtesy of Jay Hagenow.*

Middle, Page designer and columnist Jeff Vrabel plays trash-can basketball, fall 1995. *Photo courtesy of Jay Hagenow.*

Bottom, Communal french fries, fall 1995. *Photo courtesy of Jay Hagenow.*

a little less baldly. I'm for the band, but." Also among the files are handwritten reader notes the IDS staff chose to save, such as the one scribbled on the front page of a 1954 edition: "It is a disgrace to allow such a paper as this to go out. And this page is a fair example of what the Student has been for some time."

The IDS also has chronicled its perceived failings in its own pages. The recurring financial dilemmas of a student press are one common theme, as is the lack of diversity on staff and even the paper's editorial shortcomings. "Daily Student sails in sea of red ink," one April 1986 headline reads. "Summer IDS has problems—image, staff need upgrading," states a blunt headline from August 1974. In a 1964 edition, the IDS staff gave banner front-page treatment to a commentary from the paper's chief critic, history professor Michael J. Scriven: "What's right with IDS? Not much, Scriven charges."

Below left, News meeting, fall 1995. *Photo courtesy of Jay Hagenow.*

Below middle, Chris Jewell grabs a midday newsroom nap, fall 1995. *Photo courtesy of Jay Hagenow.*

Below right, Photographer Matt Stone edits photos at the light table, fall 1995. *Photo courtesy of Jay Hagenow.*

Read between the lines of newsprint, though, and the long-standing story of the IDS is about the push to get better—at the job, at the craft, at getting along with the people working just as hard alongside you. The IDS staff, it seems, is blessed with a lust for getting better but cursed with the awareness that it is not there yet.

With perfection perennially out of reach, we instead lived the full range of human experience through this one campus institution: persistence, pressure, humor, romance, perfectionism, laziness, apprehension, anger. Delight.

In one photo Jay shot near deadline, I hover over a pasted-up page, holding my hair out of my eyes with my left hand and gripping a blue proof marker in my right. In the next frame, I have caught Jay photographing me. Still holding back my hair, I stare at the camera with an expression of . . . surprise? Annoyance? Exhaustion?

The woman in that photo is so young, she has not yet discovered what a little eyebrow grooming can do to frame a face. The sports editor whose football is locked in her desk? In a few years, she will marry him. But in this moment in backshop, all that matters is the single page before her—and letting it go by deadline.

The history of the IDS is made up of hundreds of millions of moments like this one, and we could not begin to collect them all. But we hope you see yourself in these pages—not just in your era, but in the faces, hearts, front pages, disappointments and successes of those who came before and after you.

We hope that when you hold these few frames of IDS history up to light, you can see their magic.

—Amy Wimmer Schwarb, BAJ 1998

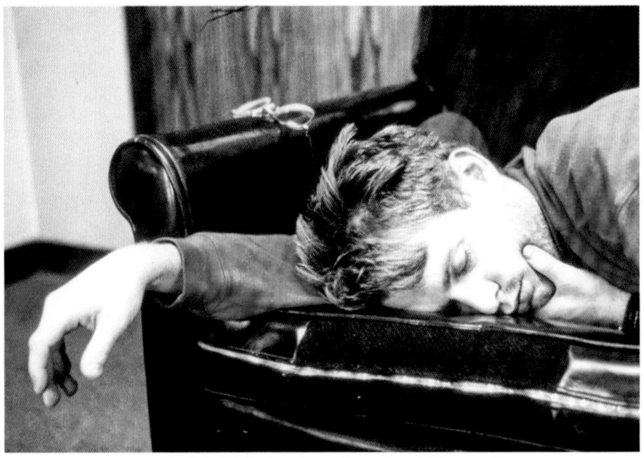

Acknowledgments

By design, newspapers are an ephemeral product. Over the course of a day, they transition from a crucial source of information to being destined for the recycling bin. But the stories contained within their pages remain valuable long after the day has ended, as a time capsule of what we were doing, thinking and feeling at a particular point in time.

It was our pleasure to unearth some of the thousands of names, faces and events that have shaped IU and the IDS over the decades, and to preserve them—both for the people who will remember them fondly (and not so fondly), and for future generations. Some of the front pages chosen for the book contain language and images that are racially and culturally insensitive. They were selected because they provide a historically accurate glimpse into the mores of student journalism and society during that time.

Additionally, several selections in this book are reprinted as they originally appeared in the IDS. Even though the IDS was operating on a daily deadline and we were not, we resisted the urge to correct copy, so misplaced commas and other minor errors are preserved here.

A generous grant from the IU Office of the Bicentennial was critical to bringing this project to life. We would also like to give special thanks to the IDS alumni who contributed original essays, photos and artifacts to this book. As former IDSers ourselves, we knew we were tapping into an alumni base of talented, devoted, motivated professionals who care deeply about the IDS. When we asked, they delivered, and this project would not have been possible without them.

We also offer heartfelt thanks to these individuals:

Laresa Lund, Jamie Zega and Matt Rasnic, interns hired through our IU Office of the Bicentennial grant, who served as our on-site coordinators, assisted with the design of the book cover and helped us access the reservoir of research when we could not be on campus.

Bradley Cook, Carrie Schwier, and the staff at the IU Archives, who helped us collect and document front pages and images and directed us to the best resources for IDS history.

Malinda Aston, Susan Elkins, Greg Menkedick, Jim Rodenbush and Ruth Witmer of the IDS professional staff, whose institutional knowledge and resource suggestions were invaluable.

The late Marjorie Smith Blewett, for not only her contemporary guidance on important moments in IDS history, but also for her loving care as a de facto IDS historian for decades. With the help of her daughter, Shayne Laughter, Blewett also helped us fact-check before her death in February 2019.

Ron Johnson and Owen Johnson, who had long envisioned a project similar to this one. Their early research helped shape the final product.

Several members of the university community who helped this project reach fruition: Peggy Solic and the team at IU Press; Emily Harrison and Anne Kibbler of The Media School; and Jennifer Gentry of the IU Alumni Association.

Our colleagues on the IU Student Publications Alumni Board, the recipient of the Bicentennial grant, who deputized us to complete the project: Michael Auslen, Kevin Corcoran, Dennis Elliott, Anne Haddad, Beth Moellers, MJ Slaby, Sara Brazeal and Jeff Vrabel.

The families of late IDS staff members Winston Fournier, Mary Monroe, Robert C. Pebworth and J. Dwight Peterson, who granted permission for their memories to be repurposed in this book. The personal reflections these alumni shared during past IDS anniversary events are stored with dozens of others at the IU Archives.

The IDS writers whose student work was selected for reproduction in these pages: Hannah Alani, Jane Charney, Jay Hagenow, Andy Hall, Pat Hanna, Jerry Hicks, Stu Huffman, Ginny Krause, Curtis Krueger, Alberto D. Morales, Christin Nance, Eve B. Rose, Steve Sanders, Ed Sovola and Donald R. Young. (Based on its cadence and the fact that it was published when he was IDS editor in chief, we also believe Ernie Pyle wrote the unsigned editorial featured in Chapter 2.)

Edie Schwarb for her microfilm and Arbutus research.

Dan Shortridge and Angie Basiouny for copyediting us on a tight deadline.

And finally, we reserve our biggest thanks to the generations of IDS staff—student and professional, from both the editorial and business sides—who make us proud to be part of the legacy.

—Rachel Kipp, BAJ 2002
Amy Wimmer Schwarb, BAJ 1998
Charles Scudder, BAJ 2014

INDIANA DAILY STUDENT

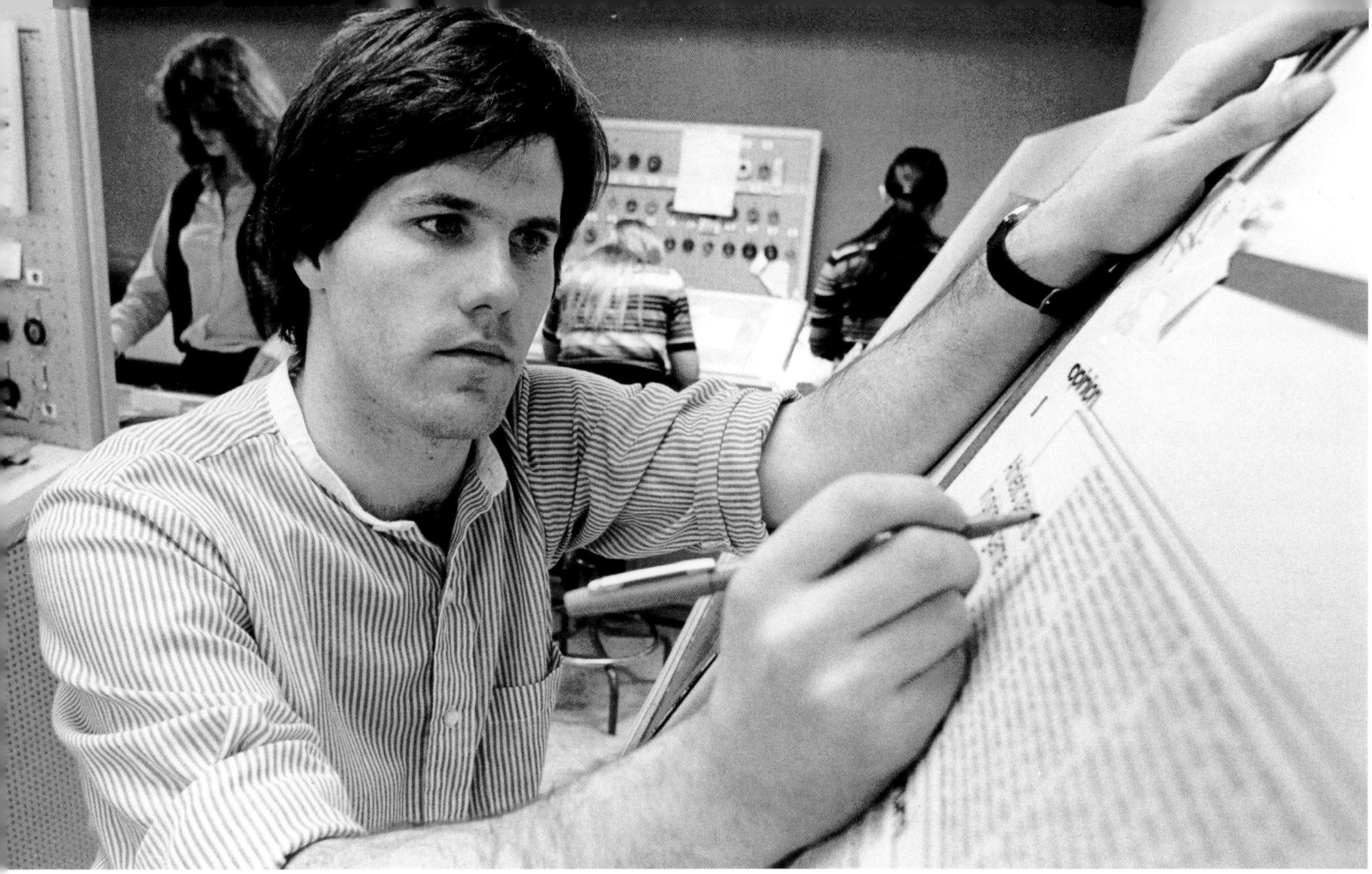

Spring 1980 IDS Editor-in-Chief Thomas French edits page proofs. *Photo courtesy of Indiana Daily Student.*

Introduction

'ALLEGIANCE TO NO FACTION': A HISTORY OF THE IDS

During the summer of 1979, IU student Tom French, an Indianapolis native who had attended the Indiana State Fair for years, became intrigued by one of its more outlandish attractions—the World's Largest Hog competition. He set out to write about it for the Indiana Daily Student.

French had always considered the Largest Hog event "weird," wondering why someone would take the trouble to raise an animal so enormous that its legs literally could not support its weight. His editors at the IDS urged him not to do the story, as it was not a serious subject. "By that point I had written hundreds of serious stories and had been bored to tears by most of them," French recalled. "My question was: What's wrong with once in a while writing something that people actually want to read?" He went to the fair, observed the winning hog and traveled to the farm in Elwood, Indiana, where it had been raised. Through his reporting, he learned that the story was "really about the American obsession with super-sizing everything. I became convinced that it had something to do with the vastness of the American landscape and American ambitions."

The article won first place that fall in the features category in the Hearst Journalism Awards Program for college students, earned French a trip to the championship in San Francisco and helped him land a job with the St. Petersburg Times. Nearly 20 years later, French—today a professor of practice in journalism for The Media School at IU—won the 1998 Pulitzer Prize in feature writing and a Sigma Delta Chi award for "Angels & Demons," a series that explored the murder of an Ohio woman and her two teenage daughters. The work became a seminal piece of narrative journalism; fellow Pulitzer recipient Anne Hull of the Washington Post said French's series long dominated the craft and served as "a model for the rest of us to follow."

The Pulitzer and all that followed could never have happened without French's association with the IDS. "It was the best learning experience I ever had and one of the greatest times in my life," said French, who also served as the newspaper's editor in chief. "I never really understood how much freedom we had to make mistakes, take chances and do outrageous things."

Ernie Pyle as a student, circa 1921. *P0022819, IU Archives.*

Years before French's investigation of the state fair's odd attraction, another IDS reporter and future Pulitzer Prize winner, Ernie Pyle, heard news that IU's 12-man baseball team had been invited to play a series of exhibition games in Japan. "I've just got to go," the wanderlust-struck Pyle told a friend. Pyle obtained permission from the dean, borrowed $200, and, with three of his fraternity brothers, secured jobs on the ship taking the baseball squad to Japan. Pyle wrote his parents that he possessed "a pretty level head, so there is not the slightest cause to worry about me. I have trotted around this old globe considerably, and I think I should be pretty well qualified to handle myself wisely."

The junior from Dana, Indiana, made sure to mail to the IDS articles about his experiences, including pieces on a storm that sailors told him was "the worst they had ever seen on the Pacific with the exception of a typhoon," and his duties as a bellboy, including carrying ice and water, shining shoes, delivering packages, drawing baths, and tending to the "innumerable queer wants of the passengers." Pyle and his fraternity brothers even managed to help a young Filipino stowaway evade detection and make his way onto American soil.

French's idiosyncratic hog story and Pyle's audacious Japanese trip would no doubt have delighted the original editors of The Indiana Student, which appeared on Feb. 22, 1867, the same year the IU Board of Trustees voted to allow women to attend classes. In its first issue, editors Henry C. Duncan, Robert D. Richardson and Henry C. "Sol" Meredith solemnly proclaimed the publication owed "allegiance to no faction," and was "subservient to no personal motives of exaltation, pure in tone, seeking the common good, partial and guided by a spirit of truth and justice." In that same issue, they also invented a fictional meeting at which President Andrew Johnson, writer Washington Irving, newspaper editor Horace Greeley, publisher James Gordon Bennett, journalist Henry J. Raymond and editor George D. Prentice gathered to determine a name for the IU publication.

Among the possibilities considered was the "Bloomington Regulator," with one of its principal objects to "regulate society, regulate literature, regulate students, regulate the faculty, regulate public exhibitions, regulate Bloomington; in short, it was to be a regulator in the fullest sense of the term." The article noted that Raymond in particular believed "The University Lightning Rod" would be fitting, as it would be the "means of silently conducting all the superfluous gas generated in the fruitful craniums of certain 'smart students,' either to immortal glories in the skies, or . . . to its more appropriate place, the dominions of Pluto beneath the earth." The men also pondered such names as "My Policy Gazette" (Johnson's choice), "Collegian, "Review," "Banner," "Mirror," and "Bummer." Finally Raymond, "by a heroic stretch of imagination and herculean wielding of brain power," came up with "The Indiana Student." That first issue also included a puckish notice informing students they should bear in mind that marriage notices would be "inserted free of charge," and a piece advocating for campus improvements (a familiar theme for subsequent IU student newspapers), especially the building of a "walk from the campus gate to the college. Many of our citizens have been deterred from attending performances at the college, in consequent of the deep mud through which they were compelled to wade."

Throughout its more than 150 years of existence, the IDS has changed with the times and technology—from the hot-metal typesetting days of the Linotype machine to scanners and computers, and today breaking news on mobile phones in readers' pockets. The newspaper has fought to maintain itself economically and reflect its audience throughout its lives—as a for-profit venture for its editors; as a newspaper owned by the university and used as a laboratory to train journalists; and as an independent publication employing students of all types with its editor-in-chief selected by a publications board that includes professional journalists and students. "These are our students on display," noted Trevor Brown, former dean of the IU School of Journalism. "Obviously at times they disappoint us. At other times they thrill us with the quality. But that's no different from a professional newspaper."

Mottos used by the IDS have reflected the changes in journalism over the years, with the paper in 1914 using "Best in the Middle West," in 1929 "He Serves Best Who Serves the Truth" and "'Tis the Truth that Makes Man Free," and in the 1990s, "You Are the News." The work produced by the newspaper has often been honored with national awards, including numerous Pacemakers from the Associated Collegiate Press, and over the years IDS alumni have earned for their articles and photographs a number of Pulitzer prizes in a variety of categories. Before the Indiana Student made its appearance in 1867, other universities had already started publications offering literary outpourings and news, including the Dartmouth Gazette in 1800, followed by the Asbury Review, the Yale Courant and Harvard Advocate. The Bloomington campus had seen two other attempts at collegiate journalism, including publications from the 1840s titled The Equator and The Athenian, the latter of which was sponsored by the Athenian Society, a literary group. The Indiana Student's appearance on Feb. 22, 1867, was likely not an accident, as its editors might have taken advantage of the pomp associated then with commemorating George Washington's birthday, including a campus tradition whereby students burned their Latin texts of Horace or buried "Calculus" in late-night ceremonies. Newspaper staff in its early years consisted of editors from the senior class, with junior class members as "associates," sophomores serving as office boys, and freshmen relegated to the "printer's devil" role, doing the mundane and grubby jobs associated with publishing in that era.

Although the first issue of the IU newspaper had lampooned its naming with its fanciful committee, the truth was more prosaic, with Duncan, Richardson and Meredith, joined by three other unnamed students, meeting to come up with a name for their creation. Reminiscing about the newspaper's start, Duncan noted that those gathered "puzzled our brains . . . in names beginning with 'A' and running to 'Z,' but no name appeared suitable until the big senior from Cambridge City—'Sol' Meredith—put his giant intellect to bear on the subject, struck an attitude, and sang out 'Student'—'Indiana Student!' And so it was christened."

The four-page, three-column, privately owned newspaper struggled to find its way, alternating between monthly and semimonthly publication, and sometimes disappearing for months at a time. "It started out under rather unfavorable circumstances," Duncan remembered, "but by hard work we managed to make both ends meet, barring a little deficit the members had to foot. But then the honor!" Meredith could always be counted on to provide local news, but sometimes he wandered afield in his writing into areas, Duncan noted, "not very suitable for a first-class paper." Although Richardson possessed writing ability, and could beat anyone on staff "on criticism," said Duncan, he could also be "inclined to be sarcastic." As for his own contributions to the Indiana Student, Duncan would only say that they often spurred Cyrus Nutt, the university's fifth president, to invite the young student to his office for a heart-to-heart chat.

Taken over in 1870–71 by the by the Athenian and Philomathean Literary Association, two literary societies, the Indiana Student went out of business in 1874, beset with financial problems and supposed pressure from IU President Lemuel Moss, who believed that IU should be a school of arts and no more. For the next eight years, students had to rely on Bloomington newspapers for news about campus activities. That changed with the arrival of a transfer student from Butler University, Clarence L. Goodwin, who sought to revive a campus newspaper. He partnered in the endeavor with a former IU student, William Julian Bryan, then teaching in Virginia. (Bryan later served as IU president from 1902 to 1937, when he was known as William Lowe Bryan after he and his wife took each other's names following their marriage in 1889.) "He brought with him the courage and conviction to start new things," Bryan said of Goodwin. "And since reawakening the professional schools would have been a bit out of line for him as a student, he brought baseball, The Student and lecture bureau to the campus." With help from IU librarian William W. Spangler, who served as business manager, the monthly 28-page Student set out to not only provide "some means of recording the doings of the alumni," but also provide "an esprit de corps to our students which they would not otherwise possess."

William Lowe Bryan's senior portrait, 1884. *P0073981, IU Archives.*

The paper underwent some rocky times, with ownership changing hands among various editors, as well as being taken over by the IU Lecture Association and the university librarian for a time. The university did finally offer a class in reporting in 1893 taught by professor Martin W. Sampson, with four students being instructed for two hours a week on such subjects as "accounts of fires, accidents, crimes; reports of lectures, entertainments,

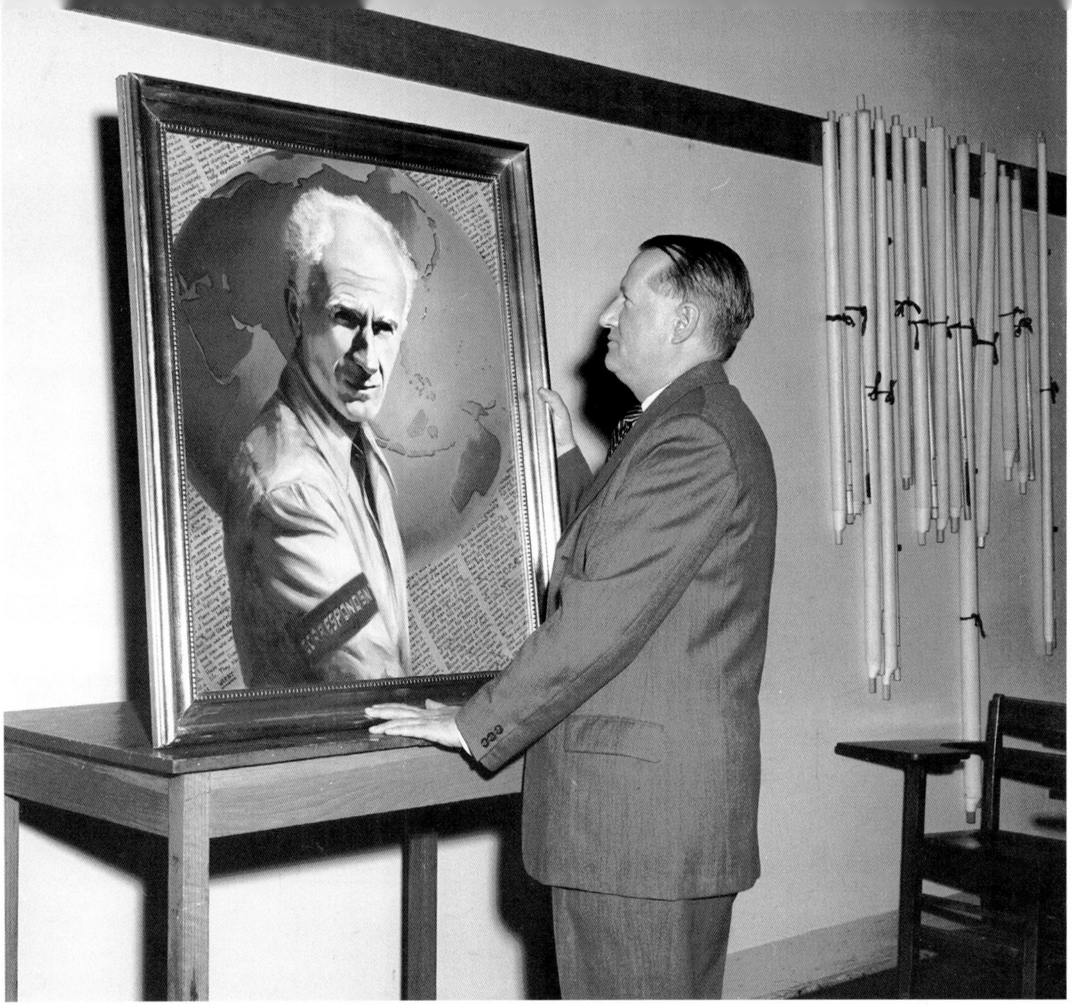

John Stempel, head of the Department of Journalism from 1938 to 1968, with a portrait of Ernie Pyle in 1953. The two were IDS staff contemporaries; both were editors in chief. *P0027093, IU Archives.*

public meetings; interview; study of daily and weekly newspapers." The class had disappeared by 1898. The paper finally was placed on solid footing under the editorship of Salem, Indiana, native Walter H. Crim, who in the fall of 1898 received permission from the IU Board of Trustees to change the name to the Daily Student (It did not become the more familiar Indiana Daily Student until 1914.) and publish it five afternoons a week; printing was done at the Bloomington World-Courier building. In the 1900s, student editors received 15 credit hours for the work, but the university dropped the policy in 1906, and applicants for the job suffered a considerable drop. Journalism courses were again offered at IU in 1908 and were taught by Fred Bates Johnson, a former Indianapolis reporter. At the end of the 1910–11 school year, Joseph W. Piercy, formerly of the University of Washington, came to IU as head of the Department of Journalism. (Piercy retired in 1938 and was succeeded by John E. Stempel, who had worked on the IDS in Pyle's era as a news editor and editor in chief and later served as a copy editor at the New York Sun.)

On May 5, 1910, after years of squabbling among editors about finances, most of the student and faculty stockholders of the Daily Student donated their holdings to the IU Board of Trustees. By this time, the newspaper had become a laboratory for journalism students, with a cast of rotating editors to provide experience to more students. In September 1914 the operation moved into new headquarters, occupying half of what had been the university's power plant. (After World War II, a Quonset hut provided room for the news staff. The journalism department and newspaper finally moved into Ernie Pyle Hall in 1954.) Four pages of six columns each were published every morning except Sunday; during World War I, to conserve paper and power, the IDS halted publication on Mondays.

By 1920 the IDS added news from the Associated Press, which came every night via a 15-minute phone call from Indianapolis, with full AP service established in 1931. Also in the early 1920s, the newspaper started an Indiana State Fair edition (Pyle served as the first editor in chief), with 10,000 copies printed and distributed free to those attending the goings-on at the fairgrounds in Indianapolis. Reflecting on the publication's centennial in 1967, Marjorie Smith Blewett, a former IDS editor in chief and a 1948 IU graduate, noted that the state fair edition ended due to financial difficulties in 1955, but those who worked on it were fond of recalling "the week of dusty typewriters, finding features among the many fair personalities, covering the horse show, and the livestock competitions, watching the style show in the Women's Building, and carrying on a running banter with Purdue students working in that school's building down the street."

Furnishings were by no means plush in the newspaper's editorial offices. Martha Wright Myrick, a 1932 graduate whose father, Joe Wright, helped run the journalism department with Piercy, recalled a cluttered city room equipped with a horseshoe-shaped desk that served as a workspace for the newspaper's rewrite men and headline writers. "I remember sitting on those rickety wooden folding chairs in front of an equally rickety typewriter batting out my story for the next after a concert or recital or whatever I had covered that night," she recalled. Students could be interrupted at any time by a faculty member storming into the office to point out an error in someone's copy. Glen Stadler, a 1936 graduate, never forgot one day when J. Wymond French, the newspaper's faculty adviser, burst out of his office to tack on the bulletin board a notice pointing out a gross error: "NEVER, NEVER, NEVER write 'TURN DOWN' when you mean 'REJECT!'"

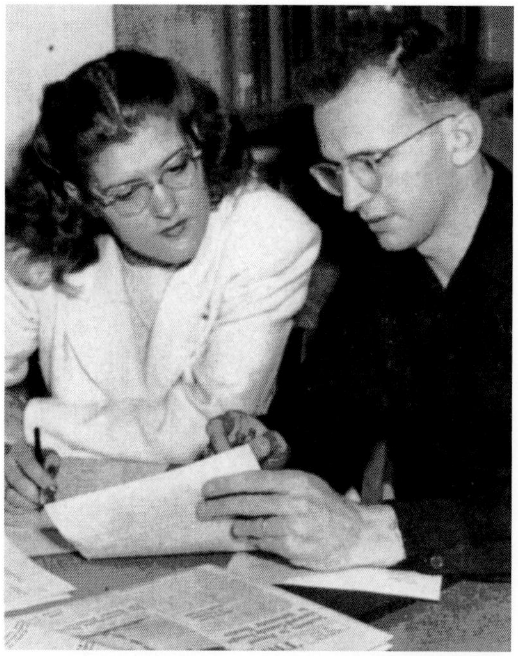

Editor-in-Chief Marjorie Jean Smith, later Marjorie Smith Blewett, with Managing Editor Lee Hirsch, 1948. *P0030392, IU Archives.*

Seeing their byline first appear in print was a cherished memory for many alumni. J. E. O'Brien, BA 1937, who went on to work at the Indianapolis Times and Indianapolis News, achieved his first byline as a freshman after receiving a tip from Henrietta Thornton of IU's publicity office. O'Brien interviewed Charles Hornbostel, the university's famed middle-distance runner, about one of his

A new printing press is set up in 1954 in Ernie Pyle Hall. *P0054950, IU Archives.*

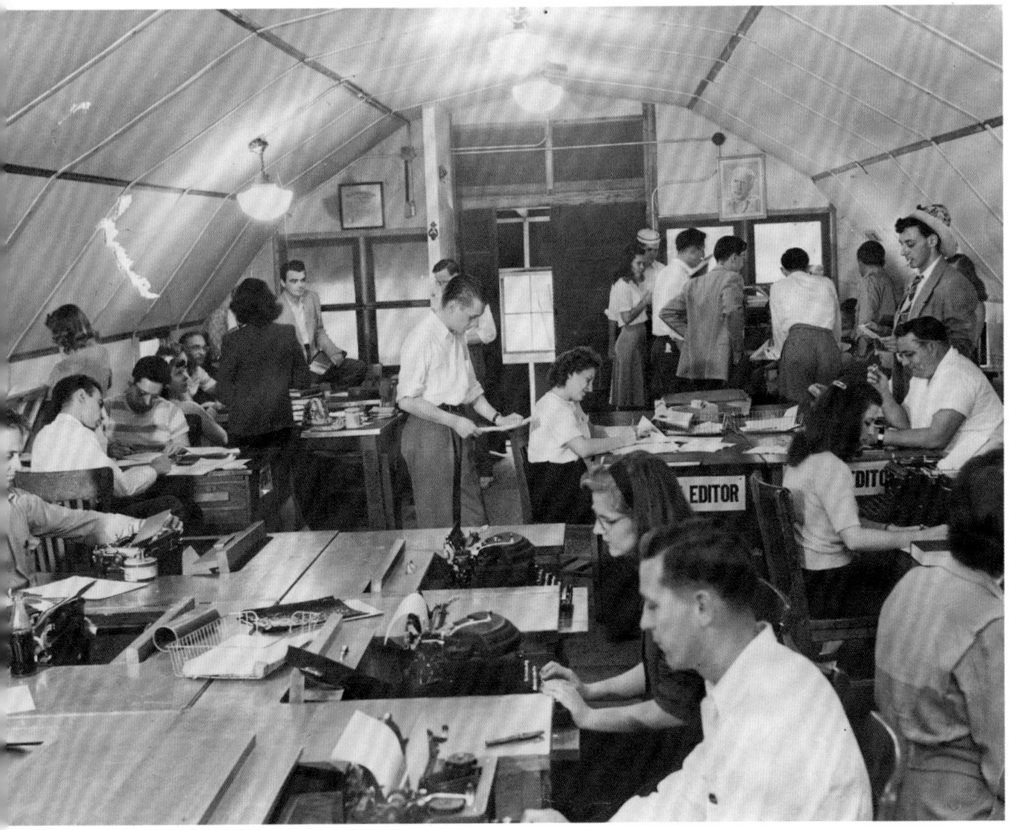

IDS newsroom in the Quonset Hut, fall 1947. Later generations of staff would remember this space as "The Shack." *P0024817, IU Archives.*

ancestors, who had also been a runner. With "some trepidation," O'Brien took his story to J. Wymond French. "He read it without changing a word, marked the paragraphs and penciled my byline atop the story," O'Brien recalled. "I then asked if I could join the staff. To my surprise, French said I could." O'Brien spent three years at the IDS working in a variety of jobs, including editors in chief. His most satisfying one was serving as night editor, as that post selected what stories appeared on the front page and which received the biggest play. Although French never questioned the night editor's news judgment, "the marked-up front page he posted on the bulletin board the next morning usually made the night editor wince," remembered O'Brien.

As part of their education under Stempel, Blewett and others on the staff had to learn how to set type by hand. The process seemed almost miraculous to G. Patrick "Pat" Siddons, who, after serving with the U.S. Army in the Pacific during World War II, had enrolled at Purdue University to study electrical engineering before realizing his writing skills were a better fit for IU. Siddons fondly recalled the heady feeling he "got from putting words on paper, the thrill of watching the Linotype operator create words in metal, and of watching that old flat-bed press crank out copies of a paper that actually contained stories I had written." The days of the flatbed press ended in 1964, when the IDS became an offset newspaper. By the middle of the 1970s, computers arrived, and reporters typed their stories on special typewriters before feeding them into a scanner that transferred the information to a digital file on a computer that could then be edited before being sent to the production room for layout. In October 1996 the IDS entered the internet age with the appearance of an online edition.

Among the major changes to the IDS, none may have been bigger than the one that occurred in 1969, when, as part of a change in the curriculum, journalism students were no longer required to work on the newspaper as part of their studies. The IU Board of Trustees also made the newspaper an enterprise of the university—still owned by IU, but without offering financial support. "It was a time of activism on campus," said Blewett, who had joined the journalism department in 1965. "Everyone was trying to get their hands on it—student government, every kind of side group, every activist group. You really realized how valuable it was when you saw that all those people wanted it. . . . We had to fight to hold on, to mold the paper as an independent paper."

Jack Backer of the Niles (Michigan) Star became IDS publisher in 1969. Dennis Royalty, a 1971 graduate, recalled that Backer often told the staff, "Progress is crisis-oriented," and gently pointed out what the fledgling journalists "could have done better while championing our success." Backer died from cancer in 1976, and eventually Siddons, who had gone on to become Bloomington bureau chief for the Louisville Courier-Journal, accepted the publisher job and returned to IU in 1978.

Siddons said that Backer had put "the Daily Student on the lips of all the college media advisers around the country. . . . Jack Backer built the ship. All I had to do was make sure that it was steered in the right direction." He did so until his retirement in 1989.

One of the many lessons Siddons attempted to impart to the IDS staff from the beginning was that "you may be young, you may be students, you may be nonprofessionals, you may still be learning the tricks of the trade, but I want this to be as professional a paper as it can possibly be. I think they took pride in seeing how professional that they could make it."

Siddons recalled one occasion with a student reporter who came to him excited that he had a scoop involving an alleged conflict of interest by a university employee. As the newspaper's adviser, Siddons could see no such conflict, and even considered the story possibly libelous. In spite of Siddons' concerns, the student seemed determined to proceed and have his article published. "I said, 'That's your prerogative, but will you do me a favor?' Siddons recalled. "He said, 'What's that?' I said, 'Would you tell me the day before when it's going to run in the paper so I can resign? Because I don't want to have to defend you in a libel suit.'" The story never appeared in the IDS.

Controversy, of course, has been part of the IDS since its inception, including angry Iranian students demanding the newspaper drop its AP wire service in favor of Reuters; accusations that the newspaper did not reflect the diversity of the student body; a decision in the early 1980s to halt free distribution in residence halls and switch to all-paid circulation; and the newspaper's move as part of the new IU Media School from Ernie Pyle Hall to Franklin Hall in the summer of 2016.

A year after the move from Pyle Hall, the newspaper underwent two major changes. In the spring of 2017, facing a projected financial loss of $250,000 for the fiscal year, the IDS reduced its print frequency from five days to two days a week, Mondays and Thursdays. "While we continue to serve readers and advertisers in print, we have grown and expanded our digital coverage," said Ron Johnson, then-director of IU Student Media—the title now used for publisher of the IDS and the Arbutus yearbook. "Our student journalists produce great content, and our goal is to keep evolving to get content where readers and advertisers need it." Additionally, Johnson announced he

IDS Publisher David Adams with student staff members David De Camp, Amy Wimmer and Dara Kates, 1996. *Photo courtesy Amy Wimmer Schwarb.*

IDS Director of Student Media Ron Johnson with Spring 2009 IDS Editor-in-Chief Michael Sanserino. *Photo by James Brosher.*

would resign at the end of the same year, but Media School Dean James Shanahan removed Johnson from his position a month early in a cost-cutting move.

With all the changes in journalism and at IU since the IDS first appeared in 1867, one thing has remained constant—the dedication of the students who have chosen to work on the newspaper. It has been that way from the Roaring '20s to the internet age. For example, in the spring of 1929, reporters and editors were working on the next day's issue when, at about 10 p.m., the lights in the newsroom went out. "The power house, which was right adjacent to the Daily Student office, was on fire," said Robert Pebworth, who worked as the night editor. "We went out and by that time, the firefighting equipment had come, and inquiries of what the devil to do."

Eventually, the staff gathered all of the type and moved it to the Bloomington World to be printed. Pebworth recalled that the staff finished making up the paper at 7:30 in the morning and, despite the fire, it was out and delivered by 8:30. "We had a sense of a team concept," he said. "We came from different backgrounds, with different interests, but we got swept up in trying to put out a good newspaper."

Seventy-nine years later, another IDS editor, Carrie Ritchie, a 2008 graduate, arrived at Ernie Pyle Hall on her first day as spring editor to discover that the newsroom had no power. "This presented a sizable challenge considering we did everything on computers," Ritchie said. "I remember huddling on the back steps of the building with my staff members, trying to think of a viable alternative." They ended up squeezing into a computer lab at the IU Memorial Union for several hours until power was finally restored at Ernie Pyle Hall.

Ritchie noted that a number of students, not too happy about returning to school after a long break, would have "complained about being in cramped quarters, trying to put out the first paper of the semester. But not this group. Instead, my colleagues were laughing, working with writers who had come in to edit their stories and genuinely enjoying each others' company." Her experience that day proved to her (as Pebworth's adventure probably had in 1929) that she had made the right choice in choosing journalism as her career. "I wanted to be part of a profession that proved people can accomplish anything with a little bit of teamwork," she said. "I think of that day often, especially when I hear people question the future of journalism. I know it will survive as long as we all work together, like IDS staffers did that day and for more than a century before that."

—Ray E. Boomhower, BA 1982, MA 1995

FOR FURTHER READING

"Indiana Daily Student to Mark 125 Years of Headlines, Bylines," Indiana University News Bureau, February 17, 1992.

Marjorie Blewett, "The First 100—The Hardest? The Indiana Daily Student Celebrates Its 100th Birthday on February 22; Controversial Student Newspaper 'Cussed and Discussed' Throughout Long Career," Indiana Alumni Magazine, February 1967.

Marjorie Blewett, "The Daily Student 100 Today: Still Has Credo of First Issue," Indiana Daily Student, February 22, 1967.

Ray E. Boomhower, profile of Tom French, Indiana Journalism Hall of Fame Golden Anniversary Induction Banquet program, October 24, 2015.

Thomas D. Clark, Indiana University: Midwestern Pioneer (Bloomington: Indiana University Press, 1970–1977).

Olivia Clarke and Andrew Moulton, "130 Years of Covering the Campus: The 'IDS' Celebrates its 130th Birthday Saturday," Indiana Daily Student, February 21, 1997.

Gillian Gaynair, "Celebrating 125 Years of the Indiana Daily Student," Indiana Daily Student, February 21, 1992.

Lee G. Miller, The Story of Ernie Pyle (New York: The Viking Press, 1950).

J. E. O'Brien, "J. E. O'Brien Reminisces about the Daily Student in the 1930s," Newswire, Fall/Winter 2002.

James A. Woodburn, History of Indiana University (Bloomington: Indiana University, 1940).

"A Century of Journalism: Memories," Indiana University Media School, http://mediaschool.indiana.edu/journalismcentennial/memories/.

IN THE WORLD, ON CAMPUS, AT THE NEWSROOM

Jamie Zega, BAJ 2018

1867 The Indiana Student publishes its first issue.

1867 The United States purchases Alaska from Russia.

1869 The Suez Canal opens.

1874 The newspaper suspends publication and is later revived in 1882 by Clarence L. Goodwin and William Lowe Bryan, who would become the 10th president of Indiana University in 1902.

1875 Lemuel Moss becomes the sixth president of IU.

1883 A fire destroys Science Hall at Seminary Square, and the university purchases 20 acres of land from the Dunn family to rebuild campus.

1884 David Starr Jordan becomes the seventh president of IU.

1888 Cream and crimson are chosen as IU's official colors.

1891 John Merle Coulter becomes the eighth president of IU.

1893 Joseph Swain becomes the ninth president of IU and the first born in Indiana.

1897 Florence Reid Myrick Ahl becomes the first female editor of the paper.

1901 IU plays its first intercollegiate men's basketball game in Indianapolis and loses to Butler, 20–17.

1901 Queen Victoria, the longest-reigning British monarch to date, dies.

1902 Former IDS Editor-in-Chief William Lowe Bryan becomes 10th president of IU.

1903 Orville and Wilbur Wright take flight for the first time.

1910 The IU Board of Trustees take over ownership of the Student, and the Department of Journalism uses the paper as a learning lab.

1911 The Department of Journalism is established.

1914 Archduke Franz Ferdinand is assassinated, leading to the outbreak of World War I.

1914 The paper becomes the Indiana Daily Student.

1915 The Turkish government arrests and kills several hundred Armenian intellectuals, an action considered the beginning the Armenian genocide.

1917 Bolshevik revolutionary Vladimir Lenin incites the Russian Revolution.

1918 An armistice is signed with Germany, effectively ending World War I.

1920 IU establishes the School of Commerce and Finance, now the Kelley School of Business.

1920 The 19th Amendment is ratified, granting suffrage for women in the United States.

1922 The first Indiana State Fair Edition is published with Ernie Pyle as editor.

1923 The first IDS Stylebook is created and edited by Editor-in-Chief John Stempel and Managing Editor Nelson Poynter.

1924 Nellie Showers Teter becomes the first female university trustee.

1925 IU and Purdue play their first Old Oaken Bucket football game.

1929 The stock market collapses on Black Tuesday, beginning the Great Depression.

1932 Construction is completed on Indiana Memorial Union.

1932 IU offers bachelor's degree in journalism for the first time.

1938 Former IDS Editor-in-Chief John Stempel becomes the leader of the IU Department of Journalism.

1938 Herman B Wells becomes the 11th president of IU.

1939 Germany invades Poland to begin the Second World War.

1940 The IU men's basketball team wins its first NCAA tournament.

1941 Construction is completed on the IU Auditorium.

1941 The IDS runs an extra edition Dec. 7 after the Pearl Harbor attacks. During World War II, the IDS would have 13 consecutive female editors.

1942 The IDS celebrates its 75th anniversary.

1944 Ernie Pyle is awarded an honorary doctorate of human letters after winning the Pulitzer Prize for correspondence.

1945 Ernie Pyle is killed on Iejima during the Battle of Okinawa.

1945 The Axis powers surrender on the European and Pacific fronts to end World War II.

1947 Alfred Kinsey establishes the Institute for Sex Research at IU, now known as the Kinsey Institute.

1947 India gains independence from British rule.

1948 The IDS begins working from the Shack, a surplus World War II Quonset hut.

1949 IU desegregates women's residence halls.

1951 IU Student Foundation stages first Little 500.

1952 Queen Elizabeth II takes the throne.

1953 IU men's basketball team wins second national title.

1953 The Korean War ends with an armistice.

1954 IU dedicates Ernie Pyle Hall.

1961 Yuri Gagarin is the first man to go to outer space.

1962 Elvis J. Stahr, a former U.S. Army secretary, becomes the 12th president of IU.

1963 President John F. Kennedy is assassinated in Dallas.

1964 "I Want to Hold Your Hand" by the Beatles reaches the top of the U.S. charts, setting off Beatlemania in the U.S.

1964 President Lyndon B. Johnson signs the Civil Rights Act.

1967 The IDS celebrates its centennial.

1968 Civil rights leader Martin Luther King Jr. is assassinated in Memphis, Tennessee. Two months later, presidential candidate Robert F. Kennedy is also killed.

1968 The men's football team plays in the Rose Bowl, the men's swimming team wins the NCAA championship, and Joseph Lee Sutton becomes the 13th president of IU.

1969 IU completes construction on the Main Library, now the Herman B Wells Library.

1969 The IDS is chartered as an independent entity separate from the Board of Trustees.

1969 Jack Backer becomes the first full-time publisher of the IDS.

1971 John William Ryan becomes the 14th president of IU.

1972 Five men break into the Democratic National Committee headquarters, beginning the Watergate scandal that would define Richard Nixon's presidency.

1972 IU's Mark Spitz wins a record seven gold medals at the Munich Olympics.

1973 Ernie Pyle Hall closes for renovations, so the IDS moves its operations to the old Delta Zeta house until 1976.

1973 The U.S. Supreme Court decides in Roe v. Wade that a woman's right to abortion falls within her right to privacy.

1974 The Department of Journalism becomes the School of Journalism but remains housed within the College of Arts & Sciences.

1975 Saigon falls to North Vietnam, ending the Vietnam War.

1976 The Apple Computer Company is founded.

1976 IDS publisher Jack Backer dies at 41.

1976 The Hoosiers go undefeated through the regular season and the NCAA tournament.

1978 Pat Siddons is named publisher of the IDS and Arbutus.

1979 Margaret Thatcher becomes the first female prime minister of the United Kingdom.

1981 The IDS adopts a paid-circulation model.

1981 The IU men's basketball team wins a fifth national championship.

1982 Female enrollment at IU outnumbers male enrollment for the first time.

1986 The space shuttle Challenger explodes 73 seconds into its flight.

1987 The men's basketball team wins its fifth national title the same year Thomas Ehrlich becomes the 15th president of IU.

1988 The IU Student Foundation launches first Women's Little 500.

1989 Dave Adams becomes publisher after Pat Siddons retires.

1989 Student protestors are killed in China's Tiananmen Square.

1989 The Berlin Wall falls.

1991 The Soviet Union dissolves.

1992 The IDS celebrates its 125th birthday.

1994 Apartheid comes to an official end in South Africa.

1994 The IDS is inducted into the Associated College Press Hall of Fame.

1994 Myles Brand becomes the 16th president of IU.

1995 The IDS becomes a free publication again.

1996 The Indiana Digital Student launches online. It is now known simply as idsnews.com.

1997 Diana, Princess of Wales, dies in a car accident in Paris.

1998 The IDS newsroom undergoes major renovations.

1999 A white supremacist shoots and kills graduate student Won-Joon Yoon near campus.

2000 Herman B Wells dies.

2000 Myles Brand fires men's basketball coach Bob Knight, causing uproar throughout campus.

2001 Nearly 3,000 people are killed during the terrorist attacks of Sept. 11.

2005 Hurricane Katrina devastates New Orleans and other parts of the Gulf Coast.

2005 Vice President and Bloomington Chancellor Kenneth R. R. Gros Louis approves the revised IDS charter that is still in use today.

2006 The IDS joins Facebook.

2007 Director of Student Media David Adams dies, and Nancy Comiskey is named interim director.

2007 Adam W. Herbert becomes the 17th president of IU.

2007 Apple releases the iPhone.

2007 Michael McRobbie becomes the 18th president of IU.

2008 Men's basketball coach Kelvin Sampson is ousted amid an NCAA recruiting scandal and is replaced by Tom Crean.

2008 Ron Johnson becomes director of student media.

2008 U.S. Sen. Barack Obama becomes the first African-American elected president of the United States.

2009 School of Environmental and Public Affairs professor Elinor Ostrom becomes the first woman to be awarded the Nobel Prize in Economics.

2009 The IDS joins Twitter.

2010 Protests erupt in North Africa and the Middle East, sparking the Arab Spring.

2011 The IDS launches its mobile app.

2011 U.S. forces discover and kill Osama bin Laden in Pakistan.

2012 The university launches its online degree program, IU Online.

2012 Twenty children and six adults are killed at Sandy Hook Elementary School in Newtown, Connecticut.

2013 The Board of Trustees votes to create The Media School, combining the School of Journalism, Department of Telecommunications and the Department of Communication and Culture.

2013 Two bombs are detonated at the finish line of the Boston Marathon, killing three people and injuring hundreds.

2015 In a landmark Supreme Court ruling, same-sex marriage is legalized in all 50 states.

2016 The IDS moves to Franklin Hall with the rest of The Media School.

2017 Students and alumni gather to celebrate the 150th anniversary of the IDS. Weeks later, Ron Johnson resigns.

2018 Jim Rodenbush becomes new director of student media.

2020 IU celebrates its bicentennial.

1867–1914

The Indiana Student made an inauspicious debut Feb. 22, 1867, with a fictionalized explanation of the origin of its name and a front-page plea for subscriptions. Its future remained questionable—and its publication schedule erratic—for years. But as its 50th birthday approached and the university made the Student its own, the newspaper found its voice—and in 1914, it added a middle name: Daily.

Above, The first known IDS staff photo, 1894–95. *P0080981, IU Archives.*

Left, Students reading the IDS, 1914. *P0080984, IU Archives.*

REFLECTION

In the Beginning

Right, P0024087, IU Archives.

Below top, IU faculty, circa 1867. *P0033853, IU Archives.*

Below bottom, IU's first female student, Sarah Parke Morrison, was admitted in 1867, the same year the newspaper published its first edition. *P0027561, IU Archives.*

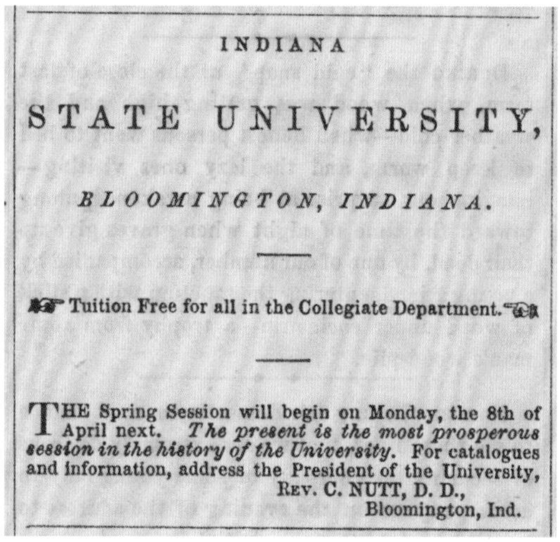

INDIANA

STATE UNIVERSITY,

BLOOMINGTON, INDIANA.

Tuition Free for all in the Collegiate Department.

THE Spring Session will begin on Monday, the 8th of April next. *The present is the most prosperous session in the history of the University.* For catalogues and information, address the President of the University,
REV. C. NUTT, D. D.,
Bloomington, Ind.

Adapted from "Indiana Daily Student Is 100 Years Old," published in the Winter 1967 edition of The Review, the alumni magazine of the IU College of Arts and Sciences.

Had those IU students of 1867 realized that 100 years later someone would be poring over their first issue seeking "news," perhaps they would not have given such a flippant account of how they chose their paper's name. Their page one story was a satire, and it wasn't until more than four years later that one of the founders wrote a serious account of it in a letter to his successors on the staff.

Its first editorial committee was Henry C. (Leatherwood) Duncan, Robert D. Richardson and Henry C. (Sol) Meredith. It was Mr. Duncan who wrote the descriptive letter, amusingly enough to correct an error in which the paper had reported he had visited campus. He then lived at Emporia, Kansas. He recalled how six young men were gathered in a room in the Fee Building:

"We puzzled our brains, all of us, in names beginning with 'A' and running to 'Z,' but no name appeared suitable until the big senior from Cambridge City—"Sol" Meredith—put his giant intellect to bear on the subject, struck an attitude, and sang out 'Student—Indiana Student!'" And so it was christened.

Fraternity politics entered into the editorial committee selection, too, for Mr. Duncan recalled that through some political maneuvers, the Betas had one on the staff, Richardson, and the Sigs had two, Meredith and Duncan.

"It started out under rather unfavorable circumstances," Mr. Duncan wrote, "but by hard work we managed to make both ends meet, barring a little deficit the members had to foot. But then the honor!

"That year we managed to get up a spicy paper generally. 'Sol' was excellent on locals, though sometimes he got off things not very suitable for a first-class paper, as for instance, the 'vegetable poetry' and the 'Ode to the Lady Hill.' Bob was a good writer, but inclined to be sarcastic. He could beat any of us on criticism. As for my own productions, about all they ever did was to get an invitation to spend an hour with Dr. Nutt . . .!"

Considering how those first editors struggled to select a name for the fledgling paper, it is interesting to note that over the years it kept the word Student but switched around the rest of the name at the fancy of the editors. In 1882 it was The Indiana Student, in 1894 it became The Student, then in 1898 it was Daily Student. It put The before the name in 1903, was back to The Indiana Student in 1912 and finally in 1914 settled down to The Indiana Daily Student.

—Marjorie Smith Blewett, BA 1948

THE INDIANA STUDENT.

VOL. I. INDIANA STATE UNIVERSITY. No. I.

BLOOMINGTON, FRIDAY, FEBRUARY 22, 1867.

The Indiana Student.

TERMS:

The Student will be furnished at the following rates:

Single copy, one college year (40 weeks)	$1 50
Single copy, one college year	0 50
Single numbers	0 10

☞ All orders should be addressed to "*The Indiana Student*, Bloomington, Indiana."

☞ Subscriptions invariably in advance.

A Want.—There is badly needed, at the present time, a walk from the campus gate to the college. Many of our citizens have been deterred from attending performances at the college, in consequence of the deep mud through which they were compelled to wade. This could be remedied at a small outlay, and should be attended to at once, if we desire to keep up our reputation; all it needs is some one to take hold and it can be put through. Who will make the move?

Serenade.—We had scarcely assumed the position of "quill driver," till we were honored with a serenade by the Bloomington String Band, which discoursed a "concord of sweet sounds" at our window, to the very great delight of all within. Come again; our window is always open.

How "The Indiana Student" was named.

THE idea having entered the fertile craniums of some of the more knowing ones of the students of Indiana University, that the public was sustaining a great loss from the non-existence of a literary magazine of some character, in which the genius and talents of these hopeful objects of the State's care and parental solicitude might be displayed; and this idea was the more indelibly impressed, in view of the fact that the citizens of Bloomington, though generally noted for their energy and enterprise, had not, as yet, succeeded in establishing an organ, in the columns of which, a student or literary man, who had any respect for himself or regard for his reputation as a writer, would be willing for his productions to appear. A meeting was accordingly convened in the office of a distinguished representative of the legal fraternity, in Bloomington, at which the following great literary lights were present: Hon. Henry J. Raymond, Geo. D. Prentice, Washington Irving, James Gordon Bennett, Andrew Johnson and Horace Greeley. The meeting was organized by calling Horace Greeley to the chair.

After a prolonged discussion on various topics, in which much learning, prophetic statesmanship and literary research were displayed, the chair announced that the first thing in order was to select a name for the paper, and suggested for the consideration of the meeting, the name of the "Bloomington Regulator," and urged as a reason for its adoption, that it would be one of its principal objects to regulate society, regulate literature, regulate students, regulate the faculty, regulate public exhibitions, regulate Bloomington; in short, it was to be a regulator in the fullest sense of the term. Washington Irving proposed the name of the "Prairie Flower," as it would indeed be a rare gem, and no doubt be highly prized by the young ladies. James Gordon Bennett proposed the name of "The Elevator;" for, said he, it will be the means of elevating everybody in general and ourselves in particular. Geo. D. Prentice proposed to call it the "Indiana Draw'-er," draw being a very popular word with certain classes, and the name would thereby be constituted an element to its success. Henry J. Raymond thought "The University Lightning Rod" exceedingly appropriate, as it would undoubtedly be the means of silently conducting all the superfluous gas generated in the fruitful craniums of certain "smart students," either to immortal glories in the skies, or perhaps, to its more appropriate place, the dominions of Pluto under the earth. His majesty, Andrew, earnestly insisted on the singular appellation of "My Policy Gazette," strenuously adhering to the principle that all "Big Things" are controlled by policy. The meeting was frequently interrupted by some disorderly persons who had assembled in the room immediately overhead, and just at this stage of the proceedings, the learned assembly was brought to a dead halt, by a deafening racket and confusion proceeding from the room in which said persons had congregated, and indicating that a regular midnight carousal of a "Host" of jolly "Good Tipplers," was being held. His majesty suggested that the interruption arose from a set of jolly fellows, his friends and boon companions, who were celebrating some important event over a bottle of inspiration, and moved that a committee of one be appointed to negotiate with them for a portion of their inspiration, as something of the kind was absolutely necessary to a successful accomplishment of the object of the meeting. The committee was about to proceed to perform his duty, when it occurred to Horace Greeley that the aforesaid disorderly persons were a camp of the Temperance Host and if the learned assembly depended for inspiration from that source, they would experience an exceedingly dry time of it indeed. The confusion having subsided, the meeting, with great mortification and disappointment, resumed its labors. A volume of names, both great and small, were proposed, such as "Collegian," "Review," "Banner," "Mirror," "Bummer," etc., and each rejected as inappropriate. After much deliberation it was agreed that it should be "The Indiana and something else," but as to what the something else should be no one could decide, until Henry J. Raymond, by a heroic stretch of imagination and herculean wielding of brain power, was delivered of the word "Student," which was unanimously adopted, and the author, for the wise sagacity, great foresight and transcendent genius displayed in originating this name, was subsequently elected one of its editors. The learned assembly having thus succeeded in its prime object, adjourned, and as the result, we have, appearing in flying colors, "*The Indiana Student.*"

Neile.

It is our intention, after the present issue, to double the size of our paper, if the patronage it receives at the hands of the public will justify us. This is to supply a need which has long been felt in our midst. If persons will take hold of the matter and aid us by their subscriptions, we promise to supply them with a first class college paper.

Marriage notices inserted free of charge. Students will please bear this in mind.

P0024018, IU Archives.

Indiana  Student.

VOL. 7. INDIANA STATE UNIVERSITY. No. 7.

Scribimus indocti doctique.

BLOOMINGTON, INDIANA, FEBRUARY 2, 1874.

TERMS:

[INVARIABLY IN ADVANCE.]

One copy, one year $2:00
One copy, one term, ... :75
Single Copy .... :05.

For a club of five outside of the University one copy will be given free.

RATES OF ADVERTISING:

¼ Column, one term .... $3 50.
⅛ Column, one term .... 2,00.
Card, one term .... 1 0?
Local Notices, per line, each insertion, ... 0.10

All business orders, communications intended for publication, exchanges, letters, etc., should be addressed to the *Indiana Student*, Bloomington, Ind.

AGASSIZ.

Not to his native Pays de Vaud,
Fringed with its Alpine glaciers wan;
Not to the footless peaks whose snow
Dazzled his childhood has he gone.

Not to the goatherd's gloaming call
Turned he to listen, ringing clear;
Not to the "*Ranz des Vaches*," of all
Strains most sweet to the Switzer's ear.

Tender the voice was, nor in vain
Ever to him its least behest:
"Tired out spirit, wearied brain,
Into my quiet come and rest."

Even as once our Poet said,
Long had he traversed paths untrod,
Finding in signs none else had read—
Many a hieroglyph of God.

Meekly from Nature's lips he learned,
Tracking her steps from shore to shore.
Secrets o'er which his soul had yearned,
Marvels she never had told before.

How at her hints his heart would stir,
Still on her shy suggestions bent,
Whether through seas he followed her,
Whether o'er breadths of continent.

Toilers for self might take the fame
Waiting to crown their toilings so;
Careless of ease, or wealth: or name,
All that *he* asked was leave *to know*!

So as he bowed with drooping head,
Patiently conning the tasks she set,
Softly the teacher stooped and said:
"Now that thou knowest thine alphabet

"Come from this narrow, cosmic rule,
Straitened through ignorance, blight, and curse.
Home to thy Father's grander school,
Into His boundless Universe."

[Selected.

Reminiscences of Indiana University.

Another misfortune befell the University in 1854. At midnight on the 15th of April, the citizens of Bloomington were awakened by the ringing of bells, and the cry of fire. On looking out, they were horrified at the sight of the main College Edifice enveloped in flames. The building was consumed with its entire contents, including a very valuable college library, and the libraries of the Literary Societies. In these libraries there were nearly ten thousand volumes. This was the darkest hour in the history of the University, for this calamity seemed irreparable. The most devoted friends of the University were ready to yield to despair, and give it up for lost. But, at length, better counsels prevailed; and it was resolved to continue the University, and to take immediate measures for the erection of a new building. Through the exertions of Dr. Daily and other members of the Faculty, and leading citizens, the people of Bloomington and Monroe county were induced to rally to her rescue. They came forward, and responded nobly in a subscription of ten thousand dollars, for the erection of a new building; and the remainder of the funds necessary for the completion of the edifice were borrowed from the Sinking Fund of the State of Indiana. Soon there arose upon the ruins of the old building one of the most beautiful and commodious college edifices, at that time, to be found in the West.

In the midst of these struggles, application was made to Congress for relief, by Gov. Joseph A. Wright and other leading men of Indiana. In response to this application, Congress donated to the University a quantity of public lands, equal in area to an entire Congressional township,—that is, twenty-three thousand and forty acres. These lands were to be selected from those belonging to the General Government in Indiana, and still remaining unsold, by commissioners appointed for this purpose. Hence these selections were made in different sections of the State. The General Assembly passed an act providing for the sale of these lands, and they were placed upon the market. From the proceeds of the sale of these lands, the endowment fund was increased from sixty thousand dollars to eighty thousand.

The following changes have taken place in the corps of instruction in the University since 1853. The Rev. Robert Milligan, A. M., filled the chair of Mathematics from 1852 to 1854, when he was transferred to the Professorship of Natural Science, which had been left vacant by the resignation of Rev. T. A. Wylie, A. M., who had accepted a similar Professorship in the Miami University, at Oxford, Ohio. The Rev. Elisha Ballantine, A. M., of Richmond, Va., was elected to the chair of Mathematics. In 1856, Daniel Read, LL. D. resigned the chair of Ancient Languages to take charge of a Professorship in the Wisconsin University at Madison; and Prof. Ballantine was transferred to the chair of Ancient Languages, and Daniel Kirkwood, LL. D., who at that time was President of Delaware College, was elected to the Professorship of Mathematics and Civil Engineering. Professor Milligan having resigned in 1855, Rev. T. A. Wylie, A. M., who had been absent two years, filling the Professorship of Natural Science in the Miami University, Ohio, was re-elected to his old chair of Natural Philosophy and Chemistry, and immediately entered upon the duties of his professorship.

The Faculty, as thus organized in 1856, continued unchanged for nearly three years. They were as follows:—Rev. Wm. M. Daily, D. D., LL. D., President, and Professor of Mental and Moral Philosophy and Belles Lettres. Rev. T. A. Wylie, Professor of Natural Philosophy and Chemistry. Rev. Elisha Ballantine, A. M., Professor of Ancient Languages. Daniel Kirkwood, LL. D., Professor of Mathematics. Jas. Woodburn, A. M. Preceptor of the Preparatory Department.

On the 1st of January, 1859, Dr. Daily resigned the Presidency of the University; and Professor T. A. Wylie, A. M., took charge of the institution as Acting President until July following; when the Trustees elected John H. Lathrop, LL. D., who had, for several years been Chancellor of the Wisconsin University, but at the time of his election he was discharging the duties of a Professor in that institution. From the beginning, up to this period in the History of the University, the duty of Lecturing each Sabbath afternoon devolved upon the President. But as Dr. J. H. Lathrop was not a minister, he found this duty too burdensome, and desired to be relieved from it. The Trustees accordingly established another Professorship, called the Chair of English Literature, and elected Rev. Henry B. Hibben, A. M, to that chair, with the understanding that he would be responsible for the Sabbath Lectures. These duties Professor Hibben performed until July, 1860.

At the Commencement in July, 1860, Dr. Lathrop was inaugurated as President, and immediately tendered his resignation, which was accepted. The reason why Dr. Lathrop resigned at the time he did, was the fact that he had just been elected to the Professorship of English Literature, in the University of Missouri, at a salary of two thousand dollars per annum; whereas, at Bloomington, in the Indiana State University, it was only fourteen hundred. The vacancy thus created was filled by the election of the Rev. Cyrus Nutt, D. D., who had been Acting President of Asbury University for two years, and was then Professor of Mathematics in that institution. Dr. Nutt accepted the Presidency thus tendered him, and entered immediately upon the discharge of the duties of his office.

[To be continued.]

The Scientists.—Scientific men are around with trowels, knives, saws, and hammers, experimenting. As long as they dig into the ground or break chunks from boulders there is no particular harm done. But some of them cut off cat's tails to see what they are made of, and lift off the tops of dog's heads to see their brains beat. This is a very interesting performance, to the scientific chaps, and would probably afford a great deal of wholesome recreation to the dogs and cats were they not unhappily prejudiced. An aged agriculturist from Stony Hill, told us this morning that he saw a dog stumble while running across a field, and that the top of its head flew off, and rolled into a hole and was lost. He went over and examined the animal and found that this piece had been sawed off, and stuck on again in a bungling manner, with the result recorded. The dog died before he could find the piece. Something still more remarkable than this is the saving of a dead man by replacing his brain with one taken from a live man. The man who thus gave up his brain not only refused to take three pairs of gate hinges and a screw driver for his intellect, but obligingly held a candle while the operation was going on. Country people who take scientific men for boarders should enclose their heads with hoop iron before going to bed.—*Ex.*

Go and see a Photograph of Dubuf's "Prodigal Son," at the Book Store.

P0079384, IU Archives.

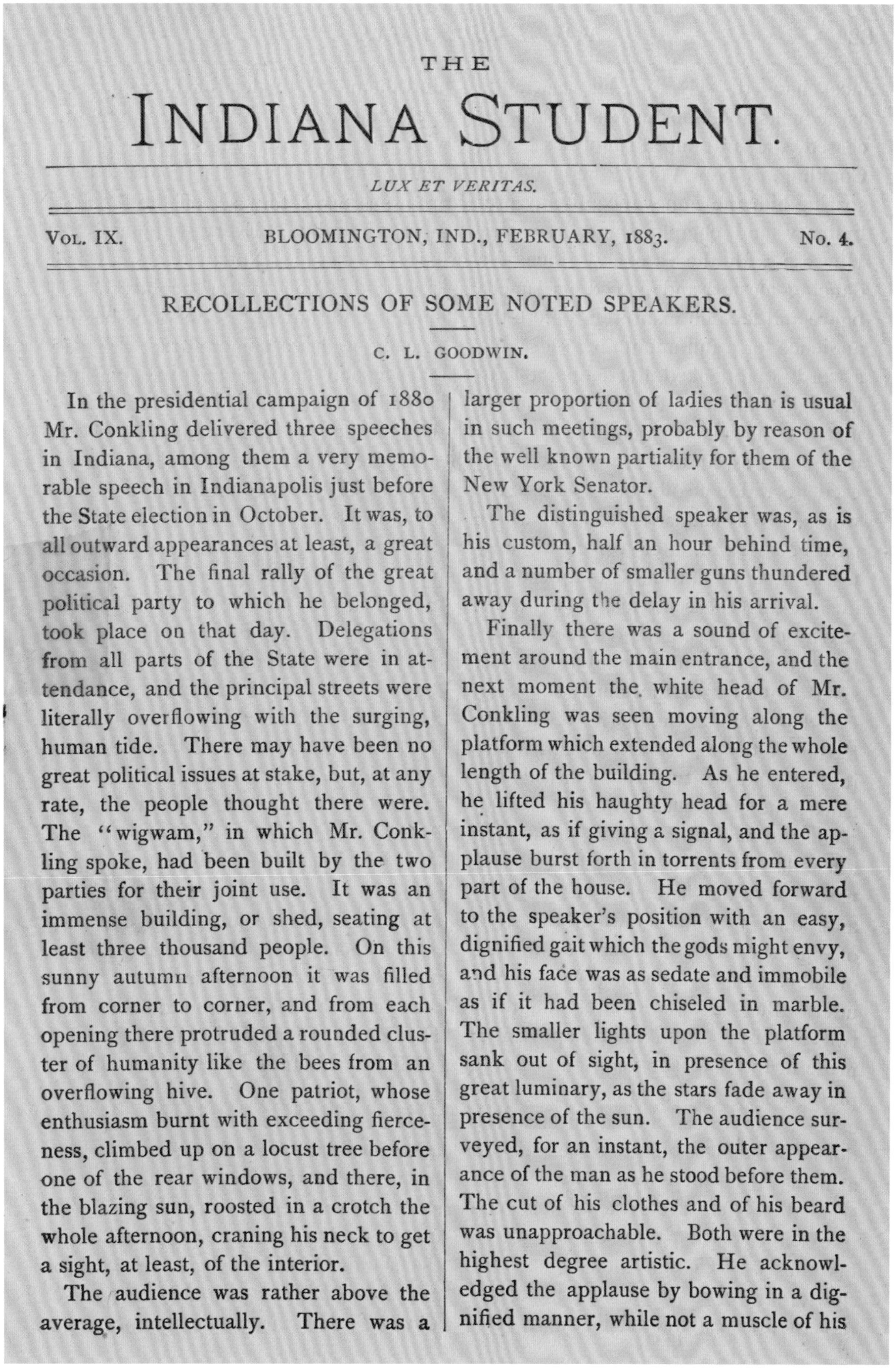

THE

INDIANA STUDENT.

LUX ET VERITAS.

VOL. IX. BLOOMINGTON, IND., FEBRUARY, 1883. No. 4.

RECOLLECTIONS OF SOME NOTED SPEAKERS.

C. L. GOODWIN.

In the presidential campaign of 1880 Mr. Conkling delivered three speeches in Indiana, among them a very memorable speech in Indianapolis just before the State election in October. It was, to all outward appearances at least, a great occasion. The final rally of the great political party to which he belonged, took place on that day. Delegations from all parts of the State were in attendance, and the principal streets were literally overflowing with the surging, human tide. There may have been no great political issues at stake, but, at any rate, the people thought there were. The "wigwam," in which Mr. Conkling spoke, had been built by the two parties for their joint use. It was an immense building, or shed, seating at least three thousand people. On this sunny autumn afternoon it was filled from corner to corner, and from each opening there protruded a rounded cluster of humanity like the bees from an overflowing hive. One patriot, whose enthusiasm burnt with exceeding fierceness, climbed up on a locust tree before one of the rear windows, and there, in the blazing sun, roosted in a crotch the whole afternoon, craning his neck to get a sight, at least, of the interior.

The audience was rather above the average, intellectually. There was a larger proportion of ladies than is usual in such meetings, probably by reason of the well known partiality for them of the New York Senator.

The distinguished speaker was, as is his custom, half an hour behind time, and a number of smaller guns thundered away during the delay in his arrival.

Finally there was a sound of excitement around the main entrance, and the next moment the white head of Mr. Conkling was seen moving along the platform which extended along the whole length of the building. As he entered, he lifted his haughty head for a mere instant, as if giving a signal, and the applause burst forth in torrents from every part of the house. He moved forward to the speaker's position with an easy, dignified gait which the gods might envy, and his face was as sedate and immobile as if it had been chiseled in marble. The smaller lights upon the platform sank out of sight, in presence of this great luminary, as the stars fade away in presence of the sun. The audience surveyed, for an instant, the outer appearance of the man as he stood before them. The cut of his clothes and of his beard was unapproachable. Both were in the highest degree artistic. He acknowledged the applause by bowing in a dignified manner, while not a muscle of his

P0068158, IU Archives.

THE

INDIANA STUDENT.

LUX ET VERITAS.

VOL. IX. BLOOMINGTON, IND., MAY, 1883. No. 7

COLLEGE DAYS.

'83.

Soft and low,
  Come and go,
Dreamy and sad they flow,
  Out of the past,
Into the past,
  Notes of the long ago.

Passing along,
  Last of the throng,
To memory's sacred care,
  Ye college days,
Taking your ways,
  Gently and sadly there,

Ill or well,
  The future will tell
How we have used you here.
  Happy or sad,
You shall make us glad,
  Happy or sad, you are dear.

O, golden days,
  Into the ways
Of truth, your light has shone.
  Light us the way
Unto the day,
  When the Unknown is known.

P0079385, IU Archives.

Infant IDS Lives Again as Dr. Bryan Reminisces

This story originally appeared Oct. 10, 1954, to mark the formal dedication of Ernie Pyle Hall as the new home of IU's School of Journalism.

By Ginny Krause

The "Grand Old Man of The Student" (and of Indiana University)—President-Emeritus William Lowe Bryan—brought memories to life this week as he reminisced of his own newspapering days.

Some 70 years have passed since President Bryan (he'll be 94 on Nov. 11) was editor of The Indiana Student. That was in 1882–'84, but you forgot you weren't there—as he vividly described the "revival" days of the campus paper.

On Feb. 22, 1867 (as all who ever passed a news quiz know), The Student first appeared, with Sol Meredith and Robert Richardson as editors. It continued to publish monthly under auspices of the junior and senior classes. And then, in 1875, publication stopped.

Dr. Bryan, backgrounding the reason for the breakdown, said that "President Moss, who headed the University from 1875 to 1883, was in many respects a great man, but he had a different idea of education than most." President Moss felt I.U. should be a school of arts, and no more.

"President Moss was a great preacher," Dr. Bryan said, "but preaching alone doesn't accomplish anything."

Dr. Bryan smiled, as if remembering, then continued: "Something happened in 1882 which changed things at Indiana University. And that something was—Clarence L. Goodwin, who had arrived from Butler as a junior in 1881. He brought with him the courage and conviction to start news things. And since reawakening the professional schools would have been a bit out line for him as a student, he brought baseball, The Student, and a lecture bureau to the campus."

At this time W.L. Bryan was teaching in Virginia.

"Had I stayed on campus," he reflected, "I would have been a junior. I also was busy working on a Virginia country weekly—setting type." And with a twinkle in his eyes, he related how he "set up half the paper one week when the boss was away and printed it. This should almost make me eligible for Sigma Delta Chi, don't you think?" (Incidentally, President Bryan was initiated by the Indiana chapter on March 17, 1928.)

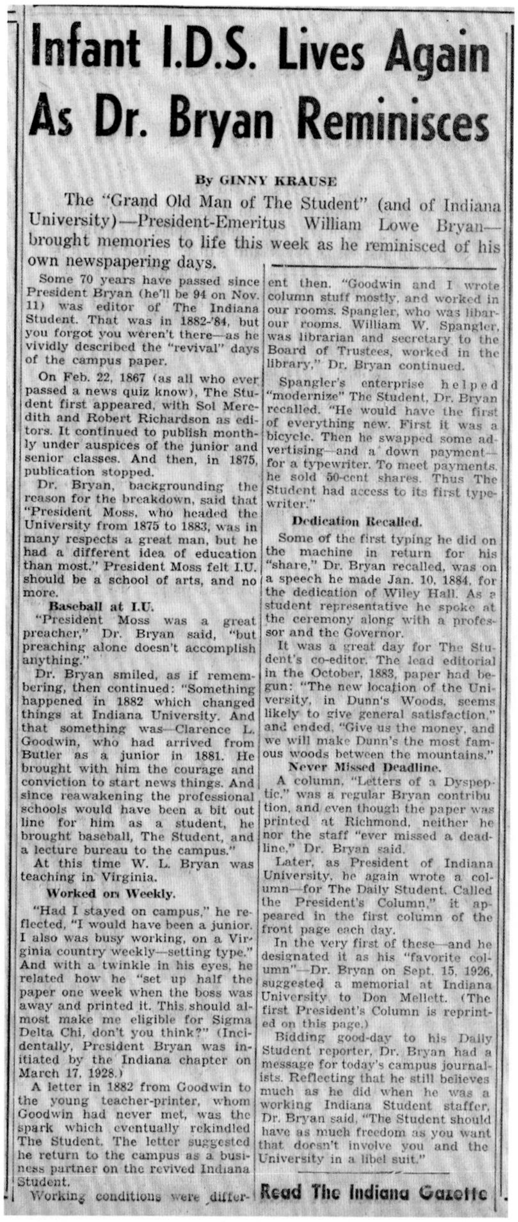

Infant I.D.S. Lives Again As Dr. Bryan Reminisces

By GINNY KRAUSE

The "Grand Old Man of The Student" (and of Indiana University)—President-Emeritus William Lowe Bryan—brought memories to life this week as he reminisced of his own newspapering days.

Some 70 years have passed since President Bryan (he'll be 94 on Nov. 11) was editor of The Indiana Student. That was in 1882-'84, but you forgot you weren't there—as he vividly described the "revival" days of the campus paper.

On Feb. 22, 1867 (as all who ever passed a news quiz know), The Student first appeared, with Sol Meredith and Robert Richardson as editors. It continued to publish monthly under auspices of the junior and senior classes. And then, in 1875, publication stopped.

Dr. Bryan, backgrounding the reason for the breakdown, said that "President Moss, who headed the University from 1875 to 1883, was in many respects a great man, but he had a different idea of education than most." President Moss felt I.U. should be a school of arts, and no more.

Baseball at I.U.

"President Moss was a great preacher," Dr. Bryan said, "but preaching alone doesn't accomplish anything."

Dr. Bryan smiled, as if remembering, then continued: "Something happened in 1882 which changed things at Indiana University. And that something was—Clarence L. Goodwin, who had arrived from Butler as a junior in 1881. He brought with him the courage and conviction to start news things. And since reawakening the professional schools would have been a bit out line for him as a student, he brought baseball, The Student, and a lecture bureau to the campus."

At this time W. L. Bryan was teaching in Virginia.

Worked on Weekly.

"Had I stayed on campus," he reflected, "I would have been a junior. I also was busy working, on a Virginia country weekly—setting type." And with a twinkle in his eyes, he related how he "set up half the paper one week when the boss was away and printed it. This should almost make me eligible for Sigma Delta Chi, don't you think?" (Incidentally, President Bryan was initiated by the Indiana chapter on March 17, 1928.)

A letter in 1882 from Goodwin to the young teacher-printer, whom Goodwin had never met, was the spark which eventually rekindled The Student. The letter suggested he return to the campus as a business partner on the revived Indiana Student.

Working conditions were different then. "Goodwin and I wrote column stuff mostly, and worked in our rooms. Spangler, who was libarour rooms. William W. Spangler, was librarian and secretary to the Board of Trustees, worked in the library," Dr. Bryan continued.

Spangler's enterprise helped "modernize" The Student, Dr. Bryan recalled. "He would have the first of everything new. First it was a bicycle. Then he swapped some advertising—and a down payment—for a typewriter. To meet payments, he sold 50-cent shares. Thus The Student had access to its first typewriter."

Dedication Recalled.

Some of the first typing he did on the machine in return for his "share," Dr. Bryan recalled, was on a speech he made Jan. 10, 1884, for the dedication of Wiley Hall. As a student representative he spoke at the ceremony along with a professor and the Governor.

It was a great day for The Student's co-editor. The lead editorial in the October, 1883, paper had begun: "The new location of the University, in Dunn's Woods, seems likely to give general satisfaction," and ended, "Give us the money, and we will make Dunn's the most famous woods between the mountains."

Never Missed Deadline.

A column, "Letters of a Dyspeptic," was a regular Bryan contribution, and even though the paper was printed at Richmond, neither he nor the staff "ever missed a deadline," Dr. Bryan said.

Later, as President of Indiana University, he again wrote a column—for The Daily Student. Called the President's Column," it appeared in the first column of the front page each day.

In the very first of these—and he designated it as his "favorite column"—Dr. Bryan on Sept. 15, 1926, suggested a memorial at Indiana University to Don Mellett. (The first President's Column is reprinted on this page.)

Bidding good-day to his Daily Student reporter, Dr. Bryan had a message for today's campus journalists. Reflecting that he still believes much as he did when he was a working Indiana Student staffer, Dr. Bryan said, "The Student should have as much freedom as you want that doesn't involve you and the University in a libel suit."

Read The Indiana Gazette

P0079415, IU Archives.

William Lowe Bryan presents a photo of Clarence LaRue Goodwin to the president of Sigma Delta Chi. Together, Bryan and Goodwin rekindled the IDS. *P0033451, IU Archives.*

A letter in 1882 from Goodwin to the young teacher-printer, whom Goodwin had never met, was the spark which eventually rekindled The Student. The letter suggested he return to the campus as a business partner on the revived Indiana Student.

Working conditions were different then. "Goodwin and I wrote column stuff mostly, and worked in our rooms. Spangler, who was librarian and secretary to the Board of Trustees, worked in the library," Dr. Bryan continued.

Spangler's enterprise helped "modernize" The Student, Dr. Bryan recalled. "He would have the first of everything new. First it was a bicycle. Then he swapped some advertising—and a down payment—for a typewriter. To meet payments, he sold 50-cent shares. Thus, The Student had access to its first typewriter."

Some of the first typing he did on the machine in return for his "share," Dr. Bryan recalled, was on a speech he made Jan. 10, 1884, for the dedication of Wiley Hall. As a student representative he spoke at the ceremony along with a professor and the Governor.

It was a great day for The Student co-editor. The lead editorial in the October, 1883, paper had begun. "The new location of the University, in Dunn's Woods, seems likely to give general satisfaction," and ended, "Give us the money, and we will make Dunn's the most famous woods between the mountains."

A column "Letters of a Dyspeptic," was a regular Bryan contribution, and even though

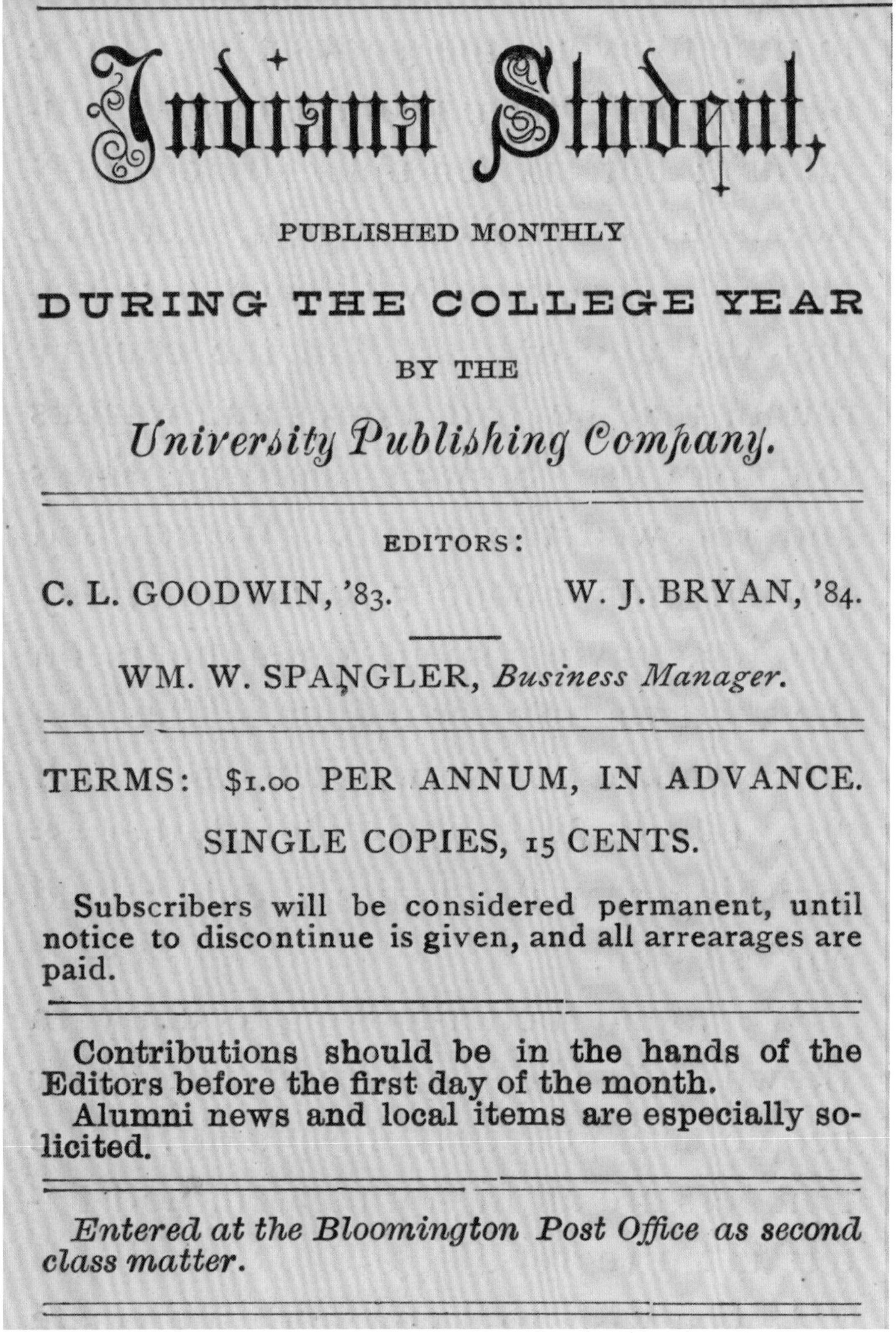

Indiana Student,

PUBLISHED MONTHLY

DURING THE COLLEGE YEAR

BY THE

University Publishing Company.

EDITORS:

C. L. GOODWIN, '83. W. J. BRYAN, '84.

WM. W. SPANGLER, *Business Manager.*

TERMS: $1.00 PER ANNUM, IN ADVANCE.

SINGLE COPIES, 15 CENTS.

Subscribers will be considered permanent, until notice to discontinue is given, and all arrearages are paid.

Contributions should be in the hands of the Editors before the first day of the month.
Alumni news and local items are especially solicited.

Entered at the Bloomington Post Office as second class matter.

IDS masthead, 1884.
P0080202, IU Archives.

"The Student should have as much freedom as you want that doesn't involve you and the university in a libel suit."

the paper was printed at Richmond, neither he nor the staff "ever missed a deadline," Dr. Bryan said.

Later, as President of Indiana University, he again wrote a column—for The Daily Student. Called the "President's Column," it appeared in the first column of the front page each day.

In the very first of these—and he designated it as his "favorite column"—Dr. Bryan on Sept. 15, 1926, suggested a memorial at Indiana University to Don Mellett.

Bidding a good-day to his Daily Student reporter, Dr. Bryan had a message for today's campus journalists. Reflecting that he still believes much as he did when he was a working Indiana Student staffer, Bryan said, "The Student should have as much freedom as you want that doesn't involve you and the University in a libel suit."

THE

INDIANA STUDENT.

LUX ET VERITAS.

VOL. IX. BLOOMINGTON, IND., JUNE, 1883. NO. 8.

A RECORD OF THE COMMENCEMENT OF '83.

Commencement is the gala day of the college world. If there is anything worth while recording, it must be this. If there is any field for a college journal to occupy it is here. And so while papers, broad and small, have flapped their printed wings a little over it, it remains for us to prepare this moderately full account of this Commencement, and dedicate it to the CLASS OF '83.

THURSDAY, JUNE 7th.

The festivities began with the following programme:

FIRST ANNUAL EXHIBITION OF INDIANA UNIVERSITY SCIENTIFIC SOCIETY.

"Mazurka de Kew," *Shuloff*—Mrs. A. Armagnac.

The Ferments - F. W. Cook, Jr., Evansville, Indiana.

Evolution of the Vertebrates—G. B. Kalb, Bellefontaine, Ohio.

"Playful Rockets"—Cook Bro's, Evansville, Indiana.

Methods of Teaching Chemistry—Lizzie Long, Columbus, Indiana.

The Senior Tramp—C. L. Goodwin, Bowling Green, Ky.

There was no attempt to give a conventionally "fine performance." Our Universatory laboratories are full of young men and women, who are pushing forward with rapid strides into the fore-front of the various departments of Science. A candid examination of the actual work done, and the opportunities offered would show, that they are not anywhere excelled. This exhibition attempted simply to represent this department, and the attempt was successful. Mr. Goodwin's account of the Senior Tramp appears in the STUDENT.

THE SENIOR TRAMP.

C. L. GOODWIN.

What I shall say of the Senior tramp in Kentucky and Tennessee will necessarily be from a somewhat personal standpoint. I wish to be understood as speaking for the whole party, and if any member of the party does not like it, I can't help it. He or she will have to settle it with me afterwards.

There will doubtless be things omitted from this account that ought to have been put in, and things put in that ought to have been omitted. The best accounts of the social features of the trip will be found perhaps in the note books of the young ladies.

Moffett could best present the political part of it, Stevenson the theological, and Swain the scientific.

The present account cannot be classified either as "fish, fowl or flesh" but a

P0079386, IU Archives.

THE

INDIANA STUDENT.

LUX ET VERITAS.

VOL. IX. BLOOMINGTON, IND., SEPTEMBER, 1883. NO. 9.

How shall we compass the largeness of our calamity? If it were simply a matter of bricks and plaster, we could count the dollars which it cost to buy them and build them into the house we know. If it were only a question of temporary inconvenience in college work, we could count the days until a worthier building should rise above the ashes of this. But when we try to estimate the total measure of this disaster, we forget the shell, comely as it was, and think only of the treasures within. Here is the scientist's rosary. These are the beads with which science prays. These books are the walls of the student's sanctuary. God struck them with his red staff, and called to them out of the thunder, and they are gone. Let us be still.

P0079388, IU Archives.

THE

INDIANA STUDENT.

LUX ET VERITAS.

VOL. XIII. BLOOMINGTON, IND., MAY 16, 1887. No. 12

ONE DAY AT INDIANA UNIVERSITY.

[A LETTER TO THE EDITOR OF THE INDIANAPOLIS JOURNAL.]

The people of Indiana feel pride in all its institutions. They are proud of its wealth; of its rich mines; of its fertile fields; of its diversified productions of the farm and factory; proud of the prowess of its soldiers in war and of the love of law and order of its citizens in peace. They are proud of the nice balance of parties which is so sensitive that at no time in the last thirty years has any party leadership defied the people's moral sense, their convictions of political right, without being rebuked by political overthrow at the next ensuing election. They are proud, too, of its achievements in literature and science; of its scholars and poets; of the line of eminent statesmen, who, from the admission of the State into the Union, have at all times occupied the front rank as patriots, as leaders, orators, and jurists. They are proud of the unequaled prudence of management which has secured to the State the largest common school fund of any state in the Union; and they are proud of a system of common schools of unsurpassed excellence.

But in the wise and comprehensive policy adopted by the fathers, it would be too much to expect that no mistake should be made; it would be surprising, indeed, if no improvement could be hoped for in any direction. Connecticut has Yale; Massachusetts, Harvard; Michigan, Ann Arbor; New Jersey, Princeton, and each of these institutions chiefly owes its greatness to the generous, fostering care with which the State or its people, or both, have augmented its resources, sustained its efforts, and bestowed upon it patronage. Indiana, too, has its State University, of which its people have a right to be proud; not, indeed, for the size and number of its buildings, for they are too small and too few, but which, nevertheless, well merits the patronage of the State and the generous support of the people.

Would it be too harsh a criticism to be made by one who shares in the common civic pride of the great Commonwealth, that in the past the State benefactions have lost their best effects by too great diffusion? Would it be too much to say that it would promote the interests of higher education, of riper

P0079390, IU Archives.

The Indiana Student.

VOL. XVI. BLOOMINGTON, INDIANA, APRIL, 1890. No. 7

The Indiana Student.

Published Monthly during College Year

EDITORS AND BUSINESS MANAGERS.

WALTER W. FRENCH, '91. EDWARD O'DONNELL, '90

ASSOCIATE EDITORS.

H. W. MONICAL, '90.	WATSON NICHOLSON, '91.
JOHN A. MILLER, '90.	MINNIE FARIS, '91.
ELLA CORR, '90.	NED DYE, '91.
C. S. THOMAS, '91.	JOSEPH GILES, '94.

TERMS:—$1.00 per annum, in advance; $1.25 if not paid within three months. Single copies 15 cents.

SUBSCRIBERS and local advertisers will be considered permanent until notice to discontinue is given, and all arrears are paid

CONTRIBUTIONS should be in the hands of the editors before the first of the month. Alumni news and local items are especially solicited.

Entered at the Bloomington Post Office as second-class matter.

IT HAS not been the custom of THE STUDENT this year to criticise. We have refrained from it because we know that complaining people are always disagreeable. But occasionally we see some things that greatly tempt us to express a modest opinion through our columns. College students are not expected to be perfection in refinement and culture but they are expected to approach somewhat nearer to it on all occasions and under all circumstances than a crowd of barbarians. It has been the source of a feeling of disgust to many this year that a certain few of our students have seen fit to make themselves very conspicuous at some of the entertainments given at the Chapel by taking a back seat and guying the performers, keeping up a hideous noise with hands and feet and whistling and yelling. There is nothing so utterly unbearable and disgusting. It is not to be looked upon as a joke or as fun. It is the extreme of rudeness and undoubtedly shows a lack of culture and refinement.

Whoever goes to an entertainment for the purpose of being entertained and of behaving himself has a perfect right to be there. But if he goes for the express purpose of creating a disturbance and of embarassing the performers he had better stay at home.

Such conduct may have been considered all right once. But college society has developed into something higher and better. Now it is considered rude and ungentlemanly and should not be tolerated. It is to be hoped that it will not be practiced any more.

THE State oratorical contest was held at Indianapolis on April 11. Each college sent in quite a large delegation and the hotel corridors were crowded with college students. The annual meeting of the Oratorical association was held on the afternoon of the 11th at the New Dennison hotel. The most interesting matter before the convention was the re-admission of Indiana University to the State association. This was accomplished without any opposition though there was some anticipated. The University being admitted her delegates were allowed to participate in the work of the convention. Several minor changes were made in the constitution. The following officers were elected:—

President—A. E. Wiggam, Hanover.

Vice-President—F. C. Brewer, Wabash.

Treasurer—C. S. Thomas, State University.

Recording Secretary—R. P. Davidson, Butler.

Corresponding Secretary—E. L. Hendricks, Franklin.

P0069137, IU Archives.

Above, Florence Myrick (center, in chair) and the IDS staff, 1897. *P0021542, IU Archives.*

Below, IDS masthead, Dec. 4, 1897. *P0080198, IU Archives.*

Facing, P0080154, IU Archives.

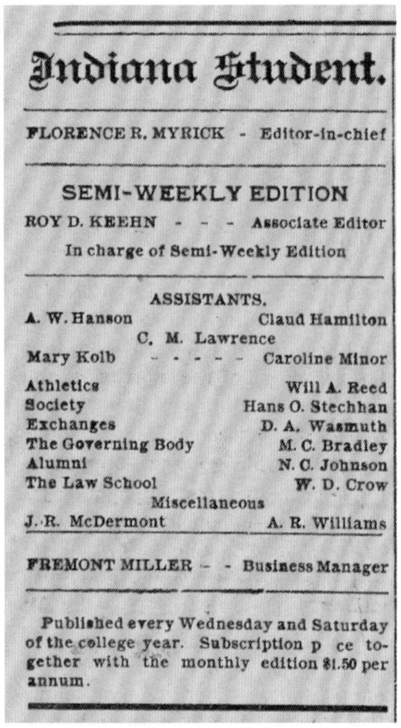

Indiana Student.

FLORENCE R. MYRICK - Editor-in-chief

SEMI-WEEKLY EDITION

ROY D. KEEHN - - - Associate Editor

In charge of Semi-Weekly Edition

ASSISTANTS.

A. W. Hanson Claud Hamilton

C. M. Lawrence

Mary Kolb - - - - - Caroline Minor

Athletics Will A. Reed

Society Hans O. Stechhan

Exchanges D. A. Wasmuth

The Governing Body M. C. Bradley

Alumni N. C. Johnson

The Law School W. D. Crow

Miscellaneous

J. R. McDermont A. R. Williams

FREMONT MILLER - - Business Manager

Published every Wednesday and Saturday of the college year. Subscription p ce together with the monthly edition $1.50 per annum.

PROFILE

Florence Myrick Ahl, BA 1899
First Female Editor in Chief of the IDS, 1897

When the IU School of Journalism marked its centennial in 2011 by creating the Distinguished Alumni Award, Florence Myrick Ahl, the first female editor in chief of the IDS, was inducted in the inaugural class of honorees. This remembrance is reprinted from the Distinguished Alumni Award program.

In 1897, Florence Reid Myrick became the first woman editor in chief of The Student, the forerunner of the Indiana Daily Student. She graduated in 1899 with a degree in English. She was a member of the Kappa Alpha Theta sorority.

After graduation, she married Thomas Ahl, and together they reared five children. In 1916, the Indiana University Alumni Quarterly published a class note about Ahl, quoting from a letter she had sent with a submission to the university's Register of Graduates. "Observe I have left occupation unfilled," she wrote. "I have five children, ranging from 12 to 21 months. I do all my own work. Somehow there seems no adequate term to describe my occupation."

Yet Ahl and her husband both were community leaders in Centerville, Indiana, near Richmond. Thomas was active in Wayne County Republican politics, and Florence was founder and for many years board president of the Centerville Public Library. She was president of the Centerville Woman's Club; a charter member of the Collegiate Club; and chair of the county flower show. Her obituary even made note of her garden as "one of the show places of Centerville."

And her interest in writing and news apparently continued. She was a charter member of the local chapter of the Scribblers, a women's club whose members were authors and newspaper writers.

Ahl died in 1946.

The Student.

VOLUME XXIII. INDIANA UNIVERSITY, NOVEMBER 20, 1897. NO. 17

PICTURES IN LIBRARY HALL

Of Men Once Promitently Connected with Indiana University.

Probably not one student out of every twenty now attending Indiana University can tell anything about the great men of the University whose pictures are now hanging upon the walls of the Library. For the benefit of the student body therefore we give a short account of the lives of these men.

The first picture, just above the European History Reserve shelves, is that of Dr. Richard Dale Owen. who was Professor of Natural Science from 1863 till 1878. He was born near New Lanark, Scotland, Jan. 6, 1810 and received his early education under a tutor, later at the Grammar School, Old Lanark. He spent three years studying at Halfwyl, Switzerland sailing for America with his father in 1897. He received his certificates of citizenship from Gen. Willliam H. Harrison He served in both the Mexican and Civil wars but resigned his Lieutenant Colonelship in 1863 and accepted a professorship in Indiana University, Between the Mexican and Civil Wars he was Professor of Natural Science in the Western Military Institute of Kentudky. From 1863 to 1867 he was Professor of Natural Philosopy and Chemistry, from 1857 to 1879, Professor of Natural Science. During this time he taught principally Geology, Mineralogy, and Chemistry but on account of a vacancy in the Modern Language Department, he taught German and French for a time. . He was assistant to his brother, David Dale Owen, in the U.S. Geological Survey of Minnesota, 1859—60. He also made a Geological survey of Indiana and some Geological examinations, of New Mexico, Arizona, North Carolina and Tennessee. He contributed largely to periodicals after his resignation in 1897. A religious spirit was always manifested by him, due to his mother's influence, but his father's scepticism and opposition to christianity had some effect upon him. While in Bloomington he became a member of the Presbyterian Church.

He died March 25, 1890, at his home in New Harmony from poison taken accidentally while engaged in Philosophical studies.

The next picture is that of the first president of Indiana University, Dr. Andrew Wylie. He was born in Western Pennsylvania, April 12, 1789.

He was accustomed to hard farm work when a boy and received a common school education at times when he could best be spared from the farm. For a number of years he farmed and spent his evenings in hard study. At the age of fifteen he entered Jefferson College, Cannonsburg, defraying his expenses by teaching, and passed through with great honors, graduating in 1810 with first honors. Immediately upon . graduation, he was elected tutor and a year later, president of the college by a unanimous choice of the trustees.

In 1817, he accepted the presidency of Washington college, Washington, Penn., and in 1829, was called to the presidency of Indiana University.

He had two characteristics of a good teacher;—learning and the power to communicate it to his students. As a writer he was clear and terse, shown by his Baccalaureates and published writings. He published a treatise, "Sectarianism is Heresy,"an"English Grammer," and some translations from Plato. He died Nov. 11, 1851.

The third picture on this wall is of Theophilus Adam Wylie. He was born Oct. 8, 1810, in Philadelphia, Pa. His early education was received in the English Academy of Dr. S. W. Crawford, his classical education in the school of Wylie and Engles, Philadelphia. He entered the Junior class of the University of Pennsylvania at its reorganization in 1828. His father was elected Professor of Languages at the same time. He graduated in 1830 receiving the degrees of A. B. and A. M. In 1836 he was offered the professorship of Natural Philosophy in Indiana University In 1852 he accepted the professorship at Miami University, but two and a half years later he returned to Indiana University and taught languages for a time. His active service continued till 1886 when he received the honorary title "Emeritry." He receivea the degree of D. D. from Miami University, Monmouth, and Princeton and L. L. D. from the University of Pennsylvania. His death occured in the summer of 1895.

The picture of Elisha Ballantine is placed above the door of the Seminary room. He was born Oct. 11, 1809, at Schodack Landing on the Hudson, N. Y. He was well trained at home, in the primary school, and the University, In 1828 he graduated from Ohio University, at Athens, Ohio and studied at Union Theological Seminary, Va. In 1834-35 he studied at Halle and Leipsic, Germany.

His life was spent in the service of the church and education. From 1840 to '43 he had charge of a congregation in Prince Edward county Va., and from 1848 to '52 was pastor of the First Presbyterian Church in Washington D. C. In 1850 he was elected Professor of Mathematics in Indiana University and two years after to the chair of Languages. In 1863 he resigned and accepted the position of Secretary of the American Board of Foreign Missions. In 1866 he was Professor of Hebrew in Lane University, Cincinnatti, O In 1867, he returned to Indiana as Professor of Greek. From that time till his death he was connected with the University as Professor and Professor Emeritus. He was highly esteemed by all who knew him and came as near having a faultless character as any of the human family. He stood in the first rank as a literary man and a scholar. He resigned his professorship in 1878 but in 1884, on the resignation of Dr. Moss, the acting President, Dr. Jordan was chosen to fill the vacancy and Prof. Ballantine was made vice-president and Professor of Greek. These positions he held till his death, March 31, 1886. On that morning he conducted chapel exercises as usual. While engaged in his usual work in the garden in the afternoon he was taken suddenly ill, retired to the house where he died in the presence of only his daughters.

The picture in the middle of the rear wall is of James Darwin Maxwell, who was a trustee of the University from 1858-1892. He was born, May 19, 1815, at Hanover, Ind., and graduated from the University with the degrees A. B. and A. M. He received his M. D. degree from Jefferson Medical College, Philadelphia. In 1836 he taught in Mississippi College. Returning to Bloomington he studied and practised medicine with his father. He was Secretary and President of the Board during his services for the University.

The third picture on this wall is that of probably the best known man of them all, Daniel Kirkwood. He was born in Hartford Co., Maryland, Sept. 27, 1814. In 1834 he attended an academy at York, Pa., and afterwards taught there. He removed to Lancester, Pa. and was Principal of the High School for some time. In 1839 he was Principal of the Pottsville Academy and it was while here that his "Analogy in the Periods of Rotation of the Primary Planets" was first published, bringing him into prominent notice both in this country and Europe. In 1851, he was chosen President of Delaware College, Newark, Del., and in 1856 was selected Professor of Mathematics in Indiana University, which position he held till 1886, excepting two years during which time he was at Jefferson College, Cannonsburg, Pa., in charge of Mathematics and Astronomy. He was a frequent contributor to scientific journals and in 1851 was made a member of the American Philosophical Society. He has published a number of papers on Astronomy all of which are held in highest regard by authorities. In 1886 he resigned and received the title of Emeritus Professor. He removed with his wife to Riverside, Cal., in 1886 where he died in the summer of 1895.

List of Students—1897

(With Bloomington and Home Addresses)
By M. C. BRADLEY.
(Continued from last issue.)

Curry, John A. 420 W 5th, Farmersburg.
Curtis, Geo Wm, Mt. Vernon.
Dailey, Chas Gutelius, 110 E 4th, Bluffton
Damand, Dottie Ann, E 3rd, Swan
Davis, Chas Gideon, 315 E 6th, Sheridan,
Davis, Edward Sherman, 402 N Lincoln, Gosport
Davis, Edward Wolfe, 209. E 5th, Rising Sun
Davis, Exum Woodard, 410 W 2nd, Elizabethtown.
Davis, Lissa, 410 W 2nd, Elizabethtown
Davis, Maud Helen, 315 E 6th, Thorntown
Davis, Thomas Johnson, 331, S Grant, Ft Wayne
Dewalt, Eva M, 3.0, N Walnut, Salem
Dewalt, Nora Ethel, 309 N Walnut, Salem
DeBruler, Geo Riley, 400 E 5th, Evansville
Deist, Henry Conrad, 710 Atwater Ave, Bloomington
Delay, Dora Carver, E Atwater Ave, Lima
Denny, Wingfield Aug, 8th and Lincoln, Campbellsburg
Derbyshire, Grant Ellsworth, 523 E Smith Ave, Cowans
Dickey, Chas Milton, 342 S Walnut, Tipton
Dickey, Harry Spence, 342 S Walnut, Tipton
Dill, Georgiana, 322 E 4th, Bloomington
Dillon, Wm J, 315 E 5th, Elnora
Dinsmore, Wylie N, Bloomington
Doddridge, Geo, 414 S College Ave. Bloomington
Dodds, Flora E, W Third, Bloomington
Dodge, Jamie Sayre, 323 S Grant, Elkhart
Dodson, John Christian, 415 E 2nd, Tell City
Donnellson, Chas A, 402 N Lincoln, Orleans
Duff, Raymond Battman, 210 E 4th, Kassuth
Duncan, Antoinette. 417 W 5th, Bloomington
Dunham, Mary, E 4th, Richmond
Dunn, Mable, 538 E 4th, Bloomington
Dyer, Fred Evert, 303 E 6th, Worthington
Early, Wm Irwin, 321 S Grant, N Liberty
East, Daisy, 408 W 1st Bloomington
Edmondson, Emma, 300 S Lincoln, Bloomington
Edwards, Frank Elder, 322 E 4th, Knightstown
Edwards, Lillie, 521 N Washington, Bloomington
Ek, Chas Marion, 3rd and Dunn, Cassville
Elliott, Roy Howe, 201 E 7th, Glenwood
Ellison, Robert S, 225 S Walnut, Greenfield
Ensle, Eva Katherine, E 3rd, McCutchanville
Erskine, Levi, 729 Atwater Ave, McCutchanville
Evermann, Ord, 303 Cottage Grove Ave, Burlington
Emison, Samuel McClellan, 216 W 2nd, Vincennes
Farlow, Arthur Joseph, 331 S Grant, Paoli
Farmbrough, Alice, 315 E 6th, Frankfort
Faught, John B, S Dunn, Vincennes
Farmer, Wm Burton, Bloomington
Fear, Carl, 515 W 6th, Frankfort
Felbaum, Emma, Dayton
Felbaum, Tillie Christine, Dayton
Felton, Albert Jacob, 435 S Grant,
Ferguson, Chas Wiley, 342 S Grant, Petersburg
Petersburg
Fertich, Mable Clare, 120, E 4th, Bloomington
Field, Leonard 202 E 5th, Bloomington
Fields, Jesse Barton, 214 E 6th, Bloomington.
Fleshman, Aquilla Dura, 419 E 6th, Valley City
Fletchall, Eugene D, 219 S Walnut, Poseyville
Fogleman, Mary Ida, 511 E Smith Ave, Mooresville
Foltz, Gertrude, 601 N Morton, Ben Davis
Forkner, Geo Donahue, 213 S Col Ave, New Castle
Foster, James Russel, 626, W 6th, Worthington
Foster, John Andrew, 409, E 7th, Kendallville
Fox, Jno Winford, 408, E 4th, Emison
French, Ralph Wilson, 201 E 7th, Solitude
Fritsch, Rudolph Fred, 508 E 6th, Evansville
Fryer, Clarence Elmer, 331 S Grant, Ft Wayne
Frazier, Jas W, 334 S Grant, Alexandria
Fuller, Maude Warren, 311 E 6th, Vincennes
Fullerton, James Masa, Mounts
Gardner, Frank, 821 S Washington, Leola,
Garretson, Laura Caroline, 221 E 6th, Pendleton
Garten, James Edwin, 213 S Grant, Odon
Gatch, Willis Dew, 515 E 3rd, Aurora
Gentry, Jay Gould, 416, E 2nd, Rockport
Gibbs, Ellis Burke, 729 Atwater Ave, Gaston
Gillespie, Chas Dale, 209 E 8th, Elwood
Glenn, Olivar Edmuns, 300 E 6th, Moorefield
Gold, Earl Thomas, 631 Fess Ave, Lawrenceburg
Goodbody, Alfred Boyce, Colonia
Gough, Cale Robert, 3rd and Dunn, Booneville.
Gough, Eugene Harrold, 323 S Grant, Booneville.
Cottage, Gainesville, NY
Graham, Wm, 201 E 7th, Bloomington
Grant, Otto Eugene, 631 Fess Ave, Columbia City
Gray, Harry, 308 E 5th, Galveston
Gregory, Chas Elmer, 508 E 4th, Alexandria
Gregory, Helen, 216 W 2nd, Bloomington
Greeson, Fred Lincoln, 502 E 3rd, Otto
Grimes, Irwin Lorenzo, 559 S Lincoln, Smithville
Grimsley, Frank Schnutt, Gosport
Griffiths, Sara Helen, 203 E 7th, FtWayne.
Gunnerson, Mrs. Adair Dickson, Bloomington
Gunnerson, Wm Cyrus, Bloomington
Guthrie, Chas Evart, 220 E 6th, Bloomington.
Guthrie, Michael Beck, 220 E 6th, Bloomington
Haas, Harriet Rosenthal, 115 E 8th, Tipton
Haas, Albert Rosenthal, 342 S Walnut, Tipton
Haggerty, Melvin Everitt, 302 E 5th, Bunker Hill
Hall, Augustus, Delphi
Hall, Hal L, 415 S Dunn, Center Square
Halstead, Benj Howard, 409 E 5th, Petoskey, Michigan
Hamacher, Herbert Ray, 710 Atwater, Henryville
Hamilton, Claud McDonald, 203 S Walnut, Huntington
Hamilton, Frank M, 303 E 6th, Zanesville.

(Continued on fourth page)

THE STUDENT.

INDIANA UNIVERSITY

VOL. XXVI. BLOOMINGTON, INDIANA, SATURDAY, APRIL 6, 1901. No. 154

WOMAN'S EDITION OF DAILY STUDENT.

A Publication of Merit Devoted to the Indiana University Women.

The much heralded Woman's Edition made its debut today with illustrated pages and the taking label, "Published by the University Women." It contains sixteen pages, and belongs to the realm of six dimensions space, a dimension in each of the departments of Literature, Athletics, Locals, Alumni, Organizations, and Music and Drama.

To speak of the paper in a general way no publication that has ever appeared in the field of Indiana University can equal the Woman's Edition in freshness and freedom from colloquialism and the select quality of its articles.

It is dedicated primarily to the Woman's Building and the leading article is a complete and well written resume of the plan of the women for raising the building fund. The story "After the Alumni Banquet" is a little on the convential order but very clever. The story "In the Library" and the sketch, "The University Spirits Visit" and the article "The Modern College Girl" would do credit to a magazine of larger pretentions Of course the Co-eds are to be exonerated for "A New Girl at Bloomington" as money is the root of all evil and one pernicious article only emphasizes the excellence of the edition as a whole.

The editorial departments are all well sustained.

Following is the staff;

Emma R. Munger . . . . . . Editor-in-chief
Sara V. Hanna, May Ethel Strong . . . . Associate editors
Julia H. McClellan, Myrtle E. Mitchell . . Business Managers

STAFF

Stella Vaughn . . . . Local
Olive F. Morehouse . . . . Athletics
Mrs. Maud Van Zandt Davis . . . . Alumni
Lydia E. Gemmer . . . . Organizations
Anna G. Cravens . . . . . Music and Drama
Maude Showers, Mary E. Coleman, Rebecca Swayne . . . . Advertising
Katharine M. Rogers . . . . Circulation

Arthur C. Moore, '04, of Summitville, Ind., is pledged to Kappa Sigma.

Money Subscribed.

Mrs. Swain has announced that the following donations to the Woman's Building fund have been made.

Showers Bros., Bloomington, $1500.

Chas. L. Henry, Anderson, $1000.

Women of Bloomington, $1000.

Joseph and Frances M. Swain, $1000.

Miscellaneous subscriptions of Woman's League members, $500.

Total, $5000.

Formal request for subscriptions has not yet been made.

THE Y. M. C. A. SOCIAL.

Association Extends Welcome to New Students and Enjoys Evening of Games.

About forty students found their way through the rain last night to Kirkwood Hall to attend the opening reception given by the Young Men's Christian Association. After becoming acquainted with each other, a football tossing contest was engaged in, the two teams being captained by George Heady and E. V. Shockley, Heady's team gained the supremacy by a score 4 to 3.

Lemonade and vanilla wafers were served after which all joined heartily in the college song and yells. The old-fashioned spelling match aroused considerable interest. Sides were chosen by W. E. Hanger and Geo. Teter and after a severe contest the prize was carried off by Geo. Teter. At about 10:30 the company disbanded, fully convinced that a "Stag Social" is a good thing even on a rainy night

---

Messrs. Rucker, Cauble, Kramer, Keeney and King will orate at the Gym the evening of April 17. The contest is to select a representative for Indiana in the Central Oratorical League, which will be held here May 17.

Mr. A. J. Yoder, of Topeka, Ind., matriculated Fall '91, has re-entered the University.

Track Athletics.

The track is being rolled and put in first class condition, preparatory to active work next week. Captain Neher has had the men out the past week doing distance work. Teter, Matthews, Lockridge, Runyan, Shields and Shockley have been running a quarter or more each day. Roudebush, Shields and Smith are working on the hurdles and Elfers is beginning his outdoor work. Prospects for the track team are bettered by the addition of Lockridge, Teter, and Rector. The Class Meet this spring will be the closest ever held and will furnish many surprises.

Purdue State Champions.

The News of yesterday contains a picture of the Purdue basket ball team who now lay claim to state championships. During the season they defeated Wabash twice, and both Butler and Indiana University. While the rules governing basket ball state that championships can not be decided except by a series of two games in three or three in five, Purdue has easily shown her superiority in playing eleven games without sustaining a defeat. They scored, in all, 368 points to their opponents 120.

Some non est Inventuses.

Our exchange number of the Woman's Edition.

—

The base ball knockers.

—

The sun.

—

A smile on the visage of twelve leading underclassmen.

—

The local editor.

—

The Hoosier lit.

—

The Freshmen who attempted to get a "corner" on Woman's Edition.

THE 'VARSITY TAKING SHAPE

Candidates Improving Form and Feeling For Positions. Weather Drags the Season.

On account of the rain there was no practice last night on the ball field. Rain is a good thing for the field as the layer of clay rolled on the diamond yesterday will be rendered solid for practice next week. The squad needs every hour of practice it can put in however, being composed of material which needs only practice to develop it.

Boyle and Thornton are both in good pitching form. An experienced baseball man who saw them working out on the diamond said that Indiana was equipped as well in pitching material as any of the Western college teams. Miller the candidate for catcher has shown considerable ablity although this is the first year he has appeared in college baseball. Darby, Stant and Phillips are candidates for the bag, number one. Darby and Stant have the requisite height for that position and are experienced players. Phillips can field a ball well and seems to be a strong hitter. Black, Wright and Shaw are trying for second. All are good men and have experience. Clevenger, Chandler, Rucker, Thomas and several others are out for short stop and 3rd base positions. Sutphin is back in the field again with Hutchinson Quick, Swan, Scott, McMasters and Allen looking for jobs.

There is much rivalry and if the student body comes up with a little enthusiasm the men on the field will do their part.

The Victor Herbert Orchestra which will give a concert here the latter part of this month is ranked as one of the greatest orchestras of its class in America. Miss Fannie Bloomfield Zeister is the soloist and she will be heard in a Concerto at the appearance here of the orchestra.

P0080156, IU Archives.

January 14, 1908

The Daily Student.

VOL. XXXIII. NO. 64 INDIANA UNIVERSITY, TUESDAY, JANUARY 14 1908 TWO CENTS.

PEACE = WITH = PURDUE!

SHELDON ANNOUNCES SEASON'S SCHEDULE

Cream and Crimson Has Formidable Program For Remainder of Season.

Coach Sheldon came back from Chicago with his pockets full of dates for basketball, baseball and track teams. He has secured contests with some of the strongest teams in the west, including several of the Conference schools. The baseball schedule is especially good and if the crimson can win most of the games scheduled, it will be a strong claimant for honors. Several track meets have also been scheduled, one of which with Northwestern, will be held on Jordan Field.

The schedules in full follow:

BASKETBALL.

Jan. 18: State Normal here.
Jan. 25: Illinois at Champaign.
Jan. 28: DePauw here.
Jan. 31: Northwestern here.
Feb. 3: Rose Poly here.
Feb. 7: Purdue at Lafayette.
Feb. 11: DePauw at Greencastle.
Feb. 15: Marion Club at Indianapolis.
Feb. 21: State Normal at Terre Haute.
Feb. 22: Rose Poly at Terre Haute.
Feb. 26: Purdue here.
Feb. 1: Culver vs. Indiana Freshmen at Culver.
Feb. 8: Purdue Freshmen vs. Indiana Freshmen here.

BASEBALL.

April 11: Illinois at Champaign.
April 25: Northwestern here.
May 11: Purdue here.
May 14: Chicago at Chicago.
May 16: Northwestern at Evanston.
June 2: Purdue at Lafayette.
June 6: Illinois here.

Besides these dates, two games will be played with Notre Dame, State Normal, Rose Poly and DePauw.

Track meets will be held with Illinois, (indoor at Champaign); Purdue (indoor here and outdoor there); Northwestern (outdoor here). The football schedule so far includes games with Chicago, Wisconsin, Illinois and Purdue.

Harlan B. Rogers, '09, has been elected captain of Wisconsin's basketball team.

EXCLUSIVE COURSE GIVEN

Librarian Jenkins Starts a Class in Bibliography.

The new course in Bibliography and Reference Problems is being patronized to the entire satisfaction of Librarian W. E. Jenkins. The course is mostly laboratory work, and because the instruction is mainly personal and individual, a large attendance is not desired. The class has been divided into two sections, one meeting Friday, at four p. m., the other Saturday, at ten a. m. It is a one-hour course, and will be under the instruction of the Librarian and his staff.

The work will consist largely of an introduction to the use of books and of library routine, and is intended primarily for students who wish to learn enough of library methods to enable them to make the proper use of books in large collections. Stress will be laid upon research work, and methods of cataloguing. The Dewey systems of classification, book notation, national and subject bibliography and reference materials will be studied.

The course is open to only those students who have had one year each of French and German.

Wellesley College announces that the Alice Freeman Palmer fellowship of $1250 a year, will be awarded in June to a woman graduate of an American college of approved standing.

BRIGHTER AND BREEZIER

Arbutus Editor to Make His Book Surpass Former Publications.

Charles E. Lookabill, manager of the Arbutus, announces that the work in all departments is progressing nicely. The work was begun earlier this year than previously and Mr. Lookabill states that every possible means to surpass all former editions is being used. The intention of the editors and managers is to make this year's issue more of a feature book. More cuts will be used and more departments represented.

The fraternity, sorority, club

(Continued on page two)

STRUT STARS TO SHINE

Interest Grows in Attraction at Harris-Grand Monday.

The feature of the night of Monday, January 20th, is to be Strut and Fret's presentation of "David Garrick," the famous old eighteenth century classic. Kenneth Gorrell, of well established Strut and Fret fame, is to play David Garrick and his interpretation of the part is said by those who have seen the rehearsals, to be better than anything he has ever tried on the University stage. Other stars are Miss Hilda Palmer, who appears in the very pretty role of Ada Ingot, Irwin McCurdy, and C. E. Woods as Squire Chivy.

"DAVID GARRICK."

David Garrick .. Kenneth Gorrell
Mr. Simon Ingot, Erwin McCurdy
Ada Ingot ...... Hilda Palmer
Mr. Smith .... Clifton Williams
Mr. Browne .... J. G. B. Jones
Mr. Jones ...... Clyde Sanders
Mrs. Smith .... Edith Holloway
Miss Araminta Brown .... Rose Hassmer
Squire Chivy ...... C. E. Woods
Thomas .... Robert C. Hill
George .... Ralph Rawlings
Servants, etc.

"A WOMAN'S WONT."

Mr. Harwood .. Clifton Williams
Mrs. Harwood .... Mary Sample
Henry Harford .. Ralph Rawlings
Jessy Harford ...... Lelia Todd
James .... Clyde Sanders
Lucy .... Elsie Ashby

COMMENDS M. SAMPSON

Cornell Sun Speaks Editorially of Indiana Man.

In an editorial way the Cornell Daily Sun has this to say of Prof. Martin Wright Sampson, formerly head of the Department of English of Indiana, who has been appointed to an Acting Professorship of English Literature at Cornell University:

"During his twelve years of service at Indiana, Professor Sampson succeeded in developing his department to a high degree of efficiency. Instruction both in literature and composition was

(continued on page 2.)

TRUCE IS EFFECTED AND GAMES BOOKED

Indiana to Meet Old Rivals Once More in All Branches of Sport.

Indiana and Purdue will meet again in all branches of athletics. The first game will be in basketball, Feb. 7th. at Lafayette.

Coach Sheldon met Athletic Director Nicol of the Boilermakers at Indianapolis yesterday and satisfactory dates were arranged in basketball, baseball and track sports. The Cream and Crimson will also meet the Old Gold and Black on the gridiron, but the date will not be selected until after the Conference decision on the seven game question.

This step is one for which the students of both schools have been waiting for some time, and it will do more than anything else to revive athletics in this state. Since Wabash cast her lot with the smaller schools, a contest between Purdue and Indiana became almost imperative. The interest aroused will not be confined merely to students, and alumni of the two schools, but a larger number of high school stars will be drawn to these two institutions. Probably one of the main reasons of the management for resuming athletics lay in the financial condition of both treasuries. A game between these two schools will attract a larger crowd than any other on the schedule.

The arrangements made by Coach Sheldon provide for two basketball games, one to be played at each of the schools. A contest will also be held here between the freshman fives. This will be pulled off on February 8th. An indoor track meet will be run off in the gymnasium here, while the crimson will journey to Lafayette for an outdoor meet some time in May. Two baseball games complete the list of dates.

Illinois University has an annual jollification after exams called the Post Exam Jubilee. It consists of the performance of stunts by the various organizations, each one limited to fifteen minutes, and may take on the nature of anything that will drive away care and relieve the strain of exams.

P0079394, IU Archives.

THE INDIANA STUDENT

PUBLISHED DAILY AT THE STATE UNIVERSITY.

VOL. XXXIX. NO. 60. BLOOMINGTON, INDIANA, TUESDAY, JANUARY 6, 1914. ESTABLISHED 1867.

READY FOR GAME WITH ILLINOIS

Berndt Hopes For Good Showing in Initial Contest Tonight.

WHITAKER IS ELIGIBLE

Nine Men Make the Trip; Captain To Be Picked.

Jan. 6 Illinois at Champaign
Jan. 12 Wisconsin at Bloomington
Jan. 17 Northwestern at Evanston
Jan. 24 Earlham at Bloomington
Jan. 30 Earlham at Richmond
Jan. 31 Ohio State at Columbus
Feb. 7 Illinois at Bloomington
Feb. 9 Purdue at Lafayette
Feb. 13 Northwestern at Bloominton
Feb. 23 Minnesota at Minneapolis
Feb. 24 Wisconsin at Madison
Feb. 28 Ohio State at Bloomington
Mar. 3 Purdue at Bloomington
Mar. 7 Minnesota at Bloomington

Coach Berndt and his band of nine hopefuls left this morning for Champaign where the first conference game of the season for the Crimson will be staged tonight. Although prospects are none too bright, Berndt is holding out all kinds of hopes that his men will show something in the game with the Illini. This game will be the initial conference game of the season for both schools and for this reason a hard fought game of the season for both schools and for this reason a hard fought early-season battle may be expected.

All of Indiana's hopes for a winning team this season are built on last year's Freshman team. Witn not a single veteran on the squad Coach Berndt is forced to develop an entirely new team. He has confidence is the men who are working under him and expects to have a quintet that will win games for the Crimson before the season is under way many weeks.

Illinois Is Prepared.

Illinois is better prepared to go into the game tonight than the Crimson. Three old men are on the squad and Coach Jones is depending on them to do much of the work in this game. Edward Williford was elected captain of the team just before vacation and he is expected to star at his position at forward. Kircher, one of the veterans, will play the other forward, and Duner will work at one of the guards.

As a final workout for the men before this game, Berndt used a long practice at basket shooting, dribbling and passing. Then to close the evening's practice, a stiff scrimmage was put on, the Whites winning over the Reds by the score of eighteen to one. The members of the Whites will start the game tonight.

Whitaker Will Play.

Hopes went up a few notches last night when Frank Whitaker was declared eligible. Whitaker took a special examination yesterday afternoon and Coach Berndt was notified late last night that the star of last year's Freshman squad was up in his studies. He is expected to be the mainstay in stopping the Illini in their rush toward the basket. Whitak in their rush toward the basket. Whitaker has a style all of his own when it comes to playing the guard position and should be able to give the forwards of the Gold and Blue considerable trouble.

Gilbert will start as center. He has the height and speed to develop into a good center for Berndt. In the scrimmage last night, he made two exceptionally good shots at the basket and landed both of them. Kirkpatrick has been picked to star as a guard. He plays the game much the same as Berger of Wisconsin, who starred for that crew for several years. Maxwell will play

Continued on page 4

LANGUAGE CONVENTION

During the Christmas vacation, Dr. P. A. Barba and Prof. A. F. Kuersteiner of the Departments of German and Romance Languages attended the convention of the Central Division of the Modern Language Association of America at the University of Cincinnati. Doctor Barba read a paper before the convention on the subject, "German Immigrant Literature." In his paper he compared the German literature in the fatherland with that produced by the writers of German descent in this country.

Professor Kuersteiner was a member of the executive committee which made a report on simplified spelling that has attracted considerable attention. The committee declared as favoring simplified spelling and asked that the matter be taken up by the Language association. Although the committee's report did not so state, this would be equivalent to taking the matter from under the supervision of the Simplified Spelling Board

The committee also reported in favor of establishing courses in Mediaeval Latin in the universities and colleges of the country. At the present time this branch of Latin is almost wholly neglected. Prof. H. W. Gilmer of the Latin Department stated yesterday that he favors this movement

NEW TERM BRINGS CHANGES IN FACULTY

Dr. Badertscher, Miss Hess and Miss Knapp Are New Members

The new term opens with many new faces among the faculty. Probably the greatest change is in the English department. Professor Richard Rice has returned after a leave of absence last fall term. He spent the time visiting with his relatives in Europe. Miss Cecelia Hennel of the English Department has resigned. She was married during the holidays and leaves shortly with her husband for his bee-ranch in Wyoming.

Dr. Warner Fite, who has been substitututing during the last term at Leland Stanford University returns again to the philosophy department. The department of anatomy has a new member in Dr. J. D. Bardertscher. Doctor Badertscher comes from Cornell where he took his Ph. D. degree and where he has been an instructor for the last three and a half years. He graduated with the degrees of A. B. and A. M from Ohio University at Athens, Ohio. The school of education has expanded its courses in home economics. Miss Abigail Hess, a graduate of the University of Illinois, and who for the last few years has been teaching at the state university at Bosman, Montana, will give courses in cookery. A well equipped and modern cooking laboratory has been installed in Wylie Hall.

Miss Ethel Knapp is the new assistant cataloguer at the library. Miss Knapp, who is a sister of Miss Winifred Knapp, is a graduate of Wooster College of Ohio and obtained her library training at Western Reserve University. She comes to our library from the Public Library of Mt. Vernon, Ohio, of which she was librarian.

A new course will be introduced at the library this term for those students who intend to take up library work. It will be a five hour course, three hours to be given under the direction of Miss Ethel Knapp, to cataloguing and the other two to miscellaneous library activities. The course will be made as practical as possible.

ASK SAM NO MORE

Samuel Hockman, more familiarly known to University students as Book-Nook Sam, is now employed as a clerk in Huder's drug store, Pennsylvania and Washington streets, Indianapolis. Sam was manager of the Book-Nook for the past two years.

NOTICE—1917

Coach Berndt has issued his call to freshman basketball men and the yearlings will report Wednesday afternoon at four o'clock in the gymnasium.

The History Club will meet Thursday night at 7:30 o'clock at the Phi Gam House

STUDENTS UNITE WITH FACULTY FOR STRINGENT SOCIAL RESTRICTIONS

General Approval of Action of Student Affairs Committee Prohibiting All "Modern" Dances.

ORGANIZATIONS LIMITED TO ONE DANCE A TERM

The tango, hesitation, "Texas Tommy" "kitchen sink," "one step," "Pump handle" and the other so-termed "modern" dances are dead at Indiana University after a short life of one term. These same modern dances are breathing their last in practically every large university as well as in many of the larger cities of the country.

The dances are stringently prohibited as the result of the action recently taken by the Student Affairs Committee regulating all University social functions. The action of the Committee come, as a climax to the agitation against these dances that was waged during the past term by various members of the faculty and of the student body, and by the Indiana Student.

The Regulations

1. Number of dances. That each class be permitted to have one dance per year; that the Booster's Club, the Press Club, the Skeleton Club, the Demurrer Club, the Woman's League and the Pan-Hellenic Council be permitted to have each on dance per year; that the Union be permitted to have two dances per year; that fraternities, men's clubs, sororities, and women's clubs be limited to one dance each per term—either formal or informal; that other organizations not herein enumerated must take application to the Advisory Committee before reserving a date on the University Calendar.

2. Chaperones. That all large parties in the Student Building or in halls down town must have at least ten chaperones, who shall be approved by the Dean of Women not later than three days before the affair.

3 Floor Committee of Students. It is advised that at each dance there should be a floor committee of not less than three students who should introduce themselves to the chaperones of the dance and asist them in every way possible.

4. Time of Taking Effect. That these rules become effective at the beginning of the Winter term, 1914, and that they ahall be in effect hereafter as the other rules relating to social affairs.

The action of the Committee was also to the effect that waltzes, two steps and the Boston without the dip, only will be permitted.

Menace to Good Society

"I am very much in favor of the action taken by the Student Affairs Committee regarding the social life here in the University," said President Bryan last night in an interview regarding the recent action of the Committee. "In fact," said Dr Bryan, "I talked with the Deans and the Committee before the action was taken and this is in accord with what I recommended I am no expert on the dance question," he continued, "but I do know that there is a right and a wrong way to conduct a dance and that the way the new dances were danced here last term made them a menace to good society. I think that the new regulations will go a long way to raising the social standard of the University."

Dean Hogate, chairman of the Student Affairs Committee, in explaining the action taken said: "There is no disposition on the part of the University authorities to entirely forbid dancing It is desired only that dances shall be limited in number and confined to proper dances, that the sensibilities of no one may be shocked This is demanded not only by the University authorities, but by the best society. The Student Affa Committee believes the great body of students will accord heartily The effort to conform to the rules at at Union dance was most gratifying."

Dean Rawles, when interviewed, said that the dance question had been left to the student body but that since it had shown no desire to take definite action, the University authorities had deemed it their duty to step in and take the needed action. "By this action the voice of the University is raised against the "modern dances." This was the only means by placing the University above criticism in a position where it could be seen as definitely favoring the mainteance of a high social standard."

Posture That Is Wrong.

Dean of Women De Nise, after having spent the holidays conferring with other University women on the dance question said that the opinion that she had to express was practically the same as was held by everyone to whom she had talked

"It is not so much the matter of the steps of the new dances that has caused the agitation against them as it is the posture used in dancing them. I think it is an advisable thing to simplify the dance and the social problem here and to use the more conservative dances until the agitation against them over the country is ended. After the dances have been made proper and the objectionable practices done away with the dances that become established in good society will be used here. I do not believe that all the agitation is due to the steps of the dances but to the posture used in dancing them" she said, "that either makes or mars them. If we could correct the posture it would, I believe solve the whole problem and standardize the dance."

George Henley, chief of the Student Marshals, in commenting on the new rules, said: "My opinion is and has always been that the new dances if danced properly are all right, but the way that they were danced here last term made them vulgar in the extreme and made the action of the Student Affairs Committee necessary. I believe that if a professional dancing teacher could be procured and the dances taught properly that in time the dances could be made prettier by them and at the same time just as respectable as the dances were when nothing but the plain waltz and two-step were danced I am mighty glad," he said, "to see the action limiting the number of dances for a term and believe that it will meet with no objection as a majority of the organizations dance but once a term."

Miss Grace Montgomery, President of the Woman's League, in interview this morning said: "From what I know of the general sentiment of the League as expressed in their last meeting I believe that it is heartily in accord with the more stringent regulations. It was the general feeling that while the new dances were graceful and fine if done correctly, the dances as generally done are ugly and wrong. We will support the Committee."

The agitation against the "modern" dances that brought about the action of the committee was begun before they were introduced here last fall. The Student Affairs Committee believed advisable at that time to place the matter of regulating the dances in the hands of representatives bodies of the University for their action. A meeting was called by President Bryan and Dean Rawles of two representatives from each fraternity to consider the question but no specific action was taken other than endorsing the action taken by the Women's Council. The Women's Council in acting on the matter adopted rules that failed to work out when tried. The University authorities seeing no other alternative took up the question at that time and the rules that will govern social events in the future are the results of their deliberations

STRUT AND FRET.—Strut and Fret meeting Wednesday 4 P. M. in Kirkwood 21 to select cast for "Strife." Important!

GEORGE HENLEY, President.

OLIPHANT'S ESCAPE

Missing death by less than five minutes was the experience of Glen Oliphant, '17, on December 29, while visiting his parents at Vincennes during the holidays. This unique happening occurred in connection with the explosion of the Indiana Creek Mine, near Bicknell, Ind., which resulted in the death of three miners, and the serious injury of several others.

Young Oliphant, with his father, was working on the night shift in the mine and about 3 o'clock Monday morning the two men came to the surface, after completing their work, preparatory to returning home. In mine parlance, they had completed five "cuts" and did not, on account of the nearness to quitting time, start an additional "cut."

Accordingly, they left their work, and in less than five minutes after the cage brought them to safety the explosion occurred. Glen Oliphant notified C. L. McQuaid, manager of the Indiana Creek mine, of the accident and with his father carried on heroic rescue work.

Oliphant is a member of the Sigma Nu fraternity and received a good start in Freshman football when his ankle was broken He is a brother of Purdue's Oliphant. He returned to school Sunday night for the Winter term.

FIFTEEN CHOSEN FOR UNION NOMINATING BOARD

Election To Be Held Monday, January 12.

Professor Samuel B. Harding, Lawrence Bock, Donald Bose, Halbert Bybee, Preston Cox, John DeLong, George Hyslop, H. V. Hornung, Bruce McCullough, Alvah Miller, Fred Meyers, Dwight Park, James Robinson, Ralph VanValer, and Arthur Voyles, were chosen by the board of directors of the Indiana Union, at a meeting last night, as the fifteen men of whom the members are to chose five for the nominating board. This election will be held Monday night January 12, at the first open meeting of the new year.

The selection of the fifteen men is in accordance with the constitution of the Union which provides that one week before the January open meeting the board of directors shall chose one member of the faculty and fourteen students as candidates for the nomination board. The members of the Union, at the January meeting elect five of these as the nomination board. This board in turn nominates the officers of the Union.

Aside from the election of the nomination board, an enter tainment of unusual significance will be given at the meeting next Monday night. The entertainment committee has not anounced definite plans but promises something entirely new and original. At a recent meeting of the board of directors it was decided to open the Union barber shop until 10 o'clock on Saturday nights. This will take effect Saturday.

MONON WRECK

The Monon train service was badly crippled late Sunday afternoon on account of a freight wreck at Putnamville, between Limedale and Gosport South bound train No. 5, due here at 4:20 o'clock arrived at 8:40 with about one hundred Indiana students. All traffic was held up for four hours until a temporary track was built around the wrecked train.

North bound train No 6, leaving here at 11:20 a m was detoured over the Vandalia tracks from Gosport via Indianapolis to Limedale. The wreck occurred at Putmanville at about 11:30 o'clock Sunday morning. Ten cars were derailed and several of them were demolished The accident was assigned to a broken arch bar on one of the loaded cars

NOTICE.

Meeting of the staff of the Indiana Student at 1 P. M. today in Kirkwood 21. All expecting credit must be present.

YALE REQUIREMENTS

Katherine M. Tinsley '15, har reentered the university after one term's absence.

BOOKS CHEAPER BY NEW DECISIONS

Holding of Supreme Court Cuts Cost of Many Texts.

OVER TEN PERCENT SAVED

Admission of Books to Parce Post Means Further Cut.

Hinging on a recent decision handed down by the Supreme Court, which was announced during the holidays, the students of Indiana University will be able to purchase their books at a lower price. This was the statement yesterday afternoon of N. O. Pittinger, manager of the Co-operative Book store. This new regulation, however, will favor the students of the School of Medicine largely.

Mr. Pittinger explained that the decision was given in the old Macy case which has been hanging fire for more than ten years. Publishers of certain books, especially books used by the medical students, have prohibited the retailers to offer their product for less than the list price. As a result, a test case was presented in the Supreme court a number of years ago by merchants opposed to this plan.

"According to the ruling," said Mr. Pittinger, "We are able to offer the Lewis and Stohr Histology for example, which is listed at $3.00 for $2.70 at a discount of ten per cent. The physiology text book is also sold at a price reduced from the list price. We sold 25 physiology texts today and on the total number, received $10 less than we would have under the old system."

When asked concerning books used by the law students and students in the College of Liberal Art, Mr. Pittinger said that the publishers of books of that type had never adhered to such stringent rules regarding the sale of their books below list price.

Another saving in book buying will be inaugurated March 1, with an added change in the parcel post regulations. At present, when a single book is wanted that is not in stock it is necessary to pay expressage on the article. Under the new parcel post laws, books can be sent through the mails at a small cost which will mean a saving to the buyer of from ten to twenty cents.

REEVES DEATH.

Death again invaded the ranks of Indiana University students when Bruce Reeves, age 21, and son of Mr. and Mrs. J. M. Reeves of 527 south Lincoln street, died December 21. His death was due to heart failure and lung trouble. He is survived by his parents, three sisters and one brother.

Reeves had been in bad health for some time but despite this fact attended the university He had sophomore standing and was majoring in chemistry. He was a young man of excellent habits and well liked by all his friends. He was a member of the First Methodist Church

The funeral services were held December 24 and the body now rests in a vault in the Rose Hill cemetery where it will be kept until Saturday when interment will take place. J. M. Reeves, the father, is one of the superintendents of construction work at the Panama Canal and was unable to return to Bloomington for the funeral services.

HARRIS POLITICAL MANAGER

N. K. Harris, '15, who was a candidate for editor-in-chief of The Indiana Student last term, has accepted the task of handling the publicity work for Charles T. Akin of Carlisle, Indiana in Mr. Akin's campaign for the democratic nomination for congress from the second district. Mr. Harris hopes to re-enter school for the spring term. Mr. Akin is the father of C. T. Akin, Jr., who entered school last term and who will also be out of school this term to assist his father.

P0079137, IU Archives.

The Course in Journalism

The early 20th century saw journalism education find its footing at IU, and as the program evolved, so did its connection to the IDS. The IU Board of Trustees became the owner of the paper, entrusting its operation to a new journalism department created in 1911. With the new owner came a new name: Indiana Daily Student, used in the nameplate for the first time Sept. 29, 1914. This story about IU's first journalism course originally appeared in the 1908 Arbutus.

The Course in Journalism was added to the curriculum of Indiana University during the year 1907–1908, the work being under the direct supervision of Fred B. Johnson, late of the Indianapolis News. A natural friendliness towards any work that would make the University of broader service to the State of Indiana, coupled with the persistence of the Indiana Press Club resulted in the establishment of this course.

For the last few years newspaper editors have been holding out their inducements for the college trained men. They have been willing to take them straight from college with little or no newspaper experience in order to get men of college and university type. The greater is their interest, therefore, in men, trained not only in general university work, but also in special newspaper work. Hence with practically all newspaper editors, this course in newspaper work—or course in Journalism as it is called—has met with approval.

The work of the course this year, divided into three terms, has been practical, in so far as practicability was possible. Two aims have been fundamental—the development of the news instinct and the writing of the newspaper "story." Perhaps as to the latter phase of the work has the course been the more successful. In the Fall term the members of the class—most of them students who had had some small town experience—worked to develop the straight news story—the happenings of every-day town and University life. They were guided by the instructor in the handling of such stories in the best newspaper way.

In the winter term the class took up for special work the so-called "feature" story, the story with the intrinsic interest, aside from its timeliness or immediateness. In the Spring term the so-called "human interest" story was taken up. This is the hardest kind of newspaper writing to do successfully and the members of the class probably averaged up with the ordinary newspaper staff in this kind of work.

Throughout the year special lectures were given by well-known newspaper men on the different phases of the newspaper work, as it touched each of them most intimately. Not only did the members of the class get the immediate value of their experience but they were brought into contact with the men who have done, are doing and will do things in the newspaper business.

Next year the practice work that has been given this year will be continued and in addition there will be as much work on the history and theory of newspapers and newspaper experience.

Arbutus coverage of IU's first journalism class. *Photo courtesy of the Arbutus.*

Everybody Goes to Chicago Saturday. Maroon the Maroons

THE INDIANA DAILY STUDENT

Yell Practice Every Day This Week--3:30 P.M. Everyone Out.

VOL. XL. NO. 1. BLOOMINGTON, INDIANA, TUESDAY, SEPTEMBER 29, 1914. ESTABLISHED 1867.

ALL EYES TURNED TO CHILDS AND CHICAGO

Preparations For Big Excusion to the Windy City Have Been Completed.

YELL PRACTICE DAILY

Jordan Field Scene of Much Activity in Anticipation of Maroon Game.

With the DePauw game already a matter of history, all eyes are now turned to the annual game wifh Stagg's Maroons at Chicago next Saturday. The time honored train load of rooters, University band, and old time enthusiasts, are again planning to take advantage of the Monon's reduced rates and will follow Childs' men into the enemy's territory. No fewer than 500 Indiana followers are expected to be on the Crimson sideline when the signal is given for the start of the 1914 Conference football eason.

All arrangments have already been for the annual trip, the one thing remaining to be done is the drumming up of the old crowd. The train will leave Bloomington Friday morning at 11 o'clock and will reach the Windy City at 5 o'clock the same evening.

Mr. Humston, the Monon passenger agent, has promised a special vestibuled train carrying both a parlor and dining car. The returning train will leave Chicago at midnight Saturday and will be equipped with Pullman sleeping cars.

The fare for the round trip is three dollars.

Season book tickets holders will be admitted to the game by paying an additional fifty cents. The regular admission will be one dollar and a half.

Special Car for Squad

Coach Childs and the members of the team will go via the excursion train in a special car reserved for the squad. It is probable, however, that a few of the members of the team will make the trip Thursday evening, in order to get a good rest before going into the game.

The Boosters' Club has arranged for yell practice this afternoon at 3:30 o'clock on Jordan Field. Ralph Thompson will be on the field to lead the yelling and to familiarize the freshmen with the Indiana yells. President Thornburgh, of the Boosters' Club, stated yesterday that much time would be given this week to the matter of efficient and concerted rooting.

TO BE UNIVERSITY PHYSICIAN

Dr. J. E. P. Holland has been elected University physician to succeed Dr. C. P. Hutchins, who resigned in August. Dr. Holland will assume the medical duties of Dr. Hutchins, Mr. Kase having the charge of all physical training work.

Dr. Holland will also have charge of physical examinations for all Freshmen men and women. He will also make all medical examinations for the students entering athletics of any kind, also giving medical advice to any student who may be ill, during his office hours at the University. He will not take charge of serious cases of sickness as University physician.

His office hours will be from 1 to 3 P. M., for men in the men's gymnasium, and from 3 to 4 P. M., for women in the Women's gymnasium. Dr. Holland will render his services free to all students.

DR. S .E. MEEK DEAD

Dr. S. E. Meek B. S. '84, M. S. '86 and Ph. D. '91, of Chicago, and well known among scientists of the country, died last summer. Dr. Meek spent one year with Dr. C. H. Eigenmann making scientific investigations in Panama. He was connected with the Field Museum at Chicago, at the time of his death. His wife was formerly Miss Ella Tourner of Bloomington.

RED BOOK NAMES

The student list for the directory in the Red Book will be placed on the desk of the University Library Thursday for the insertion of telephone numbers and changes of addresses. Please see that your name is spelled correctly and tha your phone number is in its proper place. This list will be mailed to the publisher Saturday evening. Every phone number of both professor and student is wanted on this list. The new professors who have been selected since the publication of the schedule are requested to place their names on the directory list of instructors. Cooperate with the Y. M. C. A. and the publishers in getting this useful directory out early, by seeing that your name is correct.

MANY NEW NAMES WILL APPEAR IN FACULTY LIST

French, Latin, English, History, Philosophy Economics and Zoology Departments Filled

NEW PUBLIC SPEAKING MAN

Since the closing of school and the announcement of changes in the faculty made by the secretary to the trustees, a number of new men and women have been added to the teaching force of the University, taking the places of members who are on leave of absence. Prof. S. E. Stout has been selected to fill the vacancy as head of the department of Latin. Miss Lillian G. Berry has been acting head of that department for the past year. Prof. Stout is from William Jewell College, Missouri. He is a graduate of Princeton and has been taking graduate work at Chicago.

In the French department, the vacancies of Dr. Frank Germann and Miss Frances Latzke have been filled by M .Pierre LeCoq and Miss Daphne Hoffman, daughter of Dean Hoffman. Prof. LeCoq is from St. Brieue, France and has spent several years in this country. Last year he was instructor in French at Drury College Springfield, Mo. Miss Hoffman, is a graduate of Indiana in 1912 and took her master's degree at Wellesley College in 1913. Last year she was instructor in Latin at the Bethany School of Topeka, Kas. Miss Latzke probably will return to France.

New Law Professor

The School of law will have a new man this year to take the place of Prof. Throckmorton, who resigned last year, to go to Western Reserve. John L. Baker, Indiana A. B. '10, has arrived to fill the vacancy. Professor Baker is a graduate of Miami University and has been practicing law in Indianapolis for the past year.

J. A. Hess has returned from a year's study abroad. Mr. Hess will teach in the German department. Mr. Hess has some interesting stories of the war in Europe, having left Marbourg Germany on Aug. 17, witnessing the mobilization of troops for the front.

Dr. Mildred Hoge, received her Ph. D. degree from Columbia University this year, will fill the position of C. E. Wilson in the Zoology department. Dr. Hoge is a graduate of Goucher College in Baltimore. Mr. Wilson will be an instructor in the zoology department in the Agriculture College of Mississippi.

Dr. Warner Fite will take leave of absence this year, his place being filled by Dr. W. B. Elkin, of Cornell University. Dr. Elkin received his doctor's degree at Cornell and has taught here before, substituting for Dr. Bryan, when he was in the department of Philosophy.

Simon D. Twining has been appointed instructor of Economics. Last year he was a teaching fellow in the same department.

As yet no one has been selected to fill the vacancy of Dr. E. E. Jones, who resigned to go to Northwestern University.

Dr. Robert G. Withington has become a member of the English de-

(Continued on Page Four)

"The Wizard from Yale"

CLARENCE C. CHILDS

Clarence C. Childs, Indiana's new football coach, has an enviable record as a coach and all round athlete. Coach Childes began his athletic career playing half-back on a preparatory school eleven for seven years before entering Yale. At Yale he made the 1911 Varsity, in regular position at left guard. Years before that he played a tackle position. Mr. Childs is a graduate of Yale in 1909 attending the law school until 1911.

In 1911, he made the trip across to London with the International track team, winning points in the hammer-throw against Cambridge and Oxford Universities. In 1912 he was selected to go to the Olympic games at Stockholm, America's representative in the hammer throw. He won third place in this world contest. While yet abroad he went to Berlin and Paris, where he beat French and German records in the same event. Last year he was head coach of Wooster College, Ohio.

MISS RUBY E. C. MASON IS NEW DEAN OF WOMEN

Successor to Miss DeNise Was Educated in Canada and Has Studied Abroad Several Years.

POPULAR AT WARD-BELMONT

Arriving in te city several days ago, Miss Ruby E. C. Mason will act as Dean of Women, succeeding Miss Carrie Louise DeNise, who resigned that position last June. Miss Mason is living with her mother at 728 E. Third street.

Miss Mason comes to Indiana from Belmont College at Nashville, where she has acted as dean of women for the last three years. Her home is in Canada, in which country she received her education. She is a graduate of the University of Toronto, having received her master's degree there also. She has studied abroad several years in noted schools in France and Germany. She is a sister of the late Prof. John Mason of Toulane University.

Miss DeNise, who was succeeded by Miss Mason, has been dean of women at Indiana for three years and will probably spend the coming year abroad.

In the selection of a new dean, the University trustees took into consideration the popularity and success Miss Mason enjoyed at Ward-Belmont College in Nashville, Tenn.

THREE INDIANA MEN ON FACULTY OF MAINE U.

John C. Mellett, Earl Keyes and Floyd Ramsey Members of the Faculty.

'OSITIONS OFFERED TO FOUR

Three Indiana graduates, John C. Mellett '12, Earl Keyes, '13 and Floyd Ramsey, '14, have taken positions in the faculty of the University of Maine, a remarkable showink for one university. Positions were offered to five Indiana men. Russell Sharp was forced to decline the offer to the English department of that school owing to the illness of his mother.

Mr. Mellett will be head of the department of Journalism and will be associate prrfessor of English. He was ed. of The Indiana Student during his senior year here. He has been working in New York and more recently has been connected with The Indianapolis News. He is a member of Emanon.

Mr. Keyes wil take a position in the public speaking department. While in school he was well known for his oratorical ability. He assisted in the public speaking department here and was a member of several debating teams also.

Mr. Ramsey will hold an instructorship in the department of Physics. He took his master's degree in the physics department here last June.

GREEN CAPS, FRESHMEN!

"As it is the law and custom at Indiana University for every member of the freshman class to wear the official green cap every time he appears on the University campus, the class of 1918 will take notice and appear on the campus in their green caps at once."

This was the sentiment and resolution of the Traditional Committee which met to consider the carrying out of the traditions and customs of Indiana University. The committee will formally present rules for every freshman within a short time. Smoking on the campus is also forbidden by this committee of representative students.

INDIANA WINS OPENING GAME FROM DEPAUW

Methodists' One Chance to Beat The Crimson Nipped in the Bud by Score of 13-6

ARCHIE AND "MICKEY" SCORE

(Neal Welch)

Indiana squelched DePauw's one big chance to come out with a win over the Crimson Saturday afternoon when Coach Childs' crew smashed through the Methodist line for two touchdowns while the Bogle men crossed the line only once. Both sides failed to kick the first goal. Capt. "Mickey" Erehart was successful in his second attempt, making the final count 13 to 6.

Like all early-season games, Saturday's contest served only to show up the strong and weak places in the offense and defense. It showed that Coach Childs will have little to worry about in the backfield, but that the line must be built up considerably to withstand the attack of the three Conference games that come in a row on the next three Saturdays.

Through DePauw's Line

With the two Ereharts, Capt. "Mickey" and Archie, at the halves, Whitaker at quarter and Williams at full, the backfield tore through the DePauw line for repeated gains. Of this quarter, Archie Erehart is the only one who is seeing his first days on a varsity eleven. "Mickey" is now going through his third year as is Williams. Whitaker had his initial season last year. Scott, last year's full back, has returned to the ranks and will probably be ready for duty in the Chicago game.

Not in a number of years has DePauw been represented by as much strength as the Methodists displayed against the Crimson. DePauw followers looked to their men to put up a stiff battle with a slight possibility for a win, but with the count tied at the end of the first half all of these hopes became brighter.

A penalization in the closing minutes of the fourth quarter against DePauw for roughing put the Crimson within striking distance of the goal on the winning counts. With the ball on the 34 yard line, Sharp got his team mates into a hole by slugging and the ball was put on the 49 yard line leaving Indiana just one yard to go.

"Mickey" Erehart took the ball within six inches of the line. "Mickey" was called through again, but the DePauw line displayed some of the stuff the Hoosiers did against Illinois in front of the Illinois goal last year and held. Archie plunged through the remaining few inches of ground for the second and last touchdown. Mickey kicked gaol.

Indiana Scores in Four Minutes

Indiana's first touchdown came in four minutes after the ball was put into play. It took the Crimson exactly nine plays to get the ball over the line after Capt. Erehart carried the ball 50 yards on the kickoff. This touchdown was made on straight football, all of the plays smashing through the line for good gains.

DePauw's lone touchdown took a little longer time than the Crimson's. It was made much the same as Indiana's, straight line plunges aginst a line that seemed to be unable to get together sent the ball straight down

(Continued on Page Four)

INDIANA UNION STARTS YEAR'S WORK TONIGHT

Directors Will Make Plans For The Operation of a Student Moving Picture Show

TO ELECT VICE-PRESIDENT

Dr. Howe and Dr. Campbell are Assisting the Board on Entertainment Series.

President Stump of the Indiana Union will call a meeting of the directors at 6:30 o'clock tonight. Final plans for a picture show will be made and the program for the entertainment series will be finished. Sucessors to "Micky" McCarty, first vice-president, Walter B. Jones will also be chosen.

The program for the Enterainment Series will be completed and ready for publication in a very few days, according to members of the committee. Dr. W. D. Howe and Dr. C. D. Campbell are assiting the entertainment committee.

The Union will operate a moving picture show for the benefit of the students and people of Bloomington. Mr. Stump stated this morning that it is not known where the pictures will be shown or on what nights. The auditorium of the Student building will probably be used for that purpose. The show will not be operated more than twice a week. Five cents admission will be charged. According to the plans of the Union, the show will have to be self-supporting and any money in excess will be used for other student purposes. It is the intention of the board of directors to so organize the picture show that no money need be withdrawn from the regular income of the Union.

The barber shop is ready open for student business in the "old stand," with Al Hughes still in charge. A new man from Indianapolis is helping him.

Genial Jim Potter, the wizard of the billiard balls, is greeting his old friends and meeting the new students in the Union pool room.

FOUR FOREIGNERS HERE

Two Registered From The Philippines and Two From China

Four new foreigners have put in their appearance at Indiana thus far, two men having registered from the Philippines and two from China, all of whom have either attended or have graduated from university in their own countries.

Juan Santos and Felino de la Merced of Manila, P. I., and Bulacan, P. I., were in the summer school, having come from Washington D. C., where they took special tutoring in the English language.

Santos is a graduate of two universities, receiving his A. B. degree at San Juan de Letran Univesity and his L. L. B. at Escuela de Derecho University. He arrived in the United States six months ago and has fairly mastered the English language in that time.

Mereed is studying for his L. L. B. degree also and has had experience in teaching English in the English University at Manila. He atended the universities of Manila and Escuela de Derecho.

Chow Chi Pang and Miao En Chao are the names of the two from China. They arrived in this country along with 95 other Chinees students who are attending colleges here.

Chow is studing towards a civil engineering degree. He will spend four years here taking a general science course. Miao is working for a bachelor's degree. Both men attended the American High School at Peking. Miao attended St. John's Univesity in his native country for a while.

Clyde Kellam '14 will teach this year, having taken a position as wa principal in the Kokomo schools.

P0080157, IU Archives.

1915–1938

Some of the most famous names to come out of the Indiana Daily Student—Ernie Pyle, Don Mellett and Nelson Poynter—were on staff during the teens and early 1920s. At the depth of the Great Depression in 1932, graduates worried about whether they would find jobs but also collected IU's first-ever journalism degrees. Two key figures began their tenures in 1938: publisher John Stempel, who had served on staff with Pyle and Poynter, and Herman B Wells, who was named the University's 11th president.

The reporting and editing staff in the newsroom, circa 1924. Photograph by Charles Gilbert Shaw. *P0033901, IU Archives.*

Returning from War to a Time of Growth

"It has been my privilege to have lived and participated in the establishment and growth of Indiana University, not only into a leading educational institution in the state of Indiana but throughout the nation and the world."

November 11, 1918 the Armistice was signed ending World War I. I was fortunate to be one of the soldiers who was able to return to Indiana University promptly and complete my senior year.

Professor J.W. Piercy, head of the Department of Journalism, appointed me editor in chief on March 26, 1919. The publication had carried on throughout World War I, and I found it on a firm foundation so it wasn't difficult to continue building for the future.

Important headlines in the spring 1919 edition were as follows:

"1,375 Register for Spring Term"

"Plans for Reception of Battery F of Rainbow Division"

"Enrollment Increases to 2,000 with Return of Soldiers"

"Student Self-Government Lost by 29 Votes"

"Three Hundred Students Graduate in 1919 Class"

It has been my privilege to have lived and participated in the establishment and growth of Indiana University, not only into a leading educational institution in the state of Indiana but throughout the nation and the world. A great contributor to the growth of Indiana University has been the growth of the IDS from a department of the University to one of the leading schools of journalism in the nation.

—J. Dwight Peterson, BA 1919, LLD 1966, wrote this recollection in 1977 for the paper's 110th birthday. He died in 1990.

J. Dwight Peterson. *P0078380, IU Archives.*

November 25, 1919

Victory Edition

THE INDIANA DAILY STUDENT

10 Pages Today

VOL. XLIX.—NO. 51. BLOOMINGTON, INDIANA, TUESDAY, NOVEMBER 25, 1919. ESTABLISHED 1867.

Indiana Defeats Pride of East

INDIANA CUTS FIGURE IN GREAT GRIDIRON UPSET OF 1919 SEASON

Crimson Team Outplays Powerful Syracuse Combination in Homecomers' Game Saturday. Visitors Helpless Before the Fierce Offensive of Stiehm's Players as Indiana's "Gamest Eleven" Sweep the Eastern Champions off of their Feet in a 12 to 6 Score. Opponents Unable to Gain Consistently Against Crimson Defense.

RECORD BREAKING CROWD OF ROOTERS ATTEND GAME

Probably the greatest gridiron upset in the country for the season of 1919, and one of the most profound upheavals of dope in the history of the collegiate game, occurred on Jordan Field, Saturday afternoon when Indiana's "gamest eleven" swept the powerful Syracuse machine off its feet and won by a 12 to 6 count.

The feat of the Crimson eleven in downing the team which rightfully claimed premier honors in the East, was a tremendous surprise, but it came about by no fluke. The heavy invaders were out-generaled and outplayed from start to finish; they were rendered almost helpless by the sheer fierceness and brilliance of the Crimson attack and defense. The playing of Coach Stiehm's men Saturday was the most finished sample of gridiron prowess that has been seen on Jordan Field for years.

Eight Thousand Spectators.

Every man and woman in the record throng of eight thousand people who packed the bleachers, were pulling with all their heart and soul for the team, and the players knew it. The team realized that never before had a Crimson eleven received such support, and this realization was no small factor in the victory.

The inspiration of the band and the incessant roar of organized rooting was magnificent. Every seat in the enlarged bleachers was filled long before the referee's whistle announced the kick-off of the great inter-sectional gridiron classic.

Start of Game.

The visiting players, all fine-looking athletes, and most of them veritable giants in stature, were the first to appear on the field. The Orangemen ran through a series of signals in true championship form, appearing exceedingly powerful. They were given a round of applause.

Indiana's seventy-five piece R.O.T.C. band then marched around the gridiron, lead by the peerless drum-major, Eddie Brackett. Just as it halted before the south bleachers to play "Indiana," the Crimson squad trotted on the field and was given an ovation. Then followed a round of organized cheering.

Captain Minton won the toss and chose the east goal for Indiana. The contest was called at 2:10 by Referee Davis. As had been expected, Captain Minton, Kyle and Mathys, three of Indiana's regulars were unable to start the game because of injuries.

The Syracuse coach sent in all of his regulars at the start, expecting them to smother Indiana early in the game so that he could use his second and third-string players. The opposing lineup included Captain Alexander, All-American guard of last year; and Ackley, quarter, and Schwartzer, end, both regarded as All-American timber for this fall.

Indiana Scores Touchdown.

The initial play was an inauspicious one for Syracuse. Gulick, left tackle, kicked-off out of bounds. The ball was returned and this time his kick was received by Williams, who made a return of ten yards. Bowser was given the ball for the first Indiana play, but failed to gain through the line. Ross, on the next down, went through for five yards, and Faust smashed the heavy Eastern line for four more. Leonard then punted to Ackley, who made a return of five yards.

Syracuse was given the ball, but the touted backs were made helpless by the iron defense of the Stiehm combination. Abbott managed to traverse a scant yard and Abbott failed to gain. The visitors were offside and lost five yards. Ackley tried an onside kick, and it was Indiana's ball again in mid-field. Faust proceeded to gain five yards off-tackle, but Bowser failed to gain on the next down.

It was at this juncture that the decisive play of the contest came. Williams, from mid-field hurled a perfect forward pass to Donovan, who eluded two tacklers and raced forty yards across the Syracuse goal line for a touchdown. The Crimson rooters went wild with joy. Risley missed the try-at-goal. Time was called out for Donovan, who sprained his ankle in falling over the goal line. He was forced to retire from the game, and Bell took his place at end.

Williams made five yards through center, but Indiana was penalized for being off-side. Williams again made five yards. Two attempted forward passes, Williams to Bell, were incomplete. Faust made an on-side kick, placing the ball in Syracuse's possession on their own ten-yard line. Ackley punted to Faust, who made a five-yard return. Bowser broke through for a full seven yards. Ross failed to gain and Williams and Faust lost ground on the next downs. The pigskin went over to the visitors, who again were unable to gain on three downs. Ackley started to punt, but Bell broke through the Syracuse defense and blocked the kick. Pope recovered the ball and carried it five yards. Williams went around right end for five yards, and Bowser made first down by two smashing line plunges. Indiana was penalized for off-side play, and Ross was unable to gain on two downs. At this point, with the ball on the twenty-three-yard line, Indiana scored again. Risley was given the ball for a place kick, and he

(Contined on page 10.)

THE SMILE OF VICTORY

ELLIOTT RISLEY, Tackle.

EVERY MAN ON TEAM GAVE ALL HE HAD

Crimson Players Win Syracuse Game Because of Determination to Defeat the East.

SIX PLAYERS GRADUATE

Mumby, Faust, Hiatt, Wiley, Pope and Bowser Wear Moleskins Last Time for Indiana.

If it is required that individual stars be named of the men who played on the opposing teams here Saturday, several must be mentioned. For Syracuse, the work of the following stood out above that of their teammates: Alexander, guard; Ackley, quarter; and Schwarzer, end. For Indiana, the following men starred: Mumby, Donovan, Risley, Bell, Pierce, Lorhei, McCaw, Faust, Leonard, Pope, Williams, Bowser and Ross.

The Orange team, swept off its feet by the sheer ferocity of the Crimson onslaught at the very outset of the fray, came back like the champion that it was, and fought stubbornly for the honor of Syracuse. The Syracuse coach and his players found this Indiana eleven to be several times stronger than they had expected it to be, but this over-confidence was dashed to pieces in the first five minutes of play. The All-Americans and conquerors of the East found that they had met their match in Stiehm's proteges, and upon this realization, they battled as they never had before. Defeat at the hands of Indiana meant their downfall as proud claimants to Eastern grid honors for the season of 1919, besides the humiliation of being downed at the hands of a team which stood almost at the foot of the Western Conference. Therefore, from the time Donovan made that first glorious touchdown, the Orangemen threw their all into the fight, and the Indiana team deserves its greatest glory from the fact that it defeated a champion-

(Continued on Page 6)

R.O.T.C. BATTALION CELEBRATES VICTORY

Major O'Brien Dismisses Unit After Expressing Appreciation of Spirit Shown by Men.

PLAN LARGE PICTURE

Picture of Battalion Will Be Made Next Tuesday—New Features in Military Department.

The entire R. O. T. C. battalion was dismissed after a very short drill and other exercises today in order that its members might celebrate the victory of the Indiana football team.

The unit was formed as usual in front of Assembly Hall at 1 o'clock. Companies were taken to their respective drill grounds and given a very short drill. Thef reshmen companies were put through the "overseas" extended order drill and the sophomores were given a little preliminary work in the new bayonet exercise.

Stiehm Addresses Men.

Following the short drill, the battalion was marched to Assembly Hall. Here they were first addressed by Coach Stiehm who thanked the men for their support of the Indiana team during the year mentioning especially the Centre College game and the loyalty and spirit shown in last Saturday's game.

Major O'Brien spoke to the men and thanked them for the part they played in backing the team and in helping create the greater college spirit that is prevalent at Indiana this year. He rferred to the R. O. T. C. games that had been played during the year as being examples of real spirit. He further complimented the R. O. T. C. men in the University band and made the remark that several Syracuse men had told him that it was the best band they had seen this year.

Progress of R. O. T. C.

He spoke of the progress of the R. O. T. C. unit this year and mentioned

(Continued on Page 6)

CRIMSON LEAVES THE DOORMAT TO GAIN A PLACE IN THE SUN

Indiana Breaks Into the Limelight in the Last Game of the Season and Upsets the Football Dope of the Year in a Great Intercollegiate Girdiron Struggle Between the East and the Middle West. Eight Thousand Rooters Burst Into a Pandemonium as Game Ends in Mid-field After Orange Attack of Forward Passing is Halted.

VICTORY BRINGS A NEW ERA TO INDIANA ATHLETICS

Indiana 12 and Syracuse 6—that was the result when the pride of the East met the "doormat" of the Middle-West in a great intercollegiate gridiron game here on old historic Jordan Field Saturday afternoon. As the last rays of a glimmering sun were cast on a contest which had held everyone of the eight thousand on edge for three hours, old "grads", former students, friends of the University, citizens of Bloomington as well as students, burst forth into a pendemonium.

All that was before that crowd of students and alumni as they hurtled the fence and onto the field was carried before it in its eager rush. Above the bobbing heads and shoulders of bleacherites broke loose, were carried Coach Stiehm and his squad of Crimson fight. None were so dignified or sedate as not to give a whoop and break loose with some antic betokening the pride of an Indiana revived—the joy of a victory over one of the strongest teams beyond the Allegheny mountains, the rock-ribbed home of football.

College Gossip.

For some days to follow will college gossip be centered about how Indiana defeated Syracuse. No number of times since the game Saturday has the contest from kick-off to the finish been played all over again, each play in detail. In the spirit which spells the doom of Indiana as the "doormat" of the Conference comes the realization of a new era in Indiana University athletics, where Crimson teams will be feared and respected as Syracuse has learned to respect and fear the Middle West since last Saturday.

To upset the dope of the 1919 football season is a feat but rarely accomplished by any team at the last moment. In more or less true form are games won on the gridiron and champions decided for seasons. But in the East and the Middle West a new complexion was given to football ability by the result of the Indiana-Syracuse game. The East had the game "cinched" and the Middle West fully expected the Crimson to lose the game. Yet something turned the trick.

The Spirit Prevailed.

It as the evening before that the men students of Indiana together with men of the faculty and alumni had gathered for Indiana's Centennial Pow-Wow. Before that banquet was started that body of men stood with bowed heads in a few minutes of silent prayer for the Crimson team. A few minutes before the game was called on Jordan Field it is understood that a house of girls on East Fourth street had spent a few minutes in silent prayer for the Crimson team. Again in the last few minutes of the game as Syracuse began its last effort with a variety of forward passes toward the Crimson goal, just how many silent prayers were offered will never be known. But the Crimson won—whoever believes in silent prayer may do so, the fact remains that the Syracuse offensive was halted in mid-field.

"Hail to Old I. U."

The spirit of prayer was felt as the University chimes played "Hail to Old I. U." before the game started and during the first half. As the first notes were heard across Jordan Field every Indiana University rooter rose and with bowed head remained standing until the last note died away over the gridiron.

In contrast to this hush was the ever present rooting of the bleachers. The Crimson players coming onto the field were greeted with a noisy demonstration and the University band of seventy pieces rang out with "Indiana, our Indiana". Not a one lost his voice in the rooting and the person who failed to cheer throughout the period of the game was the exception. Cheers followed the boy around the gridiron as he led a goat typified as Syracuse's goat. The north and the south side of the field yelled against each other and a few minutes after the game began, when Donovan made his run across the Orange line with the first Crimson touchdown with the Syracuse super-men in a mad chase to down him, the eight thousand rooters resembled bedlam thrown into a frenzy. When Risley kicked his two goals from placement, on all sides of the field the rooters rose again and danced on the bleachers.

Operators Kept Busy

In the newspaper stand the click of seven operators were kept constantly at work sending returns of the game to many sections of the country. Two wires were connected with New York, one for the Associated Press, one for Indianapolis, one for the Western Union, one for Syracuse University and one to Chicago. This is the first time that an Indiana football game has attracted so many newspaper men and operators to Jordan Field to keep close tab on the progress of a game of football.

Saturday evening as the band headed the procession of students throughout the down-town streets on a celebration of jollity, business came to a standstill to watch the "howling host". Not since the days when Indiana beat Purdue had the towns

(Continued on Page 6)

CAPT. ROSCOE MINTON, Half.

P0078532, IU Archives.

COMPLETE FAIR PROGRAM FOR TODAY IN THIS ISSUE

STATE FAIR EDITION

THE INDIANA DAILY STUDENT

STATE FAIR EDITION

VOL. LI. NO. 2. STATE FAIR GROUNDS, INDIANAPOLIS, IND., TUESDAY, SEPT. 5, 1922. ESTABLISHED 1867.

PURDUE UNIVERSITY HAS LARGE EXHIBIT AT 1922 STATE FAIR

12 Departments In Agriculture, Dairy Products And Home Economics On Display.

MODEL FARM ILLUSTRATED

State Chemists' Department Points Out Noxious Weeds—Poultry Colony Included In Show.

To educate rather than to advertise is the purpose and plan of the two exhibits by Purdue university at the State Fair, according to officials in charge of the display. The display, which is under the general direction of G. M. Frier, director of Purdue exhibits and short courses, is divided into 12 departments.

Ten of the departments, covering strictly agricultural subjects, are displayed in the building directly west of the Coliseum, while the other three departments covering home economics and dairy products are in the Oliver Chilled Plows building on the north side of the midway.

Spoor Farm Displayed.

The central exhibit of the agricultural group is that of the department of farm management, with Mr. Walter Kell and Mr. Robertson in charge. Included in this are models of the Spoor farm at Salem, Ind. One model shows the run-down condition of the farm when taken over by Purdue two years ago. The second shows the farm as it is today and a third shows the farm as it will be ultimately when work of rehabilitation is completed.

Each departmental exhibit stresses one point, and shows it in as simple a manner as possible so that the observer can grasp it readily. The purpose is to educate and no attempt is made to show all the work being done in each department.

The state chemist's department, in charge of A. A. Hansen, has on display the 19 weeds declared noxious by recent action of the legislature. They are shown so that the farmers can identify them easily.

Give Pointers on Feeding.

The effects of certain kinds of feeding are shown in the exhibits of the department of animal husbandry under Mr. John Swab and of the poultry department under Mr. Jones, Mr. Fitting, Mr. Williams and Mr. Ed Gannon. Included in the poultry department is a model chicken colony.

The department of botany is in charge of Dr. C. T. Gregory and K. E. Beeson, with T. J. Davis and G. M. Sterrett in charge of the department of entymology. Horticulture is in charge of Fay Gaylord, and soils and crops in charge of R. S. Thomas and W. A. Ostrander. The veterinary exhibit under Dr. F. L. Walkey and Dr. Roberts, displays several common diseases, and conditions which cause these diseases which may be avoided with care.

Show Women How to Save on Clothes

In the annex exhibit, the home economics department has a display of millinery and clothing made by students in the department and by women in the state who took the two-day millinery courses offered in several counties. The aim of the exhibit is to show women how to save clothing expenses by making their own. Miss Lella R. Gaddis is in charge, assisted by Miss Helen Virginia McKinley and Miss Nelle F. Flaningham.

Use of dairy products as food and the relative value of milk, butter and cheese is stressed in the dairy products exhibit, with John Wann of the Purdue Extension division, in charge. Recipes for various dishes in which dairy products are used, are furnished free to visitors.

"Hot Dawg, Some Fair," Say Concessionaires

"What ya' say, oh wa' ya' say, a nice juicy hamburg," "Right over here, you're not hungry, just thirsty! Lemonade is what you want, right here the real stuff, ten cents," "Hone cone taffy, melts in your mouth like ice cream in your pocket," "Hey, hey try some cotton candy, your money back if you don't like it." "Look! look! chicken sandwich, reg-lar meal, 25 cents, only 'fourth of a dollar!" And so run the deafening cries of the concessionaires on the fair grounds.

The barbecue lunches, church chicken dinners, hot dog stands, candied apples and merry-go-rounds are the yearly symbols of the State Fair. But without all these along with lost children, proud exhibitors and a thousand and one amusing sights a fair wouldn't be a fair.

RIVALRY IN STOCK JUDGING CONTESTS IS AT HIGH PITCH

Boys' Calf Club Awards Feature First Day—Kenneth Whistler's Calf Wins.

HORSE JUDGING IS CLOSE

Poultry, Cattle and Horse Judging To Continue Thruout the Week—Entry Lists Overflow.

Unusual interest and enthusiasm were manifested at the Coliseum yesterday morning when Indiana State Fair visitors crowded the building and the adjoining new horse show barn to witness the initial awarding of blue ribbons for live stock.

The judging of cattle, which occupied the entire morning, tested the ability of the judges, as all the classes were filled with the best blooded stock of Indiana and surrounding states.

Awards Hotly Contested.

The Boys' Calf club awards, the feature event of the first day's judging, was one of the most hotly contested events of the day. In each of the three events, the Shorthorn, Hereford and Aberdeen-Angus, deliberation by the judges was necessary before the winner could be chosen.

In the Calf club contest for Shorthorns and Polled Shorthorns, Carl Max Oldham, of Wilkerson, Ind., was declared the winner. A prize of $35 was awarded by the Indiana Board of Agriculture, with a like amount paid by the Indiana Shorthorn and Polled Shorthorn Breeders association.

Kenneth Whistler, of Buck Creek, was awarded the $35 prize in the Aberdeen-Angus Calf club contest. After the three winners had been chosen in the three different breeds, Whistler's animal was declared the champion steer of the Calf club by the judges of the contest.

In the Hereford contest Richey McCay, of Lafayette, was declared the winner. He was awarded a $35 prize by the Indiana Board of Agriculture, with another $35 award by the Indiana Hereford breeders.

Horse Judging Starts.

Horse judging, which started in the afternoon, like the cattle contests, was close and interesting thruout, and the large number of entries in all the contests made the event of much interest to the farmers and other visitors at the new show horse barn.

Poultry, cattle and horse judging will continue thruout the week, and officials and judges predict that the following days will see the large entries continue and that interest will continue at the same high pitch thruout.

John Wesley Cari, '85, is state supervisor and inspector of high schools in Kentucky. His address is 728 Shelby Street, Frankfort, Ky.

SIDESHOWS "MAKE" INDIANA'S FIRST STATE FAIR BACK IN '52

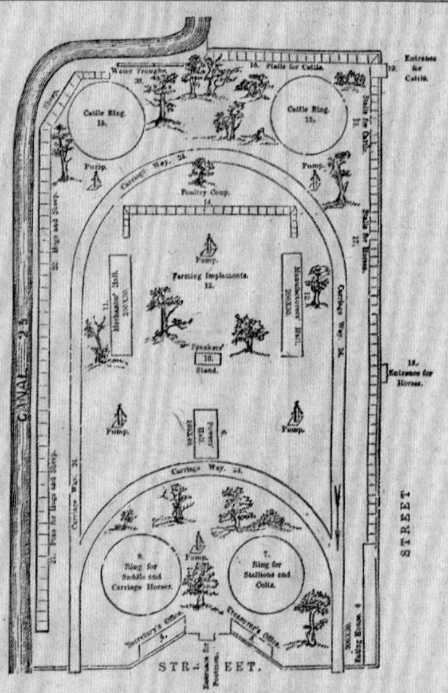

FIRST STATE FAIR GROUNDS.

An agricultural exhibit with a superabundance of sideshows.

That was Indiana's first state fair, staged at Indianapolis 'way back in 1852. The fair opened in Military park on Oct. 19 and continued thru Oct. 25.

In contrast to the present commodious quarters for exhibitors at the fair the first fair provided only 53 stalls for sheep and hogs, 71 stalls for cattle and horses, and 29 coops for poultry. Two buildings, Mechanics Hall and Manufacturers Hall, each 250x30 feet in dimensions, were then thought to be the last word in exposition buildings. The only other structures on the grounds were Powers' Hall, 100x40 feet, a small speakers' stand in the center of the grounds, and small offices at the gates for the secretary and treasurer of the Fair association.

Free Drinks Provided.

Altho the fair officials were able

(Continued on Page Eight)

Program For Today

DAY

Chamber of Commerce and Old Soldiers' Day.

Judging of Clydesdale horses, short horn and Holstein-Friesians cattle; Purdue students judging contest of Milch and Angora goats; judging of Poland-China and Chester White swine.

State horseshoe tournament.

Better Babies contest.

Balloon race, 16 entries, afternoon.

Automobile and airplane shows all day.

Music program—Women's building.

"Pop" Geers driving Sanardo, world famous pacer, in exhibition mile.

Races afternoon, with vaudeville and acrobatic exhibition before grandstand.

Band concerts, morning, afternoon and night.

EVENING

Hippodrome and horse show in Coliseum starting 7 p. m. with parade of live stock.

Fireworks spectacle and pageant, "The Heart of China," in front of grandstand.

LUSTY HOOSIER INFANTS COMPETE IN BABY SHOW

Annual Sweepstakes For Heirs Apparent Draw Hundreds To Woman's Building

Little babies, big babies and cute babies.

Babies of all kinds and sizes are entered in the Indiana Baby contest which opened yesterday. The contest is being held on the second floor of the Woman's Building, with Dr. Ada Schweitzer, director of the division of infant and child hygiene of the state board of health, in charge.

The contest is being held in the immense Rainbow room, as the staff in charge designates the artistically decorated room. Rooms are provided for the mental tests and for dressing and undressing.

The babies are divided into two classes, those from one to two years in one, and those from two to three years of age in the other. The necessary preliminary registration of babies closed on Aug. 2, but so much interest has been shown since the opening of the fair that arrangements will be made to accommodate more babies next year, according to Dr. Schweitzer.

Dr. James C. Carter, nationally known authority on baby care, is chief examiner, Dr. Bernard Larkin is eye examiner and Dr. John W. Carmick is ear, nose and throat examiner. Nurses from the Fletcher sanatarium are in attendance as assistants.

A wealth of literature regarding child care is available to all visitors, and posters containing valuable information and statistics on Indiana babies, are displayed on the walls.

That Indiana mothers are heartily in favor of the baby contest is shown by the number of eager mothers who have brought their young hopefuls to be examined but many of the young heir apparents of Hoosierdom protest vigorously to the process of examination.

Purdue Runs Concession To Pay Team's Expenses

Purdue's dairy cattle judging team will have part and possibly all of its expenses to the national dairy show paid by the proceeds of a concession operated by the Purdue Dairy club at the State Fair.

Each year teams in judging the various classes of stock represent Purdue university at the various national and international shows. Members of these teams are required to bear personally the expense of training for these contests and their expenses to the contests. The Dairy club is working to obtain funds so that the entire burden of expense will not rest on the team members.

FLYING ACROSS CONTINENT.

Jacksonville, Fla., Sept. 4.—Lieut. James H. Doolittle, army aviator, hopped off from the beach at Mebtume at 10:03 o'clock tonight for a flight by airplane to San Diego, Cal., which he hopes to reach in time for dinner tomorrow night. He plans only one stop, at Kelly Field, San Antonio, Tex., for fuel.

FORMER CONGRESSMAN DIES.

Manchester, N. H., Sept. 4.—Former Congressman George Hazelton, 90, died at Chester, N. H., today. He had represented the Milwaukee district in congress for two terms and had been U. S. attorney for one term.

WEATHER.

Indiana—Generally fair and continued warm Tuesday and Wednesday.

1922 AUTOMOBILE DISPLAY OUTSHINES FORMER SHOWS

Manufacturer's Building Has Display of 51 Different Makes of Cars.

Outshining all previous expositions the state fair auto show opened yesterday with 98 exhibitors demonstrating their wares. The manufacturer's building was filled to capacity with cars and accessory exhibits and everything was shined and polished to the last degree, in fact the entire building took on the air of an art exhibit.

Among the unique exhibits on display was the first automobile, invented, designed and built by Elwood Haynes at Kokomo in 1893. It is now the property of the United States government and up until a short time ago was on exhibition at the Smithsonian Institution, National Museum, Washington, D. C. Mayor Shank's car was also on exhibit by the LykGlas Auto NeRual System.

Fifty-five Makes Shown.

Fifty-five different makes of cars and trucks are exhibited, with several models of each make on display. All the latest types of passenger cars and trucks are shown, with many new features and improvements in the accessory line. A 20-piece orchestra will furnish music in the building during the entire week.

John Orman, manager of the show, predicts the greatest attendance ever had at an Indiana auto show. "With the farmers of practically the entire state known to be in a happy mood with general prosperity ahead for most of them, a large crowd from the rural districts is expected every day of the show," Mr. Orman said. "The dealers as a class feel sure that these people will come and will be in the market for cars for fall delivery." The show will continue all week.

Taylor Exhibit Interests Matrimonially Inclined

The married, those contemplating matrimony and those who are still hopeful find in the exhibit of the Taylor Furniture company more than usual interest, since an artistically furnished bungalow constitutes the exhibit of this company.

The living room is furnished in Karpen overstuffed furniture with blue predominating in the decorations. Lamps of the floor and table variety add to the effectiveness of the room. A sun-room, in which the plain grey walls are set off by gay cretonnes, opens from the living-room. All other rooms are furnished in the same detailed manner.

HIPPODROME ACTS TO HOLD COLISEUM STAGE EACH NIGHT

May Wirth, World Famous Equestrienne, Will Head Attractions.

CERVONE'S BAND TO PLAY

Parade of Livestock To Open Programs of Musical, Aerial and Other Acts of Merit.

May Wirth, world's best known equestrienne, will head the hippodrome attraction every night in the Coliseum on the fair grounds. She heads a group of circus acts booked by the management thru the United Fair Booking association of Chicago.

The program includes writers, singers and aerial performers. Music will be furnished by Cervone's Band of Philadelphia. This organization is making its first appearance in Indiana.

A parade of classy live stock at 7 o'clock will open the program each evening. The hippodrome acts will be under way by 8 o'clock.

A touch of musical comedy will be injected into the program by Bert Earle, a musical entertainer of long experience, and his eight girls. Earle is a master of the banjo and has toured the world playing that instrument. He and his troupe have appeared on the Keith and Orpheum vaudeville circuits in recent years.

The Murat Temple Chanters, of Indianapolis, who made a hit on last year's program, will appear each evening.

Aerial and athletic acts will be furnished by the two Jordan sisters, aerialists, the three Melvins, acrobats, and the diving Ringens.

Finks' comedy mule circus will lend a flavor of the sawdust ring to each evening's performance. The troupe includes three highly educated mules, a pony, eight dogs and a monkey. Five persons are required to handle these animals.

Skit To Be Presented Tonight By Girls' School

"A Main Street in Any Town," is a skit to be presented tonight in the Woman's Building by the Girl's State Fair school. The play will be in two acts, the first a street scene and the second a beauty parlor. The good and bad points in street costumes will be portrayed by the girls, showing harmony in color and line. Correct lines and ornaments for hats will be depicted as well as the most becoming way to wear a hat.

Coiffures suitable for all occasions will be dressed by the instructors, using the girls as models.

I. U. JUNIORS RUN STAND.

Lyndall Foster, '24, of Tipton, and Barrett Woodsmall, '24, of Indianapolis, are conducting a "hot dog" stand on the grounds. Foster and Woodsmall are juniors in Indiana University and members of the Phi Delta Theta fraternity.

1922 FAIR VISITORS CROWD UNIVERSITY EXHIBIT BUILDING

Departmental Exhibits Prove of Interest To People of State.

MOVIES ARE SHOWN DAILY

Demonstration of Nurses One of Most Interesting Displays of Instructive Program.

With exhibits from every department, Indiana University opened its doors at the State Fair Monday to show the people of Indiana thru practical demonstration what their State University is doing. This is the first year that Indiana University has ever had an exhibit at the State Fair.

One of the most interesting exhibits is a demonstration of the Indiana University School for Nurses, with Miss Nellie G. Brown, Miss Helen Farrell and Miss Katherine Shea, all of the Robert W. Long Hospital staff, in charge. The booth is arranged as a miniature ward. It has two ward beds, a bassinette, a model of an infant patient and a model of an adult patient.

Demonstrate Sick Room Care.

The demonstrations, which last from 10 to 12 each morning, 2 to 4 each afternoon and 7:30 to 9:30 each evening, show the various parts of nursing procedure. The routine care of the patient, making of beds, with and without patients in them, washing and care of the baby and any other special care of patient that any spectator wishes to see, are all shown.

The botany department, at the right entrance of the building, has an exhibit of especial importance to farmers. In its exhibit is a complete demonstration on wheat rust and the barberry bush. Information is given by those in charge as to the control and eradication of wheat rust. Microscopic slides of wheat rust are also shown.

Corn Products Displayed.

There is also a chart demonstrating the products and uses of corn. Another phase which will be of interest is the "Mutt and Jeff" corn. The department is able to control the height of the corn stalk and will explain to those interested how the growth of corn may be controlled.

The exhibits of the physics department and the department of military training are proving fascinating to many visitors. The physics department is demonstrating a machine used during the world war to locate airplanes. The United States government has loaned the University one of these machines for the study of the velocity of sound. The demonstration at the fair shows how the U. S. army made use of these machines to locate enemy airplanes.

In the department of military training Capt. R. H. Neely is showing the different types of small guns used in the world war. The exhibit includes a one-pounder, a trench mortar, a Browning machine gun, a Browning automatic rifle and a U.S. army .30-calibre magazine rifle.

Show Movies of Campus Life.

A cool spot where one may enjoy moving pictures has been provided in the University exhibit. Thru the courtesy of L. D. Kohlmeier, of the Kolograph company, the University will show continuously moving pictures of University life. Most of the scenes were taken this summer and show the activities of the various departments of the University. Five reels are being shown. Big oscillating fans provide a constant breeze so that visitors may view the University pictures in comfort.

Hoosier Pigs, Cows, Horses Break Fair Entry Records

With more than 10,000 entries in the various exhibits, displays in the State Fair this year have reached a new high point and the predictions of officials that the 1922 event was to be the biggest in fair history have been realized.

Entries in the hog, cattle and horse departments total 6,600, or 1,100 more than last year when there were 5,500 entries. Even the new horse barns erected this spring have proved inadequate. Room could not be found in the barns for three carloads of horses which arrived yesterday from the Iowa State Fair.

The poultry exhibit includes 3,300 birds this year.

The Monon railroad reported that it had set in on the grounds forty more carloads of freight than ever before. Even the concession stands are so thick that no great freedom of motion is allowed the crowds.

The Indiana Daily Student Being Given Away At Fair

This issue of the Daily Student is an example of the practical work taught in the journalism department at Indiana University. Fifteen thousand copies of the paper will be printed daily, and will be distributed FREE to visitors on the fair grounds.

This is the first time in history that a college paper has been issued at a state fair.

The Indiana Daily Student is the official publication of the department of journalism of Indiana University.

The paper is edited and published daily thruout the school year by students in the department.

The Indiana Daily Student is recognized as one of the six leading college dailies in the United States.

P0078828, IU Archives.

Above, The staff of the 1927 State Fair edition. P0077829, IU Archives.

BEHIND THE STORY

An Innovative—and Dusty—Tradition

Described as "the outstanding innovation of the year" by the Arbutus, the 1922 Indiana State Fair edition began a tradition that would last for more than three decades. Editor-in-Chief Ernie Pyle and his staff relocated to the fairgrounds in Indianapolis to produce five editions, each six to eight pages, that included fair news, state and national headlines and publicity pieces promoting IU. A 1954 article credits longtime advertising manager W.L. Reeves with the idea to produce a state fair edition, which was designed to be self-sustaining through ads sold to businesses in Bloomington and Indianapolis. Thousands of copies were distributed on the fairgrounds each year. In those first papers in 1922, headlines included "Rivalry in stock judging contests is at high pitch" and "Lusty Hoosier infants compete in baby show."

As editor, Pyle "didn't talk much, but got his work done good and fast," O.A. Miller, who worked in the backshop of the first state fair paper, told the IDS in 1954.

In 1925, a front-page story invited fairgoers to stop by the IU exhibit to watch the "actual work of typesetting and make-up" of the next day's paper. In the early 1950s, a special edition was added to cover the Lake County Fair in northwest Indiana. The 1954 article on the state fair tradition recalled some of the lengths reporters went to while reporting the most exciting fair news in Indianapolis: "In 1953,

Ginny Krause wanted the inside story on a girly show, so down the Midway she went to apply for a job. Decked in feathers, she got her story . . . and had fun doing it." The following summer, reporter Jerry Lyst experienced "the thrill of his life" when he raced down the track as the passenger of a stunt driver.

Top stories for the first state fair edition of 1947 included a stunt cyclist critically hurt in a "thrill show" and coverage of the first-ever "Hoosier Hymn Sing." The editor in chief that September was Marjorie Smith, later Marjorie Smith Blewett, who went on to become the journalism department's placement director from 1969–90 and de facto historian.

The staff worked from a room at the IU building on the fairgrounds, right off the dirt track used by horses. "The dust was that thick—there was no air conditioning," Blewett said in an interview for this book. "I took a dress for every day because it got so dirty and there wasn't a laundromat." She recalled how John Stempel, who was on staff when the first state fair edition came out in the 1920s and would go on to be IDS publisher and chair of the journalism department, worked ahead of time to gather evergreen stories about IU and Bloomington to fill the pages alongside the fair news the staff covered live. "A man from the AP who ran a telex machine took his week vacation and worked for us sending stuff down to Bloomington, where the managing editor put together the paper," Blewett said. "I don't think I did anything right that week—you know, how [Stempel] wanted it."

In the mornings, papers would be trucked to Indianapolis and within a few hours "it would be all over the fairgrounds," Blewett said. "Talk about a great PR thing—but I'm sure the fair cleaning crews hated it."

It's in the Air

This unsigned editorial originally appeared Sept. 5, 1922. It was most likely written by Ernie Pyle in his time as editor in chief.

Nearly everyone who has ever attended Indiana University will tell you there is no place in the world like Indiana. They sometimes attempt to explain that statement but they cannot.

Strangely enough, in their attempt to explain, they fail to mention the assets of the school usually mentioned by its boosters.

They have nothing to say about the remarkable professors whose fame seems so much greater in the outside world than it does to the students who work under them. They do not mention the buildings or equipment or the many advantages carefully compiled in the school catalog. They do not gather together and present facts which a logical speaker would use in convincing folk that this was a great school.

Ex-students recognize the value of all these things, recognize their argumentative value. But when they ejaculate that there is no place in all the world like Indiana, they are thinking about something else. They are thinking of spring days when the campus is bursting with fragrance, vivid with the color of blossoms and new leaves, and when the moon is bright—it is undeniable that spring is nowhere in the world as it is in Indiana.

They are thinking about the autumn evenings when dusk has settled and the last cheers have died out over Jordan Field and another football game has become a memory, another football game which may or may not have been a victory but which was a courageous fight by Indiana men whom everyone in school knew and liked.

They are thinking of 'pep' meetings and mass meetings and pow-wows in which Indiana men sounded the ancient battle cry, where sheepish football captains tried to make speeches before a howling crowd of students and equally wild old grads, and where the old songs gave at the same time a sudden impulse to tears and an elaborate thrill down the backbone.

They are thinking about hundreds of wholesome, pleasant people who were their friends.

They are thinking something about Indiana, which none of them could ever express in words.

These persons who make each broad unqualified statement about Indiana say that they have since tried out living in many other places but that somehow the tang is missing. Other schools can contain nothing after such moments. Other schools seem to lack the facilities to produce those thrills which certainly can come within but four years of a lifetime.

These are the feelings of those who have been here and have left. Perhaps it is foolish and sentimental, but they will affirm it is the truth.

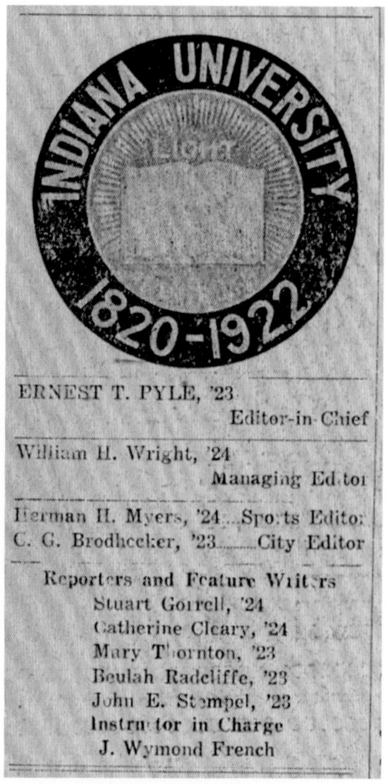
INDIANA UNIVERSITY
1820-1922

ERNEST T. PYLE, '23
Editor-in-Chief

William H. Wright, '24
Managing Editor

Herman H. Myers, '24 ... Sports Editor
C. G. Brodhecker, '23 .... City Editor

Reporters and Feature Writers
Stuart Gorrell, '24
Catherine Cleary, '24
Mary Thornton, '23
Beulah Radcliffe, '23
John E. Stempel, '23
Instructor in Charge
J. Wymond French

Masthead and staff editorial from Sept. 5, 1922. The editorial was likely written by Editor-in-Chief Ernie Pyle. *IU Archives.*

Cloudy and Unsettled Today; Thundershowers Sunday.

THE INDIANA DAILY STUDENT

Crimson-Purple Track Meet on Jordan Field, 2:30 o'Clock.

VOL. LII, NO. 145. BLOOMINGTON, INDIANA, SATURDAY MORNING, MAY 3, 1924. Established 1867.

$25,000 Fire Razes D. U. House

24 Men Homeless After Second Blaze of Year at Third Street Lodge

A fire thought to have originated from a gas heater in the basement of the Delta Upsilon fraternity house, on East Third street, at 11:40 o'clock last night, left 24 members homeless this morning. The loss was estimated at $25,000, most of which was covered by insurance.

No one was in the building when the fire started, according to John Lordan, '24, who sent in the alarm.

When the firemen arrived the entire lower floor of the building was in flames. The fire was spreading rapidly to the east side of the house, driven by a stiff wind from the west. Three streams of hose were played upon the blaze, but were ineffective until the structure collapsed. Three of the firemen narrowly escaped injury when a section of the east wall fell.

Practically all of the furniture on the first floor was removed by early arrivals, but very little clothing and other personal belongings of the members could be saved from the second floor which was enveloped in smoke almost at the start.

Crowd Gathers Quickly.

At the time the fire was discovered streets were frequented by students returning home from dances and other social engagements. Many were attired in formal dress, but in the excitement convention was forgotten as all made a helter-skelter rush toward the vicinity of the red glow illuminating the sky. Coeds forgot University rules and remained at the scene until it was evident the blaze was beyond control.

Most of the fraternity members did not arrive at their former home before the blaze practically had destroyed the building with all its contents. A check-up of members was hurriedly made and the tenseness of the situation was increased when two men could not be found. They were later accounted for, however.

The 24 occupants were invited by other fraternity men to make temporary quarters at the various houses over the campus.

The house was the property of the Delta Upsilon Alumni Association, of which James H. Warner, '15, instructor in chemistry, is president. Preliminary plans to build a new home some time ago were dropped.

Lordan Gives Alarm.

John Paul Lordan, '24, who discovered the blaze, had been sitting in a machine parked at the side of the S. A. E. house for nearly half an hour when, he said, the crackling flames in the D. U. house to the east attracted his attention. No flames, however, were issuing from the building, he asserted. He ran to the house and a glance within revealed nearly the entire lower floor filled with flames. The blaze was concentrated in the northeast corner.

Receiving no answers to shouts sent through the burning structure, Lordan dashed across the street to the S. A. E. house and called the fire department. Members of the neighboring fraternity, meantime, closed windows in the burning building and made sure that no one was imprisoned. Smoke had penetrated every nook of the interior, and the men did not venture into the dormitory, although several made quick entries to rescue property. The piano and phonograph were among the larger articles saved.

Second Fire This Year.

This was the second fire that had threatened to destroy the Delta U house this year. A defective fireplace on the main floor caused a $200 loss at 1 a. m. on Jan. 8. The entire loss of the first fire, members of the fraternity stated, was covered by insurance. A student bucket-brigade held the blaze in check until the fire department arrived. By that time, however, the flames had eaten their way through the second floor. An entire section of flooring and wall plastering had to be replaced because of the damage.

WOMEN'S CLUBS WILL GATHER HERE FOR DISTRICT MEETING

Mrs. T. J. Louden To Greet Representatives Wednesday at Convention.

8 COUNTIES REPRESENTED

Session To Be Held at Methodist Church—Business Meeting To Begin at 10 A. M.

Eight counties will be represented here Wednesday, May 7, when the Second District Federation of Clubs of Indiana meets at the First Methodist Church in its sixteenth annual convention. The county chairmen and the counties they represent are: Mrs. W. L. Evans, Daviess; Mrs. A. M. Beasley, Greene; Mrs. H. M. George, Knox; Mrs. W. J. Reynolds, Martin; Mrs. Fred Seward, Monroe; Mrs. J. E. Robinson, Morgan; Mrs. W. B. Peden, Owen, and Mrs. Amelia Crowder, Sullivan. Mrs. E. D. Farmer of Bloomington, is secretary and treasurer of the district.

A song, "America the Beautiful," will open the session at 10 a. m., immediately after registration of the visitors. Mrs. T. J. Louden of Bloomington, will greet the assembly, to which Mrs. J. R. Riggs of Sullivan, will respond. Reports and general federation news will follow. In the afternoon a conference of county chairmen will be held. Immediately following this, Winifred Merrill will give a violin recital, accompanied by Professor Skjerne. Mrs. O. M. Pittenger and Mrs. H. H. Young will give talks, these to be followed by election of officers, after which the convention will witness the Foundation day pageant on the campus.

Mrs. T. J. Louden is chairman of the reception committee, which is composed of officers of the Local Council of Women, president of Cycle Literary Club and presidents of all clubs affiliated with the local council.

On the registration and credentials committee are Mrs. F. H. Batman, Mrs. J. B. Vos, Mrs. H. H. Jeffers and Mrs. E. D. Farmer. Mrs. Clay Beard, Mrs. J. E. Luzadder and Mrs. Roy Sappenfield constitute the luncheon committee, and Mrs. Oden Smith, Mrs. B. F. Adams and Mrs. A. P. Campbell comprise the resolutions committee.

FEE PAYMENTS SLOWED BY DEADLINE EXTENSION

Activity of Arbutus Buyers Suffers Relapse After Thursday's Rush.

Arbutus fee-paying at the bursar's office progressed slowly yesterday. A line of students reaching to the corridor of Maxwell Hall had beseiged the cashier's window Thursday.

Although the deadline for paying the fee was extended until next Saturday, it appears that a large number of students plan to wait until the last day, according to assistants in the bursar's office.

By paying the fee early in the week, time will be saved the students and congestion in Maxwell Hall will be avoided, it was pointed out. About half the juniors and seniors have received receipts thus far.

SCORES

College.
Wabash 10, Notre Dame 6.
N.A.G.U. 11, Earlham 6.
Purdue 6, Northwestern 5.

American Association.
Indianapolis 7, Milwaukee 3.
St. Paul 6, Toledo 4.
Columbus 9, Minneapolis 4.
Kansas City 5, Louisville 4.

American League.
Washington 6, New York 4.
Chicago 3, Cleveland 2.
Boston 11, Philadelphia 0.
St. Louis 4, Detroit 1.

National League.
New York 7, Boston 4.
Philadelphia 7, Brooklyn 6.
Cincinnati 4, Chicago 3.
Pittsburgh 3, St. Louis 2.

Democrats Sound Rally Call for Mock Convention, May 13

Campus Jeffersonians To Choose Party Nominees in Assembly Hall—Van Osdal, Gerhart, Manley To Name State Chairmen This Week.

Political interest, already at high ebb because of the recent Republican Mock Convention and the approaching primary elections, was augmented yesterday by the announcement of campus Democratic leaders that followers of Jefferson will assemble by delegations in Assembly Hall a week from Tuesday to make their choice of national party nominees.

Nathan Van Osdal, '24; Morgan Gerhart, '24, and Gertrude Manley, '24, will select the state chairman, who in turn will choose state representatives this week. Professors Walter E. Treanor and Paul V. McNutt will act as faculty advisors to the committees and assist in selecting candidates for nomination.

National Secretary May Come.

Charles Greathouse, secretary of the national Democratic committee, tentatively has accepted an invitation to attend the convention. Other prominent Democrats from the city and state probably will witness the moot selection of the presidential and vice-presidential candidates for the fall election, according to club officials.

No charge will be made for admittance to the convention hall. All costs of staging the affair will be taken care of by the "slush fund" of the local Democratic Club, it was explained by members of the committee on arrangements.

DOWNEY ELECTED.

Springfield, Mass., May 2.—David G. Downey of New York, was elected chairman today by the committee on episcopacy of the Methodist Episcopal conference here.

2 POLITICAL TALKS SCHEDULED TODAY

Rolla Morgan To Speak for Johnson, Ryan To Plead Toner's Cause.

Two political meetings today, both Republican, will close the campaign in Monroe county.

County Attorney Rolla Morgan will speak at the court house this afternoon at 2:30 o'clock on behalf of Hiram Johnson, Republican candidate for president. Morgan is filling the date that Johnson was scheduled to fill, but which was cancelled because of the senator's illness. Attorney Morgan also will review the qualifications of Republican county aspirants, he stated last night.

Oswald Ryan of Anderson, will address a meeting at the court house tonight at 8 o'clock. Ryan will speak in the interest of the candidacy of E. C. Toner, Republican candidate for governor of Indiana. Ryan is delivering addresses throughout the state in behalf of Toner, and the local talk will be his closing speech before the primary.

Bryan To Return Today From Purdue Celebration

President William Lowe Bryan, who is attending the semi-centennial celebration held at Purdue University May 1-3, will return today.

Dr. Bryan spoke at a banquet Thursday night in honor of Purdue alumni. Provost S. E. Smith was the official representative of the University at the celebration.

KATE MILNER RABB TO AID IN UNVEILING MEMORIAL MARKER

Indianapolis Writer To Represent Historical Society at Exercises Wednesday.

Kate Milner Rabb, '86, and President William Lowe Bryan will remove the veil from the bronze tablet erected to mark the site of the first University building, on the high school campus, on Foundation Day, Wednesday, May 7, at 2:30 p. m.

Mrs. Rabb, author of "The Hoosier Listening Post," daily feature in the Indianapolis Star, will represent the Indiana Historical Society. She was a member of The Daily Student staff while in college. Dr. Bryan is also a member of the historical society.

Fesler To Speak.

James William Fesler, president of the board of trustees, will make a speech of acceptance in behalf of the University. Professor James A. Woodburn, retiring head of the history department and president of the historical society, will preside at the unveiling ceremonies.

Registrar John W. Cravens, under

(CONTINUED ON PAGE SIX)

JUDGES "SNOWED UNDER" WITH NAMES FOR PARK

Owing to the deluge of names submitted in the contest to christen the city park near the Cascades, the park board will not be able to announce the winner of the joint prize offered by the park board, the Chamber of Commerce and The Daily Student, until next week. The quality of many of the suggestions was one factor in delaying the decision of the judges.

More than 100 students and citizens of Bloomington have entered the contest, many of the number submitting two and even more names for the new park. The park to be named is a tract of 62 acres located on the Dixie Highway near the Cascades. It is considered one of the beauty spots of the state.

Politicians in Feverish Rush as Tuesday Primaries Near

Party Chairmen Predict Record Vote — Heated Fights on for Control in Both County Organizations — Law Enforcement League Influence Seen.

(By Donovan A. Turk)

Politicians, big and small, famous and oblivious, will put finishing touches on pre-election maneuvers today, and begin the impatient ordeal of waiting to hear whether or not the umpires have announced them safe at first base or called "out" in the Indiana primary election next Tuesday.

Predictions of a record vote of at least 10,000 are forecast by county chairmen of both Republican and Democratic parties. The alleged Klan and anti-Klan factions in each party and the relative strength of each; the fight within the Democratic party between the present county chairman, Mrs. Chester Evans, and Fred Campbell, chief of police, for control of the county organization; a similar scramble in the Republican ranks between the present county chairman, Frank Gentry, and Rolla Morgan for the helmship; the influence of the Law Enforcement league in the campaign; and the large number of aspirants for the various offices warrants the assertion that a record vote will be polled, the chairmen stated.

Shows Probable Winners.

Considering these numerous influences on the voter, the following deductions are presented as reflecting the sentiment of Monroe county citizens in the voting Tuesday:

Calvin Coolidge will pile up a 4-1 advantage over Hiram Johnson in the county in the Republican contest for president. The Californian is expected to poll between 700 and 900 votes. Ed Jackson is slated to win the Republican nomination for governor, shading Samuel "Lew" Shank and Edward Toner in the order named. Carleton B. McCulloch

(CONTINUED ON PAGE SIX)

OSCAR M. VOORHEES ADDRESSES MEETING IN COMMERCE HALL

General Secretary of Phi Beta Kappa Shows Prominence of Members.

CITES SOCIETY'S GROWTH

Visiting Official Has Held Present Position for 22 Years.

Acclaiming the leadership of Phi Beta Kappa among Greek-letter fraternities, emphasizing the encouragement it lends scholarship and reviewing its history, Dr. Oscar M. Voorhees, general secretary of the United Chapters, spoke in Commerce Hall last night under the auspices of the local chapter.

In addition to citing its latest achievements, Dr. Voorhees told of the earlier history of the society from its beginning at William and Mary's College on Dec. 5, 1776. In part he said:

"From those early days Phi Beta Kappa has grown until there are now 99 branches or chapters, as they are called, in as many of the leading colleges and universities of the land. Nearly 60 years ago women began to be admitted to membership. They could be accorded this privilege because Phi Beta Kappa had come to be recognized as an honorary so-

(CONTINUED ON PAGE SIX)

GUILD WILL SERVE AS NOTARY FREE TODAY

Professor Announces Hours at Which He Will See Student Voters.

Special hours for notary services to absent voters will be observed today, Professor F. H. Guild announced yesterday. The office hours are from 10 to 12 M., from 1 to 2 p. m. and from 6:30 to 7:30 p. m.

Only those student voters living close to Bloomington may yet make application for absent voters' ballots, Professor Guild explained, for clerks cannot mail ballots to voters after the second day before election.

All ballots must be back to the clerk of the voters' county on Tuesday so ballots should be sent in as soon as possible. Special hours for Monday are to be posted on the bulletin board in front of the political science department.

Educational Society Initiates 17 Pledges

Phi Delta Kappa, honorary educational fraternity, initiated 17 pledges Thursday night at a dinner in the Student Building. Professor J. A. Williams of South Dakota State Agricultural College, spoke on the early historyof the fraternity.

The initiates were as follows:

Seniors—William M. Boyd, R. A. Breman, Paul Burcker, Charles Callais, R. P. Chambers, F. A. Davis, E. L. Klinger, Virgil Miller, Harley Talley, E. C. Utley, W. F. Wright.

Post graduates—L. F. Durks, F. A. Haison, Denman Kelly, R. E. Layman, L. B. Mull, Z. N. Smith.

COOLIDGE WOULD EXCLUDE "INELIGIBLE" IMMIGRANTS

President Favors Barring Aliens Inadmissible To United States Citizenship.

(By Associated Press)

Washington, May 2.—President Coolidge announced to callers today his endorsement of the proposal that immigrants ineligible to citizenship be excluded from the United States. Efforts to obtain alteration of the immigration bill in this respect were said to be designed merely to phrase the new policy in the most courteous manner possible.

Information was withheld as to what steps were contemplated by the state department if congress approved the suggestion that exclusion be deferred for a period after the other sections of the bill are in operation.

SENATE VOTES TO OPEN TAX RETURNS TO PUBLIC

(By Associated Press)

Washington, May 2.—Tax returns were voted open to public inspection today by the senate as Republican insurgents and Democrats combined in the first major attack on the revenue bill.

The publicity proposal was bitterly fought by Republican organization leaders who were willing to have inspection of the returns by certain congressional committees. Disposing of a series of other proposals, the senate cleared the way for the opening tomorrow of the contest on the income tax schedule, the heart of the bill.

BRANCH CONSIDERS APPOINTMENT OF SMITH AS INVALID

(By Associated Press)

Indianapolis, May 2.—Governor Branch regards the appointment of Oscar Smith as a member of the public service commission to succeed Oscar Ratts as invalid, due to the fact that former Governor McCray, who named Smith, resigned before the appointment became effective, it was said today.

The governor will await the opinion of U. S. Lesh before taking any action. Ratts, who is in possession of the office, transacted official business of the commission as usual today. He attended the regular Friday afternoon conference of the commissioners.

Smith also attended the conference but no business was transacted while he was present.

Logan Studies Rock From Well Beneath Ocean Floor Level

Geology Professor Analyzing Samples of Soil for Every Five Feet of Drilling at Greentown.

Lacking but four feet of being 4,000 feet in depth, the deepest well in Indiana at Greentown, daily is yielding soil for the rock-study investigations of the region which Dr. W. N. Logan of the geology department, is completing.

Taking samples of the rock and soil at each five feet of depth, Dr. Logan has pushed his studies until he now has reached the crystalines, a rock formation which is lower even than the sedimentary rock which forms the ocean floor. The second deepest well in the state is the one at Cloverdale, which is 3,400 feet deep. Next is the Portland well, 3,269 feet in depth.

The Greentown well originally was sunk in a search for oil and natural gas, Logan explained. The venture was a failure and the drillings were turned over to him. The aperture at the top is 30 inches wide. As the shaft sank deeper, the hole narrowed and at the bottom is only four inches in diameter.

BUTLER WITHDRAWS.

Washington, May 2.—Will M. Butler, selected by Coolidge for the Republican national chairmanship, today announced his withdrawal from the race for senator from Massachusetts.

UNION TO CONSIDER ADDING MEMBER OF FACULTY TO BOARD

New Slate of Officers To Be Installed at Session Monday Night.

TREASURER WILL REPORT

Committee Promises Program of Music, Entertainment—To Supply Smokes.

Constitutional revision designed to change the method of election and providing for the selection of an additional faculty member of the advisory board will be proposed at a meeting of the Indiana Union at the Student Building Monday evening at 7:30 o'clock.

Officers voted upon several weeks ago will be installed at the meeting, which will be in the form of a smoker. Music and entertainment will comprise a part of the program, and Herman Wells, retiring treasurer, will report on the finances of the organization in the past year.

Section 4 of Article 7 of the constitution has been revised as follows:

The nominating committee shall nominate one candidate, who in every case shall be a bona fide member of the Union, for each of the four offices, the two faculty positions on the board of control, the alumni position and the trustee position, and twice the allotted number of positions for student directors. At least three nominees for the new board of control shall have been members of the old board. This committee shall publish its list of nominations in The Daily Student at least two weeks before the annual election in April.

Changes in this section are that an additional member of the faculty shall be elected to the advisory board and that there shall be two candidates for each position on the student board of directors.

Music Week Programs Here Will Begin Sunday Morning

First Presbyterian Church Plans Special Service at 10:30 o'Clock—Friday Musicale Will Be Guests at Kitson's Kuntry Kabin in Afternoon—Concerts Arranged.

Three programs tomorrow will usher in National Music Week in Bloomington. Sunday morning a special service is planned at the First Presbyterian Church; Sunday night, music will compose the service at the First Methodist Church, and Sunday afternoon at 3 o'clock the Friday Musicale will be entertained with a concert at Kitson's Kuntry Kabin. Members of the musicale, their husbands and members of the three junior organizations sponsored by the society will be guests there of Mrs. H. T. Kitson, president-elect.

All musical organizations of the city will co-operate with the University School of Music and Bloomington High School in the musical events of the week. The annual spring concert of the Bloomington Choral Society, under the direction of R. O. Heyne, will be presented Monday night, and other programs will be given each day.

The following program will be given Sunday:

I.
Talk — Professor Guido Stempel

II.
Vocal Solos
(a) Trees — Rafbach
(b) Spring Song — Becker
Mrs. Glenn MacDaniel

III.
Piano Solo
Barcarolle in G minor — Rubenstein
Lee C. MacCauley

IV.
Vocal Solos
(a) Down in the Forest — Ronald

(CONTINUED ON PAGE SIX)

Chorus To Rehearse Monday Afternoon

A compulsory rehearsal of the University chorus will be held at Mitchell Hall Monday at 4 p. m. instead of Tuesday, Professor Edward B. Birge announced yesterday.

P0078530, IU Archives.

THE INDIANA SUMMER STUDENT

Unsettled—Probably Showers or Thunderstorms.

VOL. XV. NO. 171. BLOOMINGTON, INDIANA, TUESDAY, JULY 27, 1926. ESTABLISHED 1867.

RETURNS ON MILLION INVESTED REACH $17,000,000

The often-quoted accusation that parents of today send their children to school so they will not have to work as hard as father and mother did, is an acknowledgement in itself that a college education increases one's earning power. While the aim of a college education is not primarily to increase a man's earning power so that he will not have to work so hard nor so long, yet increasing an individual's earning power is an asset to the individual and to the community of which he is a part.

Not only does an education enable the individual to make more money at his chosen occupation, but it gives him wider knowledge and greater adaptability which enable him to change occupations if economic reasons make it desirable. In a rapidly changing civilization such as ours such adaptability is very desirable.

These two facts, aside from the increased power of enjoying life, would make a college education worth all it costs the individual and the state.

Statistics worked out recently support the generalizations made above. One investigation shows that an uneducated laborer earns $20,000 in a lifetime while a high school graduate will earn $40,000 during his lifetime.

Another investigation gives the cash value of a high school education as $33,000 and that of a college education as $72,000.

The average college graduate will earn at least $20,000 more in a lifetime than the non-college man. According to this, we find by multiplying this sum by the number of graduates from the University last year, 877, that the state realized $17,540,000 on its investment in the University in the form of increased earning power. The state appropriated last year $1,365,000 to Indiana University.

BUT MOST COLLEGE PEOPLE FEEL THAT THIS MONEY VALUE RETURN FROM THE INVESTMENT IS INSIGNIFICANT COMPARED TO MANY OTHER RETURNS MADE.

Our commonwealth is far happier because of the college men and women within its borders. They make it a better place to live.

The University supplies most of the state's physicians, dentists and surgeons. It trains the majority of its teachers and nurses. It supplies many of its lawyers and business men.

The mental and physical health of its citizens depend in a very vital fashion on University graduates.

Two hospitals are connected with the institution which care for thousands of sick. The value of restored health can never be calculated.

What investment has the state made to gain this return?

THE SUM OF $1,365,00 WHICH IT SPENT LAST YEAR WAS SMALL COMPARED TO THE RETURN.

The total receipts of all Indiana's universities and colleges both public and private in 1924-25 were $7,671,362.

State-supported universities and colleges alone in Illinois, Iowa, Minnesota, Ohio and Michigan each receive more than this.

IT WILL TAKE MORE THAN TWICE THE APPROPRIATION NOW MADE TO PUT THE STATE'S UNIVERSITIES ON AN EQUALITY WITH THOSE OF ITS NEIGHBORS.

INDIANA UNIVERSITY MUST HAVE FROM THE NEXT LEGISLATURE AN ANNUAL APPROPRIATION OF $2,865,000.

A state which spends $112,600,000 for luxuries can afford a paying investment of $2,865,000 for higher education.

Bids on New Theater To Be Opened Friday

Bids for the construction of a new theater near the University will be opened Friday morning, M. D. Wells, one of the promoters, announced yesterday. Several contractors have copies of the plans and specifications made by John L. Nichols, architect. Work on the new building is expected to begin soon after the contract is let, it was said.

TO ADDRESS EXCHANGE CLUB

Members of Exchange Club will hear Mr. Howard, superintendent of the Indiana State Reformatory at Pendleton, at their regular meeting at the Graham hotel today noon.

TWO CENTERS OF SCHOOL TO HAVE DISPLAYS AT FAIR

Indianapolis Unit's Plans Not Completed—Many Exhibits Planned.

STAFF OF 65 IN CHARGE

Huge Cut Watermelon Will Represent State's Richness.

The Indiana University exhibit for the State Fair at Indianapolis, Sept. 4-11 inclusive, will include exhibits from both the local and Indianapolis units of the University. One of the feature exhibits will be that of the Bureau of Business Research and the Indiana Development council. This exhibit will consist of a large watermelon which will be cut and will contain in the heart a representation of the richness of Indiana in agriculture, industry, natural resources and transportation. The caption for this exhibit will be "Help Cut the Hoosier Melon—See What Lies in the Heart of Indiana."

A committee composed of Provost S. E. Smith and Robert E. Neff, administrator of the University hospitals, is working out the details for the exhibits from the Robert W. Long and James Whitcomb Riley hospitals, the Nurses Training School and the School of Dentistry. These details will be announced later.

Exhibits from Bloomington will include exhibitions from the science group including botany, chemistry, astronomy, zoology and possibly a few other science departments; the Latin, journalism, mathematics and geology department; the extension division, and a library exhibit.

Museum Is Planned.

The Latin department will have museum to illustrate early Roman civilization. Pottery, household utensils and various other things gathered from excavations in anci-

(CONTINUED ON PAGE FOUR)

AUTOISTS ATEMPT DRIVE OVER DIXIE

Road at Dr. Prow Hill Left Almost Impassable—Work at Standstill.

Several motorists braved more than a quarter of a mile of rough roadway yesterday to use the Dixie highway to Martinsville, it was reported. The road has been left torn up at the Dr. F. J. Prow hill, in cutting it down, making passage almost impossible.

Contractors working on the road have promised that the highway will be open to traffic Aug. 1, but with that date less than a week away, the fear was expressed yesterday by motorists that it would be considerably longer before the road will be open for traffic. Later it was announced by John Williams, director of the state highway commission, that the road would be opened the beginning of the fall semester.

Some of the drivers who attempted the "rough going" at the hill yesterday got cold feet after going part of the way and turned back. Not much has been done to improve the road at the hill in the last several weeks, it has been said, because of the inability of contractors to keep workmen on the job.

No Promises Kept.

It has been pointed out by a number of citizens that the promise has been made several times to have the road ready for use, and that each time the date has passed without doing so. A doubt has been raised as to whether the road will be passable by the time of the football season in the University. Business men point out that thousands of dollars were lost to the city last November and hundreds of persons were kept away from the dedication of the Stadium because the Dixie was closed. The opinion has been expressed that unless work progresses more rapidly than it has in the past that the road still will be closed this fall, and that the experiences of last football season will be repeated.

MUSIC ON PROGRAM.

A 20 minute musical program to be presented by Esther Edmondson, '27, Olive Hillerman, '29, and Miss Florence Massey will be given before members of the Rotary Club at the regular luncheon tomorrow noon at the Graham hotel. The program will be under the direction of Mrs. Ward G. Biddle.

Students go to Winona for Embryology Course

The six weeks' course in organic chemistry ended here Friday, the course being followed by the four weeks' course in embryology which began this week at the Biological Station at Winona Lake. Fourteen students have transferred to the Biological Station, according to information from the bursar's office.

Nine of these are members of the class of '26. They are Berna Moore, Kenneth Schwartz, Arthur Kiess, John A. Schram, George E. Moses, Albert Held, Park Huffman, J. C. Brown and R. E. Stout. The other students who have gone are Harry C. Harvey, PG, George E. Ray, '27, D. C. Moffett, PG, James Pebworth, '27, and Ben Butler Raney, '29.

FEELING TOWARD U.S. IS EXPLAINED

Dr. Charles W. Harris Tells of French Sentiment Because of War Debt.

The causes for the feeling prevalent in France that the United States should cancel the war debt was analyzed by Dr. Charles W. Harris, Presbyterian student pastor, in his lecture on "France and Frenzied Finance" Sunday morning at the Presbyterian church.

The most fundamental cause for this feeling, Dr. Harris said, was the fact that France bore the brunt of the battle and because of the nation's devasted lands many Americans favored the cancellation of the debt. During the war France received war material from the United States at very low costs and the French people can not understand now why they can not continue on the same basis, he said. Since the close of the war the French political troubles were described as being so keen that the government has been unable to accomplish anything. United States as France's creditor was blamed for this, it was said. Dr. Harris characterized the country as the extravagant daughter of the League of Nations. The more the franc fell in value the more the nation spent.

United States, Dr. Harris said, has a real duty to perform to France. It is unfortunate, he said, because Senator William E. Borah, chairman of the foreign relations committee, has his "ears to the presidency" and, therefore, refuses to be interested in nations other that the United States. Dr. Harris thought that the debt should not be canceled but should be made so low that it would not be difficult for France to pay.

Winifred Smith Spends Week-end With Parents

Winifred Smith, '24, now with L. S. Ayres and company, of Indianapolis, spent the week-end with her parents, Mr. and Mrs. U. H. Smith. Miss Smith was returning from a month's trip through the West and Canada. While in California she attended the national convention of Kappa Alpha Theta sorority.

Miss Smith was on the staff of The Daily Student for three years, both as reporter and copy editor. Since graduation she has been with L. S. Ayres intending to specialize in advertising in connection with retailing. At present she is in the book department.

PROF. WRIGHT SAYS FACULTY SHOULD INSPIRE STUDENTS

Upholds Instructors at Third Annual Educational Dinner.

ROYALTY MAKES REPLY

Covers Laid for 208—Prof. Franzen Acts as Toastmaster.

That the faculty should be an inspiration to the students in finding their place in life was the thought carried out by Prof. W. W. Wright, of the School of Education, in his talk, "We, The Faculty," at the third annual education dinner held last night at the Christian church.

In behalf of the faculty, he with some knowledge of psycho-analysis which was imparted to him by another faculty member, was able to judge the courses students had taken by their peculiar manner and also the instructor they had been exposed to.

In answer to this Paul Royalty defended the students in his talk, "We, The Students." He told of his various attempts at finding a suitable speech for the occasion and was finally advised to bluster around for three minutes and his audience would readily guess the sherade "He's a Student."

Tirey Plays.

Ralph N. Tirey gave two mandolin solos which were well received. The first was "A Medley of Old Familiar Songs" and "Sextette From Lucia." Mrs. Lola Vawter sang two selections which were "Answered," by Perry and "Trees," by Kilmer. In addition to this Mrs. Pha Curtis sang. "The Scrap Iron Quartet" entertained and the audience learned how and under what circumstances it was organized.

The decorations for the occasion consisted of toy balloons of various colors floating gayly over the tables, but on close inspection it was found that each guest was expected to manipulate his fork with a balloon tied to it. The tables were arranged to form the letters I. U. and cut flowers were used on the table.

Covers were laid for 208 guests. Prof. Carl G. F. Franzen, of the School of Education, acted as toastmaster for the occasion. W. H. Sumrall lead the community singing. Dean H. L. Smith gave the address of welcome.

Moody Gives Up Claim to Leadership in Race

DALLAS, Tex., July 26.—(A.P.)—Attorney-general Dan Moody early tonight relinquished claim to a majority vote in the Democratic nomination for governor of this state.

Interest in the returns waned in view of the announcement by Governor Ferguson that she would not contest the nomination with Moody if he led in the primary race. Moody lacked 1,279 votes of a majority on the face of present returns. The returns tabulated tonight were Moody, 560,954; Ferguson, 352,425; and Davis, 110,113.

Death of Artist Is Mourned

Many tributes have been paid to Theodore C. Steele, honorary professor of painting in the University, by members of the faculty and others who knew the artist. The following are some of the many tributes that have been paid him:

John W. Cravens, registrar—The death of Dr. Theodore C. Steele removes from the faculty of Indiana University one of its most beloved members. The esteem in which he was held was shown by the granting of the highest honor the University bestows, the degree, Doctor of Laws, which was given him ten years ago. In the Library annex of the University which will be completed in two weeks is a large section set aside as a studio for Dr. Steele. While most of Dr. Steele's paintings in recent years glorified Brown county scenery, many of his most beautiful ones were made on or near the campus of the University. Above the fireside in Dr. Steele's Brown county home are the words, "Every morning I take off my hat to the beauty of the world," and this sentiment was his guide and inspiration. His work and associations at Indiana University will always remain as outstanding features in the life of the institution.

H. L. Smith, dean of the School of Education—Mr. Steele's death is a lamentable loss to his acquaintances, to the University, to the state and to the nation, but to them all his enviable life has been an inestimable gain. As only rare spirits in all time have succeeded in doing, he has in his most modest and unassuming way perpetuated his influence in the art he patiently and intelligently put upon canvas and is the art that he most successfully embodied in his appealing life and in his lovable personality.

Prof. W. O. Lynch, acting head of the history department. It was a great thing for Indiana University just to have Mr. Steele on the campus because of his fine character and fine artistic ability. Nothing that the University has done in recent years has been appreciated more by me than the bringing of Mr. Steele to reside at the University and carry on a part of his work here.

Dr. Burton D. Myers, assistant dean of the School of Medicine—I have known the artist, Theodore C. Steele, nearly 15 years. I had visited him in his interesting home and studio in Brown county more than ten years ago and had been charmed by his agreeable personality, the simplicity of his life coupled with

(CONTINUED ON PAGE FOUR)

FLASHES

By the A.P.

PARIS, July 26.—Premier Poincare's newly formed cabinet having agreed on a ministerial declaration will go before the chamber of deputies tomorrow and demand that the government be given power to solve the financial difficulties of the country by decrees instead of by measures which would have to be debated in the chamber of deputies.

It is indicated that Poincare has decided to let ratification of the American and British loan treaties go over for the present time. This is taken to mean that Premier Poincare will not seek foreign credit to rehabilitate the franc.

SAN FRANCISCO, Calif., July 26.—A federal grand jury here tonight returned an indictment against Col. Ned M. Green, deposed several days ago as prohibition agent. The grand jury was in session only three and one-half hours. Col. Green was charged with the misappropriation of governmental liquor and misconduct in office.

ONE ACT PLAY ON CONVO PROGRAM

Cast of Students To Present "Suppressed Desires" Tomorrow.

The convocation program tomorrow morning at 9:40 o'clock will include two scenes of one-act play, "Suppressed Desires," to be given at Assembly Hall, it was announced yesterday by Prof. L. R. Norvelle. Katherine Consulas, PG, is directing the play. The final rehearsal will be held tonight.

The theme of "Suppressed Desires" is built around the Freudian theory of psycho-analysis. It portrays the situation in which Henrietta Brewster becomes thoroughly saturated with Dr. Freud's interpretation of dreams and as an apostle of the theory, attempts to separate her married sister from her husband. The higest point of complication comes when Henrietta is informed that her husband and sister have a suppressed desire for each other. She is later forced to repudiate the theory of psycho-analysis.

The part of Henrietta is played by Zula Stevens, and that of Stephen, her husband, by J. R. Davis, PG. Mabel, the sister of Henrietta, is interpreted by Ervia Garrison, PG.

This is the next to the last convocation of the Summer Session. The last convocation program will be given Aug. 4 by the Colored Male quartet, of Knoxville College, Knoxville, Tenn.

13 FIRMS TAKING PART IN EXHIBIT

Educational Supplies and Books on Display in Student Building.

Representatives from 13 firms that are participating in the educational exhibit being held in the Student Building all this week now are arranging their exhibits and demonstrating their supplies. Several others are expected to come later. They are showing material which will be of interest to principals, superintendents and high school teachers. This will be the largest display of its kind ever put on by the Summer Session office.

One of the most interesting displays is a projection machine shown by the Keystone View company. This lantern can be operated in a room in daylight without darkening the room. Stereographs and stereoscopes also are included in the display.

The E. C. Atkins company is showing a collection of saws for all kinds of cabinet work. Textbooks for common schools, teachers' books and a special pictured encyclopedia are the main features of the exhibit of the Laurel Book company and the F. E. Compton company.

The American Book company is showing textbooks for use from the elementary grades to college. Charles Scribner's sons also are showing books. Rand McNally and company has a general line of textbooks, maps and globes.

Elementary and high school texts and several professional books of special interest to teachers are being shown by Houghton-Mifflin company. The Spencer Lens company is showing microscopes, microtomes and other scientific instruments and also a visual instruction library.

Last Tribute To Be Paid T. C. Steele This Afternoon at His Summer Home

THEODORE C. STEELE

—Courtesy Indianapolis Star.

SEPT. 22, 1847—JULY 24, 1926

Ashes To Be Buried Among the Hills He Loved at "The House of the Singing Winds"—Evans Woollens, of Indianapolis, To Speak—Classes Will Be Dismissed From 3-4 O'clock, Hour of Funeral.

RITES ALSO IN CAPITAL

Artist Had Been Honorary Professor Since 1922 on Invitation of University.

A TRIBUTE TO STEELE.

As a tribute to the memory of our friend, Dr. Theodore Clement Steele, there will be no classes during the hour of the funeral services (3-4) on Tuesday afternoon, July 27.

William Lowe Bryan.
H. L. Smith, director of the Summer School.

Among the hills he loved, the rustic country he had made famous, the remains of Theodore Clement Steele will be buried this afternoon at 3 o'clock. Simple services will mark the passing of this man, painter, friend and honorary professor of painting in Indiana University since 1922. The funeral services will be open to faculty members and friends of the artist.

His ashes will be buried beneath the oak trees at his home, "The House of the Singing Winds." Evans Woollens, president of the Art Association of Indianapolis, long a friend of the painter and Mrs. Steele, will speak a few words.

The University he had honored by his association with it will pause during the hour of the funeral out of respect and as a tribute to a revered member of its faculty. The body was taken to Indianapolis yesterday to the Flanner and Buchanan mortuary for cremation, and where a short, private funeral service was read at 4 o'clock.

Mr. Steele's death came as a shock, even to those who knew it was almost too much to hope for his recovery. He had been in failing health last winter while engaged in his art work here in the University, and had observed a diet then in the hope that it would tend to improve his health. In June with Mrs. Steele he went to the Robert Long hospital in Indianapolis to undergo observation for a month.

About three weeks ago he and Mrs. Steele returned to "The House of the Singing Winds" after his trouble had been located and diagnosed. The hope was expressed at that time by Mrs. Steele that his recovery would be rapid and that he would be able to return to his work in the University in the fall. It was reported then that he was better, but visitors calling were not permitted to disturb him.

His condition gradually grew worse in the last week, and Friday it was reported that he was in a critical condition and that he was dying. The end came at 8:30 o'clock Saturday night and was caused by a stoppage of the gall duct.

Immediately after word of his

(CONTINUED ON PAGE FOUR)

Portraying the Face of Nature Claimed Undivided Thought of Theodore C. Steele

(The following article about T. C. Steele is taken from the February issue of The American Magazine of Art, 1926, and was written by Alfred Mansfield Brooks. Mr. Brooks formerly was head of the department of fine arts here before going to Swarthmore College. The article is entitled "The House of the Singing Winds." Editor's note.)

In the outskirts of Belmont, a minute hamlet of Brown county, an Indiana county remarkable for its hill scenery and notable because of the small harm civilization has yet worked within its confines, lives the landscape painter, Theodore Steele. Year on year has this delightful artist's reputation been quietly growing, Steele himself characteristically unmindful of the fact, for him Arnold's lines speak truly,

"Labor which in lasting fruits
outgrows far
Noisier schemes, accomplished
in repose,
Too great for haste. Too high
for rivalry."

To portray the face of nature, and to interpret her smiling or her weeping mood, her glory and her simplicity does, and for many years has claimed the artist's undivided thought. To him she has long spoken the language of "rememberable things," and, just so long, has he been schooling his deft fingers to record these things upon canvas. Perfectly, although his work, does he make plain the meaning of one of the most extraordinary comments ever made upon the art of landscape—Amiels, "all landscape implies a state of mind." This comment is extraordinary because it goes straight to the heart of the matter laying bare the fact that the poet and the painter of landscape do, and necessarily stand upon common ground as far as emotion and comprehension condition their respective arts.

In one small territory, but on many canvases has this man, poignantly responsive to nature's ceaselessly changing moods, painted o'er and o'er the hills to which his eyes are always lifted and from which, to judge by his successes, help never fails him. So absorbed has he become in his work, the complete portraiture of seasons it might be

(CONTINUED ON PAGE FOUR)

Landscape Canvases of Dr. Steele Noted for Their Poetic Charm, Mellow Coloring

(The following article appeared in The American Magazine of Art, Noverber, 1924, and was written by Mary Q. Burnet. The title was "Indiana University and T. C. Steele." Editor's Note.)

The aim of the Department of Fine Arts of Indiana University is to lead students to an appreciation of the beautiful rather than become artists. Art will soon become instinctive and an essential part of life when an opportunity is given youth of America at our state universities to meet and know great artists and their work. Such a plan has been inaugurated and found feasible and fruitful at Indiana University.

Theodore Clement Steele, M.A., A.N.A., LL.D., was invited by the trustees of the University, in 1922, to become honorary professor of painting and maintain a studio on the upper floor of the library building for six months in the year. This studio is open to students at certain hours. Dr. Steele does not offer any courses in art but welcomes the many students who eagerly use this unusual privilege. Occasionally he gives informal art talks. He is at the University not to teach or lecture, but to point as he would in his own studio, that the benefit of his presence, may be a new and precious experience in the student body.

The result accomplished is a sympathetic understanding of the beauty of nature by seeing familiar places about the campus transferred to canvas and become pictures—pictures that are understood and comprehended by youth who have rarely, if ever, visited gallery or museum. Robert Browning has said, "We love first, when we see them painted, things we have passed, perhaps a hundred times, nor cared to see."

The students will return to their sequestered home having gained two excellent things if not more; an appreciation and laudation of nature and that there is a definite beauty all about them, in distant hills and nearby valleys, in the low-hanging clouds of an approaching storm, in the tender green of early springtime and in the same trees all russet and umber in autumnal glory. The country, that has hitherto seemed prosaic and uninteresting, now becomes interesting and dramatic, holding all possibilities, for

(CONTINUED ON PAGE FOUR)

MORE GET POSITIONS

Several Graduates Assigned To Schools for Next Year.

Another list of graduates who have accepted positions as teachers for the coming year has been announced from the registrar's office.

Annabelle Stair will teach French at Frankfort. Bernice Galloway will instruct in Latin in the Griffith High School. Dorothy May Heller will teach mathematics at Mt. Pleasant, O.

A. E. Botkins will act as principal in the Lowell High School. Carolyn Hirschy will fill the same position in the Berne High School.

Elizabeth Clements will teach home economics at Mt. Vernon. Mary Catherine Martin will teach mathematics and Latin at Shirleyville. Ralph Mahan has accepted a position in the Vincennes High School as a history teacher while Ezra Macey will act as principal of the elementary schools in Vincennes. Esther Pearson will teach history at Greentown.

P0079144, IU Archives.

INDIANA EXPECTS HER STUDENTS TO DO THEIR DUTY

THE INDIANA DAILY STUDENT

Cloudy Today, Followed by Rain Tomorrow.

VOL. LVI, NO. 75. BLOOMINGTON, INDIANA TUESDAY, DEC. 21, 1926. ESTABLISHED 1867.

LOYALTY CONVO SET FOR 10 A. M.

The President's Column

TO THE STUDENTS OF INDIANA.

I hear you sing: We will fight for the Cream and Crimson, for the Glory of old I. U. If you fight as you ought it will not be for the selfish glory of old I. U. alone. If you fight as you ought it will be for a cause in which all our neighbor institutions are in necessary alliance with us. If you fight as you ought it will be for ideals to which no good man can be an enemy.

Fight for this state. Fight to make it great. Great in its institutions. Great in its men. Great in its life. Fight for that. Sing for that. And old I. U. will have its share of the glory of Indiana.

—WILLIAM LOWE BRYAN.

DEVELOPMENT OF ADVANCED STUDY, COMMERCE NEED

Enlarged Staff, Smaller Classes, More Courses Asked by Rawles.

LIST OF WANTS IS GIVEN

Three Courses Were Omitted Due to Lack of Men Last Year.

(By W. A. Rawles.)

The greatest need of the School of Commerce and Finance is an opportunity to develop more thoroughly the advanced work for undergraduates and graduates. In order to do this it is necessary to relieve professors of much of the routine incident to the more elementary work; to enlarge the staff of teachers so as to reduce the size of classes and the teaching load, and to provide for additional courses in accounting, business finance, marketing, risk-bearing, banking, transportation, public utilities, land economics, a co-ordinating or correlating course in the senior year and research work. Three courses heretofore scheduled were omitted last year because of insufficient man power.

The school should be able to retain efficient men on the staff by paying larger salaries. The school needs additional funds to bring prominent business men here to address and counsel with students.

Industry and business are becoming more complex and sensitive, requiring a higher standard of training and more fundamental knowledge of administrative principles and practices.

That there will be an increasing demand for graduates of the School of Commerce and Finance seems evident when it is realized that there are more than 75,000 persons in Indiana engaged in business as proprietors and as administrative and executive officers. The urgent need for trained young men to take the places of these older men as they retire seems quite apparent and furnishes a justification for the existence of a collegiate school of business in Indiana.

It is clear that the School of Commerce and Finance is not yet meeting the demand on the part of our young men and women for training along business lines. We have had requests from various persons and groups of business men for more extended courses in public utilities, for courses in the field of real estate, for a course designed to prepare young men as commercial secretaries, for more extended courses in merchandizing, for a course of study in fiduciary work, for the further development of our research and graduate work. These courses can not be introduced or expanded because of lack of funds.

Statistical Knowledge.

The need for more generous provision for research and graduate work is emphasized not only because of the direct benefit to the economic interests of the state but also for the raining of young men in the analytical methods now being used in progressive business concerns.

The School of Commerce and Finance is the only school in the state that has been recognized as having such standing as to entitle it to membership in the American Association of Collegiate Schools of Business. Therefore, it seems worthy of such support that it may offer adequate training in business to the young men of Indiana so that they may not be forced to incur the added expense involved in seeking such training outside the state.

For the foregoing reasons the School of Commerce and Finance is asking for more generous support.

DR. MYERS SHOWS NEEDS OF INDIANA MEDICAL SCHOOL

Budget Increase Necessary To Maintain Adequate Number of Doctors.

CROWDED AT PRESENT

Fewer Physicians in State Now Than in 1914—Average Life Rate Given.

(By Dr. B. D. Myers, Assistant Dean of the School of Medicine.)

The fundamental need of the School of Medicine is an increase in buildings and budget that will make possible the maintenance of an adequate supply of doctors of medicine for Indiana.

The Indiana University School of Medicine has experienced a rapid growth in the last seven years. Available space in existing buildings is not merely occupied; it is crowded to the limit! In 1919 we had 200 students in the School of Medicine; in 1925-26 we had 376 students in the School of Medicine, an increase of 88 per cent., nearly double the rate of increase in the country as a whole.

Freshman enrollment has grown from 43 students in 1919 to 116 in 1925-26; that is, the number of students increased in seven years, two and seven tenths times, while the departments of anatomy and physiology, which give all the work of the freshman year of medicine, have together today a staff of six above the rank of assistant instead of seven above the rank of assistants as in 1919.

Staff Numbers Less.

While freshman enrollment has grown from 43-116 the staff has decreased from seven to six. The salary of two temporary instructors was combined to get one assistant professor. This leaves us not only with space crowded to the limit, but with an unfairly small instructional staff, an unjustly heavy, pedagogically unsound, teaching load. We must have relief both by way of additional space and by way of material increases in instructional staff.

But you may ask, is there need in the state for more doctors than are now being graduated? The answer is, that there are 750 fewer doctors in Indiana today than there were in 1914. Of the doctors in the state today each must care for 162 more persons on the average than in 1914.

The number of Indiana men being graduated in all schools of the United States totals about 100 a year, so that in the next ten years we would add 1,000 doctors if all these men came back to Indiana, which they do not. But of the 4,251 doctors in Indiana in 1925, 1,106 were 60 years of age or more. So the probability is that, whereas we have lost 750 doctors in the last ten years, we shall probably loose not fewer than 250 in the next ten

(CONTINUED ON PAGE FIVE)

Visions of Greater Indiana To Be Carried By Workers

Increased Appropriations To Mean Increased Faculty, Higher Salaries, New Buildings, General Improvements—University Interests Committee To Be Permanent Organization.

Visions of a greater Indiana can be seen as thousands of workers for Indiana University start on the project of carrying the needs of the school to the people of the state.

Increased appropriations will mean valuable additions to the faculty, higher salaries for many professors now here who might be induced by increased remuneration to go elsewhere, adequate facilities in new buildings for an increasing enrollment, a general modernizing of the present structures and many other improvements that would add greatly to the appearance of the campus.

The Indiana University Interests committee is to be a permanent organization. If additional appropriations are made for the next two years by this legislature it is expected that it will set a precedent for later legislatures so that state schools will be provided for adequately in the future.

Plans Outlined.

Appropriations for next year would start a 10 years' building program which would help put Indiana University on a level with other state schools in the North Central group. The outline for buildings to be erected in the next decade on the Bloomington campus, at a cost of about $4,000,000, includes a power plant, an addition to Wylie Hall, building for the School of Education, an addition to Owen Hall, a building for geology, zoology, botany and museum, group of small buildings including an addition to Science Hall for the use of the physics department, an auditorium, an administration building, building for the School of Music and a journalism building.

In addition several buildings would be constructed for the Indianapolis schools at a cost of $2,200,000. These would include completion of the medical school building, additional wards for the Robert W. Long hospital, a psychiatric clinic, an out-patient building, a therapeutics building, one for environmental medicine and a clinical building.

To Repair Buildings.

If additional appropriations are made by this legislature, the money will be available next October and much could be done next year. The first item in the program for next year provides $90,000 for repairs to buildings and general improvements including additional walks and driveways. Repairs would cover painting, plastering, carpenter work and

(CONTINUED ON PAGE FIVE)

DEAN POINTS OUT GREATEST NEEDS OF MUSIC SCHOOL

Merrill Cites Crowded Condition and Student Emigration to Other States.

(By Dean B. Winfred Merrill.)

The question should be: "The Need of the State of Indiana for the School of Music," a question answered at once by the crowded condition of the school and further answered by the emigration of hundreds of students who take their millions of dollars to other states to spend—millions that should be kept at home to build up our own institutions and cut down the taxes of our own people.

The School of Music is crowded to its limit, taking care of 93 regular degree students and 1,007 students in classes. It can accommodate no larger number with its two small buildings and meager equipment, and faculty of eight.

Other Schools Get Hoosiers.

In response to my inquiry as to how many Indiana students he has, the president of a music school in a neighboring state writes, "According to our records we have 360 students enrolled here from the state of Indiana." A school in New York City writes, "In reply to your letter I have to tell you that we have six students from Indiana enrolled this year. We will be glad to enroll 60 next year if they are of the same quality as this year's brand." This comes from an endowed school of the highest rank, but can we afford to let this fine brand of students disappear from our midst?

More letters from bordering states report 40, 76, 98 and 150

(CONTINUED ON PAGE SIX)

CONTRIBUTIONS OF $49.27 RAISE CHEER FUND TOTAL TO $211.01

Last-Minute Donations Cause Short Extension of Time on Drive—Baskets of Food, Clothing To Be Bought for Poor With Money.

With contributions amounting to $49.27, the total amount of The Daily Student Christmas Cheer Fund reached $211.01 last night. The close of the drive was set for that time but last-minute donations to the Cheer Fund will be received this morning at The Daily Student office, Vivian Crates, '28, director of the drive, announced yesterday.

Mrs. Mary Waldron, executive secretary of the Associated Charities, expressed her appreciation at the kindness and generosity of the University student body, instructors, friends and townspeople who helped make the Fund a success. The money will be turned over to Mrs. Waldron who will send baskets of food, clothing and useful gifts to the needy families of Bloomington.

Although last year's fund exceeded this year's total by $59.74, it is thought the numerous campus drives for money prevented students and others from contributing as liberally as they otherwise would have done.

Christmas Cheer Fund contributions are as follow:

Previous contributions	$161.74
Varsity pharmacy	5.00
Princess theater	5.00
Harris Grand theater	5.00
Memorial Hall	4.88
Solicited at cafeteria	4.21
Kappa Delta	2.41
Sullivan and East	2.00
E. M. Davis	2.00
Carter and O'Haver	2.00
Jenkins poolroom	2.00
Residence Hall	1.80
Sigma Pi	1.53
Delta Gamma	1.41
Bedford Sudburn	1.00
Felix J. Brown	1.00
Ralph E. Esarey	1.00
Miss Ivy L. Chamness	1.00
Wiles' Drug store	1.00
Anonymous	1.00
Arbutus poolroom	1.00
Nick and Pete	1.00
William Adkins	.50
Diana Sweet shop	.50
Laura Ashbaucher	.50
Robbins Shoe store	.50
Total contributions	$211.01

FIRST ESSENTIAL FOR DISTINCTION IS FACULTY--STOUT

College of Arts and Sciences Must Have Efficient Teachers.

NEED LIBRARY, MUSEUM

Larger Funds Permit Sister Schools To Outstrip Indiana.

(By Dean S. E. Stout.)

The first essential for distinguished work in the College of Arts and Sciences is the faculty. No amount of equipment can make a college great unless it has a great faculty. Students will come unsought, for they need what we have to offer. Buildings and equipment can be bought, or can even, in a measure, be dispensed with without absolutely destroying the efficiency of our work. But a high order of talent for the faculty must be sought, and we must be able to keep teachers who have proved their value. To be able to search out such teachers and draw them to Indiana University, to give them such facilities for carrying on their work as will make their efforts worth while and bring them the satisfaction of discovery and mastery which they crave, and to provide a decent support for them and their families—these make possible the making of a great school in which the state can justly take pride.

Library Inadequate.

We are inadequately supplied with books. We have at present 180,000 bound volumes and catalogued pamphlets. As a select library it ranks well with any in the country that have cost no more. But that it is painfully inadequate

(CONTINUED ON PAGE SIX)

Powerful, Compact Group Organized To Guide Work

Every Student on Campus, Alumni, Friends Co-operating To "Sell" Worth and Needs of State's Educational Institutions to Hoosiers.

Indiana University's needs are to be presented to the citizens of the state by one of the most powerful, compact organizations ever formed in the history of the school.

Every student on the campus working in co-operation with alumni associations and friends of the University have mobilized an army that will fight to keep Indiana on a par with other states in regard to higher education.

General chairmen, district chairmen, and county chairmen of the University Interests committee have so organized the work to be done that every student in the University has a certain task to do during the campaign. From a somewhat intangible perspective, the object of the movement has become a very realistic, definite proposition.

Hilbert Rust, '27, and Dorothy Donald, PG, were appointed Nov. 19, by President William Lowe Bryan to head the two divisions of the committee. James Elliott, '27, and Vivian Crates, '28, are vice-chairmen of the organization. W. A. Alexander, librarian, and director of four successful memorial drives, is chief advisor to the committee.

Executive Committee Formed.

Early in the organization of the committee need was felt for the advice and co-operation of the student body as a whole. The result was the appointment of an all-campus executive committee, composed of campus leaders representing every phase of student activity. This group helped direct the first moves of the committee and gave advice on matters affecting the further organization of the committee. A publicity committee also was appointed to aid in keeping the project before the public.

Men and women chairmen of each congressional district in the state were selected Nov. 17 by the general chairmen with the advice of the executive committee. Women district chairmen also are chairmen of their home counties but this is not so in the case of the men heads. The main functions

(CONTINUED ON PAGE SIX)

BAND NOTICE.

Members of the University band will assemble at Maxwell Hall at 9:45 a.m. today without uniform, Capt. G. C. Cleaver in charge announced yesterday. All bandsmen will be excused from classes at 9:40 a.m., according to President William Lowe Bryan.

RAILWAYS, BUSSES TO CARE FOR RUSH

Extra Cars, Two Special Trains Will Carry Students Home Tomorrow.

VACATION SCHEDULE.

The Christmas vacation will begin at 11 o'clock Wednesday morning, Dec. 22. The first hour classes will recite at 8-8:50; second, 8:50-9:30; third, 9:45-10:20, and fourth, 10:30-11:00.

The rules pertaining to absences both before and following the vacation will apply. Any student absent from class Wednesday morning, Dec. 22, or Tuesday, Jan. 4, will have one-half hour's credit deducted from his total credit for the semester.

WILLIAM L. BRYAN.

Two special trains, extra coaches on the regular trains and extra cars on two bus lines will carry University students homeward tomorrow at the exodus for the Chirstmas vacation. The vacation will start at 11 a.m. Classes will be resumed Jan 4.

Special trains to Indianapolis and Lafayette will leave the Monon station at 11:30 a.m. The one to Indianapolis will make a non-stop trip over the Monon and Pennsylvania routes. The Lafayette special will stop at Greencastle, Roachdale, Ladoga, Crawfordsville and Linden.

(CONTINUED ON PAGE SIX)

INTEREST HEADS PROMISE MOST IMPORTANT, INSPIRING GATHERING EVER HELD HERE

CONVO TO BE HELD TODAY.

Tuesday, Dec. 21, convocation begins at 10 o'clock. The 10 and 11 o'clock classes are dismissed. The 8 and 9 o'clock and all afternoon classes meet as usual. I hope that all members of the University will attend.

Wednesday, Dec. 22, classes meet as follows:

8 o'clock	8:00-8:40 a.m.
9 o'clock	8:50-9:30 a.m.
10 o'clock	9:40-10:20 a.m
11 o'clock	10:30-11:00 a.m.

WILLIAM L. BRYAN.

DEAN H. L. SMITH OUTLINES NEEDS OF EDUCATION SCHOOL

Space, Salaries, Staff, Scholarship Funds Should Be Augmented.

(By Dean H. L. Smith.)

In common with the other departments of the University, the School of Education is in dire need of additional funds to carry on a broad scope of educational service. The following statement sets forth a few of the outstanding needs of the School of Education in Indiana University.

(1.) The need for a home. The members of the department are shuttle-cocked about the campus for places in which to hold classes. This condition provides no sense of stability or security for classroom work. An Education building would go far to relieve this situation and also to relieve that of other departments, situated in the building where the education offices are now located. Of the 91 classes in education this semester, not a single one is being held in space controlled by the School of Education. All education classes have to be held in odd spaces temporarily free from occupancy by other departments which control the recitation space. Space is needed for the Bureau of Co-operative Research. Only one room is devoted to this now and it is a very small room. Space is needed for the teaching and clerical staff offices for graduate student's research work, for laboratories, for seminar rooms, and for experimental school purposes on the campus. Space also is needed for an education museum,

(CONTINUED ON PAGE TWO)

LAW SCHOOL ASKS $80,000 ADDITIONAL NEXT TWO YEARS

Money Would Provide for Only Minimum Needs, McNutt Says.

REPORT IS SUBMITTED

Faculty Found To Be Paid Less Than Average in North Central Group.

(By Dean Paul V. McNutt.)

The most important responsibility in politically organized society is the efficient administration of justice. This responsibility rests on the legal triumvirate, the bench, the bar and the law school. The successful discharge of this responsibility involves and demands the highest degree of co-operation and intelligent effort. The future of the state, which in theory at least, represents politically organized society, depends in no small measure on the administration of justice. Therefore the welfare of the legal triumvirate is of deep concern to the state. The state needs a law school of high distinction.

In addition to this need there is also a duty. Public education is a necessity in a government such as ours. The state has undertaken the business of education. It is a governmental function. The first state constitution provided that "it shall be the duty of the General assembly, as soon as circumstances will permit, to provide by law for a general system of education ascending in regular gradation, from township schools to a state university."

The law school is a part of that University, and it has been a part of every University deserving the name since the very beginning. If public education is anything but a name, then it is the duty of the state to give adequate support to that school and to the University of which it is a part.

Oldest West of Alleghenies.

The Indiana University Law School, established in 1842, is the oldest law school west of the Allegheny mountains. It is a member of the Association of American Law Schools and is rated "Class A" by the American Bar association. It does all the editorial work on the Indiana Law Journal, the of-

(CONTINUED ON PAGE FOUR)

MANY ORGANIZATIONS OF STATE INDORSE INTERESTS CAMPAIGN

Methodist Church Conference, American Legion, Tri-Kappa Sorority, Kiwanis, Rotary Clubs and Chamber of Commerce Adopt Resolutions.

(By George MacKnight.)

Among the many organizations of the state that have adopted resolutions in favor of the Student Interests campaign are the Methodist church conference, the department of Indiana, American Legion, Kappa Kappa Kappa sorority, Kiwanis clubs of Indiana, Rotary clubs and Chambers of Commerce.

A large number of newspapers and magazines have carried editorials in favor of the movement. Among them are the Indianapolis Times, Indianapolis Star, the Indianapolis News, Indiana Farmer's Guide, Hartford City News, Indianapolis Union Labor News, Bloomington World, Bloomington Telephone, Bloomington Star, Indianapolis Union, Lafayette Leader and Bedford Times.

Legion Resolution.

The resolution of the American Legion is:

Whereas the American Legion has declared that the adequate education of youth is one of the few paramount duties of an enlightened government and has selected education as one of its primary interests in carrying out its Americanism program, and

Whereas equality of opportunity is the birthright of every American child, and

Now, therefore, be it resolved by the department of Indiana, American Legion, that we heartily indorse and lend strength to the movement to give adequate support to our institutions of higher learning and call on the members of the legislature and the Governor to perform their manifest duties in this regard, to the end that the children of Indiana may have educational opportunities equal to those of any other state."

Expression of the need of action on the matter, a Kiwanis resolution said, "Be it further resolved that we fully approve the support of our state institutions of higher education with a generosity comparable to that of oher states."

An ediorial from the Indianapolis Star of Oct. 2, "Link With Student Body," points outs, "In summarizing a table showing the

(CONTINUED ON PAGE SIX)

Meeting To Be First Act of Greatest Play in Which Students Take Part — Jack Hastings, Memorial Regiment Head, To Preside.

SHORT SESSION PLANNED

Budget Committee Members of Legislature May Be Special Guests.

(By Fred Foster.)

When the chimes ring out "Hail to old I. U." this morning at 10 o'clock, students wil wind their way to the Men's gymnasium to the most important assembly of loyal backers of Indiana University ever held in the history of the school.

The most inspiring convocation of all time is promised by chairmen of the University Interests committee. A short program has been planned. All speeches will be limited to five minutes and the affair will last not more than an hour and 15 minutes, chairmen promised.

As some vast river of unfailing source, the University Interests committee will be a permanent organization devoted to the cause of placing the University on the same level with other great universities, was the sentiment expressed by speakers last night at the banquet at the University Commons given for all chairmen of the committee. Practically all county and district chairmen were present at the meeting and last admonitions to know the excellencies and needs of the University were given.

Confident of Students.

The first act of the greatest play in which students should hope to take part as far as the University is concerned, was the way Hilbert Rust, '27, men's chairman, described the convocation to be held this morning. President William Lowe Bryan asserted he has the strongest confidence in the students who are to go out over the state to present the needs of the school to Indiana's people.

Jack Hastings, of Washington, Ind., president of the Memorial regiment, will preside at the convocation. All speakers wil talk of the work of the committee in general and also tell of their own department or school in particular.

Dean B. W. Merrill, of the School of Music, will be the first speaker on the program. He will be followed by Dr. Charles P. Emerson, dean of the School of Medicine; Dean H. L. Smith, of the School of Education; Dean S. E. Stout, of the College of Arts and Sciences, and Dean William A. Rawles, of the School of Commerce and Finance.

First Speech Here.

Dr. Frederic R. Henshaw, dean of the School of Dentistry, will make his first talk to the student body at Bloomington. Next in order of speakers are Dr. B. D. Myers, assistant dean of the School of Medicine, and Zora G. Clevenger, director of athletics. Prof. Lionel D. Edie, of the bureau of business research of the School of Commerce and Finance, who has made an exhaustive study of conditions in

(CONTINUED ON PAGE FIVE)

I. U. FACES STARVATION

In this column during the last month we have printed facts about the worth and needs of the state schools which might be of use in the campaign of education of the citizens of the state.

With this issue, the column will be suspended. In this Student, the deans of the various schools have written about the needs of their schools. Read these articles, attend the Loyalty Convocation and be ready to tell the people of your community that without aid from the legislature, the state schools face starvation.

P0078531, IU Archives.

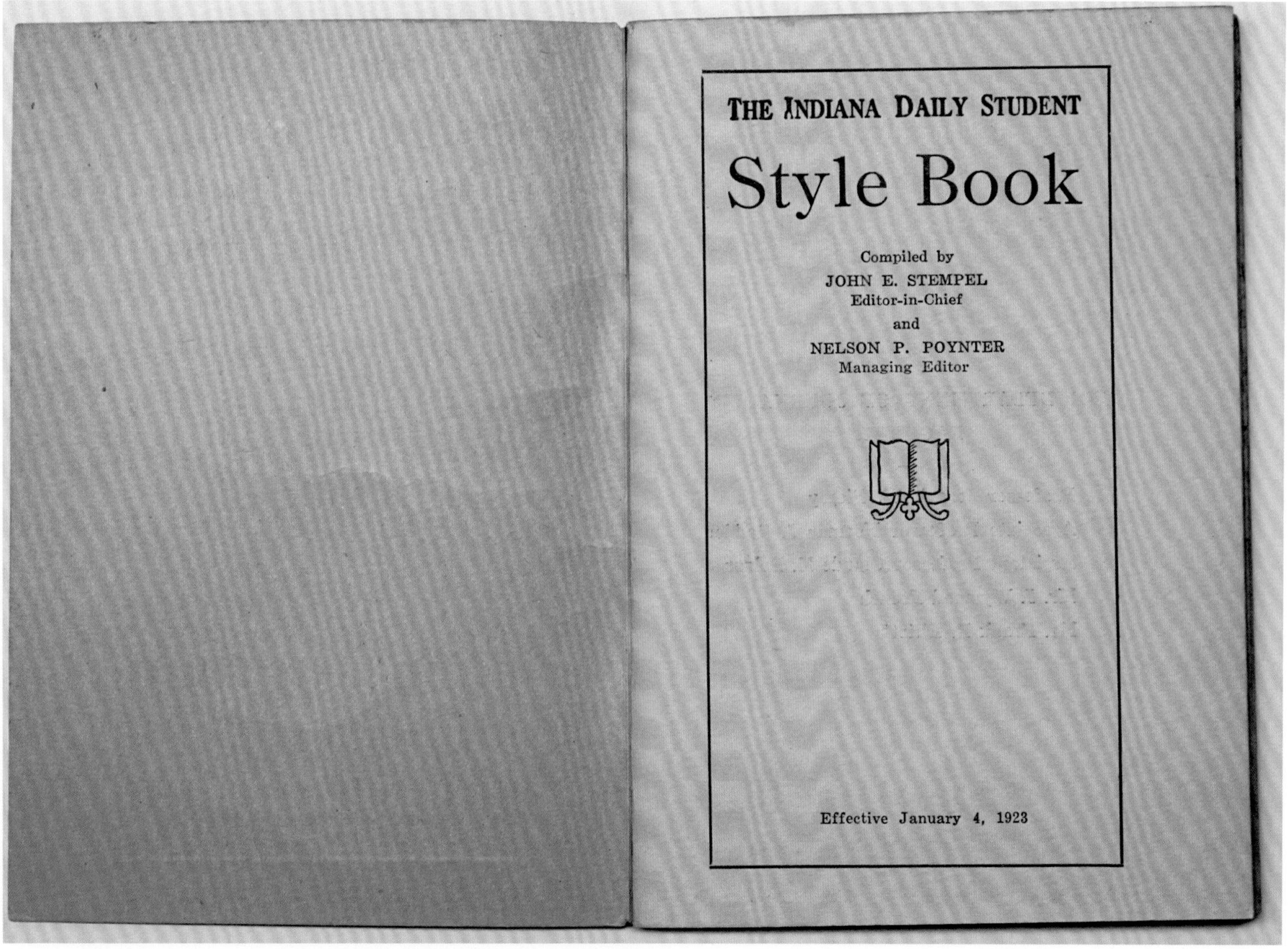

Title page of what is believed to be the first IDS stylebook. *Photo courtesy of Ruth Witmer.*

BEHIND THE STORY

The Keepers of IDS Traditions

Now yellowed with age, what is likely the very first IDS stylebook is dated Jan. 4, 1923. It was compiled by then-Editor-in-Chief John Stempel, who would go on to chair the journalism department and become publisher of the IDS, and then-Managing Editor Nelson Poynter, who went on to found what would become the Poynter Institute and Congressional Quarterly and serve as publisher of the St. Petersburg Times. The first volume became the template for the dozens that would follow, and each volume would set the style for fonts, headlines, cutlines, titles, sports summaries and more. Staffers were reminded of the double consonants in "accommodate" and to never, ever put a period after the B in Herman B Wells.

The stylebooks contained sections on the history of the IDS and job descriptions for each position, from reporter to telegraph editor. There were hints for proofreaders ("You are the last person who has an opportunity to catch an error"), sections on libel ("Catch the little things") and at least one on staff discipline ("When there is work to be done, work").

In 1923, Stempel and Poynter had this advice for reporters: "Terseness is the best quality you can develop besides accuracy.

IDS stylebooks through the years. The booklets contained job descriptions, staff rules, guides to style and grammar and more. *Photo courtesy of Malinda Aston.*

Shun 'fine writing.' Use the same words that you would use in talking to a friend." They also reminded reporters that in writing articles for the next morning's paper, "The only thing that WAS done TODAY is the work of the milkman or other early risers or prowlers." They encouraged copy editors, whom they called "the backbone of The Daily Student's style," to "challenge every word and every statement in the story you pick up. Under no circumstances take anything for granted."

Pat Siddons, who served as publisher from 1978 to 1989, rechristened the volumes "guidelines," reasoning in one edition that they were not just stylebooks, but also the carriers of the "history and traditions of what once was called 'The World's Greatest College Daily.' "

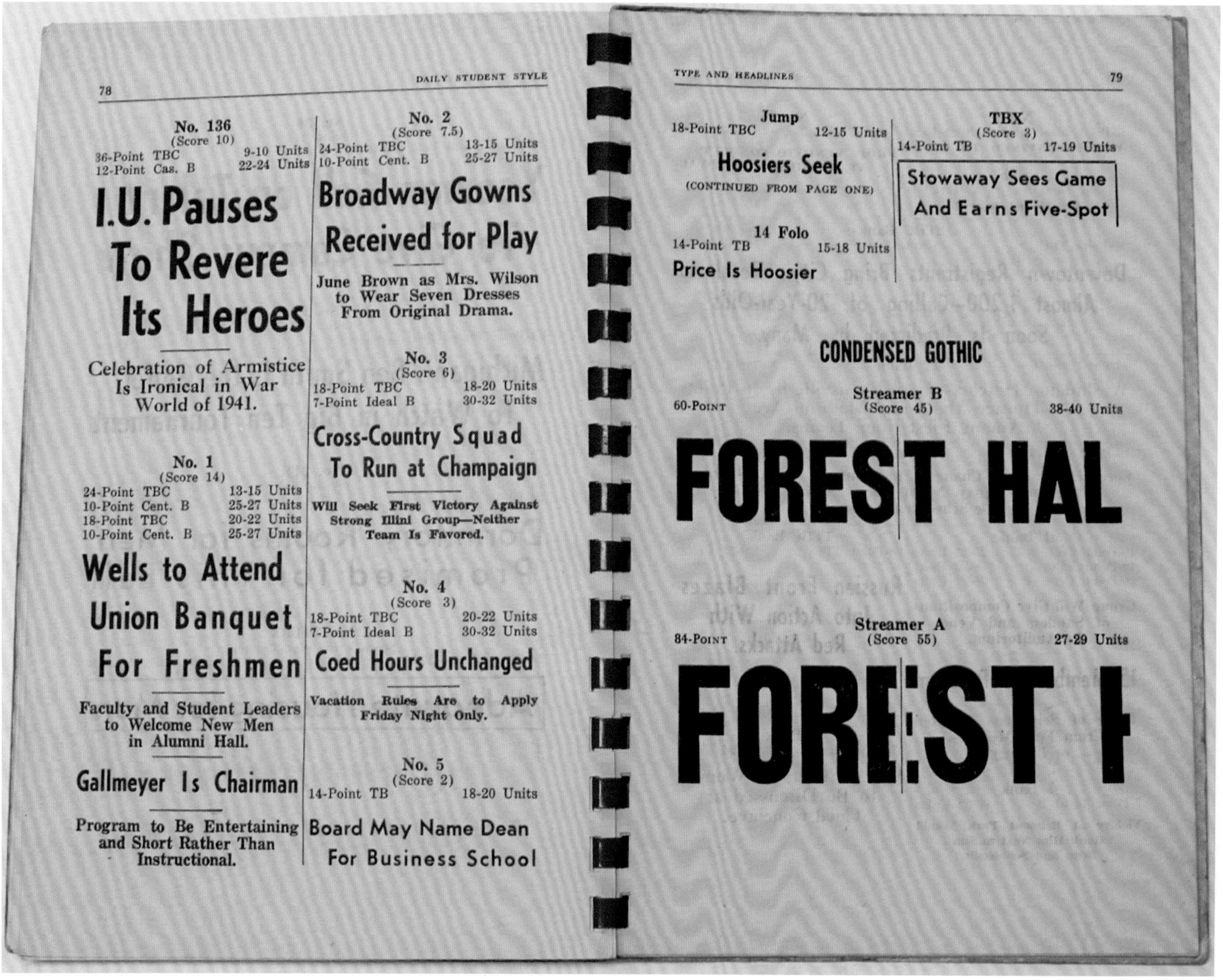
78 DAILY STUDENT STYLE

No. 136
(Score 10)
36-Point TBC 9-10 Units
12-Point Cas. B 22-24 Units

I.U. Pauses
To Revere
Its Heroes

Celebration of Armistice
Is Ironical in War
World of 1941.

No. 1
(Score 14)
24-Point TBC 13-15 Units
10-Point Cent. B 25-27 Units
18-Point TBC 20-22 Units
10-Point Cent. B 25-27 Units

Wells to Attend
Union Banquet
For Freshmen

Faculty and Student Leaders
to Welcome New Men
in Alumni Hall.

Gallmeyer Is Chairman

Program to Be Entertaining
and Short Rather Than
Instructional.

No. 2
(Score 7.5)
24-Point TBC 13-15 Units
10-Point Cent. B 25-27 Units

Broadway Gowns
Received for Play

June Brown as Mrs. Wilson
to Wear Seven Dresses
From Original Drama.

No. 3
(Score 6)
18-Point TBC 18-20 Units
7-Point Ideal B 30-32 Units

Cross-Country Squad
To Run at Champaign

Will Seek First Victory Against
Strong Illini Group—Neither
Team Is Favored.

No. 4
(Score 3)
18-Point TBC 20-22 Units
7-Point Ideal B 30-32 Units

Coed Hours Unchanged

Vacation Rules Are to Apply
Friday Night Only.

No. 5
(Score 2)
14-Point TB 18-20 Units

Board May Name Dean
For Business School

TYPE AND HEADLINES 79

Jump
18-Point TBC 12-15 Units

Hoosiers Seek
(CONTINUED FROM PAGE ONE)

14 Folo
14-Point TB 15-18 Units

Price Is Hoosier

TBX
(Score 3)
14-Point TB 17-19 Units

Stowaway Sees Game
And Earns Five-Spot

CONDENSED GOTHIC

Streamer B
60-Point (Score 45) 38-40 Units

FOREST HAL

Streamer A
84-Point (Score 55) 27-29 Units

FOREST I

While the early editions of the stylebook devoted many pages to the trials and tribulations of the telegraph and linotype machines, the versions from the Siddons years hint at the digital revolution that was to come, with sections on "how to cope" with computers.

As Siddons wrote: "It's important to remember that no matter what space-age techniques we use to get the paper out, the goal is unchanged from that of the first IDS in 1867, which proclaimed itself to be a paper 'owing allegiance to no faction, subservient to no personal motives of exultation, pure in tone, seeking the common good. . . .' "

Headlines page from the 1942 IDS stylebook. *Photo courtesy of Ruth Witmer.*

REFLECTION

Tight Times, Newspaper Extras and a Brush With Ernie Pyle

Robert C. Pebworth.
P0078379, IU Archives.

It was my privilege to work on the IDS for four years, serving as editor the fall semester of 1930. Those were tough economic times, and the grand old paper had to fight to maintain its existence. We couldn't afford the then-new and expensive AP teletypewriter service, so we picked up an envelope of AP wire story tissue copies on the Greyhound bus arriving from Indianapolis at 6 p.m. and then took a 20-minute telephone call from AP in Indianapolis to receive our "late" state and national news.

Since you couldn't fill with lengthy wire service copy, you—by necessity—covered the campus, the town and the county with the result we produced a newsy morning paper that was bought and read by many beyond the campus. As youngsters we thought it was tough competing against the "pros" on the Bloomington World, Telephone and the weekly Star. In reality, it was the greatest training ground a fledgling newspaper staff could have.

By God, we weren't just boasting when we said we produced the World's Greatest College Daily!

A few memory highlights:

The night the campus power house—then located adjacent to the IDS building which snuggled up to the Dunn cemetery—caught fire about 8 p.m. The electricity went off about 8:30, killing the linotypes. By midnight, we had moved forms, type already set and copy to the Bloomington World near the square, and at 8 a.m. we hit the street with a complete six-page paper.

"By God, we weren't just boasting when we said we produced the World's Greatest College Daily!"

Then, the late-winter weekend when we convinced the administration we could produce at a profit a "Sunday extra" to cover four varsity teams each with a strong bid to win a Big Ten championship on that one Saturday night. We helped sell the ads, sent out reporters at our own expense and waited. All four teams lost—but William Howard Taft died at 8 p.m., so we produced a "Great Man dies" extra that sold out in two hours.

And one very personal memory possibly appropriate: In the spring of 1932—the depth of the Depression—those of us heading out into the world were scratching for any possible newspaper jobs. John Mellett—brother of Don and Lowell—had been a godfather to me during my campus days, and he said, "Write Ernie Pyle (the managing editor then of a Washington, D.C., paper). Tell him I told you to write and that I said you were good." I did as instructed, and about a week later received a cryptic reply from Ernie Pyle, which said in essence: "Today I had to let go two good newspaper men because I couldn't afford to pay them. If you think you are as good as you and John Mellett say you are, come over to see me."

Regretfully, at that time I couldn't afford what surely would have been an interesting but non-productive interview.

—Robert C. Pebworth, BA 1932, wrote this recollection in 1977 for the paper's 110th birthday. He died in 1994.

The PRESIDENT'S COLUMN

Candidates for the First Professorship in Indiana University.

William Lowe Bryan

THE INDIANA DAILY STUDENT

Unsettled Today, Probable Local Thunder Showers; Rain Thursday and Colder.

VOL. LIX, NO. 34. BLOOMINGTON, INDIANA, WEDNESDAY MORNING, OCT. 30, 1929. ESTABLISHED 1867.

University Plans Drive for Building Funds

Baynard R. Hall, who was himself the first professor in Indiana University, writes in THE NEW PURCHASE (Woodburn edition, pp. 264 and following) of some of the men who tried to secure that position.

One man, hearing that a chair was to be filled, offered to furnish his own chair. One asked for the place because he needed the money; another because he had taught common school for years and deserved promotion. A Mr. James Jimmey heard that algebra was to be taught, and though he had never heard of it, felt sure that he could learn "before school took up." Mr. Jimmey further proposed to "board students at one dollar a week and find everything, washing included and will black their shoes three times a week to boot." The candidacy of Mr. Solomon Rapid is reported as follows:

" 'I heerd, sir, you wanted somebody to teach the State school, and I'm come to let you know I'm willing to take the place.'

" 'Yes, sir, we are going to elect a professor of languages who is to be the principal, and a professor—'

" 'Well, I don't care which I take, but I'm willing to be the principal. I can teach sifring, reading, writing, jogger-free, surveying, grammur, spelling, definitions, persin—'

" 'Are you a linguist?'

" 'Sir!'

" 'You of course understand the dead languages?'

" 'Well, can't say I ever seed much of them, though I have heerd tell of them; but I can soon larn them—they aint more than a few of them I allow?'

" 'Oh! my dear sir, it is not possible—we—can't—'

" 'Well, I never seed what I couldn't larn about as smart as any body—'

" 'Mr. Rapid, I do not mean to question your abilities; but if you are now wholly unacquainted with the dead languages, it is impossible for you or any other talented man to learn them under four or five years.'

" 'Pshoo foo! I'll bet I larn one in three weeks! Try me, sir—let's have the furst one furst—how many are there?'

" 'Mr. Rapid, it is utterly impossible; but if you insist, I will loan you a Latin book—'

" 'That's your sorts, let's have it, that's all I want, fair play.'

"Accordingly, I handed him a copy of Historiae Sacrae with which he soon went away, saying, he 'didn't allow it would take long to git through Latin, if 'twas only sich a thin patch of a book as that.'

"In a few weeks, to my no small surprise, Mr. Solomon Rapid again presented himself; and drawing forth the book began with a triumphant expression of countenance:—

" 'Well, sir, I have done the Latin.'

" 'Done the Latin!'

" 'Yes, I can read it as fast as English.'

" 'Read it as fast as English!!'

" 'Yes, as fast as English—and I didn't find it hard at all.'

" 'May I try you on a page?'

" 'Try away, try away; that's what I've come for.'

" 'Please read here then, Mr. Rapid;' and in order to give him a fair chance, I pointed to the first lines of the first chapter, viz; 'In principio deus creavit caelum et terram intra sex dies; primo die fecit lucem,' &c.

" 'That, sir?' and then he read thus, 'in prinspo duse cree-vit kalelum et terum intra sex dyes—primmo dye fe-fe-sit looseum,' &c.

" 'That will do, Mr. Rapid—'

" 'Ah! ha! I told you so.'

" 'Yes,—yes but translate.'

" 'Translate?!' (eyebrows elevating.)

" 'Yes, translate, render it.'

" 'Render it!! how's that?' (forehead more wrinkled.)

" 'Why, yes, render it into English—give me the meaning of it.'

" 'MEANING!!' (staring full in my face, his eyes like saucers, and forehead wrinkled with the furrows of eighty)—'MEANING!! I didn't know it had any meaning. I thought it was a DEAD language!' "

STUDENT IS SEVERELY ILL.

Dwight Mullin, '32, was taken to the city hospital with an acute case of appendicitis last night.

MOTION PICTURES WILL BE SHOWN AT CONVO TODAY

Pathe Educational Reels on Travel, Foreign Customs To Be Given.

WILL GIVE THREE FILMS

Scenes of Arabia, Mongol Life, and "Earthquakes" To Be Portrayed.

Three Pathe educational films produced under the direction of Harvard university professors will be shown at convocation this morning. The films are being furnished by the University's bureau of visual instruction. The titles of the reels are: "Wanderers of the Arabian Desert," "The Mongols of Central Asia" and "Earthquakes."

"Wanderers of the Arabian Desert" was produced under the direction of Dr. Ernest A. Hooton and Dr. Edward Reynolds, of the division of anthropology at Harvard. It is one of a series of ten films showing the development of various parts of the world's civilizations. The picturesque, war-like Arab is shown as he lives in his home in the fertile country in the Arabian desert with the famous Arabian horse. The customs of the women and their work of making tents and cooking also are portrayed.

Earthquakes Explained.

"The Mongols of Central Asia" is a picture made by a member of the famous Roy Chapman Andrews expedition into Asia, showing the peoples of the upland steppes of Mongolia.

The use of animated drawings to explain the origin of tectonic earthquakes, and to differentiate the types of wave motion which they involve makes the picture, "Earthquakes" interesting and free of technical terms. The subject is introduced by reference to the great earthquake in Japan in 1923, and explanation is given as to nature, causes and effects of earthquakes, with a special reference to the types of wave motion accompanying a quake and the methods of recording seismic phenomena. Seismographs are shown in operation, and their mechanism is carefully explained.

I. U. COED VOTERS HEAR MRS. LOUDEN

State Officer Discusses Objects and Progress of League.

"The League of Women Voters has been, since its organization ten years ago, an educational as well as a legislative factor. The object of the league is to instruct women how to use the ballot intelligently, to foster education in citizenship, and to promote efficiency in government," Mrs. T. J. Louden, state vice-president of the League of Women Voters, said at the first meeting of the campus league held last night at Commerce auditorium.

Mrs. Louden gave a brief history of the organization and told of its growth since its beginning in 1919. The league is not a political organization but urges its members to go into the political party of their choice, and is absolutely non-partisan, Mrs. Louden said. It has been instrumental in bringing about new laws, particularly those in which women are interested, she pointed out.

Jane Gottman, '30, president of the group, told of the organization of the league, which is a branch of the state and national leagues. Miss Gottman introduced the other officers who are Jessie Borror, '30, vice-president, and Katherine Hougland, '30, secretary and treasurer. A committee will be appointed to decide on a regular time and place for meeting, Miss Gottman said.

Representatives present from the city league were Mrs. Thomas Nicholson and Mrs. D. R. Major.

BLUE KEY TO MEET.

Members of Blue Key will hold their regular noon luncheon today in the Reserve room of the University cafeteria, Richard Jones, '30, president, announced Tuesday. The members will gather as soon after 12 o'clock as possible, Jones said.

"Go West, Young Man," Applies in This Case

CHICAGO, Oct. 29—(AP)—Oscar Hammerstein, famed producer of musical comedies, passed through Chicago today on his way to Hollywood to take his money "where the public is willing to pay."

"You can't be a fool," said the veteran producer. "The talking pictures have done terrific damage to the stage. I put $300,000 into every musical comedy and take a chance on losing, but in a movie you can't lose."

Hammerstein said his first musical comedy for the talking pictures would mark the return to the screen of Dorothy Dalton, his wife. Next year, he said, he planned to put the first grand opera into talkies.

ADVANCED HONORS TO BE CONFERRED ON 60 GRADUATES

Faculty Members Pass on List of Candidates for Degrees.

Sixty candidates were recommended for advanced degrees by members of the faculty at a meeting Tuesday afternoon. The list includes 9 candidates for Ph.D. degrees, 41 for A.M. degrees and 10 for M.S. degrees. These honors will be awarded Thursday night by the board of trustees.

The students who will receive Ph.D. degrees are: Fred E. Brengle, Troy C. Daniels, Donald E. Gorseline, Richard S. Harter Earl A. Johnson, Robert L. Shelley, Sister Gertrude Smith, William H. Sumrall and Chan-Sain Young.

Receive Masters Degree.

Candidates recommended for the degree of master of arts are: Fred L. Anderson, Martha A. Bateman, James C. Benne, Olive R. Beckington, Enoch N. Brindley, Sherman G. Crayton, Grace M. Custer, Lillian M. Dinius, Estella R. Dodson, Forrest R. Groff, William J. Gunkell, William T. Hammond, Hazel Howe, Mrs. Mary H. Keever, Jean Arthur Lambert, Elizabeth J. Lane, Flora E. Leach, Clifford Lineback, Lewis B. Lockwood, Sister Mary Ruth Lucey, Dudley B. Lutz, Alice E. McKeehan, Andrew C. Mahaffay, John D. Mossler, Wilford P. Musgrave, Margaret Newby, Archie M. Pender, Lemen E. Pickett, Charles E. Pittenger, Bessie F. Power, Elizabeth A. Rechenberg, Elmer C. Robbins, John C. Romey, Otto Shaw, Franklin V. Thomas, Horace M. Trent, Nelson R. Van Cleave, Anna E. Wilcox, Edna L. Willis Alson EA Wrentmore and Shepherd Young.

Those approved to receive the degree of master of science are: Riley L. Case, Emma G. DeLay, Merrill T. Eaton, Clarence B. Forkner, Audley M. Brossman, Walter A. Krick, Dewey Manuel, Walter L. Myers, Howard R. Noe and Noel C. Ware.

ALUMNI ASSOCIATION RELEASES QUARTERLY

October Issue Contains Book Reviews, News of Graduates, University Notes.

The October edition of the University Alumni Quarterly, a magazine published by the Indiana Alumni association, and edited by Miss Ivy L. Chamness, '06, has just been released.

The magazine is divided into four parts. The first part contains articles entitled, "The Spell of Modern Egypt," by Vernon Brinson Schuman, '26; "Jim Bridgers' Old Trading House," an account dealing with the history of Fort Bridger, Wyo., by Robert S. Ellison, '00, and articles giving accounts of the 1927 Foundation Day exercises and of meetings held by county alumni associations.

The second section of the magazine contains news of the University and several articles pertaining to deaths of several prominent alumni. Section three is devoted to book reviews and literary notes. One of these reviews is written by Roy Tower, of the English department, on Theodore Dreiser's book, "Dreiser Looks At Russia." The last division contains alumni notes.

TO ATTEND MEETING.

President William Lowe Bryan will go to Indianapolis Friday to attend the meeting of the state board of education.

Wall Street Tense as Market Takes Second Drop

Associated Press Photo

The above is a scene taken along Wall street, New York, as tense and curious throngs gathered when the second sensational drop within five days rocked the securities markets in the country. The three men pictured in the insets were leaders in a giant bankers' pool which was formed following the first panic late last week. The failure of this pool to stabilize the market brought the second flurry Monday. The bankers pictured are: W. C. Potter (left), president of the Guaranty Trust company; Thomas W. Lamont, (center), senior Morgan partner, and Charles E. Mitchell (right), chairman of the Chase National bank.

I. U. UNION BOARD NAMES PEBWORTH AS NEW MEMBER

Group To Sponsor Gridgraph Saturday and Hold Dance Friday Night.

Robert C. Pebworth, '31, was chosen to membership on the Indiana Union board at a regular meeting of the board held last night in the Student building, according to announcement made by Franklin K. Mullin, '30, president. Pebworth takes the place of Howard Heslett, ex-'31.

In view of the increasing interest in football that has been created during the past two weeks, members of the board last night agreed to sponsor a Gridgraph showing of the Minnesota-Indiana game on Saturday afternoon in Assembly hall. Since there are few stations that will broadcast the game and since there is no "B" team scheduled for Saturday, a large crowd of students is expected.

Considerable time was spent in discussing the active campaign for the collection of unpaid pledges to the Memorial Union building. President Mullin instructed members to meet with W. A. Alexander, faculty advisor of the student campaign, at 4 o'clock Thursday afternoon to plan for the canvass of alumni and former students in Bloomington.

Orchestra Secured.

Jack Berry's orchestra, of Indianapolis, has been secured to play for the open dance Friday night of this week although this date was reserved formerly by A. W. S. Through arrangements between the two groups the Union is to have the use of Assembly hall.

Members of the board voted to cancel the dance scheduled for the Friday night before the Purdue game so that the play, "College Widow," could be shown on both Thursday and Friday nights of that week.

Membership in the Union board is full with the addition of Pebworth and it is probable that no new members will be added until next spring. Pebworth is a member of Alpha Tau Omega fraternity, one of the night editors of The Daily Student, sports editor of the 1930 Arbutus, member of Sigma Delta Chi, international honorary journalistic fraternity, and is a member of Skull and Crescent, honorary sophomore organization.

A CORRECTION.

In Tuesday's issue of The Daily Student a mistake was made in the announcement of the lecture to be given by Prof. John L. Geiger, of the Music school, on the Boston Symphony orchestra. The time for the lecture should have been tonight at 7 o'clock instead of last night as it was published. The lecture will be given in Mitchell Annex.

Campus Journalists Hear Les Gage Talk

Les Gage, promotion manager and sports editor of College Humor, gave a short talk to members of Sigma Delta Chi, international professional journalistic fraternity, at a luncheon Tuesday noon. Mr. Gage, formerly publicity director of Wisconsin university and one-time captain and all-Western basketball player, spoke on "Publicity Work with National Publications."

In his talk Mr. Gage discussed his publication and explained how manuscripts, cartoons and jokes are received. He discussed, also, the relationship between the editorial and advertising policies of College Humor. While discussing publicity, Mr. Gage told members of the journalistic group that great opportunities in this field now await the college graduate with large concerns and publications.

Frank R. Elliott, publicity director of Indiana university, also gave a short talk at the luncheon.

CITY TEACHERS HEAR NOMINEES FOR MAYOR

Candidates Discuss Political Issues Before Instructors of Public Schools.

Republican and Democratic candidates for mayor in the coming city election appeared before the City Teachers' federation Tuesday afternoon at the high school auditorium and discussedpolitical questions which members of the faculty submitted to the two parties.

Hale Bradt, assistant principal, gave a short introductory address in which he explained the purpose of the meeting and introduced the chairmen of the Republican and Democratic parties who in turn introduced their candidates, Charles Edgar Suggs, Democrat, and Joseph Campbell, Republican, who gave the principal addresses.

HIGH SCHOOL BOY HELD

Woodrow Adams, 18, Is Arrested as Hit and Run Driver.

Charged with being a hit and run driver, Woodrow Adams, 18 year old Bloomington high school student, was arrested Tuesday night by J. A. Lucas, sheriff of Morgan county, on a warrant issued by the Morgan county court. Adams was taken to Martinsville, and if unable to furnish bond will be placed in the Morgan county jail.

Adams is charged with having run down a man near Martinsville Friday and to have driven on without stopping. The man was injured seriously and is still in a critical condition.

OFFICE BEING COMPLETED.

The new Gothic office on the balcony of the girl's gymnasium in the Bloomington high school is being completed this week.

FIRST INTRAMURAL DEBATING TEAMS OPEN COMPETITION

Affirmative Wins Majority of Victories on Question of Sophomore Pledging.

Two negative victories won by Alpha Chi Omega and Delta Phi Sigma in an overwhelming majority of affirmative victories marked the first round of the intramural debates last night in which 20 teams participated. The debates were held at the houses of the negative teams on the subject, "Resolved that no student should be allowed to pledge to any social organization until he has received 30 hours of general credit in this University."

Four meets scheduled for last night failed to be held when three were postponed and Sigma Chi forfeited to Alpha Tau Omega. Phi Beta Delta won over Delta Upsilon; Kappa Delta over Delta Zeta; Residence hall over Beta Sigma Omicron; Sigma Kappa over Delta Gamma; Acacia over Sigma Alpha Epsilon; Gamma Eta Gamma over Sigma Nu; Phi Delta Theta over Beta Theta Pi; Sigma Alpha Mu over Phi Kappa Psi; Harrill and Partner over Lambda Chi Alpha; Delta Phi Sigma over Theta Chi, and Alpha Chi Omega over Kappa Kappa Gamma.

Debates between Delta Chi and Delta Tau Delta, Alpha Omicron Pi and Zeta Tau Alpha and Sigma Pi and South hall, were postponed.

Alpha Chi Omega and Delta Upsilon were the winners of last year's intramural debate contest. The cups which are now in the possession of these organizations will be given permanently to this year's winning teams.

TRUSTEES WILL HOLD FALL MEETING TODAY

Board Will Consider Plans for Power Plant, Chemistry and Union Buildings.

The University board of trustees will hold its annual fall meeting today to discuss all campus improvements. The proposed enlargement of the Power house will be voted on and plans for letting the contract will be made.

Complete plans for the new Chemistry building will be presented to the board today by Robert Frost Daggett, of Indianapolis, architect in charge, and will be voted on and changed if necessary.

Data on the location and plans for the new Union building will be presented. A sketch of pledges and the money paid in will be read.

All financial reports for the University and its divisions are to be presented to the board today. A complete list of financial expenditures and gains is presented each year.

Unpaid Pledges Are Target For Proposed Committee

Missing Air Express Flies Into Airport Under Own Power

Strategy of Pilot Doles Saves Passengers and Crew From Injury.

ALBUQUERQUE, N. M., Oct. 29.—(AP)—Fighting a snow storm most of the way to Albuquerque from Trechado, Ariz., James E. Doles, pilot, and his co-pilot, Allan C. Barrie, brought the last Western Air Express plane, No. 113, safely to the Albuquerque airport this afternoon under its own power.

He put the plane down at Trechado, and he and his cargo spent the night there to await clear weather. Trechado is about 75 miles southeast of Gallup, and is only about five miles south of the country of treacherous lava beds and extinct volcanoes.

"It was through the cleverness of Pilot Doles that a landing was made and we escaped injury. Doles ran into the storm but kept cool. He circled and searched the limited area visible and finally sighted a small clearing in some heavy timber land. He headed for this spot and brought the plane down safely," Dr. A. M. Ward, a passenger, said.

"There was a cabin nearby which provided us refuge for the night. Of course, we had no way of communication with the outside world regarding our safety," he added.

COEDS TO RECEIVE VOCATIONAL HELP

Florence Jackson, of Wellesley College, Will Advise Freshmen.

Miss Florence Jackson, consultant to the personnel bureau of Wellesley college, will have personal conferences with freshman coeds about the choice of a profession, from 8 a.m. to 12 m. and from 2 to 4 p.m. next Monday and Tuesday, and will speak at the freshman dinners to be given by Dean Agnes E. Wells on the same days.

For 14 years, Miss Jackson was the director of the appointment bureau of the women's educational and industrial union of Boston, during which time she acted as lecturer and vocational consultant for women at a number of colleges and universities.

Those who desire conferences may make an appointment at Dean Wells' office. Fifteen minute conferences are being arranged. Before talking with Miss Jackson, coeds must fill out a paper which will be considered during the appointment. This will include points to be considered in the discussion of an occupation.

Invitations to a dinner for freshman girls next Monday and Tuesday have been sent out and Dean Wells has asked anyone who has not been invited to call at her office. Miss Jackson and Prof. W. W. Wright, of the School of Education, will speak at the dinner Monday night. Miss Jackson and Prof. E. L. Yeager, of the Psychology department, will speak at the dinner Tuesday night.

The date for a reception given by Dean Wells for new students will be announced later.

New York Firm Crashes In Stock Selling Orgy

NEW YORK, Oct. 29.—(AP)—The gigantic wave of selling that has swept through every stock exchange in the country brought its first failure today in the collapse of the brokerage firm of John J. Bell and company, members of the New York Curb exchange.

The wave of selling that struck the country's security markets was felt in all groups of bonds listed on the New York stock exchange, and the Associated Press combined average showed a decline of three-quarters of a point. Only the United States government issues showed any degree of steadiness.

TEACHING AT MISHAWAKA.

Ruth Bugbee, '29, is teaching Latin at Mishawaka.

Advisory Board To Select General Drive Chairman, Section Leaders Today—$800,000 Is Goal of Students—May Consider Union Building Site.

Preliminary plans for the organization of students to collect approximately $800,000 in unpaid pledges to the Indiana Memorial Union Fund during the Thanksgiving vacation, were made at a meeting held in the office of W. A. Alexander, librarian and faculty advisor of the campaign, Tuesday afternoon. George F. Heighway, alumni secretary; Franklin K. Mullin, '30, president of the Union board, and Janet Johnston, '30, president of A.W.S., met with Mr. Alexander.

A general chairman of the campaign will be chosen today. In turn, county chairman under whose personal control the campaign will be conducted during the vacation, will be chosen.

An advisory board composed of ten representative students will meet this afternoon in Maxwell 23 to select a general chairman and the heads of the men's and women's groups, in hope of getting county organizations created by Friday, so that the drive proper can be in full swing before the Thanksgiving vacation begins. The advisory board that is to back the general chairman is composed of the following members: Theodore Dann, PG; Max Sappenfield, '30; Richard Wall, '30, Pauline Hindsley, '29; Joe Smith, '30; Franklin K. Mullin; Elizabeth King, '31; Doris Scripture, '30, and Marthalou Gray, '32.

May Select Building Site.

The site for Indiana's gigantic Memorial Union building, the last of three great structures to be erected on the campus through voluntary subscriptions in memory of the University's war dead, is expected to be decided here today by the University board of trustees.

Meeting with the trustees this morning will be J. Carlisle Bollenbacher, architect, of Chicago, and the managers of the Iowa State and Ohio State unions, it was learned last night.

Construction will begin as soon

(CONTINUED ON PAGE THREE)

RED CROSS ROLL CALL WILL BEGIN

Dean Smith, Miss Biglow To Speak at Opening Meeting Nov. 8.

The thirteenth annual roll call of the American Red Cross will be launched in Bloomington with a meeting at the city hall Nov. 8, according to plans for the drive announced Tuesday. Dean H. L. Smith, of the School of Education, and president of the Monroe county chapter of the Red Cross, and Miss Alida Biglow, Indiana field representative from national headquarters, will be the principal speakers at the meeting. Chairmen, solicitors and all others interested in the drive are urged to attend the meeting.

Dr. Frank D. Hope, former commander of the local post of the American Legion, has been named chairman of the drive which will end Nov. 28. Under his directorship will be a corps of solicitors from the American Legion, the Legion Auxiliary, the Business and Professional Women's club and volunteers.

Dean Paul V. McNutt will make the first announcement of the drive at the dinner to be given in his honor by the American Legion and the Rotary club Wednesday night.

BAPTIST LEADER DIES.

CLIFTON SPRINGS, N. Y., Oct. 29.—(AP)—The Rev. John Roach Straton, one of the world's outstanding champions of fundamentalism, died here today of a heart attack, aged 54. Dr. Straton, as pastor of Calvary Baptist Church in New York, became famous for his support of William Jennings Bryan at the Scopes trial in Dayton, Tenn., in 1925, and for his debates with William A. Brady, Broadway producer.

P0078731, IU Archives.

HE SERVES BEST WHO SERVES THE TRUTH

THE INDIANA DAILY STUDENT

WEATHER
Rain and Warmer

VOL. LXI. NO. 110. BLOOMINGTON, INDIANA, WEDNESDAY MORNING, MARCH 2, 1932. ESTABLISHED 1867

KIDNAPERS TAKE LINDBERGH BABY FROM HOME

Famous Infant Disappears From Nursery Crib, Clad Only in Sleeping Clothes

Parents Are Unable To Give Information Concerning Abduction—Police Throw Dragnet Over Roads—Note Is Found.

(By Samuel Blackman, Associated Press Staff Writer)
(Copyrighted, 1932, Associated Press)

HOPEWELL, N. J., March 2.—(Wednesday)—(AP)—Charles Augustus Lindbergh Jr., 20-months-old son of the flying colonel, was kidnaped last night from his nursery in the Lindbergh country home near here.

He was spirited away in a dark green Chrysler sedan registered in the name of Herbert W. Allen, of Margate, N. J., and reported to have been stolen in Atlantic City, police said.

The car contained two men, who stopped at least two persons prior to the kidnaping and asked directions to the isolated Lindbergh home.

Within an hour after Colonel Lindbergh himself telephoned the first alarm, police squad cars blockaded every Jersey road for miles.

They had orders to stop any suspicious persons or cars.

The child, clad in a blue sleeping robe, was put to bed at the usual hour, 7:30 p.m. At about 10 p.m. someone peered into the nursery. The crib was empty.

The first newspaperman to reach the home was an Associated Press reporter, who ran a mile over muddy, rut-cut roads to reach a phone to send the first direct news from the residence.

Search Grounds.

Colonel Lindbergh bare-headed as usual, was pacing the grounds, while troopers and detectives went over the place with flashlights, seeking clues.

Mrs. Lindbergh, who telephoned the news to her mother, Mrs. Dwight W. Morrow, at the Morrow home in Englewood, N. J., was inside the house but was shielded carefully from newspapermen. A close friend of Mrs. Lindbergh said that she was expecting another child within three months.

The house glowed with lights, a butler appeared at the door, obviously distraught, but he, like his employers, refused to make a statement.

The police, dashing pell-mell to the place, were delayed by the mud-soaked roads. It was an hour before they reached the house, which is perched amidst the Sourland hills, on the second highest eminence in New Jersey.

At the Morrow home in Englewood, it was said Mrs. Morrow had not decided whether to leave at once to be with her daughter.

First News.

The first police news of the crime came in the following blunt teletype message:

"Colonel Lindbergh's baby kidnaped from Lindbergh home at Hopewell, between 7:30 and 10 p.m. Boy, 19 months (his age actually is 20 months) dressed in sleeping suit. Search all cars."

For the next hour it was virtually impossible to get telephonic communication with the Lindberghs. One call brought the response—"No one has time to talk!"—and finally the chief operator said she had orders to refer all inquiries to the police, who had no announcement to make.

As news of the kidnaping filtered through the friendly countryside—all Lindbergh's neighbors are farmers—lights began to glow in the hills and many came to the place to volunteer aid in the search.

The Lindbergh baby, probably the most famous infant in the world, is described as a golden-haired replica of his famous father. He is chubby, with blue eyes and curly hair.

His nursery, filled with every possible device for childish joy, is in the right-hand corner of the second floor of the big house.

The window near his crib, which was open when his nurse went into the room, is 30 feet from the ground.

Note Found.

On the window sill, police said, a note was found, and, though they would not divulge its contents, it was indicated that it contained a demand for ransom.

A three-piece ladder was found a hundred feet from the house, as if it had been dropped in a hurry, and police believe this was used to reach the window.

The window of the nursery looks out on the private road which links the estate with the outside world,

(CONTINUED ON PAGE THREE)

The President's Column

Concerning Washington

William Lowe Bryan

I

Lies.

Lies are never harmless. Lies are alive. Lies grow. Lies spread like the seeds of a disease. Consider these lines from Beaumarchais: **Bazile.** Slander, sir? You hardly know what you despise. I have seen the best of men nearly crushed under it. Believe me that there is no vulgar wickedness, no horror, no absurd story, that one cannot make the idle residents of a great city believe if he go about it in the right way. At first, a slight rumour, skimming the ground like the swallow before the storm, **pianissimo,** it murmurs, and twists and leaves behind it its poisonous trail. So-and-so hears it and **piano piano** slips it gracefully into your ear. The evil is done, it sprouts, crawls, travels on, and **rinforzando** from mouth to mouth, it goes on at the deuce of a pace; then, suddenly, I know not how, you see slander arising, hissing, swelling, and visibly growing. It rushes forward, extends its flight, whirls, envelopes, tears, bursts, and thunders, and becomes a general cry, a public **crescendo,** a universal chorus of hate and denunciation. Who the devil could withstand it?

Washington did and does withstand calumnies such as few men have had to endure. The lies came from venal politicians. They came from jealous, treacherous officers of his army. Now men of like quality crawl through old sewers in search of lies against Washington which they can sell.

He was not and he is not crushed under those slanders. But they did and they do harm. They made it harder for Washington to win the war. They made it harder for him to establish this Republic. They make it harder now "to mould our nation into the likeness of its greatest hero."

II

Hypocritical Praise.

It is a most certain fact which we know even if Quintilian and Emerson had not said so that a man speaks more loudly by his character than by his words. Children as well as older ones quickly see through fine phrases to the man. And when they see that the man is a living denial of his phrases, what he says of most fine and pious drives them to revolt. So the orator who is himself a "whited sepulchre full of iniquity and hypocrisy" when he builds a monument of words in honor of Washington and "garnishes his tomb" with praise ranks with the liar as the enemy of all the best for which Washington stood.

III

Platitudes.

A platitude is a truth so old and tried and dried that it rattles. The manifold virtues of Washington, the countless stories of his goodness and greatness, the hundred and ten "Rules of Civility and Decent Behavior in Company and Conversation" which George transcribed into his copybook—all these fine things may be banged about the ears of a boy until he longs to be a pirate if only to escape being like "Georgie, the perfect little gentleman."

A man who grew to be almost as famous as Franklin tells how as a boy he was made to hate that model of perfection. "Franklin's maxims," he says, "were full of animosity toward boys. Nowadays a boy cannot follow out a single natural instinct without tumbling over some of his everlasting aphorisms. And that boy is hounded to death and robbed of his natural rest because Franklin said once in one of his inspired flights of malignity: "Early to bed and early to rise makes a man healthy, wealthy and wise." Therefore, oh you orators and preachers and you my fellow teachers who this year all across the land recite the excellencies of Washington, let us not forget that our praiseful reiterations may turn into a ding dong of rebellion-rousing platitudes.

IV

Truth.

"Paint me with my warts," said one great man. "Tell the truth," said another when gossip had picked up a story against him that was true.

(CONTINUED ON PAGE THREE)

DIRECTORS CHOOSE NOMINATING GROUP IN M'NUTT CLUB

Barr, Ryall, Jones, Forkner Appointed on Committee.

A nominating committee consisting of Ross Barr, '32, chairman; Catharine Ryall, '32; Robert W. Jones, '32, and William Forkner, '32, was appointed at a meeting of the board of directors of the McNutt-for-Governor club in the Student building Tuesday afternoon. This committee will select the membership and entertainment committees of the organization some time during the coming week.

Paul Jasper, '32, president of the club, presided at the meeting and outlined future programs and the membership drive which is to be launched immediately. State politicians and political leaders will be brought to the campus to speak in meetings in behalf of McNutt's campaign. Dean McNutt also probably will speak at one of these meetings in the near future, it was said.

Each member of the board was given a number of application blanks with which to enroll new members for the club. The fee for membership in the organization is 25 cents, the money to be used in obtaining speakers and paying other expenses in backing the campaign. Any one on the campus is eligible for membership whether or not he is of voting age. The number of members, now approximately 100, will be increased, it is hoped, to 500 through the drive, Jasper said.

100 ARE SEEKING RESEARCH AWARDS

Graduate School Receives Applications for Ten Fellowships.

Approximately 100 applications for research fellowships have been received this spring by the Graduate school, according to an announcement made Tuesday at the office of the school. These applications, together with others which are expected, will be considered by the Graduate council, which is headed by Dr. Fernandus Payne, dean of the Graduates school. Ten of the applicants will be selected for the fellowships.

Applications have been received from almost every state and several foreign countries including Germany, Denmark, Scotland and the Philippines. The requests have been for fellowships in the following subjects: music, botany, psychology, German, chemistry, English, history, mathematics, geology, philosophy, economics, entomology, zoology and physics. The total number of applications filed is expected to exceed the number of last year.

The awards, which amount to $600 a year, plus exemption from payment of the contingent fees for the school year 1932-1933, are made on a competitive basis. The scholarship and research abilities as well as the research problem which has been started by the applicant are considered in selecting the recipients.

To Address Coeds Today

Dr. Bessie Leach Priddy, dean of women at the University of Missouri, who will speak before University women students today at the required mass meeting in Assembly hall.

VISITING MISSOURI DEAN TO DISCUSS "DEMANDS ON THE COLLEGE WOMAN"

Dr. Bessie Leach Priddy To Speak at Required Mass Meeting This Afternoon—Dean Wells, A.W.S. Officers Also To Speak.

"Twentieth Century Demands on the College Woman" will be the subject of the address which Dr. Bessie Leach Priddy, dean of women at the University of Missouri, will deliver before the required coed mass meeting at 4 p.m. today in Assembly hall, it has been announced.

Dean Priddy will speak of the demands on the college woman as she has seen them through her wide experience on the faculty and executive staffs of high schools and colleges. In addition to her duties along professional lines, Dr. Priddy has been active in civic and social life in the state of Michigan. She is the mother of three children.

Dean Priddy began her teaching career as principal of schools in Capron, Ill., after her graduation from Adrian college, Adrian, Mich. When her husband died, Dr. Priddy returned to the teaching profession, combining teaching in the Adrian high school with advanced work at Adrian college. In 1915 she was made assistant professor of history at the Michigan State Normal college, Ypsilanti, and two years later she became dean of women at the school. In 1923 she accepted the position as the dean of women at the University of Missouri and an associate professorship on the history staff.

In addition to Dean Priddy's speech at the mass meeting, the program will include reports from officers of the A.W.S., and a short talk by Dean Agnes E. Wells on the bicentennial program which she attended Feb. 22 in Washington, D. C.

J. J. Gallaway To Lead Geology Discussion

An open discussion on the subject of "Making a Living in Geology" is to be led by Prof. J. J. Gallaway of the Geology department at a meeting of Sigma Gamma Epsilon, honorary geology fraternity, in the Geology library, Thursday evening.

Robert Bates, PG, president of the organization, said that the meeting will be open to all students interested in geology. A short business meeting, starting at 7 p.m., will precede the discussion.

Pianist Will Make Initial Appearance Here on March 16

The return to America this year of Ignac Jan Paderewski, world-famous pianist and composer, who will appear here in a concert March 16 in the Men's gymnasium, marks his eighteenth tour of the United States. His schedule includes a three-months' season with forty concerts. His performance here, which will be a number in the music activities series, will be his initial visit to Bloomington.

Travelling with Paderewski on his present tour are Lawrence Fitzgerald, his manager; Eldon Joubert, who looks after the transportation and takes care of the pianos; Marcel, the valet-masseur whose task is to take care of his master's physical condition and clothes; two Pullman porters, and a special chef.

Paderewski first came to the United States 40 years ago. He made his debut in 1887 in Vienna. In 1890 London hailed him as the great pianist of the age and the following year, during the season of 1891-92, he took America by storm. Today he stands at the pinnacle of his art. The world knows of his great achievement both as a musician and a statesman. Few men have had a career so rich in dramatic experiences as this great personality.

Paderewski still holds the rank of Minister Plenipotentiary at Large of the Republic of Poland, which office gives him the right to travel on a diplomatic passport and to represent his country at official functions.

Dr. J. A. Woodburn Predicts Great Future For University; Admires Recent Changes

(By Donrabelle Ritchey)

"There are greater things ahead for Indiana university, and what we have now may seem small 50 years hence," according to Dr. James A. Woodburn, professor emeritus of the University History department, who is visiting friends on the campus for a few days. Dr. Woodburn came here from Indianapolis where he addressed a meeting of the Indiana Society of Sons of the American Revolution last Thursday night and also attended the lecture given by Winston Spencer Churchill Saturday night.

"Since my retirement there have been many changes on the campus and I have noticed them from year to year, as I make frequent visits to the University," Dr. Woodburn said. "For athletics we have the Stadium and the new Fieldhouse. There is our fine Memorial hall for the girls and the splendid new Chemistry building, and now just being finished is the new Union building which is an ornament to the campus, and it will prove to be of great use in the years to come. These fine memorial enterprises will be very gratifying to all who have contributed toward their realization.

Recalls Lone Hall.

"I naturally contrast our campus and extensive plant as they are today with the one lone building we had in my college days at the south end of College avenue," he said. "These great changes and this wonderful growth that we have made have grown out of service, loyalty, devotion and sacrifice. I am sure the Indiana youth of today will

(CONTINUED ON PAGE THREE)

Company "G" Leads In Attendance Contest

With a rating of 585.6 out of a possible 600, Company "G" had the highest rating in the company attendance contest in the University R.O.T.C. unit, Feb. 2-25, according to Colonel O. P. Robinson, commandant of the unit.

Company "I" was second over the same period of time with a percentage of 583.2, and Company "D" was third with 581.1 per cent.

CHINESE RETREAT AS JAPS OCCUPY CITY OF TACHANG

Invaders' Planes Bomb Shanghai-Nanking Railway.

SHANGHAI, March 2.—(P)—Japanese drove the Chinese army at Shanghai into retreat today and were reported to have occupied Tachang, four miles west of Kiangwan.

Six Japanese airplanes at about the same time bombed and said they cut the Shanghai-Nanking railway near Kunshan, 35 miles west of Shanghai, in pursuance of a threat to destroy it if the Chinese continued to bring in re-inforcements.

On the North thousands of fresh Japanese re-inforcements, just off ships in the Yangtze river, were attempting to advance southward for a great encircling movement.

Over Chapei, at the Shanghai end of the battle front, artillery of both sides pounded each other's positions. Weakened by a battering assault which lasted from dawn till dusk yesterday, the Chinese fell back to the South, fighting for every foot of ground.

Japanese headquarters announced that during yesterday's action the whole line between Kiangwan and Miaochungchen, a distance of about two miles, had been advanced from three-fourths of a mile to a mile.

The Japanese seemed to be well started on their plan to pinch the strong Chinese positions in Chapei between attacks from the North

(CONTINUED ON PAGE THREE)

NUSSLEIN DEFEATS TILDEN, 6-2, 6-4

German Champion Beats U.S. Star in Match Played at Fieldhouse.

William T. Tilden II, claimant of the world's professional tennis championship, bowed to Hans Nusslein, German champion, 6-2, 6-4, last night in the Fieldhouse before a crowd of 2,000 spectators.

Tilden, flashing at times the form that carried him to the pinnacle of the racquet game, could not match the steady playing of his young German challenger, and was bested in straight sets.

The present world's professional title holder, however, did score on many occasions with his bullet-like service.

In the other singles match, Albert Burke, French star, downed Roman Najuch, Polish ace, 7-5, 6-4. The latter, however, displayed unusual agility for a large player.

In the doubles play, Tilden and his partner, Burke, bowed to Nusslein and Najuch, 3-6, 6-3, 6-2.

FRESHMAN MEDIC CLUB TO HEAR DEANS FRIDAY

Dr. W. D. Gatch and Dr. B. D. Myers, deans of the Indiana university School of Medicine at Indianapolis and Bloomington, respectively, will address the members of the Skeleton club, organization for all freshman medical students, at a meeting at 7 o'clock Friday night in the Chemistry auditorium.

Dr. Myers will give a report on the meeting of the Congress on Medical Education, which was held recently in Chicago. Dr. Gatch has not yet announced his subject.

This is the first of a series of meetings the Skeleton club is sponsoring this semester to bring prominent physicians here to address students in the Medical school future meetings. The program committee consists of the following: James M. Leffel, '32; Stanton Bryant, '32; George W. Macy, '32; Samuel Kaplain, '32; Elvin Fitzsimmons, '32, and Edna C. Kirch, '33.

ASSISTANTS TO MEET.

Sophomore assistants of the Arbutus staff will meet at 4 p.m. today in the Arbutus office, it was announced Tuesday by Naomi Ragains, '33, secretary-treasurer of the 1932 Arbutus board. It is important that all of the Sophomore assistants attend the meeting, Miss Ragains said.

To Conduct Band

Prof. Paul S. Emrick, director of music at Purdue university, will conduct the concert played by the Purdue band at 8 o'clock tonight in the Men's gymnasium. The concert will take the place of the regular convocation program.

PURDUE BAND TO MAKE LIFE MERRY AT I. U. TONIGHT

Concert To Be Presented in Men's Gymnasium at 8 o'Clock.

Playing a miscellaneous program of concert music, the Purdue university band, under the direction of Paul Emrick, will be presented at the convocation entertainment at 8 o'clock tonight in the Men's gymnasium. Miss Fern Gray will be featured as soprano soloist with the band. There will be no admission charge.

The Indiana university band will enter the gymnasium first this evening, playing "Hail to Old Purdue," followed by the Purdue organization playing "Indiana, Our Indiana." The visiting musicians will be introduced by President William Lowe Bryan.

The first selection will be Chopin's "Polonaise Militaire." It is one of several polonaises written by Chopin.

The first movement of Schubert's "Unfinished Symphony in B minor" will be the second number. This masterpiece of Schubert's was written in 1822 at Vienna for the Musical Society of Gratz, which had elected him as an honorary member. The composition is a favorite of musicians and music lovers the world over.

Miss Fern Gray, soprano, will sing "Solveig's Song" from Peer Gynt Suite by Grieg. The composer based the idea of the suite on Ibsen's drama, "Peer Gynt."

The band will play Strauss' "On the Beautiful Danube," as the fourth number on the program. This selection is the most famous of all the dance compositions written by Richard Strauss.

The concluding selection will be "Overture to Egmont, Op. 84," by Beethoven, played in its original setting.

At the conclusion of the concert, the Purdue and Indiana bands will unite in playing "The Star Spangled Banner."

TODAY ON THE CAMPUS.

Noon—Euclidean Circle in Sinclair studio for Arbutus picture.
12:40 p.m.—Y.W.C.A. cabinet in Y.W.C.A. offices.
4 p.m.—Women's mass meeting in Assembly hall.
6 p.m.—Sphinx club at Kappa Sigma house.
7 p.m.—Phi Chi at Delta Chi house.
7 p.m.—University chorus in Mitchell hall.
7:30 p.m.—Alpha Phi Omega in the Y.M.C.A. rooms of Student building.
8 p.m.—Convocation in Men's gymnasium. Concert by Purdue university band.
8 p.m.—Iota Sigma Pi in Chemistry 201.

PUBLIC MAY HEAR SYMPOSIUM TALKS

No Admission To Be Charged at Religious Discussion Monday.

The symposium on religion, which will be held next Monday evening in Assembly hall, will be open to any one interested and no charge will be made for admission, it was announced Tuesday by William McFadden, student pastor of the First Methodist church, and president of the Campus Religious council, which is sponsoring the symposium.

Notices have been sent to all members of the faculty informing them of the coming symposium and urging their co-operation in the advancement of the program, McFadden said.

There are three representatives from each of the groups responsible for the existence of the Campus Religious council in the personnel of the council. The groups that sponsor the council are as follows: the Wesley Foundation of the First Methodist church, the Westminster Foundation of the First Presbyterian church, the First Baptist church, the First Christian church, the University Lutheran church, the St. Charles Catholic church, the Jewish Students' union, the Y. W. C. A. and the Y. M. C. A.

Prof. Coon, After Studying Life, Works Of W. W. Fowler, Starts Work on Volume

Returning at the beginning of the semester from a seven and one-half months' study in England and Rome of the life and works of W. Warde Fowler, eminent classical scholar and author who served at Oxford university approximately 50 years, Prof. R. H. Coon of the University Latin department now is engaged actively in writing a biography of Fowler.

Dr. Coon, who is a former student of Dr. Fowler at Oxford, became interested in the preparation of the memorial volume after consultation with J.A.R. Munro, rector of Lincoln college, Oxford, and literary executor to Fowler. Munro and other representatives of Oxford, together with members of the Fowler family, gave Dr. Coon full access to all the writings of the distinguished English author. These writings include 12 unpublished papers. Through conferences with former colleagues and friends of Fowler at Oxford, Cambridge and in London, the Indiana university classicist was able to collect a large mass of material, from which will come the biographical volume.

Spends Month in Rome.

Dr. Coon spent about a month in Rome, during which time he went over the ground covered in Fowler's classical writings. He was able to verify from a check on recent excavations and archeological findings, the scrupulous fidelity with which Fowler pictured ancient Rome.

Fowler wrote books on Roman religion and history and produced interpretations of Vergil which have gone all over the world. One of Fowler's best known works, "The City-State of the Greeks and Ro-

(CONTINUED ON PAGE THREE)

P0079138, IU Archives.

June 13, 1932

MEMORIAL DEDICATION EDITION

HE SERVES BEST WHO SERVES THE TRUTH

THE INDIANA DAILY STUDENT

WEATHER
Partly Cloudy

VOL. LXI, NO. 182. BLOOMINGTON, INDIANA, MONDAY MORNING, JUNE 13, 1932. ESTABLISHED 1867.

'32 CLASS TO GRADUATE TODAY

The President's Column

The Pleasant Story of the Hospitality of a Hospitable Man.

(From The Letters of William James, edited by his son.)

—William Lowe Bryan—

He allowed his conscience to be constantly burdened with a sense of obligation to all sorts of people. The list of neighbors, students, strangers visiting Cambridge, to whom he and Mrs. James felt responsible for civilities, was never closed, and the cordiality which animated his intentions kept him reminded of every one on it.

And yet, whenever his wife wisely prepared for a suitable time and made engagements for some sort of hospitality otherwise than by hap-hazard, it was perversely likely to be the case, when the appointed hour arrived, that James was "going on his nerves" and in no mood for "being entertaining." The most comradely of men, nothing galled him like having to be sociable. The "hollow mockery of our social conventions" would then be described in furious and lurid speech. Luckily the guests were not yet there to hear him. But they did not always get away without catching a glimpse of his state of mind. On one such occasion,—an evening reception for his graduate class had been arranged,—Mrs. James encountered a young man in the hall whose expression was so perturbed that she asked him what had happened to him. "I've come in again," he replied, "to get my hat. I was trying to find my way to the dining-room when Mr. James swooped at me and said, 'Here, Smith, you want to get out of this Hell, don't you? I'll show you how. There!' And before I could answer, he'd popped me out through a back-door. But, really, I do not want to go!"

FESLER SELECTED TO SUCCEED SELF BY ALUMNI BODY

Indianapolis Attorney Again To Represent Graduates on Board of Trustees.

James W. Fesler, Indianapolis, who has served as a member of the Indiana university Board of Trustees since 1902, was re-elected by alumni of the University at a meeting Saturday morning in the Alumni room of the Union building to succeed himself for a term of three years as president of the Board, having held that office since 1919.

Mr. Fesler, a member of the law firm of Fesler, Elam and Young of Indianapolis, was selected unanimously by the nominating committee as a token of appreciation of the work he has performed for the University.

Prof. Robinson Chairman.

Prof. J. J. Robinson of the Law school was named chairman of the meeting by the alumni group. Following the report of the nominating committee naming Mr. Fesler as the only candidate to succeed himself, George F. Heighway, chair-

(CONTINUED ON PAGE THREE)

CRIM, GROSS INITIATED INTO SIGMA DELTA CHI

Indiana Newspapermen Inducted Into Scribes' Fraternity Preceding Supper.

William J. Gross, ex '18, editorial writer for the Ft. Wayne News-Sentinel, and Walter H. Crim, '02, editor and publisher of the Salem Republican-Leader, were made associate members of Sigma Delta Chi, national professional journalism fraternity, at initiation services in the organization's den Sunday afternoon.

Following the services, the group had supper in the Colonial tea room of the Union building. The guests were U. H. Smith, University bursar; Frank Elliott, publicity director of the University; Prof. J. W. Piercy, head of the Journalism department, and Professors J. A. Wright and J. W. French, also of the Journalism department; Ray Mullin, '31; George Flowers of the Ft. Wayne News-Sentinel, and C. E. Van Valer, superintendent of the University Press.

Building To Be Dedicated Today

CEREMONIES TO BE HELD FOLLOWING CLASS REUNIONS

Golden Book of I.U.'s War Veterans To Be Opened This Afternoon.

F. E. BRYAN TO PRESIDE

President of Alumni Association Will Be in Charge of Program.

TODAY will be a memorable day in the history of Indiana university. It will be made such by the dedication at noon of the $600,000 Memorial Union building, the third structure of the $1,600,000 gift of students, alumni and friends of the University. The dedicatory ceremonies will be held in beautiful Alumni hall, immediately following the alumni luncheon and class reunions.

At 1 o'clock this afternoon, the huge Golden Book, containing the names of University graduates and former students who have performed military service for their country, will be opened. The ceremony will be performed as a part of the tableau which is to conclude the dedicatory services.

More than 4,000 students, alumni and friends of the University are expected to attend the ceremonies.

The dedication program will be opened with an overture played by the University orchestra. Frederick E. Bryan, president of the Alumni association, will preside. W. A. Alexander, director of the Memorial Fund campaign and University librarian, will introduce John S. Hastings, who is chairman of the dedication exercises.

Orchestra To Play.

The University orchestra will be heard in a number of musical selections, following which General John

(CONTINUED ON PAGE THREE)

SEVEN ACTIVITIES PROGRAMS CHOSEN

Dean Merrill Announces Result of Student Vote.

Seven headline programs were announced last night by Dean B. Winfred Merrill of the School of Music as the results of the ballot count for the events in the 1932-33 Music Activities series.

The tentative program for the season includes performances by Joseph Iturbi, Spanish composer and one of the most celebrated of modern piano artists; Albert Spaulding, noted violinist; Cornelia Otis Skinner, writer and monologuist; Don Cossack and his Russian Male chorus; the New York Women's orchestra, conducted by Ethel Leginska; the Budapest Stringed Quartet, and Clairbert, soprano, and d'Arkor, tenor, both prominent European singers, appearing together on one concert program.

"The artists have not been engaged yet," Dean Merrill said, "but we are certain that we can get those who have been selected by the vote of the University students and faculty."

GRADUATE MARRIED.

The marriage of Mary Keller, M.D., '32, to Hamilton Ade, '30, both of Lafayette, took place in the United Brethren church of that city recently. The bride and groom left on a short wedding trip shortly after the ceremony. They will be in Bloomington for the Commencement exercises today.

The Memorial Union Building, North View

—Photo by Sinclair

The Memorial structure as it appears from East Seventh street, with Jordan river in the foreground. The terrace and Bookstore may be seen on the left and Alumni hall on the right.

DR. WILLIS GATCH ELECTED MEDICAL DEAN BY TRUSTEES

Dr. Emerson, Former Head, Assumes Research Professorship.

At the meeting of the Board of Trustees Saturday, Dr. Willis D. Gatch was elected dean of the Indiana University School of Medicine at Indianapolis. Doctor Gatch has been acting dean for the past year, taking the place of Dr. Charles P. Emerson who has been abroad on an important medical mission as a commissioner on the Committee of Evaluation of the Mission Movement under the auspices of the Rockefeller Foundation. Doctor Emerson has been elected research professor in the Indiana University School of Medicine and will return sometime this month.

A contract was made with Mrs. Belle Kinney, a sculptress of New York city, for a bronze replica of the bust of Colonel Richard Owen which is in the rotunda of the State House at Indianapolis. Professor Owen was a soldier and was in charge of the Confederate prisoners held at Indianapolis. These soldiers and their descendants presented this bronze bust to the State of Indiana for the kind treatment that Colonel Owen gave them while they were prisoners of war at Indianapolis. Colonel Owen was professor of Natural Philosophy and Chemistry from 1863 to 1867 and was professor of Natural Science and Chemistry from 1867 to 1879 in Indiana university.

Rev. Shannon Emphasizes True Education in Sermon

Chicago Pastor Charges 1932 Graduates To Develop a Continuously Christianized Individuality at Baccalaureate Services.

Emphasizing that true education means that each individual must win his own full-orbed individual being out of the infinite being of personal reality named God, the Rev. Frederick F. Shannon, pastor of the Central Methodist Episcopal church of Chicago, addressed members of the 1932 graduating class at the Baccalaureate services last night at the First Methodist church.

Dr. Shannon introduced the theme of his sermon, "Blue Ribbon Humans," with an illustration of a young girl who entered a mustang pony in a hurdle jumping contest, which the unpedigreed pony won over thoroughbreds to receive a blue ribbon. The illustration was used to suggest some of the values which are capable of being won by educated and blue ribbon humans in the school of life.

Heredity Marks Individual.

"There is, first of all," Dr. Shannon said, "the blue ribbon of Christianized individuality. Whatever else we may say of the mustang pony, called Aviator because of his jumping skill, we must confess that he was a marked individual in the horse kingdom. There is a long story back of his singularity. For instance, there is the fact of heredity. The mustang, a semi-wild horse, was imported to our Western prairies by the Spaniards in the Sixteenth century. There is also the factor of environment to be considered. Wild, untamed, having no master, as the Spanish word mustang implies, Aviator had his setting amid wide prairies and under many-colored skies.

The Telling Difference.

"Yet neither heredity nor environment can tell the whole story of a horse or a human. Even within clearly defined laws of mechanism, which govern in the organic and non-human orders, there is a certain element of freedom. Much more, then, in the organic, animal and human realms there is at work a majestic volitional power which, under God, accounts for the difference in the caveman and the cultured Christian," the speaker said.

"True education, then," Dr. Shannon proposed, "means that each of us must win our own full-orbed individual being out of the infinite being of personal reality named God. We must cleave our way, so to speak, through opposing walls of matter, energy, heredity and environment into the unfailing presence of the infinitely near and dear God and Father in whom we live and move and have our being. And to do this there must needs be a continuously Christianized individuality."

March From Campus.

The Baccalaureate procession, including the speaker, officers of the

(CONTINUED ON PAGE THREE)

RECORD-BREAKING CROWD OF ALUMNI EXPECTED TODAY

Union Building Dedication, Class Reunions Are Leading Attractions.

Dedication of the new Union building and reunions of 16 classes are expected to attract a record crowd of alumni to the campus today, George Heighway, Alumni secretary, said last night.

An elaborate program to entertain visiting graduates has been arranged, and hundreds of contributors to the Memorial fund are expected to attend the festivities even though their classes are not scheduled to hold formal reunions.

Band To Play.

Following the alumnae breakfast at 7:30 o'clock this morning, the University band will present a concert on the terrace of the Union building. Union board members will be on hand to guide visitors through the building for inspection. An art exhibit on the first floor of the Student building also will be open to visitors.

At 11 o'clock this morning, the James A. Woodburn room in the Bookstore will be dedicated, with Dr. William Lowe Bryan officiating at the services. Immediately thereafter, the official raising of the flag on the Union building tower will take place.

Luncheon in Hall.

Members of the classes holding reunions will assemble on the terrace of the Union building and

(CONTINUED ON PAGE THREE)

The History of the Memorial Campaign

(Editor's Note: No one had more to do with the initiation and organization of the Memorial Campaign than Prof. James Albert Woodburn. Following is a brief history of the campaign written by him.)

(By James Albert Woodburn)

In my recent visit to the University I was very favorably impressed with the new Union Building. It is imposing from the outside, commodious and pleasing within. Every alumnus will find pride in it and will rejoice that he has had a part in bringing it to pass.

The Bookstore is beautiful, a credit to its designers, and, with its new and enlarged accommodations, it will prove in years to come one of the most attractive utilities upon the campus. The building will be a great and useful social centre, and already the residents on the campus are wondering "how we ever got along without it." I recall that it was the same way when the Student building first came into use. Such is the spirit of growth; we expand as we acquire.

The University has now realized and brought to completion the three units of the Memorial campaign, as originally planned. May I recall a little of its history?

It was only ten years ago when we reached the subscription goal of one million dollars for the Memorial buildings. Among the students at that time the cause was led by the memorable class of 1922, and no one then on the campus will ever forget the joy and elation that came when, at the midnight hour, the goal was reached in the final subscriptions. There was a jubilee and a shout of victory.

This success was the outcome of previous efforts and plans. For some time prior to 1920 the University was planning to celebrate the centennial anniversary of its founding. It was hoped that an Alumni Memorial Fund would be raised by 1920 as a donation to the University. The University had not been the recipient of large gifts. As early as 1916 the Alumni Council, in a meeting at Indianapolis which I attended, recommended the following:

1. "That a fund of not less than $1,000,000 be raised, to be known as the 'Centennial Memorial Fund.'

2. "That the chief purpose of the fund be the enrichment of the life of the University, the strengthening of the alumni movement, and the promotion of the University's educational progress."

The project had in view the proper celebration of the University's centennial year, the anniversary of the founding of one of the oldest state universities west of the Alleghenies.

There were differences of opinion as to the needs for which the money should be used. Fellowships for worthy students, a sustaining endowment for the Alumni Quarterly, Halls of Residence, a University Commons, a new Union Building, a Stadium, and other causes were urged by their advocates. It was not easy to come to an agreement as to what first things should come first.

The War came on, and that put all things else aside. It was not until 1921 that the movement was rejuvenated. I had then the honor to be President of the Alumni Council, and it fell to my lot to draw

(CONTINUED ON PAGE THREE)

Commencement Exercises Also Will Mark Closing Of Construction Program

Degree Candidates, Faculty Members, Trustees, Speakers To Meet on Dunn Meadow at 4.15 P.M.—Band To Lead Procession.

AT THE traditional sunset graduation exercises in the Memorial stadium today, 766 members of the class of 1932 will receive degrees from Indiana university. This will be the University's one hundred-third Commencement exercises. Approximately 250 seniors who will be graduated in October will bring the total of the 1932 class to more than 1,000 members.

The candidates for degrees, faculty members, trustees and graduation speakers will meet on Dunn Meadow at 4:15 p.m. for participation in the induction ceremony of the seniors into the Alumni association, after which the Commencement procession will form, led by the University band playing "Hail to Old I.U.," and file from Dunn Meadow across the military review grounds to the Memorial stadium.

Will Lead Procession.

President William Lowe Bryan and the Commencement speakers, General John T. Thompson and Dr. Ernest H. Lindley, will lead the procession, followed by the members of the Board of Trustees, the deans of the various schools and the faculty members. The candidates for degrees, grouped according to schools, which will be designated by Cream and Crimson silk flags and the school colors, will follow in this order: College of Arts and Sciences, candidates for the A.B., candidates for the A.B. with distinction, candidates for the A.B. with high distinction, candidates for the B.S. in medicine, and the B.S. in home economics; School of Commerce and Finance, candidates for the B.S. in commerce, followed by candidates for the B.S. in commerce with distinction and with high distinction.

School of Education, candidates for the B.S. in education and those candidates for the B.S. with distinction, candidates for the M.S. in education and the candidates for the Ed.D. in education; School of Music, candidates for the B.P.S.M. degree and candidates for the B.M. degree; School of Law, candidates for the LL.B., the J.D. and the LL.M. degrees; School of Dentistry, candidates for the degree of D.D.S.; Training School for Nurses, candidate for the G.N. degree; School of Medicine, candidates for the M.D. degree and those for the M.D. degree cum laude; Graduate school, candidates for the A.M., the M.S. and the Ph.D. degrees.

Approximately 250 students who have not completed requirements for graduation but who will be candidates for degrees in October will be permitted to participate in the Commencement exercises, and

(CONTINUED ON PAGE THREE)

MRS. WALDRON TO BE HONOR GUEST AT BREAKFAST

Mrs. Sembower To Be Toastmistress at Annual Alumnae Affair.

Dr. Mary A. Waldron, '20, Bloomington, will be the honor guest at the thirteenth annual alumnae breakfast at 7:30 o'clock this morning in Alumni hall of the Union building. Each year some distinguished alumna is honored and her name is not announced until the morning of the breakfast. Mrs. C. J. Sembower, '01, also of Bloomington, will be the toastmistress for the event.

Mrs. Waldron, who is in charge of social service work in Bloomington, received the A.B. degree from the University in 1920 at the age of 63. The following year she received the A.M. degree, and at the age of 66 she was decorated with the hood of a doctor of philosophy.

Holds Unique Honor.

She is the only person in the history of the University to be granted three academic degrees after the age of 63. She began her college study in 1916 at the age of 59. "Social Legislation in Indiana," an entirely original work and the first research to be made on the subject, was the title of Mrs. Waldron's thesis for the doctor's degree.

Mrs. Waldron also has studied in the University Law school and was admitted in 1922 to practice in the Monroe county circuit court. In granting her the Ph.D. degree, In-

(CONTINUED ON PAGE THREE)

COUNCIL PRAISES INDIANA ATHLETES

Alumni Body Also Elects Officers—To Announce New Members Today.

Resolutions of commendation of Indiana university athletes in winning eight team championships in four different sports and including three national titles during the past year were passed at the Alumni council meeting held in the Woodburn room of the Union building Sunday afternoon, according to Jack Hastings, '24, president of the council.

Seven new members of the council who were elected by ballots sent by mail will be announced at the Alumni business meeting at 10 o'clock this morning, it was stated. Members whose terms expire this year are Everett Sanders, '07, Washington, D. C.; Permelia Boyd, '04, Deputy; Earl Blough, '99, Pittsburgh, Pa.; Matthew Winters, '15, Indianapolis, and Hiram E. Stonecipher, '20. Arthur B. Stonex, '06, Goshen, who was a member of the council, died in July 1929.

The present officers of the council were re-elected as follows: John S. Hastings, '24, Washington, president; Walter Crim, '02, Salem, vice-president, and Mrs. C. J. Sembower, '01, secretary. Arrangements were made for the next meeting of the council to be held on Oct. 17, 1932, in Indianapolis.

The council also passed resolutions commending J. Carlyle Bollenbacher, Chicago architect and Indiana alumnus, and his firm for the architectural excellence of the new Union building.

INCREASE IS EXPECTED IN SUMMER ENROLLMENT

Inquiries Indicate Few Hundred More Students Will Attend Than in '31.

The large number of inquiries received recently regarding the Summer session, which will open Wednesday, indicate that the enrollment will exceed the number enrolled last summer possibly by a few hundred, according to Emmett W. Arnett, secretary to the director of the School of Education. Last year's total enrollment was 2,016.

A recent canvass of campus organizations revealed that 23 per cent more members of these groups will take summer work than last summer.

Matriculation, registration and enrollment will take place on Wednesday and classes will begin the following day. The nine weeks' session will close August 10, the same day the special three weeks' session will begin.

P0030111, IU Archives.

HE SERVES BEST WHO SERVES THE TRUTH

THE INDIANA DAILY STUDENT

WEATHER
Generally Fair.

VOL. LXIV, NO. 14. BLOOMINGTON, INDIANA, THURSDAY MORNING, OCTOBER 4, 1934. ESTABLISHED 1867.

Sloppy Fielding Leads Tigers To 8-3 Defeat At Hands of Cardinals

Dizzy Dean Victimizes Detroit Sluggers in Initial Tilt of "Blue Ribbon" Classic—Rowe, Hallahan May Match Slants in Today's Contest.

DETROIT, Oct. 3.—(AP)—The front line of the Tigers' defense, the iron-man infield that they heralded as the "Battalion of Death," crumbled and fell back in wild disorder, spreading nothing but doom to Detroit's hopes as the rampant St. Louis Cardinals poured through gaping holes to sweeping victory in the first skirmish of the 1934 World championship baseball battle.

Five errors by this jittery Tiger infield in the first three innings, most of them the kind of mistakes that a sandlotter would have been ashamed of, enabled the National league champions to take quick command of the proceedings and then smash the remnants of Detroit's resistance with a powerhouse attack by Joe Medwick, slugging outfielder who tied a World series record with four straight hits, including a home run.

The final score was 8-3 and the verdict, overwhelmingly in favor of the clouting Cardinals as they coasted to victory behind the effective pitching of the celebrated Jerome Herman (Dizzy) Dean, king of the National league's pitchers, signalized the fact they are still riding the crest of the wave that carried them to a sensational belated triumph in the pennant race over the New York Giants.

Rowe, Hallahan Slated.

It isn't all over, of course, on the basis of one game. The Tigers may pull themselves together overnight, with the jitters and tension of the first big strain behind them. They are a better club than they looked today and they still have their pitching ace, the sensational Lynwood (Schoolboy) Rowe to count upon. Rowe is slated to pitch tomorrow, with Bill Hallahan, a southpaw and 1931 World series hero, picked to take up the sharpshooting for the Cardinals instead of the anticipated choice, young Paul Dean.

The elder of the famous pair of pitching brothers lacked his customary control and yielded eight base hits, including a booming home run by Hank Greenberg in the eighth inning, but he was seldom in anything resembling real danger or called upon to bear down against the desultory Detroit attack. Dizzy had his "fire ball" when he needed it, however, and he was content largely to ride along behind the steadily increasing lead that his team-mates piled up.

Three Pitchers Used.

Against Alvin (General) Crowder, Fred (Firpo) Marberry and Elon (Big Chief) Hogsett, the Cardinals banged out 13 hits, capping the climax of the rout with a four-run drive in the sixth that chased Marberry from the box. This settled any lingering doubt about the outcome, as Dean himself led the onslaught with a rousing two-bagger, although the Tigers had already tossed away most of their chances in one of the most ragged exhibitions ever witnessed in a championship game.

Crowder yielded only six hits in the five innings he worked, including Medwick's fifth inning home run. With a tight defense, that big wallop might have represented the only run off him, but the "General" retired for a pinch hitter and his successors were promptly belted all over the park. Marberry lasted only two-thirds of an inning and Hogsett, a southpaw, gained control of a hopeless situation only after being pasted for a double by Bill Delancey, Cardinal catcher, which brought in the last two St. Louis runs.

OFFICIALS OF TAPS WITHHOLD PLEDGING

Forced to work until late last night because of what was termed extraordinary talent in the record turnout of applicants, officials of Taps, junior dramatic organization, announced at a late hour that pledging of students to the organization would be withheld until this afternoon.

Originally it was announced that pledges would be named immediately after the tryouts last night in Assembly hall.

Pledges named today will be inducted into Taps in the near future, Verlin Stephens, PG, president, said.

Grad To Speak

Sherman Minton, LL.B. '15, who will be the principal speaker at the district Democratic rally here tonight.

COALITION AWAITS CHANGE IN RULES

Party Believed To Have Replaced Ray Miller on Slate.

Declining to make known the identity of their new senior vice-presidential candidate, Coalition leaders attempted to keep activities of their party as vague as possible last night as they marked time until action expected to be taken by the Student Affairs committee this afternoon permits them to file a candidate for the office.

A tentative arrangement last night called for a meeting of the Student Affairs committee today, at which time it is expected that an amendment will be passed to the election rules permitting Coalitionists to file a candidate in the place of Ray Miller, former office

(CONTINUED ON PAGE THREE)

TODAY ON THE CAMPUS.

12 noon—Blue Key meeting in Union A, B and C.

12 noon—Phi Delta Phi luncheon, Colonial tearoom of Union building.

3 p.m.—Meeting of Pershing Rifles, Rooms A and B of Union building.

4 p.m.—Women's Panhellenic association meeting in East parlors of Student building.

4 p.m.—Terpsichorean meeting in Student building auditorium.

6 p.m.—Dinner for Republican Campus club, Room E of Union building.

3:30 p.m.—Meeting of I.I.A., Town Hall room of the Union building.

7 p.m.—Meeting of Indiana Union Board, Union Board room of Union building.

7 p.m.—Frills and Furbelows tryouts in East parlors of Student building.

7 p.m.—Nu Sigma Nu meeting, Rooms A and B of the Union building.

7:30 p.m.—El Ateneo Espanol meeting, Rooms C and D of the Union building.

8 p.m.—Meeting of Y.M.C.A. cabinet, Whittenberger room of the Union building.

8 p.m.—Annual Military smoker at Sigma Chi house.

I.U. GRAD SEEKING SENATORIAL TOGA TO SPEAK TONIGHT

Seventh District Democrats To Hear Shay Minton at B.H.S. Gym.

Sherman Minton, '15, New Albany, Democratic candidate for United States senator, will address townspeople, students and followers from over the Seventh Congressional district at 7:30 o'clock tonight in the Bloomington high school gymnasium in what is expected to be the keynote rally of the present campaign as far as this city is concerned.

Minton's reputation as a speaker, coupled with the fact that he is a University graduate, is expected to draw a large crowd to the meeting. Several State and party officials are expected to be present, including Omer Jackson, Democratic state chairman.

To Arrive From Vincennes.

Minton is expected to arrive in this city at about 4:30 o'clock this afternoon from Vincennes where he was scheduled to speak last night. Before going to the gymnasium, he will be met at the Graham hotel by a reception committee composed of the following: Ward G. Biddle, state senator and director of the Union building; Paul L. Feltus, University trustee; Robert E. Myers, Monroe county Democratic chairman, and Mrs. C. J. Sembower, Seventh district vice-chairwoman.

He will be escorted to the scene of the rally by a drum and bugle corps from the Burton Woolery post of the American Legion. After speaking, Minton will be entertained by World war veterans at the National Guard armory on South Lincoln street. This gather-

(CONTINUED ON PAGE THREE)

COMMITTEE CHOOSES ATHLETIC MANAGERS

At a meeting of the Managers Selection committee held last night in the Woodburn room of the Union building the following students were chosen to act as student athletic managers for the 1934-35 school year:

Basketball: senior manager—Charles E. Schaab; junior managers—Carl Seibel and Frederick B. Hanna.

Baseball: senior manager—Robert Steele; junior managers—Robert Holthouse and William S. Brown.

Track: senior managers—John Ax and John Grimsley; junior managers—Philip Lawrence, John L. Slick and Hugh Highsmith.

Wrestling: senior manager—Walter B. Keaton; junior managers—Joel Weber and Alfred Ciesar.

Swimming: senior manager—Edwin Steers; junior manager—Wendell Tombaugh.

Another junior manager for swimming will be chosen later in the season.

Smoker Will Be Given By Scabbard and Blade

A smoker for all advanced course Military students and reserve officers will be given by Scabbard and Blade, honorary military fraternity, at 8 o'clock tonight at the Sigma Chi house. All officers attending are asked to wear uniforms, according to Charles M. Carman, '35, captain of the organization.

Short talks will be given by Prof. Fowler V. Harper of the Law school and officers of the Military department. All juniors in Military are especially invited, Carman stated.

TO HONOR FACULTY WIVES.

The wives of the new members of the University faculty will be guests of honor at an informal tea to be held by the Faculty Women's club at 3 p.m. Thursday, Oct. 11, in the East parlors of the Student building. Mrs. S. E. Stout will be chairman of the meeting, which will be the first held by the club this year.

Wins Series Opener

Jerome "Dizzy" Dean, mainstay of the St. Louis Cardinals' pitching staff, who set the Detroit Tigers down, 8-3, Wednesday at Detroit. (Associated Press Photo)

APPROACHING WAR FORESEEN BY HEAD OF LABOR GROUPS

SAN FRANCISCO, Oct. 3.—(AP)—A call to the workers of the world to 'unite solidly in order to prevent what seems to be an approaching war" was voiced before the American Federation of Labor convention today by William Green, its president.

Green introduced John Stokes of London, fraternal delegate from the British Trades Union congress, who told the convention "the Socialist principle has become the obvious and sole solution of our economic and industrial crisis."

Organized workers were warned by Joseph A. Padway, Milwaukee labor attorney, against dropping their weapons in any industrial truce with employers. He criticized the Department of Justice and the National Labor board for alleged unfairness to labor.

William Dunn of Toronto, fraternal delegate from the Canadian Trades Union congress, said there appeared to be a growing number of workers in the United States "who realize such slogans and catch phrases as 'rugged individualism' are only in the economic wool pulled over the eyes of the workers to blind them from their true social position."

Green declared it was "the purpose and spirit of the workers of the world to see that war never occurs again."

"We abhor war in all its forms," he added. "We cannot allow those mad with lust for power to have their way.

"We hope the relationship between the labor organizations of the various countries will grow stronger and stronger."

Last Semester 'A' Students Announced by Registrar

Names of 85 Undergraduates and 32 Postgraduates Are Listed on Honor Roll.

The names of 117 students who made "A" grades in the work of the second semester of the past school year were announced recently by John W. Cravens, University registrar. Only 85 students merited positions on the honor list for the same period last year.

Eighty-five of the honor students were undergraduates and 32 postgraduates. The freshman class was represented with 20 "A" grade students, the sophomore class with 25, the junior class, 23, and the senior class, 17.

Bloomington high school, with 19 graduates who won places on the "straight A" roll, leads the high schools of the State. Columbus high school and Technical high school of Indianapolis have three graduates each on the list. The following high schools are represented by two each: Washington; Lincoln, Vincennes; Bradford, Pa.; Shortridge, Indianapolis; Anderson; Jefferson, Lafayette; Bloomfield; George Washington, Indianapolis; Muncie; Seymour; Central, Ft. Wayne; Logansport, and Pittsfield, Mass.

Two Made 20 Hours "A".

Two students, Saul Bernat, PG, Indianapolis, and Helen Turley McGaw, '35, English, made "A" grades in 20 hours of work. Eight students who received "A's" in 18 hours of work are as follows: Vivien Greenberg, '37, Bradford, Pa.; Rondal M. Huffman, '37, Bloomfield; Jean McGriff, '37, Detroit, Mich.; Joseph Dee, '36, Gary; Howard Broderick, '35, Pittsfield, Mass.; Norman E. Parnell, '35, Indianapolis; Louise Wylie, '35, Bloomington; Leander Bulliet, PG, New Albany, and James E. Hatfield, PG, Washington.

The following students were on the honor list for both semesters last year: William Arbuckle, PG, Rockville; Harriet Bachman, '37, Syracuse; Saul Bernat, PG, Indianapolis; Donald Binkley, '35, Bloomington; Margaret Bittner, '35, Bloomington; Elizabeth Bobbitt, '36, Oak Park, Ill.; Howard Broderick, '35, Pittsfield, Mass.; Samuel E. Brown, '34, Peru; Paul Butze, '36, Evansville; Libin T. Cheng, PG, Nanking, China;

James Coon on List.

James Coon, '36, Bloomington; Marion Fidlar, PG, Vincennes; Herschel Gier, PG, Bloomington; Sarah Goodman, '36, East Chicago; Virginia Hitchcock, '35, Isabel Hogue, '37, Vincennes; Marietta Houston, '37, Salem; Rondal Huffman, '37, Bloomfield; Gordon

(CONTINUED ON PAGE THREE)

BOARD OF AEONS.

Members of the Board of Aeons will hold a special meeting at 12:25 p.m. today to consider a matter of immediate importance.

John Sembower, PG, president.

"My Football System Is as Legal as Ever---" Bo Answers Critics

Team Goes Through Paces as Usual—Crimson Mentor Opens "Bag of Tricks" in Preparation for Conference Opener.

(By Arv Rothschild)

Drilling feverishly on deceptive passing, punting and defensive tactics, Indiana's Scrappin' Hoosiers engaged in a spirited workout Wednesday afternoon as the opening Conference encounter of the season against Ohio State's powerful aggregation loomed threateningly on the gridiron horizon.

Bo McMillin, realizing the necessity of developing a powerful combination that can offset the weight advantage the Buckeye eleven will hold Saturday, worked untiringly with his Crimson warriors on new formations and tricky strategems with which he hopes to hold Francis Schmidt's burly crew at bay.

Holds Secret Practice.

Following the preliminary drill, the gray-haired mentor took his players into Memorial stadium for a secret practice on the new plays which he has formulated for the Ohio State game. A picked freshman team was sent against a varsity eleven and executed Ohio State offensive maneuvers. Another part of the varsity resumed work on McMillin's new plans and went through a dummy scrimmage.

"Ohio State has some of the finest material in the Conference," stated the Hoosier coach. "We know that we are going into the game as the underdogs, but if our boys give the best man power possible, we will continue hoping until the final whistle." McMillin added that the Indiana supporters should not expect too much of their team in this game, since the opposition will be a good deal tougher than the opponents of the initial contest.

COUNCIL TO DISCUSS 1934-35 RUSH RULES

Dean Wells Will Relate Her Observations at Panhellenic Meeting.

Applications and violations of the 1934-35 Panhellenic rush rules will be discussed at a meeting of the Panhellenic council to be held at 4 p.m. today in the East parlors of the Student building, Mary Rachel Ward, '35, president of the council, said last night.

Miss Estella M. Whitted, instructor in the English department and chairman of the committee on the observation of rules for rush, will report the findings of her committee. Dean Agnes E. Wells will express her opinion of the new rules as they were practiced this year. She also will explain the functions of the Hoosier Art Salon association to the group for the purpose of promoting membership in the enterprise.

The Panhellenic council is made up of the president, one representative active member and one representative alumna of each sorority on the campus.

Instructors in Spanish To Speak at Meeting

Three members of the Spanish department, Prof. Agapito Rey, Richard Sherman and Glen Willbern, instructors, will speak before members of El Ateno Espanol, Spanish club, at a meeting of the organization at 7:30 o'clock tonight in the Union building.

All students of Spanish are urged to attend, it was announced by Ross Sanford, '37, president of the club. A plan for requiring certain language qualifications for membership in the organization will be discussed.

ADDRESSES SCOUTS.

Dr. Will Scott of the Zoology department spoke on "Success in Scouting Compared With Success in the University," before members of Alpha Phi Omega, honorary scouting fraternity, and 12 guests last night in the Whittenberger room of the Union building.

FLANAGAN TO HEAD LIST OF SPEAKERS AT RALLY TONIGHT

Campus Club To Hear Republican Candidate for Appellate Court.

Reversing the order of the old "bromide," Dan Flanagan, Ft. Wayne, Republican candidate for Appellate court judge of the Northern Indiana district, will speak tonight on the theme, "The Republican Party May Be Out But Not Down," at the Republican dinner-meeting to be held at 6:15 o'clock in Assembly hall.

Flanagan will relate the highlights of his political career, flavored with anecdotes and personal experiences. He also will give brief biographical sketches of Republican candidates running for election this fall.

The part local party workers are to play in the campaign will be considered at the meeting. Students who have not yet registered are urged to do so any afternoon this week in Maxwell 25, Tom Martin, '35, publicity chairman, stated last night. Registrations may be made between the hours of 3 and 5 p.m.

Tickets for tonight's banquet may be procured from Jack Root, PG, president of the club.

APPLICATIONS DUE FOR SPHINX AWARD

Club To Give $100 Scholarship to Outstanding Junior Man.

Applications for the $100 Sphinx club scholarship, which is awarded annually to an outstanding male member of the junior class, should be filed immediately in the dean of men's office, Henry Snyder, PG, president of the club, urged last night. All juniors excepting members of the Sphinx club may apply for the award.

The scholarship is awarded on the basis of prominence in student affairs, scholarship and character. The scholarship fund is raised from the receipts of the Waiters' ball, which is sponsored by the Sphinx club at the beginning of each fall semester.

The selection committee for this year is composed of Dean C. E. Edmondson, chairman; Dean C. J. Sembower; Dr. W. J. Moenkhaus of the Medical school and U. H. Smith, bursar.

PHONOGRAPH RECORDS WILL BE MADE TODAY

Recordings of readings, lectures, vocal renditions and instrumental interpretations will be made from 10 o'clock this morning to 7 o'clock tonight in Alumni hall by the Fairchild Electric Recording company, Dean B. Winfred Merrill of the Music school announced last night.

Any student desiring to make a phonograph record should obtain an appointment with Dean Merrill at his office before going to Alumni hall, he said.

The selections will be recorded instantaneously, and the completed record may be heard immediately. These metal records are permanent, and vary in size from six to twelve inches in diameter, it was said.

Recording prices range according to the size and playing time of the record wanted. Dean Merrill suggested that all numbers be timed carefully before being recorded.

TICKET SALESMEN.

Today is the deadline for Blanket hop ticket salesmen to check in their unsold tickets and money. This may be done at any time during the day in the Journalism building, between 8 a.m. and 5 p.m.

McMillin Used Present System in Former Clashes With Big Ten Schools, Without Question, While Coaching Kansas State Aggies.

(By James O. Leas)

That Coach Alvin (Bo) McMillin's widely heralded five-man backfield system of offense "is as legal today as it ever was and will be employed against Ohio State Saturday" when the Indiana football team opens the 1934 Conference season against Francis A. Schmidt's powerful Buckeyes was made known in no uncertain terms late last night.

Interviewed by representatives of The Daily Student, the Hoosier mentor was asked if he had learned of the discussion that his unorthodox style of play had created at a meeting of the Indiana Officials' association last Monday and of the dispatching to Major John L. Griffith, Big Ten commissioner of athletics, of the umpire's card which McMillin had handed an official at last Saturday's game to explain the peculiar line-up of the Crimson eleven.

McMillin said that on the various occasions when it had been questioned, his system of offense had been declared legal by the National Football Rules committee. "I used it twice against Purdue—in 1929 and 1932," Bo said, "and neither Purdue's nor any other Big Ten officials questioned its legality."

Peden Questions System.

The card clarifying the McMillin system had been submitted to Bert Coffin, who officiated at the Ohio university-Indiana game, after Don Peden, Bobcat coach, had questioned the legality of the unfamiliar formation. Prior to the start of the game, Peden had appealed to the officials, presenting a diagram, allegedly Indiana's, of the position of the eleven players. The officials agreed that the formation shown in the diagram was illegal.

However, McMillin pointed out that the drawing shown by Peden was not an accurate one. Just before the game, the Hoosier coach explained the Crimson lineup to the corps of officials who, with the exception of Coffin, readily gave it their approval. Coffin, while allowing the game to be started, alone remained skeptical.

It was McMillin's belief that had Peden approached him instead of the officials with his question concerning the Hoosier shift, it would have been explained satisfactorily. Peden, who is said to have told his gridmen before they left their locker room that Indiana was going to use an illegal shift, left the field when Bo made his explanation to the officials.

The Crimson lineup under the former Centre college star includes two fullbacks, right and left, and only one guard. The rules state that seven men must be on the line of scrimmage when the ball is snapped. Accordingly, one of McMillin's five backs drops into the line just before the center passes the ball. "If they want to call him the other guard," asserted Bo, "they can for all I care."

Regarding the flare-up and suggestion of illegality, McMillin said, "I don't know who raised all the stink, but it's the bunk."

DON PEDEN THINKS SHIFT OF PLAYERS IS ILLEGAL

COLUMBUS, Ohio, Oct. 3.—(AP)—The new shift designed by Bo McMillin for his five-man backfield

(CONTINUED ON PAGE THREE)

Ohio State-I.U. Tickets May Go On Sale Today

Tickets for the Indiana university-Ohio State football game at Columbus Saturday are expected to arrive today, L. L. Fisher, ticket agent, announced last night. After being checked, they will be placed on sale in the University ticket office in the basement of the Bookstore.

A total of 250 tickets has been ordered and will be on sale for $1.80, including State and Federal taxes, Fisher said.

P0078473, IU Archives.

February 16, 1935

HE SERVES BEST WHO SERVES THE TRUTH

THE INDIANA DAILY STUDENT

WEATHER
Snow and Colder.

VOL. LXIV, NO. 84. BLOOMINGTON, INDIANA, SATURDAY MORNING, FEBRUARY 16, 1935. ESTABLISHED 1867

Man Dead, 2 Students Badly Hurt In Crash

HAUPTMANN SIGNS FIRST PAPERS AS STEP FOR APPEAL

Convicted Slayer Will Be Taken to State Prison Today.

RIGIDLY DENIES GUILT

Admiration for Lindy Led to Judgment Against Him, Prisoner Asserts.

BULLETIN.

NEW YORK, Feb. 15.—(AP)—The New York Daily News in a copyrighted interview with Bruno Richard Hauptmann tonight quoted the convicted slayer of the Lindbergh baby as saying that the late Isador Fisch, Bronx furrier, "must have been implicated" in the crime.

FLEMINGTON, N. J., Feb. 15.—(AP)—Charles S. Walton Sr., foreman of the jury which convicted Bruno Richard Hauptmann, said tonight the jurors will meet Sunday at the home of Mrs. May Brelsford, juror No. 10, to discuss the offer of a theatrical promoter for a vaudeville tour.

FLEMINGTON, N. J., Feb. 15.—(AP)—Bruno Richard Hauptmann swore his innocence anew and perfected the first step for an appeal late today, on the eve of his removal to a cell in the state's prison at Trenton six steps from the death chamber.

"Before God, I swear I have nothing whatever to do with the kidnaping and murder of this child and that I know nothing whatever in connection with the crime," he said in a statement dictated to Miss Laura Apgar, secretary to Associate Defense Counsel C. Lloyd Fisher.

"Miscarriage of Justice.

"I also swear that I know nothing in connection with the ransom money other than as I told it on the witness stand at Flemington. I feel that a grave miscarriage of justice occurred."

He said he felt "very sorry" for the bereaved Colonel and Mrs. Charles A. Lindbergh, parents of the kidnaped and slain child and said he believed "the great admiration of the American people for the bereaved father swayed their judgment against me, and I believe it likewise swayed the judgment of the jury."

Hauptmann was restless await-

(CONTINUED ON PAGE THREE)

DAMES CLUB GROUPS TO MEET NEXT WEEK

Four groups of the University Dames club will hold meetings next week, Mrs. Frederick Neel, president of the organization, announced Friday.

The music group will meet at 2:30 p.m. Monday in the East parlors of the Student building to discuss the lives and works of French composers of the eighteenth century. At 7:30 p.m. Monday the book group will hear Mrs. Paul Overman review "The Luck of the Road," by Ruth Sawyer. Mrs. Fred Steele will be the hostess to this group at her home.

Mrs. J. H. Ravencroft will entertain the sewing group at 2:30 o'clock Tuesday afternoon at her home and at 2:15 o'clock Wednesday afternoon the bridge club will hold its weekly meeting in the East parlors of the Student building.

CHAPERONS WILL MEET

Group To Discuss Coeds' Scholarship Today.

Means of improving the scholarship of coeds who have been placed on probation this semester will be discussed at the monthly meeting of sorority chaperons at 10 a.m. today in Dean Agnes E. Wells' office.

Lists of organized freshman coeds who failed to make required grades last semester and also a list of coeds who will continue on probation from last semester will be turned over to the respective chaperons by Dean Wells.

Crimson Sharpshooters Hope To Avenge Early Season Defeat by Wisconsin Five

Seeking its sixth Big Ten victory in defense of its position at the top of the Conference, Indiana's Crimson basketball team will invade the home of the Wisconsin Badgers at Madison, Wisc., tonight for a return battle with the only quintet that has been able to repulse the Hoosiers in the current Big Ten campaign.

With the Big Ten race in its home stretch, Indiana's chance to get a crack at the Conference crown hangs in the balance at Madison tonight. Most of the practice time this week has been spent in polishing an offensive attack that is designed to pierce the Badger defense, which, although not seeming to function to the degree of perfection that it did earlier in the season, is considered by Coach Everett Dean to be one of the best in the Conference.

ALL WISCONSIN-I.U. TICKETS ARE SOLD

MADISON, Wisc., Feb. 15.—(Spl.)—Forty-eight hours before the time scheduled for the Wisconsin-Indiana cage encounter here Saturday night the university fieldhouse was sold out, according to Harry Schwenker, ticket manager. "A total of 8,735 ducats for the Conference net fray were dispensed," Schwenker stated, "and we are expecting to turn back about 4,000 at game time."

Badgers Win First.

When the Badger five came to Bloomington for the first encounter between the two teams, it combined a smooth-working passing machine with a tough defense to give the Hoosiers a 30-23 setback. At present Wisconsin is resting in second place in the Conference standing, having lost only to Purdue and Northwestern.

Monday night the Crimson will tangle with the Purdue Boilermakers at Lafayette in what, to Indiana and Purdue followers, is the most important tilt of the season regardless of Conference standings. But with the two State teams standing at the top of the heap, the fans already have bought every available seat in the Jefferson high school gymnasium at Lafayette and are expecting one of the hardest battles of the year.

The Lambertmen have lost only to the Illinois five, which nosed them out, 37-36, at Champaign. These teams meet in a return tilt tonight at Lafayette, and the Boilermakers will have a chance to avenge their defeat.

Coach Lambert, Purdue mentor, is expected to start the same combination against Indiana that was successful in downing Fordham and Temple last week-end. At the forward positions will be Kessler and Downey, with Seward at the pivot post and Cottom and Shaver as the guards. Lambert recently shifted Cottom from one of the forward assignments where he led the Conference in scoring last year to floor guard to team with Shaver. Kessler has been the outstanding scoring threat of the team to date and now stands fourth in the Big Ten with 70 points.

Probable Starting Lineups

INDIANA	Pos.	WISCONSIN
Kehrt (c)	F	DeMark
Stout	F	Preboski
Fechtman	C	Stege
Gunning	G	McDonald
Walker	G	Poser

Lost in Disaster

Warrant Officer Ernest Daily (above), radio operator on the dirigible Macon, was one of the two men missing after the giant craft crashed into the Pacific ocean. The other missing man was a mess sergeant. (Associated Press Photo)

THOM TO STAKE TITLE MAY 3 IN ENCOUNTER WITH CYCLONE BURNS

Coach W. H. (Billy) Thom, world's junior middle weight champion, will stake his title in a feature bout with Cyclone Burns on the night of May 3 in the annual sports show in Louisville on the eve of the Kentucky Derby, according to an Associated Press dispatch from Louisville.

Forsaking boxing for wrestling as the bill of fare this year the promoters offered a card including the following titleholders: Lord Patrick Landsdowne Finnegan, welterweight; Leroy McGuirk, light heavyweight, and Billy Thom, middleweight.

STUDENTS TO DISCUSS CREED DISCRIMINATION

Using an outline recommended by the International Council of Religious Education as the basis for its weekly discussions this month, the student class of the First Presbyterian church will hold its discussion at 9:15 o'clock Sunday morning on the subject, "What Discriminations Do Jews and Catholics Face?" The Rev. Douglas Vernon will lead the class.

The outline, which has been prepared especially for Protestants, deals with their relationships with Jews and Catholics. It has been drawn up to be used by classes in preparation for Brotherhod Day, Feb. 24, which has been designated by the National Conference of Jews and Christians.

Italy Prepares Herself For War With Ethiopia

ROME, Feb. 15.—(AP)—Italy's military machine tonight continued without interruption to turn out soldiers for possible hostilities in Africa as another note arrived from Ethiopia's emperor blaming Italy for frontier aggression.

The first detachments of the projected expeditionary force were ready to sail from Southern Italian ports tomorrow night. The total number of men en route to Eritrea and Italian Somaliland may reach 15,000 by the end of the week.

Any student who has moved or who did not give his complete address at the time of registration should report to the registrar's office immediately.
John W. Cravens, registrar.

HOUSE IN UPROAR AS REPUBLICANS STAGE WALKOUT

Rift Occurs After G.O.P. Amendments Are Rejected—Legislative Machinery Is Halted Unless Representatives Return.

INDIANAPOLIS, Feb. 15.—(AP)—Republicans in the House of the Indiana General Assembly bolted this afternoon in protest over the $50,000,000 budget bill and had not reached any decision tonight as to whether they will return next Monday.

Should they decide not to return, legislative machinery would be stopped, since they are sufficient in number to break a quorum. There are 65 Democrats and 35 Republicans in the House and it takes 67 members to make a quorum.

The walkout came after the Democratic majority had voted down almost a score of amendments offered by the Republicans. The Republican amendments proposed to lop off approximately $2,000,000 of the recommendations made by the State Budget committee which drafted the bill.

Quorum in Doubt.

The bill finally was advanced to second reading after the total appropriations contained in it had been increased $98,986.86. The budget for the next biennium now is fixed at $50,429,042.86 under the terms of the measure.

The measure was advanced over the protests of Representative James M. Knapp of Hagerstown, Republican floor leader who stayed to object to any further action on the ground that a quorum was not present.

Representative Knapp charged that the presiding officer on two occasions ruled that he saw a quorum "when actually 34 Republican members and seven Democratic members were absent—or 41 members."

SHORTRIDGE DEFEATS BLOOMINGTON, 24-23

Trailing for three quarters of one of the most hectic games played in the high school gymnasium this year, the Shortridge (Indianapolis) Blue Devils staged a last-minute rally to down the Bloomington high school Panthers, 24-23, last night in the final home encounter of the season for the local quintet. The Shortridge reserves defeated the Panther Cubs, 21-17, in the curtain raiser.

ERECTION OF NEW I.U. BUILDING IS ALMOST CERTAIN

Construction and Equipment Would Cost About $400,000.

PROBABLY TO BE STONE

Chicago Firm Prepares Preliminary Plans for New Structure.

(By John W. Cravens, secretary of Indiana university)

It was good news that Senator Ward G. Biddle telephoned from Indianapolis Friday when he informed President William L. Bryan that the House had passed the Senate bill making it possible for Indiana university to erect an administration building that would cost, including equipment, $400,000. The bill passed the Senate last week under Senator Biddle's guidance, and there was little opposition. In the House the vote was 72 to 19. This small number in opposition shows the high regard our law makers have for Indiana university.

The building will doubtless be made of stone, and while there has been no official action taken as to its location it is generally believed that it will occupy the site now occupied by Assembly hall. Approximately $350,000 will be used for the building and $50,000 will be used for equipment.

$120,000 To Be Gift.

The new building will be financed by the Government and the University. Of the $400,000 the Government will make a straight out gift of 30 per cent or $120,000, and will loan the University 70 per cent or $280,000 on a long term basis of probably 30 years. The exact terms of the loan will be revealed in a short time by the Government. These gifts and loans are a part of the Government's recovery program.

There is no greater building need at Indiana university than an administration building. It is needed to furnish adequate rooms that are absolutely fire-proof. In two former major fires at Indiana university priceless records and equipment were destroyed, and the buildings now used for administrative purposes are far from fire-proof.

Firm Prepares Plans.

The firm of Lowe and Bollenbacher of Chicago has prepared preliminary plans for the new structure. The chief need is for accommodations for the administrative offices now inadequately supplied in Maxwell hall. The new quarters will provide ample rooms and filing space for all officials now in Maxwell hall and in Assembly hall. As to any additional space remaining that will be determined when the architects submit their plans and estimates of final cost.

While it is not certain when work will begin on the new structure, it is believed that the plans will be pushed as rapidly as possible and actual construction will begin this spring. Unless there will be unlooked for delay the building should be ready by Jan. 1, 1936.

ANOTHER "WONDER FIVE"—CRY OF FRANKLIN COLLEGE STUDENTS

Striking Students Demand More Athletic Scholarships, Optional Chapel—Class Rooms Empty, Professors Idle as Campus Is "Picketed."

FRANKLIN, Feb. 15.—(AP)—A group of Franklin college students today formulated for submission to President William Gear Spencer a resolution setting forth their demands for more scholarships to benefit athletes.

The students, who went on strike yesterday, asserted that only in this way can the college obtain material to make another "Wonder Five" basketball team such as the institution had in 1922, '23 and '24.

The striking students also object to compulsory chapel. Dismissal of Richard A. Cox of Lebanon, who was said to have made a careless remark concerning the school, also is reported to have stirred campus sentiment.

"For Good Of College."

"We are striking for the good of Franklin college," said one student. "We are not going in for any 'mob stuff,' but are merely protesting against the college program. We need more college spirit which has been lacking. We are going to give our basketball team a big send-off."

Coeds and men students alike milled around the campus main entrance today. "Pickets" were stationed at the doors of various buildings. Class rooms were empty and professors idle.

Blame Compulsory Chapel.

R. H. Sellers, chairman of a committee composed of board members, asserted "it all simmers down to the start of compulsory chapel attendance two years ago and lack of understanding between the students and officials."

The petition to be submitted to President Spencer seeks the award of gift scholarships "in order that the athletic record of the college may be improved." The Franklin basketball team during the current season has had only a fair record.

The college, a Baptist institution, has an enrollment of about 250 students. It was established in 1834.

BILLIARD CHAMP WILL GIVE EXHIBITION TODAY

Charles Peterson, nationally known billiard champion, will give an exhibition on the "how and why of billiards" from 9 a.m. to 5 p.m. today in the billiard room of the Union building. Admission to the exhibition will be free.

A representative of the National Billiard association, Peterson is being brought here under the auspices of the Indiana Union. His appearance here was arranged by the Union officials to stimulate interest in the International Collegiate Billiard tournament to be held March 8 in the Union building. Mr. Peterson, founder of the tournaments, will include in his exhibition demonstrations of shots that can be legally used in the tournament play.

COMPASS DELAYS FLIGHT.

LOS ANGELES, Feb. 15.—(AP)—A recalcitrant compass requiring gradual adjustments delayed Wiley Post's altitude test flights over Union air terminal today until tomorrow, thus advancing the probable time of his take-off on a projected 7 to 8 hour stratosphere flight to New York to Sunday morning at the earliest.

Cue Expert

Charles Peterson, nationally known fancy shot billiard champion, who will give an exhibition today from 9 a.m. to 5 p.m. in the billiard room of the Indiana Union building.

HORNBOSTEL TO RUN IN HALPIN HALF-MILE AT NEW YORK MEET

Charley Hornbostel, one of Coach E. C. Hayes' most famous trackmen, who has added more laurels to his long string of accomplishments in his Eastern appearances this winter, will run again tonight in the Halpin half-mile, one of the feature events of the New York Athletic club's sixty-eighth indoor track and field meet.

Hornbostel, fresh from two dazzling speed performances at the Millrose meet last week, will enter tonight's race as a strong favorite. His strongest rival, Elton Brown of the Kansas City A. C., has withdrawn because of a severe cold. Brown, unbeaten thus far on the indoor boards, was expected to prove a keen competitor to the Hoosier runner.

High School Basketball Scores

Jeffersonville 29, Martinsville 21.
Mitchell 24, New Albany 12.
Frankfort 22, Delphi 13.
Anderson 32, Bedford 19.
Lafayette 44, Greencastle 34.
Orleans 26, French Lick 20.
Shelbyville 19, Technical (Indpls.) 16.
Jasper 26, Princeton 20.
Salem 30, Seymour 28. (Overtime)
Vincennes 27, Central (Evansville) 23.
Richmond 35, Connersville 18.
Elwood 30, Broadripple (Indianapolis) 19.
Manual (Indpls.) 35, Warren Central 20.
Washington (Indpls.) 21, Cathedral (Indpls.) 20.
Mishawaka 24, Winamac 19.
Muncie 31, Newcastle 20.
Tipton 26, Alexandria 25.
Michigan City 36, Riley (South Bend) 25.
Marion 44, Huntington 32.
Oolitic 26, Spencer 22.
Crawfordsville 28, Franklin 25.
Rushville 35, Columbus 31.
Memorial (Evansville) 21, Tell City 20.
Bosse (Evansville) 25, Reitz (Evansville) 16.
Central (S. Bend) 29, Laporte 28.
Wabash 29, Hartford City 12.
St. Mary's (Anderson) 37, St. Andrew (Richmond) 10.
Logansport 23, Kokomo 16.

EXTRA

A Bloomington merchant was killed, two students were injured and a taxicab driver suffered a broken leg in an automobile crash at the corner of Fifth and Lincoln streets at about 1 o'clock this morning.

George Dean, 40, proprietor of a local drug store, died while he was being rushed to the hospital in an ambulance immediately after the accident.

Injured.

James Hawes, '35, 215 East Third street, suffered serious internal injuries but hospital attaches said early this morning that he is expected to live.

Winifred Robertson, '38, Memorial hall, was badly cut and bruised about the head and shoulders.

Lloyd Trisler, driver for the Hoosier taxicab company, suffered a broken leg when he was thrown from his car by the force of the impact.

The crash occurred as the cab was driving toward the Bloomington business district. George Dean, driver and sole occupant of the other car, was headed south on Lincoln street.

The two cars crashed, swerved and separated. Both were badly damaged.

All Were Unconscious.

All four of the victims were unconscious when picked up by the crowd which immediately gathered about the scene of the accident. All were rushed to the Bloomington hospital.

The two students were riding in the back seat of the cab, and the impact hurled them both against the inside of the car. The cab driver was thrown out the door of his cab and pinned under it as it overturned at the curb.

Indications were that both cars had been traveling at a moderate speed, and that the cab driver failed to see Dean coming out of the side street until he was almost upon him.

Trisler, 28 years of age, was employed by the Hoosier Cab company, and lives at 721 South Lincoln street. He is married but has no children.

From Columbus, Angola.

Hawes is a resident of Columbus, Indiana. Miss Robertson lives at Angola.

Police were investigating the cause of the accident early this morning, but had given no indication as to its result as The Daily Student went to press.

ITALIAN NEWS BUREAU SCORES UNITED PRESS

ROME, Feb. 15.—(AP)—The Government Press bureau said today it had sharply rebuked the United Press for sending out a story regarding a non-existent ultimatum by Italy to Ethiopia.

The bureau said it also had rebuked the United Press for sending out a telegram concerning the Associated Press in which it was stated "The Italian government officially warned the Associated Press correspondent in Rome that the Military Secrets act would be invoked against the Associated Press if its false reports continued." The bureau termed this United Press story as "really unethical."

Heilman To Lead Talk On Munitions Probe

William Heilman, '37, will lead a discussion on "The Revelations of the Munitions Investigation" at 6:30 p.m. Sunday at Westminster Inn. The subject was the topic of an address made recently at Indianapolis by Senator Gerald P. Nye of North Dakota.

University students who will take a leading part in the forum are Alice Jane Binkley, '35, Lucille Houpt, '37, Ida Lucille McKinney, '37, William Doolittle, '36, and Clifton Weisheit, '38. The forum is open to any one who wishes to discuss the topic.

Mayor Berndt Answers Daily Student Charges

(By Mayor A. H. Berndt)

There are certain facts in connection with the fire at the Delta Tau house which should be known and recognized, which if known will prevent any fair-minded person from laying the blame of the loss on the fire department. In the first place, a woman employe of the fraternity informed members of the fraternity that she smelled smoke, and upon investigation, two boys went to the basement and found that a fire was in progress, after which they returned upstairs and returned with buckets of water to extinguish the flames. But upon their return, they decided that the fire had made such headway that an alarm should be given. The first thought was that a messenger should be sent to the gymnasium and notify members there who were attending the basketball game. The alarm that came to the fire department was phoned in by one of the women cooks who ran to a neighbor's house. During all of this time the flames were growing larger and spreading. Within eight minutes after the alarm was received the department had reached the fire and had laid two lines of hose and were in a position to use water if there had been any way by which they could get into the basement. At the same time, firemen had rushed to the basement with chemicals, and found that a gas pipe had broken and a long flame of gas fire was further impeding their chances of entering the basement. Twenty minutes after the first call, a second call was sent to the department and another truck was sent to the fire, and a third line of hose was laid. Your paper states that "it was 45 minutes before more than one line of hose was put into action."

It must not be overlooked that firemen and citizens worked hard and long to pry an iron grate loose which had been sealed into the foundation on the back side of the building. If so much time had not been required to get into this basement window doubtless a different story would be told today. Even with gas or smoke masks the city firemen could not have entered the basement to fight the fire.

At 6:30 in the evening, Virgil McCall, a student, passed the Delt house on his way to the basketball game and witnessed a group of boys in the yard discussing the smell of smoke or frie, and 60 minutes after that time an alarm was sent into the department. It is only reasonable to believe that the fire in the basement had made considerable headway during that length of time. Raymond Renaker, living next door north of the Delt house, watched proceedings from the time the fire was discovered, and he states that in no way ought the fire department be blamed for the loss of the house, because citizens and firemen together did everything humanly possible to save the building. Dean Clarence Edmondson of the University, who is a member of the fraternity, was on the scene and agreed that the department was not to blame for the loss of the property. Every neighbor in the immediate vicinity, including myself, is most sorry for the fraternity. And I might say that all neighbors have a very kindly feeling toward the Delta

(CONTINUED ON PAGE THREE)

P0079013, IU Archives.

MELLETT MEMORIAL DEDICATION ISSUE

HE SERVES BEST WHO SERVES THE TRUTH

THE INDIANA DAILY STUDENT

WEATHER
Partly Cloudy.

VOL. LXIV, NO. 124. BLOOMINGTON, INDIANA, FRIDAY MORNING, APRIL 19, 1935. ESTABLISHED 1867

Journalists Will Honor Memory of Don Mellett, Martyred Editor, Today

Slain Editor To Be Honored Today

Don Mellett (above), former Indiana university student and editor of a Canton (O.) newspaper, who was slain by racketeers during an editorial campaign which he was waging, will be honored today when the University chapter of Sigma Delta Chi dedicates the Don Mellett den in the Union building.

Son of Newspaper Hero To Unveil Bronze Plaque In Sigma Delta Chi Den

Lee A White of the Detroit News Will Give Principal Address on Dedicatory Program—Undergraduates, Associates To Be Initiated.

To pay tribute to a newspaper editor slain by gangsters he was opposing, noted journalists from throughout the Middle West will assemble on the Indiana university campus this afternoon for the dedication of the Don Mellett Memorial den in the Union building and the annual Sigma Delta Chi State Founders' day banquet.

Sponsored by the Indiana university chapter of the professional journalistic fraternity and the Department of Journalism, the Mellett dedicatory ceremonies will begin with the unveiling of a plaque in the Sigma Delta Chi room, renamed the Don Mellett Memorial den in honor of the Canton, Ohio, editor and former University student.

To Hold Services.

Initiation services for associate and active members of Sigma Delta Chi will be held at 4 p.m. and 5 p.m., respectively, in the Town Hall room on the third floor of the Union building. The plaque will be unveiled by Don Mellett, elder son of the militant editor, at 6 p.m. President William Lowe Bryan will speak at the unveiling of the plaque. The widow and other immediate members of the Mellett family will attend the ceremonies. The dinner is scheduled for 6:30 p.m. Delegates from the Indianapolis alumni, Purdue, DePauw and Butler chapters of Sigma Delta Chi will attend.

Lee A White, member of the editorial staff of the Detroit News and a past national president of Sigma Delta Chi, will make the Mellett dedicatory and Founders' Day address at 8 p.m. in Union A, B, C and D. Although the banquet will be closed to all but Sigma Delta Chis and visiting newspapermen, the address by Mr. White will be open to the public.

Cook To Preside.

Robert A. Cook, president of the Indiana university chapter of Sigma Delta Chi, will preside at the Founders' day dinner, and brief talks will be made by James A. Stuart, managing editor of the Indianapolis Star and a past national president of Sigma Delta Chi; Prof. J. W. Piercy, head of the Department of Journalism, and James C. Kiper, national executive secretary of the fraternity who will represent John Stempel, national president of Sigma Delta Chi.

Prof. Arthur Leible of the English department, a member of the organization, will read a poem which he has written and dedicated to the memory of Mellett, whom he knew intimately.

Undergraduates who will be initiated into the fraternity are: J. E. O'Brien, '37, Gordon Parks, '35, Stuart Van Dyke, '35, Harry Walterhouse, '35, John Thomson, '35, and Lloyd Wilkins, '37.

11 Associates Named.

Eleven Indiana newspaper men who will receive associate membership in Sigma Delta Chi are: Robert Tucker, dramatic critic, and John P. Edmison of the editorial staff of the Indianapolis Star; Wayne Coy, formerly editor and publisher of the Delphi Citizen and now director of the Governor's Commission on Unemployment Relief; Walter S. Greenough, vice-president of the Fletcher Trust company in charge of public rela-

(CONTINUED ON PAGE THREE)

S.D.X. NOTICE!

Active and associate members of Sigma Delta Chi will meet at noon today in the Colonial tearoom.

Tickets for the Sigma Delta Chi State Founders' day dinner may be secured throughout the day at the Union desk.

Student Is Re-signed As Campus Cop Finds Road Marker in Room

The bitter memories of a moment of vandalism probably came back to a University student Thursday as he stood in a pouring ran digging a post hole at the corner of Third and Walnut streets.

Walt Peterson, campus policeman, accidently wandered into the student's room and discovered among the interior decorations the seven-foot "Nashville–Columbus–North Vernon" road sign which had been missing for several days from the corner of Third and Walnut streets.

Accompanied by Peterson, the student had to return the sign to its former place, dig another hole and replace the sign while Jupe Pluvius showed no mercy.

REGISTRAR'S RECORDS SHOW THAT CONVICT WAS NOT I.U. STUDENT

Careful investigation Thursday of records on file in the registrar's office failed to disclose any evidence that George Donald Dillon, college student convict who recently was sentenced to four years' imprisonment in Colorado on charges of burglary, ever attended school here. Dillon told Judge Henley Calvert that he "attended Indiana university in 1928."

Dillon was arrested last month in Greeley, Colo., after an exchange of gunfire with a policeman. Dillon said that he had resorted to robbery and theft for several years so that he might continue his college education.

He admitted having previously served a term in the Indiana State penitentiary, after which he went to Colorado and entered an engineering school.

'Let Demilitarized Rhineland Alone,' Great Britain, Italy Warn Germany; Borah Dubs Council 'Spineless Tool'

Hitler Sends Diplomatic Protest to British Against League's Censure of Reich's Rearmament.

BERLIN, April 18.—(AP)—Great Britain and Italy, it was revealed tonight, have warned Germany she must let the demilitarized Rhineland alone.

Ambassadors of the two powers yesterday presented their joint Stresa decision to maintain the status quo in the Rhineland, and Germany met that with a "sizzling" diplomatic protest to Great Britain against the League of Nations censure of the Reich's rearmament.

Nevertheless, Nazi officials today were inclined to look upon yesterday's action at Geneva more calmly, partly because the British and Italian ambassadors, in response to pointed questions, gave the foreign office assurances of their governments' intention to fulfill their obligations under the Locarno treaty.

May Issue Protest.

While the foreign office strove to pour oil on troubled waters and the press received instructions to handle the situation with gloves, Reichsfuehrer Adolf Hitler left his Bavarian mountain retreat and went to Munich to confer with party leaders and close advisors over the form his answer to the League Council's indictment shall take.

A formal and sensational protest was expected to issue tomorrow or Saturday from the Munich conference, in which Foreign Minister Konstantin Von Neurath and Joachim von Ribbentrop, Hitler's arms experts, are participating.

Senator Introduces Bill Designed To Prevent American Money Going Into Foreign War Coffers.

WASHINGTON, April 18.—(AP)—Riled by the League of Nations demand that Germany comply with the Versailles treaty, Senator William E. Borah today denounced the council as the "spineless tool" of a few European nations and then introduced a bill to prevent American money from going into foreign war coffers.

Taking the Senate floor during the afternoon, Borah thundered of the League:

"Nothing in the history of this institution better illustrates that it is not an independent body for peace, but a spineless tool in the hands of a few nations to do what those nations elect."

Is Foe of League.

A stern foe of the League from its inception, the senior Republican on the Foreign Affairs committee declared:

"This institution should no longer pretend to be an independent body seeking by independent methods to advance the cause of peace."

Borah's attack echoed through the chamber at the conclusion of a speech by Senator Lewis of Illinois, Democratic whip, criticizing members of the League for demanding that Germany live up to her treaty obligations while they continue to disregard "obligations they have contracted with the United States."

The bitterness of Borah's criticism of the League was paralleled by the language he employed in a statement accompanying a bill proposing to shut off private loans to foreign nations.

His proposal would supplement the Johnson act which already bars loans from this government to other nations delinquent in their obligations to the United States.

To Give Address

Lee A White (above), a member of the editorial staff of the Detroit News and a past national president of Sigma Delta Chi, who will deliver a dedicatory address for the Mellett memorial den at 8 o'clock tonight in rooms A, B, C and D of the Union building.

200 LIMIT PLACED ON RESERVATIONS FOR A.W.S. DINNER

Lena Madesin Phillips and Irma E. Voight To Be Guest Speakers.

Only 200 reservations will be available for the formal A.W.S. convention banquet Thursday night, April 25, in Alumni hall where Miss Lena Madesin Phillips, one of America's most outstanding business women, and Miss Irma E. Voight, dean of women at Ohio university, will be the guest speakers.

Governor and Mrs. Paul V. McNutt, Judge and Mrs. Walter S. Treanor of Indianapolis and President and Mrs. William Lowe Bryan will be the guests of honor. Other invitations have been sent to faculty and administrative officers, deans and heads of departments and their wives. The remaining reservations, at $1.25 a plate, will be open to townspeople and students. Persons wishing to attend the banquet are urged to make their reservations as quickly as possible, Dean Agnes E. Wells stated Thursday.

Have Made Reservations.

Seventy-six official delegates and thirty-one additional representatives from schools throughout the United States have already made reservations for the convention, and 11 deans and assistant deans of women have accepted invitations to attend. Dean Wells will be hostess at a breakfast for the visiting deans Thursday morning, April 25, at her home. Mrs. Sanford F. Teter, member of the University Board of Trustees, will entertain the deans at luncheon Thursday noon.

The deans and assistant deans

(CONTINUED ON PAGE THREE)

CAPTAIN MARSHALL TO LEAVE R.O.T.C.

I.U. Officer Notified of Transfer to Station in New York.

Official orders notifying Captain Floyd Marshall of the University Military department of his transfer to the Plattsburg Barracks army post in northern New York were received Thursday at the Military office. Captain Marshall will report at his new post June 30.

Captain Marshall has been a member of the University military faculty for six years, the maximum period of service for army officers detailed to college and university R.O.T.C. duty. Marshall is a graduate of Indiana university, a former member of the football team and of The Daily Student staff. He has served as coach of the rifle team and as faculty adviser to Scabbard and Blade, honorary military fraternity.

Captain Koger M. Still of Fort Benjamin Harrison has been detailed to replace Captain Marshall here. Captain Still will join the faculty on or before June 30.

BIDDLE WILL ATTEND BUYING CONFERENCE

A co-operative purchasing system that would lower the cost of school supplies for students will be considered at the first annual buying conference of the National Association of College Bookstores to be held April 23-26 in New York, Ward G. Biddle, manager of the University bookstore, said last night.

Mr. Biddle, who will attend the conference, explained that a great saving is expected to be made to students through this plan. Although college bookstores on the Pacific coast have been using this method for the past eight years, this is the first time that it has been considered in the East.

Fifty-six manufacturing companies have rented space in the Hotel McAlpin to display their goods at the conference. Approximately eighty members of the National Association of College Bookstores will send representatives to the conference, which is under the direction of Donald Lyman of the Columbia university bookstore.

DEANMEN TO FACE PURDUE OUTFIT AT LAFAYETTE TODAY

15 Players Will Leave by Auto at 10 o'Clock This Morning.

ADLER SLATED TO HURL

Fuzzy Himmelstein Is Only Regular From Last Year in Lineup.

Attempting to add baseball to the long list of sports in which Indiana teams this year have trounced their oldest and bitterest foe—Purdue—the Crimson diamond crew will battle the Boilermaker nine at 4 o'clock this afternoon at Lafayette in the first contest of a two-game series.

Coach Everett Dean and 15 Hoosier pastimers will leave Bloomington by auto at 10 o'clock this morning. Another performer, shortstop Fuzzy Himmelstein, only regular from last year in the starting lineup, will join his teammates in Lafayette, going there from Indianapois. Bob Adler, star sophomore hurler, will start on the mound for the Deanmen. Willard Kehrt probably will relieve him before the encounter is ended.

All Sophs But One.

Indiana's beginning array will consist of all sophomores with the exception of Himmelstein. Steve Kubic will be behind the plate, Adler in the box, Bill Baise at first base, Russell Grieger at second base, Kenny Payne or Tom Brady at third base, and Torchy Holmquest, Kenny Gunning and Babe Hosler in the outfield. Other men who will make the trip are catcher Harlow Redding, pitchers Vic Roberts and Willard Kehrt, infielders Jim Hendricks and Herb Queisser, and outfielder Heinie Wahl.

Coach Ward (Piggy) Lambert has a veteran nine at Purdue this season that may prove too tough for the Hoosiers' rookie outfit. The Gold and Black crew has triumphed in the majority of its engagements so far this year, boasting a double-header victory over Butler and a win over Notre Dame among its accomplishments.

DEBATE FINALISTS TO MEET TUESDAY

Misses Hillix, Fenn To Form Negative Team Against Van Dyke, Ashby.

Elizabeth Hillix, '36, and Jane Fenn, '37, debating the negative side of the question, "Resolved, That the present system of relief is detrimental to the best interests of the American people," will meet the team of Stuart Van Dyke, '35, and Robert Ashby, '38, in the finals of the Intra-University debate Tuesday evening, April 23, as a result of the semi-finals held last night in Alumni hall.

The coed combination downed the team of Murray Strauss, '38, and Sydnor Shatz, '38, while Ashby and Van Dyke won on a forfeit from the team of Herbert Backer, '36, and Arthur Sachs, '37.

The finals in the debate, which is being sponsored by Phi Delta Gamma, honorary forensic, dramatic and journalistic fraternity, will be held at a regular Union open forum Tuesday, April 23. Both the winners and the runners-up will receive keys—gold to the winning team and silver to the runners-up.

Late News Flashes

DISORDER IN BULGARIA.

SOFIA, Bulgaria, April 18.—(AP)—A feverish day of arrests, cabinet resignations and incipient disorders was climaxed tonight as Premier Petko Zlateff's entire government resigned, and King Boris immediately commissioned Zlateff to continue until another cabinet can be formed.

MRS. BECKER WINS.

WASHINGTON, April 18.—(AP)—The bitterly contested fight for president generalcy of the Daughters of the American Revolution ended tonight in complete victory for Mrs. William A. Becker of Summit, N.J.

RAPS PRESIDENT.

ATLANTA, April 18.—(AP)—Referring to President Roosevelt as "an extreme radical," Governor Eugene Talmadge today predicted a third party ticket in the 1936 general election.

FROWNS ON EXTRA SESSION.

INDIANAPOLIS, April 18.—(AP)—Governor Paul V. McNutt tonight asserted that, in his opinion, there is "no great public demand" for a special session of the Indiana Legislature.

FEARS HAUPTMANN SCANDAL.

NEW YORK, April 18.—(AP)—Asserting he feared a "national scandal," Edward J. Reilly today urged the New Jersey State Bar association to investigate the handling of Bruno Richard Hauptmann's defense fund.

JEFF SEEKS NET COACH.

JEFFERSONVILLE, April 18.—(AP)—School board members here said tonight they had arranged a conference for Saturday with Frank Barnes of Flora, to discuss closing a contract with him as Jeffersonville high school basketball coach.

NO EMBARRASSMENT HERE!

CHICAGO, April 18.—(AP)—President Robert M. Hutchins of the University of Chicago, which lately has been the target of "Red" charges, declared in a radio address late today he had "never been able to find a red professor."

Freshmen Engage Sosnik

Noted Composer and His Band To Play for Mardi Gras Ball To Be Held April 26.

Harry Sosnik, former maestro at the Edgewater Beach hotel in Chicago and master of music ceremonies at the A. and P. Gypsy Carnival at the World's Fair, will play for the second annual Freshman Mardi Gras ball to be held from 9 p.m. to 1 a.m. April 26 in Alumni hall.

Simultaneously with the signing up of this famous "name" band, possible nominations for the freshman Princess have begun to circulate through the campus. Six sororities already have designated their choices of possible nominees. The Phi Mu's, Alpha Chi's, Theta's, Kappa's and Pi Phi's are raking their outstanding freshmen over the coals in order to sift out a possible winner.

Ten Backers Necessary.

Before a candidate may be nominated she must have her name backed by ten freshman men who must present ten ticket stubs at the Union desk. These stubs will be held by officials until the poles open for election at which time the stubs will be refunded to the original holders. Tickets for the Mardi Gras ball will be placed on sale at the Union building desk at 8 o'clock this morning. The ball will be open to all students. The deadline for the filing of nominations will be at noon, Tuesday, April 23.

DISCUSSES "MERCURY."

The history of the movements of the point in the orbit of the planet Mercury which is nearest the sun, was discussed last night by Prof. K. P. Williams of the Mathematics department before members of Sigma Xi, honorary scientific fraternity.

FIFTH ANNUAL STATE MATHEMATICS MEET WILL BE HELD TODAY

Winners of the fifth annual State high school mathematics contest, sponsored by the University Extension department in co-operation with the mathematics section of the State Teachers' association, will be selected today at the final round of the competition which will be held on the campus.

One hundred five contestants, 53 of whom are entered in the algebra division and the remainder in the geometry division, will compete in the final round. Gold, silver and bronze medals will be awarded to the winners of first, second and third places, respectively, in the algebra division. Geometry winners will not be announced until Monday.

Examinations will be held at 10 a.m. today in Assembly hall and sectional awards will be given at a luncheon at noon in the University cafeteria. Mathematic pupils, their teachers and parents will be entertained with a tea at 2:15 p.m. at the home of President and Mrs. William Lowe Bryan.

The committee in charge of the contest includes A. M. Welchons, Technical high school, Indianapolis, chairman; Mrs. Adela Bittner of the University Extension division; Clarence Lane, Lafayette; Walter C. Shriner, State Teachers college, Terre Haute; H. N. Whittern, Muncie, and Arthur Sims, Lebanon.

NOMINATE MEMBERS.

Blue Key, honorary upperclassmen's fraternity, held a luncheon meeting Thursday for the purpose of nominating new members for the organization. The nominees will be voted on at the next meeting of the group.

Medical Organization Installs New Officers

Lynville A. Baker, '36, was installed formally last night as president of Theta Kappa Psi, honorary medical fraternity, at the organization's annual installation meeting in Union A and B. Robert Bridgeford, '37, Gordon Bailey, '37, and A. Lee Hickman, '37, were installed as vice-president, secretary-treasurer and historian, respectively.

Lester Renbarger, Chester Conway, Howard Stellner, Gilson Hild and Paul Pentecost, all of the University Medical school in Indianapolis, made short talks at the meeting. The organization will meet again May 2.

Music To Herald Holy Day

Bloomington Churches Will Unite in Observance of Good Friday—To Hold Union Services.

A dramatic musical interpretation, musical numbers by choirs, trios and quartets will be presented in six Bloomington churches today in observance of Good Friday and Holy week. Three afternoon services including a Union service at the First Christian church and five evening services will be given.

Pastors from seven churches will make 20-minute addresses at a three-hour Union service at the Christian church from noon to 3 p.m. on the theme "The Words of the Cross." Pastors that will speak are: the Rev. William A. Binkley, McDoel Baptist church, "Word of Mercy;" the Rev. J. W. Meloy, United Presbyterian, "Word of Promise;" the Rev. R. O. Pearson, Fairview Methodist, "Word of Compassion;" the Rev. Charles B. Schwartz, First Presbyterian church, "Word of Loneliness;" the Rev. Frank Messersmith, "Word of Suffering;" the Rev. Douglas Vernon, Westminster Inn, "Word of Triumph," and the Rev. C. Howard Taylor, First Methodist church, "Word of Confidence." A male quartet, composed of Walter Woodburn, Judge Donald A. Rogers, James Damrell and Arthur Livingston, will sing two numbers. Mrs. Otto Rott will sing "Sweet Peace," and Prof. Douglas Nye will present "Oh Love That Will Not Let Me Go."

To Hold Mass.

A mass at 8 a.m. and the mass of the "Presanctified" at 9 o'clock will open Good Friday services at the St. Charles Catholic church. A three-hour service, or "Tre Ore," will be given from 1 to 3 p.m. with Father Zeller of New York speaking on the "Crucifixion." Father

(CONTINUED ON PAGE THREE)

P0079014, IU Archives.

'He Died for the Republic'

This selection was adapted from an article that originally appeared Oct. 10, 1954, to mark the formal dedication of Ernie Pyle Hall as the new home of IU's School of Journalism.

By Donald R. Young

Pride can be a virtuous thing—and it can be deadly.

Donald Ring Mellett was murdered while trying to build a community of which he could be proud.

With pride, mixed with shock, President William Lowe Bryan urged that a tablet memorializing Don Mellett be placed on campus.

With pride, such a plaque was dedicated in the Sigma Delta Chi room in the Union Building on April 19, 1935. The plaque was moved to Ernie Pyle Hall last week—to the new Don Mellett Auditorium.

And only pride in her husband and his work could bring Florence Mellett to say many years after his death: "We need more crusaders!"

It is with pride that we recall Don Mellett's story again.

Not a pleasant story, it is an inspiring one, as it unravels from Elwood, Ind., through a college campus and inky print shops to a modern-day "shot heard round the world" and the death of a hero.

Today, on Indianapolis' north side, lives a woman with Don Mellett's story to tell.

Don Mellett was born Sept. 26, 1891, one of seven sons of The Elwood Gazette's publisher. Four months later, the paper recorded the birth of a boy named Wendell L. Wilkie. The two became fast friends.

Eventually both reached the IU campus. Don's main interest was newspaper writing. He became editor of the IDS.

In those days an editor could point a sympathetic finger to a campus gasping for water in a repeatedly drought-stricken community and suggest that maybe IU should be moved to Indianapolis.

This was Don Mellett's first crusade and it brought quick retaliation from Bloomington merchants. The campus is still here, but the city's water problem went relatively unsolved until only recently.

Also to Bloomington came Don's wife Florence, whom he met at Shortridge High School. The young couple moved into a small house in the 500 block of East Kirkwood.

Illness caused by over-exertion as a cross-country runner forced Don to leave school a semester before he'd have graduated in 1914, but he stayed long enough to become a charter member of the Rho chapter of Sigma Delta Chi.

Mrs. Mellett recalls they moved several times—to Brown County, Bloomington, Indianapolis, Columbus. Don wrote all this time and for a while owned The Columbus (Ind.) Ledger.

In 1923, the Melletts and their four children moved to Akron, Ohio, where Don became The Press advertising manager. There he met James M. Cox, former Ohio governor, Democratic candidate for President in 1920 and owner of a newspaper chain. He was looking for someone to inject new life into his Canton paper.

Mrs. Mellett says that "at the same time, Don was offered a newspaper job in Cleveland, but Mr. Cox persuaded him to take the Canton post. Certainly, we did not know of the situation there and if Mr. Cox did, he didn't say anything."

As editor of The Canton Daily News, Don found that the city's "leading" gambler had an office in the police station. Policemen

Don Mellett, circa 1924.
P0021483, IU Archives.

IDS Publisher John Stempel, at right, helps hang a memorial plaque to Don Mellett in September 1954 at Ernie Pyle Hall. *P0027098, IU Archives.*

themselves kept open the bootleg-liquor traffic. The underworld, in short, controlled all the vices and the city government.

Opening his editorial fire, the new editor named persons, places, events. First indication that the gangster rulers were squirming came in February 1925, Mrs. Mellett recalls.

"We were going out for dinner. While Don was shaving, the phone rang, and I answered. A man asked if we were going to be home that evening. I said no. He replied that if we knew what was good for us, we wouldn't leave. Then he hung up. From that moment, we lived in agony."

Then Don Mellett received offers of bribes. He replied by publishing them. There were more threats—and more stories and editorials.

On Thursday July 15, 1926, the Melletts returned late from a dinner party. The children were asleep.

"I was fixing coffee when Don decided to go out and drive our car into the garage. It was God's will," Mrs. Mellett recalls.

Don Mellett never got back to the safety of the kitchen door. For firing two bullets into the body of a man against whom he had no personal grievance, a 23-year-old "trigger man" was sentenced to life imprisonment.

Lee A. White of the Detroit News wrote on the Mellett case:

"If ever there was doubt of Don Mellett's campaign, that doubt died with him. Not merely because an outraged society could never let such a crime go unavenged, not merely because the press could never permit itself to be gagged and manacled and scourged. But because there are no defeats for honesty, integrity and high purposefulness, however long the victory may be delayed. Truth set on foot is in itself victory, even though the fruits of that victory may be posthumous."

HE SERVES BEST WHO SERVES THE TRUTH

THE INDIANA DAILY STUDENT

THE WEATHER
Fair and warmer today; Saturday fair with rising temperature.

VOL. LXVI—NO. 137. INDIANA UNIVERSITY FRIDAY, MAY 7, 1937. BLOOMINGTON, INDIANA, ESTABLISHED 1867

GIANT SKY LINER EXPLODES; 30 DIE

Air Monarch Falls in Flames

—Associated Press photo

Germany's giant skyliner, the Hindenburg, which slumped to the Lakehurst, N.J., dirigible landing field a shattered and flaming mass of twisted wreckage Thursday afternoon, is shown above as she landed at Lakehurst on a previous transatlantic trip.

Dirigible Ripped Apart By Hydrogen Blast in Stern; Falls in Flames

Hindenburg Disaster Occurs as Ship Approaches Mooring Mast—Ground Crew Narrowly Escapes.

LAKEHURST, N.J., May 6.—(AP)—Her silvery bulk shattered by a terrific explosion, the German air liner Hindenburg plunged in flames at the U.S. Naval air station tonight, with indications at least one-third of the 99 aboard perished.

As minor explosions continued to tear her twisted aluminum skeleton and ribboned fabric hours afterward, estimates of the death toll were conflicting and duplicating.

Harry A. Bruno, press relations counsel for the Zeppelin company which operated the luxurious modern dirigible, said that 64 of the persons aboard her on her maiden 1937 voyage here had been reported saved. He listed 20 passengers and 44 of the crew as survivors.

Timothy W. Margerum of Lakewood said there were already 40 corpses in the Naval station's garage which had been hurriedly transformed into a morgue. Many of the dead were horribly burned by the oil red flames. Margerum reported others were dying. Hospitals for miles around were filled with the injured.

The Navy department in Washington said it was advised at least 48 persons were killed.

Gas Cell Blamed.

An explosion of the No. 2 gas cell toward the stern of the ship was named as the cause of the disaster by state aviation commissioner Gill Robb Wilson, who called the blast "strange." The highly-inflammable hydrogen gas billowed into fierce flame as the explosion plummeted the ship to the airfield. Ground spectators said crew members in the stern of the ship "never had a chance" to escape.

The disaster struck without the least warning. The ship had angled her blunt nose toward the mooring mast, the spider like landing lines had been snaked down from her belly and the ground crew had grasped the ropes from the nose, when the explosion roared out scattering ground crew and spectators like frightened sheep.

Had Waved Gaily.

The passengers, who were waving gaily a minute before, from the observation windows that slit the belly of the dirigible, were so stunned they could not describe later what happened. Some jumped to the sandy landing field along with members of the crew. Others seemed to have been pitched from the careening sky liner as it made its death plunge.

The heat drove back would-be rescuers, so it could not be determined for how many the Hindenburg made a burning tomb. Fire departments from nearby communities converged on the field and soon had streams of water playing on the broken airliner. The flames still enveloped the outline of the ship, apparently feeding on the fuel oil supply which the Hindenburg carried for her Deisel motors.

Somewhere in the glowing furnace were the two dogs, 340 pounds of mail and the ton of baggage which she had aboard.

31 Accounted for.

Thirty-one survivors were accounted for in hospitals and other places in the Lakehurst area at 8:45 p.m. (C.S.T.)

F. W. von Meister, vice-president of the American Zeppelin Transport company, the General U.S. agents for the German Zeppelin Transport company, the Hinden-

(CONTINUED ON PAGE THREE)

Scribes Set May 24 for 'Razz' Fete

Theta Sigma Phi To Put Feminine Audience "on Pan" at Banquet.

Members of the local chapter of Theta Sigma Phi, professional journalistic sorority, will present their annual "Razz" banquet at 6 p.m. Monday, May 24, in Alumni hall, Eleanor Jones, '37, president of the group, announced Thursday.

Invitations to the banquet, at which the exclusively feminine audience will be "put on the pan" by Theta Sigma Phi members, will be sent to approximately 400 outstanding University coeds within the next few days, according to Mrs. Jane Harrison Pierce, chairman of the ticket committee.

Will Write Script.

The script for the affair, which will include satirical skits and individual "razzes," will be written by Jean McGriff, '37, Charlotte Lowey, '37, Marjorie Finkbiner, '38, and Mary Aldred, '39. Properties committee members are Miriam Meloy, '38, Mary Pence, '38, and Virginia Gilberg, '37.

Martha McKenna, '37, and Helen Weatherwax, '38, will comprise the food committee, and Miss Gilberg and Miss Aldred will be in charge of reservations for the banquet.

Rural WPA Work May Be Limited

Kloeb Suggests Operations Be Discontinued for Seven Months of Year.

WASHINGTON, May 6.—(P)—A proposal to abolish the Works Progress Administration's operations in rural areas seven months of the year went before Congress today.

Representative Kloeb (Dem.—Ohio), on the basis of a survey made in the farming district he represents, told a House appropriations subcommittee he believed WPA could be suspended in 2,000 counties of the United States from May to Dec. 1 "without injury."

The Ohioan said if his suggestion were adopted relief expenditures for the year beginning July 1 could be held "substantially below $1,000,000,000."

The House Committee which received Kloeb's proposal is considering President Roosevelt's request for $1,500,000,000 to finance next year's relief.

The Day In Brief

Campus—

Theta Sigma Phis set "Razz" banquet for May 24 (this page).

Tri Delts win top honors in annual sing (this page).

Contributions to Bryan Scholarship trust vault to $15,000 total (this page).

National—

Thirty die in German dirigible explosion (this page).

State—

Union secretary asserts that Indiana Railroad workers did not take written vote on strike (page 6).

Sports—

Michigan State downs University courtmen, 8-1 (page 5).

RELEASED ON BAIL.

NEW CASTLE, Ky., May 6.—(P)—Brig. Gen. Henry H. Denhardt was released on $25,000 bail today after a jury reported it was hopelessly deadlocked on whether or not he shot to death his fiancee, Mrs. Verna Garr Taylor, 40.

Chemistry Group To Hold Services For 17 Tonight

Purdue Professor To Address Phi Lambda Upsilon at Formal Banquet.

Seventeen chemistry students will be inducted into Phi Lambda Upsilon, honorary chemistry fraternity, at the initiation banquet to be held at 6 p.m. today in the Colonial tearoom of the Union building, John R. Morris, PG, secretary of the organization, announced Thursday. Dr. E. F. Degering of the Purdue university chemistry department will be the principal speaker at the banquet.

The 17 men who will be initiated are: R. J. Ballard, '38; H. S. Barnaby, '38; Malcolm D. Bray, '38; Urban Collignon, '38; Robert Gillespie, '38; R. W. Stephenson, '38; Morris Zukerman, '38; L. A. Blatz, '37; William T. Couter, '37; Charles Inman, '37; Thedford Dirkse, PG; Henry Fischbach, PG; Floyd Kauffman, PG; Russell Sperry, PG; R. A. Johnston, PG; Vincent E. Parker, PG, and Harry Afflerbach, '37.

Dr. Degering's talk, which will not be open to the public as had been announced previously, will be based on the subject, "Laboratory Gadgets and Accessories." The talk will be illustrated with lantern slides and will deal with the various phases of research work done at Purdue.

MAY EVICT STRIKERS.

ANDERSON, May 6.—(P)—Sheriff Harry Gossett and his deputies are expected to serve eviction notices tomorrow morning on striking employes of the Indiana Railroad who assertedly have been picketing and occupying the traction system's power plant and shops here since the walkout began nearly seven weeks ago.

Dirigible Explosion Echoes 'Round World

Disaster Brings Comments From Executives in Berlin, Washington.

From records in Washington last night the Associated Press gleaned the information that 18 major dirigible disasters have occurred during the last 23 years. Of the ill-fated airships, three were owned by the United States—the Akron, the Macon and the Shenandoah. Approximately 350 persons were killed while only 94 escaped death in the aerial accidents.

While in Indianapolis to attend an American Legion executive committee meeting, Col. J. Monroe Johnson, assistant secretary of commerce in charge of air commerce, said last night he "would not even speculate on the effect the Hindenburg explosion might have on American participation in transatlantic air service."

In Washington, Chairman Royal S. Copeland of the Senate committee investigating air safety, said he would order the committee investigator to begin an inquiry "at once" into the disaster to the German airliner Hindenburg.

From Galveston, Tex., President Roosevelt, learning of the disaster to the dirigible Hindenburg at Lakehurst, N.J., last night sent a message to Chancellor Hitler in Berlin expressing his "deepest sympathy" to the German government.

Coronation bound, 70 persons, watching their bags "weighed in" for the outgoing trip of the giant airliner at midnight, said they would not believe the Hindenburg had exploded. One man cried, "They're kidding—it's their idea of a joke."

Once convinced by newspaper-

(CONTINUED ON PAGE THREE)

Men's Glee Club To Take Part in Hoosier Festival

Second Annual Musical Will Be Staged Next September at State Fair.

The University Men's Glee club, directed by Prof. D. D. Nye of the Music school, has been selected to participate in the second annual Hoosier Music festival to be staged next September at the State Fair in Indianapolis.

After appearing on the Fair grounds for morning programs, the glee club will fill afternoon and evening engagements on the stage at the Lyric theatre in Indianapolis. Arrangements for the glee club's bookings were made by Dr. Frank Elliott, University publicity agent, and Frederick E. Green, director of the University band.

Another highlight of the musical show will be concerts by a 125-piece band, which is to consist partly of members of the University band. Other bandsters are to be outstanding musicians selected from high schools throughout the State.

Guest conductors for the band presentations are to be Dr. Frank Simon, well-known leader of the radio-famed Armco band, and Dean B. Winfred Merrill of the University School of Music.

Sorority Presidents Accept Amendment To A.W.S. Constitution

Members of the House Presidents' association at a meeting Thursday voted to accept the amendment to the A.W.S. constitution recently submitted to them by the A.W.S. Council. The ruling, which was observed in the election in March, was omitted in the 1936 revision of the constitution.

The amendment provides that in A.W.S. elections freshman coeds shall vote for one organized and one unorganized class representative, the sophomores and juniors shall vote for two organized and two unorganized class representatives and that all women students shall vote for a candidate for the presidency.

Preceding the business session of the meeting, Mrs. John H. Mueller addressed the group about her experiences encountered while traveling in Europe.

COUNTY SCHOLARSHIPS.

Indiana university students who have made outstanding records may apply for appointment to County Scholarships. Blanks for application may be had May 12 at the registrar's office and should be filled out and filed with Dean Rothrock no later than May 22.

Finding a 'Second Bryan' Is Tough Job, Feltus Says

Seeking a man to fill the office of President William Lowe Bryan, who has played such an integral part in the development and progress seen by the University during the last 35 years, is no easy assignment, according to Paul Feltus, member of the University Board of Trustees.

"There is no doubt that the presidency of Indiana university is a much desired post," Mr. Feltus said Thursday, "and the trustees now are receiving letters recommending men from every part of the country, but the board will not be in any hurry in its selection. The man finally selected must be the "right man" and to fill President Bryan's place with a man worthy of that position is no overnight job."

Through extensive investigations now being carried on by Judge Ora L. Wildermuth, member of the Board of Trustees from Gary, numerous names of capable men already have been proposed and placed on record, it was learned Thursday.

Following the Foundation day morning services Wednesday, a committee of trustees, including Mrs. Sanford A. Teter, John S. Hastings and Mr. Feltus, conferred with Dr. Walter A. Jessup, Foundation day speaker, on the subject of selecting a new president. Asked to suggest a possible candidate for the administrative office, Mr. Jessup replied, "I don't know quite the man for you."

Delta Delta Delta Wins First Place In Sing Program

Delta Taus Lead Fraternity Groups of Larger Division.

Phi Mu, Phi B. D. Score

Organizations Top Contestants in Smaller Division—Awarded Cups.

By VELMA WOLFE

Delta Delta Delta, social sorority, was named first place winner among the 10 sororities and fraternities who competed last night in the larger division of the seventh annual all-University Sing. Delta Tau Delta led the six fraternities entered in the event and was awarded the Dean B. Winifred Merrill silver loving cup.

Phi Mu sorority and Phi Beta Delta fraternity won cups which were donated this year by the Y.W.C.A. and Y.M.C.A. for the outstanding groups in the smaller numbered divisions.

Given Honorable Mention.

Honorable mention was given to Kappa Kappa Gamma sorority and Beta Theta Pi fraternity in the larger division. No honorable mention was announced in the smaller division.

The annual songfest, sponsored jointly by the Y.W.C.A. and Y.M.C.A., was held on the main steps of the Student building which were illuminated by two large spotlights.

Judges for the affair were: Miss Ada Bicking of the Arthur Jordan Conservatory of Music, Indianapolis; Prof. H. C. Montgomery, Wabash college; Prof. Lowell M. Tilson, Indiana State Teachers college, Terre Haute; Prof. Glenn M. Seitz, Franklin college, and Profs. D. D. Nye and E. B. Birge of the University School of Music.

During the intermissions Robert Dilts, '38, played one of the required numbers, "The Bells of St. Mary's" on the chimes. Virginia Gilberg, '37, and William Harvuot, '38, were co-chairmen of the affair.

Pershing Rifles To Attend Meet

Drill Unit Will Leave Today for Review at University of Illinois.

Attired in newly pressed uniforms with brightly shined brass, 50 cadets of the University company of Pershing Rifles, special drill unit, will leave Bloomington at 9 o'clock this morning for Urbana-Champaign, Ill., to compete in the Pershing Rifles regimental drill meet tonight and Saturday. The affair is to be held on the campus of the University of Illinois.

Other participants in the annual competitive review of the first and third regiments will be from the University of Illinois, University of Cincinnati, Michigan State college, Ohio State university, University of Dayton, Western Kentucky State Teachers college and the University of Kentucky. Indiana university is the headquarters for the third regiment.

Darrel Burnett, '37, and Howard Hawkins, '38, lieutenant colonel and adjutant respectively of the third regiment, are in charge of arrangements for the event. Officers of the local company are Max McCaslin, '37, captain; Joe D'Enbeau, '38, sergeant, and Paul Mielke, '38, first lieutenant.

DEAN PAYNE RETURNS FROM BUSINESS TRIP

Dean Fernandus Payne of the Graduate school returned to the campus Thursday from a week's business trip to Chicago and Colorado. While in Chicago, he attended a meeting of the American Association of University Professors.

Dean Payne's trip to Colorado included an inspection tour of the Colorado State college, Greeley, Colo., in connection with his work as chairman of the classification committee of the Association of American Universities.

Swingmaster

JIMMY CATHCART
. . . Tonight's Union Maestro

'Pickaninny' Pianist To Perform Tonight At A.W.S.-Union Hop

Cathcart Will Feature Marvin Chandler at Dance in Alumni Hall.

Diminutive 7-year-old Marvin Chandler, half of the Chandler twin song and dance duet that twice before has entertained campus groups at the Union building, will appear with Jimmy Cathcart and his band at the Union-A.W.S. dance from 9 to 12 o'clock tonight in Alumni hall.

Little Marvin, who, in spite of his extreme youth, taps the "ivories" in true rag-time style, will play the piano with the band and do several tap dance routines, Hal Lieber, '38, business manager of the orchestra, said Thursday. Marcella Chandler, the other half of the duo, will not be with her brother, Lieber stated.

Residents of Bloomington.

The twins are colored residents of Bloomington and are well known in this city as child entertainers. They received the approval of a capacity crowd of University students Wednesday night at the Foundation day birthday party held in Alumni hall. They also entertained on the program of "Club Hi-Hat," cabaret show, which was held April 30.

Jimmy Cathcart, '38, will bring the big "bull" fiddle to the front tonight in another feature of the dance, when he gives his own interpretation of "Dinah." "Warpy" Waterfall, '39, has dressed up an old tune for re-presentation by making a new arrangement of "If I Could Be With You One Hour Tonight."

The dance tonight is the first of three Union-A.W.S. dances to be held during the remainder of the semester. A dance is scheduled for next Friday night and the annual post-prom dance will be held Saturday night, May 22, the Union-A.W.S. dance committee has announced.

University Budget To Be Considered By Board Monday

Trustees Will Review Pension Plan for Faculty, Administrative Officers.

Chief among the University administrative issues that will be presented for consideration at the scheduled meeting of the University Board of Trustees Monday are the budget for the 1937-38 school year and the faculty retirement plan, which would pension all faculty members and administrative officers reaching a stipulated age.

President William Lowe Bryan has worked untiringly during the past few months, conferring with department heads and compiling the budget data into tables and forms suitable for presentation to the trustees at their meeting Monday.

Adoption Is Doubtful.

According to Paul Feltus, member of the Board of Trustees, it is not likely that the budget will reach formal adoption Monday. A substantial increase in State appropriations and the intricate task of preparing a financial arrangement that will supply the needs of the pension plan will require additional consideration at the board meeting in June, Feltus explained.

Prof. Raleigh W. Holmstedt of the School of Education, active chairman of the faculty pension plan committee, listed Thursday the outstanding features of the plan, as accepted last semester by a unanimous vote of the faculty.

Through a joint contribution arrangement the faculty and University each will contribute half the necessary funds. Although the committee has not definitely agreed to admit all University employes as beneficiaries of the plan, arrangements at present provide for a 5 per cent deduction from the monthly salaries of all participants, an equivalent amount being contributed by the University.

ACACIA PLEDGES KOCH.

Acacia, social fraternity, last night announced the pledging of Elmer Koch, '39.

Bryan Scholarship Fund Soars Over $15,000 Mark

The William Lowe Bryan Scholarship and Fellowship fund Thursday increased to more than $15,000, according to an incomplete report released last night by Otto Grant, '37, co-chairman of the student executive committee which proposed the plan.

With only five of 21 social fraternities and less than half of the sororities reporting incomplete returns, the solicitating was beginning to get under full way after the first period of a day and a half, Grant said. In order to bring the movement to an end within the planned period, members of the executive committee were unanimous last night in urging all of the 200 student workers to file pledge cards as soon as possible in the Bryan fund office of the Union building.

Of 275 student pledges selected at random from Thursday's returns, the average contribution amounted to $24.26. Later contributions from unreported students are expected to keep the figure near the first day's average of $25.

Commenting on the apparent confusion among students regarding the manner of pledging, Grant last night gave The Daily Student the following statement. "I wish to make clear that this is a voluntary contribution and that each student in pledging should arrange his payments in a manner most convenient to him."

P0035363, IU Archives.

HE SERVES BEST WHO SERVES THE TRUTH

THE INDIANA DAILY STUDENT

THE WEATHER
Cloudy and cooler, showers in east, south portions today; Thursday fair, warmer.

VOL. LXVII—NO. 109.——Z 174. INDIANA UNIVERSITY WEDNESDAY, MARCH 23, 1938. BLOOMINGTON, INDIANA ESTABLISHED 1867

WELLS TAKES UNIVERSITY HELM

A. E. Morgan Dismissed From TVA

Ousted Chairman Ready To Resist Roosevelt Order

Fight Expected in Courts, Congress—H. A. Morgan Elevated.

WASHINGTON, March 22.—(AP)—President Roosevelt summarily dismissed Chairman Arthur E. Morgan of TVA from office today, precipitating what many believed would be a bitter controversy in the courts and in Congress.

For Morgan, long engaged in controversies with other directors of the public power agency, was ready to resist the Chief Executive's order, and critics of TVA at the capitol were eager to bare the agency's innermost secrets in a congressional investigation.

Vice-Chairman Elected.

Mr. Roosevelt elevated Vice-Chairman Harcourt A. Morgan to the chairmanship. He has aligned himself with Dictator David E. Lilenthal in opposing the policies of Chairman Morgan. In informed sources, it was said the vacancy of the board might be filled tomorrow, possibly by the appointment of James L. Fly, now TVA's general counsel.

At any rate, Congress will be notified officially of Chairman Morgan's removal tomorrow. Mr. Roosevelt said he wuld send a message embodying the record of his recent personal investigation of the TVA row and incorporating an opinion by Attorney General Cumings citing his authority for his action.

Even before receiving the message, however, legislators were quick to praise or blame the President tonight. Senator Bridges (Rep.-N.H.) said the dismissal was an act of "the typical dictator," while Speaker Bankhead declared it was "thoroughly justified."

"Well, That's That," Is Morgan's Comment

YELLOW SPRINGS, Ohio, March 22.—(AP)—A terse "Well, that's that!" was Arthur E. Morgan's comment today on his removal at TVA chairman.

He indicated he would take no immediate steps to oppose the President's action.

Only a few hours before, he had precipitated his removal by again bluntly defying President Roosevelt's authority to oust him.

Mr. Roosevelt had given Morgan until 2:30 p.m. today to state "any reason" why he should not be removed, and at that hour the raw-boned, six-foot engineer, 59 years old, was in his shirt sleeves chopping trees at his home here.

"No action on my part is necessary," he said as the deadline passed.

U.S. Sends Panay Bill to Japanese

WASHINGTON, March 22.—(AP)—The United States requested Japan today to pay $2,214,007.36 for the Panay incident.

The bill was itemized as follows:

Property losses—$1,945,670.01.

Deaths and injuries—$268,337.35.

Three Americans died and two-score persons were injured as Japanese planes bombarded the U. S. Gunboat Panay and three Standard Oil tankers last Dec. 12. The Panay sank, and the tankers were sunk or beached.

COPS END SOUR RENDITION OF "SWEET ADELINE"

NEW CASTLE, March 22.—(AP)—Musical criticism as the New Castle Police department writes it:

"Call to — avenue, 1:55 a.m. . disturbance. A quartet doing wrong by 'Sweet Adeline.'

"Selection ended by officers Ocker and Dinkins."

Auction Block Will Feature Spring Styles

A special group of spring coats and hats will be featured at the second auction of unclaimed articles from the Bookstore's Lost and Found department from 3 to 4:45 o'clock this afternoon in the Commons. Charles Sparrenberger, law '38, again will serve as auctioneer.

Two ladies' spring coats and a man's sport coat are to be placed on the block along with an automatic pencil, a pair of pigskin riding gloves, an umbrella, a pair of Oxford glasses, notebooks and costume jewelry.

Students may inspect articles at the department and request that certain ones be auctioned off, Harold W. Jordan, manager of the Bookstore, said Tuesday.

'Hasty Pudding' To Run 2 Nights

First Experimental Theatre Play Will Have Premiere Tonight.

"Hasty Pudding," first of a series of original plays to be staged this semester by the Experimental theatre, will be presented two nights, instead of one, as previously was announced. The first performance will begin at 7 o'clock this evening in Kirkwood 41. The second will be given at the same time Thursday.

According to L. Foster Harmon, director of the Experimental theatre, the change has been made in order that more persons may see the play.

"Hasty Pudding" is a broad comedy written by Robert Maloy, '38, in the style of eighteenth century plays. It is a burlesque of the complicated and involved plots written during that period with the characters drawn after the pronounced types so popular in drama then.

The cast includes George Rauch, '41; Gaylord Allen, '39; Kay Kerrick, '40; Mary Susan Stull, '41; Forrest Comrie, '41; Patricia Shane, '41, and Vivienne Weiss, '40. All persons who have season books for the University Theatre, and all students enrolled in courses in the Division of Speech are invited to attend. There will be no charge for admission.

Indiana On the Air

WIRE 1400 kilocycles Today

4-4:15 p.m.—Indiana University Variety Show.

Vera Mae Massey, '41, will present a dramatic interpretation of Amy Lowell's poem, "Patterns." There will be a musical accompaniment played by Dick Shores, '39.

Bob Lee, PG, is to be the announcer.

April 1 Is Set As Deadline for Board Petitions

Union Nomination Papers Required To Have 50 Signatures.

Nomination petitions of students desiring to be elected to the three remaining positions on the Union Board should be filed before April 1, Edwin H. Ham, '38, president of the Board, said last night.

Two candidates of at least junior standing in the University and one candidate of sophomore standing are to be named in the election which will be held April 6. All members of the Union, men students of the University in good standing, are eligible to vote in the election.

50 Signatures Required.

The petition of any student for candidacy is to be signed by at least 50 Union members. The petition is a request to place a student's name on the Union election ballot and is to be signed by the student filing for election. The candidate is required to attach a notarized statement saying each signature on his petition is authentic and that each signer is a member in good standing of the Union.

After receiving the endorsement of the University registrar that the petition is correctly made out and that the student is of the standing stated, the petition is to be filed with the president of the Union Board or sent to him in a sealed envelope left at the Union desk.

Reservations Due Today for Annual Theta Sig Banquet

Coeds who would see the feminine elite of the campus panned and roasted at the Theta Sigma Phry Cooking school Thursday night in Alumni hall should make reservations by noon today at the Chi Omega house. Approximately 400 coeds are expected to attend the tenth annual Razz banquet sponsored by Theta Sigma Phi, professional journalistic sorority.

Only when "the 400" are "done-in to a turn" will their hopes for revenge rest in the tongue of Doris Seward, '38, who will serve the return razzberries on Miss Lotta Dough, noted "coking" expert, and her assistants. "It'll burn 'em up," was Miss Seward's only comment Tuesday when questioned as to the nature of her comeback.

As a final serious note in the evening's festivities, a senior ring will be awarded to an outstanding senior coed elected on the basis of scholarship, character and leadership.

SEEK TO BUY BRIDGE.

WASHINGTON, March 22.—(AP)—A bill introduced today by Representative O'Neal (Dem.-Ky.) would authorize Kentucky to purchase the Louisville municipal bridge over the Ohio river between Louisville and Jeffersonville, Ind.

Audience Lauds Sevitzky In Music Series Finale

With two encores and repeated curtain calls the Indianapolis Symphony orchestra under the direction of Fabien Sevitzky completed the 1937-38 Music Series last night with a concert before approximately 1,500 music enthusiasts.

In spite of the unusual length of the first number, the audience seemed consistently attentive and pleased with the orchestra's interpretation of the Kalinnikoff symphony.

Before playing the Suite from "Peter Ibbetson," Sevitzky made the following announcement concerning the selection: "This suite was especially arranged by the composer upon my request because I am so fond of the opera. In January he arranged it and you now have the privilege of hearing it for the first time—anywhere!"

Perhaps the most popular selection on the program was "Moto Perpetuo," a composition portraying the state of perpetual motion. The effect was achieved by a technically difficult violin solo played by the first violins.

In response to repeated curtain calls, the orchestra offered two encores, "Govotte" by Lully and "The Blue Danube" by Strauss. Sevitzky then thanked the audience for the flattering reception and expressed the hope that he and the orchestra might return next year.

Eleventh and Youngest

University President Herman B Wells

Writing Quality Depends Upon Public—Jackson

200 Hear Noted Author at Theta Sigma Phi Alumnae Luncheon.

We will have greater fiction writers in America only when the reading public is ready for them, Margaret Weymouth Jackson, noted Indiana author, told more than 200 women faculty members and townswomen Tuesday at the annual spring luncheon sponsored by the alumnae chapter of Theta Sigma Phi, professional journalistic sorority.

If we would have a new literary form in fiction, if we would alter literary tradition to make it conform to the world as we know it, the one group that can bring about this change is composed of the women who buy and read magazines, the writer said. As long as women are satisfied with the stereotyped forms of modern fiction, we cannot change our literary conceptions, Mrs. Jackson explained.

Speaking on "Fiction in the Making," Mrs. Jackson analyzed several of her own stories, discussing their construction and how they originated. The measure of talent a writer has cannot be controlled, she said, but is endowed from sources outside oneself. When a writer has used his measure of talent to the extent of his ability, it does not matter that he is not a great writer, for there is no immediate measure of judging what is or is not great, Mrs. Jackson explained.

Alumnae To Show Engel Art Exhibit

An exhibit of 25 watercolors and 20 photographic portraits by Mr. Harry Engel of the Fine Arts department will be shown during April at the Art institute of Ft. Wayne under the auspices of the Ft. Wayne alumnae chapter of Pi Beta Phi, social sorority.

Several of the pictures which Engel exhibited at the Bookstore this year will be included in the display. Photographs of Walter E. Treanor, judge of the United States Circuit Court of Appeals at Chicago, and Hanya Holm, modern dance artist who appeared on the campus in February, will be shown. Watercolor landscapes of Southern Indiana scenes also will be included.

Mrs. Walter E. Thornton, Ft. Wayne, is chairman of the exhibit.

F.D.R. TO VACATION.

ABOARD ROOSEVELT TRAIN, March 22.—(AP)—President Roosevelt travelled southward tonight for a ten-day rest at Warm Springs, Ga.

A.A.U.P. Discusses Leaves With Pay

Chapter Will Circulate Questionnaire To Sound Out Faculty Opinion.

The University chapter of the American Association of University Professors discussed the plan of leaves-of-absence with pay at its March meeting Monday night. The chapter decided to send out questionnaires to the general faculty asking opinions on the plan.

The questionnaire, which will include queries on the amount of pay, the length of absence and the rank of those entitled to pay if the proposed plan is adopted, will be discussed at the April meeting.

The A.A.U.P. has 14,000 members who are teachers in 523 schools in the United States. The group is considered to be one of the most forceful agencies in the country in shaping policies and influencing academic trends. With all schools and departments represented, the University chapter has 137 members.

Rebels Advance; Fear Italian Aid May Be Recalled

HENDAYE, France, at the Spanish Frontier, March 22.—(AP)—The Spanish Insurgent Aragon offensive was speeded up today amid reports that British-Italian negotiations would bring withdrawal of Italian troops from Insurgent forces.

Insurgents sent word they had driven Government troops from five barricaded trench lines at Valdcalgorfo and resumed their drive toward Catalonia and the Mediterranean coast.

The object of Generalissimo Francisco Franco's drive is to separate Catalonia, the northeast portion of Spain, from the rest of Government-held territory.

His troops launched a heavy attack today in the sector about 10 miles southeast of Alcaniz and some 35 miles from the sea. Insurgents asserted Government troops suffered 2,000 casualties in hand-to-hand fighting.

Withdrawal of Italian troops, they said, would not mean that German and Italian guns, planes and other armaments and equipment would be withdrawn. German and Italian military advisers likewise were expected to remain.

SAYS CZECHS WILL RESIST.

PITTSBURGH, March 22.—(AP)—Dr. Jan Papanik, Czechoslovakian consul in Pittsburgh, warned today that any attempt by Reichsfuehrer Adolf Hitler to interfere in Czechoslovakia "will be met with stubborn resistance."

"But there will be no war unless Germany starts it," he added.

Youngest President Ever To Direct I.U. Chosen by Trustees

Former Business School Dean Succeeds William Lowe Bryan, Who Retired Last July—Selection Culminates Year's Search by Board.

Herman B Wells Tuesday became the eleventh president of Indiana university—the youngest in the school's history. He was chosen unanimously by the Board of Trustees after a 17-minute session in the Trustees' room in the Administration building.

Wells served as acting head since last July and before that was dean of the School of Business Administration.

The election was the culmination of a year's search in which hundreds of candidates from all parts of the country were interviewed in an attempt to select a successor to President Emeritus William Lowe Bryan, who retired last July after serving at the helm of the University for 35 years.

Following is the Board's official announcement.

"Herman B Wells is this day elected president of Indiana university.

"With great expectations, we invite him to great responsibilities. His observed experience, practical wisdom, admirable temperament and high ideals give conspicuous assurance of enduring achievement. With trust in him, we have confidence in the future."

The new president made the following statement:

"I have a deep sense of the great responsibility which the position carries. But I likewise appreciate the vast opportunity which it offers for service to my beloved alma mater and to the people of the state of Indiana.

"During the past few months, I have enjoyed the wholehearted co-operation and support of Dr. Bryan, the Board of Trustees, my advisory committee, the alumni and friends of the University and the faculty and student body; and I acknowledge with gratitude that co-operation. In the months and years to come, I shall strive to merit the continued co-operation of these same persons and groups and shall give all of my energy to the maintenance of Indiana university's great heritage of educational leadership."

Is 35 Years Old.

Thus, at 35, President Wells becomes the youngest chief executive of a state universtiy and the seventy-first Indiana university man to become head of an institution of higher learning.

Past presidents of the University since its organization as a college in 1828 are: Andrew W. Wylie, 1829-1851; Alfred Ryors, 1852-1853; William Mitchell Daily, 1853-1859; John H. Lathrop, 1859-1860; Cyrus Nutt, 1860-1875; Lemuel Moss, 1875-1884; David Starr Jordan, 1884-1891; John Merle Coulter, 1891-1893; Joseph Swain, 1893-1902, and William Lowe Bryan, 1902-1937.

Hold Press Conference.

At a press conference Tuesday morning, Ora Wildermuth, president of the Board, said that the more the Trustees searched for a

(CONTINUED ON PAGE TWO)

Page Diogenes

BEDFORD, March 22.—(AP)—Benjamin Payton, 16-year-old boy who said he had hitchhiked from Mitchell, ten miles south of Bedford, was admitted to the Lawrence County jail today when he produced papers signed by Thomas J. Wood, Mitchell justice of the peace, committing him to jail for eleven days on assault and battery charge.

Appointment Comments

Statements secured Tuesday from various administration heads, faculty members and townspeople indicate the genuine admiration and respect with which President Wells is regarded. The following statements were made after the selection of the new president.

President Emeritus William Lowe Bryan: "The selection of Dean Wells as president of Indiana university gives me great satisfaction. Since the decision was made a member of the Board has said to me that after interviews with more than 20 persons east and west who were recommended by eminent advisors, they found Dean Wells peer of the best of them. I trust the wisdom of that judgment.

"I have come to know that Dean Wells has a clear vision of what a university is for. A university president is lured in every direction to establish new, popular fields of work. President Wells will not be led astray by such temptations. He will consider the old and the new with wise deliberation so as to put the strength of the University vigorously behind those things which are truly fundamental.

"It will be a great pleasure to me to join with all the members and friends of the University in hearty support of President Wells in the great work to which he has been called."

Dean W. D. Gatch of the Indiana University School of Medicine: "I am delighted by the appointment of Mr. Wells. The trustees could not have done better. In the past year, Mr. Wells has demonstrated beyond a doubt his ability to bear the great responsibilities of the presidency of the University. He has shown a sympathetic understanding of the affairs of the Medical center. I am pleased to have the appointment go to an Indiana man who will cherish the fundamental traditions and qualities of the University."

W. A. Alexander, Indiana university librarian: "I am very much pleased that Herman Wells has been elected president of our University. The Trustees could not have made a wiser choice. He has so many qualifications for the position, that I feel sure his election will be accepted with favor by faculty, students, alumni, and by citizens generally."

Dean H. L. Smith, School of Education: "The faculty of the School of Education is happy to join the other faculties in congratulating Acting - President Wells on the signal honor that has come to him in his election to the presidency of our University. The opportunities connected with the future guidance of Indiana university are great indeed. The responsibilities are of vast significance. We pledge our support to President Wells in his efforts to advance the influence of Indiana university, and we believe that under his leadership our institution will continue to grow in importance as a leader in State and National educational circles."

Dean Bernard C. Gavit of the Law school: "As a friend I am happy over this deserved promotion. As a member of the University community, I am confident that the one right man has been found for the presidency. He has high and significant ideals as to what the University should be and he has the ability to make those ideals effective. I am sure that under his leadership, Indiana university will be developed into one of the outstanding schools of the country."

Prof. R. E. Cavanaugh, director of Indiana University Extension division: "Trustees of Indiana university could have made no better choice. President Wells has proved his ability in every phase of University work. As a student he was outstanding, as a teacher he was popular and successful, as a dean he brought his school to a high ranking position among the country's schools of business administration and as acting president during the past nine months he has guided the University program with rare good judgment and tact. The success of President Wells is assured, for in addition to his high personal qualifications for the position, he has the solid support of the faculty, the Trustees and the people of the State, all of whom he knows so well. Indiana university will prosper under the administration of President Wells."

Dean S. E. Stout of the College of Arts and Sciences: "In the short time that President Wells has been guiding the course of the University as acting president he has shown fine qualities of leadership in a difficult situation, and has won the hearts of faculty and student body. His appointment will meet with universal approval. He will have behind him at once a unity of support and enthusiasm that a stranger could only have won slowly. His work in the School of Business Administration has been the outstanding development in the University in the last two years. I look forward confidently to equal success in his administration of the University as a whole."

Dean B. W. Merrill of the School of Music: "I am happy to know that after this interim the University has a head, a strong executive, who can carry it on in its new growth in the service of the State. It is a great opportunity."

Dr. G. D. Timmons, secretary of the Indiana University School of Dentistry and assistant to the dean of the school: "The faculty of the Indiana University School of Dentistry has been informed this morning of the appointment of Dean H. B Wells as president of Indiana university and we wish to state that we, as a body, are highly gratified over this selection. In the year that has elapsed since Dean Wells took over his duties as acting president of the University he has proved his worth in every capacity and the faculty of this school looks forward towards great progress in the advancement of Indiana university under his splendid direction."

Dr. Matthew Winters, president of the Indiana University Alumni association: "As president of the Indiana University Alumni association, I want to congratulate the Trustees of Indiana university upon their selection of H. B Wells as president. He brings to

(CONTINUED ON PAGE TWO)

Prof. Snoddy Explains Change in Viewpoint Of Harvard Scientist

The change in the psychological thought of Prof. Karl S. Lashley of Harvard university was the theme of an address given Tuesday by Prof. George S. Snoddy of the Psychology department. The discussion was the sixth in a series of lectures sponsored by the department.

The change referred to by Prof. Snoddy dealt with the turn of Prof. Lashley from the mechanical to the thinker school of psychology. Prof. Snoddy said this change was brought about by the influence of C. J. Herrick, a contemporary psychologist.

Prof. Snoddy explained Lashley's aversion to teaching, saying Lashley would rather spend his time doing research work than instructing classes.

P0055934, IU Archives.

1939–1954

The World War II and post-war years were a time of seismic change for the world. Immediately after the bombing of Pearl Harbor, men began to serve in the armed forces, leaving women to run the newsroom. Thirteen consecutive female editors oversaw the coverage of major events, including D-Day and V-E and V-J Days. The staff said goodbye to a cherished friend in Ernie Pyle—but nine years after his death, would celebrate the opening of a brand-new journalism building dedicated in his memory.

The newsroom in 1942.
P0037428, IU Archives.

56,000 Crowd Fairgrounds To Set New Sunday Record

THE EIGHTEENTH ANNUAL STATE FAIR ISSUE OF
THE INDIANA DAILY STUDENT

VOL. LXVIII—NO. 173—Z 174. INDIANA UNIVERSITY MONDAY, SEPTEMBER 4, 1939. BLOOMINGTON, INDIANA ESTABLISHED 1867

THE WEATHER
Fair today and tomorrow with possible showers late today.

1914 RE-ENACTED IN EUROPE

Small, Fast Field Slated for Horseman Futurity

Spectators Fill Stands To View 'Lucky' Teter

Grand Circuit Racing And Live Stock Judging Begin Today.

Peak Crowds Expected

Lieut.-Gov. Schricker Speaks To Unions—Crowds Are Orderly.

By DICK BEAVANS

Despite the threat of inclement weather late in the day, 56,000 thrill-seeking Hoosiers stormed the Indiana State Fairgrounds for "War Veterans' Day" Sunday, setting a new Sunday attendance record and assuring the success of the first half of the double Labor Day holiday, featuring the bang-up exhibition by "Lucky" Teeter and his daring crew of "Hell Drivers."

As judging of live stock and poultry in open classes and five days of Grand Circuit harness racing begin today, Fair officials expect attendance to surpass all previous Labor Day records. The day's headline event will be the three-year-old Horseman Futurity trot, with an estimated purse of $3,160 at stake.

Grandstand Filled.

With 11,500 spectators filling the Grandstand to its capacity Sunday, an additional throng of almost equal dimensions stood in awe about the infield and along the track as the "Hell Drivers" drove their mechanical mounts through a gruelling pace of motor car acrobatics.

First item carded on Sunday's program was the Sunday School session at 9:30 a.m. in the auditorium of the Indiana University building, which was presided over by Lieut-Gov. Henry F. Schricker.

Horse Show in Evening.

For evening entertainment, the Fair offered the Horse show and judging of heavy draft horses in the Coliseum and a presentation of the stage show, "Belles of Liberty," and fireworks before the Grandstand.

In observance of "War Veterans' Day," visitors were treated with afternoon and evening concerts at the Grandstand and in the Coliseum by the American Legion all-state band and with a parade about the Midway by the Tilford H. Harpole American Legion Post Drum and Bugle corps.

Additional music was furnished about the grounds by the Newsboys' band of the Indianapolis News and the Lions Club all-State band. High school and University musicians played at the Hoosier Music Festival in the Indiana University building.

Though clouded skies held down the number of heat prostrations, cases handled at the Red Cross Emergency hospital mounted to a

(CONTINUED ON PAGE THREE)

CARRIER BOYS ATTEND FAIR.

Among Sunday's visitors to the Fairgrounds were 50 carrier boys of the Washington Herald, attending the Fair as guests of their "boss," Paul Bausman, editor and publisher of the Washington Herald and president of the State Associated Press.

New I.U. Song Makes Its Debut With Fair's Music Festival Band

Students at Indiana university as well as the institution's old grads will have a new song to learn this fall, Russell P. Harker, Frankfort attorney, and I.U. alumnus, having composed and written words for a song which will be known as "Indiana Victory."

Members of the University School of Music faculty and Director Frederick E. Green of the University Band believe the new composition, which has been published by the Thornton W. Allen Co., of New York, publishers of such widely known college songs as "On Wisconsin," Michigan's "Victors" and "For the Honor of Old Purdue," will become as popular as Harker's "Indiana, Our Indiana," written in 1912. The new song is receiving its initial tryout by the Hoosier Music Festival Band in the Indiana university auditorium at the State Fair.

The composer of "Indiana Victory," a former member of the Indiana legislature, is a native of Portland, Ind., and received his A.B. degree from the University in 1912 and his LL.B. degree in 1913. During his student days from 1911 to 1913 he served as director of the I.U. Band which then was composed of 30 members who received no credit for their work. It was while acting as band director that he arranged the now well-known "Indiana, Our Indiana," the melody of which has been taken over by many high schools of the State for their school song.

Indiana University Building

Basketball Combines With Medicine To Draw Throngs to I. U. Exhibit

Presenting everything from basketball rule demonstrations and stage shows to medical research and emotion measurement, Indiana university's building at the State Fair has been jampacked with visitors during the first three days of the Fair.

A stage show, sponsored by the University, is continuous from 9 a.m. to 9 p.m. each day. A one-act play written by Paul Boxell, '40, the plot which is based on the fair, is being offered. Members of the University Theatre are the actors. Portions of the continuous stage shows are being carried on the radio by WOWO of Ft. Wayne and WIRE of Indianapolis.

Exhibits have been arranged representing many departments of the University. Dr. Paul Weatherwax, professor in the Department of Botany, is exhibiting a hybrid corn which will

(CONTINUED ON PAGE THREE)

State Fair Program Today

LABOR DAY

Livestock

Horses—Grooms Contest and Gold Medal Colt Club, judged in Coliseum.

Cattle—All open steer classes, judged in Coliseum.

Sheep—Wool, and Gold Medal Lamb Club judged in Sheep Arena.

Swine—Yorkshire and Fat Barrows, judged in Swine Arena.

Poultry—Judging in Poultry Building.

GRANDSTAND

Afternoon—Grand Circuit Races, Vaudeville.

Night—Stage Show, "Belles of Liberty" and Fireworks, 7:45 p.m.

COLISEUM

Day—Purdue students judging cattle, 8 a.m.

Night—Horse Show, Parade of Champions, Band concert, 7:15 p.m.

Heavy Draft—Geldings or mares, pairs, four years and over, judged at 7:30 p.m.

BROADCASTS

WFBM broadcasting from studio west of Administration Building.

WIRE broadcasting from studio.

WLS broadcasting from Prairie Farmer Booth in Grandstand.

WOWO broadcasting from stage in Indiana University Building, 1:30-2 p.m.

MUSIC

Indianapolis News Newsboys Band—News Tent.

Indianapolis Concert Band.

Lions' All-State Band.

Hoosier Music Festival, Indiana University Building.

EXHIBITS

Manufacturers' Building and Machinery Field Exhibits open until 10:00 p.m.

Education Exhibit open all day.

Model Farm Home open all day and evening.

Purdue University Exhibit open all day.

Conservation Department Exhibit open all day.

Indiana University Stage Show day and night, I.U. Building.

Style Show—Women's Building, 10:30 a.m.-2:30 p.m.

Johnny J. Jones' Rides and Shows open until 10 p.m.

175 Musicians Play Daily in Hoosier Festival

High School Players Live In Junior Activities Center.

Some 175 musicians from 136 Indiana high schools have been selected for the Hoosier Music festival this week at the Indiana State Fair, which is conducted annually under the joint auspices of Indiana university and the State Board of Agriculture. Band and orchestra directors of these high schools have been invited to nominate candidates from among their musical organizations for the festival.

The festival is one of the well-known features of the Fair and selection for participation in it is regarded as a high honor for high school musicians. Four scholarships to the University's School of Music will be awarded on the basis of proficiency shown by the high school musicians selected for the festival.

Frederick E. Green, director of the Indiana university band, will supervise the festival and Robert J. White, supervisor of music in the East Chicago schools, will be conductor of the orchestra, and Joseph A. Cremelspacher, music supervisor of the Crawfordsville schools, conductor of the festival band.

Festival participants will be housed this year for the first time in the new permanent buildings making up the State Fair Junior Activities center, which is located in the northwest section of the exposition grounds and consists of three buildings—two dormitories, one for boys and one for girls and each housing 750 persons, connecting with a central auditorium and exhibition hall building. At the center, also will be housed the Indiana Board of Agriculture Girls' Home Economics school and the 4-H Club members who yearly attend the Fair under the sponsorship of Purdue university. All the occupants will receive their meals prepared there under the supervision of trained dietitians during the Fair.

Musicians selected for the music festival will appear daily as a part of the stage program in the auditorium of the Indiana university Exhibit building, at the Grand Circuit races and the Fair's evening horse show.

NO TAIL LIGHT.

Everett Harrold of Gaston was fined $2 in Muncie city court for driving a horse-drawn wagon without a tail light.

Find Your Way Around the Fair

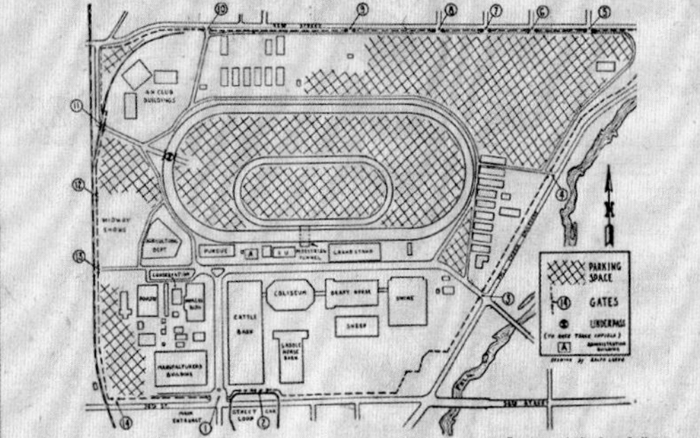

Courtesy of Outdoor Indiana.

Liner With 1,400 Refugees Is Torpedoed And Sunk As New World War Begins

BULLETIN
By The Associated Press

The Cunard White Star liner Athenia was torpedoed and sunk today off the Hebrides. It was bound from Glasgow to Montreal carrying 1,400 passengers—more than usual because of the numerous refugees aboard, many of whom slept on cots. In Washington the ship was said to be carrying "mostly Canadians and some Americans."

Britain and France went to war Sunday against Germany. They kept the pledges they made to Poland to see her through.

It is 1914 all over again; in most of Europe the guns must roar again.

Britain waited just 15 minutes beyond the deadline of her last ultimatum to Germany, that said in effect: Take your troops out of Poland or we fight.

And then Prime Minister Chamberlain, his old voice trembling in the most fateful address of all his long career, told the Empire:

"We are at war with Germany!

"I am certain right will prevail."

France, her mighty legions ready, followed suit automatically. Thus, the two great allies of the first world war take the field yet again against Germany.

12 Millions Under Arms.

It will mean more than a dozen million men under arms, it may mean the most widespread death and destruction in all history; it will mean billions of dollars to feed the guns; preparation alone for war cost the world a billion and a half dollars a month.

Meanwhile, the United States moved swiftly to invoke the neutrality act.

GREAT BRITAIN—Following Chamberlain's announcement of England's entrance into the war, King George broadcast an appeal to his empire to stand fast in this hour of conflict.

"We have been forced into a conflict," said the slender, youthful appearing monarch. "We are called with our allies to meet the challenge of a principle, which if it were to prevail would be fatal to any civilized order in the world." Meanwhile, Queen Elizabeth, who captured the attention of millions of Americans this summer while visiting the United States this summer, listened from another room.

The Duke of Windsor—former King Edward VIII of England—waited eagerly on the Riviera to start a plane flight home, British sources said. It was said that the Duke was in almost constant communication with London. If the Duke returned to his native land, his American wife the former Wallis Warfield, was expected to accompany him.

Eden in New Cabinet.

Two of Chamberlain's appeasement foes—Anthony Eden and Winston Churchill were taken into the new British war cabinet. Eden will serve as Dominions secretary and Churchill will be First Lord of the Admiralty.

The British Admiralty denied the accuracy of a report picked up by the Mutual broadcasting system in a short-wave broadcast from Paris that the $20,000,000 German Liner Bremen had been captured by the British Navy.

(CONTINUED ON PAGE THREE)

90 of 100 Say No!

Ninety out of 100 Hoosiers attending the State Fair Sunday believe that this country should not enter the second World War at the present time.

Fifty-eight think we should not send supplies to the Allies.

But 54 believe that this country should enter the war if the allies appear to be losing.

Most of those interviewed were emphatic in giving a negative answer to the first question. "The odds against Germany are overwhelming enough," as one elderly man phrased it, seemed to express majority opinion of the 1939 State Fair-comers.

Schricker Sees 4-H Display As 1939 Fair's Highlight

By LIEUT. GOV. HENRY F. SCHRICKER, Commissioner of Agriculture of Indiana

All my life I have been interested in agriculture and for the last two and a half years as Commissioner of Agriculture I have had an official interest in the agriculture of our State that has given me a new conception of the true greatness of our own Hoosier State.

Each of the past three summers I have traveled in many parts of the State, and I have never found the interest in our great State Fair that I have found this year. The advance sale of half-price tickets—200,000 of them—is the largest we have ever had, and I have been especially pleased that thousands of city folks as well as farm folks have bought these tickets. This sale assures our crowd and the success of the Fair.

This interest goes beyond mere attendance. Our exhibits are more numerous than ever before. Our good Hoosier folks are supporting this Fair not only by attending but by exhibiting the best from farm, home and factory. It takes the vast variety of things one sees at the State Fair to really "make"

(CONTINUED ON PAGE THREE)

3-Year-Olds Top Today's Card at Fairground Oval

2-Year-Old Trot and Pace Races Conclude Labor Day Crowd.

By TOM MILLER

A small but brilliant field of six of the nation's finest 3-year-old trotters will feature a stellar five-race speed program in the $3,160 Horseman Futurity at the Fairground track this afternoon. Also scheduled for today's activities are two 2-year-old races, one for pacers and one for trotters.

The Claypool Hotel 2:08 pace has been dropped because the roll was not filled, but the high number of entrants in the 2-year-old pace and the 2-year-old trot forced officials to divide each into two divisions with split purses. The division in those races will give harness-racing enthusiasts a full afternoon of the sport.

The closeness in performances of the Horseman Futurity entries make that race, second richest of the week's Grand Circuit racing, loom as a wide-open affair. As drivers sent their charges through their last workouts, several horses in the field were the object of much attention from the "rail-birds."

Athlone Iosola Great, owned by Leo McNamara of Indianapolis and to be driven by the city's own Sep Palin; Ned Abbey of the Good Time Stable, Goshen, N.Y.; Voltina, bay filly of Ben White, Lexington, Ky.; and Lyrmite, the brown filly of Thomas Berry of Lexington are all highly-regarded in pre-race predictions.

The races will be for two heats with a third heat to be run if the race is not decided by the first two trips around the mile oval. The track appears fast and veteran horsemen called it faster than the Good Time track at Goshen, N.Y., the scene of the famous Hambletonian.

In the 2-year-old trot the division of the field will send seven horses to the wire in the first di-

(CONTINUED ON PAGE THREE)

Henry Schricker Denounces War

"We want America to stay out of war and we do not want to sacrifice a single American boy or girl in war," declared Lieut. Gov. Henry F. Schricker during his address at the Sunday-school services conducted in the Indiana university building at 9:30 a.m. Sunday morning, and broadcast over radio station WIRE.

Instead, said Lieut. Gov. Schricker, "we want to make useful citizens of Indiana boys' and girls and to make them worthy of the great state of Indiana which they love."

Again the world is at war, Schricker said. Again the world has forgotten God and is seeking to destroy everything built up since 1918. Children in America are attending the great State Fair while the children in England are seeking refuge from the industrialized centers, he added.

"I thank God that I live in Indiana," concluded Lieut. Gov. Schricker.

Prior to Schricker's address, music was provided by a chorus made up of girls from the Home Economics school at the fair, and William Broom, a member of the staff of the University's music festival. Frederick E. Green, director of the famous "Marching Hundred," offered the opening prayer. John Marks, a 4-H club member of Clay county presided during the services.

P0078795, IU Archives.

December 10, 1940

HE SERVES BEST WHO SERVES THE TRUTH

THE INDIANA DAILY STUDENT

THE WEATHER
Cloudy to partly cloudy and considerably colder today; Wednesday generally fair.

VOL. LXX—NO. 59——Z 174. INDIANA UNIVERSITY TUESDAY, DECEMBER 10, 1940. BLOOMINGTON, INDIANA ESTABLISHED 1867

GENE WHITE TO LEAD '41 BO-MEN

British Capture 1,000 Italians in Egypt

RAF Rains Bombs On German Bases In South France

By The Associated Press

Britain's desert forces in a dawn strike at Italian invaders of Egypt had captured 1,000 prisoners by dusk Monday night, killed the Italian commanding officer and seized his assistant, the British command announced.

Fighting continued late last night possibly heralding a full-scale offensive by Britain in Egypt against Marshal Graziani's legions camped for three months 70 miles inside Egypt from Libya at the coastal base of Sidi Barrani.

Italian Command Shakeups.

The British attack coincided with military command shakeups in Italy, and newly announced Greek victories over the Fascists in Albania. A Greek government spokesman declared the entire Italian right wing north of Porto Edda had crumpled and that Greek troops also had secured new successes in northern Albania with the capture of strategic mountain peaks.

Against the German half of the Axis, R.A.F. pilots in Britain reported they rained explosives on or near Nazi submarines moored in the Bordeaux dock basins in southern France Sunday night.

The Egyptian operations came while London's bomb-wearied millions rallied from an all-night deluge of 700 tons of German explosives and 100 tons of fire bombs—an assault which the Germans described as the heaviest yet in the air siege of Britain.

500 Prisoners From Sidi Barrani

Dispatches from British desert forces said 500 prisoners were tak-

(CONTINUED ON PAGE TWO)

Fuehrer Speaks To Nazi Workers

Exactly a month after announcing Germany was strong enough to meet any combination of nations in the world, Adolf Hitler spoke to the workers of the Reich early today.

The Fuehrer's speech came close on the heels of the heaviest attack yet launched against London—Sunday's night raid on London.

None of the three major American radio networks carried the rebroadcast of Hitler's speech which was at 4 a.m. this morning. The Mutual Broadcasting company, however, recorded it and will carry it later today.

Since the speech was delivered after The Daily Student went to press, it is not known what the Fuehrer's speech was about. In reports last night the Associated Press said that it was expected Hitler would devote at least part of the address to reminding workers that Germany has delivered smashing blows in past months against London's war industries without receiving in return any approximation of similar bombardment.

Lacking any formal occasion for a talk, such as a special anniversary, observers could only speculate that something special was in the wind, including the possibility that he might announce aid to Italy in what has developed into a tough assignment against Greece.

Bookstore Receives Prof. Benns' Work

The University Bookstore recently has received copies of "Europe's Return to War," written by Prof. F. Lee Benns of the Department of History, and published on Dec. 2 in New York by F. S. Crofts and Company. Prof. Benns' study, a work of 120 pages, discusses the background, causes and course of the Second World war down to Nov. 15, 1940.

According to the author, it aims to blaze a pathway for readers through the bewildering succession of events which have occurred in Europe and the Far East since 1938.

The book is provided with five maps to illustrate the course of events, and has a five-page annotated bibliography for those who wish to read further on special topics.

Debaters Lose To Ohio

An Indiana debate team composed of Wayne Minnick and Len Bunger, both '42, was defeated Friday by an Ohio State university team on the Columbus campus. Indiana's debaters took the negative side of the topic, "Resolved, That the Powers of the Federal Government Shold Be Increased."

I. U. TEAM AT CAPITAL.

Bunger, Paul Bard, Minnick and William Robinson, all '42, debated last night before a speech class at the Indianapolis Extension Division. The class is taught by Robert Huber, director of debate.

"Joes" To Select Water Follies Queen From 35 Coeds in Commons Wednesday

Thirty-five queen aspirants will parade before the critical eyes of the Commons joeing crowd at 3:15 o'clock Wednesday afternoon in the first elimination of the Dolphin club's Water Follies Queen contest.

The 10 girls selected by ballot will enter the final competition at the afternoon performance of the Water Follies Saturday, Dec. 14. The coed topping the other nominees will rule with two attendants, the runners-up, at the evening performance.

Two Judges To Officiate.

Two of the judges in the final selection will be Bud Sawin, coach of the Rivera club at Indianapolis, and E. C. Hayes, University track coach. The two other judges have not yet been chosen. The winner will receive a trophy and her picture will appear in the Arbutus.

The candidates are:

Anna Shalkelford, Pat Fletcher, Mary Kelly, Pat Failing, Jean Shoemaker, Mary Giovanni, Marthada Vaughn, Jean McKee, Verna Taylor, Mary Alice MacCaa, Anna Lippencott and Winifred Brown, all '44.

Jean Shavinger Named.

Also, Jean Shavinger, Jane Shavinger, Barbara Brown, Margery Hasbrook, Emily Jean Clements, Virginia Thomas, Judith Jones, Irene Sanders and Martha Barnett, all '44.

Also, Carol Keene, Bettye Reckner, Marjorie Vale, Margaret Nunn, Elizabeth Hutchings, Dorothy Shimp and Inge Pelikan, all '43, and Mary Ellen Hines, Jane Pulley, Ardelle Welter, Carolyn Campbell and Mary Jane Funk, all '42.

'Leading' Women To Attend 18th Matrix Table Tonight

Prominent women of the University and of Bloomington will meet at 6 p.m. today in Alumni hall to hear Evelyn Eaton, author of "Quietly My Captain Waits" address the 18th annual Matrix Table.

Miss Evelyn Eaton.

Miss Eaton, who has been brought to the campus from Williamsburg, Va., where she is engaged in gathering material for her third historical novel, will reside at the Union building during her brief stay here.

Informal Reception.

Following the dinner and her talk on "Writing the Historical Novel" Miss Eaton will be the center of attraction at an informal reception also in Alumni hall.

Dark and vivacious, the bearing of Evelyn Eaton in part may explain her vivid depiction of Mme. Louise Guyon de Freneuse, the daring heroine of her best seller. Since Miss Eaton has spent her life cultivating an acquaintance with many different lands, that also may have assisted her in painting this French woman in the New World.

Men in Balcony.

Since many men have expressed their desire to hear Miss Eaton's talk, but are strictly taboo on the ground floor, the balcony will be thrown open to men only, Miriam James, '41, president of Theta Sigma Phi, sponsoring organization, announced.

Miss Eaton's most famous work, "Quietly My Captain Waits," which is now on display in the University Bookstore, is at the present time being prepared for motion pictures. Movie rights to the story were purchased for $40,000 while it was still in manuscript form.

Miss Bond, '36, Becomes Bride Of Dr. Weimer

Mrs. Arthur M. Weimer.

The marriage of Miss Mary Elizabeth Bond, '36, and Arthur M. Weimer, dean of the School of Business, was solemnized at 11 o'clock Saturday morning in the McKee chapel of the Tabernacle Presbyterian church in Indianapolis with the Rev. Roy Ewing Vale, pastor of the church, officiating.

Attending the couple were Miss Doris Decker, '36, and Croan Greenough, personnel director and assistant to the President. Only relatives and close friends were present at the wedding.

After the ceremony Mr. and Mrs. Weimer left for a brief trip to Chicago. They will be at home at 511 North Fess avenue in Bloomington after Jan. 1.

The bride, daughter of Mr. and Mrs. Starner Bond of Oaktown, was a teacher in the Mishawaka high school until her marriage. While on the campus, Mrs. Weimer was a member of Alpha Lambda Delta, freshman women's scholastic honorary; Le Cercle Francais, French club; the English club, the A.W.S. council, the International Relations club, Pi Lambda Theta, national education fraternity for women, and Phi Beta Kappa, scholastic honorary.

MRS. WEATHERWAX AWAY.

Mrs. Fannie Weatherwax, secretary and assistant to the dean of women, is on a vacation until Dec. 26. Mrs. Weatherwax will visit her sister, Mrs. Alice Howe, at Franklin, spend a week in Chicago and also visit Mr. and Mrs. Carl Moore of Gary.

Negroes To Sing Songs of Slaves At Convocation

Program To Be at 4 P.M.—Classes Will Meet at Regular Time.

The joy, pathos and religious devotion of original negro slave songs and spirituals will fill Alumni hall, when the Fisk Jubilee Singers from the Negro University at Nashville, Tenn., interpret the songs of their race at convocation at 4 p.m. Wednesday.

Originated in 1871 to raise money to save their school, the Fisk Jubilee Singers have made theirs

The Fisk Jubilee Singers will give the weekly convocation program which will be at 4 p.m. this Wednesday instead of at the usual time. Classes will meet at the regular daily hours, as no time allowance will be made for the convocation, according to W. S. Bittner, Associate Director of the Extension Division.

a history of performances before royalty and with symphonies. The members of the group that will sing on campus are direct descendants of the first Singers.

In 1875 the original group returned to Fisk university to dedicate Jubilee hall, named for them and built with the money they had earned singing. They had been received in the White House by the

(CONTINUED ON PAGE TWO)

Greenough-Decker To Be Married Soon

The approaching marriage of Doris Decker, '36, and William Croan Greenough, '35, personnel director of the University, has been announced by the bride-elect's parents, Mr. and Mrs. Adrion Decker of Decker. The wedding will take place in the near future.

The engaged couple were attendants at the recent marriage of Dean Arthur M. Weimer of the School of Business, and Mary Elizabeth Bond, '36, of Oaktown.

Miss Decker, a school teacher in the Bridgeton high school, is a graduate of Indiana university and a member of the Pi Beta Phi sorority

Mr. Greenough, son of Mr. and Mrs. Walter S. Greenough, 556 East Fall Creek boulevard, Indianapolis, was graduated from Indiana university and has the M.A. degree from Harvard university. He is a member of the Phi Kappa Psi fraternity and Phi Beta Kappa, honorary scholastic society.

Qualifications For Ideal Man Told by Coeds

A mental picture of the "Ideal Man" was presented to Y.M.C.A. members, who attended a supper Sunday evening at the Acacia house, by an open panel group of Y.W.C.A. members. The group was composed of Mary Jane Straub, '41, Millie Cox, Lois Armstrong, Joan Veit, and Jane Hudson, all, '42.

According to the speakers, ribald humor, "lines," and first date "smoochers" are definitely taboo. The girls gave another hint to the wise. When asking a girl for a date, the asker should not blunder by questioning, "What are you doing Friday evening." Ladies prefer the "Are you busy?" approach.

Tips to the Dateless.

A "tip" to the boys who "just can't get dates." The following formula, the girls decided, is sure to put any boy on the social blacklist: "Be conceited; devote all your time and attention to other women while on a date; talk about yourself all evening and interrupt her while she is speaking. This formula is sure to make you unpopular with the girls."

And to the boys who haven't been dating because financial conditions are "pretty tough," the following words of encouragement should prove enlightening. "We enjoy inexpensive dates just as much as we do extravagant affairs," quoted one member of the panel group.

Phi Betes Not Required.

Although most of the girls conceded the point that their "dates" should be intelligent, they added that they didn't expect hem to be in he "Phi Bete" class.

Barbara Johnson, '42, Pi Phi pianist, played Claude Debussy's "Clair de Lune," after the discussion. Vera Mae Massey, '41, closed the program with a reading entitled "The One On My Left."

THERE AIN'T NO JUSTICE.

Harold (Red) Zimmer, University halfback, played in all eight of Indiana's football games this year without injury.

The gridiron season over, he went out for intramural basketball and suffered a broken bone in his right foot.

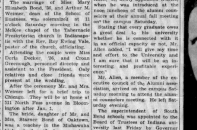

Frank Allen, New Trustee, Greets Alumni Counselors

"I consider my appointment quite an honor," said Frank E. Allen, '16, newly appointed trustee, when he was introduced at the noon luncheon of the alumni counselors at their annual fall meeting on the campus Saturday.

Stating that every graduate owes a great deal to his university whether he is connected with it in an official capacity or not, Mr. Allen added, "I will give my time and effort to the University and I am sure that it will be an interesting and profitable experience."

Mr. Allen, a member of the executive council of the Alumni association, arrived on the campus Saturday morning to attend the alumni counselors meeting. He left Saturday evening.

The superintendent of South Bend schools was appointed to the Board of Trustees of Indiana university last Friday by Governor M. Clifford Townsend upon recommendation of the State Board of Education. He succeeds Val Nolan who died Oct. 1 and whose term expires July 1, 1941.

(CONTINUED ON PAGE TWO)

Frank E. Allen.

NOTICE

Will the members of the following organizations please go to the Dexheimer-Carlon Studios sometime today and make arrangements to have their pictures on the organizations page in the 1941 Arbutus: Sphinx club, A.W.S. council and Y.W. C.A. council.

Lawyers To Hear Evens

Prof. Alfred Evens of the School of Law will speak to lawyers of Indianapolis and surrounding counties this afternoon and evening at the Legal Institute on the Law of Evidence at the World War Memorial building, Indianapolis.

The Institute is conducted by the Lawyer's association of Indianapolis.

Bill Smith Named Honorary Captain At Sports Dinner

Gene White, junior guard who kicked the field goal that won the Purdue game, was elected captain of the 1941 football squad and Bill Smith, '41, was elected honorary captain for the 1940 squad by football lettermen at the annual winter sports banquet last night in Alumni hall.

Gene White.

* * *

Bill Smith.

Almost 500 students, faculty members, alumni and football fans met to fete the varsity and freshman football teams and the National Collegiate champion cross-country team at the annual dinner sponsored by the Indiana Union.

Van Orman Praises Teams.

Introducing F. Harold Van Orman, president of the Van Orman hotels and principal speaker for the occasion, Ned Reglein, PG, toastmaster, asked Mr. Van Orman why his face was so red. Mr. Van Orman later admitted that he had acquired too much sun under a sun lamp in his attempt to appear masculine before Coach Bo McMillin.

Between his stream of rapid-fire repetoire and his embarassing questions to high University dignitaries, Mr. Van Orman congratulated the football and cross-country teams on their success of the past season and invited the 18 graduating gridders and the four graduating harriers to come to him for a job in the hotel business.

"The hotel business needs educated, well-reared boys like you," he said. "And when you are away from this great institution, out in the world, carry with you the thought of the great future of America."

Speaker Jokes With "Hermie."

Addressing President Herman B Wells in regard to the State Budget committee which was at the banquet, he said in a more humorous vein, "Herman, if I don't get you twenty million I'm a piker. Why, I even know enough on those guys to get you thirty."

(CONTINUED ON PAGE TWO)

Phi Beta Kappa Sets Dinner Date

The 17 seniors elected to Phi Beta Kappa last week will be initiated into the scholastic honorary at a dinner Dec. 16 in the Union building. The new members and those elected into the society at the 1940 Commencement will be guests.

Initiation services will follow the dinner, which 100 persons are expected to attend. The charge to the initiates will be given by Prof. Prescott W. Townsend of the Department of History, president of Phi Beta Kappa.

Assisting in the initiation ceremony will be Prof. Ford P. Hall, head of the Department of Government, vice-president, and Prof. Cecilia Hendricks of the Department of English, secretary.

At 8 o'clock the annual president's address will be delivered by Prof. Townsend in the Chemistry auditorium. His subject will be "Imperialism and Revolution in Ancient Rome." This talk will be open to the public.

Reservations for the dinner must be made before Dec. 15, Prof. Hendricks said. Tickets are on sale at the Union desk.

Union Will Entertain Service Men Tonight

Prof. J. J. Robinson of the Law School will speak at a smoker given for Union service workers at 8 o'clock tonight in the Men's lounge of the Union building, according to Hanly Hammel, '42, chairman of the Personnel committee.

A motion picture on Pan-American diplomatic relations, called "Good Neighbors," will be shown in addition to Prof. Robinson's talk on "The Framing of the Constitution of the Indiana Union," Hammel said.

All men students who have done Union service work are invited to attend. There will be refreshments and cigarettes, Hammel said.

Oceanides Water Pageant To Be Built Around Fairy Tale of the "Frog Prince"

A search for a bracelet of a princess will take place at 8 o'clock Wednesday night in the women's pool in the Student building when Oceanides, women's swimming honorary, presents its annual water pageant. The water stunts, races, relays, ballets and diving exhibitions by members of the club will be built around the fairy story of the "Frog Prince."

The princess, played by Mary Stuart Hayes, '41, loses her bracelet while playing on the edge of a lake. The loss causes her great sorrow and the king's jester, Marie O'Dowd, '42, carries the news to the princess' father, the king, portrayed by Ruthe Edwards, '43.

Search For Bracelet.

Because the princess will not be comforted until her bracelet is found, the king announces that his daughter's hand will be given in marriage to the one who retrieves the bracelet from the lake. One by one the king's attendants dive into the lake to search, but none of them are successful.

Finally a huge frog, played by Ada Schuelke, '41, leaps into the pool and brings up the bracelet, dropping it at the princess' feet. The king offers many things to the frog but he wants only the hand of the princess. As the princess shrinks in horror the frog tears off his headdress and appears as a handsome prince. The grand finale of the pageant ends with the entire cast retiring to the palace for a wedding feast.

Cast of Pageant.

The king's attendants are Ruth Baecher, Elmyra Holmdohl, Betty Nicholls, Madylon O'Dowd, Lenora Wilkinson, and Ruth Youll, all '41; Alma Freyn, Doris Trogdon and Emily Zankl, all '43; Jane Gaff, Jane Hudson, Marcile Irle and Jeanette Pass, all '42, and Marjorie Hasbrook, Jean Hilbert, Gertrude Knelleken, and Jean McKee, all '44.

The maidens are Nelda Johnson and Georgia Vorgang, both '41.

Christmas Arias by Concert Herald University Yuletide

By JUNE ROWLAND.

Music of familiar Christmas arias, sacred chorales and choruses filled the air Sunday afternoon—all of which seemed to herald the University Christmas season with the Choral Union presenting its annual concert in the Men's gymnasium.

To the audience who heard the ever-popular works from Bach's "Christmas Oratorio" and Handel's "Messiah," the concert was not new. For, traditionally, during the last 18 years, some chorus of the University has sung the whole, or parts of "The Messiah" during the Christmas season. The first performance was directed by Professor-Emeritus Edward B. Birge of the School of Music in 1922.

The audience Sunday heard again the beauty of the composite themes with their distinct counterpoint and the elaborate melodies of the aria. The chorus of 225 members sang with the skill of a much-reheased group. Their carrying power, tone color and effective control provoked much applause.

Each soloist might be singled out, for the individual performances were as unique as were their selections. To Betty Grimsley, '43, contralto, fell the task of "soloing" first. In her first presentation and throughout the program, Miss Grimsley sang with perfect sureness and command.

Bryant Millikan, '41, baritone, sang with clear-cut articulation the solo in the "Fantasia on Christmas Carols" by R. Vaughan Williams. Warren Wooldridge, '43, tenor, sang another difficult recitative with ease. Pure, clear tones were characteristic of both Naomi Bosworth, '43, and Elizabeth Haupt, '42, the soprano soloists.

True to a custom begun more than two centuries ago when the first audience who heard Handel's "Hallelujah Chorus" rose spontaneously to its feet, the audience Sunday did likewise. An informal note came at the close of the program, when the singers, also spontaneausly, sang Christmas carols as the audience left the gymnasium.

Few of the audience probably knew that the group which sang had rehearsed together less than an hour, for it was only during

(CONTINUED ON PAGE TWO)

P0070622, IU Archives.

Winston Fournier, center, and the editorial staff, including Anne Douglas, third from right, and Dan Holthouse, far right, in November 1941. *P0024014, IU Archives.*

Facing, In the custom of newspapers at that time, an extra was considered an extension of the most recent edition, which explains why the IDS Pearl Harbor extra was dated the day before the Pearl Harbor invasion. *P0036156, IU Archives.*

REFLECTION

The 'Lucky Coincidence' That Led to a Historic Extra

"When we started shouting out the "War Declared" headline . . . the band quit playing and instruments were put aside and the musicians joined in buying our papers . . ."

The biggest event that fall, of course, was the extra edition a gang of us put out—under the wise guidance of John Stempel—on Pearl Harbor Sunday, Dec. 7, 1941. When the news first came on the radio, several of us immediately gravitated to the little red IDS building and called Stempel to see about an extra. He said OK if he could round up a backshop crew, which he did. A lucky coincidence was the fact that someone forgot to turn off the heat under all the linotype pots for the weekend, so we had hot metal right off. Otherwise, it would have taken too long to get hot metal and there would have been no Extra. (It was normal custom to turn off the pots on weekends.)

All the reporter and editor types turned into newsboys as soon as the old web-type flatbed press started turning out the papers. As I recall, Dan Holthouse and I got the first hundred copies off the press and hastened to the Commons to hawk our wares. (In those days the Commons was always jammed on Sunday evening as Warpy Warterfield's band played, etc.) When we started shouting out the "War Declared" headline—set in wooden "second coming type"—the band quit playing and instruments were put aside and the musicians joined in buying our papers: price five cents.

Dan and I got back to the press for more papers before all the guys had gotten their first batch. We sold a lot of papers that night and we were one of the very few papers in the state to publish a Pearl Harbor Extra.

A few days later I resigned as editor because the Draft Board was insistent, and Anne Douglas became the first woman editor of the IDS. (*Editors' note: The first female editor was Florence Myrick Ahl in 1897.)*

—Winston Fournier, BA 1946, wrote this recollection in 1977 for the paper's 110th birthday. He died in 2007.

War Declared

EXTRA THE INDIANA DAILY STUDENT **EXTRA**

VOL. LXXI—NO. 60——Z 174. INDIANA UNIVERSITY SATURDAY, DECEMBER 6, 1941. BLOOMINGTON, INDIANA ESTABLISHED 1867

JAP BOMBS KILL 350 AT PEARL HARBOR

+ + +

Honolulu Center Of Jap Attack

NEW YORK, Dec., 7.—(A.P.)—Three hundred and fifty men were killed by a direct bomb hit on Hickman Field, an NBC observer reported tonight from Honolulu.

In addition to these casualties from an air raid by planes which the observer identified as Japanese, he said three U. S. ships including the battleship Oklahoma, were attacked in Pearl Harbor.

HONOLULU, Dec. 7.— (AP) —Japanese bombs killed at least seven persons and injured many others, three seriously, in a surprise morning aerial attack on Honolulu today.

Army officials announced that two Japanese planes had been shot down in the Honolulu area.

The dead, not immediately identified, included three caucasians, two Japanese and a 10 year old Portuguese girl.

Several fires were started in the city area, but all were immediately controlled.

Gov. Joseph B. Poindexter proclaimed M-Day emergency defense measures immediately in effect. He appointed Eduard Doty in charge of the major disaster council.

The M-Day proclamation established civilian-military control of traffic and roads, and permits the Governor to issue food ration regulations.

Spray Streets With Bullets.

First reports said 10 or more persons were injured when enemy planes sprayed bullets on the streets of Wahiawa, a town of around 3,000 population, about 20 miles northwest of Honolulu.

This report indicated the aerial attack was aimed at points on the island of Oahu other than Honolulu and the heavily fortified Pearl Harbor Naval Base.

The attack ended at about 9:25 A.M. (1:55 P.M. CST) lasting for approximately an hour and 15 minutes.

Witnesses said they counted at least 50 planes in the initial attack, which the army said started at 8:10 A.M. (2:40 P.M. CST).

The attack seemed to center against Hickam field, huge army airport, and Pearl Harbor, where the islands' heaviest naval fortifications are located.

Wave on Wave of Bombers.

Wave after wave of bombers streamed through the cloudy sky from the southwest, shattering the morning calm.

Perhaps the first to die was Bob Tyce, owner of a civilian airport near Honolulu, who had started to spin the propellor of a plane when the enemy came over one plane swooped down, machine guns blazing, and Tyce fell dead.

Most of the attackers flew high, but a few came low. Five came down to under a hundred feet elevation to attack Pearl Harbor. An oil tank there was seen blazing and smoking. Others apparently headed directly for Hickam field to drop bombs.

There was no immediate statement by military officials as to whether any service men were killed or injured, or as to property damage at military and naval posts.

See Rising Sun Emblem.

Spectators said they saw the Japanese Rising Sun emblem on the low flying planes.

Japanese Consul General Sajao Kita said he believed the bombing was "by United States Army planes on maneuver."

When told there were dead and wounded as the result

(CONTINUED ON PAGE THREE)

—EXTRA—

TOKYO, Dec., 8 (Monday) –(A. P.)– Japanese Imperial headquarters announced at 6 A.M. today that Japan had entered a state of war with the United States and Britain in the western Pacific as from dawn today.

MANILA, Monday, Ded., 8.—(A.P.—There were no signs of war and Manila was quiet at 5:25 A.M. today—3:25 P.M., C.S.T., Sunday).

Lieut.-Gen. Douglas MacArthur, commander of U. S. forces in the far east, was advised officially of the attack on Pearl Harbor and placed his entire command on the alert.

WASHINGTON, Dec. 7.—(AP)—The White House announced that Japan had attacked Guam.

WASHINGTON, Dec., 7.—(A.P.)—The White House announced at 2:22 P.M. CST today that an army transport carrying lumber rather than troops had been torpedoed 1,300 miles west of San Francisco. This placed Japanese naval action well east of Hawaii, toward the mainland.

There was no information whether the transport had been sunk or whether there was loss of life among the crew.

BERLIN, Dec. 7.—(AP)—A German spokesman declared tonight there could be no reaction from Germany to the announced Japanese air attack on Pearl Harbor until all sides of the case were at hand.

"We cannot comment," the spokesman said, "until full and exact details of the Japanese as well as the American statements are available."

(CONTINUED ON PAGE THREE)

Lieut.-Col. Shoemaker Says No Change In Program Here

By LIEUT. COL. R. F. SHOEMAKER

It does not now appear probable that any material change will occur in the military program at the University as a result of the Japanese crisis. It will be remembered by many that at the outbreak of the first World War, the campus was largely taken over by the War Department with the establishment of the Student Army Training Corps. This step was made necessary because of the urgent need for officer personnel. Largely through the operation of the R.O.T.C. installed shortly after the termination of the War, this situation does not now exist and at the present time approximately 100,000 Reserve officers are on active duty.

Many students will want to know what effect this crisis may have on the acceleration of the provisions of the Selective Service Act and particularly as it may apply to those who have been granted deferment for various reasons. It is regretted that a specific opinion cannot be given, the one logical conclusion appearing to be that only the development of time will furnish that answer.

WITH GRIM FACES Secretary of State Cordell Hull, special envoy Saburo Kurusu (right) and Ambassador Kickisaburo Nomura are shown as they appeared yesterday in Washington while still attempting to settle the Pacific question peacefully.

Cabinet To Meet At 8:30 Tonight

WASHINGTON, Dec. 7.—(AP)—The President decided today after Japan's attack on Pearl Harbor and Manila to call an extraordinary meeting of the cabinet for 8:30 p.m. tonight and to have congressional leaders of both parties join the conference at 9 p.m.

Mr. Roosevelt, the White House said, "is assembling all the facts as rapidly as possible and in all probability he will, as quickly as possible, make a full, informative report to Congress, probably in the form of a message."

At the time of his decision for a special meeting of the cabinet and congressional chieftains, Mr. Roosevelt was conferring with his war and navy secretaries and the Army chief of staff, Gen. George C. Marshall.

Presidential Secretary Stephen Early said that the meeting would emphasize international affairs rather than military strategy. He emphasized that for the time being Mr. Roosevelt was not calling in chairmen of the Senate and House Military and Naval committees.

WELLS PLEDGES FULL I.U. AID

Commenting on the Japanese attack on the U.S. Naval Bases at Pearl Harbor and Manila, President Herman B Wells said: "The news of the attack is tragic and terrible. It seems fantastic that Japan would take such a step. Indiana university, through the one hundred and twenty years on its history, has always done its full share in every national crisis and may be expected to do so again."

+ + +

U. S. Wins First Battle Is Report

By The Associated Press

Japan attacked the United States today, striking by air at the great Pearl Harbor Naval Base at Honolulu, and latest reports indicated that the United States had won the first battle in the new world war.

A bulletin from Honolulu said a naval engagement was in progress off that famed island playground, with at least one black aircraft carrier in action against Pearl Harbor's defenses.

Planes Battle Over Honolulu.

The British radio also reported that a "foreign warship" had begun bombarding Pearl Harbor.

Aerial dogfights raged in the skies over Honolulu itself as American warplanes rose to give battle to the Japanese invaders.

In Washington, the White House announced that a U. S. Army transport, carrying lumber rather than troops, had been torpedoed 1,300 miles west of San Francisco—thereby placing Japanese naval action well east of Hawaii, toward the United States mainland.

Damage to Base Unknown.

An N.B.C. broadcast from Honolulu said the Japanese attack had inflicted untold damage on the U.S. naval base at Pearl Harbor and on the city itself.

Several Japanese planes were reported shot down.

First reports from Honolulu said at least two formations of nine four-motored black bombers, marked with Japan's rising sun insignia, flew over Honolulu.

On the Pacific coast, the army and navy went onto an immediate war-time basis. All leaves were cancelled, all furloughs revoked. Every man was ordered to report to his post.

Announcing the President's action for the protection of American territory, Presidential Secretary Stephen Early declared that so far as is known now the attacks were "made wholly without warning—when both nations were at peace—and were delivered within an hour or so of the time that the Japanese ambassadors had gone to the state department to hand to the secretary of state Japan's reply to the secretary's memorandum of the 26th.

Promptly, Navy officers said that long prepared counter measures against Japanese surprise attacks had been ordered into operation and were "working smoothly."

And within a few minutes, the War department ordered all military personnel in this country into uniform.

There was a disposition in some quarters here to wonder whether the attacks had not been ordered by the Japanese military authorities because they feared the President's direct negotiations with the emperor might lead to an about-face in Japanese policy and the consequent loss of face by the present ruling factions in Japan.

Stephen Early, presidential secretary, said that as soon as the information of the attacks on Manila and Hawaii was received by the War and Navy departments it was flashed immediately to the President at the White House. Thereupon and immediately the President directed the Army and the Navy to execute all previously prepared orders looking to the defense of the United States.

Kichisaburo Nomura, the Japanese ambassador, and Saburo Kurusu, the special Japanese envoy, were at the State department at the time of the White House's announcement of the attacks.

The two Japanese went to see Secretary of State Hull at 1:35 p.m. (EST) and remained about 20 minutes.

They handed to the secretary Tokyo's reply to the statement of principles which he gave to them on Nov. 26.

After their departure, the State department announced that Hull had informed the Japanese that a document presented by them was "crowded with infamous falsehoods and distortions."

Mr. Spriggs says this is a mistake. No. 397 was omitted in numbering. Mary Bradley Oct. 6, 1944

HE SERVES BEST WHO SERVES THE TRUTH

THE INDIANA DAILY STUDENT

THE WEATHER
Fresh winds and considerably cooler Tuesday.

VOL. LXXII—NO. 398—Z 174. INDIANA UNIVERSITY TUESDAY, JUNE 6, 1944. BLOOMINGTON, INDIANA Established, 1867.

INVASION ON!

ALLIED TROOPS LAND IN FRANCE

Nazis First to Tell Of Activity on Coast

(The first indication that the invasion was on was a dispatch shortly after 12 o'clock this morning, quoting the German broadcasts. The highlights of this early dispatch, which was not confirmed until shortly after 2:30 a.m., Bloomington time, follows.)

LONDON, June 6 (Tuesday) — (AP) — Three German news agencies tonight flashed word to the world that an Allied invasion of Western France had begun with Allied parachute troops spilling out of the dawn skies over the Normandy peninsula and sea-borne forces landing in the Le Havre area.

There was no immediate Allied confirmation.

The Germans also said that Allied warships were furiously bombarding the big German-held French port of Le Havre at the mouth of the Seine River, 100 miles west of Paris.

German shock troops, the broadcast said, also were hurled against Allied troops rushing ashore from landing barges.

Le Havre lies 80 miles across the channel from the British coast. It is approximately 600 miles southwest of Berlin, a little more than the distance separating the Nazi capital from the Red Army lines in the East.

BUT WITH MUSIC.

LONDON, Tuesday, June 6—(AP)—The German-controlled Calais radio came on the air today with the following announcement in English:

"This is D-Day. We shall now bring music for the (Allied) invasion forces."

Dunkerque and Calais Bombed.

Dunkerque and Calais, just across the channel coast from Britain and 150 miles northeast of LeHavre, were under attack by strong formations of bombers, D.N.B. said.

The Berlin radio said lated that "combined Anglo-American landing operations against the western coast of Europe from the sea and air are stretching over the entire area between Cherboug and Le Havre."

Eisenhower's Instructions

LONDON, June 6—(AP)—A spokesman for Gen. Dwight D. Eisenhower, in a London broadcast, told the people living on Europe's invasion coast today that "a new phase of the Allied air offensive has started" and warned the to ove imnland to a depth of 35 kilometers (about 22 miles).

In a special broadcast over the B.B.C., directed to France and other coastal countries, the spokesman said:

"A new phase of the air offensive has started. It will affect the entire coastal zone situated not less than 34 kilometers inland from the French coast. People will be advised by special announcements dropped from Allied planes.

"The attack will take place less than one hour later. As soon as the warning has been given, the following orders are to be followed:

"First, leave the town at once.

"Second, choose such a route out of town as to avoid the main road.

"Third, leave on foot only carrying essentials.

"Fourth, go to the country at least two kilometers from town.

"Do not assemble in groups which might appear to be troop concentrations."

The broadcast advised the people to keep as far as possible away from roads and railroad lines and to take nothing with them they cannot carry personally.

The spokesman concluded with the advice that those able to leave the 35-kilometer coastal belt should do so at once, adding that those who cannot leave now must do so when the Allies give warning.

Planned for Four Years

Allied Command Has Built Machine to Retaliate.

By PAUL KERN LEE
Associated Press Foreign Staff

The Allied invasion of western Europe, largest and most daring such undertaking in the history of warfare by any standards, is the result of nearly four years of careful, methodical preparation.

Hardly had Britain's army in France been snatched from seemingly certain destruction at Dunkerque than plans for the eventful return were being laid.

For the time being Britain had to content herself with the all-out defense of her home islands against the German aerial blitzkrieg. Mid-September, 1940, was the high point of that battle. Air attacks continued, but it was from that period that the Germans themselves realized their aerial losses were greater than the results warranted.

German Plans Fail.

It was in that time, too, that some sort of German invasion of Britain was nipped off. Stories trickling out months and even years afterward told how hundreds of German invasion barges had been caught and sunk by the R.A.F. Officially, both Britain and Germany kept mum, but it was obvious that a hastily-prepared invasion program had failed. It served as a warning to Britain that spur-of-the-moment invasion could not succeed.

Britain proceeded slowly.

The commandos were organized, and for years developed their technique in a series of hit-skip raids against the German-held continent, gathering information, damaging enemy installations, keeping the Nazi garrisons in a constant state of alertness and alarm.

With American entry into the war after the Japanese attack on Pearl Harbor, Dec. 7, 1941, the pace quickened from a creep to a gallop.

Americans Join British.

In January, 1942, American troops landed in northern Ireland. They were there for one purpose: To prepare for the ultimate invasion of Europe. Soon they extended to Britain itself; their numbers were constantly augmented.

The Americans formed their own commando-like striking force, the Rangers.

In August, 1942, combined forces, mostly Canadian, stormed ashore at Dieppe, France.

The Dieppe adventure since has been officially dismissed as a raid in force, a sort of rehearsal, in which it was not intended to remain on the continent.

Dieppe Raid Showed Strength.

Whatever its purpose, it definitely showed the Allied command that the German defenses of western Europe were very strong, stronger perhaps than had been imagined.

After spending all day on the enemy coast, the raiders withdrew. Their casualties had been heavy. Possibly, had the German defenses proved weak or asleep, the invasion might have stemmed immediately from Dieppe. As it was, the Allies continued their preparations and chose other fields for immediate action.

In November the Americans and British invaded French North Africa. They came from Britain and the United States. Their timing was nearly perfect; their plans were neatly laid and closely followed; they worked with the

(CONTINUED ON PAGE THREE)

Along Invasion Coast

THIS MAP OF the French channel coast and the Low Countries locates important railway lines and principal cities from the French port of Cherbourg on the west to the big German port of Hamburg on the east.

'One Up and Two to Go,' Roosevelt Tells People

WASHINGTON, June 5—(AP)—Hailing the capture of Rome with the jubilant phrase "one up and two to go," President Roosevelt declared tonight that the aim now is to drive Germany "to the point where she will be unable to recommence world conquest a generation hence."

Mr. Roosevelt, in a nation-wide radio broadcast, cautioned that this struggle with the Nazis would be tough and costly, and that the day of Germany's surrender "lies some distance ahead."

Whether his reaffirmation that the fight would be pressed until Germany surrenders was a reply to the recent speech of Pope Pius XII was not stated. The Pope asserted last week that the idea that the war must end either in complete victory or complete destruction is a stimulant toward prolonging the conflict and expressed hope for an early peace.

Assures Pope's Freedom.

Speaking of Rome as the great symbol of Christianity, the President declared "it will be a source of deep satisfaction that the freedom of the Pope and of Vatican City is assured by the Armies of the United Nations."

But he declared that no thanks are due Hitler and his generals "if Rome was spared the devastation which the Germans wreaked on Naples and other Italian cities."

"The Allied generals maneuvered so skillfully," he said, "that the Nazis could only have stayed long enough to damage Rome at the risk of losing their armies."

"Our victory," Mr. Roosevelt asserted, "comes at an excellent time, while our Allied forces are poised for another strike at Western Europe—and while armies of other Nazi soldiers nervously await our assault. And our gallant Russian Allies continue to make their power felt more and more."

(CONTINUED ON PAGE THREE)

Day of Decision In Bloomington

Rome had fallen. It would be a full moon. It was ripe, psychologically and meteorologically, for the invasion, said the armchair strategists yesterday.

Most of them had gone to bed—lulled by the beautiful moonlight and the first really cool night in days—when the first inkling that something was afoot came over the Associated Press wires into The Student office shortly after midnight.

For two hours The Student staff stood first on one foot and then on the other. The Germans were telling the story. Detail by detail they built up the picture. Washington was mum. London reported only Gen. Eisenhower's instructions to the European underground to be prepared.

Then a message. An important announcement would be made at 2:31 a.m., Bloomington time.

Seconds after 2:31 a.m. came the flash:

LONDON—EISENHOWER'S HEADQUARTERS ANNOUNCES ALLIES LAND IN FRANCE.

The invasion was on.

Today Bloomington churches will be open for all who would pray for American success. Bloomingtonians will pray—and work—and work and pray. The Day of Decision is here.

Liberators Sink Jap Destroyer

ADVANCED ALLIED HEADQUARTERS, NEW GUINEA, June 6—(AP)—Liberator bombers sank a Japanese destroyer in the Halmahera Sea and probably destroyed another off Manokwari, headquarters announced today.

Havre Area Is Center Of Attack

SUPREME HEADQUARTERS, ALLIED EXPEDITIONARY FORCE, June 6—(AP)—Gen. Dwight D. Eisenhower's headquarters announced today that Allied troops began landing on the northern coast of France this morning strongly supported by naval and air forces.

Text of the communique:

Under the command of Gen. Eisenhower Allied naval forces supported by strong air forces began landing Allied armies this morning on the northern coast of France.

The Germans said the landings extended between Le Havre and Cherbourg along the south side of the bay of the Seine and along the Northern Normandy coast.

Parachute troops descended in Normandy, Berlin said.

Berlin first announced the landings in a series of flashes that began about 6:30 a.m. (11:30 p.m. Central war time).

The Allied communique was read over a transatelantic hookup direct from General Eisenhower's headquarters at 2:32 a.m. (Central War Time) designated "Communique No. 1."

A second announcement by S.H.A.E.F. said that "it is announced that Gen. B. L. Montgomery is in command of the army group carrying out the assault. This army group includes British, Canadian, and U.S. forces."

Le Havre Shelled.

The Allied bulletin did not say exactly where the invasion was taking place, but Berlin earlier gave these details:

Allied naval forces, including heavy warships, are shelling Le Havre. "It is a terrific bombardment," Berlin said.

Allied parachute troops floating down along the Normandy coast were landing and being engaged by German shock troops.

Other Allied units were streaming ashore into Normandy from landing barges.

Asks a Full Victory.

In a special order of the day issued to all soldiers, sailors and airmen under his command, Gen. Eisenhower said:

"We will accept nothing except full victory."

Eisenhower told his men they were "embarking on a great crusade toward which we have striven these many months," and warned them that they were facing a tough, well-prepared enemy.

Berlin said the "center of gravity" of the fierce fighting was at Caen, 30 miles southwest of Le Havre and 65 miles southeast of Cherbourg.

Caen is 10 miles inland from the sea, at the base of the 75-mile-wide Normany peninsula.

Heavy fighting also was reported between Caen and Trouville.

One of Berlin's first claims was that the first British parachute division was badly mauled.

Montgomery in Charge.

General Montgomery, hero of the African desert, was leading the assault of the Allied liberation Army.

No other Allied commanders were announced, for the thousands of battle-trained Allied troops, although Gen. Omar Bradley has been in command of American ground forces in England for several months.

Bradley participated in the Tunisian victory.

Thousands of battle-trained American, British and Canadian troops hurled themselves at Hitler's western defenses after months of preparation.

(CONTINUED ON PAGE THREE)

P0022967, IU Archives.

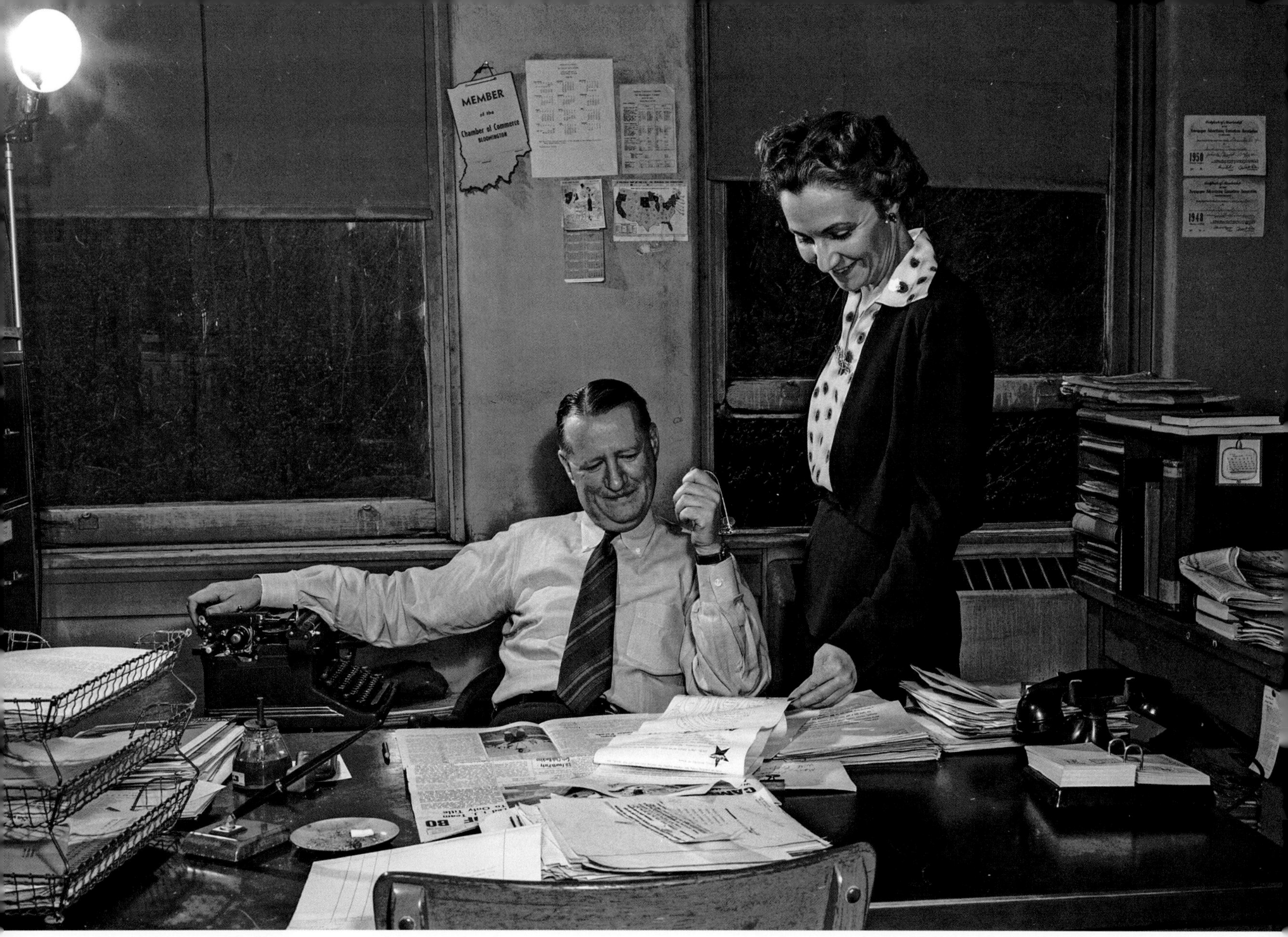

IDS Publisher and journalism department head John Stempel in 1952. *P0077735, IU Archives.*

PROFILE

John E. Stempel, BA 1923
Chairman of the journalism department, 1938–1968

This selection was adapted from an article that originally appeared Jan. 22, 1982, after Stempel's death.

By Curtis Krueger

John E. Stempel led IU's journalism department through three decades that witnessed major changes in communication methods.

Stempel, who retired from IU in 1968, taught students who later became reporters at The New York Times, The Wall Street Journal, the Los Angeles Times and the Chicago Tribune.

Stempel's career at IU spanned 30 years in which television, radio and new technology transformed journalism into a profession different from the one he entered in 1917 as a part-time reporter for the Bloomington Evening World.

As chairman of the journalism department from 1938 to 1968, Stempel also oversaw operations of the IDS, then a laboratory newspaper.

He directed the journalism department's efforts to add photography management and other courses that kept pace with the changing communications field. But as a teacher, he earned a reputation for adhering to the traditional principles of proper grammar and style.

"You better get it right or you will be selling apples on the street corners," Stempel often warned his students.

IDS publisher Patrick Siddons, a 1950 IU graduate and student of Stempel's, said his former teacher will be remembered for his "insistence on truth, fairness, accuracy and a dogged pursuit of the story."

In his editing class, known on campus as a tough course, Stempel instituted weekly news quizzes and other assignments that built his reputation as a stern instructor.

"I always took the position," he recalled in 1980, "that any student who could get along with me could get along with any managing editor in the country."

"He just taught that editing course like a very gruff city editor," David Weaver, IU associate professor of journalism, said.

Richard Gray, dean of the School of Journalism and Stempel's successor, said Stempel "devoted his life and energy to the study of journalism as a respected academic discipline."

Gene Miller, a 1950 IU graduate and former student of Stempel's who has won two Pulitzer Prizes for reporting at the Miami Herald said, " 'St. John,' we called him behind his back; yet hardly anyone believed him saintly, I suggest he was."

Stempel, a Bloomington native, worked alongside his friend Ernie Pyle at the IDS and became editor in chief before he graduated in 1923. He did graduate work at Columbia University.

As a professional journalist, Stempel worked for the Bloomington Star, the New York Sun and the Easton (Pa.) Express. He was author, with Norman Radder, of "Newspaper Editing, Headlines and Make-up." He wrote several magazine articles and after retiring, was a freelance newspaper consultant.

Stempel was awarded the Indiana Newspaperman of the Year Award in 1968 and was admitted to the Indiana Journalism Hall of Fame in 1970.

HE SERVES BEST WHO SERVES THE TRUTH

THE INDIANA DAILY STUDENT

THE WEATHER
INDIANA—Cloudy and warmer Tuesday. Wednesday partly cloudy and warm.

VOL. LXXIV—NO. 48——Z 174. INDIANA UNIVERSITY WEDNESDAY, NOVEMBER 8, 1944. BLOOMINGTON, INDIANA Established, 1867.

ROOSEVELT WINS FOURTH TERM

Ernie to Receive Degree at Convo

Writer to Visit Campus for Ceremony Monday.

Ernie Pyle, most widely read writer of the present war, will return to the University campus Monday to receive from his alma mater the honorary degree of doctor of humane letters.

President H. B Wells announced yesterday the decision of the faculty and Board of Trustees to grant to the noted war columnist the first honorary degree of its kind ever awarded by the University. Simultaneously George F. Heighway, alumni Secretary and chairman of a special committee, announced that the degree would be conferred at a special convocation at 11:15 o'clock Monday morning in the Auditorium.

Ceremony Plans

Plans for the ceremonies, as made public yesterday, provide for an academic procession, music by the University Concert Band under the direction of Gerald Doty, and formal award of the degree.

The ceremonies also will include acceptance by the University of the Boris Chaliapin portrait of Pyle, recently presented by Time Magazine through P.I. Prentice and Roy Larsen, publisher and president, respectively, of the publication. This portrait was used as the cover design by Time last July.

At Monday's ceremonies the portrait will be presented formally by a representative of Time and accepted on behalf of the University by John S. Hastings, of Washington, Ind., a member of the board of trustees and college mate of the famous columnist.

Classes Dismissed

All University eleven o'clock classes will be dismissed and all University offices will be closed for

(CONTINUED ON PAGE THREE)

OPEN HOUSE

The coeds of Forest Hall will honor Miss Draper with an informal open house tonight after the Convocation. Miss Draper will be an overnight guest at the Forest Hall.

Original Sketches To Be Presented By Ruth Draper

Tonight's Convo Audience to Hear Monologuist in Auditorium.

By MILDRED WYATT

Ruth Draper, the mistress of monologue, will make her first appearance at Indiana University at the fourth Convocation at 7 o'clock this evening in the Auditorium.

A grand-daughter of the late Charles A. Dana, one of the most prominent figures in the history of American journalism, Miss Draper follows her illustrious grand-father's stlye in her presentations. Her character sketches are simple, strong, clear, and "boiled down."

Her repertoire includes more than two dozen sketches which evoke more than a hundred characters. The mere remembering of her many interpretations, however, is far from being Miss Draper's most notable achievement. She writes all her sketches herself. Her most remarkable characteristic is the control she has over the different moods and personalities she assumes every ten or fifteen minutes.

With seeming ease, Ruth Draper removes one shawl, thus ceasing to be the tragic Dalmatian peasant vainly seeking her husband in a New York hospital, and then dons another to become the wife of an old sea captain, gossiping with her neighbor on the porch of a cottage in Maine, and again with a lace scarf promptly turns into a timid Italian girl meeting her lover in the shadow of a tourist-infested cathedral.

This slight mechanical adjustment plus the facial and vocal changes create the completeness of each characterization. At the final curtain the stage is teeming with people as real to the mind's eye as Miss Draper's solitary figure, alone visible, in the flesh.

PARCEL POST TO ITALY

WASHINGTON, Nov. 6—(AP)—Limited parcel post service to Italy has been resumed, the Foreign Economic Administration announced today.

440 Jap Planes Lost In Driving Manila Raid

U.S. PACIFIC FLEET HEADQUARTERS, PEARL HARBOR, Nov. 7—(AP)—The fury of American naval air power, sweeping into the heart of the Philippines for the second consecutive day, destroyed 249 Japanese planes, sank a destroyer and an oil tanger, and damaged four other warships, Admiral Chester W. Nimitz reported late Tuesday.

The airmen ran their two-day total of planes destroyed in the Manila and ajacent areas to 24, including nine men-of-war.

To the south of the regions swept by the naval fliers, Gen. Douglas MacArthur's liberation forces were fighting one of the toughest battles of the Leyte campaign. Elements of four Japanese divisions were putting up a bitter struggle. Yank heavy artillery was hammering the Nipponese in the Ormoc trap on the west coast.

The Admiral's communique said 3rd Fleet carrier planes followed up Saturday's attack by blasting Manila harbor shipping and widespread airfields on Luzon Island Suday. In the Saturday strike they sank a submarine chaser, probably sank a heavy cruiser, and damaged a light cruiser and three destroyers. In addition to the warships and tanker bagged Sunday, three cargo vessels were sunk and others damaged.

Clark Field, north of Manila, was hit hard. Three oil storage areas were left in flames.

Of the planes destroyed at Clark and a half dozen other Luzon dromes in two days, 113 were shot down and 327 destroyed on the ground. The Admiral added "many others were destroyed on the ground by strafing."

WAR Briefs

VOSSENACK BATTLE RAGES.

LONDON, Nov. 7—(AP)—American and German troops were locked tonight in a struggle for the center of the German town of Vossenack in Hurtgen Forest, with powerful Nazi reinforcements battling fiercely to bar the road to Cologne and the rich Rhine Valley only twenty miles away.

After five days of see-saw fighting, Lieut. Gen. Courtney Hodges' 1st Army doughboys tonight held half of the mile-and-a-half-long town, and the Germans were solidly entrenched in the other half.

EASTERN FRONT QUIET.

LONDON, Nov. 7—(AP)—Fighting along the winding Eastern front slackened generally today—twenty-seventh anniversary of the Russian revolution—with Moscow announcing only that "there were no essential changes on the front," and that yesterday sixteen German

(CONTINUED ON PAGE THREE)

County Republican Sweep Indicated

Gov. Dewey Leads Three to Two Over Roosevelt

12 Out of 42 Precincts Hand in Returns from Voting.

By JAMES WRIGHT

A clean sweep for the Republican Party in Monroe County seemed imminent early today on the basis of returns from twelve of the forty-two precincts.

Gov. Thomas E. Dewey led President Roosevelt almost three votes to two. Dewey received 2,305 ballots; Roosevelt, 1,610. In the last election, five Republican presidential votes were cast for every four Democratic votes in Monroe County.

Senatorial Race.

In the long-term senatorial race, Homer E. Capehart led Henry F. Schricker by 429 votes, while William Jenner, Republican candidate for short-term senator, lead Cornelius O'Brien 2,262 to 1,504.

Also in the returns Samuel Jackson trailed Ralph Gates by 291 votes in the guberinatorial race, and Gerald Landis led Arthur Greenwood by 338 votes for Repreesntative of the Seventh Congressional District.

Comfortable Margins.

County offices led their opponents by comfortable margins. As expected, Judge J. Frank Regester was running ahead of the Democratic ticket, but behind Q. Austin East, his Republican opponent for judge of the Circuit Court.

The other leading candidates were Robert McCrea for prosecutor; Robert Miller, for joint senator of Monroe, Brown, and Green Counties; George W. Henley for State representative; T. Nolin Welch for County Auditor; Mrs. Thelma Gilmore for treasurer; Albert H. Skirvin for sheriff; Dr. Ray Borland for coroner; John Stapleton for surveyor; and Ira Robinson and Clyde Holmes for County Commissioners.

Perry 6 was the first precinct to submit its full report to the election board at the Courthouse, followed almost immediately by Marion 1.

Monroe County Vote

President
(12 precincts out of 42)
Thomas E. Dewey (R)........2305
Franklin D. Roosevelt (D)....1610

Senator (Long Term)
Homer E. Capehart (R)......2140
Henry F. Schricker (D)......1711

Senator (Short Term)
William Jenner (R)..........2262
Cornelius O'Brien (D)........1504

Governor
(8 precincts out of 42)
Ralph E. Gates (R)..........1293
Samuel D. Jackson (D)........1002

Congress
Gerald Landis (R)...........1273
Arthur Greenwood (D).........935

Prosecutor
(7 precincts out of 42)
Robert McCrea (R)...........1148
Floyd Cook (D)...............703

Judge
Q. Austin East (R)..........1016
J. Frank Regester (D)........850

State Senator
Robert Miller (R)...........1136
James E. Cullum (D)..........695

State Representative
George Henley (R)...........1142
W. O. Lynch (D)..............688

Auditor
T. Nolin Welch (R)..........1132
Leon Chitwood (D)............700

Treasurer
Thelma Gilmore (R)..........1168
Wm. Paul Campbell (D)........675

Sheriff
Albert H. Skirvin (R)........1132
Ray H. Stephens (D)..........717

Coroner
Ray Borland (R)..............1148
Charles R. Easton (D).........691

Surveyor
John T. Stapleton (R)........1131
William J. Burch (D)..........705

Commissioner, First District
Ira E. Robinson (R)..........1108
William J. Hubbard (D)........715

Commissioner, Second District
Clyde Holmes (R).............1106
J. Leroy Swarthout (D)........709

DEWEY LEADS STATE

Democratic Candidates Benefit by Heavy Scratching.

INDIANAPOLIS, Nov. 8—(AP) — Gov. Thomas E. Dewey, Republican nominee for president, increased a slender lead over President Roosevelt early today in slowly accumulating returns in Indiana but other Democratic candidates were running counter to the Dewey trend.

With 2,357 of 4,016 precincts reported, Dewey led the President, 539,826 to 495,522.

Both Gov. Henry F. Schricker, Democratic nominee for U.S. Senator, and U.S. Senator Samuel D. Jackson, Democratic gubernatorial entry, were benefitting from heavy scratching, Schricker particularly.

Example of Scratching.

Allen County, a Republican stronghold, was an example of the scratching differential in Schricker's favor. Here Homer E. Capehart, the Republican Senate nominee, ran 1,123 votes behind Dewey in the first thirty precincts reporting. In sharp contrast, Schricker was topping President Roosevelt by 864 votes, even though his total was less than Capehart's.

Tabulations at 4:45 a.m. showed:

Senate—(long term) — 2,207 precincts: Capehart, 475,468; Schricker, 481,222.

Senate—(short term)—1,573 precincts: William E. Jenner (R) 330,794; Cornelius O'Brien (D) 288,088.

Governor—2,166 precincts; Jackson, 470,788; Gates, 470,822.

(CONTINUED ON PAGE THREE)

Democrats Take Necessary Seats For Senate Grip

Eight of 13 Needed to Retain Control Assured; Fish Loses to Bennett.

WASHINGTON, Nov. 8—(Wednesday)—Eight of thirteen seats needed by the Democrats to retain control of the treaty-ratifying Senate were assured early today, while eight Republican House places—among them that of Rep. Hamilton Fish—tumbled to administration forces.

Looking toward peace and creation of a world security organization, the importance of congressional control was stressed by both parties in the campaign. Senator Harry Truman, President Roosevelt's running mate, called openly for the defeat of eight Republican senators he dubbed as "isolation-

(CONTINUED ON PAGE THREE)

Associated Press returns on the 435 House of Representatives seats at 4 a.m., C.W.T., showed:
Democrats elected, 161. (Present Congress, 214; vacancies, 5).
Republicans elected, 62. Present Congress, 212).
Progressives elected, 1. Present Congress, 2).
American Laborites elected, 1. Present Congress, 1).
Farmer Laborites elected, 0. Present Congress,1).
Contsest undecided, 210.

FRANKLIN D. ROOSEVELT

Presidential Vote by States

As compiled by The Associated Press at 3:30 a.m.

	1940 Totals Roosevelt Dem.	Willkie Rep.	Total Precincts	Units Reprtg.	1944 Totals Popular Vote Roosevelt	Dewey	Electrl. Vote Rvlt.	Dewey
Alabama	250,726	42,184	2,300	1,088	115,094	25,403	11	—
Arizona	95,267	54,030	438	180	22,808	15,491	4	—
Arkansas	158,622	42,121	2,087	593	48,895	18,240	9	—
California	1,877,618	1,351,419	14,850	8,260	807,382	615,576*	25	—
Colorado	265,554	279,576	1,663	585	64,750	79,991*	—	6
Connecticut	417,621	361,819	169	169	434,841	391,349	8	—
Delaware	74,599	61,440	250	192	45,791	34,382	3	—
Florida	359,334	126,158	1,472	600	148,354	67,597*	8	—
Georgia	265,194	23,934	1,735	587	172,276	29,499	12	—
Idaho	127,842	106,553	845	400	48,466	42,900	4	—
Illinois	2,149,934	2,047,240	8,737	6,250	1,508,618	1,276,425	28	—
Indiana	874,063	899,466	4,016	1,436	338,091	356,872	—	13
Iowa	578,800	632,370	2,463	1,456	290,937	312,998	—	10
Kansas	364,725	489,169	2,742	1,291	93,674	167,441	—	8
Kentucky	557,222	410,384	4,282	2,823	321,857	255,677	11	—
Louisiana	319,751	52,446	1,871	518	120,786	29,148	10	—
Maine	156,478	163,951	527	610	138,988	153,734	—	5
Maryland	384,546	269,534	1,327	1,267	283,223	265,787*	8	—
Massachusetts	1,076,522	939,700	1,852	978	473,141	407,177	16	—
Michigan	1,032,991	1,039,917	3,843	1,116	234,023	323,597	—	19
Minnesota	644,196	596,274	3,703	922	230,031	192,754	11	—
Mississippi	168,267	2,814	1,683	695	77,150	5,488	9	—
Missouri	958,476	871,009	4,519	3,254	492,445	474,741*	4	—
Montana	145,698	99,579	1,175	391	49,908	39,866	4	—
Nebraska	263,677	352,201	2,046	929	82,953	131,559*	—	6
Nevada	31,945	21,229	299	231	17,420	15,586	3	—
New Hampshire	125,292	110,127	296	276	96,415	91,318	4	—
New Jersey	1,016,808	945,475	3,647	2,368	591,335	607,404	—	16
New Mexico	103,699	79,315	902	340	38,017	30,259	4	—
New York	3,251,918	3,027,478	9,121	8,462	3,064, 913	2,770,565	47	—
North Carolina	609,015	213,633	1,921	1,384	413,141	177,624	14	—
North Dakota	124,036	154,590	2,251	297	19,743	19,526*	4	—
Ohio	1,733,139	1,586,773	8,872	5,901	928,158	1,012,498	—	25
Oklahoma	474,313	348,872	3,672	3,129	333,308	262,895	10	—
Oregon	258,415	219,555	1,845	903	73,145	75,138	—	6
Pennsylvania	2,171,035	1,889,848	8,197	7,037	1,517,365	1,470,333*	35	—
Rhode Island	182,182	138,653	261	260	158,814	114,108*	4	—
South Carolina	95,470	1,727	1,282	663	65,770	3,648	8	—
South Dakota	131,362	177,065	1,949	1,128	57,102	79,608	—	4
Tennessee	351,601	169,153	2,300	1,926	230,350	150,774	12	—
Texas	840,151	199,152	254	224	505,617	107,240	23	—
Utah	154,277	93,151	870	316	49,445	33,380*	4	—
Vermont	64,269	78,371	280	245	53,916	71,428	—	3
Virginia	235,961	109,363	1,712	1,493	213,876	128,510	11	—
Washington	462,145	322,123	3,164	760	114,163	74,001*	8	—
West Virginia	495,662	372,414	2,796	1,140	168,349	132,471	8	—
Wisconsin	704,821	679,206	3,094	2,022	398,511	432,193	—	12
Wyoming	59,287	52,633	673	364	18,311	20,541	—	3
Total	27,243,466	22,304,755	130,353	77,359	15,771,666	13,594,740	395	136

* Soldier vote in all but ten states is being counted with the civilian vote cast yesterday. In the ten states the vote will be counted as follows: California, Nov. 24; Colorado, Nov. 22; Florida, Nov. 8; Missouri, Nov. 10; Nebraska, Dec. 1; North Dakota, Dec. 5; Pennsylvania, Nov. 22; Rhode Island, Dec. 5; Utah, Nov. 12; Washington, Dec. 5.

Vote Magic Aids President to Sail Over Opposition

Early See-Saw Struggle Ends as Roosevelt Takes 34 States.

By THE ASSOCIATED PRESS

The vote-getting magic of Franklin Delano Roosevelt won him a fourth term in the White House today, and continued leadership in the vast unfinished business of war and peace.

Thomas Edmund Dewey, youthful New York Governor who declared in vain that "it's time for a change," conceded defeat at 2:15 a.m. (C.W.T.).

Said Dewey at a news conference in New York:

"It's clear that Mr. Roosevelt has been re-elected for a fourth term."

Falls Behind.

The Republican nominee had fallen farther and farther behind in tabulations pouring in during the early morning hours after a see-saw struggle in early counting. The ballots of nearly 27,000,000 Americans showed, at the time he gave up:

For Roosevelt, 14,411,965.
For Dewey, 12,165,763.

State after state had slipped away from Dewey. Roosevelt took command of thirty-four, with an electoral count of 395. Dewey had only fourteen, with 136 votes, at the time he announced it was all over.

Unmistakeable Trend.

Even before Dewey conceded the trend had been unmistakeable.

At Hyde Park the President told his neighbors late in the evening that it looked like another victory. Supporters carrying red flares flocked into the grounds of the world famous squire of Dutchess County.

All over the country, except in the cornbelt, Roosevelt went out ahead when the election score sheets were halfway finished. The President got the Solid South and all five border states. He was far ahead in the Mountain and Western States, and he had a comfortable edge in the East and Northeast.

Safe Victory.

There was an outside chance that soldier votes would change some State decisions. But the Roosevelt victory was safe.

In eight of the eleven states counting their service ballots belatedly, the outcome could be changed. Seven of the eight, with ninety-nine electoral votes, were on Roosevelt's side.

At a midnight celebration with his neighbors at Hyde Park, N.Y., President Roosevelt had said it looked like he would win. Sidney Hillman, also celebrating, with his C.I.O.-P.A.C. followers at a New York City hotel, declared:

Reaffirm Confidence.

"The American people have reaffirmed the faith and confidence they repose in a great American and an outstanding leader by voting to return President Roosevelt to office."

In the Congressional races, Demo-

(CONTINUED ON PAGE THREE)

Associated press returns at 4:30 a.m. C.W.T. Wednesday, from 85,593 of the country's 130,810 voting units showed the popular vote:
Roosevelt, 17,262,463;
Dewey, 15,083,592;
Total, 32,346,055.

Because of the Ernie Pyle convocation on Monday, November 13, 11 o'clock classes will not meet on that day.
H. T. Briscoe,
Dean of Faculties.

HALL ACCOUNTS.
All hall accounts payable on a two payment basis will be due this week. A penalty of $1.00 for the first day and $ .25 for each additional day will be assessed for failure to pay as scheduled.
Vice-President and Treasurer.
W. G. Biddle.

WELLS HAS OPEN HOUSE.
President H. B. Wells will have Open House for students in his office between the hours of 2:30 and 5 o'clock this afternoon.

P0078443, IU Archives.

'The Hurt Has Become Too Great'

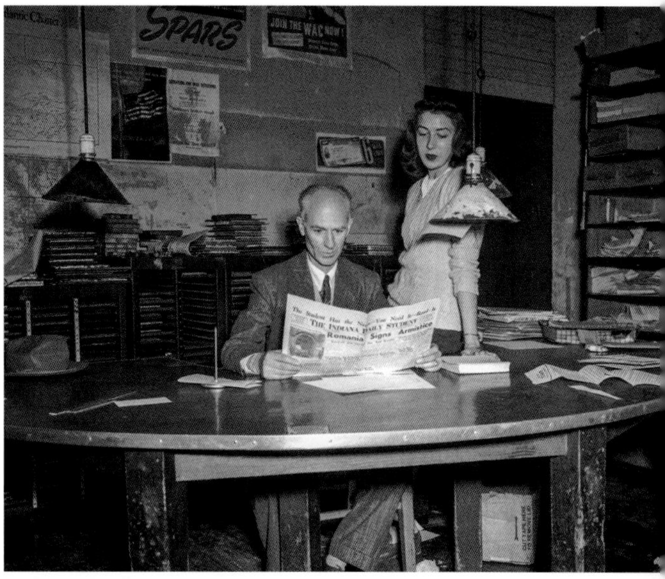

Ernie Pyle reads the paper while sitting in "the slot" during his last visit to campus in November 1944 while Patricia Krieghbaum looks on. *P0029070, IU Archives.*

This selection was adapted from an article that originally appeared April 28, 1945.

By Ed Sovola

It is with sadness that we write this belated tribute to Ernie Pyle. He was killed on Ie Island near Okinawa, April 18. Publication of the IDS during that final exam week was stopped. It is tragic that the newspaper on which Ernie worked while at school could not report his death and our sorrow.

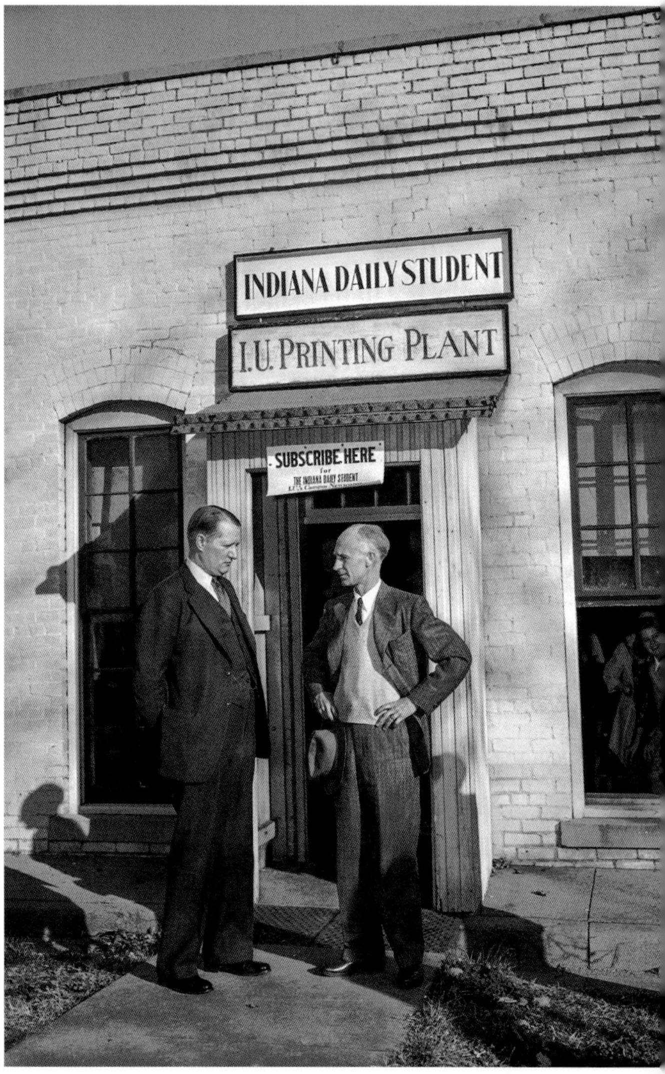

Ernie Pyle, right, and publisher John Stempel standing outside the IU Printing Plant, which also housed the newsroom, in 1944. *P0029072, IU Archives.*

To eulogize of Ernie Pyle's work and life in flowery language would certainly be odious to one who loved simplicity and scorned ostentation. His greatness came from honesty and sensitivity towards little things. He wrote as he lived. He lived as he believed. He died while reporting "his war."

G.I. Joe's greatest friend wrote as he left the European theatre of operations, "I do hate terribly to leave right now, but I have given out. The hurt has finally become too great. All of a sudden it seemed to me that if I heard one more shot or saw one more dead man, I would go off my nut."

Ernie didn't go off his nut. After a brief rest he steeled himself to go out to the Pacific. Ernie exemplified the highest tradition of newspapermen. To report the 5 W's—who, when, what, where, why—Ernie went to see, touch, hear, and live with death, mutilation, hunger, and ironically, man's nobility and self-sacrifice. His death from a Japanese bullet closed the fountainhead of news which could be anywhere little people and Ernie were. He died doing his job. He died doing it well. Ernie would have wanted it that way.

To think of Ernie, one cannot help but wonder what quality made him great. Why was he loved by so many little and big people?

Ernie was great because he hated war and loved peace and progress. He was loved because he went into the bloody maw of Mars asking no favors while writing about what he hated, violence and mutilation, and what he loved, bravery and unselfish devotion. He spoke the language of G.I. Joe who faced his fate and did not flinch. He wrote of their joys and their sufferings. He wrote clearly because their joys and sufferings were his. He detracted nothing from what he saw and felt. He did not color what was not there. His keen insight and high sensitivity to all human emotions made his writing great.

Writing from the Western front he said, "As the tank continued to shoot I ducked into a doorway, because I figured the Germans would shoot back." The "human touch" of Ernie Pyle. "The hurt has finally become too great." The human heart of Ernie Pyle.

The newspaper world has lost its best correspondent. The world has lost one of its most humane citizens whose powerful pen ran dry on Okinawa. All who knew him personally of through his writing mourn his passing.

Here at Indiana University, to preserve the memory of Ernie Pyle for coming generations, a fund for an Ernie Pyle Memorial has been started. Gifts from $1 to $300 have already been received. There also has been some discussion of changing the Department of Journalism to a School of Journalism as a tribute to Ernie. Let us hope it will materialize. Ernie Pyle would like that. His work and life deserve such tribute.

To Ernie Pyle...

Ernie Pyle, the great little man, brought the war with its laughs and sorrows to millions of readers every day. He made every G.I. Joe seem like the boy next door or the fellow down the street — just with his sincere writing and his interest in the common, human things.

Now Ernie Pyle writes no more about the soldiers in France or the landings on Okinawa. But we cannot forget the great work he did in interpreting the war for us at home.

The Indiana Foundation recently received a suggestion that Indiana University alumni and friends honor Ernie Pyle by creating a memorial fund to enlarge the department of journalism here.

What better way could tribute be paid to a son of Indiana that to honor him with a memorial at the University he attended? Perhaps Ernie wouldn't have wanted any tribute at all—he was that way. But his service demands high tribute from his fellow students, his readers, and his host of friends.

Ernie Pyle was a little guy who understood the other guy—not only understood him, but wrote about him. That's why we liked Ernie Pyle, and that's why we miss him.

This editorial ran on page 4 of the April 28, 1945 edition, the first published after Ernie Pyle's death. *P0066958, IU Archives.*

V-E Tomorrow

EXTRA THE INDIANA DAILY STUDENT EXTRA

VOL. LXXIV—NO. 157——Z 174. INDIANA UNIVERSITY SATURDAY, MAY 5, 1945. BLOOMINGTON, INDIANA Established, 1867.

NAZIS SIGN SURRENDER

By THE ASSOCIATED PRESS

The war against Germany, the greatest in history, ended today with the unconditional surrender of the once mighty wehrmacht.

The surrender to the western Allies and Russia was made at Gen. Eisenhower's headquarters at Reims, France.

The British Ministry of Information announced that tomorrow will be treated as V-E Day.

The ministry said officially that, "in accordance with arrangements between the three great powers, the Prime Minister will make an official announcement at 3 p.m., (8 a.m., central war time), tomorrow.

At Washington microphones were made ready for a broadcast by President Truman. Prime Minister Churchill, after a busy day, went to see King George VI.

News of the surrender came in an Associated Press dispatch from Reims, at 8:35 a.m., central war time, and immediately set the church bells tolling in Rome and elsewhere.

In the hour before the news from Reims, Nazi broadcasts told the German people that Grand Admiral Karl Doenitz had ordered capitulation of all fighting forces, and called off U-boat warfare.

America greeted announcement of Germany's unconditional surrender with a mixture of emotions. Hilarious gayety, solemn prayer in the streets, a partial stoppage of business and an electric feeling of excitement swept from coast to coast.

New York City's reaction was a snowstorm of waste paper. "Business as usual," was the reaction from the New York Stock Exchange.

At London thousands of American soldiers in Piccadilly Circus screamed, yelled, shouted, hugged and kissed one another.

Bloomington and the campus took the early announcement calmly. City leaders were cautious about the announcement, but churches were ready for services when word is given (see Page 3).

P0036157, IU Archives.

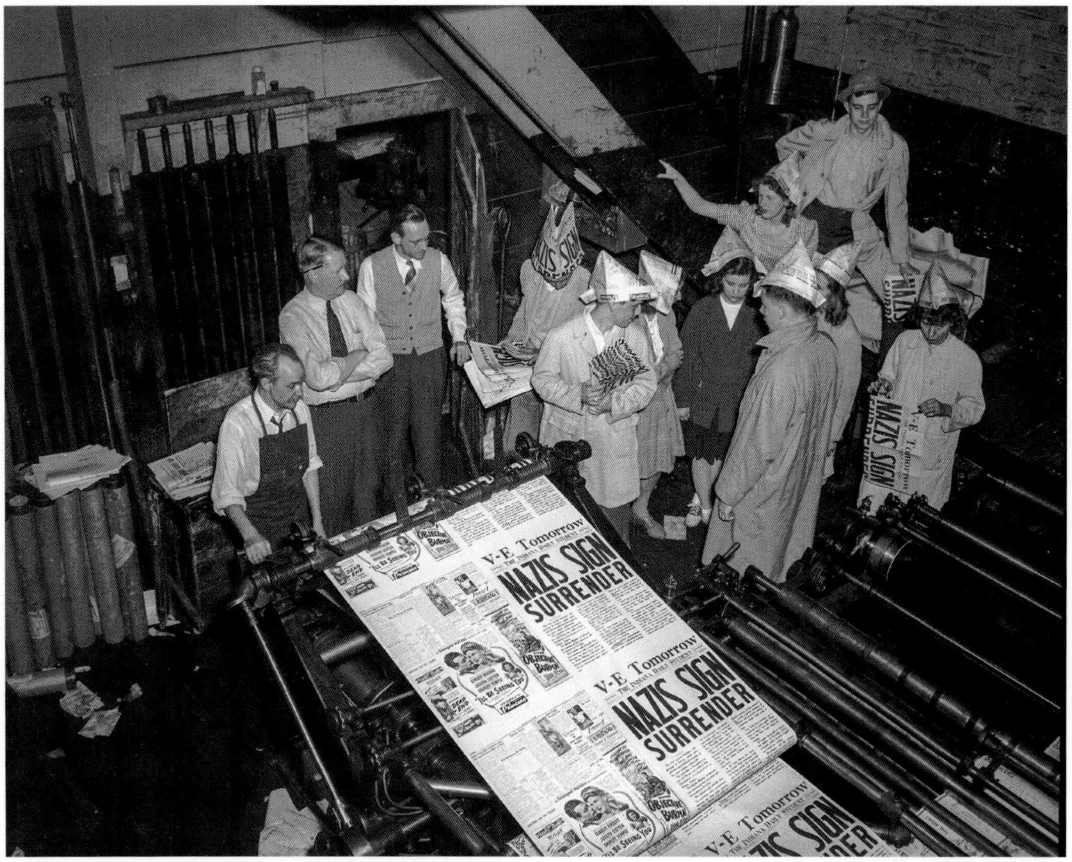

The staff gathers around the printing press as the extra announcing victory in Europe during World War II is printed in May 1945. *P0027102, IU Archives.*

REFLECTION

An 'Endless' Wait—and Then a Two-Day Nap

While I was editor, the August 1945 armistice was our "big story." With plenty of warning that the end of the war was imminent, we were prepared and ready to go to press except for the lead story. Our mentor, John Stempel, stayed close at hand.

The news finally broke and we rushed the story through. Presses were cranked up and ready to roll when notice came through that it was a false alarm. The wait until the "true" news came was endless . . . hours and hours . . . a day and a night—I can't remember how long.

Cigarette rationing was in effect and we ran out as we sat in the old IDS office, tapping our toes. It got so bad that some of us begged pipe and chewing tobacco from the pressmen to roll our own, bringing on a few green faces and squeamish stomachs.

When the armistice was finally official, our newsboys hit the streets with extras as did the whole staff. All I remember of that night was the downpour of rain, the celebrating and hysterical spirit that had grabbed the whole student body. Unfortunately, much of the next day's celebration was missed by the staff who slept around the clock for the next two days.

—Mary Monroe, BA 1946, wrote this recollection in 1977 for the paper's 110th birthday. She died in 2006.

"The wait until the 'true' news came was endless . . . hours and hours . . . a day and a night—I can't remember how long."

HE SERVES BEST WHO SERVES THE TRUTH

THE INDIANA DAILY STUDENT

THE WEATHER
Turning much colder. Snow.

VOL. LXXX—No. 74——Z 175. INDIANA UNIVERSITY SUNDAY, JANUARY 21, 1951. BLOOMINGTON, INDIANA Established 1867

I.U. TO STAGE 'LITTLE 500' BICYCLE RACE IN STADIUM

Mickey McCarty Says:

(Editor's Note: C. Walter McCarty, '15 is a member of the University's Board of Trustees. As editor of The Indianapolis News, his column, "Mickey McCarty Says" appears daily in The News.)

FELLOW I.U. ALUMNI AND TAXPAYERS: When the wily and willowy Wilcox told a small group of us Indianapolis Fourth Estaters a few weeks ago about the 50-mile bicycle race to be conducted in Memorial Stadium May 12 for the benefit of the scholarship fund of the Indiana University Foundation, it served to bring back fond memories of my boyhood days — days when I was the proud owner of a bicycle.

\+ + +

Dad owned a hardware store in Washington, D.C. (Daviess County), and as a result I was able to get my bicycle — a red (fire department red)racer — at cost. I used it to deliver my newspaper route. Incidentally, I carried both home-town newspapers — The Herald (Republican) and Sam Boyd's Democrat. I was independent politically. If the Republicans were in power, I carried The Herald and if the Democrats occupied the City Hall, I carried the Democrat. They never could accuse me of blind partisanship — not even in carrying newspapers.

\+ + +

I also used my red racer to help my high school classmate, Elmer Q. (Catchie) Oliphant, deliver The Indianapolis News to Washington subscribers in the evening. "Catchie," who later became an all-American football player, got his early athletic training in my barn, which we had fitted up as a gymnasium. He started out training to be a long-distance runner and I used to use the red racer to pace him. The family later moved to Linton and "Catchie" became a four-letter man at the Cow College up the Monon, and subsequently an all-American at West Point.

\+ + +

Before I went to Bloomington to specialize in campustry and other kindred subjects at I.U., I disposed of the red racer, part by part and wheel by wheel. That was about the time Herman B (without the period) Wells was trying out his first tricycle up at Jamestown. I was sorry later I had disposed of it. It would have come in mighty handy around the S.A.E. house, especially in "rush" season, because our boys couldn't even afford a horse and buggy like our more capitalistic neighbors, the Betas and the Phi Psi's.

\+ + +

One of my duties as a freshman at the S.A.E. house in those days —thanks to Lindsey, not Kinsey— was to go downtown to the Bloomington postoffice each morning and bring back the mail. Not being as worldly wise as I am today, I had signed up for an 8 o'clock and this meant I had to roll out of bed at the crack of dawn. Sometimes I didn't, and was then my old bicycle training would have served me in good stead.

\+ + +

However, our ebony-hued cook, old Bob, owned what was called a bicycle. So everytime I overslept I pedaled down to the P.O. and back in less time than it will take Wilcox' thirty-thee bicycle teams to do that fifty miles May 12. One of Mayor Harris' two Bloomington policemen used to caution me occasionally, as I rounded the public square, that I was exceeding the speed limit. Of course the cop never had to make an 8 o'clock like I did.

\+ + +

Another time I longed for my old red racer was after I had switched from algebra to geology, thinking the latter course would be a snap. It wasn't! Our professor was Dr. Cummings. The textbook we studied was Volume I, but Ross Bartley and I always referred to the professor as Volume 2. He knew more about the various formations of the earth than was ever found in a textbook. It was a wonderful and enjoyable course, except for one thing. Dr. Cummings always scheduled what was then known as a "Geology hike" on Saturdays.

\+ + +

Every Saturday we hiked somewhere — to Brown County, Lawrence County, or Orange County to study the various formations and caves as well as that product now known as Bill Riley's limestone. In our geology class was a very attractive Pi Phi who was some class herself. It was springtime, and, some how or other, she and I — both ardent students of nature — got into the habit of lagging far behind the others who were trying to keep up with Dr. Cummings. He warned us several times that if we couldn't stay with the rest of the class he'd have to "flunk" us.

\+ + +

On one of these occasions, I recall, he said, "Mr. McCarty, the next time we go on a hike I'm going to ask you to bring a bicycle so you can keep up with us."

It was then that I fondly wished — not for my old red racer — but "A Bicycle Built For Two."

'Wuxtra' by State Eds

This special issue of the Indiana Daily Student has been written and edited by Indiana newspapermen—many of whom are ex-editors of The Student—who returned to the campus to participate in the activities announcing the "Little 500."

The Student Foundation Committee, the management of the "Little 500" and all Indiana University wish to thank these friends and alumni for their interest and their active support of this project.

'Working Way' Unique In America—Ashton

By DEAN JOHN ASHTON
College of Arts and Sciences

One of the phenomena of American education that often amazes foreign visitors is the large number of students in our universities who pay all or most of their own way in higher education by working at a multitude of jobs while they attend schools. Another thing that amazes the visitors is that these jobs often have no relation whatever to the student's academic work.

This practice has many facts and many implications with respect to the ideal which we suggest of higher education for all who are qualified to receive it. The young man or woman whose finances are limited to what he can accumulate by working in the summer and by doing some kind of hourly work, anywhere from ten to forty hours a week, during the year, does not enjoy the same opportunity as does the student whose education is subsidized by parents or other sponsors.

It is true that the working student may learn much more of self-reliance, develop a much better sense of the value of money, and a much stronger feeling of the significance of a college education than the student who does not have to depend on outside work. These stimuli are such that the self-supporting student sometimes surpasses other student of equal abilities. But the one who has a heavy load of outside work does pay the penalty not only of less time for studying, but also of less energy for his academic work.

We need, in short, in addition to the scholarships which take into account only the academic record, scholarships which will evaluate the relationship between the scholastic achievement of the student and the amount of time he has to work to put himself through school.

Not a day passes that a member of the faculty is not reminded of the need for some type of assistance for students who but for the many hours they must spend earning their room and board, could establish outstanding academic records. I know of no faculty member who would not contribute to and assist in furthering any program which would help answer this recognized problem.

The "Little 500" race which will be conducted to raise money to "help those who help themselves" is certainly a step in the right direction. The members of the Student Foundation Committee are to be complimented for their efforts in this most worthy cause.

Cycling Teams To Be Backed By Sponsors

It appears a certainty all teams entered in the "Little 500" here May 12 will have sponsors.

A list made public yesterday by Howard S. Wilcox, director of the I.U. Foundation, contained the names of twelve organizations who have already pledged their support of one of the thirty-three teams that will make up the field in the cycling classic.

Mr. Wilcox thanked each of the sponsors for their early interest and support of the race.

The sponsors already obtained are the Standard Oil Co. of Indiana; the Gabriel Shock Absorber Co., Cleveland; the City Securities Corp., Indianapolis; Bon. O. Aspy, General Insurance—Fidelity and Surety Bonds, Indianapolis; Indianapolis Press Club; Graham Motor Sales, Bloomington; the members of the Business Research Fund, Bloomington; Carl Stockholm Cleaners, Chicago; University Chevrolet Co., Bloomington; Central Motor Parts Co., NAPA Indianapolis Warehouse; Sherwood Blue, Indianapolis, and Business and Real Estate Trends, Inc., Bloomington.

Mr. Wilcox emphasized the list of sponsors already obtained is especially heartening to the Foundation because no special effort to enlist sponsors has been made.

When the field of entries has been narrowed to the thirty-three starters, each sponsor will be assigned to one of the teams. The sponsor's fee covers the cost of his team's bicycle and entitles the sponsor to two seats in the box immediately behind the "pit" of his team.

Weimer Invites Business Alumni

The annual meeting of School of Business Alumni Association will be May 11 and 12 to enable all returning alumni to attend the "Little 500," according to Dean Arthur M. Weimer of the School of Business.

"The race, and equally as important, the cause for which the race is being staged, will certainly appeal to anyone who has ever attended Indiana University," Dean Weimer said.

He volunteered the services of every member of the School of Business, adding that he knew each of them would be more than happy to help make the race a success.

Several members of the School of Business faculty have already been named to key spots in the "Little 500" organization. Dean Weimer himself is slated to head the Timing Committee.

Business and Real Estate Trends, Inc., of which Dean Weimer is president, is sponsoring one of the starting 33 teams of the May 12 race.

The Big Wheels

THIS CARTOON, drawn by the Indianapolis Star's Pulitzer prize winning cartoonist, Charlie Werner, shows Tony Hulman, Speedway owner, waving the famous checker flag at Wilbur Shaw and President Herman B Wells.

"THE LITTLE 500"

Greatest Annual Collegiate Bicycle Race in the World
Saturday, May 12, 1951
Memorial Stadium, Indiana University
Bloomington, Indiana

BOARD OF DIRECTORS

CHAIRMAN

Byron K. Elliott, '20
Executive Vice President
John Hancock Mutual Life Insurance Company
Boston, Mass.

HONORARY CHAIRMAN

Anton Hulman, Jr.
Chairman of the Board
Indianapolis Motor Speedway

James S. Adams
Partner, Lazard Freres & Co.
New York City

George A. Ball
Chairman of the Board
Ball Brothers Mfg. Company
Muncie

F. McK. Blough
Manager, Standard Oil of Indiana
Indianapolis

Maurice L. Bluhm
President
I.U. Club of Chicago

Dr. William Lowe Bryan
President Emeritus
Indiana University

Kenneth R. Kress, '51
Lorain, Ohio

Dr. John K. Langum
Vice-President
Federal Reserve Bank
Chicago

Mayor Thomas L. Lemon
Bloomington

Robert M. Loomis
President
I.U. Alumni Association
Indianapolis

Mendel McCarty
President
I.U. Club of Indianapolis

(Continued on Page Six)

Governor Henry F. Schricker
Indianapolis

Frank V. Schwinn
Treasurer
Arnold, Schwinn & Co.
Chicago

W. Wilbur Shaw
President, General Manager
Indianapolis Motor Speedway

Mrs. Ralph W. Showalter
Indianapolis

Robert Skiles, '51
Bluffton

Smith William Storey
President
General Portland Cement Co.
Chicago

Receipts to Aid Needy Students

Indiana University will have its own "Little 500" bicycle version of the famous Indianapolis 500-mile motor Speedway classic this Spring.

The race will be run to raise funds to help students who are working their way through school, and except for the fact that bicycles and not souped-up racing cars will be used it will be the Speedway Classic in miniature.

Announced Yesterday.

The announcement of the big campus event came yesterday at a gathering in Alumni Hall presided over by Howard S. (Howdy) Wilcox, executive director of the I.U. Foundation.

The first of its kind on a college campus, the "Little 500" will be a 50-mile test of speed and endurance on the cinder running track in Indiana's Memorial Stadium Saturday, May 12.

Thirty-three racing bikes will represent the thirty-three men's housing organizations that survive the trials to be conducted in the weeks preceding the race.

Racing Pits.

There will be all the trappings of the Speedway. Each team of four riders will have its own racing pit along side the track for repairs of the bikes and for recuperation of the riders. The press and radio will occupy a "pagoda" patterned after the big track.

The same type of split-second timing gear used at the Indianapolis Speedway will be installed to keep tally of the lap-by-lap speed of each racing bike.

Speedway know-how will be there, too, in the person of Wilbur Shaw, Speedway president and three-time winner of the motor classic, who will be the pace setter on a tandem bike for the preliminary lap around the quarter-mile cinder track.

Speedway board chairman Tony Hulman will be the honorary chairman for the collegiate event.

Klein is Starter.

Waving the checkered flag will be Seth Klein, the portly official starter for every Indianapolis Speedway race since 1920.

Tommy Milton, two-time winner and now chief steward of the Indianapolis track will be the chief steward of the "Little 500."

Head of the technical committee will be Carl Stockholm of Chicago, former American Olympic bicycle racing champion.

Under the direction of Bob Skiles and Ken Kress, the sponsoring Student Foundation Committee has gained the support of all the campus organizations for the unique project. In the Hoosier state, a number of leading alumni have pledged their assistance in the sale of tickets and in securing the business and manufacturing sponsors who will underwrite the race.

Former Editors.

Enthusiastic supporters of the "Little 500" also are leading newspapermen in the state. A group of former editors of The Indiana Daily Student returned to the campus yesterday to edit today's special Sunday edition of The Daily Student. Others contributed special articles to the edition.

Wilcox pointed out that the I.U. plan of providing funds for working students comes from the realization that most scholarships favor students who can devote the major portion of their time to studies.

A unique system has been worked out to award the grants. By this system, applicants will be given points for their grade averages. Added to this will be another total of points, depending upon how many hours a week the students must devote to earning their own support. Those with the largest combined totals will be eligible for the grants. Details of the new-type scholarships will be announced later.

The entire proceeds from the race will go to the new fund being established in the I.U. Foundation, since all expenses will be paid through the sponsors of the race.

A number of special prizes will be presented to lap winners and to the leaders at the end of the race, including R.C.A. television sets and a winners' trophy for the first team to cross the finish line. All the prizes also are donated.

400 Leaders Of Student Body Hear the Story

Wells, Shoemaker, and Lemon Support Plan to Raise Funds.

By CHARLIE LYONS
Editor, The Daily Student, 1950

More than 400 student leaders gathered in Alumni Hall yesterday heard the first official announcement of plans for Indiana University's "Little 500" bicycle race in Memorial Stadium next Spring.

Howard S. (Howdy) Wilcox, executive director of the I.U. Foundation, outlined the "inside stuff" at the "kick-off" meeting in a bid to raise funds for scholarships for worthy students.

Over a brilliantly lighted stage on which sat top University and civic leaders as well as leaders of the Student Foundation committee, appeared the theme of the scholarship drive in foot-high letters, "Help Those Who Help Themselves."

Wells All For It.

President Herman B Wells told the group that he heartily endorsed the race.

"It is a great promotion. It will gain friends for the Foundation and gain funds for the scholarship drive.

"This drive will also be good for the students who come after you. I know it will be a success if you give it your co-operation."

Col. R. L. Shoemaker, Dean of Students, acted as chairman. He stressed that this drive will be the means of keeping deserving and industrious students in school.

Among Those Present.

R. E. (Danny) Dever, publicity chairman of the Little 500, introduced the dignitaries on the stage which included, in addition to President Wells, Howdy Wilcox, and Col. Shoemaker, Mayor Tom Lemon, of Bloomington; Fenwick T. Reed, assistant to President Wells, Bob Skiles and Ken Kress, president and general manager of the Little 500.; Jean Gordon, secretary; Al Moellering, vice-president, and D'Alice Coburn, director of ticket sales.

Mayor Lemon promised the co-operation of the city.

"I think it's a fine idea. What's good for I.U. is good for Bloomington."

Every Nickel for Aid.

Mr. Wilcox said that "every nickel taken in at the gate will go into the scholarship fund. Additional revenue will come from the thirty-three financial sponsors who will put up $100 per team."

Also on stage were three large R.C.A. television sets which will go as prizes to the first three housing organization teams to get over the finish line in the race.

Equally prominent on the stage

(Continued on Page Three)

T. E. (POP) MYERS
Honorary Vice-president

BYRON K. ELLIOTT
Chairman, Board of Directors

ANTON HULMAN JR.
Honorary Board Chairman

HERMAN B WELLS
Honorary General Manager

WILBUR SHAW
Honorary President

P0035364, IU Archives.

BEHIND THE STORY

Chronicling 'On-Track Feats and Off-Track Warts'

The founder of the Little 500 was no stranger to newspapers or the IDS.

Howdy Wilcox, the founder of the bicycle race that continues today, sold newspapers at age 7 to help earn his keep while his paternal grandmother was raising him. Wilcox's mother had died years before while delivering his younger sister, and father Howard Wilcox Sr.—the 1919 Indianapolis 500 champion—died when Howdy was 3 years old.

Wilcox served as IDS editor for one week in March 1942 before war service beckoned. But once he was back in the U.S. and back on campus, it wasn't long before the school paper became of use to him again.

As the executive director of the IU Foundation, Wilcox believed students who were active in university activities would graduate to become actively donating alumni. He created the IU Student Foundation to further that goal, and the group's first signature event was a bicycle race, announced via a special Sunday edition of the IDS on Jan. 21, 1951. Charlie Lyons, the IDS editor who was appointed by the shrewd Wilcox to serve as public relations director for his new organization, wrote the lead story.

Wilcox's first Little 500 would be his last, as The Indianapolis Star and News newspapers hired him to serve as personnel and promotions director. (He couldn't pass up the $12,000 salary, a boost from his $9,000 IU paycheck.) He would remain in the newspaper business until the mid-1960s, when he started his own public relations firm in Indianapolis.

The Little 500 rolled on, entrenched as not just one of the university's biggest events of the year but one of the most important at the IDS. For three decades, iconic photos of the winning team in victory circle always included a copy of the IDS, hustled quickly from the on-campus printing presses to the old 10th Street Stadium. The edition included photos from the race's early laps and the team name as the banner headline.

Howdy Wilcox with his wife and sons at the qualifications for the inaugural Little 500 in 1951. *P0023337, IU Archives.*

IU students read the Little 500 "qualifications extra" in the lead-up to the 1967 race. *P0078389, IU Archives.*

The IDS has chronicled the race's on-track feats and off-track warts, with front pages sometimes featuring the winners below the fold and police stories above. In 1988, the main headline was not about the race, but the five people arrested at a student apartment complex. Three years later, a photo of a car being overturned became the era's signature image—and the focus of a First Amendment dispute after a judge ordered the IDS photographer to hand over his shots so police could identify the suspects.

Whether you needed to know the race winner or the number of weekend arrests, the Little 500 issue of the IDS was a must-read—and still is.

—John Schwarb, BAJ 1996

WHOSE FAULT IS IT?

Bitter Herbs

By Herb Michelson

In Cleveland tonight Harry (Kid) Matthews will administer a bruising left-and-right attack to the medulla oblongata of unfortunate Danny Nardico. . .

In Columbus, Ohio, this p.m., major league baseball moguls will rack their brains to outwit one another on the trading marts. . .

Here in Bloomington this evening, in a place where people usually dance or stuff themselves over a banquet table, four gentlemen will tax their "think tanks" in an attempt to obtain answers to interrogations from sports-minded members of the student body. . .

What will come of these three thought-provoking incidents is questionable. . . Matthews will probably knock out Nordico. . . Some ballplayers will probably switch uniforms. . . And undoubtedly a number of Hoosier textbook holders will devise various schemes to either boost the I.U. football team to the nation's No. 1 spot, withdraw the school from the Big Ten, or maintain our present well-rounded athletic policy. . .

To the sporting world, the events taking place in this Hoosier home of learning take a back seat to the fight in Cleveland and the baseball conclave in Columbus. . .

However, back-seat drivers have been credited as being rather shrewd maneuverers. . .

Even if nothing but idle conversation echoes off the walls of Alumni Hall tonight, the Town Hall presentation will have proved successful. . . Perhaps some of this chit-chat will influence Prof. John F. Mee when he and his Athletic Committee form I.U.'s athletic policy. . .

If it doesn't, the student body should feel that they have helped in the formation of a "vox pop" system in collegiate athletics.

Is It Yours? Is It Yours? Is It Yours? Is It Yours?

—DAILY STUDENT PHOTOS By MARSHALL L. LINCOLN

What Kind of Program?—It's up to You

The last several weeks have seen much debate—both informed and confused—on what I.U. should do for an athletic policy that would be best for the school. Prompting this talk were the Hoosiers' inability to win regularly on the football field, the resignation of Coach Clyde Smith, and Coach Smith's explanation last week of the faults of today's big-time college football that led him to resign.

Tonight at 7:45 o'clock in Alumni Hall, the Town Hall forum, sponsored by the Union Board, will invite all thoughts and ideas on athletic policy to be brought forth into the open. Prof. John F. Mee, chairman of the faculty athletic committee, will clarify some of the issues as speaker at the forum.

The Student has attempted to throw some light on the situation by showing three possibilities for a future I.U. athletic policy:

1. The University could go all out for football and attempt to push the sport into the realm of "big-time"—a move that would surely mean Hoosier victories and championships, even though other sports might starve to death.

2. I.U. could try to balance its athletic program, with athletes in all sports getting equal attention, assuring that the University would be highly respected in all the various sports. Football, however, would not get the special allowance it needs right now out of the sports budget to rise immediately to an all-conquering position.

3. I.U. could take a definite step towards de-emphasis of athletics and "secede" from the Big Ten, whereby all the pressures and headaches caused by "big-timeness" would be eliminated, along with many sports-minded students of the future.

These issues will no doubt be part of the discussion at Alumni Hall tonight. They deserve serious consideration. The faculty athletic committee does not want to decide by itself what athletic policy the University will follow. Students, faculty members and the alumni have a part in it, too, for the University sports are a part of them.

The importance of the problem makes it mandatory for the I.U. sports follower to bring his opinions to the forum.

Town Hall Panel To Discuss Problem Tonight

Whose fault is it? This question about the I.U. sports program will be discussed at the first open Town Hall meeting tonight at 7:45 o'clock in Alumni Hall.

The discussion will center around the views of Prof. John F. Mee, faculty representative to the Big Ten and head of the I.U. Athletic Committee; Prof. Edward E. Edwards, of the School of Business and a member of the Athletic Committee; Al Moellering, Law, Chief Justice of the Supreme Court last year, and Keith Cochran, senior, president of Union Board. These men will make up the panel to be moderated by Max Graeber, senior.

Question Period.

After the discussion questions may be presented from the floor. These questions and the answers that follow will have a bearing on the athletic program in future years.

Members of the Town Hall committee who have planned this meeting are Fred Pain, senior, Union Board representative; Max Graeber, senior; Judy Abel, Susan Bassett, James Cramer, and Joe Root, all juniors, and Phil Broyles, sophomore. Mr. Broyles is general chairman of the meeting.

Poll Results.

The results of the poll taken by Town Hall this past week are:

Thirty-four per cent of the students are satisfied with the status-quo of sports at I.U.

Twenty-one per cent of the students felt that sports at I.U. should be de-emphasized.

Forty-five per cent felt that sports at I.U. should be accentuated.

This poll was answered by 360 students. It will have no direct bearing on the athletic program when it is discussed by the Athletics Committee. However, a similar poll will be taken at the meeting tonight and it will have a definite bearing on the decision made.

HE SERVES BEST WHO SERVES THE TRUTH

THE INDIANA DAILY STUDENT

THE WEATHER
Mostly cloudy and mild today with occasional showers. Tomorrow mild with showers.

VOL. LXXXI—NO. 54——Z 175. INDIANA UNIVERSITY WEDNESDAY, DECEMBER 5, 1951. BLOOMINGTON, INDIANA Established 1867

U.S. ASKS RELEASE OF FOUR AIRMEN

Aud Program To Preview Christmas

City Mayor to Add Realistic Touch To Square Scene.

The question, "I Wonder What Christmas Is Like?", will be asked one week from tonight at the annual Christmas program at the Auditorium. As in the past, the question will be presented musically.

A musical and chóreographic depiction of "Christmas on the Community Square" also will be presented. Adding to the authenticity of this theme will be the appearance of Thomas L. Lemon, Mayor of Bloomington.

The Chancel Choir, the Singing Hoosiers, the Women's Chorus, and the Opera Chorus will sing in the first section of the program. Jack De Lon, senior, tenor, will sing portions of "The Messiah," by Handel. He will be accompanied by James Serviss, PG, bass; Vera Scammon, PG, soprano, and

(Continued on Page Two)

Ol' Sol Shows

Ol' Sol put a temporary halt to the Bloomington monsoons yesterday with a reasonably pleasant day. After a night of flooded streets, the campus was comparatively mudless. The maximum temperature of the day was 57 degrees, and the minimum was 43. Temperature when 3:30 p.m. classes broke up was 51 degrees.

Inside - -

Group Selects Franzen For Foreign Survey Team

Prof. Carl G. F. Franzen, of the School of Education, has been selected to represent the North Central Association in a visit to army personnel dependents' schools in Europe and the Near East in January and part of February.

He is one of the five-member team which is to survey the dependent school situation in Germany, Austria, and Trieste. He will also observe schools in Paris, Athens, Ankara, Turkey, and London.

The dependent schools are for the children of army and civilian personel in those countries. The North Central Association accredits the schools, and Prof. Franzen said that the survey is made to see if the schools are carrying out the regulations and standards set up by the association.

Others who will go are A. J. Gibson, chairman of the W. Va. state committee of the North Central Association; Lt. Col. Dudley D. Brodie, of the operative branch of the Adjutant General's Office in Washington, D.C.; Dr. John R. Richards, special assistant to the Secretary of the Army, and J. B. Allen, of the Lillywhite office of the Commission of Education, Federal Security Agency.

The men will leave for Frankfurt, Germany, on military aircraft on Jan. 4. They will return from London as soon as the survey is completed.

Suez Fights Continue As Dead Count Rises

CAIRO, Egypt, Dec. 4 —(AP)— Egyptians and British soldiers clashed bloodily for a second day in the violence-struck city of Suez today, and the interior ministry said fifteen Egyptians were killed.

The ministry said twenty-nine Egyptians, including a child, were injured, and that one of the dead was a woman.

The British listed their losses at two wounded in the hour-long fight near a water processing plant at the edge of the city. Their communique said twenty Egyptians were reported killed, but added that this report was unconfirmed.

Taken with latest Egyptian reports of yesterday's pitched battle at Suez, the bloodiest yet in the Canal Zone dispute, the ministry's figures boosted to sixty-five the number killed in two days.

In another disorder in Cairo, seven policemen and several students were slightly injured today when students refused to disperse. The students were demonstrating against the shooting of Egyptians

(Continued on Page Two)

Demands C-47 Return

BUDAPEST, Hungary, Dec. 4—(AP)—The United States today demanded that Hungary free four crewmen and return the American C-47 transport plane which was forced down by Soviet fighters Nov. 19 while on a flight from West Germany to Yugoslavia.

Some diplomatic observers said they believed the demand would be met comparatively soon.

They pointed out that a Hungarian note yesterday and a previous Soviet news agency account charged that the plane was intended for dumping spies into Hungary, but did not accuse the four U.S. Air Force men themselves of such activities.

George Abbott, U.S. charge d'affaires since the departure last Summer of minister Nathaniel Davis, asked release of the aviators and their C-47 transport plane when he called on Foreign Minister Karoly Kiss at 2:30 p.m. today. A formal note later made the same request.

(Diplomatic officials in Washington said Abbott was not allowed to see the fliers but reported he was assured they were in Hungarian custody and in good health. They said a separate protest might go later to Moscow.)

Abbott refused to make any prediction as to whether the demand might be met, but he said Foreign Minister Kiss promised to pass it on to the proper authorities.

Minister Killed and Three Hurt In Five-Car Collision on Road 37

A Methodist minister was burned to death and three persons were injured in a five-car accident last night six miles north of the City on State Road 37.

The Rev. Braxell Roberts, 31 years old, of Route 6, minister of the Arlington Methodist Church, was thrown halfway through the windshield of his car when it was hit in the rear by one driven by Carl Reynolds, 43 years old, of 108 South Rogers street.

Reynolds was reported in "fairly good" condition in Bloomington Hospital last night.

Emil Porter, 17 years old, of Martinsville, and Martin Kinzler, 24 years old, of Indianapolis, were also taken to the hospital after the wreck. They were treated and released.

Trooper Rayborn Taylor, of the State Police, said the accident resulted from a collision a few minutes before, at about 6:20 p.m.

Four cars were stopped on the highway when the car driven by Mr. Raynolds approached from the south.

The first collision occurred when the vehicle driven by Porter skid-

(Continued on Page Six)

'Staying Young' Theme For 'The Silver Whistle'

"The Silver Whistle," the third major production of the University Theatre this season, will open Friday night at 8 o'clock. Tickets for the three-act comedy may be obtained at the I.U. Ticket Office. The play will also be presented Saturday night and Friday and Saturday, Dec. 14 and 15.

Set at a home for the aged, "The Silver Whistle" is about persons who have grown older than they are. When Oliver Erwenter, a tramp played by Joseph Golden, PG, arrives at the home, he tries to show these persons that they are only as old as they want to be.

"The Silver Whistle" made a successful run on Broadway after it opened during the 1948-49 season. The University Theatre production is under the direction of Lyle Hagan, assistant professor of speech.

Vishinsky Denies Evading Atomic Bomb Question

PARIS, Dec. 4 —(AP)— Andrei Y. Vishinsky branded as a lie today a report that he had not answered a question in the secret Big Four arms talks about whether Russia would admit inspectors as soon as atomic weapons were prohibited.

The Soviet foreign minister insisted, in an involved statement to newsmen, on immediate prohibition of atomic bombs, before an international control system is working.

Vishinsky stopped in a U.N. corrider after the Big Four session today and issued a blast at newspaper reports, based upon accounts by Western sources, that he had not given a satisfactory answer to this question yesterday by U.S. Ambassador Philip Jessup:

Will the Soviet Union admit international inspectors into its territory on the very day after the prohibition of the atomic bomb is declared?

Vishinsky fired back, in his first public comment on the talks, that "of course it is necessary to organize various measures closely connected with control." He said that if this is set forth in a convention, only people who seek to delay the prohibition of atomic weapons still would find reasons for delay, such as calling for employment of inspectors, instructing them and sending them to appropriate places.

Western diplomats said they felt this meant "no" on the question of inspection within Russia.

New Reservoir To Be Named 'Lake Lemon'

City Council Votes Unanimous to Honor Mayor.

A mayor usually isn't proud of a "lemon" in his administration.

But the Bloomington City Council last night gave Mayor Thomas L. Lemon one that he might be proud of. They unanimously voted to name the new waterworks lake, "Lake Lemon."

Mrs. Helen Zell, Clerk-Treasurer, read petitions to name the lake after the outgoing mayor. Councilman Charles H. Dunn made the motion that the lake be officially called "Lake Lemon."

Bernard Glover, Fire Chief, reported to the Council that the City Fire Department answered fifty-three alarms in November amounting to a loss of $2,550. Nineteen of the alarms were at homes.

Councilman David E. Chitwood made a motion that traffic lights be installed on West Eleanor street, three-quarters of a block

(Continued on Page Two)

Today——

—— on the campus ——

UNION - A.W.S. DANCING — 8 p.m. Rhythm Room. Music Activities Committee program from 9 to 10:30.

TOWN HALL FORUM — 8 p.m. Alumni Hall.

DEPARTMENT OF FINE ARTS EXHIBIT — All day. Gallery, Art Center. "Swiss Posters."

DEPARTMENT OF FINE ARTS EXHIBIT — All day. Main Gallery, Art Center. Edward Millman's one-man exhibit of paintings.

DEPARTMENT OF FINE ARTS EXHIBIT — All day. Library, Art Center. "The Moy-Mack Print Show."

P0079402, IU Archives.

HE SERVES BEST WHO SERVES THE TRUTH

THE INDIANA DAILY STUDENT

THE WEATHER
Partly cloudy and colder. Tomorrow fair.

VOL. LXXyII—NO. 101—Z 175. INDIANA UNIVERSITY FRIDAY, MARCH 6, 1953. BLOOMINGTON, INDIANA Established 1867

JOSEF STALIN DEAD

Group Slices 2 P.C. From I.U. Budget

By THE ASSOCIATED PRESS

An across-the-board cut of 2 per cent in Indiana's two-year budget was announced Thursday night by the State Senate Finance Committee.

The trim may mean that about $471,000 has been sliced from the operating and salary appropriations of Indiana University and that similar whacks in the budget requests of the three other State-supported colleges and universities have been made.

$3,196,000 Total Trim.

The total trimming on the full State budget amounts to $3,196,000, according to Senator Clem McConaha, of Centerville, Republican chairman of the committee.

He said most of the slice was made by knocking an average 8 per cent in salary appropriations for doctors and attendants at mental hospitals. But he added that there are enough unfilled positions in the mental hospitals to still permit substantial pay increases under the new figure.

Senate Approval Needed.

The total budget yet must be approved by the entire Senate, however. When the budget left the House last Friday, the two-year outlay totaled $605,645,738.

With the committee's recommended cut, the total budget would be only $602,449,738 with several items still to be considered.

The total amount cut on a percentage basis from the requests for the colleges and universities and other State departments was $1,900,000.

Trimmed to $23,092,000.

That might mean that I.U.'s asking of $23,563,638 for the biennium has been trimmed to approximately $23,092,000 if the cut is 2 per cent on each institution and department.

The $1,900,000 slash in funds for the colleges and universities and $1,180,000 cut in salaries for mental hospitals, with $116,000 sliced from other departments makes up the over-all amount knocked from budget so far.

Senator McConaha added that the item for State support for teacher's salaries has not been considered yet by the committee.

Senate Gets One Volunteer For U.N. Parley

Mock Conference Delegates to Discuss World Affairs.

Only one student senator volunteered Thursday night to attend a mock United Nations conference at the University of Wisconsin, March 27, 28 and 29.

Bob Frowick, president of the Student Body, said that he hoped to accompany the senator, Gary Ash, sophomore, and other senators that may sign up, to attend the meeting sponsored by the University of Wisconsin student government.

The conference will be patterned after a United Nations meeting with student government representatives from all over the country acting as U. N. delegates to discuss current world problems. Each delegate will assume the role of one of the U. N. sixty-one member nations.

The purpose of the conference, Mr. Frowick said, is to educate student leaders on U. N. and world affairs. He felt that the conference would be "very educational." He was indefinite about the cost.

In other senate business, the Bipartisan and Pogo parties were among eleven campus organizations dropped from the official list of student groups since they did not turn in rosters at the Activities Office to comply with the rules set up by the senate.

Other groups which will not be recognized officially as a campus organization include the American Civil Liberties Union, the National Association for the Advancement of Colored People, the Socialist discussion group on contemporary affairs, Delta Tau Mu, Junior Toastmasters, Dragons Head, Square and Compass, Top Hats, and Townettes.

To regain status as an official campus organization, the groups will have to comply with the rules for establishing a new organization. Until they take action, the groups will not be able to keep funds in the Treasurer's office or make use of University facilities for their meetings.

Victory Ball Will Honor Mac and Team

Women to Have Extended Hours for Union Dance.

Branch McCracken and his I. U. Big Ten basketball champions will be honored at a Victory Ball in Alumni Hall immediately after the Iowa-Indiana game Monday night.

The A. W. S. Board of Standards has extended women's hours from 10:30 p.m. to 12:30 a.m. for the free dance which will last till midnight. This will allow the students to enjoy a planned celebration.

Palmer Jenkins and his combo will play for the dance which is sponsored by the Union Board.

Danny Parker, sophomore, is chairman of the dance, and Bob Bluemle, sophomore, heads the entertainment committee.

State-wide Drop In Jobless Pay

A State-wide drop in the number of unemployment insurance claims was reported by William C. Stalnaker, director of the Indiana Employment Security Division.

During the last week of February layoffs dropped, construction and quarry work picked up, and industrial hiring continued. The State agency received 17,680 claims last week. This total was about 7,200 below that for the same week last year.

Mr. Stalnaker said the supply of manpower appeared to be decreasing, and that fewer job seekers registered in most division offices.

DISCUSS POD PRANCE — Presidents of campus honoraries discuss plans for the Pod Prance tonight sponsored by Tomahawk, independent sophomore honorary. They are; (front row, left to right) Jo Peckenpaugh, Pamarada; Col. Raymond L. Shoemaker, Dean of Students, who will help judge the dancing contests, and Betty MacLeod, Enomene. Back row, left to right, Jim Weber, Flame; Bill Dahl, Tomahawk; Ralph Jones, Falcon; Ted Pincus, Skull and Crescent; and Tom Mellman, Sphinx.

Students to Don Pods for Prance

"I miss seeing the honorary pods on campus. I used to wear one myself," reminisces Col. R. L. Shoemaker, Dean of Students.

Col. Shoemaker will be pleased tonight at the Pod Prance where pod-bedecked couples will dance to the melodies of Ed Yates and his band in Alumni Hall.

Informal Dance.

Tomahawk, national honorary for independent sophomore men is sponsoring the informal dance, which will last from 9 p.m. until midnight. The dance is open to the public.

Members of Flame Club, Sphinx Club, Skull and Crescent, Falcon Club, Pamarada, Pleiades, and Enomene will be honored at the dance, which is a part of the drive to revive pod-wearing by members of campus honoraries.

Chance to Lead Band.

Those persons who have always had a secret desire to lead a band will have their chance tonight during the Sammy Kaye-style floor show. Several dancers will be selected from the crowd to take the baton and direct the band.

Novel prizes will be awarded to the best dancers in each of four divisions, fox trot, waltz, South American, and jitterbug. Col. Shoemaker, Dean of Students; Bob Frowick, president of the Student Body, and Jo Kren, president of the Women's Residence Halls, will select the winners.

Bill Dahl, junior, president of Tomahawk, will act as master of ceremonies for the program.

Committee chairmen are: Dale Miller, tickets; Harold Cohen, decorations; Morris Wertenberger, publicity, and John Stevens, personnel, all sophomores.

Tickets will be available all day today in the Commons and tonight at the door.

N.C.A.A. Tickets On Sale Today

Three hundred special student tickets for the N.C.A.A. regional basketball playoffs next week end in Chicago are due to arrive either today or Saturday, Bob Cook, I.U. athletic publicity director, said late Thursday.

Mr. Cook said the seats would be in the end sections of the Chicago Stadium, where the tournament is being conducted. These half-price tickets are in addition to the 2000 tickets that have already been received at the I.U. ticket office, and will go on sale at 9:30 a.m. today.

The announcement of the special ticket offer came late Thursday afternoon in a phone call from Arthur Morris, N.C.A.A. tournament manager, in Chicago.

Specials in End Sections.

Mr. Cook emphasized the fact that these cut-rate tickets will be for seats in the end sections only. He said that students should not expect good seats at this rate and that the regular tickets will be in the side sections.

The Hurryin' Hoosiers will play in the second game next Friday evening against the DePaul-Miami (Ohio) victor. Holy Cross is scheduled to meet the Notre Dame-Eastern Kentucky victor in the first clash. The games are scheduled to begin at 7:45 and 9:40 o'clock.

The two losers will play the consolation game at 7:45 o'clock Saturday evening, with the championship contest slated for 9:40 o'clock.

The DePaul-Miami (Ohio) and Notre Dame-Eastern Kentucky tilts will be played on Tuesday evening in the Ft. Wayne Coliseum.

700 Reserved.

About seven hundred tickets have already been reserved for the two sessions, George Keough, manager of the ticket office, announced Thursday. He added, however, that if the demand outlasted the present supply, more ducats could probably be ordered.

Person who have already reserved tickets must pick them up by 5:30 p.m. Wednesday or their reservations will be cancelled, Mr. Keough said. That is the deadline for ticket sales on campus.

Accident Causes Major Damage

Local police reported major damage Thursday in a collision involving cars driven by Hershel A. Frye, 28 years old, of Route 8, Bloomington, and Barbara L. Smoot, 22, of Route 3, Bedford.

Both cars were going north in the 500 block of South Walnut street. Police reported no injuries.

Mrs. Fred Miller, of 1106 North Walnut Grove, reported her son's bicycle was stolen Thursday morning.

Another bicycle was recovered by police and returned to the owner, Bill Hall, son of Mr. Curtis B. Hall, of 422 Hawthorne drive.

Winter Gone?

Students slipped and skidded their way across an icy campus for the second time this week, as a 1.5 inch snowfall was recorded Wednesday night. The high for Thursday was 43 degrees, while the low was 26 degrees. At 4:30 p.m. the temperature was 41 degrees.

Today—
—on the campus—

WRESTLING MEET — Big Ten preliminaries 7 p.m. Fieldhouse.
REC NIGHT — 7:30 p.m. Student Building.
AUDITORIUM SERIES — Dudley, Maslow and Bales and Dance Company, 8 p.m. Auditorium.
RHYTHM ROOM — 8 to 12 p.m. Commons, Union Building.
FOLK DANCE WORKSHOP — 8:30 p.m. Alpha Hall.

Hogue Says Germans Treat Yanks Civilly

'Little Confidence in U. S. Strength,' Colloquy Hears.

"The attitude of the German people toward American occupation troops is one of polite civility," said Arthur R. Hogue, professor of history at Chapel Colloquy Thursday.

Prof. Hogue revealed that the German people have little confidence in the strength of U. S. forces. In the event of a Soviet attack, he said Germans feel they would fall into Russian control in one of the greatest slaughters of history.

Prof. Hogue was describing his trip through Frankfort, Bonne, Cologne, Heidelberg, Munich, Hamburg, and Berlin, as the guest of the German government.

120,000 Students.

There are sixteen German universities, six technical institutions, and twenty academies, with 120,000 students enrolled in them he said. All students have definite vocational choices when they enroll in one of these institutions, and the majority of them prefer professions over business careers. Unfortunately, Prof. Hogue pointed out, most of the libraries suffered heavily from war-time destruction.

Professors, he said, are persons of high prestige in Germany. He was once told that "A professor is not a king; he is God himself!" The German scholars impressed Prof. Hogue with their courtesy, urbanity, and fine manners.

Refugees Worst Problem.

Prof. Hogue said that the refugee problem was Germany's worst. Refugees from the Soviet-controlled Eastern sector come streaming into the Western part through the funnel of Berlin, seeking safety, he said.

There is a definite conflict, he continued, between Anglo-American and German thinking about punishment of war criminals. Germans feel that their former leaders are receiving ex post facto punishment.

As for general conditions in Germany, Prof. Hogue said that one can live a life of luxury there—if he can afford it. Germany has good food, operas, theatres, and fine hotels. Clothing, however, is difficult to obtain at a reasonable price.

Buildings Are Rubble.

The physical damage done by the war is appalling, he said. Buildings are nothing but dust and rubble, some of which is piled so high that children ski down them in the Winter.

German people, he stated, think

(Continued on Page Six)

Four Struggle to Rule World's Largest Empire

Malenkov Tops On First Round

By JOHN HIGHTOWER

WASHINGTON (AP) —The death of Josef Stalin was believed here Thursday night to have signalled the start of a contest for power among his chief followers which will have incalculable consequences for war or peace in the world.

At present, the machinery of control of the sprawling Communist Empire is believed to be technically in the hands of G. M. Malenkov and V. M. Molotov.

Malenkov has been Stalin's chief lieutenant in running the Communist party in Russia, which American oficials have long regarded as the real center of power. Molotov has been Stalin's chief deputy premier.

Future Is in Question.

What will happen now is anybody's guess. President Dwight D. Eisenhower, with all the resources of intelligence information at his command, made this clear at his news conference Thursday.

Mr. Eisenhower said that with his advisors he had considered all the possibilities of future developments and had come to what he started with—meaning that no one could definitely say what the next turn of events will be. The attitude of the United States government, he said, is one of watchfulness.

The problem in Russia is that, unlike the constitutional processes for switching authority which exist in democratic countries, there is no known orderly process for shifting control of power to new hands. Stalin may have left a political will, but if so no word of it has leaked out to date.

Malenkov Runs Ahead.

Speculation about who might be his successor has tended to concentrate primarily upon Malenkov because in the management of the Communist party he has appeared to be Stalin's hand-picked favorite. But the name of Molotov has ranked high in all considerations of this problem by American official experts on the Soviet Union. Also mentioned is L. P. Beria, who is believed to have a powerful support in the form of the secret police.

Still another figure who American experts say can not be counted out is Nicholas Bulganin, whose personal power and prestige rest upon his influence with the Soviet armed forces.

In view of the line taken by the President at his news conference, it appeared that the United States government would proceed with great caution to adjust to the new situation, keeping its policies flexible to deal with any of various possibilities. These include:

1. A continuation of the present Russian policies based on antagonism to the free world. This antagonism is expressed in the war in Korea, the struggle in Indo China and in the general aim of expanding Communist domination wherever possible.

2. A new and more truculent attitude. This could develop if Stalin's successor proved to be reckless in his expansionist policies or if he felt that intensification of the conflict outside Russia would strengthen his position at home.

3. A drastic weakening of Soviet power which might follow upon any prolonged, bitter struggle among Soviet leaders for Stalin's mantle.

4. A drastic modification of Russia's aims in the world, leading to sincere efforts to reach understandings with the free nations and bring the cold war to an end as well as finding a solution for the hot wars in Korea and Indo China.

U.S. officials generally believe that considerable time may elapse before the pattern of control in Russia is established. Their thinking is based in large part upon what happened when Lenin died and Stalin began the maneuvers

(Continued on Page Six)

JOSEF STALIN

'After Stalin' Discussed By Slavic Club

"After Stalin What?," the topic of the Slavic Club discussion Thursday night, suddenly assumed a sudden and unexpected significance.

Less than an hour before the meeting, the report of the death of Josef Stalin was announced.

Dr. Michael Ginsburg, chairman of the Department of Slavic Studies, said, "We are witnessing one of the important moments of our time. The importance of this moment lies in the fact that it is the beginning of a new era and may have tremendous consequences in Russia and the rest of the world."

Possible Bosses.

There are four men who could succeed Stalin: Malenkov, Molotov, Beria, and Bulganin. A possibility was suggested. "Triumvirates are only temporary," Dr. Ginsburg said. "Always in triumvirates, one man eventually arises to the top after much blood-letting.

"Malenkov is a person much less known to us than many other members of the Communist party. Since 1948, Malenkov has been rising constantly. He has been vice-chairman of the Council of Ministers since then," he explained.

"A symbolic privilege was given him at the nineteenth Party Congress," Dr. Ginsburg explained. "Malenkov replaced Josef Stalin as the key speaker at this meeting, the first in thirteen years. This was the first time anyone except Stalin had spoken as the main speaker at the Congress."

The Soviet press recently gave special attention to the anniversary of Malenkov's fiftieth birthday. This was the first time any birthday anniversary other than Stalin's was officially observed by the Soviet government.

'The Living God.'

"The weight that rested on Stalin's shoulders was so heavy that not even Malenkov can carry it right now," Dr. Ginsburg said. "Stalin leaves a vacuum that cannot be filled for many years. He was great because of his authority. He was the Living God whose opinion was accepted as the Supreme Truth. It will take decades to build up a reputation such as Stalin had."

"If the change goes smoothly, Communist satellites and occupied countries will live as before," Felix Oinas, instructor in slavic studies, said. "However, if there are signs of trouble in Russia, perhaps the satellites and occupied countries will come out of their hiding places and take up arms against their oppressors."

Red Premier Dies at 73

By EDDIE GILMORE

MOSCOW (AP)—Josef Stalin is dead.

The leader of the Soviet peoples died at 9:50 p.m. Moscow time (12:50 p.m. C.S.T.) after being stricken Sunday night.

To say that this nation of 200 millions will be shocked is to make an understatement. Millions of Russians already know of the death, as this dispatch is being telephoned to London at 8 a.m.

This correspondent was riding through Moscow's snowy streets, listening to his automobile radio, when the announcement came. The driver, a former Soviet army man, was so stunned he could hardly drive the car to the central telegraph ofice where all telephone calls to the outside world must be placed.

"Excuse me," he said, a trickle of tears rolling down his cheeks. "He was a real person."

That probably sums up what is in the heart of many Soviets.

Stalin had been in coma since he was stricken Sunday night, and his condition grew progressively worse. Thursday his ten physicians said his heart was faltering.

The announcement of his death was broadcast from Moscow at 4:07 a.m. Moscow time Friday—more than six hours after his doctors had given up their struggle.

The oficial announcement said:

See Obituary on Page Four

"The heart of the comrade and inspired continuer of Lenin's will, the wise leader and teacher of the Communist party and the Soviet people—Josef Vissarionovicth Stalin—has stopped beating."

Successor Unknown.

There was no immediate indication from Moscow who was taking over control of the country, but the announcement was issued in the name of the Communist party's Central Committee, the Council of Ministers and the Presidium of the Supreme Council. All these are organs which Stalin dominated, and among those next to him in power have been Georgi Malenkov, L. P. Beria, V. M. Molotov and Nicholas Bulganin.

As if appealing for unity, the official statement said:

"In these sorrowful days all the peoples of our country are rallying even closer in a great fraternal family under the tested leadership of the Communist party created and reared by Lenin and Stalin."

Malenkov Next to Stalin.

The most prominent leader of the Communist party, next to Stalin, has been Malenkov. He keynoted the All-Party Congress last October, laying down the law to all segments of the party in matters of discipline.

"The Soviet people have boundless faith in and are permeated with a deep love for their Communist party for they know that the supreme law governing all the activity of the party is service in the interests of the people," the announcement said.

The Soviet regime holds sway across a sixth of the surface of the earth—from the Baltic Sea to Bering Strait.

Illness Known Wednesday.

Stalin's fatal illness became known on Wednesday, more than two days after he was stricken in his Kremlin apartment. An official announcement issued from the Ministry of Health and signed by the ten physicians said Stalin "had a sudden hemorrhage of the brain" the night of March 1. This "affected vitally important parts of the brain" and paralyzed his right leg and arm. He lost consciousness and the power to speak.

Two more bulletins were issued — early Thursday Moscow time, and again Thursday evening only an hour and a half before the announced death hour. The third bulletin told of Stalin's failing heart.

P0079532, IU Archives.

REFLECTION

Linotype Memories

"That all-night Boress might turn into playing a Boress trick on someone. For some reason, the word never spread around the state or country. It is purely local."

What is in our memory banks? Remember what a Boress is? What does WGCD mean? Who dropped a type drawer in front of Professor Stempel? Why did Stempel sign things with "stj" in all lower case and what nickname evolved from that?

There is a word, "Boress." It is a true IU Bloomington campus word. According to Stempel's stylebook, it started back in the 1920s as a more polite way to use "bore ass." It can mean playing tricks on someone or it can be one of those late-night talk sessions that go on and on discussing everything. That all-night Boress might turn into playing a Boress trick on someone. For some reason, the word never spread around the state or country. It is purely local.

We used to call the Daily Student the WGCD. It came after the Chicago Tribune called itself WGN, World's Greatest Newspaper, and even used that for its radio station call letters. Our students dubbed our paper the WGCD, the World's Greatest College Daily. Some remember when professor Ernest Linton, who taught government, deemed it the World's Best Newspaper!

Dropped type drawers—what a horrifying memory. In the type lab, we were all supposed to learn the California Job Case so we could set headlines from all that type. Less known was that John Stempel had his typographers' union card. He went to the type lab after class and sorted out the "pied" type from our clumsy efforts—or a dropped drawer!

Get a group of journalism alumni together from about 1947 to 1950 who had Professor Walter Steigleman for feature writing. Someone will start the phrase and others will join in on "unnecessary, superfluous, redundancy." He used it so often in class we could all chant it and still do.

Stempel recalled that his use of "stj," all lower case, started when he was on the old New York Sun. He used that to mark copy he had read as different from some other initials in the newsroom. When he came back to campus in 1938 to lead the journalism program he continued to use the initials. Some students began to use the name, "Saint John." Behind his back, of course.

We can call up another memory, the drilling on Herman B (No Period) Wells. At some time, most of us put in that period and saw red marks on our work. Stempel even made sure The Associated Press used it in its stylebook as an example of being careful about eccentricities.

So many memories—Sigma Delta Chi with its Blanket Hop and Gridiron Dinner; Theta Sigma Phi with its Razz Banquet and Matrix Table dinners with prominent speakers. There was the famous Pearl Harbor issue, the only extra in town the afternoon of December 7, 1941. The news staff itself went out all over campus, shouting the big headline, "Jap Bombs Kill 350 at Pearl Harbor."

So many memories for the Linotype Generation. Or, the "Linotype Slugs." Or, maybe the "Hot Types."

—Marjorie Smith Blewett, BA 1948, wrote this essay for a 2000 special publication produced for a reunion of the "Linotype Generation," which extended from the 1930s to the 1950s.

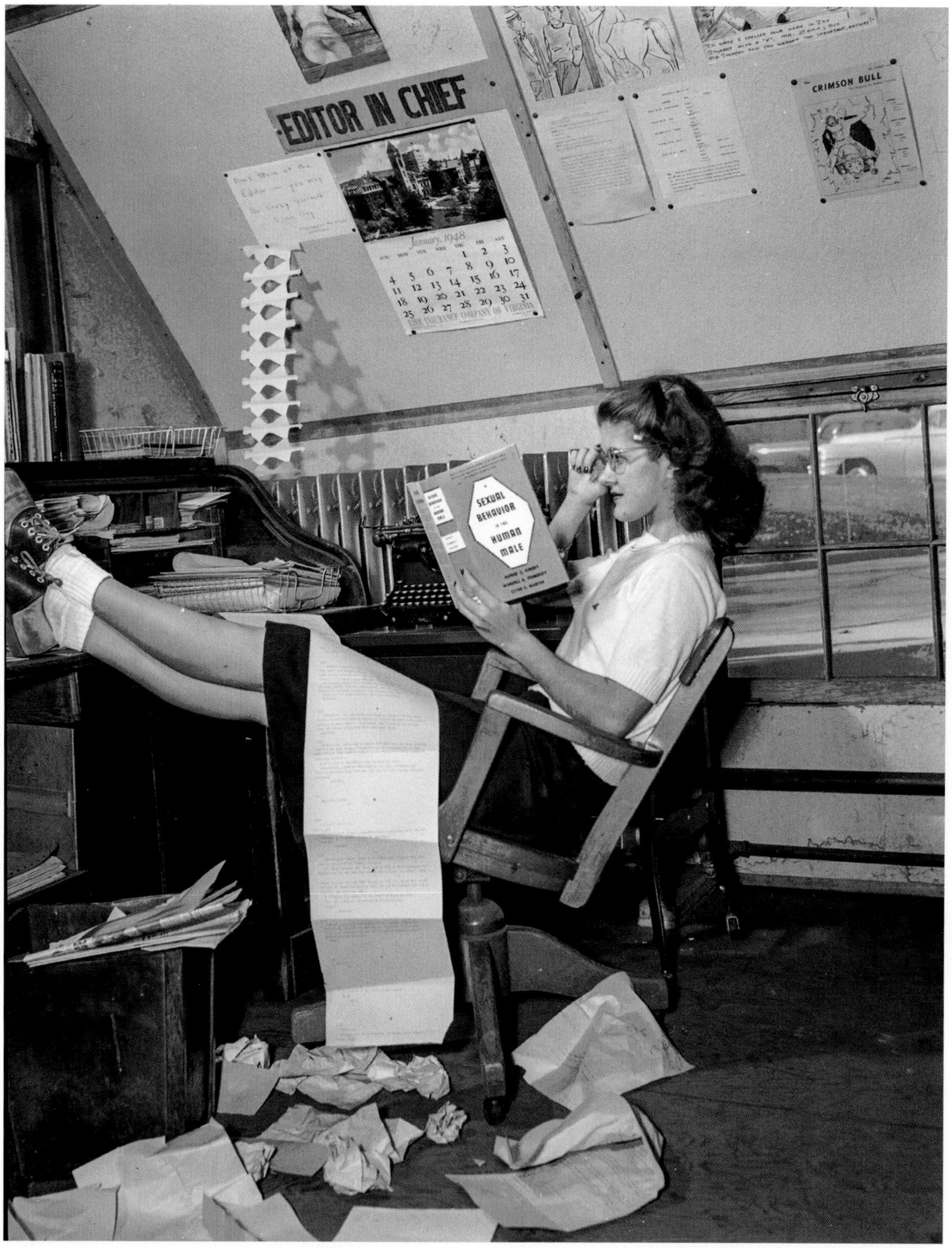

Marjorie Smith Blewett poses at Ernie Pyle's desk with a copy of Alfred Kinsey's "Sexual Behavior in the Human Male" for a 1948 Arbutus photo. She says the book was actually open to a random page of statistics. *P0041206, IU Archives.*

WE DOOD IT

THE INDIANA DAILY STUDENT

VOL. LXXXII—NO. 110—Z 175. INDIANA UNIVERSITY THURSDAY, MARCH 19, 1953. BLOOMINGTON, INDIANA Established 1867.

Hoosiers Snare N.C.A.A. Crown In 69-68 Drama

KANSAS CITY (Special to The Daily Student) — They trampled and shoved and shouted and yelled in the plush halls of the swank Municipal Auditorium . . . The players, with their towels around their heads and top coats covering their sweaty uniforms stampeded into their Continental Hotel headquarters with more ferocity than a herd of cattle.

The kids had done it . . . . they had won the fifteenth N.C.A.A. tourney. In the most breath-taking and pulse-pounding manner, Branch McCracken's tots of destiny had knocked off Phog Allen's Jayhawks, 69-68.

K.U., the Cinderella quintet of the nation, and the Hoosiers, the club few figured to wind up in the N.C.A.A. top spot, put on a brilliant exhibition.

I.U.'s victory was its second in N.C.A.A. history—in 1940 the Hoosiers knocked off another Kansas quintet, 60-42. It was the third N.C.A.A. title for a Big Ten team.

Wisconsin, the only winner besides I.U., did the trick in 1941.

Washington won the third-place consolation prize by humbling Louisiana State, 86-69, with big Bob Houbregs scoring 42 points.

The championship game had all the thrills of an A-grade movie. After Bob Leonard, fouled by Dean Kelley, of Kansas, had hit the second of two free throws, Coach Allen called his Jayhawks to the bench for final instructions.

Eyes On Clock.

The Hawks took the ball out and passed to the forecourt, watching the clock closely. Jerry Alberts, a substitute who came into the conflict when pivot-star B. H. Born was called out on personals, fired a one-hand push-shot from the side as the clock registered six seconds to play.

The ball never had a chance. It slammed against the rim amidst the groans of the partisan crowd of 10,500 and was knocked out of bounds by an unidentified Kansas player. It was Indiana's ball as the game ended.

Three New Records.

The Hoosiers will leave Kansas City Thursday morning by plane. They will arrive in Bloomington about 3 p.m.

In winning the tourney, I.U. set two team records, while the Hoosier big dog, Don Schlundt, set one mark.

As a team, I.U. broke the four-game series total-point record, which was set by Illinois in 1951 with 298 points. Washington broke that mark in the first game, winding up with 307 points. But I.U. hit the 310 mark two hours later.

More Records Fall.

The new champs also busted the four-game free throw mark of 80, which was also set by Illinois in 1951. I.U. shattered it Tuesday with 89 charity tosses and extended the new mark to 108 Wednesday evening.

Don Schlundt hit 49 free throws in the four games. This topped Clyde Lovellette's 1952 record of 35.

In the shooting column, the Hoosiers out-shot Kansas, 36.5 per cent to 32.3 per cent, and grabbed 33 rebounds to K.U.'s 29. Kansas made 26 of 34 free throws, while the Hoosiers missed 10, hitting only 19 of 29.

But the kid who saved the Hoosiers time after time was Charley Kraak, who hit a couple of baskets

(Continued on Page Three)

'Grand Slam'

INDIANA	G	F	P	T.
Kraak, f	5	7	5	17
DeaKyne, f	0	0	1	0
Farley, f	1	0	5	2
Schlundt, c	11	8	3	30
White, c	1	0	2	2
Leonard, g	5	2	2	12
Poff, g	0	0	0	0
Scott, g	2	2	3	6
Byers, g	0	0	0	0
Totals	23	19	21	69
KANSAS	G	F	P	T
Patterson, f	1	7	3	9
A. Kelley, f	7	6	3	20
Davenport, f	0	0	0	0
Born, c	8	10	5	26
Smith, c	0	1	1	1
Albert, c	0	0	1	0
D. Kelley, g	3	2	2	8
Reich, g	2	0	2	4
Totals	21	26	17	68

Indiana 21-20-18-10—69
Kansas 19-22-17-10—68

Free throws missed: Indiana—Kraak 3, Schlundt 3, Leonard 2, Scott; Kansas—Patterson, A. Kelley 2, Born 2, D. Kelley 2.

Town Goes Wild As Final Gun Decides Title

'Illegal' Walkout Sweeps Campus—Pandemonium Rules.

By THE STAFF

"It's great!"

And the campus and city went wild.

The dam burst with the bang of the final gun ending the Hurryin' Hoosier's dramatic 69-68 victory over the Kansas Jayhawks.

Through the din, Dean of Students R. L. Shoemaker spoke in a "voice heard 'round the campus."

There'll be no penalty for walkouts, he said. And in the next statement extended coed hours to 1 a.m.

Girls Start It.

Women's housing units, lead by the girls in Rogers Center and the Women's Quad, plowed through token resistance of counselors to form a cheering mass in the City's streets.

The men were out even faster.

The southeast side of the square was packed with more than 2,000 yelling, singing Hoosier fans. The Bloomington police just stood by—smiling.

It's just great," one loudly-shouting fan called above the din on the Square.

A snake dance quickly formed in the streets. And a bon fire was blazing in the midst of the throng.

Firecrackers, aerial bombs, noise makers, and horns resounded and echoed across the square.

Hunched atop a post on the Courthouse lawn, one merry, merry-maker was lighting cigars from the blazing flares that lit the square in a bluish-white light.

Police At A Loss.

City police were at a loss to control the mass of howling students and they could do little but stand helplessly in the City Hall. There was no organization within the crowd itself. The police threatened to break up the demonstration if it didn't burn itself out soon. That was at 1 a.m.

One police officer said he thought it would be a good idea to wait until all the students were in bed then get a group of "West Enders" and go out and wake up the students.

A giant bonfire flared at Walnut street and Kirkwood avenue and cars were lined up five abreast.

Fire Truck Stalls.

The Delta Upsilon fire truck stalled at the fire. The mass of cheering fans soon picked up the chant:

"No school Thursday."

In the midst of the bonfire crowd, Bob Frowick, president of the student body, led singing and what organized cheers he could manage.

(Continued on Page Three)

CAMPUS TO GREET CHAMPS

—COMPOSITE By FRED CAVINDER

ROUND THE BASKETBALL CLOCK—No matter what the time or the place, I.U.'s cagers have come through and are first in the Big Ten, first in the N.C.A.A., and certainly first in the hearts of Indiana University. Pictured clockwise from twelve noon are Phil Byers, Jim Schooley, Ron Taylor, Goethe Chambers, Paul Poff, Charlie Kraak, Burke Scott, Bob Leonard, Don Schlundt, Dick Farley, Lou Scott, Dick White, Jim DeaKyne, and Jack Wright. Surrounded by their charges are Coach Branch McCracken, assistant coach Ernie Andres, and senior manager, Ron Fifer.

Parade, Banquet To Honor Heroes

The country's No. 1 basketball team is in for a surprise today!

When their bus from Indianapolis arrives at Cascade Park, the Hurryin' Hoosiers will transfer to a caravan of shiny convertibles, and begin a parade through Bloomington and the I.U. campus. Neither Coach Branch McCracken nor any of the team is aware of the celebration planned in their honor.

The I.U. band, the University High School band, and cheering throngs of students and townspeople will join the caravan as it reaches Tenth street and College avenue about 3:30 p.m. Similar to Indian's N.C.A.A. victory celebration in 1940, the parade will wind up at the I.U. Fieldhouse.

Sponsors of Parade.

The Union Board and the Bloomington Junior Chamber of Commerce will co-sponsor the welcome-home parade. They are also honoring the team at a banquet in Alumni Hall at 6:30 o'clock tonight.

Because the University is now operating on the minimum number of classes permitted accredited institutions, classes will not be dismissed for the parade. The Departments of Army and Air Sciences and Tactics announced that they have postponed examinations originally scheduled for that time.

Parade Rolls.

After picking up its musical accompaniment and the cheering throngs at Tenth street, the parade will roll down College avenue to Kirkwood avenue. Here it will turn, march down Indiana, Third street, Jordan avenue, and Seventh avenue to the Fieldhouse.

No program has been set up for the parade after it reaches the Fieldhouse because of the banquet for the team at 6:30 p.m.

Spunky Spirit.

In 1940 when Coach McCracken brought his team home from Kansas, 2,000 spirited students greeted the team at the outskirts of Bloomington. The fifty-car parade and the celebration that followed was called "the most enthusiastic demonstration seen on the campus in recent years."

George Gamble, senior, chairman of the Union Student Spirit Committee, urged that students from each housing unit join the parade with signs and banners cheering the N.C.A.A. victors. Referring to the signs at the Sunday night rally after the Illinois game, he said that they helped tremendously to pep up the spirit in the Fieldhouse.

The plane bringing the Macmen home from Kansas City will land in Indianapolis at 1:30 o'clock this afternoon.

Fair or Foul?

Wednesday's weather, as uncertain as a two-handed push shot from forty feet out, started with .58 inches of rain early in the morning and remained cloudy all day. The high was 65 degrees the low was 48, and the temperature at 4:30 p.m. was 60 degrees.

Champions' Fete A Sell-out; 600 to Attend

Campus and City to Honor Team at Banquet Tonight.

More than 600 students and Bloomington backers of the Hurryin' Hoosiers will be out to pay tribute to the triumphant N.C.A.A. champs and Coach Branch McCracken at an honor banquet in Alumni Hall at 6:30 o'clock tonight.

The banquet is a sell-out and tickets will be available only if earlier buyers return them, Charles J. Faris, chairman of the banquet, said.

Vern Huffman, most valuable Big Ten football player in 1936, will be toastmaster. The program consists of the introduction of the team; a talk by Jack Brickhouse, Chicago radio and television announcer, and the presentation of gifts to the squad and Coach McCracken.

The Rev. Robert A. Matzke will give the invocation.

Past and present I. U. basketball players will be on hand to help fete this year's team. Four of the starting five of the 1940 N.C.A.A. championship team will be here for the banquet. They are Jay McCreary, Herm Schaefer, Bob Dro, and Marvin Huffman. The fifth member of the team, Bill Menke, was killed in World War II.

Reserve members of the 1940 team who will attend are Bob Menke, Jim Gridley, Chet Francis, and Andy Zimmer.

The banquet is sponsored by the Bloomington Junior Chamber of Commerce with assistance from the Indiana Union.

SERVICE CLUB TO ELECT.

The Social Service Club will meet to elect new officers tonight at 7:30 o'clock in Union 306. After the election, club members will see "The Social Worker," a film produced by United World Films, Inc., for the Department of State. The film depicts the life and career of a girl in social service work.

All-Tourney Team

Forward—B. H. Born, Kansas University.
Bob Houbregs, University of Washington.
Center—Donald Schlundt, Indiana University.
Guard — Bob Leonard, Indiana University.
Dean Kelly, Kansas University.
Most Valuable player—B. H. Born, Kansas University.

Kappa Kappa Psi Initiates Eight

Eight bandsmen became members of Kappa Kappa Psi, band honorary, Tuesday night in the Union Club Lounge.

The new members are Warren Hickman, senior; Julien Blackerby, James Thrasher and Robert Howes, juniors, and David Owens, Michael Danko, Larry Gentry, and Mark Beymer, sophomores.

John W. Ashton, Vice-President and Director of Student and Educational Services, was initiated as an honorary member. Dean Ashton directed the Department of Bands before it came under the supervision of the School of Music.

History Repeats Itself

'Firewagon' Wins Second N.C.A.A. Title

By JANE ZAISER

History repeated itself at Kansas City Wednesday night. I.U. won its second N.C.A.A. championship by again defeating the University of Kansas Jayhawks, 69-68.

The first time was in 1940, when the Hoosiers won the crown by downing Kansas, 60-42. It was in the first N.C.A.A. tournament final played at the Kansas City Auditorium.

This time it was closer. The Hoosiers were forced to fight all the way to the gun.

Picked Over Purdue.

Although the 1940 Hoosier basketball team was runner-up to Purdue in the Big 10, it was chosen to represent the Conference in the N.C.A.A. because of its outstanding record that season. The I.U. team won 17 of 20 games and whipped the champion Boilermakers twice.

I.U. faced Springfield College in the first game of the regionals, which were played at Butler Fieldhouse in Indianapolis. The Hoosiers won, 48-24, and as The Daily Student reported, "It was a case of the team from the state which made basketball famous showing the team from the school where the sport originated how to play the game."

The team didn't play today's high-scoring brand of basketball then. Herman Shaefer, I.U. forward was high-point man with 14 points, the largest total scored by an Indiana man during the tournament.

Downed Duquesne Easily.

I.U. easily downed Duquesne University, 39-30, to win the regionals for the Eastern half of the U.S. Duquesne never came closer than 5 points to the Indiana team.

The Hoosiers went into their final game at Kansas City as underdogs. Just before the game a telegram from Lawrence, Kans., businessmen was read over the loud speaker. The message read that to Kansas, "Indiana is just another ball club."

Coach Branch McCracken reported that this just made the boys more determined to beat the Jayhawks.

More than 500 Indiana fans gathered in Alumni Hall the night of the finals to hear the game as it was re-constructed from telegraph reports.

Bob Cook, then managing editor of The Bloomington Star, now athletic publicity director, did the reporting. The wire service was obtained so that fans wouldn't be bothered by their "fading radios."

Youth Versus Age.

The final contest was written up as a battle of "youth versus age." McCracken was then only 32 years old and was just in his third year as Indiana coach. Forest (Phog) Allen, the Jayhawk Coach, was 55

(Continued on Page Three)

Applications Open For Pamarada

Independent women with forty academic hours, a 1.5 grade average and two activities may apply for membership in Pamarada, upper-class women's honorary.

Application blanks will be available at the Student Building desk until 5:30 p.m. Friday.

Tanya Pickett, junior, chairman of the membership committee, said that members will be announced at the A.W.S. Mass Meeting Monday, March 30.

Today——

——on the campus——

CHAPEL COLLOQUY — "Security and Academic Freedom." Ralph F. Fuchs, School of Law, 11:45 a.m.; Colonial Tea Room, Union Building.

BASKETBALL RECOGNITION DINNER — 6:30 p.m.; Alumni Hall, Union Building.

ART FILM—"Five-Thousand Years of Eyptian Art"; Ray Garner 7:30 p.m.; Art Center 190.

INDIANA UNION DUPLICATE BRIDGE — 6:30 p.m. Lounge, Union Club.

DEPARTMENT OF ECONOMICS LECTURE — "Economics in Transition" Clarence E. Ayres, University of Texas; 7:30 p.m.; B. & E. 101.

DEPARTMENT OF GEOGRAPHY ILLUSTRATED LECTURE — "Finland, A European Borderland" W. R. Mead; University of London; 8 p.m.; B. & E. 100.

JORDAN RIVER REVUE—8 p.m. University Theatre.

P0025417, IU Archives.

May 20, 1953

HE SERVES BEST WHO SERVES THE TRUTH

THE INDIANA DAILY STUDENT

THE WEATHER
Fair and mild today and Thursday.

VOL. LXXXII—NO. 147—Z 175. INDIANA UNIVERSITY WEDNESDAY, MAY 20, 1953. BLOOMINGTON, INDIANA Established 1867

FORMER I. U. EDITOR KICKED OUT OF IRAN

Met Scores Again In Long 'Tristan'

By DOROTHY TEAL

The love story of "Tristan Und Isolde" took its tragic course from the heights of rapture to the depths of despair Tuesday night with the Metropolitan Opera's production of the Wagnerian drama.

Met singers won the audience's approval in a strenuous presentation which lasted more than four hours.

Outstanding in the performance was Margaret Harshaw, soprano, who took the role of the tragic heroine, Isolde. Miss Harshaw is a truly magnificent Wagnerian soprano. Her range and vocal quality enabled her to be heard above singers and full orchestra in her arias.

Miss Harshaw sang with Ramon Vinay, the Met's Tristan, the dramatic second act love duet. The climax of the opera was her rendition of the immortal "Leibestoed" (Love-Death) in the final scene.

Thebom Best Actress.

Blanche Thebom, was cast as Brangaene, Isolde's maid. Miss Thebom was probably the best actress in the cast, but I.U. audiences would probably agree that Wagner is not her best operatic type.

Mr. Vinay's best moments were in the last act, before Tristan's death. His acting and singing in this scene were convincing as the dying lover, still longing for Isolde.

The supporting roles of King Marke and Kurvenal were sung by Dezzo Ernster and Sigurd Bjoerling, respectively. The performance was conducted by Fritz Stiedry.

Staging 'Pale.'

Although some of the staging of the Met's "Tristan Und Isolde" seems a little pale alongside modern settings—like "Rigoletto's" — the Wagnerian opera can't be beaten for musical melodrama.

Wagner was a master at dramatic technique in opera, according to some critics, but he nevertheless taxes the strength of singers and orchestra alike. In many of Wagner's operas, as in "Tristan Und Isolde" the singers have to stand around on the stage and wait for the orchestra to finish a significant theme. Wagner also was the first to develop the recurring theme suggesting a character or an idea.

Three Recitals Set for Today

Two joint senior recitals and a voice recital will be presented today by students in the School of Music.

William Benton Handley, cello, and Charles Atkins, clarinet, will give a joint recital at Recital Hall at 11:30 a.m. They will be accompanied by Mary Ann Mathews and Mary LaFollette. All are seniors.

Ronald Downey, trombone, and Kenneth Duff, trombone, will present a joint recital at 11:30 a.m. in East Hall. They are both seniors. They will be accompanied by John Judd and Herman Chaloff, PG's.

Miss Shirley Vavra, PG, will present a voice recital tonight in East Hall at 8:30 o'clock.

German Department To Show Films

Four films and a set of slides sponsored by the Department of German will be shown Thursday and Friday.

Three black-and-white films, "Muehsterland," "The Bavarian Alps," and "Bavarian Forests," and one color film, "Peasant Wedding in Hesse," will be shown Thursday at 1:30 p.m. in Kirkwood 104. The films will last an hour.

Friday morning at 10:30, a set of about 100 color slides, entitled "Picture Book of Germany," will be shown in Kirkwood 3. The showing will take about an hour.

Today——

——on the campus——

AUDITORIUM TOURS—10:30 a.m. and 2:30 p.m., I. U. Auditorium.
I. U. BAND TWILIGHT CONCERT—7 p.m., South Green.
RHYTHM ROOM—8 to 11 p.m. Commons, Union Building.
BASEBALL—Indiana vs. DePauw, 3:30 p.m., I. U. Baseball Diamond.
PREVIEWS OF EDUCATION MOTION PICTURES—7 p.m., Education 125.
BIOLOGY SEMINAR—"The Protective Effect of Certain Chemicals Against Radiation Damage to Chromosomes" Herbert P. Riley, University of Kentucky, 7:30 p.m. Biology 26.
DEPARTMENT OF SLAVIC STUDIES—Presentation by students and faculty members of three plays in Russian and Ukrainian, 8:30 p.m. Recital Hall, Music Building.
"LOOK AT THE STARS"—8:30 to 9:30 p.m., Kirkwood Observatory.

Bitter Herbs Flops as Met Spear Carrier

By HERB MICHELSON

Milton Cross wouldn't have said too many nice things about me . . .

I wasn't "all met." Maybe in a little roadshow that used to cover the Keith circuit Bitter Herbs would have fit the bill . . .

But with the New York Yankees of the theatrical world, I was a flop. Somehow, someway, I was part of last night's double header of Tristan und Isolde (starting pitchers weren't listed).

Just Like Faust.

For the price of one dollar and other valuable considerations I sold my soul to the Metropolitan Opera. They grease-painted my face. They garbed me in cloaks befitting a Tenth Century Gabby Hayes. Then they told me to get out there and be "all Met."

It seems only just to point out that I was, in reality, all wet . . .

In the first act, they had me bear a flag. Trumpets sounded. Isolde did whatever any Isolde would do—with anxious breath, rapidly-thumping heart, she awaited my coming.

Chips Are Down

Wagner's heroine didn't have a thing to worry about. I was on my way. The chips were down; it was the clutch. Flag, in hand, like Horatio at the viaduct I strode out before the waiting thousands.

It was easy.

Act two found me in a new uniform. They had taken my vassal's tights from me. In my next appearance they had thrown me to the dogs—I had been relegated to the task of hunting game for Tristan. My mail was threadbare. My armor belonged in a body shop.

'Isolde Needed Me.'

But undaunted, unflinching, I carried on in the knowledge that Isolde, surely, would be in need of my services. Maybe it was the way she smiled, or perhaps it was the manner in which she flung a poisoned spear in my vicinity.

Dressed like one of Robin Hood's fraternity brothers, I once again marched onto the podium, spear in hand. Let them laugh. Wagner had it all figured out — he must have known that someday, in some theatre in some land, Michelson would be there.

Thus ended by operatic career. I'll be missed. The King of Cornwall will never be the same.

And neither will Milton Cross.

Group to Hear Forestry Plans

Members of Southern Indiana Inc. will hear an outline on a State forestry program, presented by the directors of the Indiana Forestry and Woodland Owners Association at a meeting in New Albany on June 24.

Philip H. Willkie, president of the association, said the program is to stress the importance of the forestry resoures of the State, its wood-working industries, proper handling of woodland crops and increasing the forest and industrial wealth of the State.

Pinned!

Sigma Chis Hang Lovelorn Expert Who Told Secrets.

The Daily Student's "pin expert" probably has the biggest pin on campus—but she "wooden" wear it.

In a feature in Tuesday's Student, the feminine writer, an Alpha Phi, offered the woman's view of the age-old question, "To pin or not to pin?" the author offered tips on winning elusive college jewelry.

At dinner that night a solemn group of Sigma Chis, perturbed about the story arrived at the Alpha Phi house to make a presentation.

Amid a trumpet fanfare, the feature writer's "steady," clutching a copy of the I.D.S., lifted a huge wooden replica of the Sigma Chi pin from a white satin pillow and placed it—hung by white suspenders — around the red-faced journalist's neck.

Union Board Hires First Co-ordinator

Mrs. Russell Wins New Student Post After Interview.

Mrs. Bette Russell, PG and secretary to Leo R. Dowling, Assistant Dean of Students, has been hired as the program co-ordinator for the newly-created Student Union Board.

At a meeting of the board Tuesday afternoon Phil Broyles, president, said the selection had been made after Mrs. Russell was interviewed by Lyman C. Smith, manager of the Union, and the three old-over members of the board—Mr. Broyles, Lee Marchant, and Bill Chambers, juniors.

Mrs. Russell, who has attended I. U. five years, received a B.S. degree in education in 1949. Her major subject is speech education.

At the meeting Bob Bluemle, sophomore, proposed that secretaries be obtained for all board members who wish them. It was also suggested that the board make a retreat to McCormick's Creek at the start of the Fall semester. Both proposals were tabled.

Myers to Head Finance Club

Display Reveals Activities of Club.

Jay Myers, junior, has been elected president of the Finance Club for the 1953-54 school year.

Assisting Mr. Myers will be Bob Howard, vice-president; Dane Burns, secretary, and Don Mauch, treasurer. All of the men are sophomores.

A display, showing the opportunities in the field of finance, and the activities of the Finance Club, has been arranged on the bulletin board of the main lobby in the B. & E. building.

Nathan L. Silverstein, professor of finance, spoke to the club on "Adventures in Local Real Estate Finance;" Tuesday night in B. & E. 19.

BROKEN AXLE CAUSES WRECK

WINCHESTER, Ind. (AP)—A broken axle was blamed for the derailment of twenty-three cars of a westbound New York Central freight train in Winchester Tuesday. No one was injured.

Miss Mahoney's Condition 'Very Good'

Marilyn Mahoney, freshman, is in "very good" condition after a successful operation Tuesday at the Indianapolis Robert Long Hospital, her physician reported Tuesday night.

She underwent surgery for a broken thigh bone, broken and dislocated pelvis, and a fractured ankle. These injuries were suffered in the May 9 crash which was fatal to an I.U. coed, two mothers, and a Wabash College senior.

Robert Barger and John Smiley, sophomores, injured in the same accident, remain in "very critical" condition at Bloomington Hospital.

An Associated Press release reported Tuesday that Mrs. Joseph J. Daniels has been named as administrator of the estate of her son, Michael Fairbanks Jr., killed in the same crash. No value of the estate was given.

Fairbanks was the adopted son of the late Richard Fairbanks, former publisher of The Indianapolis News.

Klibansky's Talk Rescheduled

Because of illness, Raymond Klibansky, professor of logic and metaphysics at McGill University, Montreal, Canada, will be unable to give his lecture tonight at 8 o'clock in the Bryan Room.

Prof. Klibansky was scheduled to speak on "The Fall of Constantinople and the History of Western Thought." He is well known for his interpertations of the development of Western thought, along with his editorial work.

The lecture has been rescheduled for early next Fall.

Senate Shindig Set for Tonight

Student Senate's going to a party.

Miss Marjorie Bell, associate director of student activities, will entertain the senators at her home tonight. Miss Bell told the group to come to the open house about 7 o'clock and "stay as long as you can."

At last Thursday's Senate meeting, she asked new student representatives to attend the party as well as outgoing senators.

A.W.S. Cancels Lantern Night

List to Be Made of Selected Women.

Lantern Night, the annual ceremony for previously unrecognized senior women, has been cancelled, Miss Marjorie Bell, associate director of student activities, said.

The program, sponsored by A.W.S., was to be Thursday evening. Reason for cancellation is the illness of the general chairman.

A list of women to be recognized has been partially made, and the committee is arranging to notify the selected girls next week.

Members of A.W.S. and Union Board will visit housing units during the first week of classes next Fall to explain the position of each on campus, Jane Vance, sophomore, said at Tuesday's meeting of A.W.S. Council.

Council members voted to open A.W.S. committee applications Sept. 21 to Sept. 30 of the Fall semester.

MURDER INDICTMENT GIVEN.

ANGOLA, Ind. (AP)—A county grand jury Tuesday returned a ment against Mrs. Patricia Williams, 37-year-old Angola housewife accused of the fatal shooting of her husband.

Senate Group Favors Student Honor Program

Report Says System Needs Orientation Before It Will Work.

The special Student Senate committee assigned to investigate the campus cheating problem reported Tuesday that it favors establishment of a new standing senate committee on student honor.

The group made its recommendation after studying the Faculty-Student Relations Committee report on cheating. The Senate report will be submitted for adoption at Thursday's Student Senate meeting.

The report states that at present "an honor system at Indiana University would be unworkable." Students must be oriented to such a system, the report continues. The Faculty - Student recommendation made no proposals concerning an honor system.

Preventive Measures.

The new senate committee, the report outlines, would perform preventative and informative measures concerning cheating. To carry out this program, it would operate through "organizations which are already set up and functioning in a service and character-building nature." This includes groups such as the Y.M.C.A. and Y.W.C.A., religious organizations, I.F.C., and housing councils.

According to the report, the purposes of the Senate honor committee will be emphasized especially during orientation week for matriculating freshmen. The I.U. Pilot and Freshmen Leadership Camp will also stress the objectives of the committee. This new standing committee will define the general method of correction to be used on violaters.

Standard Method.

Part two of the report recommends the establishment of a standard method of procedure throughout the entire university for reporting and handling problems of cheating.

A faculty member will report a student for cheating if he "feels the case warrents such action," the report continues. Final action in a cheating case will be taken to the Student Supreme Court.

In concluding, the senators on the special committee said that they believe an honor system can eventually be evolved on campus through close co-operation of the Student Senate, Faculty-Student Relations Committee, and Faculty Council.

DULLES IN INDIA.

NEW DELHI, India (AP)—U. S. Secretary of State John F. Dulles has arrived by plan in India.

Rained-Out Bands to Try Twilight Concert Again

The combined Varsity and Symphony Bands will try again tonight.

Weather permitting, the bands will present a Twilight Concert at 7 o'clock on the lawn in front of the south entrance of the Union.

The "Little 500 March," composed by Newell Long, assistant professor of music, will be one of the features of the program. Mr. Long will conduct the playing of his march, which is dedicated to Howard S. Wilcox, former director of the I. U. Foundation and originator of the annual bicycle race.

Daniel L. Martino, director of bands, will be conductor for this evening's concert, with Charles F. Keen, assistant director, conducting two of the numbers.

There will be four soloists for the concert. Mangham Lehr, junior, will be pianist for David Bennett's "Repartee"; and C. Dale Fjerstad, PG, will play the trumpet in "Trumpeter's Lullaby," by Leroy Anderson.

Kenneth Jolls, freshman, will play a vibraharp solo, and John C. Fenn, freshman, will take the solo part in David Bennett's "Calfskin Calisthenics."

The program is as follows:

March and Procession of Bacchus from the ballet "Sylvia" ..Leo Delibes arr. by Tom Clark
Italian in Algiers Overture ..G. Rosinni arr. by Lucien Cailliet
Merry Widow ....Harry L. Alford Novelty Concert March, Mr. Keen conducting
Repartee ....David Bennett Mangham Lehr, soloist; Mr. Keen conducting
The "Little 500" March ....Newell Long Mr. Long conducting
Cypress Silhouettes ......David Bennett
Themes from First Roumanian Rhapsody ....George Enesco arr. by Clair W. Johnson
Trumpeter's Lullaby ....Leroy Anderson C. Dale Fjerstad, soloist
Horse and Buggy ......Leroy Anderson
Vibraharp Solo ....Kenneth Jolls, soloist
El Relicario ....Padilla
Calfskin Calisthenics ......David Bennett John C. Fenn, soloist
Mississippi Suite Overture ..Ferde Grofe arr. by David Bennett
La Sorella ....L. Gallini
American Fold Rhapsody.......... ....Clare E. Grundman
Four American folk songs
Marches ....John Phillip Sousa
Black Horse Troop
George Washington Bicentennial

Training Squadron To Meet Tonight

The last May meeting of Bloomington's Flight B of the 959th Volunteer Air Reserve Training Squadron will be tonight at 7:30 o'clock in Science 214.

On schedule are two talks, three training films, and a review of current events. Lt. Col. Garwood Judah and Major Merritt Lawlis will speak on "Principles of War" and "The United Nations," respectively.

Walk Through Door at Right Time— And You May Be '53 Siwash Queen

Count Basie will crown some pretty coed queen of the 1953 Senior Siwash Friday night in Alumni Hall.

We're having no elimination contest to pick the five queen contestants for the honor," Ray Ruff, chairman of the Siwash said. "We feel that every senior deserves to be nominated," he added.

Mr. Ruff said that to be fair in picking the queen candidates the coeds will be chosen as they walk through the door into Alumni Hall. The 35rd, 153rd, 253rd, 353rd, 453rd, 553rd, 653rd, 753rd, 853rd, and 953rd senior coed to turn in her ticket to the dance will automatically be put in the court.

At 11 p.m. Mr. Basie will draw one of the numbers from a hat, and that girl will be queen of the 1953 Senior Siwash.

Must Have I.D.'s

picked up by seniors starting this

Tickets for the Siwash may be morning at the I.U. Ticket Office. Seniors must show their I.D. cards to get a ticket.

Seniors will be allowed to bring upperclassmen as their dates, Mr. Ruff said. Dress for the dance will be suits for the men and heels for the coeds.

President Wells will honor graduating seniors this afternoon in Alumni Hall at the President's Reception for seniors. The president emphasized that the reception is not formal, and that he expects seniors to drop in any time after their classes.

A free movie will be shown in B.&E. 100 tonight for seniors and their dates. The movie, a current technicolor attraction, will be shown at 7:30 p.m.

The Senior Coffee Hour in the Commons will be this Friday. It has been changed from Saturday as previously reported. Judy Kaplan and Jack Jackson, in charge of the coffee hour, said that free cokes along with the coffee will be available. Seniors must show their I.D. cards to participate in the hour. There will be entertainment

Tom Mellman, chairman of senior week announced last night that tickets for the Senior Siwash will be destributed today. They may be obtained from the Union desk after 1 p.m.

Marc Purdue Accused Of Writing 'False News'

Marc Purdue, '35, Associated Press Correspondent and former editor of The Daily Student, was expelled Tuesday from Tehran for sending abroad what the Iranian government called "false and provocative news against the interests of Iran."

A native of Evansville, Mr. Purdue has been Iran bureau chief for the AP. He is the sixth foreign correspondent to be expelled from that country since the government took over the holdings of the Anglo-Iranian Oil Co.

Mr. Purdue, who is unmarried and stands only a little over five feet tall, became an AP war correspondent in World War II because he was too small for the Army.

Was Outstanding Senior.

As a senior at I.U. he was named the outstanding journalist of 1935 by Sigma Delta Chi, of which he was a member. He participated in many other activities as a student, and was a member of Blue Key, Alpha Tau Omega social fraternity, Theta Alpha Phi (drama honorary), and Phi Delta Gamma (debating, journalism, and drama honorary).

He also worked on the Arbutus staff and the Bored Walk, predecessor of the Crimson Bull, and served as publicity director for the University Theatre.

According to the Associated Press, Hossein Fatemi, foreign minister, announced at a news conference that Mr. Purdue must leave Iran within three days. He did not explain, the government's charges.

Purdue Not at Conference.

Mr. Purdue, the AP said, was not at the news conference. He was covering a meeting of the lower house of the Iranian Parliament, where leading deputies of the opposition launched three attacks on Premier Mohammed Mossadegh. Advised of the expulsion order, he immediately notified the U.S. embassy and tried to get particulars.

When asked what Mr. Purduo had reported that was "false and provocative," the AP reports that Fatemi said it was general and gave no details.

Four hours later, two detectives, who said they had not been told the reason for the expulsion order, called at the AP office and told Mr. Purdue to report to police headquarters Wednesday. According to the AP, they said he would then be given an explanation and his exit visa.

The action against Purdue came only four days after William Oatis, another AP foreign correspondent, was freed from prison in Czechoslovakia. Mr. Oatis is now in New York after serving two years of a ten-year sentence imposed on charges he had engaged in espionage.

Served AP Since 1941.

Mr. Purdue has been a member of the AP's foreign staff since World War II, having previously worked for the news service as a correspondent in Southeast Asia and as chief of the India bureau. After his graduation from I.U. he worked on newspapers in Evansville, Fort Wayne, and San Antonio, Texas. He joined the AP at Louisville, Ky., in 1941.

Phil Clarke, Mr. Purdue's predecessor in Iran, left that country after Fatemi's newspaper, Bakhtar Embrooz, demanded that he be put on trial. Mr. Clarke was accused of "Intriguing against the government and security of the country."

In a nine-month period before that, the regimeof Premier Mossadegh expelled four other correspondents, nicluding representatives of the New York Times, Reuters News Agency, and the London Daily Express.

Prison Whets Oatis Appetite For Hot Jazz

NEW YORK (AP) — Associated Press Correspondent William N. Oatis brought back from Communist captivity an itchy foot and a hunger for hot jazz.

Mr. Oatis, whose hobby is collecting records and writing music, asked fellow newsmen Tuesday where he could find a good jazz band. Somebody suggested Eddie Condon's in Greenwich Village.

"That's Chicago style," said Mr. Oatis. "I want Kansas City jazz."

He returned to New York Monday after serving twenty-five months of a ten year prison term in a Czechoslovakian jail. He was accused of espionage, in connection with news gathering activities he said would have been routine in this country. He was released last Saturday.

Wants to See Things.

"I've never seen San Francisco and would like to see it," he said of his future plans.

His wife, Laurabelle, suggested he might like to visit New Orleans, traditional home of jazz.

"That would be heaven," Oatis agreed.

The slim, 39-year-old correspondent also plans to visit relatives in Indiana, Minnesota and Arizona.

Joking happily, he and his wife set out Tuesday to buy him a new suit to replace the one he went to prison in April 23, 1951.

He confessed he missed dressing up and also missed newspapers, the daily symbol of his trade. He said he hasn't even had a chance, yet, to read stories of his arrival home.

Tells of Vivid Dreams.

For the moment at least, Oatis is not talking of his arrest and the charges against him. He did remark, however, of the months in prison:

"I had dreams of buying a newspaper and of riding on trains. Life in prison is so drab and colorless that the dreams of people in confinement can be very vivid. The dreams make up for the lack of color.

"Sometimes they are so vivid that you have to stop and think whether it was real or just a dream."

1953 Color-Filled Arbutus Ready for Readers Today

The Arbutus is here! Students may pick up their yearbooks at the I.U. Ticket Office after 1 p.m. today.

Robert McIntire, business manager, said there will be some extra copies of the book for sale at the Ticket Office. Since the number is limited, he expects the extra copies to be gone soon.

Students picking up ordered books should present I.D.'s.

The book has a hard-finished cover of brick-red and white, with a drawing of students studying on the brick-red background. The cover drawing, like many of the drawings in the book, is in modern art.

The inside of the book is filled with color pictures. In the first section of the book are several pictures of campus scenes and students in full color. These are followed by pictures of the campus at night—in black and white to show the contrast between the night and the lighted buildings.

Titles are all done in color — brick-red, yellow, and blue. Each organization title is done in color which makes it stand out on the page.

The pictures in beauty queen section have a blue color tint. Publisher Ralph Cronin said that this color gives the queen pictures a three-dimensional appearance.

Color tints are used all through the book—even the sports shots are colored.

The pages which introduce each section are drawn in modern art. Color tints also are used in this section. Some of the sketches are comic drawings showing some phase of campus life.

Packed into the 484 pages of the book are pictures of campus organizations, campus functions, and many informal shots of campus life. Informal shots of students are included in the housing section and in the organizations section.

The editors have carried the theme, of the settled campus housing unsettled students who are unsure of what the future holds, throughout the book.

The advertising section includes pictures of students in their hometowns. Advertising is divided into city sections. Each section includes copy which gives the reader background about the city.

The books arrived late Tuesday night, and Mr. McIntire said they must be unloaded this morning and counted before distribution.

Audio-Visual Center Cancels Films

Audio-Visual Center has cancelled the regular weekly film preview sessions for the remainder of the semester.

The next weekly preview will be on June 25. During the summer session, previews will be on Thursday rather than Wednesday night. Previews will still be shown in Education Building, room 125-127.

Rain Scare

Students kept their fingers crossed as the bright sun still prevailed. After a trace of rain yesterday morning, the sun came out and raised the temperature to a high of 75 degrees. Low for the day was 55 degrees, and the 4:30 p.m. temperature was 74 degrees.

P0079398, IU Archives.

HE SERVES BEST WHO SERVES THE TRUTH

THE INDIANA DAILY STUDENT

THE WEATHER
Cloudy, Cool; Rain We Hope.

VOL. LXXXIII—NO. 32—Z 175. INDIANA UNIVERSITY WEDNESDAY, OCTOBER 28, 1953. BLOOMINGTON, INDIANA Established 1867.

Rains to Relive Scenes Of 'Greatest' Literature

Speaking great words to great music, Claude Rains will relive for the convocation audience tonight scenes from some of the greatest works in English and American literature.

Mr. Rains, known throughout the theatrical world for his exacting and interpretive characterizations, will recite from some of the outstanding literary masterpieces, including William Shakespeare's "Richard II" and "Julius Caesar," at 7:15 o'clock in the Auditorium.

Read to Music.

"Enoch Arden," written by Alfred Lord Tennyson, will be read by Mr. Rains to music especially written by Richard Strauss for dramatic presentation. Mr. Strauss wrote this music for "Enoch Arden" 30 years ago for the German actor, Max Heinrich, who read the passage with success all over Europe.

Jack Maxin will accompany Mr. Rains at the piano in this selection.

One of T. S. Eliot's most well-known works, "Journey of the Magi," will be recited by Mr. Rains to piano background. "Builders of America," with words by Edward Shenton and pianoforte arrangement by Karl McDonald will also be included in the program.

Piano Solo.

Excerpts from "The Canterbury Tales," by Chaucer and translated by Nevill Coghill, will be recited by Mr. Rains. A piano solo by Mr. Maxin, Brahms' "Edward Ballade in D minor" will round out this program of "Words and Music."

Mr. Maxin who will assist Mr. Rains in his dramatic program, is considered one of the most talented of the younger pianists. A graduate of Swarthmore College and the Philadelphia Conservatory of Music, he was chosen this year from 30 pianists to appear with Eugene Ormandy and the Philadelphia Orchestra during the current season. He spent the past Summer at the University of Colorado as a visiting lecturer for the Creative Arts Festival.

Fowler Resigns As President Of Y.M.C.A.

Badertscher Moves Into Vacant Post After Resignation.

Dick Fowler, junior, resigned as president of the Y.M.C.A. His resignation was officially accepted late Monday night at the "Y" cab inet meeting.

Ken Badertscher, senior, vice-president, moved into the presidency immediately, while Wendell Gish, senior, was elected by acclamation to fill the office of vice-president.

Express Regret.

Mr. Fowler expressed deep regret at leaving the office. However, he stated, vocational conflicts necessitated the action.

As he accepted the gavel, Mr. Badertscher said, "Dick left big shoes to fill, but I shall try my best to take over the duties of the office and fulfill them successfully."

Two Appointments.

Mr. Badertscher announced two "Y" administrative appointments. They are: Jim Ashley, junior, administrative assistant in charge of special events, and Joseph Shroyer, senior, administrative assistant in charge of the "Y Men" organization. Mr. Gish, newly-elected vice-president ,will retain his duties as administrative assistant in charge of personnel.

Mr. Fowler, who officially withdrew from the University early this week, said that his plans for the future are indefinite.

Police Report 'Spook' Pranks At New High

An I.U. student was the recipient of a property-damaging spree by Halloween "pranksters" Tuesday night as Bloomington Police sweated out the most destructive pre-Halloween period the city has ever known.

The automoble of Floyd Smith, West Hall, freshman, was stoned by unknown youngsters. Damages of approximately $80 resulted.

Mr. Smith said that he gave chase to the assailants' car, but was unable to catch them. He did get the license number of the vehicle.

The Police also reported Tuesday a series of near-tragic traffic accidents caused by "mischief bent pranksters" who Monday nght removed flares and a barrcade gaurdng a street evacuaton on North College street.

The "prank" caused four cars to fall into the deep hole within six minutes about 7 o'clock, causing major damage to three of the vehicles and minor damage to one.

Police Chief John Axom said, "We are fortunate that no one was injured," and expressed the police department's concern over the unconcerned way in which Bloomington youngsters are "having fun."

Drivers of the wrecked vehicles were recorded by police as: Otis E. Edwards, 17 years old, of Route 1; Charles E. Stephens, 35, of 725 West Seventeenth street; Arthur Brown, 41, Route 1, and Oscar Gray, 1026 West Fifth street.

Mailboxes in the rural areas around Ellettsville have suffered much punishment. Monroe County Sheriff Fred Davis said Tuesday that the mail box damage reports had been turned over to Postal Inspectors.

Three Bloomington youths were caught Tuesday and admitted to breaking 30 City street lights and smashing several plate glass store windows. Parents of the youths agreed to pay $80 each for the boys' destructive acts.

Concert Planned For Auditorium

Orchestra, Chorus to Combine Talent.

The Philharmonic Orchestra and the University Women's Chorus will give a combined concert Sunday, Nov. 8, at 3 p.m. in the Auditorium.

Prof. Ernst Hoffman, conductor of the orchestra, and George Krueger, associate professor of choral music, will direct the groups.

The combined chorus and orchestra will present "The Spinning Song," from Wagner's "The Flying Dutchman," and Burnet Tuthill's "Big River."

Mr. Tuthill is head of the music school at Southwestern College, Memphis, Tenn. His "Big River" is a story of the Mississippi River, its moods, and the people whose life the river affected.

Three orchestral numbers will be given by the Orchestra at the concert. They are "The Scherzo," from Mendelssohn's "Midsummer Night's Dream;" Ravel's "Pavne for a Dead Princess," and "Scheherazade" by Rimsky-Korsakoff.

Betty Tate, PG, will be violin soloist for "Scheherazade," Conductor Hoffman said.

Today—

—on the campus—

I.U. AUDITORIUM TOURS—10:30 a.m. and 2:30 p.m., Auditorium.
ART DEPARTMENT LECTURE—"Adventures of an Art Detective," Alfred Frankenstein—4:30 p.m., Art Center 190
"LOOK AT THE STARS,"—7-8 p.m., Kirkwood Observatory
PREVIEWS OF EDUCATIONAL MOTION PICTURES—7-9 p.m., University School Auditorium
CONVOCATION — dramatic readings by Claude Rains, 7:15 p.m., I.U. Auditorium
RHYTHM ROOM—8-11 p.m., Commons.

YOUR VARSITY SHOW PERFORMERS—Members of the Morrisonaires vocal group line up at the piano. Left to right in the front row are Ivanna Gwaltney, Nia Scopelitis, Barbara Taulman, Shirley Drew, and Jan Moore. In the bak row are Mary J. Fenton, Bonnie Stewart, Lynn Sturgeon, and Beverly Beogaholtz.

21 I. U. Showmen Work On 12-Act Varsity Show

By NANCY WAGNER

An assignment for speech class has turned into a dance act for the Homecoming Varsity Show.

Conrad Brown, sophomore, whose hobby is Indian dancing, will give a unique addition to the Varsity Show Friday night in the Auditorium. After using his hobby for a speech topic he was advised to try out for the show and was chosen.

The 12-act musical, under the direction of Dr. Kenneth O. Snapp, visiting director of bands, will combine talents of 21 student showmen into the sixth annual Varsity Show. Tickets went on sale Monday in the I.U. ticket office.

Tom Lukens, freshman, acting as master of ceremonies will introduce the acts.

To Set Tone.

The Morrisonaires, a singing group, will set a popular musical tone for the show. Trent Roberson, sophomore, will add mystery with his magic tricks and Howard Kahl will give a take-off on a French movie in an attempt to add laughs to the show.

The blending voices of the Four Counts—Vern Cressler, Bud Baker, and Dave Baker, seniors, and Al Cobine, PG, will provide popular tunes for the evening.

Impersonating pianists Frankie Carle, Eddie Duchin, and George Shearing will be Robert Aichele, junior.

Orchestra to Play.

More music will be provided by the Marching 100 stage orchestra under the direction of Kenneth Jolls, sophomore.

Dancing by Mary Martin and Joe Kazerauni, sophomore, will be among the acts. Vocal soloists will be Rene Routreau, PG, and Pat Mramer, sophomore. Jerry Tyree, freshman, will play the trumpet.

Last Call For Senior Pics

The last call for senior Arbutus pictures will be Friday. Appointments should be made immediately at Campus Studio, 110 South Indiana Avenue.

Students who will receive a degree in February, June, or August, 1954 are eligible to have their picture in the senior section of the Arbutus.

Appointments may be made by phoning City 6035 between 8:30 a.m. and noon or between 1 and 5 p.m.

N. Y. U. Offers Root-Tilden Aid

The New York University School of Law is now accepting applications for its 20 three-year Root-Tilden scholarships. The scholarships will be awarded to students interested in legal careers.

Among 54 young men now in training under the scholarships is John Ward, who received the A.B. degree in government at I.U. last June.

Mr. Ward came to I.U. from the Indiana School for the Blind, and was given the Root-Tilden scholarship in May, 1952.

Root-Tilden scholarships were made possible financially by an anonymous donor. They honor two New York University law graduates of the 19th century who later became famous. The men were Elihu Root and Samuel J. Tilden.

In effect for three years, the program is designed to educate potential leaders in public affairs.

Applications should be sent to the Dean of the School of Law, New York University Law Center, New York 3, N.Y. The deadline is in February.

City Council Votes Water Rate Boost

The City Council unanimously passed by roll call vote Tuesday night ordinances to authorize the City to issue $1,500,000 in water works improvement bonds and to increase the minimum cost of water from $1.50 to $2.25 for 3,000 gallons.

Purpose of the ordinances is to finance the City's proposed water system expansion. Also, the City Water Works must pay off a debt of $66,464.77 to the Radio Corporation of America.

A petition is to be filed for a hearing of the ordinances before the Indiana Public Service Commission. The ordinances cannot become effective nor can construction contracts be let without the commission's approval.

The ordinance calling for hikes in rates pointed out that the present filtration plant could not long meet increased water demand. The present plant, with a 3,000,000 gallon a day capacity, was built in 1926 and expanded in 1940. A planned filtration plant, to be adjacent to the old plant, will purify 6,000,000 gallons of water a day.

Lavish Ceremonies Set For Homecoming Queen

With a fanfare of trumpet blasts, the 1953 Homecoming Queen and her court will enter Memorial Staduim at 1:15 o'clock Saturday afternoon for lavish pre-game crowning ceremonies.

Five convertibles carrying the queen and her court will enter the stadium at the south west entrance and drive to the 50-yard line. Members of the Union Board will escort the coeds to the center of the field.

With another fanfare, Gov. George N. Craig will crown the queen and present her with a bouquet.

To Circle Field.

The queen and her court will be returned to their cars, circle the field once, and stop at box No. 30, where the coeds will sit to watch the game. The box, which will be decorated, is in the front row of the I.U. section in the stadium.

Male students will vote for the queen Thursday from 8:30 a.m. to 4 p.m. in Alumni Hall. The five finalists will be "on exhibit" there all day. Men will vote by numbers corresponding to the queen contestants, instead of by name.

Announce Winner Friday.

The winner will be announced Friday night at the annual Varsity show.

The five finalists, who were chosen last Thursday from a field of 41 applicants, are Marguerite VanArsdall and Mary Alice McClelland, seniors; Marilyn Morrison, junior, Sue Sackett, sophomore, and Carol Enz, freshman.

For Saturday's ceremonies, the queen and her court will wear suits and heels. For the first time this year the queen will wear a long velvet robe trimmed in white fur.

Snider Secretary Of Placement Group

J. Douglas Snider, director of the Bureau of Personnel Relations and Placements, was recently elected secretary of the Midwest College Placement Association at their meeting in Milwaukee, Wisconsin.

Composed of 362 prominent businessmen and 102 representatives of universities and colleges throughout the United States, the organization tries to bring industry and colleges to gether in their job placement work.

FLOOD LEVEL RISES.

ROME (AP)—The Po, Italy's biggest river, was rising an inch an hour toward flood level Tuesday night.

Robbins Tells Of Humor Arts In Literature

By MARILYN SCHETTER

The arts of parody and satire in American writing were illustrated Tuesday as J. A. Robbins, assistant professor of English, spoke at "Readings from Literature."

Anecdotal humor often makes legends of such men as Mathew Arnold, Henry James and Mark Twain, said Prof. Robbins at the program in the Men's Lounge of the Union.

Usually Harmless Humor.

When Mark Twain laughed at others, his humor was usually genial and harmless. At Whittier's 70th birthday anniversary dinner, however, he completely misjudged his audience and recited an amusing satire on Emerson, Holmes, and Longfellow who were guests at the dinner.

Prof. Robbins read the speech in which the frontier humor did not appeal to the staid New England writers. The toastmaster later called the speech a "bewildering blunder and a cruel catastrophe."

Noyes Next.

Explaining that a parodist selects a fault in a man and exaggerates it, Prof. Robbins read Bret Harte's parody on Whittier's "Maud Muller" and a parody on Poe's use of internal rhyme in "The Raven."

Next Tuesday at 4 p.m. Russell Noyes, professor of English, will read works of John Keats.

Roaring '20's, Dance Theme

Wayne Luby to Play Homecoming Climax.

"The Roaring '20's" will set the theme for the Homecoming Dance which will climax Homecoming day activities.

Wayne Luby and his orchestra will play for the informal dance Saturday night in Alumni Hall from 9 to 12 o'clock. Music will also be piped to the Union ABCD Rooms.

The dance is being sponsored by Union Board. Irv Rodenberg, junior, is general chairman.

Working on the decorations designed to bring back memories of "the good old days" are Madge McKiernan, Sherrill Rumbaugh, Tom O'Donnell, Jo Pierce, and Jackie Sandy, juniors, and Shad Newkirk, Ann Kaegie, Darlyne Ganz, Candace Dorsey, and Jane Allen, sophomores.

Tickets may be purchased at the entrance to the Commons or the Union Desk.

Homer Sapiens

Those Purdue students who came here to celebrate and turned their car upside down, can come back Nov. 21 and see the same thing happen to their whole darn team.

Indiana 'Chimes' Win Union Board Nod

Chimes of Indiana

The Daily Student believes "The Chimes of Indiana," by Hoagy Carmichael, should become as popular as the Alma Mater itself. We think it should be played more often at football games and other school functions.

To help make this beautiful song more familiar to the students, we are printing the words to "The Chimes of Indiana" below.

Sing these chimes of Indiana,
Hail to the Crimson hue!
Sing her praise to Gloriana
Hail to our old I. U.!
Oh, lift thy voices
Joined in loyal chorus;
Let thy hearts rejoice
In praise of those before us.
Sing these chimes of Indiana,
Ever to her be true!

Hoagy's Song A Step Closer To Alma Mater

By JERRY LYST

"The Chimes of Indiana," came one step closer to becoming the official Alma Mater of I.U. Tuesday night as the Union Board stamped its unanimous approval on a resolution favoring its adoption.

The resolution began:

"Whereas the melody of Indiana University's Alma Mater, 'Hail to Old I.U.,' is not original with this University . . ." this referred to I.U.'s use of Cornell University's song "High Above Cayuga's Waters."

Other Reasons.

Other reasons for the action were:

"Whereas many other schools have made use of this melody to the extent that it no longer is able to stand as a unique symbol of tribute to any of them and."

"Whereas 'The Chimes of Indiana' by Hoagy Carmichael is a fitting tribute to Indiana University and is worthy of being its Alma Mater, the Indiana Union Board there-by resolves that it go on record as favoring the substitution of 'The Chimes of Indiana' as the recognized Alma Mater of this University."

'Official' Through Use.

A copy of the resolution will be presented to the Board of Trustees. Fenwick T. Reed, secretary of the Board told The Daily Student Friday that he thought the paper's proposal to change the Alma Mater was a very worthwhile suggestion.

There is little information available about how the present Alma Mater was adapted. The lyrics were written by Joseph T. Giles in 1893. An investigation recently completed revealed that the Alma Mater became "official" merely through constant use.

There was little discussion of the proposal when it was read to the board by Bill Chess, junior, originator of the resolution. Mr. Chess said that he believed that the new song "should be integrated in a rather slow fashion."

Sub-committee Appointed.

Phil Broyles, president of the board, said, "The alumni might take offense if we immediately erased their Alma Mater.'

Sunday the Student Spirit Committee appointed a sub-committee to work with The Daily Student in promoting the popularity of Hoagy Carmichael's song.

The Marching Hundred will play "The Chimes of Indiana" at halftime of the I.U.-Missouri Homecoming game next Saturday.

'No Prank'

Sheriff Laments Bulldozer Theft as Trail Ends.

"It certainly isn't a Halloween prank . . . not when it involves 25 tons of machnery."

Monroe County Sheriff Fred Davis, so commented Tuesday night when asked about the disappearance of a 25-ton bulldozer, which was reported stolen from the Riley Stone Quarry near Bloomington Monday.

Sheriff Davis is calling upon his super-sleuth techniques as the mystery goes into its third day.

The bulldozer was apparently hauled away from the quarry on a low-boy trailer early Monday morning or late Sunday night Sheriff Davis said that he was able to trace the big machine as far as Glenns Valley, a town about 40 miles northeast of Bloomington.

Witnesses said they saw the mystery bulldozer being pulled on the trailer on the way to Glenns Valley, but the trail ended there.

Flame Invides 300 To Reunion Saturday

Invitations to Saturday night's Flame Club reunion have been sent to more than 300 former members of the upperclass Independent honorary, Al Kranz, senior, chairman of the reunion, said Tuesday.

Food, dancing, and entertainment will be features of the event which will begin at 8:30 o'clock at the Lili-Yen restaurant, 327 South Woodlawn avenue.

Undergraduates of Flame Club will register returning alums in the Main Lobby of the Union Building all day Saturday.

ELKHART OFFICIAL DIES

ELKHART ,Id. (AP)—Glenn R. Sawyer, Elkhart County probation officer and draft board memberf, died Monday night.

PG Describes Indian Life

By M. A. BRODHECKER

Th life and customs of the Tarahumara Indians of Mexico was the topic of a talk given by Soledad Perez, PG, at a meeting of the Folklore Club Tuesday night.

Miss Perez, a counselor at Oak Hall, is a native of Mexico who is working on a PhD. in English, with a minor in Spanish and folklore. She is also co-author of the book, "The Healer of Los Olmos and Other Mexican Lore," and has taught at Texas Western College.

The Tarahumara Indians, which Miss Perez described, live in the Northwestern part of Chihuhua, Mexico, and are quite primitive. Jesuit missionaries have had contacts with the Indians since 1645, she said, but they have had very few contacts with outside people. Some of their customs are based on Christian observances, but the natives do not know the meanings of many of the rituals, she added.

Live in Mountains.

The Indians live in the mountains and gather only for the various festivals that occur during the year. At this time they have dances, rituals, and drink "tesquino," a whisky that they make. Miss Perez stated that about the only time that they are very sociable is when they have had some "tesquino."

Dr. Remedios W. Moore, assistant to Prof. Thompson, will speak on Fillipino Folk Tales at the next meeting of the club at 8 p.m. Nov. 10, in Union 313.

Pence to Play Recital Tonight

Homer Pence, senior, will play a bassoon recital in Recital Hall tonight at 8:30 o'clock. Accompanyng hm wll be Mildred Henninger, PG.

The program will include works by Bach, Mozart, Saint-Saens and Bernard C. Heiden, associate professor of music.

Fire Restrictions Lifted Amid Rainfall Sounds

Bloomington and State fire restrictions were lifted Tuesday amid the welcome almost forgotten sound of steady rainfall.

It was the first major rainfall since early July, the weather bureau said. The soft rain that started Monday afternoon in this area continued to fall all day Tuesday, contrary to the weatherman's expectation that it would cease before noon.

Proclamations Lifted.

Mayor Emmett Kelly's proclamation of "no outside fires" in Bloomington was lifted after leaves and soil were soaked by the rain, eliminating the long persistent danger of leaf and forest fires.

Governor George N. Craig's Statewide emergency proclamation prohibiting any outside fires in State Forest Preserves and Parks, and the discarding of cigarettes from automobiles was also lifted.

More Coming.

General rainfall was reported over Indiana for a 24-hour period ending Tuesday afternoon, and moisture-hungry Hoosiers were expected to receive showers throughout Tuesday night. The rain is expected to end sometime Wednesday, but more is expected to fall Thursday and Friday in the form of light showers.

The rainfall totals for the long-lasting drizzle are well under an inch in most areas of the State, it was reported, but the amount is enough to aid ground water supplies and benefit small grain crops. State Weather Bureau authorities expressed the view that the rainfall total for the week, including expected future showers would not completely end the three-month drought. The reason for this is that most areas in the state have a six inch deficiency which cannot be made up by the present rain.

When It Rains It Drizzles

A rainfall of .88 inches dropped Tuesday temperatures to 50 degrees after weeks of hot, dry weather.

Highest temperature for the day was 63 degrees. At 5 p.m. the mercury read 52 degrees.

Higher Education Colloquy Subject

"What Are We Afraid of in Higher Education?" will be discussed by James Witte, PG, at Chapel Colloquy, Thursday, in the Union Colonial Tea Room.

Mr. Witte will present a "layman's viewpoint.' '

He contends: "We have nothing to fear in the United States from free men speaking the truth. The danger comes when we become intolerant of the unorthodox."

Persons planning to attend the discussion may bring lunch trays from the Commons to the Colonial Tea Room. Doors will open at 11:30 a.m.

Jean Felix, senior, representing Mu Phi Epsilon, music honorary for women, will present a prelude of recorded music. The program will feature Tchaikowsky's "Sixth Symphony." The discussion will begin at 12:50 o'clock.

Georgas Named Folio Poster Winner

Paul Georgas, senior, is the winner of The Folio Poster Contest, Sidney Shapiro, PG and judge of the art work submitted, said Tuesday. Mr. Georgas was awarded a prize of $10 and one year's subscription to The Folio, campus literary publication.

Participants in the contest were members of Arthur Deshaies' art classes. Mr. Deshaies, instructor in Fine Arts, and Henry R. Hope, chairman of the Department of Fine Arts, acted as advisors for the project.

COMPOSER DIES.

BERLIN (AP) — Eduard Kennekc, 68 year-old German operetta composer, died Tuesday.

P0079400, IU Archives.

The staff at work in "The Shack" in February 1949. *P0048324, IU Archives.*

FROM THE ARCHIVES

'The Shack' Still Lives . . . in Our Hearts

This article originally appeared May 29, 1954, in the last paper to be edited in "The Shack" during a regular school session.

By Pat Hanna and Stu Huffman

So long," they sang.

"It's been good to know you . . ." the journalists were singing.

But most of them had lumps to their throats.

You have to act hard-boiled. Cynical. And unsentimental.

And you have to wear trench coats with turned up collars to claim the title of "newspaperman."

You don't show emotion about anything. Especially an old building. A rickety Quonset at that.

You tell yourself it doesn't matter, that this is the last time most of the "Party Crew" will be around the Shack. Writing stories and headlines. Boressing. Arguing merits of campus issues. Talking potshots at what ails IU.

There'll be other evenings. Other journalists. Other good times.

You tell yourself that this Shack has nothing to do with it. Just a tumble-down old building. Ridiculous to think that it is responsible for the closeness of the kids who work within it.

A photo page celebrates the modern comforts of the newly-remodeled Ernie Pyle Hall in 1954. *P0079411, IU Archives.*

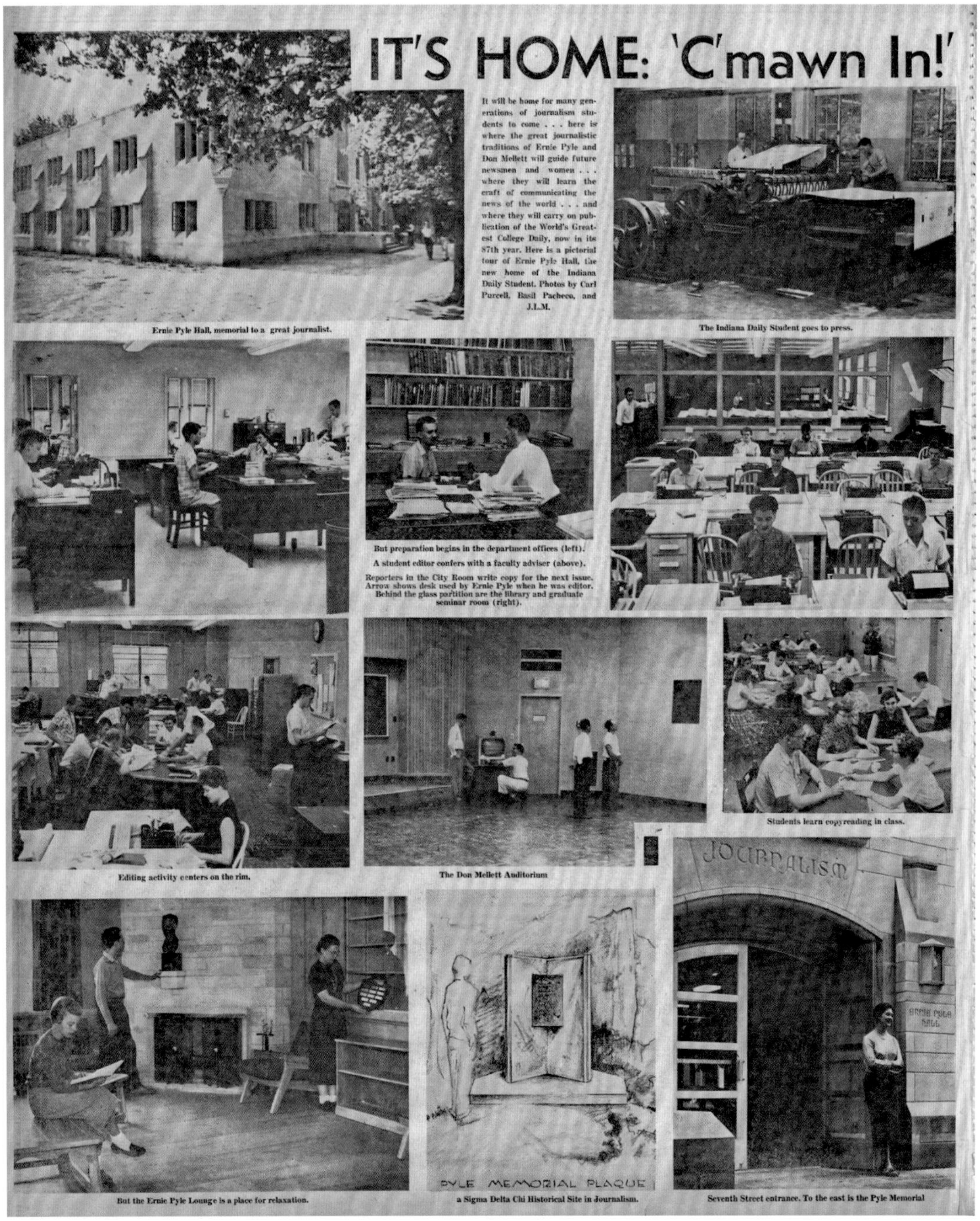

IT'S HOME: 'C'mawn In!'

It will be home for many generations of journalism students to come . . . here is where the great journalistic traditions of Ernie Pyle and Don Mellett will guide future newsmen and women . . . where they will learn the craft of communicating the news of the world . . . and where they will carry on publication of the World's Greatest College Daily, now in its 87th year. Here is a pictorial tour of Ernie Pyle Hall, the new home of the Indiana Daily Student. Photos by Carl Purcell, Basil Pacheco, and J.L.M.

Ernie Pyle Hall, memorial to a great journalist.

The Indiana Daily Student goes to press.

But preparation begins in the department offices (left).

A student editor confers with a faculty adviser (above).

Reporters in the City Room write copy for the next issue. Arrow shows desk used by Ernie Pyle when he was editor. Behind the glass partition are the library and graduate seminar room (right).

Editing activity centers on the rim.

The Don Mellett Auditorium

Students learn copyreading in class.

But the Ernie Pyle Lounge is a place for relaxation.

PYLE MEMORIAL PLAQUE

a Sigma Delta Chi Historical Site in Journalism.

Seventh Street entrance. To the east is the Pyle Memorial

It won't be so different in the new building when the IDS operation begins again next fall.

You tell the re-write man how great it's going to be over there. Luxury plus. Real plush.

No more freezing to death while writing your Big Story.

No more cussing when one leg gives way on your chair.

No more propping a chair against the back door to keep it shut against the March wind.

It will be clean. Shiny. No litter.

No battered lamp shades.

No yellowed clippings on the wall. The floor won't rock when you rush in or out. You'll be able to find the Redbook when you want it.

It doesn't really make a difference that the Shack is where you learned to write, where you made mistakes. Got chewed out. Did a good job, got "story of the day." Not much difference, you assure yourself.

Ernie Pyle's desk. They'll move that.

Walt Kelly's sketch of Pogo on the ceiling. Surely, they'll take that.

You see the panel bearing the names of past editors. You remember the half-hearted jokes they made as they printed them there on their last night "on duty." You hope they'll take that panel to the new setup, too.

"Remember the first day we came in here?"

Suddenly, you turn and hurry out the door. Past Ernie's desk. Past the bulletin board with the nasty letter to the editor. Out under the sign "Indiana Daily Student."

So long, Shack.

It's been good to know you.

In this photo from the 1949 Arbutus, Rose Ann Raper, associate editor, talks with chief editorial writer Bill Terhune. *P0048331, IU Archives.*

10c **Little 500 EXTRA** 10c

HE SERVES BEST WHO SERVES THE TRUTH

THE INDIANA DAILY STUDENT

THE WEATHER Partly cloudy with little change in temperature today and Sunday.

VOL. LXXXIII—NO. 144—Z 175. INDIANA UNIVERSITY SATURDAY, MAY 8, 1954. BLOOMINGTON, INDIANA Established 1867

SIGMA NU WINS '500'; TACKS SLOW PACE

The Sigma Nus came home champ today!

In a race marred by sabotaging tacks and occasional rain, the victory team put on the last lap kick to take the race after a last 20-lap battle between the Acacias, A.T.O.s, Delta Chi, North Hall Barons, and Phi Delta Theta.

Before 12,000 howling fans, the five teams put on a spectacular exhibition of stretch bicycle riding that carried no resemblence to last year's Friar Hall-dominated race, which was really decided after 170 laps or so.

The winning time was 18.72 m.p.h. The total time elapsed for the Sigma Nu teaw was 2 hours, 45 minutes and 35 seconds.

The weather finally cleared up toward the end of the race to give the riders sunshine and less of the strong wind that blew over the track most of the day.

In a race marred by more flat tires and yello wflags than in injuries and spills, the teams were necessarily held up while the track was scraped for the tacks by officials and workers.

As the first bomb sounded today an overcast sky let go with a few drops of rain. But few race enthusiasts panicked and by the time of the third bomb at 12:30 p.m. the sun managed to creep from behind the clouds.

President Wells standing near the speaker's platform wearing a tan trench coat looked about the crowd and waved cheerfully.

Before the big race got underway Ralph Martin, sophomore, rider for the Sigma Nu team which started in ninth spot said, "Come rain or shine, the Sigma Nu team is going to get on that bike and really go."

The consensus of opinion was the same from most all of the riders.

Gene Strauss, junior, rider for the Friars, proclaimed, "I hope we can repeat. It's going to be a good race with a lot of good times in it."

In view of the threatening skys, Don Foster, senior, K.D.R. rider, said, "Sportsmanship will be necessary at all times in order to keep the race free from accidents."

Giving the Little 500 a carnival like atmosphere with his calliope playing, Dr. H. B. Harris, Owensboro, Ky., was up front in the parade Friday night and race track today.

For his own pleasure Dr. Harris, a dentist, puts his drill and novocaine aside to play at carnivals and festivals throughout the country.

His reward — traveling expenses and helping friends, like Bill Arsstrong, executive director of the I.U. Foundation, who is also from Owensboro.

* * *

At 10 Laps . . .

The race began exactly at 1 o'clock with overcast skies. After Seth Klein, official starter, gave the riders the green flag, Acacia and the Friars quickly overtook the first-place Barons. Light showers began just after the gun.

Total time elapsed after ten laps was 7:23, and average time for the leading Delta Chi was 20.32 miles an hour.

* * *

At 25 Laps . . .

At 25 laps, Phi Gamma Delta had taken over the lead from Delta Chi, which was second. S.A.E. was third, and Todd House had moved into fourth.

The Barons had dropped down to fifth position.

Finishing out the other top ten positions were Phi Kappa Psi, Sigma Pi, in seventh position, and Dodds House in eighth place. Phi Delta Theta had dropped to ninth, and A.T.O. was in tenth.

Total elapsed time at the end of 25 laps was 18:40 and the average speed for the leading Phi Gams was 19.98 miles an hour at that time.

* * *

At 50 Laps . . .

At the end of 50 laps Delta Chi was still leading, trailed by the North Hall Barons. Acacia was in third. S.A.E. was fourth. Todd House was fifth, A.T.O. sixth. Dodds House was seventh, Phi Sigma Kappa eighth, Dunn House ninth, and Sigma Nu rounded out the top ten teams.

At this time about eight teams had picked up half-inch carpet tacks apparently strewn on the tracks. One bicycle had picked up three tacks.

Elapsed time at the end of 50 laps was 37:31. Average time for the leader was 10.99 miles an hour.

A 30 TO 40 mile an hour wind blowing from the west was hampering the riders on the north straightaway possibly slowing down the average time over previous years.

* * *

At 75 Laps . . .

At the end of 75 laps A.T.O. had taken the lead with a 19.49 mile-an-hour average. S.A.E. was second. Dodds House was third. North Hall Barons were in fourth position.

Sigma Nu was fifth. Phi Gamma Delta was sixth. Sigma Pi was seventh. Phi Delta Theta dad dropped to eight. Acacia was ninth and Delta Chi, which had led at 50 laps, was tenth.

The leading time at 75 laps was 57:44, slowed down considerably because of the yellow flag due to tacks on the southeast turn.

* * *

At 100 Laps . . .

At the half-way 100th lap the A. T.O.'s were still leading with an average of 19.05 miles an hour, slowed down considerably by tacks scattered around the track. S.A.E. was second. Sigma Nu had moved into third from fifth. Acacia was in fourth. Delta Chi had come from tenth to sixth. Phi Kappa was seventh. Phi Delta Theta was eighth. Todd House was ninth and Phi Gamma Delta was tenth.

Pole position team number one, North Hall Barons were in 12th place, preceded in the 11th place by Dunn House, followed by Dodds House in 13th place.

Last year's winner, North Hall Friars, was in 14th place and Lambda Chi Alpha was 15th.

Elapsed time at the half-way mark was one hour, 18 minutes and 45 seconds.

Last year's winners the Friars hah had three flats and one spill by this time.

Speed was beginning to pick up after 100 laps as the weather improved—the wind dying down and the coming out.

* * *

At 125 Laps . . .

At the 103rd lap, the yellow flag was dropped again as tacks and other material continued to hamper riders with more flat tires.

About 50 flats had been reported at this time. Workers started dragging the track with boards to clear some of the tacks which were causing the trouble.

Wilbur Shaw, president of the Indianapolis Speedway, and F. T. Reed, secretary of the Board of Trustees, also were clearing tacks. Mr. Reed was quoted as saying unofficially:

"The tacks didn't seem to be a mere accident."

* * *

OFFICIALS said that they were running out of tires, but were sending out for more, after using several loads changing flat tires.

Dealers in Bloomington were reported to have been contacted but tire dealers in town were said to be running out also. There was talk of calling off the race because of tire shortage but at 125 laps, the race was still on.

At the 125th lap mark A.T.O. was still leading with an 18.60 miles an hour average. Tying for second place were Sigma Nu and Acacia, fourth place, Delta Chi, and fifth place Phi Delta Theta. . .

The other top ten were Todd House sixth; Phi Kappa in seventh; Sigma Pi, eighttth; North Hall Barons, ninth, and Dodds House in 10th.

* * *

AT THE 130th LAP, however, the second place tie between the Acacia and Sigma Nu was broken when Acacia took over second place.

* * *

At 150 Laps . . .

At the end of the 148th lap, an accident between the Friar Hall and Dodds House riders took place, but they were uninjured and continued the race.

Few flats were showing up at the 150th lap, although the leading Alpha Tau Omega team came up with a flat, losing only a lap or so before getting into the race.

Quick action at the repair tent enabled them to keep their lead.

At the 150th lap the Alpha Tau Omegas still held the lead, followed in second place by Sigma Nu. Acacia was in third place, Delta Chi fourth, Phi Delta Theta fifth, and North Hall Barons moved into sixth place.

* * *

THE PHI GAMMA Delta team was in seventh place, followed by Todd House in eighth place. Dodds House, ninth, and Phi Kappa was holding on to tenth.

I THOUGHT I COULD AND I DID—The Little Red Engine from the storybook tale, "The Little Engine That Could," carried the Alpha Chi Omegas and Siga Nus to first place in the pit decorations today.

Little Red Engine Theme Wins Decoration Trophy

With the motto "I think I can, I think I can" Alpha Chi Omega and Sigma Nu chugged into the first place today as pit decoration winners.

Taking the appropriate theme of the "Little Engine That Could," the winners—backed by Cummins Engine Co.—displayed the storybook tale with a big red engine on a white background with the little engine's motto.

The Rogers West W and Rogers V combination and the Alpha Tau Omega and Chi Omegas received honorable mention.

A silver rocket on a blue background of the Rogers groups which copped honors had a late take-off. Construction began on it only this morning at 7 o'clock but was completed under the guidance of Vivian Falberg and Al Silverman, sophomores, decorations chairman. They were backed by Curry Building Supply Company.

DIAMONDS were not only a girl's best friend but were trumps in the Alpha Tau Omega and Chi Omega displays.

* * *

They were backed by the Diamond Chain Company, of Indianapolis.

Alpha Tau Omega and Chi Omega and Chi Omega chairmen were Bruce Curtis, sophomore, Jim Farrell, junior, and Betty Bullelt, sophomore.

A few repairs had to be made on the winning display when Jean Thiery, junior, accidentally fell on the design. The situation was remidied quickly by the Sigma Nu chairman, Roger Melaven, freshman, and pit workers.

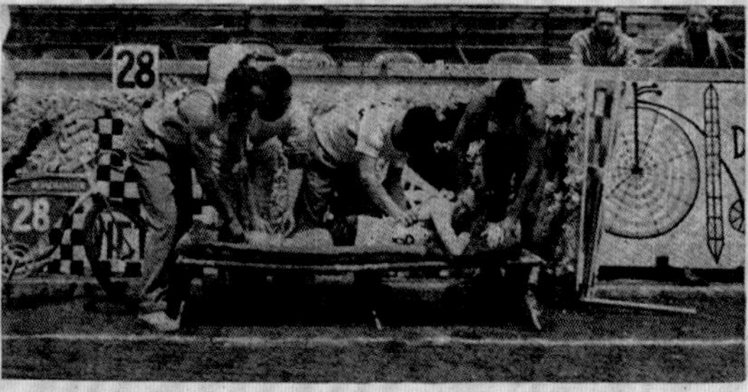

LAST MINUTE RUB DOWN—A member of the South Hall B team gets a "going over" to be assured of being in tip-top shape before flashing around the cinder oval. Fatigue and aching muscles were two of the riders worst enemics. Enemy No. 1 were the tacks which marred the hopes of many teams.

TACK VICTIM—An epidemic of flat tires marred the Little 500 today. The tacks were found on the Southeast turn and tok a toll of over 40 bicycle tires.

Tacks Mar Race

A vandalous crew of tack spreaders, who evidently did their "dirty work" before the race started, caused an epidemic of flat tires in the Little 500 today.

The yellow caution flag was out after Lap 70 until 71 and again after Lap 95 until 110.

According to unofficial reports there were at least 70 flats as a result of the tacks as fast riding cyclists continued to pick up the tacks in their tires after the last green flag was out.

As the tire supply dwindled, race officials talked of calling the event, but the backog of tires never reached the zero mark.

* * *

AT THE END of the Lap 115 there were only six tires left at the track. Officials said that they had already depleted the two-car load supply of one Bloomington merchant but were hoping to get two more carloads from another source. Spare tires were taken off practice bikes for use in the race.

The tacks appeared to be of the ½-inch carpet variety and were found scattered on the southeast turn. They seemed to be concentrated on the inside of the turn and officials instructed riders to stay on the outside.

While the caution flag was out, officials dragged the turn with boards and picked up the pointed tire piercers by hand.

Both Wilbur Shaw and F. T. Reed, secretary of the Board of Trustees, picked up tacks and pieces of metal on the southeast turn.

* * *

THE S.A.E. TEAM was an example of how the tacks played havoc with numerous teams. The S.A.E.'s were second at the end of Lap 115, but after picking up a tack they were forced out of the race.

Here's How They Stood at the End of Each Period

	At 10 Laps . . .	At 25 Laps . . .	At 50 Laps . . .	At 75 Laps . . .	At 100 Laps . . .	At 125 Laps . . .	At 150 Laps . . .	At the Finish . . .
	Time: 7:23	Time: 18:40	Time: 37:31	Time: 57:44	Time: 1 hr: 18:45			
1.	Delta Chi	Phi Gamma Delta	Delta Chi	A.T.O.	A. T. O.	A.T.O.	Alpha Tau Omegas	Sigma Nu
2.	Phi Delta Theta	Delta Chi	North Hall Barons	S.A.E.	S. A. E.	Sigma Nu and Acacia	Sigma Nu	Acacia
3.	Phi Gamma Delta	S.A.E.	Acacia	Dodds House	Sigma Nu		Acacia	A.T.O.
4.	Acacia	Todd House	S.A.E.	North Hall Barons	Acacia	Delta Chi	Delta Chi	North Hall Baons
5.	A.T.O.	North Hall Barons	Todd House	Sigma Nu		Phi Delta Theta	Phi Delta Theta	Phi Delta Theta
6.		Phi Kappa Psi	A.T.O	Phi Gamma Delta	Delta Chi	Todd	North Hall Barons	Todd House
7.		Sigma Pi	Dodds House	Sigma Pi	Phi Kappa	Phi Kappa	Phi Gamma	Phi Gamma Delta
8.		Dodds House	Phi Sigma Kappa	Phi Delta Theta	Phi Delta Theta	Sigma Pi	Todd House	Delta Chi
9.		Phi Delta Theta	Dunn House	Acacia	Todd House	North Hall Barons	Dodds House	Dodds House
10.		A.T.O.	Sigma Nu	Delta Chi	Phi Gamma Delta	Dodds House	Phi Kappa	Phi Kappa

P0081198, IU Archives.

Ernie Pyle's Career Paralleled His College Days at I.U.

Twice Ernie Plye set out for Japan, and twice he missed the big show he went out to see. Death from a sniper's bullet on Ie Shima on April 18, 1945 ended his chronicling of the Pacific war; a contract with a steamship company prevented him from landing on Japan in April, 1922, to cover the battles between the Indiana University baseball team and various Japanese nines.

This parallel between Ernie's career and his college days was the final one added to the many that John S. Hastings, '24, president of the Board of Trustees, and a college classmate of Ernie's, recounted in his address during the ceremony in which Indiana University conferred the honorary degree, doctor of humane letters, on Ernie in 1944.

Describing how life on the campus prepared him for the life of the future, Mr. Hastings recalled that Ernie was sucessively newspaper reporter and editor; he "wanted to see all the world twice"; his automobile polo playing was a forerunner of his jeep riding, and his eating of Sigma Delta Chi luncheons contributed to his later dietary difficulties. And on the campus, Ernie became noted for his lack of sartorial interest, his sensitivity often camouflaged by a veneer of roughness, his shyness yet warmth in friendship.

He entered Indiana University a shy lad from a Northern Indiana farm, and left a big man of the campus—to his classmates a glamorous figure who was to repeat the story in the years that followed.

Ernie had gone out to the Pacific not because he wanted to, but because he knew he had to. As he went, he knew that his number might be up almost any time, for he had come close to death too often. The event that shifted him from a reporter of the war to a reporter of G.I. Joe's war was the death of a soldier in the same foxhole he shared in North Africa; and the year before he died in the Pacific he had escaped severe injury when a bomb blast at Anzio threw him out of bed and across the room in his quarters at the correspondents' billet.

In the four years preceding his death, Ernie Pyle had established himself as America's most loved and best read war correspondent. His daily column was appearing in 386 daily newspapers and in almost as many weekly newspapers, and he is one of the few columnists whose work was extensively reprinted during the periods when he was on vacation.

Hoosiers take a great deal of credit for the things that made Ernie great. In presenting him the honorary degree at Indiana, Dean Fernandus Payne summed up the Hoosier pride thus:

"Born in Indiana, educated at Indiana University and the broader school of experience, a journalist with a keen sense of observation, an accurate reporter with a yen to write about common people and ordinary things which ordinary reporters pass by unseen, he is a man who has lived with the soldiers in their foxholes, on the march, in camp, and in battle, who has written of their sorrows, their joys, their hardships, their love of peace, home and family, their sense of humor, their death, and who has won our friendship and affection. By his actions and writings he has made a significant contribution to the maintenance of morale at home and at the front. In the true sense of the word he is a soldier, fighting for the freedom of mankind."

Twenty-one years before The Arbutus had printed:

"This brilliant gem which blushed unseen in Dana,
"Long since globe trotter, Student ed., Aeon, and who-knows-what,
"Still wears the same old hat, is still the same good fellow,
"Lo, this man's name heads all the lot."

The same notes have been recurrent in recent critical evaluations of Ernie's work. He never saw the review of his "Brave Men" in the magazine of Phi Beta Kappa, but it would have caused him to grin, for this unassuming little man, who had made a good aca-

(Continued on Page Two)

ERNIE PYLE HALL DEDICATION ISSUE OF

HE SERVES BEST WHO SERVES THE TRUTH

THE INDIANA DAILY STUDENT

INDIANA NEWSPAPER SESQUICENTENNIAL— 1804 - 1954

VOL. LXXXIV—NO. 20—Z 175. INDIANA UNIVERSITY SUNDAY, OCTOBER 10, 1954 BLOOMINGTON, INDIANA Established 1867.

ERNIE PYLE HALL: DREAM COME TRUE

Five Men to Get Honorary Ll.D.'s

By AL BOLIN

Amidst the pomp and ceremony of a dedicatory Convocation in the Auditorium on Sunday afternoon, five Indiana and former Indiana newspapermen—including the deans of Hoosier daily and weekly editors, and directors of three of the nation's large newspaper chains—will receive honorary Doctor of Laws degrees from Indiana University.

As the end of the Sesquicentennial of Newspaper Publishing and Printing in Indiana draws near, the faculty of Indiana University has chosen to thus honor five Hoosiers who followed in the footsteps of Elihu Stout, very first Hoosier editor. Coincidentally, the head of the company which today publishes the lineal descendant of Stout's paper, is among the LlD. recipients.

Recipients Listed.

Those receiving the honorary degrees are:

A. A. Hargrave—editor and publisher of The Rockville Republican, who recently observed his 98th birthday anniversary by walking to the office (as usual) to help his son out by writing for and editing the weekly newspaper.

Roy W. Howard—who rose from Indianapolis newsboy to the presidency of United Press in just ten years. A graduate of Manual Training High School in Indianapolis, Mr. Howard pioneered in press associations and syndicates, and now is chairman of the executive committee of Scripps-Howard Newspapers.

Frederick A. Miller—86year-old third-generation Hoosier newspaperman who started on The South Bend Tribune fresh out of high school 67 years ago, and since 1924 has been the editor, publisher, and president of the paper.

Eugene C. Pulliam — president and publisher of The Indianapolis News, The Indianapolis Star, four other Indiana and two Arizona newspapers. Among them is The Vincennes Sun-Commercial, descendant of Stout's Western Sun. At DePauw University in 1909, he helped establish the first chapter of Sigma Delta Chi, national professional journalistic fraternity.

Basil L. Walters—who started to work on the Richmond (Ind.) Palladium while still a student at Indiana University, and today is executive editor of the Knight Newspapers. He was chairman of the first Freedom of Information Committee, American Society of Newspaper Editors, and recently ended his term as presindent of A.S.N.E.

President Herman B Wells will preside at the Convocation, beginning at 3 o'clock. George Y. Wilson, organist, will play the processional, and the Rev. Joseph R. Walker, First Presbyterian Church of Bloomington, will give the invocation.

After introduction of guests by President Wells, John S. Hastings, President of the Board of Trustees and friend of Ernie Pyle, will speak on behalf of Indiana University, and Frank T. Millis, auditor of state, for the State of Indiana.

Marchington Hundred to Play.

The Marching Hundred will play two Sousa marches before C. Walter McCarty, editor of The Indianapolis News and also a member of the Board of Trustees, will introduce the Convocation speaker, J. Russell Wiggins, managing editor of the Washington Post and Times-Herald, will speak on "The Right to Know."

Conferring of degrees will immediately precede the benediction by the Reverend Walker.

Prof. John E. Stempel, Department of Journalism chairman, will present the candidates for degrees.

Claude Rich, I.U. Alumni Secretary, is chairman of the official dedicatory ceremonies.

J. RUSSELL WIGGINS

'Right to Know' Wiggins' Topic At Convocation

By JOAN EMHARDT

When the I.U. Marching Hundred swings into the strains of John Philip Sousa's "Washington Post" march at the dedicatory Convocation for Ernie Pyle Hall, there will be one man who will no doubt feel an especial thrill.

That man is J. Russell Wiggins, managing editor of The Washington (D.C.) Post, the newspaper to which Sousa dedicated his famous march. Since, the name Times-Herald has been added to hypenate the paper's nameplate.

Mr. Wiggins' address will be on "The Right to Know," an appropriate topic for the man who is chairman of the Committee on

(Continued on Page Four)

Four Seminars To 'Follow Up' Convo Address

By BILL CHUMLEY

Four seminar panels, designed to follow up the Ernie Pyle Hall dedicatory address, "The Right to Know," by P. Russell Wiggins, managing editor of The Washington (D.C.) Post and Times-Herald, will take place Sunday and Monday in the Don Mellett Auditorium of the newly dedicated publications-journalism building.

These seminars, which are all open to the public, will include leading persons from newspapers, government, business, and civic organizations. The first symposium will be Sunday evening, beginning at 8 o'clock, and three are on the agenda for Monday morning and afternoon.

The Sunday evening panelists will discuss, "What Newspapers Must Do to Keep Information Free."

Panel Members.

Panel members include Basil L. Walters, executive editor of The Knight Newspapers; Albert W. Spiers, editor of The Michigan City-News Dispatch; Frank T. Millis, Indiana state auditor, and Mayor Ivan Brinegar, of Bedford, retiring president of the Indiana Municipal League.

Monday morning at 9:30 a.m., Paul L. Feltus, editor and publisher of The Bloomington Star-Courier and an I.U. trustee, will preside over the second seminar discussing "Communications in the Modern Community."

Panel members for Mr. Feltus' seminar will be E. C. (Ned) Gorrell, editor and publisher of The Pulaski County Democrat; Frank O. Wellnitz, editor of The Elwood Call-Leader; H. B. Snyder, editor of The Gary Post-Tribune; Robert W. Lemon, manager of WTTV, Bloomington; Mrs. Frank H. Cox, vice-chairman of the Indiana Merit System Association; Mrs. Henry P. Humphrey, president of the Indiana Federation of Women's Clubs; Yandell Cline, secretary of Arvin Industries, and Leon Chitwood, secretary of Carpenters' Local Union 1664.

The first Monday afternoon seminar, scheduled to begin at 1 p.m., will discuss "Communications in Modern Business," and will be presided over by Prof. S. G. Savage.

Mr. Savage's panel members will be Howard W. Allen, vice-president of the Johns-Mansville Corpora-

(Continued on Page Two.)

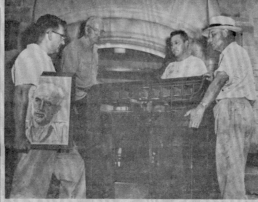

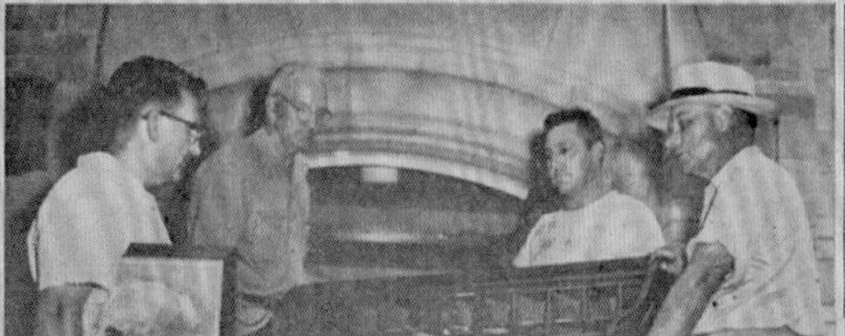

BIG CHANGE-OVER—When Ernie Pyle's desk was moved into Ernie Pyle Hall in August, the shift of operations into the new journalism building was completed—for where Ernie's desk is, there I.U. journalists are at home. Watching I.U. workmen move the desk, which was used by Ernie when he was editor of The Daily Student, is Prof. J. Poynter McEvoy, (left above). He carried in the picture of Ernie which is in the newsroom.

Journalism Department Had Agate Start

By JUDY BENJAMIN

The firm conviction that $29 a week was not enough money for one of the top reporters in Indianapolis was the real beginning of the Department of Journalism 47 years ago, although a course in "news gathering" was offered even earlier, in 1893.

Fred Bates Johnson, who was graduated from I.U. in 1902, decided that a profession in which top pay was $29 a week was not for him. He returned to I.U. to study law, and persuaded University authorities to let him teach a reporting course to help him defray expenses. Mr. Johnson offered two courses to 19 students in 1907.

Since that year, 5,100 students have studied in the department. The curriculum has expanded to 37 courses, but the philosophy—"based on the policy that a broad cultural background with some specializiation in one of the fields of knowledge is more essential than detailed work in the technique of journalism" — has remained the same.

Four Students in 1893.

But even before Mr. Johnson's course in "Reporting," four students assembled in 1893 for instructions from Prof. Martin W. Sampson in news gathering which included: "accounts of fires, accidents, crimes; reports of lectures, entertainments, public meetings, interviews, studying daily and weekly newspapers. Throughout the year, two hours a week."

Prof. H. T. Stephenson, of the Department of English, offered the course in 1895-96, and the next year his brother, Nathaniel Stephenson, a Cincinnati Tribune reporter, conducted it.

Then for 10 years there were no journalism courses, until Mr. Johnson added journalism to the curriculum to stay.

Those were the days when a budding journalist studied almost

(Continued on Page Four)

Sigma Delta Chi Initiations To Add Sixteen to Chapter

With attention focused during dedication of the new journalism building this weekend on two alumni of its chapter—Ernie Pyle, '23, and Don R. Mellett, '14—Sigma Delta Chi will initiate twelve professional and four undergraduate members into the national journalistic fraternity.

The new building has been named Ernie Pyle Hall for the Scripps-Howard war correspondent who during World War II followed G.I. Joe to his own death by a sniper's bullet on Ie Shima. The auditorium in the new building henceforth will be the Don Mellett Auditorium in tribute to the crusading Canton (Ohio) Daily News editor who was shot down by gangsters in 1926. The bronze

(Continued on Page Four)

In His Words, Such Is 'Forever An Inspiration'

Dreams do come true . . . and this weekend the dedication of Ernie Pyle Hall climaxes the long-time dreams of I.U. journalists and Administration.

Dedication Program

SATURDAY

- 10 a.m.—Indiana Associated Press Fall Meeting, Ernie Pyle Hall.
- 1:30 p.m.—Football, Indiana vs. Michigan State, Memorial Stadium.
- 4:15 p.m.—Tours of Ernie Pyle Hall.
- 5:15 p.m.—Sigma Delta Chi Initiation, The Den, Union Building.
- 6 p.m.—Journalism Alumni Reunion Dinner, Alumni Hall, Union Building.
- 8 p.m.—Fall Carnival, Fieldhouse.

SUNDAY

- 3 p.m.—Dedication Convocation, I.U. Auditorium.
- 4:15 p.m.—Dedication Ceremony. Recognition of Pyle Plaque. Cutting the Ribbon to Ernie Pyle Hall Entrance. Reception.
- 5:15 p.m.—Sigma Delta Chi Initiation, Lounge, Ernie Pyle Hall.
- 8 p.m.—Symposium, "What Newspapers Must Do to Keep Information Free."
  Ceremony at Don Mellett Plaque.
  Don Mellett Auditorium, Ernie Pyle Hall.

MONDAY

- 9:30 a.m.—Symposium, "Communications in the Modern Community." Don Mellett Auditorium, Ernie Pyle Hall.
- 1 p.m.—Symposium, "Communications in Modern Business." Don Mellett Auditorium, Ernie Pyle Hall.
- 3 p.m.—Symposium, "How Shall We Pay for Today's Mass Media?" Don Mellett Auditorium, Ernie Pyle Hall.

Ernie Pyle, the beloved Hoosier journalist, himself best described this building, which for the first time brings I.U.'s journalistic and printing activities under one roof. In 1922, while editor of The Daily Student's State Fair editions, he wrote in an editorial about the proposed Memorial Union Building, Memorial Hall, and Memorial Stadium:

"Whenever men and women in any age have achieved renown or done noble deeds that won for them the admiration and love of their fellow men, they have been immortalized by memorials. Only thru the medium of such can their lives and their work remain forever an inspiration to those that come after them. The form of memorials vary, but the instinct that has prompted their building always remained the same."

Inspiration Applied.

This weekend a limestone building with all the space, light, and adequate facilities that the Departments of Journalism, Publications, and Printing, have needed for many years becomes the scene of three-day dedicatory activities in the memory of a man whose professional life is an inspiration to all journalists. His memorial—Ernie Pyle Hall—is the practical application of the inspiration.

Actually, the new journalism hall will be officially dedicated at 4:15 o'clock Sunday afternoon, when Paul L. Feltus, member of the I.U. Board of Trustees and editor of The Bloomington Star-Courier, wields the scissors on the ribbon across Ernie Pyle Hall entrance doors on Seventh Street.

Before that and after the ceremony, however, many activities center about the dedication to make this a weekend to be remembered in the pages of Hoosier journalism history. On the weekend, newsmen will talk over freedom of information, exchange ideas on modern communications, and honor illustrious members of their profession.

It is also the "traditional college weekend." Business also enters the picture as Indiana newspapermen gather for the Fall meeting of the Indiana Associated Press. The alumni dinner is yet another event on the weekend agenda.

Sunday a Gala Day.

Sunday is the gala day, however, when, beginning at 3 p.m., the public as well as dedication guests will hear J. Russell Wiggins, managing editor of The Washington Post and Times-Herald, speak on "The Right to Know."

Immediately after Convocation, the activities will move to Ernie Pyle Hall, where the Ernie Pyle Plaque, the Sigma Delta Chi Historical Site marker, will be recognized.

With the ribbon cutting completed, the public is invited to a reception in Ernie Pyle Hall.

On Sunday night, the first of four symposiums will be conducted in the Don Mellett Auditorium in Ernie Pyle Hall. The auditorium will be dedicated at Sunday night's symposium.

This weekend will not be the first time of busy activity in Ernie Pyle Hall. Converted from the old Stores and Services Building with the addition of two new wings,

(Continued on Page Five)

Alumni Return For Big Weekend

By IRVING GROSS

THIS is what they've been waiting for! And on this biggest of big weekends for alumni of the Department of Journalism, they are returning in droves to the scene of their crimes against The Indiana Daily Student Style Book from all corners—and in between—of the United States for the dedication of Ernie Pyle Hall.

They've come home for the ribbon-cutting ceremony, dedicatory convocation, the seminars, the game and Carnival. But Saturday night, beginning at 6 o'clock, they will cut nostalgia with a butter knife at the Alumni Reunion-Dinner in Alumni Hall. The fatted calf has been killed for the occasion (Sigma Delta Chi offered up the Crimson Bull — but journalism alumni are deserving of the best, it was decided.)

Some Changes Made.

Between courses, the alumni — who have never edited a piece of copy in the lush new editorial

(Continued on Page Three)

ROY W. HOWARD
Scripps-Howard Newspapers

EUGENE C. PULLIAM
The Indianapolis Star-News

FREDERICK A. MILLER
The South Bend Tribune

A. A. HARGRAVE
The Rockville Republican

BASIL L. WALTERS
Knight Newspapers

P0080158, IU Archives.

1955–1969

In the midst of the Cold War, college campuses transformed into places of conflict and debate, and the IDS wasn't immune to the era of upheaval. Questions of student voice led to questions of editorial independence. The newspaper covered assassinations, space programs and protests, sometimes to the chagrin of university officials. By the end of the 1960s, journalists at IU were given a new charter and new responsibilities.

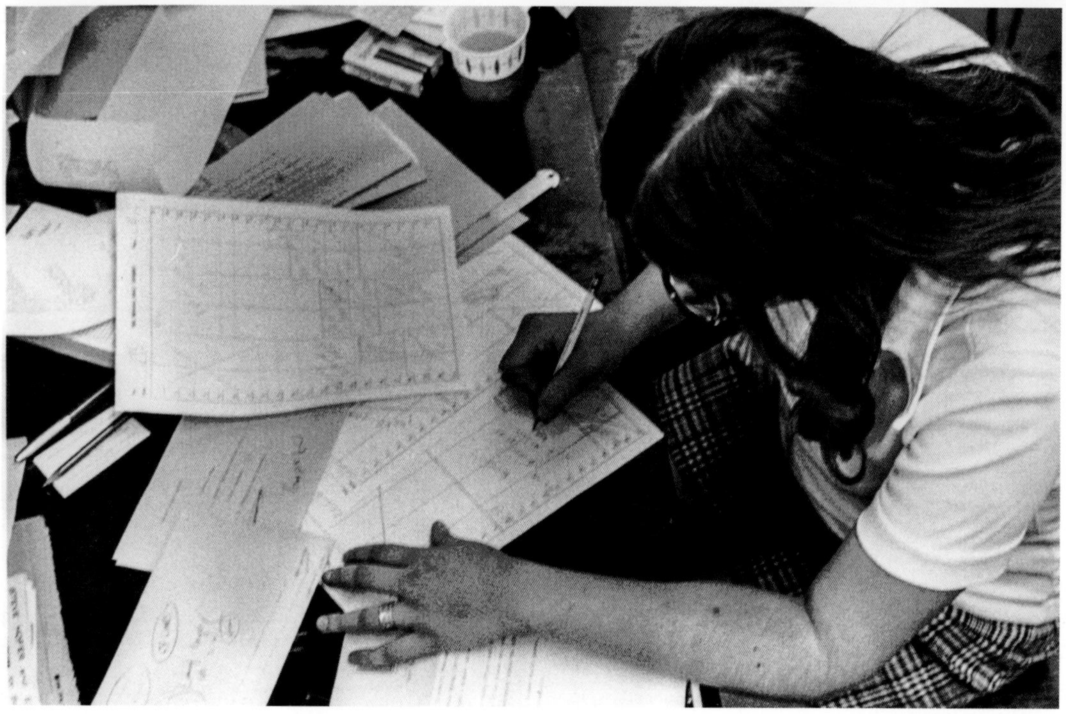

First row left, The IDS newsroom, photographed on April 2, 1958. *P0077734, IU Archives.*

First row right, The spring 1966 staff of the IDS. *P0024337, IU Archives.*

Second row left, IDS staff members (*clockwise from left*) Tom Fleming, Jerry Lyst, John Stevens, Susie Wallace and Ginny Krause in 1955. P0030150, IU Archives.

Second row right, Three staffers at work in the IDS newsroom on September 23, 1958. Photo by Elwood Martin "Barney" Cowherd. *P0027084, IU Archives.*

Bottom, A staffer lays out a page for the IDS in the early 1960s. *P0077828, IU Archives.*

This Card, That Line—Classes'll Be A Cinch After This!

—DAILY STUDENT PHOTO By HERB HOELTKE JR.

CAN I HAVE? — The Fieldhouse was bustling with students Friday roaming from table to table on the first day of enrollment.

By ROY VANETT

Faces — some new, some familiar, some excited and shining — even some bewildered with thoughts of home, or of the days ahead — was the scene at the Fieldhouse Friday morning as a new crop of frosh began winding up a week of getting acquainted with I.U. with enrollment.

It all began with a "guard" directing you by initial and time. After this it was "Hang on to those cards ... don't lose" this, or that and these and those! One would think that life itself depended upon those cards.

A warning should be given to those who think they can jump the line. This Daily Student reporter tried it and almost got the bums rush. Those boys sure were briefed well this year.

There were grads and some seniors there too, but the whole process of enrollment seemed like an everyday affair to them. Some of them had to be reminded that even grads have certain phases that can't be passed up.

Further from the entrance there were calls of "Get your cards ready ... I.D.'s — I.D.'s please," and if you didn't have one, "Over that way for a "mug" shot. About this time the pocket combs began coming from everywhere. That early morning rain really had the coeds busy! Of course those noon showers didn't help matters any either.

Later on it was, "This way, this way ,and then... go over there, or go back there, or sorry your in the wrong place."

The I.D. Process.

"Fill this out," was a familiar chant as more tables waylaid confused frosh and grads alike. At the I.D. tables, where things seem to roll right along with the photographers working production line style (almost 600 shots on a roll of that film), it was in effect, sign your name on this postage stamp, which was really the students identification card for his entire stay at I.U.

Watching the cameras snapping other students, you think to yourself, "Do I know him, or her, or am I just thinking it?" Oh, well, on to the next stop.

"What? I can't get in this section, but ... that person didn't know that she is luckier than upperclassmen who enroll late Saturday. Of course there's always the guy who got everything just as he wanted it. Perhaps next time.

Then came the call, "separate the cards — in order please," and another stop was passed. Pick up an athletic ticket blank then climb the stairs to the Men's Gymnasium.

Then it was fumble, fumble with the cards until an empty corner was found to re-arrange things and go on.

Afternoon Work Desk.

The table that "shook" everyone a little bit was that awful place called the "Afternoon Work" desk. Sometimes things are going just right then these guys say "Sorry." Oh, wll, this won't happen again, says Jane Coed, followed by snickers from the ones who know.

Along the path of the enrollment there were a few tables set up for those who became confused, or mixed up in the processes. At one table, some fellow was trying to get two cars onto the campus. Looks like the two car families are the coming thing alright.

For the frosh the enrollment was cards, cards, cards, and more to sign. The others carried one! But no one got by that big, important stop with the little PAY HERE.

At last there was daylight showing through a door — the end. But what was this, it looks like a carnival midway with "hawkers" selling their wares.

"No obligations, just sign here" .... even the politicians were there!

Finally no more stops. Next, classes. The work starts Monday. Only one thing worries me, how do I wash this ink off my hands that some zealous card checker stamped by mistake.

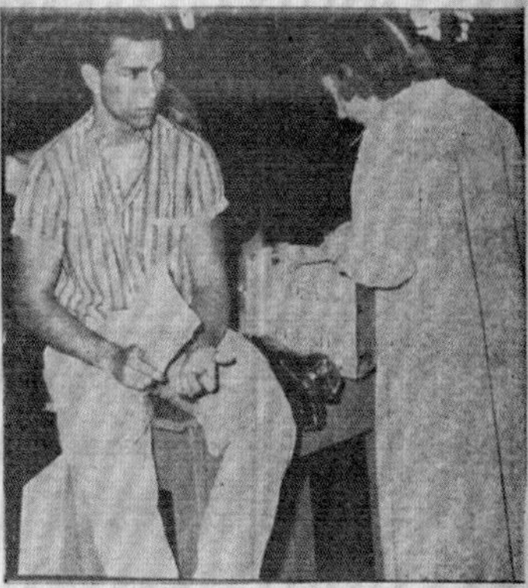

—DAILY STUDENT PHOTO By HERB HOELTKE JR.

WHAT DO WE HAVE HERE? — A popular spot during enrollment in the Fieldhouse was the Lost and Found table. Everything turned up here. Carol Robinson is looking through the found articles for something she lost. Fred Settina is resting on the table. Both are freshmen.

SECTION TWO | THE INDIANA DAILY STUDENT | SECTION TWO

LXXXVI—NO. 5—Z 175. | INDIANA UNIVERSITY | SATURDAY, SEPTEMBER 15, 1956. | BLOOMINGTON, INDIANA | Established 1867

Death Takes Miss Anderson And Kinsey From I.U. Family

Three members of the University family died during the Summer including I.U.'s founder of the Institute of Sex Research, Dr. Alfred C. Kinsey.

The other two persons who died were a leader in social service work, Miss Agnes Anderson, associate professor of social work, and Mark P. Helm, former registrar of the Indiana University School of Medicine at Indianapolis.

Dr. Kinsey, 62-year-old professor who became famous for his scientific study of human sex behavior, died Aug. 25 at Bloomington Hospital of pneumonia and a heart ailment.

Carrying an enormous workload, Dr. Kinsey worked 80 hours a week for years. He was forced to restrict his schedule because of ill health for a period before his death.

Research To Continue.

The pioneering research projects which he began are being carried on by the Institute of Sex Research, Inc. which Dr. Kinsey founded in 1947 on the I.U. campus. It is now under the direction of his co-workers, Dr. Wardell B. Pomeroy and Dr. Paul Gebhard, who act as joint directors of the Institute.

Drs. Pomeroy and Gebhard and statistician Clyde E. Martin shared equal credit with Dr. Kinsey on the title page of the best sellers published by the Institute, "Sexual Behavior in the Human Male" and the second work, "Sexual Behavior in the Human Female."

The Institute is continuing nearly a dozen additional studies and reports which Dr. Kinsey had laid out for the future including a book on which Dr. Kinsey was working at the time of his death, "Sex Laws and the Sex Offender."

Dr. Kinsey, a zoologist, won early scientific recognition for his study of the gall wasp.

His interest in sex research stemmed from his joining 11 other teachers at I.U. in giving a marriage course during the 1930's. His search for answers to questions which the students asked about sex lead him to the conclusion that existing answers were confusing and contradictory. He resolved to study sexual behavior with scientific research methods.

From a single graduate assistant paid from Dr. Kinsey's own pocket, his work grew into the Institute with a staff of 15 and a large library of sex literature in Jordan Hall valued at $200,000.

Miss Anderson Dies June 8.

Miss Agnes Anderson, who died on June 8 after an extended illness, was head of the Division of Social Service work on the Bloomington campus. She was also active in campus affairs and county, state

(Continued on Page Four)

DR. ALFRED C. KINSEY

MISS AGNES ANDERSON

Old Vic Company to Begin '56-'57 Auditorium Series

By JUDY WILLIAMS

The celebrated Old Vic Company will open the 1956-57 I.U. Auditorium series with a presentation of "Romeo and Juliet," on Oct. 15.

Harold W. Jordan, director of Auditorium programs, announced that the tour of the Broadway play, "Teahouse of the August Moon," which was scheduled on the series for Nov. 1, has been cancelled because of the release this Fall of the movie made from the show.

The Old Vic Company will also do "Richard II" by Shakespeare in a special performance for the general public Oct. 16. Tickets for this performance will go on sale at the Auditorium box office Sept. 28.

Tickets Available.

Tickets are still available for the Auditorium series, Mr. Jordan announced. Tickets may be purchased by mail order or at the box office.

London's Royal Victoria Theatre, or the "Old Vic" Company, has been a center of drama for many years. It has been the birthplace of many theatrical names and is especially known for its work in the plays of Shakespeare. The company, known for its costly productions, has come to symbolize tradition in the history of dramatic productions.

The group is touring principal cities in the United States presenting its repertory of Shakespearean plays under the sponsorship of American impressario, Sol Hurok, and The Arts Council of Great Britain.

Second Appearance.

This will be the second appearance of the English dramatic company at Indiana University. In the Fall of 1954 it gave two performances of "Midsummer Night's Dream" in the Auditorium.

Heading the list of players in the company are Claire Bloom, John Neville, Paul Rogers, Coral Browne, Rosemary Harris, Richard Wordsworth, Jack Gwillim, Ernest Hare and Wynne Clark.

Probably the best known of the players is Claire Bloom who was in motion picture performances of "Innocents of Paris," "Alexander the Great," and in Laurence Oliver's "Richard III." She also played Cleopatra in Shaw's "Caesar and Cleopatra" in an N.B.C. spectacular last Spring.

The rest of the schedule for the year is as follows:

Oct. 18—Societa Corelli, instrumental ensemble.
Nov. 15—Vienna Symphony Orchestra, Andre Cluytens, Conductor.
Nov. 26—N.B.C. Opera Company in "Madame Butterfly."
Feb. 22—Clifford Curzon, pianist.
March 6—Ballet Theatre.
March 14 — Indianapolis Symphony Orchestra, Izler Solomon, Conductor.
April 7—Jerome Hinds, basso.

COOKING GIVES LONG LIFE.

ROCHESTER, Ind. (AP)—Observing his 101st birthday Friday, onetime Fulton County Sheriff Andrew A. Gast of Akron gave part of the credit for his long life to his wife's good cooking. He and his 93-year-old wife will observe their 70th wedding anniversary Oct. 27.

Faculty Shows New Faces And New Titles

Board of Trustees Lists Promotions, Leaves of Absence.

Appointments to the faculty, appointments of department chairmen, changes in title, and leaves of absence have been acted upon by the I.U. Board of Trustees.

Charles S. Hyneman, nationally known political scientist, has been named professor of government. Prof. Hyneman was graduated from I.U. in 1923, and received his masters degree here in 1925.

He headed the departments of government at Louisiana State and Northwestern Universities, and organized the Louisiana Municipal Association for local government officials. He received the Ph.D. degree from the University of Illinois.

Dr. L. Rush Bailey, who was a member of the School of Dentistry faculty in Indianapolis in 1947-51, is professor and acting chairman of the dental school's prosthetics department. He received a D.D.S. degree from Northwestern University and formerly practiced dentistry in South Bend.

Herbert J. Muller, visiting professor at I.U. in 1953-54, is professor of English and government. He was a member of the Purdue University English faculty for 19 years.

Dinko Tomasic has been made professor of sociology in accordance with the transfer of the Institute of East European Studies to the Department of Sociology.

Robert F. Byrnes, director of the Mid-European Studies Center in New York, is professor of history. He also is a member of the staff of the University's Institute of East Europeas Studies.

William Riley Parker, one of the country's leading Milton scholars, is professor of English. Prof. Parker had been executive secretary of the Modern Language Association of America since 1947. He is the author of two books and numerous articles on Milton.

Robert W. Briggs, chief of the embryology department of Lankenau Research Institute and Institute for Cancer Research, Philadelphia, is professor of zoology.

Visiting Professors.

Keith Caldwell, former director of the I.U. South Bend Center and now visiting professor of political science at the University of California, is visiting professor of government. He also is co-ordinator of the I.U.-Thailand Public Administration Training Project.

Reidar T. Christiansen, ranked by folklorists as one of the world's top six authorities in the field, is visiting professor of folklore. He was director of the Norwegian Folklore Collection at the University of Oslo.

David Daiches, English-born author and educator, is visiting professor in the I.U. English Depart-

(Continued on Page Two)

Singers, Nickel Coffee Leave I.U. In June

Israeli Force Wipes Out Jordan Post

JERUSALEM (AP)—A 1,000-man Israeli armored force and three fire-bombing planes wiped out a police post in Jordan Thursday night, Jordan charged Friday.

A military spokesman in Amman, Jordan's capital, said 10 Jordanians were killed, 4 wounded and 4 are missing in this second big attack from Israel in three days. It was 12 miles inside Jordan.

Three of the dead were listed as civilians; the rest were police or national guardsmen.

An Israeli broadcast heard in Amman described the attack as a reprisal for the killing of three Israeli Druze tribesmen by Jordanians Wednesday.

Jordan sent a complaint to the

(Continued on Page Two.)

Wine and Women Don't Always Mix

ST. CATHERINES, Ont. — (AP)— "Let the peaches stand in your favorite wine until thoroughly penetrated," says the Ontario Peach Growers' Marketing recipe booklet. "Experiment with different wines."

The booklet usually is popular but its distribution at a meeting here last week may have set back peach consumption more than a little, the board acknowledged ruefully.

The meeting was the annual conference of the Ontario Women's Temperance League.

CHILD EATS LOCUSTS.

ROME —(AP)— Diet depends on your point of view, Dr. Margaret Mead of Britain told a world diet congress in Rome. She has just returned from Nigeria where she heard a village child complain a new teacher from a different tribe ate rats and snails. The child, Dr. Mead said, prefers locusts and caterpillars.

Summer Session Competes With Political Campaigns

By JUDY MILLER

While the nation's politicians put on their big shows at Chicago and San Francisco this Summer, and Mickey Mantle challenged Babe Ruth's all-time home run record, things were happening here at I.U., too.

Even before commencement the Singing Hoosiers and the Hoosier Queens left for their eight-week U.S.O. tour of Far East military bases. The 29 songsters, accompanied by Conductor George F. Krueger, choral director of the School of Music, and Mrs. Krueger, visited Japan and Korea and returned to I.U. late in July.

Jordan Hall Dedicated.

Jordan Hall, beautiful life-science building, was dedicated in a four-day Commencement week celebration. The dedication ceremonies were highlighted by an announcement from President Herman B Wells of a $350,000 grant to I.U. from the Rockefeller foundation. The grant will be used for genetic study.

High school junior boys, 850 strong, invaded the campus June 9 for week-long Boys' State activities.

Before leaving I.U., the class of '56 learned that the stained glass roof of the Wellhouse, long in a state of disrepair, had been finally mended and broken glass replaced.

Summer Session began June 15 with a record enrollment of 4,306 students on campus, an increase of four per cent over last Summer's enrollment. The two-day separate registration and enrollment procedure was used for the last time, and has been replaced by simpler one-operation process.

Nickel Loses Again.

The beginning of Summer Session marked the end of the nickel cup of Commons coffee. The price went up to seven cents.

The Indiana Union christened its recreation area at Bean Blossom Reservoir in July with speed boat races. Approximately 1,800 persons watched the sixty entrants race. Two weeks later students were invited to take part in a Union Sports Day Program at the recreation area.

Early in July The Indiana Daily Student announced that the Indiana State Fair edition would be discontinued. After 30 years of Fair editions, The Student was discontinued for financial reasons.

This Fall's freshmen and their parents had a chance to visit the campus for pre-Orientation programs and interviews. More than 1,000 freshmen took advantage of the programs and took their Orientation tests early.

Marching 'Hundred' Plus.

Ronald C. Gregory, new director of the Marching Hundred, announced that the band's size would be increased to 160 this Fall. New accessories are to be added to the snappy Cream and Crimson band uniforms worn for the first time last Fall.

Beverly Mattox, junior and a member of Delta Delta Delta social sorority, was named Miss Indiana and competed in the Miss Universe contest at Long Beach, Calif.

The publication of the 1956-57 volume of Who's Who was published and 94 members of the I.U. family received mention.

Mayor Tom Lemon, of Bloomington, was named by Hoosier Democrats as their candidate for

(Continued on Page Four)

Convo Series Offers Big Names

Clement Attlee, Bennett Cerf, Claude Rains, and the two Hoosier gubernatorial candidates, Harold W. Handley and Ralph Tucker, will appear on the convocation series for the coming school year.

Britain's postwar prime minister, Clement Attlee, will speak on "Today's World" in early January. Mr. Cerf, Random House publisher, will appear in mid-November to speak on the literary world.

Rains to Read.

Actor Claude Rains will present readings Nov. 11. Mr. Tucker and Mr. Handley will make campaign speeches.

"Very few universities have as fine and complete a schedule of this scope and excellence," said John H. Mueller, chairman of the convocations committee, as he described the convocation plans.

Mr. Mueller went on to explain that the planning of the coming convocations involves co-operation among all departments of the University.

"Since their content is so widely spread, every young citizen should be interested in these convocations," stated Dr. Mueller.

Most of the programs begin at 7:15 p.m. throughout the year in the Auditorium. Admission is free. The I.U. Board of Trustees sets aside an appropriation annually to finance each program.

Mr. Cerf, who is a panelist on the TV program "What's My Line?" will give a talk on the effects of movies and television on literature.

Leader of the party which he claims is "concerned with the welfare of the common man." Mr. Clement Attlee introduced socialistic policies in the British government. His talk will deal with conditions of today's world.

The world of footlights and cameras will be captured when Claude Rains, stage and screen star, presents readings. Mr. Rains has appeared in such movies as "The Deception," "Now Voyager," and "Saturday's Children." He appeared in the stage play "Sealed Cargo" in 1951.

Laurence to Lecture.

Pulitzer - prize winner William Laurence, now science editor for the New York Times, will lecture in mid-February. Mr. Laurence has written the books "Dawn Over Zero." The story of the atomic Bomb" and "The Hell Bomb," from his experience as eye-witness at the dropping of the Atomic bomb over Nagasaki.

The provisional afternoon and evening schedule for the year 1956-57 is as follows:

Oct. 30—Herbert Knapp, documentary film and lecture on Thailand, 7:15 p.m.

Nov. 7—Flor Peeters, Belgian organ virtuoso and composer, 7:15 p.m.

Nov. 11—Claude Rains, stage and screen star to present readings, 3 p.m.

Nov. 16—Bennett Cerf, publisher and columnist, to lecture on "What Are the Movies and Television Doing to Literature Today?" 7:15 p.m.

Lecture on Asia.

Dec. 5 — Albert Ravenhalt lecture on Asia, 7:15 p.m.

Dec. 7—Murl Deusing, documentary film and lecture on "Adventure in Africa," 7:15 p.m.

Jan. 8 — Earl Clement Attlee, Great Britain's postwar prime minister, to lecture on "Today's World," 7:15 p.m.

Feb. 14 — William Laurence, Pulitzer-prize winning science editor for the New York Times, to lecture, 7:15 p.m.

Feb. 17—Robert Noehren, American organist, 3 p.m.

March 8—Clifford Kamen, documentary film and lecture on "Greece," 7:15 p.m.

March 20 — Modern Dance Program, I.U. Modern Dance Workshop, 7:15 p.m.

No date set—Ralph Tucker, Democratic candidate for governor, Harold W. Handley, Lieutenant Governor, and Republican candidate for governor.

This schedule is subject to change.

P0020519, IU Archives.

HE SERVES BEST WHO SERVES THE TRUTH

THE INDIANA DAILY STUDENT

THE WEATHER
BEAT
PURDUE

VOL. LXXXIX—NO. 50—Z 175. INDIANA UNIVERSITY SATURDAY, NOVEMBER 21, 1959. BLOOMINGTON, INDIANA Established 1867

BEAT P.U.!

—DAILY STUDENT PHOTO by C. W. DANE

Charge of the Bucket-Hungry Fightin' Hoosiers

By GARY LONG

Indiana's Fightin' Hoosiers, who last won the Old Oaken Bucket from Purdue in 1947, will clash with the angry and frustrated Boilermakers in Memorial Stadium at 1:30 p.m. today in a continuation of a football rivalry rich in tradition.

Purdue has dominated the series and the Bucket since 1948 when the Boilermakers trounced the Hoosiers 39-0, but Indiana is rated its best chance to bring the Bucket back to I.U. since the Purdue string of 11 straight games without a loss began.

The Hoosiers, although young and inexperienced at the start of the season, have improved tremendously, while the Boilermakers, pre-season favorites to win the Big Ten championship, have been hampered by injuries and a weak offensive attack all year.

The Fightin' Hoosiers were a big question mark as the '59 campaign began because Coach Phil Dickens had lost much of his "Cinderella" team of last season, which surprised multitudes of football fans with a 5-3-1 record.

Inspirational Leadership.

However, Dickens' inspirational leadership and coaching worked the same miracle with the '59 Fightin' Hoosiers that it had with the team last season.

The I.U. players posted impressive victories over Illinois, Marquette, Nebraska, and Michigan, outplayed Ohio State in a scoreless tie, lost a heart-breaker to Michigan State, and also lost to Minnesota and Northwestern.

Now, the Fightin' Hoosiers would like to climax their second successful season in succession with a victory in the annual Old Oaken Bucket battle.

The Boilermakers, on the other hand, were supposed to be the team to beat in the race for the conference title and the hoped-for trip to the Rose Bowl.

Purdue Has Depth.

Coach Jack Mollenkopf, who uses unit substitution, had a team which was two-deep at every position, with a strong crop of sophomores ready to help pave the way to California. If an injury halted a first stringer, there was supposed to be a second stringer, almost as good, ready to fill the gap.

However, the Boilermaker injuries came in pairs. Not only was first string quarterback Ross Fichtner eliminated from the starting lineup for six weeks, but Bernie Allen, his understudy, was injured two weeks later and still hasn't returned to full effectiveness. BC

Purdue's All-American fullback candidate, Bob Jarus, was hurt in the third game of the season, and then, after hitting his peak in Purdue's 14-7 victory over Iowa, was struck down with a throat infection.

Laraway May Be Out.

Meanwhile, second team fullback Jack Laraway was out of the lineup off and on throughout the year. A shoulder injury last Saturday in the 29-23 Boilermaker victory over Minnesota may keep Laraway off the field today.

Despite the disastrous injuries, in the line as well as the backfield, the Boilermakers whipped Notre Dame, Wisconsin, Iowa, and Minnesota, while losing to Michigan State and Ohio State, and tieing UCLA and Illinois.

Now, for the first time since the second game of the season, Mollenkopf will be able to put his first string backfield on the field intact.

Fichtner will start today, and his tremendous performance against Minnesota last week proved that he is at full efficiency once again. He was named UPI's "Midwest Back of the Week" in his substitute role.

Although Jarus will not start, being out of shape because of the weight he lost during the battle with the throat infection, he will see action. If Jarus hits as hard as he can, the Fightin' Hoosier linemen will know whom they're tackling.

Pent-up Frustrations.

Purdue is out to loose its pent-up anger and frustra-

(Continued on Page Two)

P0078542, IU Archives.

HE SERVES BEST WHO SERVES THE TRUTH

THE INDIANA DAILY STUDENT

THE WEATHER
Fair and cooler today.
Cloudy and warmer Friday.
High today near 60.

VOL. LXXXIX—NO. 130—Z 175. INDIANA UNIVERSITY FRIDAY, APRIL 8, 1960. BLOOMINGTON, INDIANA Established 1867

TOM ATKINS WINS BY 45 VOTES

For Student Body President—By Districts

	Married	GRC	Town	Wells	Tower	Wright	Trees	Smithwood	Third	Northwest	Jordan	Total
Atkins (Ind.)	77	289	258	471	321	565	476	388	80	52	82	3,059
Dann (Org.)	32	48	118	81	225	201	35	372	617	498	787	3,014

Five-Year Control By Organized Ends

By THE DAILY STUDENT STAFF

Tom Atkins, junior, was elected President of the Student Body by 45 votes Thursday night.

He and his vice-presidential running mate, Jim Taylor, sophomore, defeated Organized candidates Mike Dann and Steve Beeler, juniors, 3,059-3,014.

The election was one of the closest in the 13-year history of student body presidential balloting as well as the first Independence Party victory in five years.

Largest Turn-Out.

The voting turn-out was the largest in history.

The triumph was recognized as a personal one for Mr. Atkins, who siphoned off 214 votes from the three usually solid Organized voting districts.

Although the Organized candidates polled heavily in their three districts, Mr. Atkins picked up a net gain of 95 votes over last year in those districts.

Mr. Atkins carried the pivotal Smithwood district by 16 votes and Tower Center by 96, while Wells Quadrangle gave him a surprisingly strong 471-80 margin.

He also carried each of the five Residence Halls districts, Town, Married, and Graduate Students.

Women Turn Tide.

Mr. Atkins' deciding gain came in the two women's centers, Smithwood and Wells Quadrangle, where he picked up a total of 536 votes over last year's Independent candidates.

Mr. Dann won only in the three Organized districts.

Mr. Atkins, waiting for the election results, sank back in his chair in the Arbutus Snack Bar and breathed a sigh of relief when the announcement of his victory reached there.

Regaining his composure, Tom asked, "Can somebody loan me 30 cents? I'd like to call my mother."

Victory Statement.

After a quick round of handshaking among the party faithfuls, Mr. Atkins released his victory statement:

"We would like to take this opportunity to sincerely thank the students at Indiana University for the vote of confidence given me and my party."

Mike Dann, reached at his fraternity house last night, said: "I am of course disappointed; nobody likes to lose. But I was beaten by a wonderful fellow to whom I pledge my wholehearted co-operation and support."

There were 832 more votes cast in this election than in last year's contest when John Nash, Organized Party candidate, defeated Dave Williams, Independent, by 562 votes.

Mr. Atkins gained votes in every district over last year's Independent candidates.

Parade Staged.

Joyous Independence backers, with Mr. Atkins and Mr. Taylor in front, staged an impromptu automobile parade around the campus when the final returns were tabulated at 10 p.m.

The Independence Party broke open a sleepy campaign almost void of issues and party squabbles and with little actual campaigning as they distributed perfume favors in Smithwood the night before the election and plastered campus property with campaign stickers before dawn Thursday.

Posters, cardboard signs on trees, election statements, and campaign literature flooding the campus Thursday morning created the first realistic campaign atmosphere during the dormant pre-election weeks.

Mr. Atkins is the first Negro to become President of the Student Body at Indiana University.

Impressive Record.

His record is an impressive one. He has served in Student Senate four semesters, has been speaker pro tem of that body and on the Senate executive committee the same period, has been president of his class, and president of the huge Men's Residence Halls Association. He was also president of his dormitory and his residence center. He is also a member of the Board of Aeons, and president of the Security Council of the Little United Nations Assembly.

Mr. Atkins is an honors program student with a 2.7 cumulative average.

Mr. Taylor, the vice-president-elect of the Student Body, has served in Student Senate two semesters, is on the Senate executive committee, has been a class officer two years, and was a page in the U.S. House of Representatives three years. He graduated as valedictorian of his class at the Page School in Washington, D. C.

The new campus officers will be sworn in by Chief Justice William Vititoe, senior, at the next Student Senate meeting April 21.

Chi Phi Victors In Quiz Bowl

Chi Phi, social fraternity, captured the traveling trophy when they defeated Kappa Sigma, social fraternity, 2200 to 950 Thursday night in the final round of the fifth annual Campus Quiz Bowl.

Members of the winning Chi Phi team were Mike Montgomery, senior, and John Craft, junior. George Carey and Bill Marshall, seniors, represented Kappa Sigma.

Both teams had a large number of supporters in the audience. Members of Chi Phi fraternity recognized their team's victory by carrying their representatives out of Whittenberger Auditorium on their shoulders.

Moderator for the evening was Dan Hoyt, junior, who compared the audience with the audience of a wedding ceremony.

"It's kinda like when somebody's getting married," said Mr. Hoyt. "Chi Phi on one side and Kappa Sigma on the other."

The Chi Phi team was the first to answer a correct question and led most of the evening. The score was Chi Phi over Kappa Sigma, 1100 to 1000, at the half-way mark. Chi Phi remained in the lead throughout the remainder of the match.

Chi Phi fraternity team members were awarded individual trophies. The traveling award, the Colonel Raymond L. Shoemaker Trophy, will be inscribed with the name of the 1960 winning team.

General chairman of the Quiz Bowl was Tom Smallwood, sophomore. Other members of the 1960 committee were Carolyn Beardsley, junior, secretary; Kathy Krause, junior, entries; Gordon Eslick, senior, and Pat Roelke, sophomore, questions; Jim Russ, sophomore, arrangements; Arnie Goldberg, sophomore, publicity; and Bob Hanning, sophomore, posters.

Strikers Show Good Conduct

One reason why the current sit-down lunch counter strikes in the South haven't been more violent is because the participating Negro students are from the milder-tempered middle and upper classes, said Prof. John T. Liell, sociology, advisor of the I.U. chapter of the NAACP, Thursday.

Speaking at a Campus Colloquy in Union Cafeteria A, he said that although provocation by whites to violence had been severe in sit-down strikes, Negro behavior had been passive and in some cases exemplary.

Pointing out the Woolworth store chain, one of those at which Negro students have staged sit-down strikes, Mr. Liell asserted Woolworth's trade had declined recently by some 17-19 per cent.

The Aid to Collegians on Trial program (ACT), which is a campus effort to financially aid Negro students arrested in these sit-down lunch counter strikes, has thus far collected about $400, Mr. Liell said.

Although ACT has been concentrating mainly on student contributions, he said, the faculty will be approached soon for support.

Communism In Cuba Can Be Met—Phillips

By Harvey Kagan

Should the Cuban government come under the "domination of international communism," Western Hemisphere republics have the "authority and ability" to counteract such a government on behalf of the Cuban people, Richard I. Phillips, public affairs officer for the Department of State said Wednesday.

Speaking on "Impressions of Latin America" in Ballantine 109, Mr. Phillips said the Declaration of Caracas of 1954 states that if a Western Hemisphere government should come under the domination of international communism, the foreign ministers of Western Hemisphere republics are to meet and decide what countermeasures should be taken.

Could Include Invasion.

Such action could include economic sanctions or invasion, Mr. Phillips said. Indeed, he said, there is no limit to the type of countermeasures which the foreign ministers might take.

However, there is reason to believe that the Cuban government will not become communist-controlled, Mr. Phillips added.

Speaking of Panama's desire to have their flag fly along side that of the United States in the Canal Zone, Mr. Phillips said that a recent Congressional "demonstration" of opposition to the Panamanian desire will "undoubtedly delay" any administration decision on the matter.

U.S. Can Aid.

On the subject of what this country can do to aid Latin America, Mr. Phillips said the U.S. should continue to expand its present programs. Such programs include, he said, loans through the Import-Export and Inter-American Development Banks, student exchanges, cushioning the impact of fluctuating prices on Latin American goods, and continued private investment in Latin America.

However, Mr. Phillips said, private investment in Latin America will depend on individual government's actions and reception to such investment.

But no matter how much the U.S. aids Latin America, Mr. Phillips said, the bulk of improvement must be made by the Latin American nations themselves.

SUPPORT FOR PORT.

OGDEN DUNES, Ind. (AP) — A plan is under way to make the Michigan City harbor a deepwater port.

Krizman Wins Table Tennis Championship

Dave Krizman, freshman, won the 1959-60 Indiana Union Table Tennis Championship tourney last night.

Four of Indiana University's top table tennis players competed against each other for the I. U. Championship and the opportunity to play a match against Jim McClure, Indianapolis, ex-world champion table tennis player.

The evening's events began with the semi-final playoffs between the four remaining I. U. players. Mac Busby, senior, and Ben Ewton, junior, played each other in the first match with Mr. Busby winning 16-21, 21-16, and 21-15.

In the second match, vying for entrance into the finals Dave Krizman and Tim Cobb, freshmen, played two rounds with Mr. Krizman's defeating Mr. Cobb by a score of 21-14 in the first and 21-17 in the second.

Final Match Played.

The two winners, Mr. Busby and Mr. Krizman, then played two rounds for the final match. Mr. Krizman became the 1959-60 Indiana Union table tennis champion by defeating Mr. Busby with a score of 21-8 and 21-9.

Ray Muston, junior, recreation director, presented the winner's trophy to Mr. Krizman on behalf of the Indiana Union. Mr. Krizman is the holder of 180 titles, among them the National Boy's Championship, Canadian National Junior Championship for two years, the Indiana State Championship for five years, and the U.S. runnerup for two years in a row.

Mr. Krizman started playing table tennis in 1950, and has a sister, Sharlene, the American Girl Champion and a member of the U. S. Olympic team, who attended I.U. last year.

Exhibition Match Staged.

After the presentation of the trophy to Mr. Krizman and Jim McClure, former holder of six national and five world championships, an exhibition match was staged. Mr. McClure, an Indianapolis manufacturer and distributor of tennis tables, defeated Mr. Krizman, winning 21-16 and 21-12.

After the exhibition match, Mr. McClure then asked for the audience's questions about the game of table tennis. Some of the questions asked concerned serving a forehand drive, and the most effective ways to hold a paddle.

Has Special Paddle.

Mr. McClure's personal paddle interested the spectators. When asked the type, he stated that he used a sandwich paddle which consists of a thin layer of sponge under the regular layer of rubber covering on the paddle surface.

Students arranging the tournament were Mr. Muston and Skip Boisson, general chairmen of the Recreation Council; Mike Norris, table tennis chairman; Mike McKenna, tourney arrangements chairman; Jeff Finn, tournament publicity chairman, and Kim Helfish, tourney director, all freshmen.

A rather large audience attended demonstrating the increasing popularity of the game on the I.U. campus.

John Nash Proud Of Achievements

"I think we've accomplished more this year than in the three previous years that I've been on campus," outgoing Student Body President John Nash, senior, said of his year in office.

He cited increased finances and a larger office as chief reasons for the improvement.

A small scholarship for the president was among his suggestions for the future. He said that the maximum value of scholarship should be about $200 so that it would not attract people who are "out for money" to the position.

He also said he planned to propose to the Student Senate that it "take a good look at the financial situation" and plan their spending carefully.

He mentioned the Board of Review for Campus Activities and the Academic Board of Review that have been recently created by the Senate.

"They are both steps in the right direction," he added.

He also said that he wanted to see the Senate newsletter and the leadership training program further developed.

Traeger Leads Union Vote

Norm Traeger and Ann Levenstein, sophomores, outpolled seven other candidates to win the remaining two positions on the 1960-61 Union Board.

Mr. Traeger had 2,066 votes in the campus-wide balloting. Miss Levenstein had 1,942.

The two winners will be installed at the Union Board installation banquet April 25.

The election results:

Norm Traeger	2,066
Ann Levenstein	1,942
Carolyn Bechert	1,553
Frank Hill	1,179
Judy McGill	1,139
Cindy Orme	1,045
Ralph Foley	900
Anne Creel	799
Pat Roelke	385

Police Quell Election Protest

A group of approximately 100 students marched on Smithwood Hall late last night, protesting the election results. Campus police quelled the demonstration shortly after they reached Smithwood. The crowd dispersed, singing segregation songs.

Today—
—on the campus—

EVANSVILLE NORTH SIDE HIGH SCHOOL CHOIR — 11:30 a.m., Music Bldg. Recital Hall.

BIG TEN UNION BOARD CONFERENCE — 1 p.m. to midnight, Union Bldg.

PSYCHOLOGY COLLOQUIUM — "The Concept of Optimal Stimulation in Learning and Motivation," Clarence Leuba, Antioch College, 3:45 p.m., Lindley 303.

YMCA-YWCA AND STUDENT CHRISTIAN ASSOCIATION SPRING LEADERSHIP CONFERENCE — 5 p.m., Bradford Woods.

HI-FI POPULAR RECORD CONCERT — 7 p.m., South Lounge, Activities Center, Union Bldg.

WFIU RADIO PROGRAM — "Image America: The Community," produced by The Fund for Adult Education and NBC, 7-8:30 p.m.

REC NITE — 7:30 p.m., Student Bldg.

EASTER PARADE ON CAMPUS —8 p.m.-12 midnight, Alumni Hall, Activities Center, Union Bldg. Fashion Show, 8-9 p.m. Dancing, 9:30 p.m.-12 midnight.

RHYTHM ROOM —8-11 p.m., Commons, Activities Center, Union Bldg.

PHILOSOPHY CLUB MEETING —"A Budget of Cross-Type Inferences," Norwood Russell Hanson, 8 p.m., Room G45, Biddle Continuation Center, Union Bldg.

FOLK DANCING — 8 p.m., Room 26 A, B, and C, Activities Center, Union Bldg.

COSMOPOLITAN CLUB INTERNATIONAL MIXER — 8-12 midnight, International Center, 111 S. Jordan.

—DAILY STUDENT PHOTO by TERRY JOYCE

VICTORY DRIVE — Tom Atkins, junior, (right) gives a victory smile during a parade Thursday celebrating his winning of the student body presidency. Looking on is his running mate, Jim Taylor, junior (left) who was elected vice-president of the student body.

Organized Candidates Sweep Class Offices

By AL HAHN and JIM POLK

The Organized Party salvaged a clean sweep of all major class offices in Thursday's election.

Chosen presidents of their classes were: Robin Pebworth, senior, Jay B. Hunt, junior; and John Raeburn, sophomore.

The Independence Party could not win a single electoral class office and will have only the two Independence directors automatically on each class council to represent them in class government next year.

Mr. Pebworth won 711-473 over Retha Biggs, Independence, junior, for president of next year's graduating class.

Mr. Hunt defeated Paul Pomeroy, sophomore, 828 - 510, and Mr. Raeburn, this year's freshman class vice-president, moved up a notch for next year by winning over Daye Sherwood, freshman, 1139-940.

The closest Independence candidate to any Organized class office victor was Dave Lawhead, freshman, who lost to the 1960-61 sophomore class vice-president, Rex Green, by 104 votes.

The distinct victories for all the Organized Party class candidates supported the analysis that the Independence student body victory was one of personal triumph for Tom Atkins, junior.

The Organized Party will again have their class presidencies. Current senior class head Bob Dabagia will serve until graduation. Joe Adams had briefly occupied the Freshman Class presidency as an Independence officer when Organized president Chuck Cain dropped from school this semester.

Independence candidates carried Smithwood—a seesaw district usually the deciding factor in class races —in each presidential contest, but a heavy party-line vote in the Organized districts carved wide wins for each Organized candidate.

The winning margin in each class presidential tussle was greater for the Organized than it was last year when the Organized lost one presidency and took narrow victories in the others despite a 562-vote endorsement for the Organized student body candidate, John Nash.

Referendum Count Delayed

Election officials delayed counting the two referendum issues on Thursday's ballot until today.

Jim Barrett, sophomore, chairman of the Student Elections Commission, said the referenda would be totaled this afternoon and forwarded to the proper authorities. Results will be listed in tomorrow's paper.

The calendar committee of the Faculty Council will meet Saturday to consider the results of the referendum on vacation and calendar preferences if the tabulations are ready, Charles E. Harrell, registrar, said Wednesday.

The committee, Mr. Harrell said, would discuss the student desires as to when to begin and end school and how long Christmas vacation should be. The decision of the committee will be referred to the Faculty Council for action sometime in May.

Students had protested a shortened vacation this Christmas. Unofficial estimates placed Thursday's referendum vote running heavily in favor of beginning school earlier in September to enable a longer Christmas holiday and ending college the last week of May.

The other referendum issue on Big Ten postseason athletic participation is expected to be sent the Faculty Council by Student Senate at a later date.

PROGRAM IN RECITAL HALL.

The North High School choir and brass and percussion from Evansville, Indiana will present a public program today at 11:30 a.m. in Recital Hall.

The group will present 17 numbers.

Independents Lose Ground In Senate

By JIM POLK

The Democratic Student Party, long regarded as a minor third party in campus politics, picked up four Student Senate seats in Thursday's elections to continue as the pivotal wheel in the campus' legislative body, as was predicted.

The new Student Senate lineup when the new Senators are sworn in April 21 will include 10 Organized Senators, seven Independence legislators, and five Democratic Students. One Senator is unattached while one seat is vacant.

The Organized Party regained the plurality in Student Senate when Democratic Students pulled surprise triumphs in two races with Independents. However, the plurality is two seats short of a majority and can wield no control without the cooperation of other Senators.

Close Victory in Tower I.

Mollie Brown, freshman, squeaked out a close victory in Tower I when the Independent vote was split between two candidates. Mohammed Hayat, grad., Democratic Student, won 114-40, over Krishna Bahadoorsingh, junior, Independence.

Judith Friedl, junior, Democratic Student, was unopposed in Town II and Nancy Dillingham, freshman, Democratic Student, was unopposed in Wells Quadrangle I.

All four Student Senate seats except the Town II had been held by Independence Senators. Town II had been occupied by Gayle Bishop, sophomore, Organized, who did not run for re-election.

Two other Democratic Student candidates made surprisingly good showings despite their defeats. Sonjia Camesasca, freshman, Democratic Student, bowed to Suzie Tripp, freshman, Independence, in Smithwood I, 206-163, and Suzette Conkle, junior, Democratic Student, lost to Steve Wheatley, sophomore, Organized, in Jordan II, 381-121.

Erb Wins Atkins' Seat.

Karl Erb, freshman, won over two other Independence candidates for the Trees Center seat held the last two years by President-elect of the Student Body Tom Atkins, junior.

Jim Grandorf, freshman, Independence, was unopposed in Wright II and Jim Russ and Sandra Platt, both Organized sophomores, were unopposed in Third Street I and Northwest II, respectively.

All three class presidency seats went to Organized nominees.

There are four Independence holdovers, four Organized, and one each Democratic Student and unattached.

Senate results:

Tower I	
Brown (Dem. Stdt.)	113
Hallert (Ind.)	107
Arney (Ind.)	66
Trees	
Erb (Ind.)	239
Mc Iwain (Ind.)	167
Pierce (Ind.)	91
Jordan II	
Wheatley (Org.)	381
Conkle (Ind.)	121
Foreign Student	
Hayat (Dem. Stdt.)	114
Bahadoorsingh (Ind.)	40
Smithwood I	
Tripp (Ind.)	206
Camesasca (Dem. Stdt.)	163

BRUSSELS TO MOSCOW.

MOSCOW (AP)— A Boeing 707 jet airliner arrived Thursday from Brussels to open Sabena Airlines nonstop service between Moscow and the Belgian capital.

PRESENTS FOR MR. K.

PARIS (AP)— A special jet plane took off for Moscow Thursday with two tons of gifts received by Soviet Premier Nikita Khrushchev during his visit to France.

Phi Kappa Psis To Open '500' Qualification Trials Saturday

Phi Kappa Psis Little 500 team will open the qualification trials Saturday at 10 a.m. at the University School track. The Phi Psis won the 1959 Little 500.

Last night the drawing for qualification times for the Little 500 teams was part of a briefing session for all riders, alternates, and team managers.

In case of rain Saturday morning, qualifications will be postponed to 1 p.m., running in the same order. If rain should continue, qualifications will be Sunday at 1 p.m. If weather prevents them then, they will be run Saturday, April 23, beginning at 10 a.m.

The 35 teams and their time of qualification are:

10:00—Phi Kappa Psi
:05—Stockwell-Unit 13
:10—Alpha Tau Omega
:15—Sigma Nu
:20—Phi Sigma Kappa
:25—Phi Delta Theta
:30—Pi Kappa Phi
:35—Elliott House
:40—Theta Chi
:45—Zeta Beta Tau
:50—Ferguson House
:55—Kappa Delta Rho
11:15—Ruter House
:20—Sigma Phi Epsilon
:25—Tower Center-A
:30—Harding House
:35—Dodds House
:40—Delta Chi
:45—Delta Tau Delta
:50—Beta Theta Pi
:55—Kappa Sigma
12:15—Lambda Chi Alpha
:20—Sigma Pi
:25—Delta Upsilon
:30—Lower Linden
:35—Sigma Alpha Mu
:40—Acacia
:45—Phi Gamma Delta
:50—Campbell-Unit 14
:55—Forest Hall
1:15—Sigma Alpha Epsilon
:20—Dunn House
:25—Sigma Chi
:30—Towers Center-B
:35—Chi Phi

P0078536, IU Archives.

October 22, 1960

HE SERVES BEST WHO SERVES THE TRUTH

THE INDIANA DAILY STUDENT

THE WEATHER
Partly cloudy, warmer Sat. Fair, mild, cloudy Sunday High 65; Low 35.

VOL. LI—NO. 30—Z 175. INDIANA UNIVERSITY SATURDAY, OCTOBER 22, 1960. BLOOMINGTON, INDIANA Established 1867

Willie Hunter, Tailback · Jeff Slabaugh, Center · Moses Gray, Right Tackle · Jack Holder, Fullback · Earl Faison, Right End · Capt. Richie Bradford, Wingback · Dave Martin, Left Guard · Jim Haas, Left Tackle · Wil Scott, Blocking Back · Tony Rocco, Left End · Larry Coleman, Right Guard

STADIUM DEDICATION AT 1:10 P.M.

Five Sophomores To Start Today

INDIANA		MICHIGAN STATE
Tony Rocco (198)	LE	Fred Arbanas (215)
Jim Haas (235)	LT	Tom Winiecki (215)
Dave Martin (210)	LG	George Azar (195)
Jeff Slabaugh (208)	C	Dave Manders (213)
Larry Coleman (205)	RG	Tony Kumiega (191)
Moses Gray (230)	RT	Mickey Walker (198)
Earl Faison (235)	RE	Art Brandstatter (212)
Wil Scott (200)	QB	Tom Wilson (178)
Willie Hunter (202)	LH	Herb Adderley (193)
Richie Bradford (168)	RH	Gary Ballman (191)
Jack Holder (185)	FB	Ron Hatcher (214)

Kickoff—1:30 p.m. (CST)
Broadcasts—WFIU (Indiana U. Sports Network), WILS, Lansing.
Expected Attendance—40,000

Five sophomores will be among the 11 Indiana University Fightin' Hoosiers taking the field at 1:30 this afternoon to do football battle with the Michigan State Spartans.

The combined dedication of the Hoosiers' new stadium at 1:10 and I.U.'s 48th Homecoming are expected to draw the biggest crowd ever to attend an I.U. football game in Bloomington.

The previous high was 33,663, for the 1948 I.U.-Notre Dame game, in old Memorial Stadium. Between 35,000 and 40,000 fans are expected today.

Want Spittoon Back.

Coach Phil Dickens' Hoosiers, seeking re-possession of the "Old Brass Spittoon," a symbol of I.U.-MSU football rivalry since 1950, expect a tough battle with the Spartans, who have lost only one game this season (to Iowa, ranked by the Associated Press as the nation's No. 1 team).

The spittoon has been on the I.U. campus only once in the last decade. The Hoosiers beat the Spartans in 1958, 6-0, when then-sophomore end Earl Faison ran 92 yards for a touchdown in the third quarter, after blocking an MSU field goal attempt. Faison also sparked the Hoosiers' losing effort at East Lansing last year, with four pass receptions good for 55 yards and the lone Hoosier touchdown.

Important to Daugherty.

The game will not count in the Big Ten standings for either team, Indiana being on probation, but it is important to MSU Coach Duffy Daugherty nevertheless. Mr. Daugherty calls I.U. "next to Michigan, our oldest regular foe among Big Ten teams."

"We want to win this game just as much as any other on our schedule and will play this week with that in mind," said Mr. Daugherty. "There will be no looking ahead." MSU plays host to once-beaten Ohio State next week.

Overpowered Notre Dame.

The Spartans are coming to Bloomington fresh from a 21-0 shellacking of Notre Dame last weekend. MSU fans are hoping for repeat performances today from two Spartans who played brilliantly against the Irish, end Fred Arbanas and halfback Herb Adderly.

(Continued on Page Two)

Card Section Meets at 1 P.M.

Card section members should enter the stadium at gates 28 and 29 before 1 p.m. today.

The members are to sit in their assigned rows although they may sit in any seats within the row.

50-YEAR PIN AWARDS.

Three Indiana University athletes of the 1910 era will return to the campus today to receive from the "I" Men's Club the coveted 50-year pin.

They are Col. Guy M. Kinman, Fayetteville, Ark., who won a letter in football in 1910; John C. Mellett, Indianapolis, also a football letter winner, and Morrell M. Shoemaker, Granville, Ohio, cross country.

Here's What's Doin' Today

1960 Homecoming Program

8 a.m.-12 N — Judging of Homecoming Decorations
9 a.m.-5 p.m. — Auditorium open to visitors featuring the Exhibit of the Arts of Thailand
10-10:30 a.m. — Concert, Michigan State University Band, Bloomington Public Square
10-12 N. — School of Music Alumni Reception, Music School
10 a.m.-12:30 p.m. — School of Law Alumni Open House and Luncheon, Law School
11 a.m.-1 p.m. — Public Luncheon, new Fieldhouse
1:30 a.m. — "I" Men's Luncheon, new Fieldhouse
12-12:45 p.m. — Exhibition Rehearsal, I.U. Marching Hundred, new Fieldhouse
1:10 p.m. — Dedication Ceremonies, Indiana University Stadium
1:30 p.m. — Football, Indiana vs. Michigan State
4-5:30 p.m. — School of Music Alumni Reception, Music School
4-6 p.m. — School of Law Open House, Law School
7:30 p.m. — Homecoming Variety Show, Auditorium
8 p.m. — School of Music Opera Theatre, "The Golden Cockerel", East Hall
9 p.m. — Play, "Charley's Aunt," University Theatre

Crash—and the Jordan Flows

When the Homecoming Queen dedicates the new stadium with a bottle of Jordan River water, it will be the second time in six months that the water has been used in dedications.

Last summer, in an impromptu dedication, I.U. dedicated its showboat, Majestic, with a bottle of water from the campus river—and the bottle refused to break. Officials finally had to use a hammer to get the water out. Hopes were expressed all over campus today that the jinx would not continue.

But, on the other hand, the showboat had a very successful season.

A Last Look at An Old Friend

By JON GAST

Indiana University will officially dedicate its new 4.5 million dollar football stadium at 1:10 p.m. today before the Hoosiers homecoming game with the Spartans of Michigan State.

Only one-half mile away, however, Memorial Stadium stands, now only an empty football battleground of the past.

It was only 35 years ago, November 21, 1925, that Indiana University President, William Lowe Bryan, and the Student Body dedicated Memorial Stadium to the war heroes of World War I.

On that Saturday afternoon, also the day of a homecoming game, the Hoosiers and Purdue Boilermakers battled to a 0-0 tie, before 14,000 fans, the largest crowd in I.U. athletic annals to that date.

Perhaps the most important game in the 35-year history of Memorial Stadium was the Hoosier-Purdue clash on November 24, 1945. The Indiana team was undefeated and needed only a victory over Purdue to clinch the Big Ten title.

Played before a record crowd of 27,000, the Fightin' Hoosiers, coached by Alvin "Bo" McMillin, annihilated the Boilermakers, winning 26-0, and captured the Western Conference championship.

Pihos Acclaimed.

Three days after the game, Coach McMillin told the Chicago Quarterback Club, "We won the first Hoosier title in our Big Ten History mainly because of the inspired play of Pete Pihos."

Pihos, an ex-paratrooper with five battle stars, was described by McMillin as "the greatest player in Big Ten history."

In the "big" game, the Boilermakers held I.U. scoreless for two quarters, but the Hoosier backfield finally started to move, behind one of the finest lines in the nation, and Pihos scored twice in the third quarter to clinch the game.

In the fourth quarter, I.U. quarterback, Ben Raimondi passed for two touchdowns and the Hoosiers ruled the Big Ten.

There were many other heroes for Indiana that day, including Taliaferio, Groomes, Armstrong, Ravensburg, Deal, Cannaday, Brown, Goldsberry, Kluszewski.

Another game at Memorial Stadium well remembered by I.U. football fans was the 1947 clash with Purdue. The Hoosiers, on the strength of Rex Grossman's fourth quarter field goal, edged the Boilermakers, 16-14.

A Good Season.

Coach McMillin, leading I.U. to five wins in eight games that autumn, felt the Hoosiers had a good season. "I believe we had a successful year, especially since we lost more men the 1946 campaign than any team in the conference," he said.

Mr. McMillin, commenting on the game, continued, "I felt that if we were going to whip Purdue in the next few years, it would have to be this season. The Boilermakers sure have got the horses. They'll be mighty hard to beat in the future," Mr. McMillin concluded.

The coach proved to be an excellent fortune teller, unfortunately for the Hoosiers. McMillin's prediction was made in 1947, and Indiana hasn't won from Purdue since.

Another classic Hoosier battle at Memorial Stadium was the 1950 game between I.U. and the Fighting Irish of Notre Dame.

Played before 34,000 fans, a record crowd, the Hoosiers, coached by Clyde Smith, crushed the Irish, 20-7.

The victory over Notre Dame was the first Hoosier conquest of the South Bend team in 44 years. Indiana has not beaten them since.

The Hoosiers gained 213 yards in rushing, compared with 93 yards picked up by Notre Dame. Bobby Robertson, I.U. halfback, practically wrecked the Irish by himself, gaining 185 yards in 18 tries, and scoring two touchdowns.

Greatest Effort Ever.

Robertson's offensive effort was the greatest individual performance in Indiana history. The eight-yard pass of I.U. quarterback Lou D'Achille to Don Luft, accounted for the the remaining Hoosier touchdown, and Indiana finished its rout of the Irish, 20-7.

Memorial Stadium once again was the scene of a fine football game involving Michigan State and the Hoosiers, on November 17, 1951.

The Spartans from East Lansing, Mich., rated as the top team in the nation that year, faced the Hoosiers, in State's last game of the season, before a Dad's Day crowd of 20,000.

Michigan State scored two quick touchdowns in the opening minutes to lead I.U., 14-0. But Hoosier fullback Pat Gedman scored on a one-yard plunge in the closing minutes of the first half, and it seemed the Spartans would carry a 14-7 lead with them to the dressing room.

Ashburner to Anderson.

However, I.U. mentor Clyde Smith, in his last season at the helm of the Hoosiers, rushed quarterback Dick Ashburner and end Cliff Anderson into the game for the last play of the first half.

Ashburner, with Spartan linemen swarming around him, faded back, and as the gun sounded, passed to Anderson for a 50-yard touchdown play. D'Achille kicked the extra point and it was I.U. 14, Michigan State 14, at half time.

The Spartans, rallying like true champions, quickly scored two touchdowns and added a field goal, apparently on the way to crushing

(Continued on Page Two)

Former Team Captains To Take Part in Program

By HUGH MOORE

Gov. Harold W. Handley and University alumni and officials will join today in dedicating Indiana University's new six-million-dollar stadium at 1:10 p.m. today.

Twenty members of the 1925 Memorial Stadium Dedication team and 53 former football team captains or their representatives have returned to take part in the ceremonies.

Remarks will be made by Gov. Harold W. Handley, President Herman B Wells, and Dr. Merrill Davis, who is captain of the 1910 team, a 50-year I-Man, and now a member of the Board of Trustees. The Reverend Elliston A. Cole, former pastor of the Trinity Episcopal Church, Bloomington, will give the dedicatory prayer.

The Homecoming and Dedication Queen will break a bottle of Jordan River water over the goalpost to dedicate the new stadium officially.

Bands to Play.

The Marching Hundred and the Michigan State marching band will play for the occasion.

Other dignitaries on the dedication platform will be Willis Hickam, president of the Board of Trustees, Prof. John F. Mee, chairman of the athletics committee, Frank Allen, director of athletics, and Everett Dean, president of the I-Men's Association.

Also, Paul Jasper, president of the Alumni Association; Tom Atkins, President of Student Government; Ted Young, of Eggers and Higgins architectural consulting firm, and Robert Hunt, of Hunt, Huber, and Nichols construction firm, Indianapolis.

Un-named.

A name has not yet been chosen for the stadium. Mr. Allen said recently that it may be a few years before the structure receives a definite name.

The first major athletic construction at I.U. since 1928, the stadium cost 6,072,860 dollars, to be paid in self-liquidating 30-year bonds. It seats 48,344 persons, all along the sidelines.

The stadium, designed by the architectural firm of Eggers and Higgins, New York, contains many new concepts in stadium design.

A Compact Stadium.

Despite its large seating capacity the stadium is compact — from the farthest corner of the stands diagonally to the farthest corner of the field is only 570 feet.

For spectator convenience, the stadium was constructed in a concave form, permitting all seats to be angled toward the center of the playing field. Also, ramps have replaced stairs to provide easy access. The architects estimate that the stadium can be completely vacated in 20 minutes.

The West stands at the highest point are 109 rows high, the East stands, 72 rows. The top of the West stands is 120 feet above the field, and the top of the press box elevator shaft, 180 feet.

The press box has space for 150 sports writers, 14 radio stations, and a large number of photographers.

35,000 More Seats Possible.

Mr. Allen said this week that seating could eventually be pro-

(Continued on Page Two)

Statistics! Stadium Has Many

Some statistics about the new stadium:
Capacity: 48,344.
Cost: $6,072,860.
Construction:
- 2,500 tons of structural steel.
- 26,000 cubic yards of concrete.
- 140,650 square yards of parking area.
- 22,070 square yards of roads.
- 47,620 square yards of walks.
- 18,313 of sodded grass.

Contractor: Huber, Hunt, and Nichols, Inc., Indianapolis.
Architect: Eggers and Higgins, New York.
Height: 180 feet (to top of elevator shaft on West stands.
West stands: 109 rows high.
East stands: 72 rows high.

P0078535, IU Archives.

THE INDIANA DAILY STUDENT EXTRA—10c

VOL. LXXXXI—NO. 150—Z 175. BLOOMINGTON, INDIANA SATURDAY, MAY 12, 1962. INDIANA UNIVERSITY Established 1867

PHI PSIS WIN!

—DAILY STUDENT PHOTO by BILL DELANEY

OFF THE SIDE EXCHANGE — Members of the Dodds House Little 500 team are shown using the off the side exchange early in the race this year. The rider on the pit side of the bike has just dismounted, and is about to be caught by a fellow team member partially obscured by the rider on the track side of the bike who is about to mount.

Record Crowd Swelters In Humid Heat at Track

The crowd came, and despite pessimistic warnings of rain, the sun still shone. A mass of hats, sun glasses, sundresses, and burmudas made its way to the bleachers and waited for the beginning of the race. Spectators sweltered in very humid 72-degree weather.

"It's a record-breaking crowd," said Bill Armstrong, executive director of the I.U. Foundation. "The attendance this year is 17,042 and last year it was 16,048.

In the heart of the stadium sat the pumping force of the Little 500. A man-made island set in a circular pool was the stage for Foundation members, who spent most of the afternoon chatting with Miss Lynda Lee Mead, Little 500 sweetheart and Miss America of 1960.

Mickey and Minnie Mouse and Pluto helped carry out the theme of the race by running around in the infield greeting people and talking to kiddies.

Colorful.

In a fashion much like that of a circus, colors played the important role of putting spectators in a happy mood.

Hanging from the goal posts were bright insignia of the Little 500 in red, white, and blue letters. Riders waited in their "shirts of many colors" with financial sponsor on the back and housing unit and coed sponsor on the front. Black and red helmets topped their outfits.

The sun reflected off the huge traveling trophy which was waiting for the winner of the race and 10 more trophies sat waiting for the 10 top teams.

National Anthem.

The excitement was high but all was still as Gerald Lang, senior, and Lorna Dallas, sophomore, sang the national anthem.

At the far west of the track a medical aid station with about four nurses stood ready for any injuries. A stand for bike repairs waited patiently.

In front of each pit was a new bike. If a rider wrecked his racer, he could immediately get a new one.

Tower.

Jerry Udall, senior, in charge of the Rules and Regulations Committee, stood in a tower in the infield to spot accidents. Multi-colored streamers decked the top of the tower.

Suffering officials had to wear warm suits.

James Pauloski, president of the Foundation in 1953, was announcer for the race. All eyes were turned his way when he said the words, "The race is on."

Celebrities Comment.

"I think the race is marvelous, just marvelous," said Juliet Prowse. Miss Prowse said she was very pleased to have been invited to appear at I.U. since she has never appeared on a college campus before.

Little 500 Sweetheart Lynda Lee Mead said, "Boy, this is some race." When asked what she thought about kissing the members of the winning team, Miss Mead said, "I'm reserving my comment until after the race is over."

Comedian Leo De Lyon, wearing a Little 500 hat and carrying a white cigarette holder, said he thought the race was very interesting but that it's hard to concentrate my interest because I'm not emotionally involved with any team."

Commenting on the Extravaganza, Mr. De Lyon said, "It was really swinging."

Although Mr. De Lyon did not attend college, he has appeared before several college audiences — "the best audiences in the world." I thought the students were getting younger and younger, but I guess I'm just getting older and older."

Mr. De Lyon will fly to his home in Los Angeles Sunday to spend seven hours with his wife and two children before leaving on a four week engagement in Australia.

Hoagy.

Watching his Kappa Sigma team and the two teams leading the race, Hoagy Carmichael said that it's the first Little 500 he's ever been to and that he's really fascinated.

Mr. Carmichael hasn't been on the I.U. campus since the Homecoming Variety Show three years ago. "All the new buildings have taken the place of my hunting grounds," he said.

Dressed in brown slacks and a brown and white checked shirt, Mr. Carmichael said that he is leaving for New York City Sunday. He lives in Beverly Hills, Calif., and his winter home is at the Thunderbird Club in Palm Springs, Fla.

Win One of Closest Little 500's in History

Phi Psis outdueled SAE today to win their fourth Little-500 race, in one of the closest finishes in the history of the race.

Led by Dave Blase, John Odusch, Frank Brunell, and Jim Berry, Phi Psi rode to the record finish before a record crowd of 17,042.

Phi Psis led at the end of 195 laps with SAE's running second by seven seconds and continued to hold the lead for the duration of the race. Official time of the Phi Psis was 2 hours, 17 minutes, 26 seconds with an average speed of 21.83 for a new race record. SAE's were nine seconds behind in crossing the finish line.

Coming in third was the Phi Gamma Delta team, followed by Chi Phi, fourth, and Acacia.

Coming in sixth, through 10th positions were Alpha Tau Omega, Beta Theta Pi, Phi Delta Theta, Edmondson II, and Sigma Nus.

The start of the race was marred by a mass pileup of riders and bicycles even before the first lap had been completed when an unidentified rider veered into the side of another.

The Theta Chi, Kappa Delta Rho, Sigma Pi, Laurel Hall I, Walnut Hall, Elliott House, and several other teams, unable to steer clear of the tangled mass, hit the cinders.

Theta Chi, by virtue of the pileup, lost four laps because of a broken chain.

Forty minutes later, the yellow caution flag went out again on the northwest turn when Lambda Chi Alpha slipped and fell, causing a collision with the Elliott House team. An unidentified cyclist, unable to avoid the crackup, sailed right over the fallen riders.

Vic Owen, captain of the Elliott House team, emerged with only minor bruises from the scuffle.

The third yellow flag went out at the end of the 95th lap as Edmondson II and Phi Kappa Theta collided on the northwest turn. Again, no serious injuries were reported. The green flag was out again a lap later.

Acacia, who had been running slightly behind the leaders, had a wreck on the main straightaway during the 112th lap and dropped back several positions. No other bikes were involved. The Acacias lost one bicylce. At the 120th lap the Acacias were running in the sixth position.

Same Time.

At the end of 105 laps, SAE and Phi Psi had the same time of 1:12:23, but the Phi Psis picked up two seconds in the next five laps to take the lead at the end of 110.

Phi Psis still led at the end of 115 laps, 120, and 125 laps with the SAE's in second place by a fraction of a second during this time. SAE took the lead by one second at the end of the 130th lap over the 1960 winners Phi Psi. Phi Gamma Delta was running third, more than a minute behind the leaders. Acacia remained in sixth.

Phi Psi's regained the lead by two seconds at the end of the 135th lap, but it was SAE again at 140 and 145 laps.

In about the 136th lap, while in third place, Allen Plumber, freshman, rider for Phi Gamma Delta, took a spill in the middle of the Northeast turn. He remounted his vehicle and rode to the pit for an exchange. Because 20 or 30 odd seconds were lost, the Phi Gams relinquished their place to the Chi Phis. In a short time, however, the Phi Gams regained the third position.

The race settled down to a three-way battle involving SAE, Acacia, and Phi Psi at the end of 30 laps. Laurel Hall and Delta Tau Delta had led in the early stages. Acacia and Phi Psi were 1-2 at the end of 35 but SAE and Phi Psi were tied at the end of 40 with Acacia third with one second.

Acacia then took over the SAE's place at the end of 45 and had the lead all to themselves at the end of 50 laps. SAE's trailed by 17 seconds, then the biggest margin of difference.

SAE still led at the end of 65, Acacia was second, and Phi Psi third. SAE still led at the end of 70 but the Phi Psis had moved up to second. It was tied at the end of 75 laps between the SAEs and the Phi Psis.

PLAYER TAKES LEAD.

FORT WORTH, Tex. (AP)—South African Gary Player, singing the praises of a red hot putter, seized the lead Friday in the $40,400 Colonial National Invitational Golf Tournament with a 36-hole total of 138.

Simic and Miss Grimsley New Foundation Leaders

Curt Simic and Karin Grimsley, juniors, will lead the I.U. Student Foundation Committee for the 1963 Little 500 Weekend.

Mr. Simic, president, and Miss Grimsley, vice-president, were appointed by William S. Armstrong, executive director of the I.U. Foundation.

Mr. Armstrong said that the two were selected because of their interest, work done on the committee this year, knowledge of the event, leadership ability, and their ability to get along with others. He expressed pleasure in looking toward the event in 1963, and confidence in Mr. Simic and Miss Grimsley to maintain the high standards set by past presidents and vice-presidents of the Student Foundation.

Mr. Simic has ridden for the Dodds House Little 500 team for the past two years. In addition to riding this year, he is a member of the Promotions Committee for the event.

Mr. Simic, who hails from Kouts, Ind., is majoring in physical education and minoring in English. He is interested in intramural athletics and was a member of the I. U. gymnastics team during his freshman and sophomore years.

Miss Grimsley is president of Pi Beta Phi, social sorority. An English major from Evanston, Ill., she has been active in YWCA and Union activities, and has served on the Freshman Camp staff. She was a member of Pleiades and Enomene, activities honoraries, and has served on the Foundation committee for the 1962 Little 500.

Here Are Previous Little 500 Winners

Little 500 winners and runners-up over the 11 year history of the race are as follows:

1951—South Hall Bucaneers
Sigma Alpha Epsilon
1952—North Hall Friars
Rogers East V
1953—North Hall Friars
Acacia
1954—Sigma Nu
Acacia
1955—South Cottage Grove
West Hall
1956—Phi Gamma Delta
Dodds House
1957—Sigma Nu
Dodds House
1958—Phi Kappa Psi
Sigma Nu
1959—Phi Kappa Psi
Sigma Alpha Epsilon
1960—Phi Kappa Psi
Sigma Alpha Epsilon
1961—Acacia
Phi Gamma Delta

—DAILY STUDENT PHOTO by JAN SANTILLI

NEXT YEAR'S BIG THREE — Bill Armstrong, center, director of the I.U. Foundation, congratulates Curt Simic, junior, and Karen Grimsley, junior, on their recent election as president and vice-president, respectively, of the I.U. Foundation for next year.

—DAILY STUDENT PHOTO by BILL DELANEY

PHOTOGRAPHERS' LAP — Most of the 33 teams entered in this year's Little 500 are shown as they round the corner at the southwest side of Memorial stadium. The teams were arranged in 11 rows of three teams each, with the fastest qualifying teams in the front rows.

How They Rode—The Top Teams at 25-Lap Intervals

At 25 Laps

1. Acacia 18:8
Phi Kappa Psi
Sigma Alpha Epsilon
Phi Delta Theta
5. Laurel Hall 1

At 50 Laps

1. Acacia 35:12
2. Sigma Alpha Epsilon
3. Phi Kappa Psi
4. Phi Gamma Delta
5. Chi Phi
6. Alpha Tau Omega
7. Laurel Hall 1
8. Walnut Hall
9. Beta Theta Pi
10. Phi Delta Theta

At 75 Laps

1. Sigma Alpha Epsilon 52:14
Phi Kappa Psi
3. Acacia
4. Phi Gamma Delta
5. Chi Phi

At 100 Laps

1. Sigma Alpha Epsilon 1:09:02
2. Phi Kappa Psi
3. Acacia
4. Phi Gamma Delta
5. Chi Phi
6. Alpha Tau Omega
7. Beta Theta Pi
8. Phi Delta Theta
9. Walnut Hall
10. Sigma Nu

At 125 Laps

1:26.10
1. Phi Kappa Psi
2. Sigma Alpha Epsilon
3. Phi Gamma Delta
4. Alpha Tau Omega
5. Chi Phi

At 150 Laps

1. Phi Psi 1:43:13
2. SAE
3. Chi Phi
4. Phi Gamma Delta
5. Alpha Tau Omega
6. Acacia
7. Phi Delta Theta
8. Beta Theta Pi
9. Walnut Hall
10. Sigma Nu

At 175 Laps

1. Phi Psis 2:0:16
2. SAE
3. Phi Gamma Delta
4. Alpha Tau Omega
5. Acacia
6. Chi Phi
7. Beta Theta Pi
8. Phi Delta Theta
9. Sigma Nu
10. Edmondson, Floor 2.

At the Finish

1. Phi Kappa Psi
2. Sigma Alpha Epsilon
3. Phi Gamma Delta
4. Chi Phi
5. Acacia
6. Alpha Tau Omega
7. Beta Theta Pi
8. Phi Delta Theta
9. Edmondson II
10. Sigma Nu

P0078534, IU Archives.

Racing Deadline

Little 500, today and for many decades, asserted itself throughout campus including the newsroom. In the early 1960s, we prided ourselves on producing a newspaper, getting it printed and to the track as fans were exiting. In those days, we printed in letterpress and in house.

The newsroom was on the second floor of Ernie Pyle Hall, all furniture including Ernie Pyle's rolltop desk painted in a uniform cream. The pressroom, domain of a single hired professional printer, was on the first floor.

Between my assignments as student government reporter and editor in chief, another favorite position was night editor. Five of us each took one day's paper a week, sat in the slot of the newsroom rim, assigned headlines, checked edited stories, decided story placement and laid out the pages. It was my good fortune, I thought, to draw the special edition for the Little 500—good training for all the deadline newspaper stories in my future.

Well ahead of the big day, I conjured in my head a page one layout with photos forming a giant "I" and stories filling in the spaces on either side of the letter's vertical bar. Contrived, yes, but I thought memorable.

The day arrived. The bicycles rolled. The pictures fell into place. The stories were as appropriate as I decided to think they were. Nervously watching the clock, I followed the page downstairs, saw it made up by our professional one-man printing operation.

Like clockwork? That clock ticked way too slowly in my frenzied mind. But eventually it all went to the old ink-blacked press. I watched heart in mouth as the first copy came off the press. Almost. It stuck. The mechanism stuttered and the web broke! Paper does tear, including the giant rolls of newsprint that thread through a printer.

I gasped. The grizzled old professional cursed (shades of things I would hear in many pressrooms) and calmly went to work while I stood by fretting. It took him awhile to rethread the webbing. But he did get the process going again.

Needless to say, the IDS got printed, and it got delivered to the track before too many fans had slipped away. I heaved a sigh of relief and thanked any staffers still around.

Came the Monday morning critique and comments meeting in Don Mellett Auditorium. Little was said about my special page one, but I allowed myself to bask in the common knowledge and seeming admiration of my colleagues for a job well done under an extreme deadline.

But pride does go before a fall, and even the little mistakes in journalism will haunt you.

As the meeting broke up, much-loved professor Chris Savage lumbered to the door, tossing back over his shoulder: "That was a great page one Holly Gooding produced Saturday."

I had forgotten to change the one line of type that identified which night editor was in charge of that issue.

—Myrna Oliver, BA 1964

IDS Editor-in-Chief Myrna Oliver celebrates the 96th birthday of the IDS. Photo by Doug Roberts. *P0077839, IU Archives.*

"But pride does go before a fall, and even the little mistakes in journalism will haunt you."

BEHIND THE STORY

The Breaking News That Shaped a Generation

Friday, Nov. 22, 1963, was pretty much a standard late November day in Bloomington. The temperature at 1:30 p.m. was comfortably cool, about 63 degrees. The sky was overcast, but dry.

I was interviewing Dean of Students Robert H. Shaffer in his Maxwell Hall office. At about 1:50 p.m., his secretary stuck her head in the office.

"Excuse me, Dr. Shaffer," she said with a voice of both alarm and disbelief. "The radio says President Kennedy's been shot, and perhaps killed."

Shaffer looked stunned. I looked up from my note pad.

"I've got to go," I said.

"Kennedy's assassination was the first in a series of events that would rock the nation."

The walk from Maxwell Hall through the Indiana Memorial Union to the IDS office in Ernie Pyle Hall took about 10 minutes. But I took a circuitous route, through the Chemistry Building and Ballantine Hall, recording the reaction of students and faculty before passing by Beck Chapel and the cemetery before entering Pyle Hall.

In the newsroom, there was little activity. Students were gathered in stunned silence around the Indiana Associated Press teletype machine as the wire service began filling in details. I sat down at a typewriter and wrote the story which appeared on the front page the next day. It was the only bylined story on the front page that day.

Kennedy's murder was one of two presidential assassinations in the 20th century. The other occurred 62 years earlier, when William McKinley was shot twice in the abdomen by Leon Czolgosz, an anarchist.

Kennedy's assassination was the first in a series of events that would rock the nation. Students in Bloomington that day would go on to fight in Vietnam. Martin Luther King Jr., the civil rights leader, was assassinated in Memphis in 1968. Kennedy's brother, Robert F. Kennedy, was himself assassinated in 1968 while campaigning for president in Los Angeles. The Ohio National Guard shot unarmed students protesting at Kent State University in Ohio.

Eight years after President Kennedy's murder, The New York Times published extensive excerpts from the Pentagon Papers, a classified Defense Department report showing the U.S. government had systematically lied not only to the American people but also to Congress about the war. By the time President Nixon was driven from office in 1974 as a result of the Watergate scandal, the unquestioning confidence that Americans had in government in 1963 had been shattered.

Arguably, the events that began with President Kennedy's assassination continue to reverberate in American politics today.

—Joel Whitaker, BS 1964, MA 1971

THE INDIANA DAILY STUDENT

THE WEATHER Rain ending this morning, becoming partly cloudy with steady or slowly falling temperatures. High in mid-30's, much colder tonight with low in 20's. Friday's high 58, low 55. Sunday outlook, partly cloudy and cold with high of 35 to 45.

VOL. LXXXXIII—NO. 55—Z 175. INDIANA UNIVERSITY SATURDAY, NOVEMBER 23, 1963. BLOOMINGTON, INDIANA 7¢ Established 1867

KENNEDY FUNERAL MONDAY NOON

Armstrong, Theatre 300, 'Lucia' still on

Bucket open house, Y lunch cancelled; Simon recital on.

Most campus events will go on this weekend despite the assassination of President Kennedy. However, some activities in addition to the Purdue game have been postponed or cancelled.

The "Louis Armstrong and His All-Stars" Pop Concert is still definitely on, Lawrence L. Davis, manager of the I.U. Auditorium said. In addition the color film, "Der Rosenkavalier," will be presented as scheduled tomorrow afternoon at 3 p.m. in the auditorium, as will be the piano recital by Abby Simon Monday at 8 p.m., Mr. Davis said.

Dean Wilfred Bain of the School of Music could not be reached last night for official confirmation on whether or not the opera, "Lucia di Lammermoor" scheduled for 8 p.m. in East Hall or the University Singers program at 8:30 p.m. tomorrow will be presented. However, Prof. Ross Allen, music, said that as far as he knows both programs will be presented.

Also definitely on is the performance in Theatre 300 of "Suddenly Last Summer" and "Ile" tonight at 8 p.m. Last night's performance was cancelled, and Friday tickets will be accepted tonight.

Steve Smith calls assassination barbaric

Steve Smith, President of the Student Body, when asked about his reaction to the assassination of President Kennedy, expressed extreme shock.

"This is a tremendous shock to me as it is to all Americans. I didn't believe such a barbaric act could occur in America today. Who would do such a thing?"

Mr. Smith expressed faith that Lyndon Johnson would rise to the occasion and carry on in President Kennedy's place.

'Bucket' clash postponed

Indiana University President Elvis J. Stahr jr. and Purdue President Fredrick Hovde announced Friday in a joint statement that the Oaken Bucket game has been cancelled until further notice.

The statement read as follows:

Indiana University and Purdue University are in agreement that their football game scheduled for Nov. 23 should be postponed because of the sudden tragedy which has struck our country. The game will be rescheduled and specific announcement of the date will be made as soon as more definite plans for national mourning become known to us.

Regular classes and related functions will be held Saturday and on other scheduled days until further notice.

Mrs. Kathryn Fagan, community leader, dies

Mrs. Kathryn Fagan, 63 years old, 1002 East First street, organizer and leader of many civic organizations, died at 6:15 p.m. yesterday at Bloomington Hospital. She had been stricken in a beauty parlor just four hours earlier by a cerebrel hemorrhage.

The widow of Sam G. Fagan, owner of Fagan Stone Mills, Mrs. Fagan was a member of St. Charles Catholic Church.

A native of Rochester, N.Y., Mrs. Fagan had been a Bloomington resident for 22 years. She was the first head of the Bloomington Community Chest, which is now the United Fund.

She organized the Monroe County Civil Defense, and served as its first director for many years. During World War II she was the director of the Bloomington USO, receiving honorary honorable discharges from both the U.S. Navy and the Marine Corps.

While Mrs. Fagan was Monroe County Chief Probation Officer, the local probation department was cited as the outstanding probation department in the state.

Active in Republican Party affairs, she had served as precinct committeewoman in Perry 13, and was a supporter of Sarkes Tarzian's renewal of the Monroe County Republican Party.

At the time of her death, she was planning some new activities for young people.

Mrs. Fagan had several letters in her files from the late William Lowe Bryan, a former president of Indiana University, praising her ability to adopt a cause and get it underway.

She had just returned on Tuesday from the funeral of her brother, Thomas Lanni, in Alexandria, Va.

Funeral services will be at 11 a.m. Monday in St. Charles Catholic Church with burial in Valhalla Memory Gardens. Friends may call at the Day Funeral Home after 12 M. Sunday.

Surviving is a brother, John Lanni, of Sun City, Ariz., and a sister, Mrs. Teresa Jordan of California.

Mexico seals borders after assassination

LAREDO, Tex. (UPI)— The Mexican government announced through its Laredo offices Friday it has sealed the Texas-Mexican border for 72 hours.

Mexican government officials in Laredo said the government closed the border because of the assassination of President Kennedy.

The spokesmen said they hoped to seal off the border to prevent any attempted getaway by the presidential assassin and persons connected with him.

TRADE PROSPECTS.

CANBERRA (AP)— Trade Minister John McEwen said prospects are bright for increased trade between Australia and Israel following the visit of an Israeli trade mission.

JOHN FITZGERALD KENNEDY

Assassin's bullets fatal to President

BULLETIN!

DALLAS (AP)—Lee Harvey Oswald, a 24-year-old dishonorably discharged Marine, was charged with the murder of President Kennedy shortly before midnight, some 10 hours after he had been arrested on another charge-of slaying a policeman.

By The Associated Press

President Kennedy's funeral will be Monday at St. Matthew's Roman Catholic Cathedral, the White House announced Friday night.

The body of the President, slain by an assassin in Dallas, Texas, yesterday noon will lie in repose at the White House today and will lie in state in the rotunda of the Capitol on Sunday and Monday.

The President's body will be taken a couple of miles to the cathedral at 11 a.m. Monday. There, Richard Cardinal Cushing, archbishop of Boston and close friend of the Kennedy family, will celebrate a Pontifical Requiem Mass at noon.

Burial site unknown.

Acting-White House press secretary Andrew T. Hatcher said he did not know where Kennedy will be buried.

—A hidden gunman assassinated President Kennedy with a high-powered rifle Friday.

Three shots reverberated. Blood sprang from the President's face. He fell face downward in the back seat of his car. His wife clutched his head and tried to lift it, crying, "Oh, No!"

Half an hour later at 1 p.m., John F. Kennedy was dead and the United States had a new president, Lyndon B. Johnson.

Suspect arrested.

Within the hour, police had arrested a 24-year-old man following the killing of a Dallas policeman. Homicide Capt. Will Fritz said Friday night witnesses had identified the man as the slayer of the policeman.

Fritz said it had not been established that the man killed the President — but it had been established that he was in the building from which the shots were fired at the time of the assassination.

Russian citizenship.

He is Harvey Lee Oswald of Fort Worth, who four years ago said he was applying for Russian citizenship. He has a Russian wife.

Capt. Fritz said Oswald was a member of an organization known as "Fair Play for Cuba."

Oswald denied that he had shot anybody.

The assassination occurred just as the President's motorcade was leaving downtown Dallas at the end of a triumphal tour through the city's streets.

Shot near underpass.

His special car—with the protective bubble down—was moving down an incline into an underpass that leads to a freeway route to the Dallas Trade Mart, where he was to speak.

Witnesses heard three shots. Doctors were not certain whether the President was struck by one or two bullets. He had wounds in the neck and head which could have been caused by one bullet.

The third shot wounded Gov. John B. Connally of Texas in the side but his condition was reported not critical.

As the gunfire rang in the street, a reporter in the caravan screamed, "My God, they're shooting at the President."

Rifle barrel spotted.

Bob Jackson, a Dallas Times Herald photographer, said he looked around as he heard the

(Continued on Page Four)

Dismal day as students hear of death

By JOEL WHITAKER

The word spread quickly around the campus.

A boy dashed into the Junior Division office at 1:30 p.m. Friday.

"The President's dead! He's been shot! I just heard it on my car radio," he said.

On the eighth floor of Ballantine Hall, an economics professor talked to one of his students.

"You can miss class if you wish. I just can't lecture today," he said.

He gave the student his exam paper from the last hourly. His hands shook.

A group of students walked out of a classroom where they'd been taking an hourly.

"The President's been shot!" was the first word that greeted them.

A girl cried.

In the Chemistry Building students walked out of classes with white faces, drawn tight. Many were trembling.

Hundreds of students crowded into The Daily Student office and other public points around the campus to hear the latest bulletins on the radio.

Everywhere you walked on campus yesterday, you heard radios blaring.

Many classes were called off.

As word the President was dead was broadcast on the radios at 2:38 p.m. Friday, tears welled up in the eyes of many girls.

The chairman of one department looked at his secretary and just nodded his head.

She buried her head in a cleansing tissue and wept.

Stahr postpones University address

President Elvis J. Stahr jr's State of the University address, scheduled for Monday at 4:30 p.m. in Whittenberger Auditorium, has been postponed, it was announced Friday night.

The postponement is a result of mourning the assassination of President John F. Kennedy.

Announcement will be made of the rescheduling of the address.

STAR GIVES PICTURES.

The Associated Press Wirephotos appearing in The Indiana Daily Student today are through the courtesy of The Indianapolis Star.

Kennedy, often mistaken as pageboy in Congress, exuded youthful vigor

It was on a freezing Jan. 20, 1961 that John F. Kennedy was sworn in as President in a ceremony of moving dignity, rooted in rich tradition as old as the country itself. He took the oath of office with his hand on a Bible that had been in his mother's family for generations.

His inaugural speech was devoted almost entirely to foreign affairs.

He set himself two goals — survival of liberty at home and peace in a world shivering in an "uncertain balance of terror."

He invited the Communist world to join in a new beginning of the "quest for peace" before "the dark powers of destruction unleashed by science engulf all humanity in planned or accidental self-destruction."

"Let us never negotiate out of fear, but let us never fear to negotiate," he said.

Inaugurated with President Kennedy was Vice President Lyndon B. Johnson of Texas. They had served together in the Senate, where President Kennedy spent eight years. Previously he had served six years in the House.

Youngest President.

John F. Kennedy at 43 years old was the youngest man ever elected President. He succeeded the oldest man ever to hold that office, Dwight D. Eisenhower, who was past 70 years old when his term expired.

(While Theodore Roosevelt was about nine months younger than President Kennedy upon becoming Chief Executive, he reached that office from the Vice Presidency as the result of William McKinley's assassination.)

President Lyndon B. Johnson, who took the oath of office Friday afternoon at the Dallas airport, is 55 years old.

Called youth advantage.

The millions of television viewers saw the image of a young, vigorous candidate, poised, cool, highly-informed, quick on his feet and, above all, possessed of a reassuring self-confidence.

When critics made an issue of his youth, President Kennedy retorted that the new problems of a new age required youth and vigor to deal with them.

President Kennedy was so young when he first went to Congress that he frequently was mistaken for a pageboy. Even as a freshman Senator he once had a similar experience. As he started to board the miniature subway car which runs between the Senate Office Building and the Capitol, a guard bawled at him:

"Stand back! Wait till the Senators are seated, PLEASE!"

John Kennedy waited.

Many political assets.

President Kennedy was boyishly handsome, carrying a slim 175 pounds on his 6-foot frame, topped by a shock of unruly chestnut hair, that was almost a trademark. He had a blue-eyed, open-faced look, a friendly smile and a studied carelessness in dress and demeanor. He talked

(Continued on Page Eight)

Johnson sworn in at Dallas airport

JOHNSON TAKES OATH — Lyndon B. Johnson is sworn in as the 36th President of the United States in the cabin of the presidential plane. Mrs. Jacqueline Kennedy stands at his side as Judge Sarah T. Huges, left, administers the oath of office. President Johnson then returned to Washington in the plane along with the body of former President John F. Kennedy.

WASHINGTON (AP) — Lyndon B. Johnson became 36th President of the United States Friday afternoon about 2:39 p.m. (EST).

The former Senate majority leader, and Vice-President under President Kennedy was sworn in aboard the Presidential jet transport at Dallas' Love Field. He then was flown to Washington.

President Johnson walked, haggard and alone, Friday night into the presidential office that now is his.

Sad journey ends.

Mr. Johnson's sad journey from Dallas, where President Kennedy was slain by a sniper, ended at 6:23 p.m. when his helicopter landed on the White House lawn. It had brought him from Andrews Air Force Base, Md.

The new President held his wife's arm as they walked down the ramp to the lawn.

He spoke with Secretary of Defense Robert S. McNamara, and McGeorge Bundy, special assistant to the President for national security affairs, who flew in with him.

Then the party walked through the rose garden to the executive offices.

Walks alone.

While others in the party stood beneath the portico outside, Johnson walked alone through the French doors and into the White House.

The 55-year-old Texas coming into the presidency after the assassination death of the President had Mr. Kennedy's high esteem and confidence.

From old political foes-within the Democratic party-they became a close working team.

President Johnson tried in 1960 for the presidential nomination. When Mr. Kennedy won, Mr.

(Continued on Page Four)

City Hall closes door; flag flown at half-staff

Bloomington City Hall was closed Friday following the announcement of President Kennedy's death. Mayor Mary Alice Dunlap said it would open Monday at the accustomed time.

"It is a sad day for the United States and the world," Mayor Dunlap said. "All of our hearts are grieved. We are all saddened by the tragedy."

Mayor Dunlap said the flag on City Hall would be flown at half-staff from today until the funeral of the late President Kennedy.

Personal tragedy stalks close-knit Kennedy clan

BOSTON (UPI)— The assassination of President Kennedy Friday was the latest in a series of personal tragedies that has stalked the close-knit Kennedy clan.

Of the nine children born to former Ambassador and Mrs. Joseph P. Kennedy, three are now dead.

Lost third child.

Little more than three months ago — last Aug. 9 — the dead President's third child, Patrick Bouvier, died 39 hours after he was born.

The president's father suffered a stroke two years ago that left him partially disabled.

The President himself narrowly escaped death during World War II when his torpedo boat was sunk in the South Pacific. He twice was hospitalized for long periods.

Strong family ties.

This recurrance of tragedy struck deeply at the Kennedys. Yet in many ways it strengthened already strong family ties.

Nowhere was the unity so evident as at the Kennedy Compound, a cluster of summer homes at the Cape Cod resort community of Hyannis Port.

There the Kennedys gathered with their wives and husbands and children during the summer and on traditional holidays.

The President had planned to come "home" to Hyannis next week to observe Thanksgiving with his parents and brothers and sisters.

JOHN B. CONNALLY

Facing, P0024027, IU Archives.

THE INDIANA DAILY STUDENT

THE WEATHER Rain or snow late today or tonight, probably continuing until tomorrow. Expected high around 40. The high yesterday was 42; low 39.

VOL. XCV—NO. 65 | INDIANA UNIVERSITY | THURSDAY, DECEMBER 16, 1965. | BLOOMINGTON, INDIANA | 2 Sections—14 Pages | 7¢ | Established 1867

Santa Wells visits on Christmas Eve

President Stahr crowns 1966 Arbutus Queen, Lana Messick, senior.

Chancellor Herman B Wells plays traditional role.

PHOTOGRAPHS BY BUD HERRON

Santa's elves help distribute candy canes.

Carolers present Christmas wreath to President and Mrs. Stahr.

Gemini nose to nose in historic rendezvous

MANNED SPACE CENTER, Houston, Tex. (AP) — Four excited U.S. astronauts culminated a tense space hunt in the lonely world of space Wednesday nudging their two spaceships into a historic rendezvous 185 miles above earth.

Gemini 6 pilots Walter M. Schirra Jr. and Thomas P. Stafford masterfully flew up for a visit with the tired, bearded crew of Gemini 7, Frank Borman and James A. Lovell Jr., then together set out on a six-hour formation flight.

The tiny spacecraft continued their twin voyages nose to nose only six to 10 feet apart.

Word from Stafford.

First word the maneuver was successful came from Stafford. He calmly reported to anxious ground controllers over a noisy communications channel shortly after 2:30 p.m. EST: "We're about 120 feet apart and sitting."

The meeting occurred high over the Pacific Ocean during Gemini 6's fourth orbit of the earth and Gemini 7's 165th.

A busy worldwide tracking network, for the first time in history keeping tabs on two spacecraft at once, came to a virtual standstill during the final breathtaking minutes of the momentous and dramatic meeting in space.

"This is the waiting time," Mission Control said as the final, tricky maneuvers to bring them only feet apart started. "It's all up to them."

Maneuvered cautiously.

Even though they were travelling 17,500 miles an hour over a 103,000-mile chase course, Schirra cautiously maneuvered the spacecraft at a relative speed of only a few feet a second nose-to-nose with Gemini 7 — not risking a collision.

"We did it," someone said over the command channels.

Thus the United States claimed title to man's greatest space adventure, one that represents another giant step in its race to put men on the moon by 1970.

If American spacemen are to return to earth once they land on the lunar surface, they must launch themselves from the moon in their excursion vehicle and rendezvous with an orbiting mothership.

Twice stalled in an attempt to become the nation's first hunter spacecraft, Gemini 6 roared off its Cape Kennedy, Fla., launch pad right on schedule at 8:37 a.m. EST.

The new kings of space travel, Borman and Lovell, took a back seat to the razor-sharp Gemini 6 crew. The Gemini 7 pilots appeared cheerful and chipper while circling the earth waiting for the big moment of meeting.

With Schirra, a cool, veteran of space travel, at the ship's controls, and Stafford, making his first rocket ride, running the onboard computers, Gemini 6's six-hour stalk of the sky appeared destined for success from the start.

Chase begins.

At the moment of blastoff, these elated words were heard from Gemini 6: "I should say. This is a real one."

The chase was on.

Nose skyward, the mighty 90-foot Titan 2 rocket roared steadily from the pad in a cloud of pink-tinted smoke. Minutes later, Schirra and Stafford got the go-ahead for rendezvous on the fourth orbit — just as planned.

RENDEZVOUS WITH HISTORY—Four, three, two, one, lift off! And Gemini 6'ers Walter Schirra and Thomas Stafford streaked off into space on a journey that would take them to within a few feet of their Gemini 7 predecessors, Frank Borman and James Lovell.

U.S. warns allies, 'beware Peking'

PARIS (UPI) —Defense Secretary Robert S. McNamara warned America's NATO allies Wednesday that Communist China will be able to hurl long-range nuclear missiles at the United States or Europe within 10 years.

Within two years Red China will be capable of striking shorter distances with medium-range rockets, he said.

McNamara described growing Communist Chinese nuclear might in an 18-minute speech to a closed session of the NATO—North Atlantic Treaty Organization—Council of Ministers. U.S. officials outlined the secretary's remarks to newsmen afterward.

British delegation sources quoted McNamara as having said that intelligence reports reaching the U.S. indicate Red China also may possess a rocket submarine capable of launching nuclear missiles. The U.S. delegation said it could neither confirm nor deny the British report.

McNamara's blunt speech came a day after Secretary of State Dean Rusk told the council the U.S. is fighting Europe's war as much as its own on the battlefields of Viet Nam.

McNamara pressed the same point home again Wednesday. But he said the U.S. has no intention of slashing its 250,000-man Army in Europe by transferring major combat units from positions there to Southeast Asia.

McNamara said he came to the council meeting with no ready-made answers to the problem of Chinese expansionism backed by nuclear weapons.

Today—

——on the campus——

PERCUSSION ENSEMBLE — George Gaber, director, 8:30 p.m., Recital Hall.

TELEVISED SEMINAR—"Basic Tools of Reliability," Obert B. Moan, 3:30 p.m., Radio-TV Studio 07.

DUTCH COFFEE HOUR — 4:30 p.m., Ballantine 004.

GRADUATE HISTORY CLUB CHRISTMAS PARTY — 6:30 p.m., Parker House.

PHI SIGMA IOTA — "Christmas Folklore," 7:30 p.m., International Center.

LINGUISTICS CLUB—"The Understanding of Language by Men and Machines," Dr. Michael Scrivin, 8 p.m., Ballantine 005.

SAILING CLUB—7 p.m., Ballantine 310.

DUPLICATE BRIDGE— 7 p.m., Kiva, Union.

I.U. economists see varied rises

The nation will continue to flex its economic muscles in 1966, but a growth rate in some sectors slightly under that of the past year is predicted by a team of I.U. business analysts.

Writing for the "outlook" edition of the monthly Indiana Business Review, the analysts see a gross national product (total goods and services) of $702.6 billion, an increase in 1965 dollars of about 4.77 per cent over the current calendar year.

However, if price increases run about 1.5 per cent, then the "real" growth in GNP will be only a little over 3 per cent, they explained.

Rise in GNP.

This rise in GNP is unfavorable when compared with the 4.5 per cent to 5 per cent boosts of the last two years, but "we have had almost five years of uninterrupted expansion and our unemployed resources are tending to become marginal; therefore, the increase we forsee can be considered a good accomplishment.'"

Elsewhere, the I.U. business analysts note:

Government purchases of goods and services will show significant increases in 1966 at all levels of the economy. Federal spending will be boosted by the Vietnamese situation and by expanded domestic programs. The combination of pressing needs and improved revenues will produce similar hikes in spending by state and local governments.

Business fixed investment, a major factor in the economy's expansion in the past several years, will continue to show healthy increases over 1965 rates. The annual growth in this sector is expected to approach 10 per cent.

Residential construction will show modest improvement through 1966. Though the number of new homes constructed will not increase appreciably, higher average outlays per unit will provide an annual rise in this sector of 4.3 per cent.

Inventory work-down.

Inventory accumulation, though positive throughout the coming year, will not approach the level of the immediate past. Business will continue into the second quarter of 1966 to "work-down" excessive inventories purchased as a steel strike hedge.

Consumer durables will show the smallest rate of growth among all the major demand sectors. Color television will continue to lead this area, but the growth in auto sales will lag. Total prchases of consumer durables will decline in the first quarter of 1966, resuming a modest growth pattern thereafter. Consumer nondurables and services will not show any marked deviation from the preceding pattern, largely because of the consistent relationship of this sector to current disposable personal income. Consumer expenditures as a share of GNP will be influenced by medicare and excise tax cuts.

I.U. study aids Indiana legislators in their proposed salary increase

INDIANAPOLIS (AP) — Pay of Indiana state legislators would be increased from the present $1,800 a year to as high as $7,500 a year under suggestions made by legislative leaders Wednesday.

(A Senate salary study subcommittee requested a report from the I.U. Institute of Public Administration. The report said the cost of serving in the legislature will continue to rise.

(The two most important points of the survey, according to John S. Waggaman, research associate, were 1) a recommendation that a Congressional ratio system be set up to establish a pay basis, and 2) that the overall salary of the legislators should be jumped to $7,800 per two years without the per diem salary instead of the present $4,820, which includes the $20 per diem salary.

(On the basis of a formula which involved 17 variables affecting legislative pay compensation, the I.U. report showed the legislators should actually get $8,478 per two years.

Commends study.

(The report commended further study of actual costs, a study of staff needs, and a $5 a day increase in the present $20 per diem expense payment.

(It said the cost of campaigning for the legislature might range from $300 to $700 in a rural district considered safe for one party to as much as $1,500 to $2,000 in a competitive urban district.)

Sen. Jack H. Mankin (D-Terre Haute), Senate president pro tem, told a salary study subcommittee he felt a $7,500 annual salary would be realistic along with per diem expense money during legislative sessions.

He said he felt the per diem payment now $20, should be eliminated for between-sessions meeting of study committees if the salary was raised to that level.

Mankin also said he will not be a candidate for any leadership position in the 1967 session, in which he will serve as holdover senator, because of the extra time and expense involved.

$8,000 luxury.

"For me this year the legislature has been an $8,000 luxury," Mankin said. He explained he felt he had lost that much in attorney fees because of the time consumed by his legislative duties.

House Speaker Richard C. Bodine, (D-Mishawaka), said he would go along generally with Mankin's salary suggestion and recommend putting the figure in the $6,000 to $7,500 range.

The two leaders disagreed on whether the 61-day biennial sessions should be lengthened, Mankin saying he opposed longer sessions and Bodine taking the view that 61 days was too short.

Mankin qualified his statement by saying special sessions on limited subject matter, such as the two held this year, might be called more frequently.

Others comment.

Bodine said he had seen too much bad legislation slip through in the crush of business which develops near the end of regular sessions.

Rep. John F. Coppes, (R-Nappanee), suggested the 61-day limitation might be interpreted to refer to 61 legislative working days instead of 61 calendar days as at present.

Rep. Otis R. Bowen, (R-Bremen), House minority leader, proposed a salary of from $4,000 to $8,000 a year and Sen. Allan E. Bloom, (R-Fort Wayne), Senate minority leader, suggested a figure around $6,000.

U.S. premiere radiates 'joy and triumph'

By JERRY HARRIS

The American premiere of the Christmas fantasy "Joyful and Triumphant" last night at the Christmas Eve on Campus program in the Auditorium was a joy for the audience and a triumph for the composer, NBC's director of music Don Gillis.

The grandiloquent medley succeeded in achieving "the big sound of Christmas," as well as some fresh approaches to the familiar carols.

The composition suffered slightly, however, in its first live American premiere, in comparison with the original recorded version.

It succeeded, however, as a completely untypical, welcome treatment of the usual hackneyed medley of Christmas carols.

Credit for this goes to the inimitable masters of the art of crowd-pleasing, the Singing Hoosiers, directed by Robert E. Stoll, instructor in the School of Music. From the rollicking "Twelve Days of Christmas" to the sacred "Silent Night," the group was always articulate and well-blended.

The percussion section of the Symphonic Wind Ensemble, directed by Dr. Ronald Gregory, director of bands, succeeded where the brasses failed. Eleven percussionists juggled 28 different instruments to achieve many of the spectacular effects of the piece while the brass had trouble with one attack after another.

BULLETIN

NICE, France (UPI)—Author W. Somerset Maugham, 91, died in a hospital here early Thursday.

Lana Messick 1966 Arbutus Queen

By DAVE McALLISTER and KAREN WEISKOPF

Lana Messick, senior, was crowned 1966 Arbutus Queen last night by President Elvis J. Stahr at the Christmas Eve on Campus dance in Alumni Hall.

Miss Messick, one of six finalists for the title, was voted the winner by an all-campus election held yesterday. Runners-up included Janelle James, Susan Sheehan, Paula Branstette, and Gina Macdonald, freshman, and Deryle Durand, junior.

Santa appears.

Prior to the crowning, Chancellor Herman B Wells made his annual appearance as Santa Claus. Aided by six "elves," he passed out candy canes to all present and bid the students a "Merry Christmas"

The finalists and their escorts, who were representatives of the Arbutus staff, the Union Board, and Blue Key honorary, followed Santa Claus into the hall. The contestants were introduced to the crowd by Dave DeJean, junior, Arbutus editor-in-chief; Joe Vogel, senior, business manager, and Dave McAllister, junior, managing editor.

Dance in 'Toyland.'

The dance, sponsored by the Union Board, featured the theme "Santa's Workshop." Alumni Hall was transformed into Toyland with candy canes and gingerbread men around the walls and giant raggedy Ann dolls and toy soldiers on stage. A revolving reflector sent multi-colored light specks racing across the walls, ceiling, and floor.

The dancing was fast and frenzied as the Fugitives blared out a throbbing beat to such tunes as "My Girl," "We Can Work It Out," and "You Were On My Mind."

The dance followed a carol serenade by about 65 shivering students on President Stahr's lawn. President and Mrs. Stahr stood before their door, and then accepted a wreath offered on behalf of the students.

P0078667, IU Archives.

THE INDIANA DAILY STUDENT

THE WEATHER Continued fair with change in temperature. High, 80 to 86, low 55 to 60. Yesterday's high, 84, low 62. Tomorrow's high around 90.

VOL. XCV—NO. 194 | INDIANA UNIVERSITY | SATURDAY, AUGUST 6, 1966. | ERNIE PYLE HALL, BLOOMINGTON, INDIANA. 47401 | 10¢ | Established 1867 Now in our 100th year

—DAILY STUDENT PHOTO By TODD CURLESS

DEMONSTRATORS LINE UP in Dunn Meadow in preparation for their march through downtown Bloomington. The 175 faculty members, students, and children began the march on the I.U. campus and worked their way down Kirkwood avenue, around the square, and then back to the campus. Following the demonstration, the marchers went to Whittenberger Auditorium for the teach-in. Throughout the march on the downtown area, demonstrators were equipped with signs protesting the war in Viet Nam. Many of the signs bore a quote by Indiana Senator Vance Hartke, "Escalation breeds escalation." The march, completed without incidents, and the teach-in were sponsored by the Committee to End the War in Viet Nam.

—DAILY STUDENT PHOTO By TODD CURLESS

JOHN BIRCH SOCIETY members greeted marchers at the courthouse square yesterday on their trip from the I.U. campus to downtown Bloomington and back. The John Birch Society was handing out leaflets explaining its cause. The organization's trailer was parked at Kirkwood and Walnut streets.

175 protestors march, debate

Marching 175-strong down Kirkwood avenue, students, faculty members, and several children demonstrated yesterday against the war in Viet Nam. The crowd overflowed the teach-in which followed in Whittenberger Auditorium, sponsored by the Committee to End the War in Viet Nam. "A long, quiet afternoon," committee and University spokesmen said, but the audience and teach-in leaders debated the war with spirit.

Kirkwood avenue and the square were lined with police and Committee "ushers" who kept traffic moving. Spectators seemed to enjoy the members of Delta Upsilon fraternity carrying "Ban the Beard" and "Send Soap" signs at the end of the parade. The DU's were not allowed to enter Whittenberger Auditorium.

The seven speakers' topics ranged from serious objections to American foreign policy and endorsement of Robert Kennedy for President in 1968, to jabs at President Johnson and other world leaders for "twisting the meanings of words."

Involvement in Asia.

Several speakers said they were "deeply ashamed and frightened" by current world problems and U.S. involvement in Asia. Applause punctuated frequent statements about U.S. policy and "military blunders" since World War II.

Dr. Irving Zeitlin, sociology, said that American military force in Viet Nam was of a more expansionist nature than China had shown in disputes with bordering Asian countries. Each succeeding talk underlined the predominant feeling that the Viet Nam was was "violating the principles and freedom we are trying to defend by fighting."

Continual laughter met Dr. Norman Rabkin's speech on English language and the war. His accusations centered on what he called the language of pious morality, which leaders of both sides use to confuse issues and skirt serious problems. His point, he said, was that euphemisms "deceive the very people who employ them."

Terms used with war.

He used terms like "Charlie," "non-Toxic gas" which he says

(Continued on Page Four)

Alexander says Watts the same

By PAM MITCHELL

Speaking out on conditions in the Watts district of Los Angeles, the status of the national DuBois Club, and the draft, Franklin Alexander gave a small press conference and then talked with about 40 students at two meetings following the anti-war "teach-in" yesterday. He called the Viet Nam conflict a "dirty, imperialist war."

Hesitant on the question of advocating outright violence, the new national president of the DuBois Club instead stressed political and economic independence for Negroes and using that power in community government to make necessary changes.

Mr. Alexander, a leader of the DuBois Club and community efforts in Watts said conditions there were no better than they were before the riots of August, 1965.

He explained the smaller rioting this March "indicated that the police are not willing to work with the people." To him the Los Angeles police were a catalyst in the 1965 insurgencies, and the lack of a hospital in the Watts district was still a main issue.

The most important thing the DuBois Club is doing in Watts now, he continued, was aligning several community groups into an organization for reform. Brought together over the hospital issue, the community elements have organized a community alert patrol, which watches policemen in action and "acts as a deterrent to the police."

Questioned repeatedly about the accusation that the club is Communist-dominated, Mr. Alex-

(Continued on Page Four)

—DAILY STUDENT PHOTO By TODD CURLESS

FRANKLIN ALEXANDER, national president of the W.E.B. DuBois Club, calmly smokes a cigarette as he addresses members of the press corps in a conference after the teach-in. Mr. Alexander came into national prominence during the Watts riots.

Dr. Andressohn dies; taught history at I.U.

Dr. John C. Andressohn, 81 years old, professor emeritus of history, died early yesterday at his home in Bloomington.

Dr. Andressohn had been a member of the I.U. faculty for 33 years before his retirement in 1955.

He was born Aug. 21, 1884, in Philadelphia, Pa. Dr. Andressohn received his A.B. from the University of Wisconsin in 1911, his A.M. degree there in 1912, and his Ph.D. in 1923. He had also studied at the Universities of Berlin and Munich.

In 1949 Dr. Andressohn was sent to Heidelberg, Germany by the U.S. Army to lecture in both English and German.

He was a member of the Association of University Professors, American History Association, and the Medieval Academy of America.

Survivors are his widow, Frieda; his brother, Carl, Dousman, Wis., and a sister, Mrs. L.H. Kottnauer, Steubenville, Ohio.

Funeral services will be held Monday at 10:30 a.m. in the Allen Colonial Chapel in Bloomington. Burial will be in Valhalla Memorial Gardens. Friends may call at the Allen Funeral Home Sunday 3-5 and 7-9 p.m.

Pollution and electrical ordinance hearings set

By LOUISE ONDRIK

Regulation of water pollution — especially with industrial wastes— and licensing of electrical workers will be discussed at public hearings of the Bloomington City Council soon to prepare for action on two proposed ordinances.

The waste control ordinance is under study by a committee headed by Councilman Harry Day.

It provides for prohibiting the use of sewers for high temperature liquids, explosive or flammable liquids or gas, wastes containing high percentages of grease, oil, or other insolubles, high acid or toxic waste, or any of a number of solid or semi-solid materials specified in the ordinance.

The Board of Works will advise industrial users of sewers about correcting unsatisfactory conditions and will be in charge of inspection.

Penalties to ensure compliance with the ordinance are provided.

Councilman Day called for a public hearing on this ordinance at the next regular council meeting, Aug. 18.

Councilman Robert Clegg is chairman of the committee studying the ordinance to license electricians and electrical contractors and providing penalties for violation.

The ordinance provides for minimum electrical requirements, examinations for competency, payment of license fees, license renewals, suspension and appeal, electrical inspections and approval, liability, and penalties.

Individuals, firms, corporations, or partnerships operating as electrical contractors or electricians would be required to have li-

The ordinance allows for payment of an initial fee of $50 by the contractor, with a $25 annual renewal fee, and sets a $10 fee for each additional person working under the contractor in the electrical field.

OBUS delegates visit with Governor

A trip to Indianapolis yesterday paid dividends for Operation Ballot for University Students (OBUS) representatives Dean Aulick, I.U. Student Body President, and Rick Levin, co-director of OBUS.

The two saw Lt. Gov. Robert Rock as they had planned and had a two hour impromptu visit with Gov. Roger D. Branigin.

Lt. Gov. Rock told the representatives that he couldn't make a formal commitment to the OBUS project. However, he likes the way it is being presented throughout the state.

As Mr. Aulick and Mr. Levin were leaving the State House after talking with the lieutenant governor, they met former Democratic state chairman J. Manfred Core. He attempted to get an appointment for them with Fred Garver, one of Gov. Branigin's aides.

While waiting to see Mr. Garver, the governor entered the lobby where they were waiting. Mr. Aulick and Mr. Levin were introduced to Gov. Branigin. He invited them into his office where the three talked informally for two hours.

The governor told the OBUS representatives that he sees nothing wrong with the ideas behind OBUS. He pointed out that one of the problems will be establishing some sort of safeguard to prevent double voting by absentee voters.

Double voting in this case would involve students voting in their home precincts and again in the county where they attend school.

To counter this problem OBUS proposes that students register by telephone or mail with their precinct registrar. The registrar would then notify the county registrar where the student is attending school that the student is properly registered and authorize him to issue that student an absentee ballot for his home county.

Mr. Aulick and Mr. Levin think that such a system will prevent double voting.

Free final fling tonight in Solarium

The IMU Board is sponsoring a free dance tonight from 8 to 11 in the Solarium.

The dance, "Summer's Last Fling," will feature the Un-Called Four.

Dress is casual.

Bishop shuts Owl's doors

The Owl was closed last night before Franklin Alexander's scheduled appearance there in the last program of the day's anti-war teach-in demonstration.

The Owl, a coffee shop located in the Wesley Foundation building, is sponsored by the Campus Ministerial Association, which had given its approval for Mr. Alexander's visit with consent of the steering committee of the Foundation. Signs on the door said Bishop Richard Raines had ordered the Owl closed, and that it would not open until September.

The Rev. Allison Hawkins, associate minister of St. Mark's Methodist Church, said last night that approval had been given for Mr. Alexander to come onto the Methodist - owned property. A church layman, he added, called Bishop Raines in Indianapolis. After the Bishop called Jim Dyer, president of the Wesley Foundation, the closed signs were put on the doors, and Mr. Alexander's sponsors were told to find another meeting place.

The Students for a Democratic Society continued the program in Union 27A. Member Peter Montague said "SDS wants students to hear national figures with something to say pertinent to our lives. I am appalled personally, and I think I speak for SDS as a group, by the contempt for our minds shown by Trustees of I.U. and the bishop of the Methodist Church. They show no faith in our ability to reason and they show no faith in our ability to think."

Five Northern Democrats bolt

Republican leadership unable to kill open occupancy provision

WASHINGTON (AP) — The House turned back a major challenge to a proposed open housing law yesterday and kept it in the 1966 civil rights bill by a vote of 198 to 179.

The Republican-led effort to kill the controversial provision was defeated after fervent pleas from the Democratic leaders and the Republican author of the propoal, Rep. Charles M. Mathias Jr. (R-Md.).

"This is not only civil rights legislation, it is moral rights legislation," Speaker John w. McCormack (D-Mass.), declared.

Majority leader Carl Albert of Oklahoma said if the proposal were killed "we will have failed in a major area of our responsibility to the American people."

Proposal was compromise.

Mathias, who offered the proposal as a compromise to a much tougher ban on housing discrimination requested by President Johnson, addressed his appeal to hsi party colleagues.

"If we hope to assume the leadership of this great nation," he said, "we cannot shirk our duty today."

However, the overwhelming number of Republicans followed House Minority Leader Gerald R. Ford of Michigan up the aisle to be counted in favor of killing the provision. The vote was just a head count, with no names recorded.

Republicans support bill.

About 25 Republicans stayed with Mathias, including Rep. William M. McCulloch (R-Ohio), the party's key spokesman on civil rights legislation.

A few Northern Democrats, three from Ohio and two from Baltimore where racial violence has broken out recently, voted with the Southern Democrats against the measure.

Vote next week.

Although the housing provision must win final approval by a roll-call vote next week, its backers feel Friday's action all but insures it will remain in the bill and be sent to the Senate.

The provision bans racial discrimination by builders, bankers, real estate agents and others in the business of selling or renting housing. Owner-occupants are not covered unless they engage in three or more real estate transactions in 12 months, in which case they would be considered to be in the business.

Owner-occupants of dwellings up to four-family size would also be exempt from the proposed law.

Weekend—

—on the campus—

Saturday

THURSDAY CLASSES MEET

SABBATH SERVICES—Conducted by the University Jewish Community, Beck Chapel, 9:30 a.m.

IMU DANCE — Solarium, Union Building, 8 p.m.

BROWN COUNTY PLAYHOUSE —"Clarence," Nashville, Indiana, 8 p.m.

SHOWBOAT MAJESTIC —"Morning's at Seven," Jeffersonville, 8 p.m.

UNIVERSITY THEATRE—"King Lear," 9 p.m.

Sunday

UNIVERSITY THEATRE—"The Glass Menagerie," 8 p.m.

BROWN COUNTY PLAYHOUSE —"Clarence," Nashville, Indiana, 8 p.m.

SHOWBOAT MAJESTIC —Morning's at Seven," Jeffersonville, 8 p.m.

Monday

CONVOCATION — Film-lecture, "Incredible Iceland," Robert Davis, Auditorium, 7:15 p.m.

CAMPUS MINISTERIAL ASSOCIATION—Studies in Religion, "The New Theology: Protestant Trends," Rev. Arthur S. Lloyd, Ballantine 109, 7:30 p.m.

P0081191, IU Archives

Happy Birthday To Us! See Section B

100 years of excellence at I.U.

THE INDIANA DAILY STUDENT

Now in our 101st year

WARMER
Cloudy, warmer today and tomorrow. High today 38-46; low upper teens. High yesterday, 33; low 12.

VOL. XCVI—NO. 96 INDIANA UNIVERSITY WEDNESDAY, FEBRUARY 22, 1967. ERNIE PYLE HALL, BLOOMINGTON, INDIANA, 47401 10¢ Established 1867

Indian voters riot in Bombay on election day

NEW DELHI, INDIA (AP) — India's ruling Congress party suffered telling losses yesterday to two rightist parties in the early hours of ballot counting following a day of severe election violence.

In two important parliamentary races in New Delhi, rightists were leading their Congress party incumbents.

Opposition led by the right-wing Swatantra party and the Hindu Jan Sangh party posed a threat to the Congress party in the assembly of the western desert state of Rajasthan, land of the princely rulers. Communists were winning the legislature in the southern state of Kerala.

The tense parliamentary race in northeast Bombay between V. K. Krishna Menon, leftist former defense minister, and Congress candidate S. G. Barve, bubbled over into street fighting involving a mob of 3,000 people. No casualties were reported.

In New Delhi, Works and Housing minister Mehr Chand Khanna was trailing M. L. Sondhi, the Jan Sangh candidate who formerly belonged to the Congress party, in the race for one parliamentary seat.

In the other prestige contest in New Delhi, Balraj Madhek, national president of the Jan Sangh, led Raghavendra Singh of the Congress prty. In all, Jan Sangh held leads in six of seven New Delhi seats in Parliament.

—DAILY STUDENT PHOTO By JOHN CHANEY

Birthday greetings

STUDENTS FROM MAGEE II of Foster Quadrangle look over the top of Ernie Pyle Hall after leaving The Indiana Daily Student a 100th birthday greeting last night. From left are Jim Kain, junior; Ken Lundgren, freshman; Frank Jakubowski, sophomore. (See Section B.)

Draft questions to be answered

Deputy draft head Rhodes first of new IMU speakers

By JUDI BURKE
Daily Student Staff Writer

The draft and its problems and implications for I.U. students will be thrown open to discussion and debate tomorrow at an open forum presided by Col. Wayne Rhodes, state deputy Selective Service director.

Col. Rhodes will speak and answer questions concerning all phases of the Indiana draft situation from 3-5 p.m. in Whittenberger Auditorium. His appearance on campus is sponsored by Union Board's Student Interests Commission.

Present draft policies, the forecast for changes, and exactly where I.U. students stand with respect to the draft will be covered during the session.

"What we are trying to do is more or less bring Gen. (Lewis B.) Hershey down to earth for I.U. students," said Rick Levin, junior and Student Interests Commission chairman.

"COL. RHODES HOPES to be confronted with particular, individual situations," Mr. Levin said, "both to clear up problems for students, and to make current developments in draft policy more easily understandable."

Tomorrow's forum is the first of this semester's Student Interests Commission-sponsored programs. Two all campus caucuses and a Roundtable Dinner are also scheduled in the future.

Mr. Levin explained that the Student Interests Commission was created to "direct attention to a long overlooked area in Union programming.

"We have two goals," he said, "one the discussion of intellectual and academic issues coufronting the University, and the other promotion of better relations among students, faculty, and administration."

Campus Caucus II, on Tuesday, March 9 from 3-5 p.m. in Whittenberger Auditorium, will concentrate on "The Role of the Left in the University."

SPOKESMEN FOR BOTH "new right" and "new left" campus factions will discuss the issues involved. Speakers representing students, faculty, and administration will conduct the program, followed by a question and answer period and an open discussion for audience reaction and debate.

Campus Caucus III, on Tuesday, April 11, from 3-5 in Whittenberger, will be concerned with campus spring elections. Candidates for Student Body president and vice-president will speak, answer questions, and participate in open audience discussion.

The commission will also sponsor a Roundtable Dinner on Sunday, March 19, at 6 p.m. in the Solarium. Patterned to a degree after the Lycea Dinners, the Roundtable Dinner will be devoted to "The Value Revolution," and its speakers will touch on such topics as academic freedom, the Sexual Freedom League, the W.E.B. DuBois Club, etc. Tickets will be available March 3 at the Activities Desk in the Union.

In addition to Mr. Levin, Student Interests Commission steering committee members include Debbie McAdams, junior; Nancy Andrew, Anne Brafford, Julie Jones, Dottie March, and Chris Perry, sophomores, and Mike Berger and Paul Helmke, freshmen. Bob Forste, junior, is Union Board adviser for the commission.

80,000 GM workers laid off in strike

DETROIT (AP) — General Motors Corp. announced last night that at least 80,000 of its workers will be laid off this week as a result of a strike at Mansfield, Ohio.

GM spokesman said the 80,000 would be laid off even if the strike is settled soon because of a parts shortage resulting from the Mansfield walkout.

"Actually," the spokesman said, "this is a conservative figure and it could go as high as 100,000."

GM HAD ANNOUNCED earlier in the day a number of layoffs affecting a half dozen of its assembly plants. The announcement last night said 22 GM assembly plants would be hit.

About 3000 of the Indiana employees will be laid off by today.

Yesterday's layoff was at the Guide Lamp Division in Anderson. Only hourly paid workers were sent home, and 3,400 others were not affected.

The Fisher Body plant at Marion announced that 1,000 workers in the shipping division would be laid off after the second shift today.

Closings of plants in Detroit, St. Louis, Arlington, Tex., and Pontiac, Mich., were called for last night. Plant sites where layoffs were scheduled included Anderson and Marion, Ind., Doraville, Ga., Columbus, Ohio, and Buffalo and Tonawanda, N.Y.

Prospects for early settlement of the unauthorized strike at a Fisher Body Division plant here remained dim. The membership of striking Local 549 met last night and decided to stay out.

Call Gripe Vine 6 to 9 p m
Monday through Thursday
(Phone 337-7974)

You're so tied up in administrative red tape you're choking to death, and you still haven't found out what you want to know? You've got a question that's been bugging you for months and your friends just laugh at you when you try to tell them about it? You need a shoulder to cry on? Call Gripe Vine, 7-9 p.m. Monday through Thursday, or write to Gripe Vine, c/o The Indiana Daily Student, Ernie Pyle Hall. We don't promise any miracles, but we'll try to help.

Today —

—on the campus—

DAILY STUDENT CENTENNIAL WEEK — DAILY STUDENT 100TH BIRTHDAY

GERMAN COFFEE HOUR —"Kaffeestunde," Ballantine 004, 3 to 5 p.m.

THE PATTEN FOUNDATION LECTURE SERIES — "The Myth of the Golden Age in the Renaissance: Ethics," Tarry Tuchman Levin, Harvard University, Ballantine 013, 4 p.m.

PHYSICAL EDUCATION FOR WOMEN DANCE DIVISION — Film "Old Chief's Dance," HPER 154, 4:30 p.m.

PHYSICS DEPARTMENT SEMINAR — "The Study of Biological Macro-Molecules by Means of X-ray Diffraction," Michael G. Rossmann, Purdue University, Swain West 119, 4:30 p.m.

ASTRONOMY DEPARTMENT COLLOQUIUM —Speaker: Grant Athay, High Altitude Observatory, Swain West 221, 4:30 p.m., Tea, Swain West 113, 4 p.m.

IMU CHESS CLUB — Hoosier Den, Union, 7 p.m.

ASTRONOMY DEPARTMENT — "Look at the Stars," Kirkwood Observatory, 7:15 to 8:15 p.m., weather permitting.

WORKSHOP BATIK — Craft Shops, Union, 7:30 p.m.

HILLEL FOUNDATION DRAMA GROUP — "Warsaw — Year Zero," by Harry Geduld, Director: James De Felice, Fine Arts Auditorium, 8 p.m.

Quiz Bowl competition tougher as teams enter second round

By CYNTHIA ENGLE
Daily Student Staff Writer

Competition is stiffening and scores are getting closer as more teams are eliminated in Campus Quiz Bowl.

Willkie Co-op defeated Phi Kappa Psi, 145-130, last night in a protest rematch. Willkie's victory in this match made the eligible for the second round of matches.

Willkie protested on a question Neil Irick, senior, started to answer in last Thursday's Quiz Bowl. Before Mr. Irick answered he identified himself, and without giving him a chance to answer the question, Dr. Herbert E. Smith, Director of Student Activities and moderator for Quiz Bowl, called his answer wrong.

AFTER THE PROTEST match the second round continued with Sigma Alpha Epsilon beating Delta Delta Delta, 80-55, Willkie Co-op over Briscoe 9A, 100-70, and Delta Chi winning over Kappa Delta Rho, 150-135.

Also Briscoe 7B defeated Phi Gamma Delta, 120-85, Zeta Beta Tau beat Landes II 130-100 and Wissler IV overcame Nichols 130-125.

These close matches were sprinkled with crazy stumpers.

Dr. Smith identified one question as easy enough for a sixth grader. "How many inches in a square foot?" (144 square inches.)

Or "Where is the duck-bill platypus found?" (Australia.)

IN THE MATCH BETWEEN Sigma Alpha Epsilon and Delta Delta Delta the Tri-Delts had a bonus True or False Question. It was "James Garfield lived weeks after his assassination, however one day his wife walked into the President's bedroom, flipped on the lights and to her horror discovered the President was dead. True or False?"

THE ANSWER WAS FALSE because there were no lights then. The Tri-Delts said President Garfield wasn't married.

Then the SAE's had to tell what the different draft classifications stood for. The only one the team identified correctly was 1-A, ready for active duty, which may say something for what they think about.

Other stumpers were "Name the seven dwarfs," (Dopey, Sleepy, Grumpy, Sneezy, Doc, Happy, and Droopy), and "Take the number of degrees in a right angle, and the number of degrees in a straight angle, and multipy this by the number of degrees in a circle." (97200.) Neither team was able to answer correctly.

ON A GEOGRAPHICAL identification question about the location of the North Pole, judges, timers, and Dr. Smith pulled out volumes of the Encyclopedia Britannica to check an answer that was finally rejected.

Mother Goose had a question in the Quiz Bowl as the ancient question about the number of travelers to St. Ives was asked. This question passed unanswered also.

Judges for Quiz Bowl were Stanley Rafalko, associate professor of Anatomy and David Bleick, English.

The third round of matches will begin tomorrow night at 7:30 p.m. in Whittenberger with Hardin vs. Martin III, Sigma Alpha Epsilon vs. Willkie Co-op, Delta Chi vs. Briscoe 7B, and Zeta Beta Tau vs. Wissler IV.

Matches in the third round will last fifteen minutes each.

CIA to withdraw aid from private groups

WASHINGTON (AP) — Director Richard Helms of the Central Intelligence Agency told senators in secret session yesterday that the agency is withdrawing financial support from some private organizations it has subsidized.

That word came from Senator Richard B. Russell, (D-Ga.), chairman of the Senate panel which supervises the CIA.

Senator Russell would not name individual organizations, but he did say it would be a mistake and a waste of money to continue any investment in the National Student Association (NSA).

Mr. Russell spoke with newsmen after a three-hour session with Mr. Helms.

Mr. Helms himself walked briskly from the meeting and brushed aside questions.

SENATOR RUSSELL TOLD NEWSMEN that in view of the publicity swirling around the CIA because of revelations that it subsidized the student association, "It might be well for the CIA to sever financial connections with a great number of organizations."

Russell said he has been aware from the start that the CIA had been channeling funds to the NSA. The NSA's supervisory board held an emergency meeting last week and said some of the group's leaders had been trapped into gathering intelligence for the CIA.

Mr. Russell said it would not have been possible to openly subsidize such groups. This would have cast doubt on the status of any Americans attending any international meeting, he said.

"SO FAR AS THE TALK that there has been anything done that impinges on academic freedom or subverts youth," he said, "that's just a lot of hogwash."

Senator Russell contended the program of helping young Americans attend world youth meetings thwarted Communist efforts to take over those forums.

"I think it was a good program," the senator said. "It probably paid a higher dividend to stop Communist propaganda than almost any other program."

Mr. Helms had gone before the meeting backed by a prediction from Senate Democratic Leader Mike Mansfield that the CIA will survive its current "period of discomfiture" with a strengthened intelligence arm.

SENATOR MANSFIELD SAID the government could allocate funds openly through the State Department and other agencies, "and state it to the world," so that Americans could atend international meetings.

Senator Robert F. Kennedy, (D-N.Y.) said the CIA operated under presidential orders when it financed student trips to foreign meetings.

"If it was a mistake, it was one of policy made in the executive branch and it should not be blamed on the CIA," Senator Kennedy told a reporter.

Mr. Kennedy said that when he was in the Cabinet as attorney general he knew the government was paying the bills for student travel abroad and he said the decision to do this through the CIA was made "at the highest levels" in the Eisenhower, Kennedy and Johnson administrations.

THE CIA'S ACTIVITY was under executive supervision at all times, Mr. Kennedy said.

Senator Stuart Symington, (D-Mo.) also said, in a separate interview, that the CIA was operating under instructions when it offered financial aid to the NSA.

"This is an operating agency and it operates under policies and instructions of others," Symington said. He declined to be more specific about who gave the instructions, but he presumably referred to the National Security Council which is headed by the President.

Symington is a member of a Senate Armed Services subcommittee which supervises the CIA.

Meanwhile, the National Council of Churches (NCC) announced yesterday in Chicago its programs have received minor financial aid in three instances from foundations linked to the CIA.

The council is the cooperating agency for 34 Protestant and Eastern Orthodox denominations that have a total membership of 42 million persons.

Dr. R. H. Edwin Espy of New York, NCC general secretary, said:

"The national council had no knowledge at any time that any of these gifts may have had any link with CIA involvement."

Dr. Espy said the council is "only too glad to cooperate to the fullest in any and all federal efforts to investigate the matter."

Former Socialist party leader Norman Thomas confirmed in New York a Washington Post story that the defunct Institute for Labor Research had received more than $1 million in CIA funds.

LUNA chairman explains change

By BRUCE GILLEY
Daily Student Staff Writer

Several changes will exist at this year's Little United Nations Assembly (LUNA), the chairman of the project said yesterday.

Judi Ruhl, junior, in charge of arrangements for LUNA this year, pointed out that the popularity of model UN's has caused more schools to sponsor them and thus decreased the number of colleges taking part at each one.

Today about 200 students from 12 other schools and I.U. will register for the 13th annual LUNA convention at I.U., Miss Ruhl said. But only about 80 of these students will be from other schools, she added.

In 1964 and other recent years, as many as 400 students, many of them from other colleges and universities, attended LUNA at I.U.

In accounting for the decrease, Miss Ruhl said that more model UN assemblies are going on at the same time as LUNA. LUNA used to be the only project teaching college students about the workings of the UN at this time of year, she added.

BECAUSE FEWER STUDENTS from other schools are taking part in LUNA this year, Miss Ruhl said, more I.U. students will be "representing" foreign countries than before.

Another change this year is that there will be three persons serving as president of the LUNA general assembly, Miss Ruhl said.

In the past, Dr. Richard F. Crabbs, special assistant for International Affairs and lecturer in government, has served as the assembly's president, Miss Ruhl said. But he is on sabbatical this year, she added.

Therefore, the LUNA general assembly will have a different president each night when it meets Thursday, Friday, and Saturday evenings, Miss Ruhl said.

Ilpyong Kim, lecturer in government, will preside Thursday, Miss Ruhl said. Donald Snow, grad., and Donald W. Zacharias, assistant professor of Speech and Theatre, will serve as president Friday and Saturday, she added. All the meetings of LUNA are open to the public, Miss Ruhl said.

AFTER REGISTRATION today at Whittenberger Auditorium from 2:30 to 6:30 p.m., the delegates to LUNA are scheduled to meet tonight for the first general meeting in Whittenberger Auditorium at 7:30 p.m.

Tomorrow, Friday, and Saturday mornings, the delegates will meet in committees similar to ones in the UN from 9 a.m. until 12 M. In these committee meetings resolutions proposed by delegates will be considered for passing.

All proceedings will follow the rules used in the real UN. During the four day LUNA session, the delegates will hear speakers discuss various aspects of international government.

Mr. Elia Torrey, who has spoken before the UN general assembly several times, will welcome the delegates this evening and explain the purposes of LUNA.

THE MAIN ADDRESS of the session will be given Friday at 7:15 p.m. in the Auditorium. Carl T. Rowan, former director of the U.S. Information Agency and now a nationally syndicated columnist, will speak at an open convocation on international affairs. Mr. Rowan's speech will be carried live on WFIU.

Saturday evening the delegates to LUNA will hear Clark Drummond, assistant director of the Collegiate Council for the United Nations, at a banquet.

I.U. cagers get help; Wildcats, Iowa lose

Hold on to your hats Indiana basketball fans 'cause things are looking better every day for the Hoosiers in the Big Ten.

They got some more help last night from a couple of clubs in the lower part of the standings—Minnesota and Wisconsin. The Gophers knocked off Iowa, 88-86 at Madison.

So, that gives I.U. a two game lead over Iowa and the Wildcats. Michigan State is still only one game back and has the chance of catching the Hoosiers.

IBEW officers pledge more strike benefits

Union officers of the International Brotherhood of Electrical Workers (IBEW) Local 2031 told strikers yesterday that more strike benefits are on the way from the national IBEW assistance council.

In a telegram to Local 2031 the national IBEW office said: "Be it resolved that financial aid other than benefits now being received shall continue until a successful conclusion is reached in the strike. A direct appeal will be made on all IBEW Westinghouse workers."

Any money the local strikers receive will be in addition to the $25 strike benefit now paid to each worker who walks a four-hour shift each week on the picket line.

Fred Haseman, president of Local 2031, had no comment concerning how much money will be given to the local or when it will start getting it.

Mr. Haseman also implied that previously published reports saying strikers wanted to go back to work were untrue.

No new negotiations have been set between the union and Westinghouse. The last series of talks were called off Thursday by federal mediators when no agreement could be reached.

I.U. to receive $199,097 in federal grants

The I.U. Foundation will receive two federal grants totaling $199,097, Senators Vance Hartke and Birch Bayh announced Monday night, in Washington D.C.

The Institute for Sex Research will use a $130,797 grant from the Department of Health, Education and Welfare. The second grant for $68,300 from the National Endowment for Arts will be used by the Educational Television Stations program service.

The grant to the Institute for Sex Research will be used in the program "Youth Cultures and Aspects of Socialization Process," said Dr. William Simon, Senior Sociologist of the Institute for Sex Research. Persons between 18 and 23 years old will be the subjects of this study of the transition from adolescence to adulthood.

THE STUDY WILL FOCUS on changes in sexual, religious, political, and academic attitudes of young persons of this age group. College students from all parts of the nation will be the main subjects of this program. However, a smaller sampling of persons who do not go to college also will be taken.

"The program will begin in the spring, and the results will be ready by the end of the year," Dr. Simon said.

The second grant will be used to develop original arts programs by educational television stations throughout the nation. It will encourage innovations in communicating the arts and will help discover new arts talent, said Duane Straub, assistant director of the educational television stations program service.

The more than 100 educational television stations throughout the nation will compete for a part of the I.U. grant which will be distributed by the Educational Television Stations Programs Service here.

P0081191, IU Archives.

Planning second semester issues of the IDS in 1967 are Craig Klugman, editor in chief; Gil Pappas, managing editor; Pam Mitchell, chief editorial writer; and Irene Nolan, assistant managing editor. *P0078395, IU Archives.*

REFLECTION

When the Editor Is Edited

The editor of the Daily Student was walking purposefully through the newsroom, his face grim. The editor, Sheldon Shafer, talked to the people who pasted up the paper. He made phone calls. He went to the faculty offices. At the time, I was working in the Ernie Pyle Hall newsroom, and I knew: Something was up, something was wrong.

It was the spring semester 1966, and, yes, something was wrong. A group of graduate students had taken out an ad opposing the Vietnam War. And then, hours before publication, the IU administration ordered it killed, partly to forestall a response from donors and legislators who would think IU was training leftists, partly because the administrators very likely also hated the message in the ad.

How could so flagrant an episode of interference happen? At the time, journalism was a department in the College of Arts and Sciences, like history and English. Almost all J-students were expected to work at the IDS, as reporters and editors. Much of our grade in some courses depended on our work on the IDS. The IDS, academically, was inextricably tied to the business of IU and its benevolent oversight.

This is a story of not only how the Daily Student has changed, but also how some things remain constant—friendships, journalistic ideals—and other things, well, let's say they mellow.

A year after the ad issue, a group of local news people—from the IDS, the two Bloomington dailies, and IU and Bloomington radio, and the correspondents from Louisville and Indianapolis papers—were invited to have a conversation with the IU president, Elvis J. Stahr Jr.

At some point, someone asked Stahr what he thought of the Daily Student. I was there as IDS editor and listened carefully to what

"This is a story of not only how the Daily Student has changed, but also how some things remain constant—friendships, journalistic ideals—and other things, well, let's say they mellow."

Stahr had to say. He first made some anodyne remark. Then he added (somewhat icily, in my recollection) that administrators wished the IDS would just publish what they said.

Later that semester, Stahr gave an important campus address. Though I don't remember what the subject was exactly, it was probably on student activism. That evening, as I was working on the stories about the speech, I got the word: Publish Stahr's text in full, word for word, as a news story.

Today, it's hard to imagine, but then, as IDS staff, we all were as beholden to the journalism faculty as history or English majors were to theirs. In the name of student independence, it was wrong. But while a few IU students and some faculty objected to the entire idea of the Daily Student as it was constituted, most of us knew nothing else.

I graduated a month or so later. Sheldon Shafer and I left Bloomington that June. I was more bitter about my experience as a student editor than my good friend Sheldon was. We went our separate ways, but we kept in touch.

After we left, a new journalism chair arrived in 1968. His name was Dick Gray, and he almost immediately began uncoupling the IDS from the department. He also changed the department to a school of journalism.

After Dick Gray died of a heart attack in 1984, the IU faculty council adopted a memorial resolution about his contributions to the university, including what he did for the IDS.

"Students were no longer required to work on the paper, nor could they earn credit for doing so," the resolution said. "Under this new arrangement, faculty no longer oversaw the Daily Student's operations, nor did they have any control over its content. The newspaper's charter forbade even the publisher to exercise control over content except to prevent obvious libel. In short, under Dick Gray's regime, student editors and reporters were to learn about freedom of the press by practicing it."

By that time, Sheldon Shafer and I had settled into our careers, his at the Louisville Courier-Journal and mine at the Journal Gazette in Fort Wayne. Like those of many student journalists, our friendship forged at the IDS lasted a lifetime. He was the best man at my wedding, I was the best man at his. His children call me Uncle Craig, mine call him Uncle Sheldon. With our kids surpassing or nearing the age of 40, they may decide to dispense with the uncle honorific.

And with time, my frustration with IU journalism faded, maybe disappeared. I've served on the IU Publications Board for over two decades. I have made friends among journalism faculty and administrators, including one, now retired, from the '60s.

Certainly, we can attribute some of this to age; it is hard to keep your anger white hot for 50 years. Some I can attribute to Sheldon's mature, level-headed outlook on his days working at the IDS. As Sheldon said when I told him I was retiring, "Nothing is forever."

But some of my changed outlook has to do with what I learned at IU and the IDS. Newspaper independence was drilled into all of us, in class and at the IDS. I was angry at the hypocrisy that Sheldon and I faced head on more than 50 years ago, and I recognized the hypocrisy for what it was because IU taught me to recognize it.

For that, of course, I am grateful, as I am for my lifelong friendship with Sheldon and others I met at the Indiana Daily Student. Yeah, the word "Daily" no longer applies to the pulp edition, and Ernie Pyle Hall is no longer its home. But, you know, what the hell, things change.

—*Craig Klugman, BA 1967*

School fire in pictures: Page 8.

THE INDIANA DAILY STUDENT

COOLER
Partly cloudy and cooler today. High, mid 50's. Low, 38 to 43.

Now in our 101st year

VOL. XCVI—NO. 122 INDIANA UNIVERSITY FRIDAY, APRIL 7, 1967. ERNIE PYLE HALL, BLOOMINGTON, INDIANA, 47401 10¢ Established 1867

EMPLOYES VOTE TO STRIKE TODAY

AWS attempting to extend women's hours

By PEGGY VLEREBOME and CAROL FIESTER
Daily Student Staff Writers

The Association of Women Students (AWS) last night moved to give freshman and sophomore women the same extended hours now granted to juniors and seniors. The action will probably result in a confrontation with the I.U. administration.

Dean of Students Robert H. Shaffer said last night that the AWS "cannot change the Trustees' rule unilaterally. We will be glad to study their recommendation."

He added that no change in women's hours could be made until the effects of extending the unresticted hours system to juniors this year could be evaluated.

AWS CONTENDED that according to its constitution it has the power to determine women's hours. The action, made at the legislative board meeting, was not a recommendation to the administration.

In previous years, changes in hours were recommended by AWS and then approved by the Board of Trustees.

Under the policy, women under 21 years old would need written parental permission, which would be put on permanent record with the counselor or housemother. Students would have an identification card that they will present upon leaving and returning to their housing units.

Students without parental permission will keep the present hours system, except in the case of a campus cultural event, registered organization activity, or emergency delay. Closing hours then will be extended.

AWS is scheduling the policy to take effect during Summer Session.

OPTIONAL SIGN-OUTS for women with unrestricted hours leaving the living unit at any time is in the proposal. This sign-out may be placed in a sealed envelope to be opened only in case of emergency. There would be no limit to the number of overnight signouts.

Lissa Purdy, AWS president, said that AWS took the stand on women's hours because it doesn't believe it or anybody can legislate moral laws. She said the responsibility of personal life lies with a woman student and her parents — not I.U.

"The AWS legislative board would like to set up the most flexible system for women so they can grow with this responsibility," Miss Purdy said. Equality between the Dean of Students and students is the question, she said.

"The only way they'll get us to not enact the policy is to take away our power— to dissolve AWS," Miss Purdy said.

One provision of the constitution that Miss Purdy says gives AWS the power states:

"All the AWS legislative powers for the self-government of women students of Indiana University are vested in and shall be exercised by the AWS Legislative Board, which derives its powers from the Board of Trustees of Indiana University through executive officers of the University."

Another provision states that all questions over the interpretation of the constitution shall be referred to the AWS Legislative Board, whose decision shall be final, subject to the approval of the Student Supreme Court and the Dean of Students.

Dean Shaffer said the recommendation would be considered by his office first and then by the Administrative Committee, composed of the four University Vice-Presidents and President Elvis J. Stahr.

He said that "It would have been helpful if it (the AWS Legislative Board) had consulted us."

Samuel E. Braden, Vice-President and Dean for Undergraduate Development, also said that the AWS Legislative Board could make a recommendation about revising women's hours.

"I'm sure it can be brought before the Trustees at their meeting April 21," he said. He added that "If it (AWS) has gotten power from the Trustees and if the Trustees have given AWS carte blanche to do this, the thing for AWS to do would be to try it. The thing to do is to present it to the Trustees."

Mrs. Virginia H. Rogers, Assistant Dean of Students, said that the "AWS Legislative Board, Miss Purdy, and their predecessors have always made proposals" instead of enactments. Although the Legislative Board said the AWS constitution gives the board the power to make such changes, Dean Rogers said "We have not changed our view of their constitution."

Even if the Legislative Board demands the enactment of the changes instead of recommending them, Dean Rogers said that "the approval of the executive officers and/or the Trustees still would be required."

The new policy would also include provisions for final week and vacation periods. Closing hours would be extended to midnight from reading day through the evening preceding the last day of final examinations.

CLOSING HOURS during vacations would be 11 p.m. for any night preceding a day of regularly scheduled classes and 1 a.m. for any night not preceding a day of classes.

"If any housing unit wants to restrict this it can," Miss Purdy said.

Miss Purdy, a former Progressive Reform Party member, said that the policy has nothing to do with any party lines.

The question of women's hours has been before AWS for three years. This policy has been in the works since before Christmas.

All three parties — PRP, Action, and Tryus — are advocating what AWS is demanding.

Panhellenic and the Inter-Residence Halls Association are on the AWS Legislative Board.

Tryus chooses Senator Gibson for No. 2 spot

By BRUCE GILLEY
Daily Student Staff Writer

Nancy Gibson, junior, was selected as the Tryus candidate for Vice-President of the Student Body last night.

Miss Gibson replaces Roger Jones, sophomore, as running mate of Marty Zohn, sophomore, for the spring elections.

TRYUS PARTY CHAIRMAN Rock Winchell, sophomore, announced the selection of Miss Gibson by the party's executive cabinet after more than 100 party members supported her at a special meeting last night.

Mr. Jones was selected unanimously at the Tryus nominating convention Monday night to run for Student Body Vice-President. However, he announced Wednesday that conditions beyond his control made it necessary for him to withdraw.

MISS GIBSON was nominated at the convention Monday by George Muncaster, junior and Student Senator from Wright Quad. She declined because she intended to serve as a resident adviser in the Halls of Residence next year. Resident advisers are not allowed to participate in Student Government.

However, at the meeting yesterday, Senator Muncaster placed Miss Gibson's name before the party again for consideration. She was again heartily endorsed by all those present.

This time Miss Gibson, who has served in the Senate for two years, accepted the nomination.

"STUDENT GOVERNMENT should not be an interest group," Miss Gibson said in her acceptance speech. "It must be a representative political action group."

Commenting on the Tryus platform, Miss Gibson said, "The campaign involves more than specific grievances and many-paged platforms full of promises."

MISS GIBSON SERVES in the Student Senafter he or she is elected, Senator Muncascial Affairs Committee. Student Body President Dean Aulick, senior, recently named her to the Student Supreme Court. Miss Gibson is also a resident of the women's academic unit and in the honors program in mathematics.

The Tryus executive committee is allowed to replace any candidate who has filed and withdraws by the party constitution, Chairman Winchell said.

Mr. Winchell said last night that the executive committee would also fill some other vacancies on the party slate. However, he did not announce any other appointments.

Discount rate to decline; credit may ease

WASHINGTON (AP) — The Federal Reserve Board approved unanimously yesterday the first decline in its discount rate in more than 6½ years. The move, which could signal a dramatic easing of credit throughout the economy, was welcomed immediately by the administration.

The drop, from 4.5 to 4 per cent, is effective today in 10 of the 12 districts which make up the Federal Reserve System, the nation's central bank.

Only the Atlanta and St. Louis districts did not seek a drop in their rates yesterday. They are expected to follow suit soon.

A LOWERING in the discount rate usually means lower interest rates for businessmen who borrow money and consumers who purchase houses, automobiles, and other goods on the installment plan.

Spokesmen for the home building and savings and loan industries said earlier this week that a material lowering of home mortgage interest rates could result within 30 days if the Federal Reserve lowered its discount.

THE BOARD said the action it took yesterday is in line with recent declines in market rates and in keeping with its policy objectives of assuring sufficient credit to provide for orderly economic growth.

The discount rate is the charge made by the Federal Reserve on funds borrowed by its member banks. Other interest rates are pegged upward from it.

—DAILY STUDENT PHOTO By DENNIS ELLIOTT

The school rifle club's

. . . ammunition, stored in the basement of the northwest wing, exploded as the fire spread through the basement. The fireman lying on the ground holds the hose down so the other fireman can soak the ammunition.

It's back to school after $2-million fire

By THE DAILY STUDENT CITY STAFF

The pupils displaced yesterday by the fire at Central Junior High School will be sent to Dyer and Bloomington High School, the Bloomington School Board decided last night.

Seventh and Eighth graders will attend Dyer grade school in the afternoon. The regular pupils at Dyer will attend school in the morning.

The ninth graders from Central will attend BHS.

Dr. Ronald Walton, superintendent of schools, said at the meeting that numerous offers were received by the school board as to where the pupils from Central could be sent.

I.U.'S OFFER to provide facilities for the students was turned down by the board, Dr. Walton said, because I.U. would have difficulty supplying educational materials for grade school students.

When students will start attending Dyer and BHS will be announced later this week or early next week, Dr. Walton said.

The fire loss at Central Junior High School was estimated last night at $2 million by Bloomington Fire Inspector Wayne Gobel.

The fire which gutted most of the 48-room building, located on the site of the original I.U. campus, was not thought to be the work of an arsonist.

"THE ONLY THING that we can definitely say at this time is that the fire did start in the stage area (of the auditorium)," Inspector Gobel said.

He added that the fire department did not know what caused the fire.

The school was inspected by the Bloomington fire inspectors last week, and was given an A-1 rating — conforming to all fire safety regulations.

The loss is covered by insurance, a school system spokesman said. The structure is insured for $1.75 million. The equipment — books, furniture, fixtures — is insured for $400,000.

THE INVESTIGATION of the fire's cause will not be completed for at least a week, according to Mr. Gobel.

Peter North, 13 years old, an eighth grader, said the fire broke out in the auditorium prop and costume department at about 7:30 a.m. He called the fire department at 7:41.

By the time the fire department arrived at 7:45, the fire had started to spread to the northwest and west wings. The auditorium is on the fourth floor of a building between the northwest and west wings.

Huge, black clouds of smoke poured onto South Walnut street by 8 a.m. The snorkel unit fought the fire in the west wing and watered down the walls of the south wing.

The fire gutted the northwest wing and destroyed the auditorium and the girls' gym. The fire then spread from the attic, according to a fireman, into the west wing and burned out the fourth floor.

The fire was officially under control at 11:20 a.m. The Bloomington Fire Department used the snorkel, an aerial truck, and six pumpers to fight the blaze. The Ellettsville department was on standby notice.

LATE YESTERDAY afternoon a wrecker came in and knocked down the walls that were in danger of collapsing.

At a little after 10 a.m., when the southeast wing was in danger of being gutted, a human chain of Central School pupils, I.U. students, and onlookers, wound up the fire escape into the fourth floor. It brought down, hand over hand, books, furniture, and equipment from the fourth floor library, classrooms, and science rooms.

At one time the volunteers threw books from the fourth floor windows to the ground. The books and equipment were loaded quickly into trucks and taken away by city Street Department workers.

The school rifle team's ammunition, stored in a basement corner of the northwest wing, started to explode at about 10:30 a.m. The police fenced off the area around the wing to keep spectators away, but the fence was taken down about 11 a.m.

500 workers to picket I.U. dorms and services

By JERRY HARRIS
Daily Student Staff Writer

About 200 members of the I.U. employes labor union last night voted unanimously to "hit the bricks" and begin picketing at 4 a.m. today.

Larry Wall, union president, estimated the effort would involve "close to 500" employes. This is about one-third of the total service and maintenance staff at I.U.

The most immediate effect of the work stoppage is likely to be a shortage of staff workers in the dormitory cafeterias today.

JACK RAY, director of personnel, said late last night that he would notify the dormitory heads of the intended strike.

"We will try to ensure that students will be served as scheduled Friday, but I can't guarantee that there won't be some problems."

Mr. Ray said that the strongest union support is in the Halls of Residence and the Physical Plant.

The members of the American Federation of State, County, and Municipal Employes (AFSCME) Local 832 voted the action after hearing Joseph Kinch, a general representative of the union's state headquarters.

"I have discouraged the local from taking this action twice before, but when they tow cars away, that's the straw that broke the camel's back," Mr. Kinch said.

ALTHOUGH THE ACTION was precipitated by the towing away of about seven employes' cars yesterday, Mr. Kinch said in answer to a question:

"It isn't just the parking problem — we don't go back to work until we get everything we've been asking for."

The employes, meeting in the Livestock Auction Barn on south Ind. 37, gave a unanimous voice vote in response to a motion by Ronald Wickens, a University employe and union member, that "we hit the bricks at 4 a.m. tomorrow."

There was not a single dissenting voice.

When asked whether he would call the union's actions a strike, Mr. Kinch said:

"YOU HEARD THE VOTE. Call it a walkout, call it a holiday, call it what you want."

According to the Conditions for Co-operation with Employee Organizations, adopted by the Board of Trustees, the administration may refuse to negotiate with any employe group which asserts the right to strike.

The AFSCME, voting at a membership meeting, disavowed its right to strike earlier this year.

Mr. Ray said the Personnel Division "would communicate with the striking employes to urge them to return to work."

"We want them at work," he said.

But according to a statement made by the Board of Trustees "the University will not continue to employ any person who participates, threatens, or encourages any strike or work stoppage."

THE AFSCME has held a position of "formal recognition" — a status provided by the Trustees which entitles an employe organization to be heard on matters of interest to the staff. The union attained that status by virtue of representing at least 10 per cent of the regularly employed staff and by disavowing the right to strike.

Mr. Kinch, who was accompanied by three other union international representatives at the meeting, said that he had twice before dissuaded local members from striking, but that he felt that he could no longer do so.

"Both the local and I am fed up with the University's stalling," he said.

HE REFERRED to the union's unsuccessful attempt last month to gain permission for an election among staff members to give Local 832 exclusive recognition as the only bargaining unit for I.U. employes.

The Conditions for Co-operation state that such an election may be conducted among "all the regularly employed employes of the common campus."

AFSCME sought to have this interpreted as applying only to about 1,500 service and maintenance workers, among whom union support is stronger than among an equal number of clerical staff.

WHEN ADMINISTRATIVE and AFSCME representatives could not agree about the meaning of the statement, the issue was referred to the Board of Trustees, which is scheduled to meet April 21.

Wells named to group to review CIA funding

By LINDA CLARK
Daily Student Staff Writer

I.U. Chancellor Herman B Wells was named yesterday by President Johnson to an 18-member special committee headed by Secretary of State Dean Rusk to review Central Intelligence Agency (CIA) financing of schools and other groups.

The committee is a result of recommendations of a different committee headed by Under Secretary of State Nicholas Katzenbach. The Katzenbach group reviewed the problems in financing groups fighting Communist propaganda abroad.

The CIA's role in subsidizing the overseas activities of some student, labor, and other private American organizations was disclosed seven weeks ago. President Johnson then ordered a halt to CIA financing of the National Student Association (NSA) and appointed the Katzenbach committee.

THE COMMITTEE on which Chancellor Wells will be a member will have several basic problems to resolve.

It must decide how to keep private and voluntary institutions free from government direction so there will be no question in foreign countries that the organizations are free. And it must be decided how Congress, which presumably will openly appropriate funds for the program, can retain some rule over government money.

The NSA sought funds from the CIA in the early 1950's, the Katzenbach committee reported, because as a leftist — though anti-Communist group—it could not get the money from other sources during the prevailing political climate of the period.

More recently, the report concluded, the American public ". . . has become increasingly aware of the importance of the complex forms of international competition between free societies and Communist states . . . Hence, it is increasingly necessary for organizations like NSA to seek support for overseas activities from open sources."

DR. KATZENBACH and the members of his committee, John Gardner, Secretary of Health, Education, and Welfare, and Richard Helms, CIA director, recommended that some sort of mechanism should be set up to openly provide federal funds for overseas operations of private organizations deserving public support.

The Katzenback committee made two recommendations, both of which were accepted by President Johnson.

The committee recommended a new policy under which "no Federal agency shall provide any covert financial assistance or support, direct or indirect, to any of the nation's educational or private organizations."

OBUS may become permanent lobby

Operation Ballot Box for University Students (OBUS) may become a permanent lobby for students as a result of a bill Student Body President Dean Aulick, senior, introduced in the Student Senate last night.

Mr. Aulick's bill proposes reorganizing and renaming the OBUS structure. After OBUS is revamped it would be known as Indiana Student Governments (ISG) and would serve as a state-wide forum for common problems of student governments.

As stated in Mr. Aulick's bill, the ISG would have two major purposes. It would further student rights through a state-wide educational program showing that students are responsible citizens. One goal of this program is lowering the legal voting age.

THE SECOND purpose would be to create a semi-annual forum to discuss typical student problems and work for solutions.

Today —

—on the campus—

HILLEL FOUNDATION — Shabbat Service, 7:30 p.m., Oneg Shabbat — Fireside Readings from Franz Kafka, read by Hillel Barzel, 9 p.m., 1515 East 10th street.

COSMOPOLITAN CLUB — International Center, 8 p.m.

I.U. PHILHARMONIC ORCHESTRA CONCERT — Tibor Kozma, conductor, I.U. Auditorium, 8 p.m.

KIVA PROGRAM — Union, 8:30 p.m.

Right, P0079135, IU Archives.

Top-ranked USC Trojans shake Hoosiers' rosy dream

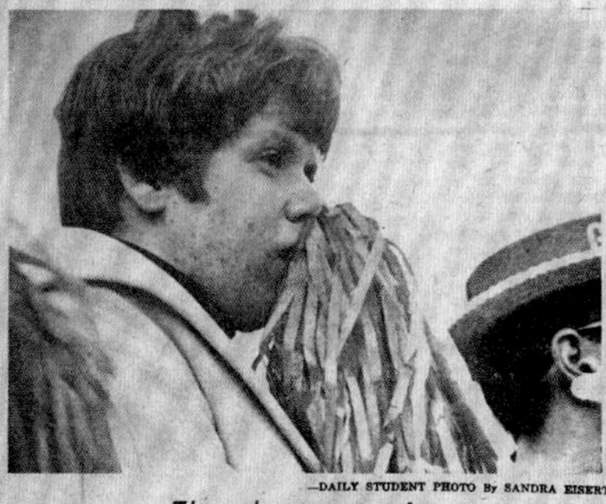

—DAILY STUDENT PHOTO By SANDRA EISERT

There he goes again

IT WAS A DISTRESSING DAY for I.U. fans, like this one, who watched O. J. Simpson score two touchdowns in USC's 14-3 victory over the Hoosiers.

By RICK ROTH
Daily Student Sports Editor

PASADENA, Calif. — The University of Southern California is to Indiana what Wellington was to warfare, what Brutus was to Caesar, what Roger Maris is to baseball, and what Gene Tunney was to boxing. Southern California is a myth destroyer.

The top-ranked Trojans shook Indiana out of its impossible dream here Monday afternoon, 14-3, before a record crowd of Hoosier dreamers.

Nearly everyone, including many residents of this smoggy Southern California city, was disappointed — but not surprised — as the Trojans toppled the Hoosiers in the greatest of all collegiate football contests — the Rose Bowl.

INDIANA'S STINGY DEFENSIVE unit did its share in holding the No. 1 ranked Trojans to only two touchdowns — the least number they've tallied in victory this year — but many little mistakes kept the Indiana offensive unit from touchdown ground.

Southern Cal's great defense had much to do with that too. It was the first time this year that Indiana was shutout in the touchdown department.

The Hoosiers gained only 79 net yards rushing against the Trojans, but still penetrated close to the goal line on several occasions.

A dropped pass in the end zone, the failure to pick up one foot in two tries, a couple of penalties, and a two outstanding Southern California defensive backs were the reasons that Indiana failed to tally a touchdown.

The reason that Southern Cal scored its two touchdowns was a man named Orenthal James Simpson.

O.J. WHO? turned out to be O.J., whew! as he rolled up 128 yards in 25 carries and scored both Trojan touchdowns against the Hoosiers. Another 45 yards that Simpson collected were nullified by USC penalties on an afternoon when the Helms Foundation selected him as Rose Bowl Player of the Year.

A record crowd of 102,946 reported to the Rose Bowl in shirt-sleeve weather, and most of them went away believers. Most of them also went away with some idea of how Indiana knocked off nine of ten opponents and won a Big Ten co-championship.

Southern California took the ball 84 yards in 13 plays the first time it got the ball and tallied seven points as Simpson rammed it over from the two.

The Trojans had the ball two more times in the first quarter, but Indiana's defense rose up and stopped the touchdown bids.

The second time USC had the ball, it marched down to the Indiana two yard line before fullback Dan Scott fumbled and Indiana's Mike Baughman recovered the ball in the end zone.

THE HOOSIERS were unable to cross the 50-yard-line in the opening stanza.

When the second quarter opened, Indiana took the ball away from Southern California on downs as Simpson was stopped for no gain on a fourth-and-inches situation.

The Hoosiers then marched to the USC 29-yard-line before the Trojan pass defense stopped the drive.

Southern California then lost six yards in three plays against the Hoosier defense and had to punt.

The punt went to Indiana quarterback Harry Gonso at the 39-yard-line, and he returned it to USC's 35 on a fine broken-field running exhibition.

The Hoosiers then marched to the Trojans' eight-yard-line, but a bread-basket pass to Al Gage in the end zone got away and Dave Kornowa had to salvage three points for Indiana on a field goal from the 17.

THE SCORE WAS 7-3 at the half, and Indiana, still tight and nervous about the game, had surprised viewers across the nation. The stage seemed to be set for another of the patented finishes.

But Indiana was in poor field position both times it got the ball in the third canto, unable to cross the mid-field stripe.

USC, meanwhile, marched 66 yards and Simpson upped the Trojans' lead to 14-3, the final score, with a seven-yard scissors step.

As the fourth quarter dawned, everyone knew that it was time for Indiana's get-'em-at-the-pass routine. And, the Hoosiers drove to the USC 37-yard-line in the opening minutes of the quarter, but a momentary injury stopped the drive.

Gonso ran over his left tackle on a second and two situation ,and, besides coming up only inches short of the first down, came up with a muscle spasm in his leg.

Gonso's understudy, junior Mike Perry, was unable to engineer the inches in two additional plays against the rugged Trojan defenders and the Hoosiers went back to the defense.

THE DEFENDERS held Southern Cal to a minus one yard in three plays this time, and again the host school had to punt. This time, Indiana went from its own 22-yard-line to Southern Cal's 19 before the drive was stopped.

With third and one on the 19, Gonso rammed up the middle for three yards and an apparent first down, but an illegal procedure penalty nullified the play. Gonso then flipped a pass to flanker Jade Butcher, but the officials ruled the Bloomington High School product out of bounds and it was fourth down and six to go for the Hoosiers.

Gonso was then nailed for a ten-yard loss as he faded back to pass. The drive was over and so was the dream as USC took the ball and moved it to the Indiana 37-yard-line before punting the ball into the endzone.

LESS THAN A MINUTE remained, and Indiana could not move the ball.

There was lots of disappointment, particularly from the bookies who had installed USC as a solid two touchdown favorite to whip the Hoosiers.

Southern California Coach John McKay called it "as good a game as we've played all year," while Indiana fans knew that it wasn't as good a game as the Hoosiers have had.

After the game, Coach John Pont vowed that Indiana will return to this mountain-nestled city in two years. In fact, he "promised the players we'll be back."

The seniors went out with their heads held high and the sophomores went out of the stadium looking back — just as a reminder of what they have told themselves they'll see in two more years.

Indiana finished the season with a 9-2 record, the best overall mark in the Big Ten, and far better than the "maybe they'll win half" record that they were predicted to attain.

THE INDIANA DAILY STUDENT

COLD
Cloudy today with possible light snow. High today 18; low tonight 0 degrees. Tomorrow sunny and cold; high of 23.

VOL. XCVII—NO. 70 INDIANA UNIVERSITY THURSDAY, JANUARY 4, 1968. ERNIE PYLE HALL, BLOOMINGTON, INDIANA, 47401 10¢ Established 1867

'Rally of appreciation' greets most exciting college team

I.U.'s Rose Bowl football team returned last night from sunny California to chilly Indiana weather but a warm Hoosier welcome. Curt Simic, assistant director of the Indiana University Foundation, was master of ceremonies at a "rally of appreciation for the greatest and most exciting team in college football" last night in the new fieldhouse.

About 3,000 Big Red fans who greeted the team in the fieldhouse heard President Elvis J. Stahr vow that I.U.'s sesquicentennial anniversary in 1970 would be started off with the football team playing in the Rose Bowl.

Dr. Stahr said Rose Bowl tournament officials who had been sponsoring the event for decades had "never been so impressed by those on the gridiron and fans of any school in competition there as they were with I.U."

J. W. (BILL) ORWIG, athletic director, revealed his pleasure at seeing I.U. fans at the Rose Bowl still standing during the final 55 seconds of the game looking for a victory.

Applause followed a statement made by Rick Roth, sports editor of The Indiana Daily Student, who said, "It takes a great winner to be a good loser — Indiana is a great winner."

Mr. Simic recognized the Marching 100, which was not at the reception because they hadn't returned to Bloomington yet, the pom pon girls, the cheerleaders, and the Student Athletic Board for their help in boosting student spirit this year.

He then introduced Chancellor Herman B Wells who received a standing ovation. "The team not only won respect from Southern California but it won the hearts of Americans from coast to coast," Dr. Wells stated. He seconded Dr. Stahr's vow to return to the Rose Bowl in 1970.

Bob Russell, a senior guard on the team expressed his feelings on the Rose Bowl. One of the greatest thrills for him was running from the dressing room while the Marching 100 was playing "Indiana" and looking into the west stand and seeing a "sea of red and white pom pon shakers."

Mr. Simic introduced Coach John Pont as the greatest coach of all time. Coach Pont called the I.U. fans "the finest people in the world." He introduced the senior members of the squad, mentioning Captain Doug Crusan, Gary Cassells and Ken Kaczmarek who were not present because they were practicing for other bowl games.

He added that he was not sure if the vow of President Stahr and Chancellor Wells was an order or a request but that he would fulfill it.

Following the introduction of Dr. Edwin H. Cady, Big Ten Faculty Representative, the cheerleaders led the crowd in the school song to end the reception.

State Budget makers reject finance plan

The State Budget Committee turned down a plan for financing a $9.2 million expansion of the joint I.U.-Purdue campus at Fort Wayne, and a $400,000 land acquisition program in Bloomington, in December.

The plan called for expansion of the Fort Wayne campus through a joint I.U.-Purdue foundation that would lease the facilities to the university.

"This means that we'll just have to re-examine the project and work out some other type of financing that would be acceptable," I.U. Business Manager Donald Clark told Bloomington Herald-Telephone reporters.

BUILT IN 1963 by the joint I.U.-Purdue Foundation, the Fort Wayne Center Building was financed by the same arrangement proposed for the expansion, Mr. Clark said. Cost of the building was $5,600,000. However, the universities had no bonding limit imposed by the legislature at that time.

The 1967 Legislature has set the bonding authority for each university. I.U. was authorized $4,262,000 and Purdue $4,975,000.

The land-acquisition program was primarily one of long-range projects, Mr. Clark said.

"WE ARE WORKING on locating a couple of buildings at the moment that could involve some land purchases. I assume we will go back with requests on specific parcels," Mr. Clark said.

By turning down the foundation financing plan, the Budget Committee said, the universities' bonding authority could be used on other projects, committing more student fees to debt retirement.

The intended campus expansion included classroom, laboratory, and office space.

IN INDIANAPOLIS, I.U. plans to remodel parts of the Medical Center, including new elevators, ceilings, and other repairs, for a total of $264,200, were okayed by the Budget Committee.

Harried Hoosiers drop trio

Indiana's basketball balloon went up and came back down during the holidays as the Harryin' Hoosiers suffered their first three losses of the season.

The Hoosiers will return home Saturday to start the Big Ten season against Minnesota after a grueling five-game road trip.

Indiana won the first two games of the trip, defeating North Carolina State in an overtime and clipping Notre Dame. The former moved the Hoosiers into fifth place in the national ranking and the latter moved I.U. up to third.

BUT, THEN, the Hoosiers went into a slump.

Favored to win the Dallas All Sports Classic, Indiana was clobbered in the opening round by Western Kentucky, 110-91, and finished last in the four-team field the following night with a loss to previously winless Southern Methodist, 91-84.

Tuesday night, the Hoosiers traveled to Detroit and took it on the chin again, 99-93.

Indiana is now 6-3, and listed among the also-rans in the national polls.

Indiana Coach Lou Watson called his charges' performance in the last three games "sluggish, listless, and flat."

"We got zoned for the first time down at Dallas," said Watson, "and we couldn't hit from the outside. Then we got behind and had to start playing catch-up basketball."

When the Hoosiers started playing catch-up, they started fouling and that cost them points and players.

INDIANA OUT-SCORED all three opponents from the field, but the foul line tally tipped the scale against the Hoosiers.

Joe Cooke, the sophomore guard, scored 30 points against SMU and 20 against Detroit, while Earl Schneider, the junior forward had his best game with a 20 point effort.

Sophomore Ken Johnson led all Indiana scorers against Western Kentucky, getting 19.

Watson says that his Hoosiers "seem to be tired." They took the day off yesterday and will have only light dress rehearsals for Minnesota today and tomorrow.

"We're just not hitting from out," was Watson's comment. He noted that senior sparkplug Vernon Payne has been good only on 11 of 44 shots from the field.

Harry (Butch) Joyner returned to the Indiana lineup at Detroit Tuesday night, and tossed in 14 points in a good comeback effort. He will start Saturday against the Gophers.

Watson says that Western Kentucky was the "finest, fastest, best-shooting ball club we've faced all year."

SOUTHERN METHODIST, according to Watson, was "just a hungry ball club that had been coming close to winning all year but hadn't quite got the job done."

"We just broke down again at Detroit," said Watson. "Both defensively and offensively we were flat, we just weren't ourselves."

Watson says of the three straight zone defenses the Hoosiers have faced that "the way to break them is to fast-break them."

But, he noted, "we're not getting out from the basket fast enough." And, Indiana is noted as having one of the physically fastest teams in the country.

"Winning Saturday will be tough for us now," said Watson, "but I haven't got my chin down on these kids yet."

The Hoosiers need to win Saturday to get off to a good start in the defense of their Big Ten basketball co-championship.

"We need to win a game now in which we hit the basket," said Watson. "Other than hitting, there's nothing we can do now. We're not going to change a thing. Joyner will be in there starting Saturday, and I just hope we can bounce back."

Spectator vacates quonset; Sutton and ax prompt move

Joseph L. Sutton, Dean of Faculties, walked into the office of the Spectator with an ax Dec. 20, and offered to help the newspaper vacate the building.

Dean Sutton explained the ax when he said, "The editor told me there were some pieces of furniture too large to get out the door. I told him I'd shorten them if I could."

Although Dean Sutton did not use the ax, the Spectator left the quonset hut near the I.U. ticket office. That afternoon the furniture and equipment were on the lawn outside the office.

The ouster ended a dispute between the paper and University officials concerning the use of University office space. The non-registration policy, instituted this fall by the University, provides for the use of University space only for organizations that are connected with a University department.

The Spectator editor, James R. Retherford, was informed that the paper could use the space only if it was sponsored by a department. The Spectator was unable to find a sponsor and Mr. Retherford was informed that the paper must vacate the quonset hut.

"I talked to those people on Dec. 5 and they agreed to move out in 15 days," Dean Sutton said. "I told them they better or I would move them out personally."

Mr. Retherford, who was not present for the moving, is under federal grand jury indictment on two counts of refusing to report for induction to the armed forces.

Today —

—on the campus—

FRENCH COFFEE HOUR — 1:30-3 p.m., Ballantine 004.
VICTORIAN STUDIES PROGRAM — Christopher Ricks, Oxford University, "Tennyson: The Passion of the Past," 4 p.m., Ballantine 013.
SAILING CLUB — 7 p.m., Ballantine 013.
IMU DUPLICATE BRIDGE — 7 p.m., Kiva, Union.
CONVOCATION — Film Lecture, Willis Butler, "Holiday in Holland," 7:15 p.m., I.U. Auditorium.
MAHLON POWELL LECTURE SERIES — sponsored by the Department of Philosophy, Paul Ziff, University of Wisconsin, "Understanding," 8 p.m., Ballantine 109.
FACULTY RECITAL — Harry Houdeshel, flute, and Walter Bricht, piano, 8:30 p.m., Recital Hall, Music.
CAMPUS CRUSADE FOR CHRIST — 9 p.m., Bryan Room, Union.

Missing staff delays Rose Bowl coverage

Lost: one campus editor, one photo editor, and numerous reporters.

The Indiana Daily Student today will not present "complete" coverage of the annual Rose Bowl classic.

We really wanted to, but we "lost" some of our personnel coming home. We hope to "find" them by tomorrow.

Actually, Margaret Craig, junior, campus editor, and John Fulton, junior, photo editor, are somewhere over the United States between Los Angeles and Indianapolis jetting home.

They called The Daily Student yesterday afternoon from Los Angeles and assured us they'll be here sometime today.

Tomorrow morning The Daily Student will complete its coverage of the Rose Bowl including, we hope, a two page picture spread. That is, if we find Miss Craig and Mr. Fulton before press time.

Just a hoax

Bomb scare delays flight with Rose Bowl tour group for five hours.

A bomb scare temporarily held up a tour flight which was scheduled to leave at 5 p.m. Tuesday from Long Beach.

The plane had been delayed for repairs about five hours after its scheduled take-off time, when a student from a group waiting for the plane shouted that there was a bomb on the plane, Hugh Hazelrigg of the I.U. News Bureau said.

The FBI was called in, as they are in all bomb scares. They asked the student who made the statement to identify himself, which he did. He admitted that it was just a hoax, Mr. Hazelrigg said.

However the plane and all the luggage had to be searched as a precaution. The search took about 2 hours. The plane took off about 12:19 a.m. this morning and arrived in Indianapolis at 7 a.m.

The FBI did not release the student's name, and he was allowed to return to Indianapolis on his flight. The Dean of Students office said they did not know if any disciplinary action would be taken against the student.

A false bomb scare is a federal offense and subject to federal prosecution, Mr. Hazelrigg said this does not mean the student will necessarily be prosecuted.

—DAILY STUDENT PHOTO By FESTUS OKE

The winner

COACH JOHN PONT addressed the crowd at the reception in the New Fieldhouse last night, and it was clear that I.U.'s fans consider him a winner all the way.

—DAILY STUDENT PHOTO By FESTUS OKE

It has begun!

WORK HAS STARTED on I.U.'s Assembly Hall on 17th street. Earth-moving equipment is first in line, making preparations for the foundations for the giant structure. The beginnings are being made between the New Fieldhouse and the New Stadium.

P0079401, IU Archives.

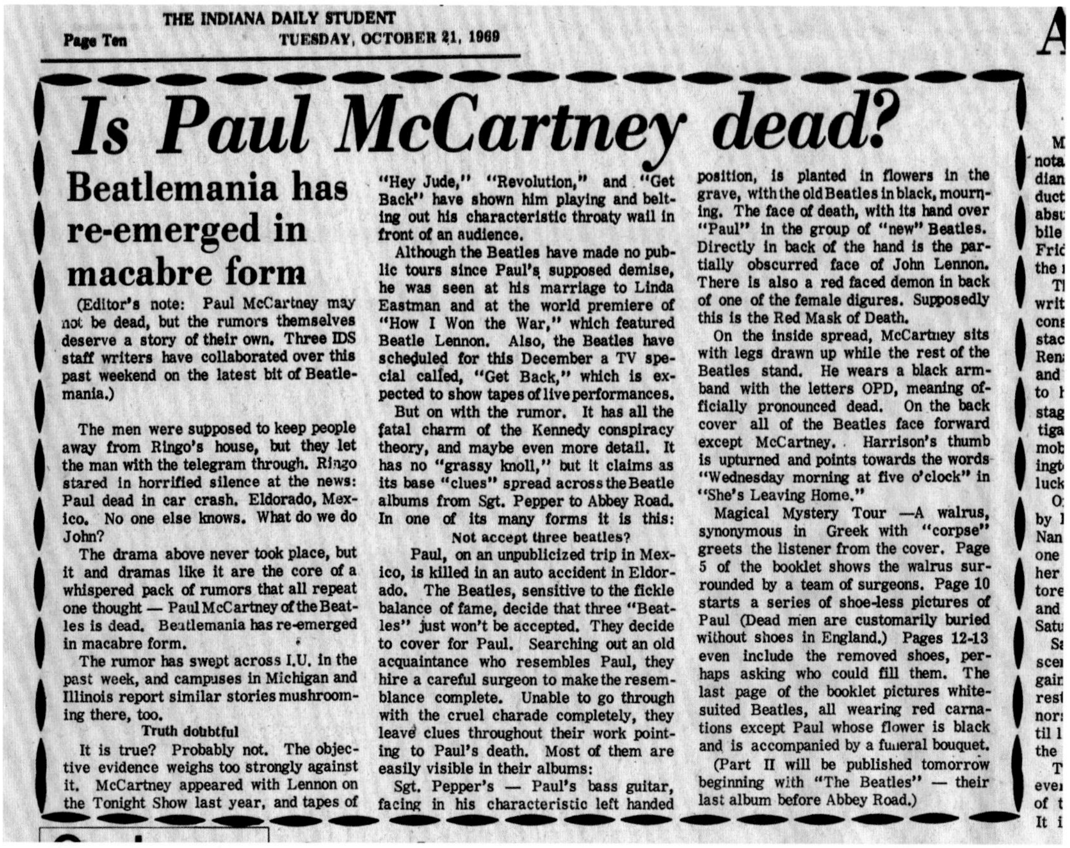

THE INDIANA DAILY STUDENT

Page Ten — TUESDAY, OCTOBER 21, 1969

Is Paul McCartney dead?

Beatlemania has re-emerged in macabre form

(Editor's note: Paul McCartney may not be dead, but the rumors themselves deserve a story of their own. Three IDS staff writers have collaborated over this past weekend on the latest bit of Beatlemania.)

The men were supposed to keep people away from Ringo's house, but they let the man with the telegram through. Ringo stared in horrified silence at the news: Paul dead in car crash. Eldorado, Mexico. No one else knows. What do we do John?

The drama above never took place, but it and dramas like it are the core of a whispered pack of rumors that all repeat one thought — Paul McCartney of the Beatles is dead. Beatlemania has re-emerged in macabre form.

The rumor has swept across I.U. in the past week, and campuses in Michigan and Illinois report similar stories mushrooming there, too.

Truth doubtful

It is true? Probably not. The objective evidence weighs too strongly against it. McCartney appeared with Lennon on the Tonight Show last year, and tapes of "Hey Jude," "Revolution," and "Get Back" have shown him playing and belting out his characteristic throaty wail in front of an audience.

Although the Beatles have made no public tours since Paul's supposed demise, he was seen at his marriage to Linda Eastman and at the world premiere of "How I Won the War," which featured Beatle Lennon. Also, the Beatles have scheduled for this December a TV special called, "Get Back," which is expected to show tapes of live performances.

But on with the rumor. It has all the fatal charm of the Kennedy conspiracy theory, and maybe even more detail. It has no "grassy knoll," but it claims as its base "clues" spread across the Beatle albums from Sgt. Pepper to Abbey Road. In one of its many forms it is this:

Not accept three beatles?

Paul, on an unpublicized trip in Mexico, is killed in an auto accident in Eldorado. The Beatles, sensitive to the fickle balance of fame, decide that three "Beatles" just won't be accepted. They decide to cover for Paul. Searching out an old acquaintance who resembles Paul, they hire a careful surgeon to make the resemblance complete. Unable to go through with the cruel charade completely, they leave clues throughout their work pointing to Paul's death. Most of them are easily visible in their albums:

Sgt. Pepper's — Paul's bass guitar, facing in his characteristic left handed position, is planted in flowers in the grave, with the old Beatles in black, mourning. The face of death, with its hand over "Paul" in the group of "new" Beatles. Directly in back of the hand is the partially obscurred face of John Lennon. There is also a red faced demon in back of one of the female digures. Supposedly this is the Red Mask of Death.

On the inside spread, McCartney sits with legs drawn up while the rest of the Beatles stand. He wears a black armband with the letters OPD, meaning officially pronounced dead. On the back cover all of the Beatles face forward except McCartney. Harrison's thumb is upturned and points towards the words "Wednesday morning at five o'clock" in "She's Leaving Home."

Magical Mystery Tour —A walrus, synonymous in Greek with "corpse" greets the listener from the cover. Page 5 of the booklet shows the walrus surrounded by a team of surgeons. Page 10 starts a series of shoe-less pictures of Paul (Dead men are customarily buried without shoes in England.) Pages 12-13 even include the removed shoes, perhaps asking who could fill them. The last page of the booklet pictures white-suited Beatles, all wearing red carnations except Paul whose flower is black and is accompanied by a funeral bouquet.

(Part II will be published tomorrow beginning with "The Beatles" — their last album before Abbey Road.)

A clip from the October 21, 1969, edition of the IDS. *P0080189, IU Archives.*

REFLECTION

From Bloomington to Abbey Road

Rumors about the death of the Beatles' Paul McCartney, inspired by the Abbey Road and Sergeant Pepper album covers, were rampant in the late '60s. I believe it was the fall of 1969 when a few of us at the Daily Student sat around the newsroom at Ernie Pyle Hall and discussed whether these rumors were true.

I suggested that we send a telegram to Apple Records to simply point-blank ask the question. "They have to answer us," was my belief. The telegram was sent, and we were sure there would be a reply the next day. No reply was ever sent.

More than 30 years later, I was waiting for an elevator at Tribune Tower in Chicago when a reporter asked me, "Did you go to Indiana?" When I answered yes, he said, "It must be you!"

He was referring to a telegram published in "The Beatles Anthology," which had just been released. Sure enough, there was the telegram (in difficult-to-read reverse type) on page 341. I couldn't believe that Apple had stashed that telegram away in its archives.

I never had seen the telegram, which was signed, "Alan Sutton, Indiana Daily Student, Bloomington, Ind." My final words are evidence of a college journalist's confidence (hubris?). "Urgent reply requested."

Tribune columnist Mary Schmich had fun with this in a Jan. 14, 2001, column titled, "Writings from the past live on—much like Paul McCartney."

—Alan Sutton, BA 1970, wrote this recollection in 2011 for the 100th anniversary of the journalism school.

Kennedy Asks That Indianapolis Crowd Pray For King Family

On April 4, 1968, U.S. Sen. Robert Kennedy was in Indianapolis, campaigning for the Democratic nomination for president. That evening, after news broke that Martin Luther King Jr. was killed in Memphis, Kennedy addressed a crowd with an impromptu speech that is remembered as one of his best of the campaign. This story, reported from Indianapolis, originally appeared April 5, 1968. A number of Kennedy's words are misquoted in this early report.

By Jerry Hicks

INDIANAPOLIS — With tears streaming down his cheeks, Sen. Robert F. Kennedy (D-N.Y.) asked the people at a rally for him last night to say a prayer for the family of Dr. Martin Luther King, "and for our nation."

Dr. King was shot and killed last night in front of his motel in Memphis, Tenn., 90 minutes before the senator's speech.

Sen. Kennedy told a crowd of about 3,000 persons, half of them Negroes, "for those of you who feel hatred, violence, and revenge, I can sympathize with your bitterness because I had a member of my family shot. He, too, was shot by a white man."

Screams came from the audience when Sen. Kennedy announced Dr. King's death. "What we need is not a division of the races with hatred and violence, but love, wisdom, and compassion for one another as Dr. King understood, whether they be black or white."

Sen. Kennedy said that this is not an end to the violence, but that "the majority of whites and blacks of this country want to live together, want justice for all human beings, in all our lands."

With quavering voice, Sen. Kennedy asked that persons put down signs supporting his campaign while he made his remarks. Sen. Kennedy said at Weir Cook Airport preceding the address, "He (Dr. King) dedicated himself to justice, and love between fellow human beings. He gave his life to that principle. I think it is up to us, his fellow citizens, and public officials to follow that dream, to try to end the divisions so deeply rooted in our country, and remove the stain of bloodshed from our land."

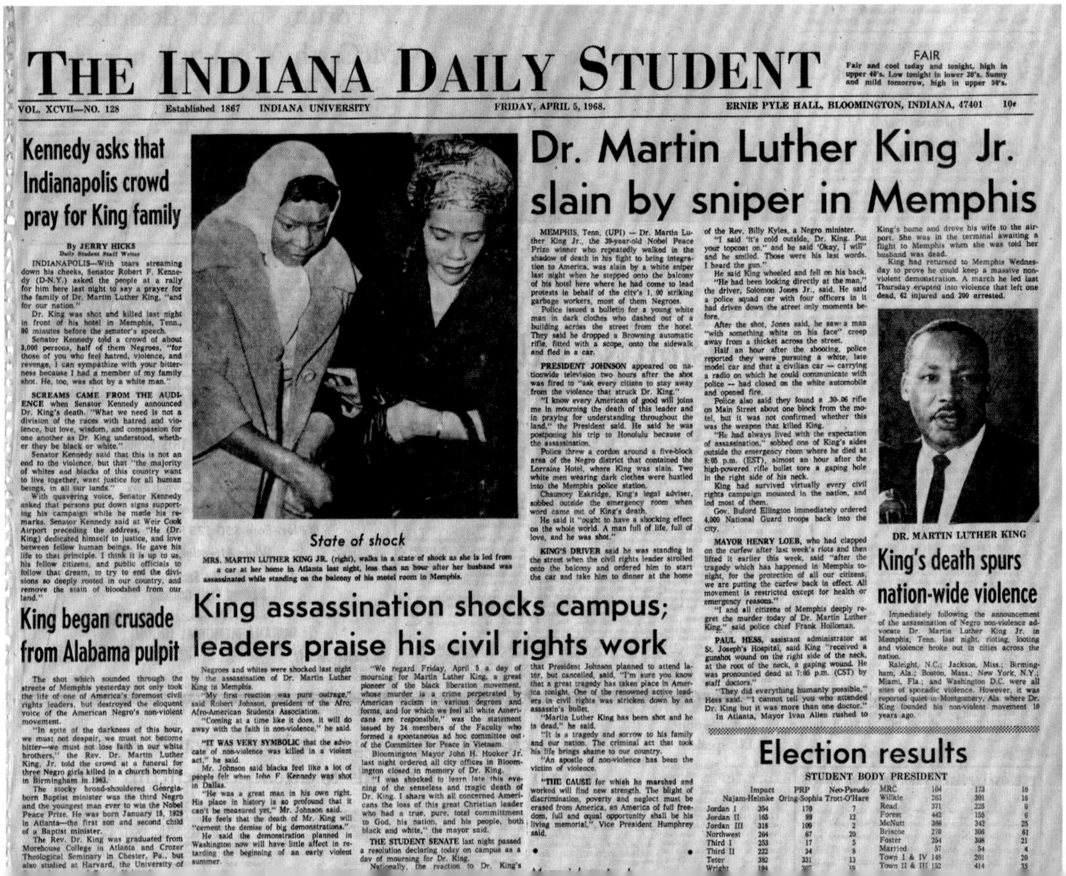

THE INDIANA DAILY STUDENT

FAIR
Fair and cool today and tonight, high in upper 40's. Low tonight in lower 30's. Sunny and mild tomorrow, high in upper 50's.

VOL. XCVII—NO. 128 Established 1867 INDIANA UNIVERSITY FRIDAY, APRIL 5, 1968. ERNIE PYLE HALL, BLOOMINGTON, INDIANA, 47401 10¢

Kennedy asks that Indianapolis crowd pray for King family

By JERRY HICKS
Daily Student Staff Writer

INDIANAPOLIS—With tears streaming down his cheeks, Senator Robert F. Kennedy (D-N.Y.) asked the people at a rally for him here last night to say a prayer for the family of Dr. Martin Luther King, "and for our nation."

Dr. King was shot and killed last night in front of his hotel in Memphis, Tenn., 90 minutes before the senator's speech.

Senator Kennedy told a crowd of about 3,000 persons, half of them Negroes, "for those of you who feel hatred, violence, and revenge, I can sympathize with your bitterness because I had a member of my family shot. He, too, was shot by a white man."

SCREAMS CAME FROM THE AUDIENCE when Senator Kennedy announced Dr. King's death. "What we need is not a division of the races with hatred and violence, but love, wisdom, and compassion for one another as Dr. King understood, whether they be black or white."

Senator Kennedy said that this is not an end to the violence, but that "the majority of whites and blacks of this country want to live together, want justice for all human beings, in all our lands."

With quavering voice, Senator Kennedy asked that persons put down signs supporting his campaign while he made his remarks. Senator Kennedy said at Weir Cook Airport preceding the address, "He (Dr. King) dedicated himself to justice, and love between fellow human beings. He gave his life to that principle. I think it is up to us, his fellow citizens, and public officials to follow that dream, to try to end the divisions so deeply rooted in our country, and remove the stain of bloodshed from our land."

State of shock

MRS. MARTIN LUTHER KING JR. (right), walks in a state of shock as she is led from a car at her home in Atlanta last night, less than an hour after her husband was assassinated while standing on the balcony of his motel room in Memphis.

Dr. Martin Luther King Jr. slain by sniper in Memphis

MEMPHIS, Tenn. (UPI) — Dr. Martin Luther King Jr., the 39-year-old Nobel Peace Prize winner who repeatedly walked in the shadow of death in his fight to bring integration to America, was slain by a white sniper last night when he stepped onto the balcony of his hotel here where he had come to lead protests in behalf of the city's 1, 00 striking garbage workers, most of them Negroes.

Police issued a bulletin for a young white man in dark clothes who dashed out of a building across the street from the hotel. They said he dropped a Browning automatic rifle, fitted with a scope, onto the sidewalk and fled in a car.

PRESIDENT JOHNSON appeared on nationwide television two hours after the shot was fired to "ask every citizen to stay away from the violence that struck Dr. King."

"I know every American of good will joins me in mourning the death of this leader and in praying for understanding throughout the land," the President said. He said he was postponing his trip to Honolulu because of the assassination.

Police threw a cordon around a five-block area of the Negro district that contained the Lorraine Hotel, where King was slain. Two white men wearing dark clothes were hustled into the Memphis police station.

Chauncey Eskridge, King's legal adviser, sobbed outside the emergency room when word came out of King's death.

He said it "ought to have a shocking effect on the whole world. A man full of life, full of love, and he was shot."

KING'S DRIVER said he was standing in the street when the civil rights leader strolled onto the balcony and ordered him to start the car and take him to dinner at the home of the Rev. Billy Kyles, a Negro minister.

"I said 'it's cold outside, Dr. King. Put your topcoat on,' and he said 'Okay, I will' and he smiled. Those were his last words. I heard the gun."

He said King wheeled and fell on his back.

"He had been looking directly at the man," the driver, Solomon Jones Jr., said. He said a police squad car with four officers in it had driven down the street only moments before.

After the shot, Jones said, he saw a man "with something white on his face" creep away from a thicket across the street.

Half an hour after the shooting, police reported they were pursuing a white, late model car and that a civilian car — carrying a radio on which he could communicate with police — had closed on the white automobile and opened fire.

Police also said they found a .30-.06 rifle on Main Street about one block from the motel, but it was not confirmed whether this was the weapon that killed King.

"He had always lived with the expectation of assassination," sobbed one of King's aides outside the emergency room where he died at 8:05 p.m. (EST), almost an hour after the high-powered rifle bullet tore a gaping hole in the right side of his neck.

King had survived virtually every civil rights campaign mounted in the nation, and led most of them.

Gov. Buford Ellington immediately ordered 4,000 National Guard troops back into the city.

MAYOR HENRY LOEB, who had clapped on the curfew after last week's riots and then lifted it earlier this week, said "after the tragedy which has happened in Memphis tonight, for the protection of all our citizens, we are putting the curfew back in effect. All movement is restricted except for health or emergency reasons."

"I and all citizens of Memphis deeply regret the murder today of Dr. Martin Luther King," said police chief Frank Holloman.

PAUL HESS, assistant administrator at St. Joseph's Hospital, said King "received a gunshot wound on the right side of the neck, at the root of the neck, a gaping wound. He was pronounced dead at 7:05 p.m. (CST) by staff doctors."

"They did everything humanly possible," Hess said. "I cannot tell you who attended Dr. King but it was more than one doctor."

In Atlanta, Mayor Ivan Allen rushed to King's home and drove his wife to the airport. She was in the terminal awaiting a flight to Memphis when she was told her husband was dead.

King had returned to Memphis Wednesday to prove he could keep a massive non-violent demonstration. A march he led last Thursday erupted into violence that left one dead, 62 injured and 200 arrested.

DR. MARTIN LUTHER KING

King's death spurs nation-wide violence

Immediately following the announcement of the assassination of Negro non-violence advocate Dr. Martin Luther King Jr. in Memphis, Tenn. last night, rioting, looting and violence broke out in cities across the nation.

Raleight, N.C.; Jackson, Miss.; Birmingham, Ala.; Boston, Mass.; New York, N.Y.; Miami, Fla.; and Washington D.C. were all sites of sporadic violence. However, it was reported quiet in Montgomery, Ala. where Dr. King founded his non-violent movement 10 years ago.

King began crusade from Alabama pulpit

The shot which sounded through the streets of Memphis yesterday not only took the life of one of America's foremost civil rights leaders, but destroyed the eloquent voice of the American Negro's non-violent movement.

"In spite of the darkness of this hour, we must not despair, we must not become bitter—we must not lose faith in our white brothers," the Rev. Dr. Martin Luther King, Jr. told the crowd at a funeral for three Negro girls killed in a church bombing in Birmingham in 1963.

The stocky broad-shouldered Géorgia-born Baptist minister was the third Negro and the youngest man ever to win the Nobel Peace Prize. He was born January 15, 1929 in Atlanta—the first son and second child of a Baptist minister.

The Rev. Dr. King was graduated from Morehouse College in Atlanta and Crozer Theological Seminary in Chester, Pa., but also studied at Harvard, the University of

King assassination shocks campus; leaders praise his civil rights work

Negroes and whites were shocked last night by the assassination of Dr. Martin Luther King in Memphis.

"My first reaction was pure outrage," said Robert Johnson, president of the Afro, Afro-American Students Association.

"Coming at a time like it does, it will do away with the faith in non-violence," he said.

"IT WAS VERY SYMBOLIC that the advocate of non-violence was killed in a violent act," he said.

Mr. Johnson said blacks feel like a lot of people felt when John F. Kennedy was shot in Dallas.

"He was a great man in his own right. His place in history is so profound that it can't be measured yet," Mr. Johnson said.

He feels that the death of Mr. King will "cement the demise of big demonstrations."

He said the demonstration planned in Washington now will have little affect in retarding the beginning of an early violent summer.

"We regard Friday, April 5 a day of mourning for Martin Luther King, a great pioneer of the black liberation movement, whose murder is a crime perpetrated by American racism in various degrees and forms, and for which we feel all white Americans are responsible," was the statement issued by 24 members of the Faculty who formed a spontaneous ad hoc committee out of the Committee for Peace in Vietnam.

Bloomington Mayor John H. Hooker Jr. last night ordered all city offices in Bloomington closed in memory of Dr. King.

"I was shocked to learn late this evening of the senseless and tragic death of Dr. King. I share with all concerned Americans the loss of this great Christian leader who had a true, pure, total committment to God, his nation, and his people, both black and white," the mayor said.

THE STUDENT SENATE last night passed a resolution declaring today on campus as a day of mourning for Dr. King.

Nationally, the reaction to Dr. King's death that President Johnson planned to attend later, but cancelled, said, "I'm sure you know that a great tragedy has taken place in America tonight. One of the renowned active leaders in civil rights was stricken down by an assassin's bullet.

"Martin Luther King has been shot and he is dead," he said.

"It is a tragedy and sorrow to his family and our nation. The criminal act that took his life brings shame to our country.

"An apostle of non-violence has been the victim of violence.

"THE CAUSE for which he marched and worked will find new strength. The blight of discrimination, poverty and neglect must be erased from America, an America of full freedom, full and equal opportunity shall be his living memorial," Vice President Humphrey said.

Election results

STUDENT BODY PRESIDENT

	Impact Najam-Helmke	PRP Oring-Sophia	Neo-Pseudo Trott-O'Hare
Jordan I	354	170	7
Jordan II	165	99	12
Jordan III	318	109	2
Northwest	264	67	20
Third I	253	17	5
Third II	222	34	8
Teter	382	331	13
Wright	194	307	19
MRC	104	173	10
Willkie	263	301	16
Read	371	225	5
Forest	442	155	6
McNutt	366	342	25
Briscoe	270	306	61
Foster	254	308	21
Married	57	54	4
Town I & IV	148	201	20
Town II & III	152	414	35

P0078440, IU Archives.

April 25, 1968

THE INDIANA DAILY STUDENT

SLIGHTLY SUNNY
Mostly sunny and warmer Thursday. High 53-61; low 35-39. Little chance for rain today.

VOL. XCVII—NO. 136 Established 1867 INDIANA UNIVERSITY THURSDAY, APRIL 25, 1968. ERNIE PYLE HALL, BLOOMINGTON, INDIANA, 47401 10¢

—DAILY STUDENT PHOTO By JOHN HILLERY

Glad to meet you, Senator

STUDENTS YOUNG AND OLD gathered at the Bloomington Airport yesterday to greet Senator Robert F. Kennedy as he arrived here on his campaign tour for the May 7 primary. After spending most of the afternoon in Bloomington, Senator Kennedy continued through southern Indiana to Louisville late last night.

RFK suggests aid changes

By JERRY HICKS
Daily Student Staff Writer

Senator Robert F. Kennedy (D-N.Y.) told a capacity crowd in the Auditorium yesterday that the U.S. should not give more aid to a country threatened internally than that country is capable of using itself.

Senator Kennedy was in Bloomington for more than three hours yesterday, continuing his campaign for the Democratic nomination for President. He is entered on the May 7 Indiana primary.

Competitor Senator Eugene J. McCarthy spoke at the Auditorium last Thursday. The third candidate in the primary, Gov. Roger D. Branigin, will be in Bloomington Saturday.

Accompanying Senator Kennedy was Col. John Glenn, first astronaut to orbit the earth. Mrs. Ethel Kennedy, the Senator's wife, did not accompany him although she has been with him most of the Indiana campaign.

SENATOR KENNEDY made brief remarks at the Monroe County Airport and at the RCA plant. After his address in the Auditorium the senator went to the Poplars Midtown Motor Inn to speak to the Monroe County Democratic Women's Club, a gathering of his campaign workers, and a group of mothers of asthmatic children.

Speaking from a prepared text at the Auditorium, Senator Kennedy called the South Vietnam government corrupt and unstable.

He proposed that when the central interests of the U.S. are not directly threatened, "We should give no more assistance to a government against any internal threat than that government is capable of using itself, through its own agencies and instruments."

"WE CAN HELP them," he said, "but we cannot, and we should not, try to do their job for them."

The growing force in the world is not communism, nor capitalism but nationalism, Senator Kennedy said.

"Vietnam has proven that all the might and power of America cannot provide nor create a substitute for another government, or for the will of another people."

VIETNAM IS NOT THE LAST challenge the U.S. will face abroad, Senator Kennedy said, but "Vietnam is only Vietnam — it will not settle the fate of Asia, nor of America, much less the fate of the world."

The danger has not passed for the nations of Asia and Africa, he said. The governments of these nations are unstable and the U.S. should help these nations with their efforts.

"But we cannot continue, as we have too often, to identify the United States with the preservation of a particular internal order within those countries," he said.

On China, Senator Kennedy said the U.S. should maintain its vigilance until China's internal revolution runs its course. He called the Chinese record of instigating internal revolutions one of failure. Containment of Chinese expansion should principally come from Japan, India, Indonesia, Pakistan and the Soviet Union, he said.

Senator Kennedy's formal remarks were interrupted 12 times by applause.

DURING A QUESTION-answer period he brought mixed emotions when he called for abolishing college draft deferments.

He smiled after seeing his proposal was unpopular with half his college audience and asked "Would you like to know why I'm against college deferments?"

"The draft program we are pursuing is inequitable and unfair," he said. "The burden of the war is primarily on the poor." The war not only takes away from programs which would aid the poor, he said, but those in Vietnam are by and large poor people."

Col. Glenn brought applause when he said that young people are "through putting up with sham and hypocrisy."

He said he was encouraged by seeing youth participate in American politics.

"It's not who you are interested in but the fact you are interested," he said.

Floor governors told to start planning visitation policies

An administrative committee met yesterday in the office of John W. Snyder, Vice President and Dean for Undergraduate Development, to discuss the initiation of the new visitation policies.

Todd Kendall, president of Inter-Residence Halls Association, said he is telling floor governors to "start making plans now." Mr. Kendall said pending the approval by IRHA Presidents Council, which meets Sunday night at 9 p.m., the administrative committee has given the go ahead to plan for the new visitation policies.

Mr. Kendall said he was confident that the new policy would pass the Council.

THE ADMINISTRATIVE COMMITTEE that discussed the policy yesterday was comprised of Dean Snyder; Robert H. Shaffer, Dean of Students; Dr. Elizabeth Greenleaf, assistant dean of students and director of counseling activities in the residence halls; Herbert E. Smith, associate director of student affairs and director of fraternity affairs, and Mrs. Virginia Rogers, assistant dean of students.

Also, Todd Kendall; Jack Wickes, president of Inter-Fraternity Council; Ted Najam, Student Body President, and Anita Silvey, president of Pan Hellenic Council.

The program will be started on an experimental basis, said Mr. Kendall, with no ending date. He said he hopes it will be started procedurally by May 1.

The administrative committee gave Dean Shaffer the authority to stop visitation anytime something should go wrong.

DEAN SHAFFER told the IRHA he would consult with them before taking any action to stop visitation, if the need should arise.

The procedure the administrative committee released for obtaining approval of visitation policies for individual floors in the residence halls follows.

The unit will submit its plan to the Board of Governors of the residence hall. The governors will review the proposal for legality and vote on it. The president of the residence hall will then initial the proposal and send it to the Counselling and Activities office. There Dr. Greenleaf and Mr. Kendall will give the proposal final approval. If Dr. Greenleaf is not available to approve the proposal Thomas Hennesy, associate director of counseling and activities, will consider it in her place.

Kennedy's crowd warmer than day

By JERRY HICKS
Daily Student Staff Writer

The winds blew strongly yesterday and the temperature barely touched 50 degrees.

But the crowds turned out to greet Senator Robert F. Kennedy (D-N.Y.) who came to Bloomington in his campaign to win the May 7 Indiana presidential primary.

Stepping from his plane at noon yesterday, and running about half an hour behind schedule, he headed for the fence at the Monroe County Airport to greet local citizens and eight busloads of children from Grandview Elementary school.

He rode in an open car to the RCA plant on the south edge of Bloomington to speak to factory workers and college students who had followed him.

HE TRIED TO SHAKE as many hands as possible everywhere he went. When he reached the I.U. Auditorium where he was to give his main address, he stopped backstage to shake hands with several members of the faculty.

He waited quietly, scanning the Auditorium crowd, while he was being introduced. He spotted a newsman he knew who has been on the campaign trail with him. The newsman called out to him "Senator, your hair's a mess."

The Senator smiled and brushed the shock of hair out of his way.

HIS MAIN ADDRESS was of serious tone, but he delighted his audience with light remarks.

The Auditorium audience gave Col. John Glenn, former astronaut who was with Senator Kennedy, a burst of applause when he was introduced. Senator Kennedy afterward said that "I thought your appleause for Col. Glenn was much too long."

He said that 3000 buttons he had asked his brother, Senator Edward Kennedy (D-Mass.) to get for him with his picture on it came back with Edward's picture on it.

"I told him it was too late for him to enter the race. People would consider him ruthless," Senator Kennedy said.

The audience howled when he said that he had already been contacted by George Hamilton, movie actor who had dated Lynda Bird Johnson.

"HE CALLED to ask for my daughter's telephone number."

At the RCA plant Senator Kennedy told the crowd that he supported unions, but he was surprised to see the unfavorable reaction of the audience when he said he knew what the unions had done for Bloomington. He came back with, "Well, I know what they have done for this community."

When he saw his words still had not made a hit he said, "I know what they've done for Indiana, now how's that?"

One student booed him at the Auditorium when he called for an end to draft deferments.

"BOO YOURSELF," he said smiling.

At one point during his speech he received applause from a hesitant few.

"Well are you going to clap or aren't you?" he said smiling again.

After he had answered several questions following his address, I.U. officials stood up to end the questions and to thank the audience for coming. But Senator Kennedy shook his head and shoved his hands out for them to let him answer more questions, to the delight of his audience.

He continued handshaking at the Poplars Midtown Motor Inn after his speech.

Senator Kennedy left Bloomington about 3 p.m. to go on a seven city campaign tour in Southeastern Indiana for the rest of the day.

—DAILY STUDENT PHOTOS By JOHN FULTON

SENATOR KENNEDY'S hand motions varied as his speech ranged from international to domestic issues in an address at the I.U. Auditorium yesterday.

Estimated 60 faculty members to cancel classes for strike

"I wish I knew how many of my instructors were going to be gone Friday," said William Riley Parker, chairman of the English department, when asked how many faculty members in his department had called off classes because of the student-faculty strike.

The strike, sponsored by Committee to End the War in Vietnam (CEWV) is against the war in Vietnam. The Faculty Committee for Peace in Vietnam will participate in the strike, but no one seems to know just how many faculty members will actually be involved. Canceling of classes is being done on an individual basis.

DR. ROBERT KLAWITTER, assistant professor of English and a member of the faculty strike committee, said he was not sure how many in the department would be striking. But he said he expects at least 60 faculty members to strike and said many would be from the English department.

"The English department is still known for its radical professors," he said.

Mark Ritchey, grad., a teaching assistant in history, said more than 60 professors will strike.

"A lot of professors will not hold classes because many of them will not cross a picket line on principle," he said.

BYRUM E. CARTER, Dean of the College of Arts and Sciences, has urged department heads to see that classes are in session Friday.

Monroe Democratic Women hear gubernatorial hopeful

Richard C. Bodine, Indiana House minority leader and contender for the Democratic nomination for governor, was in Bloomington yesterday to address the Monroe County Democratic Women at their luncheon at the Poplars.

At the luncheon, he spoke briefly about the upcoming gubernatorial race and his candidacy. He suggested that the governor's election should be held in years other than presidential election years to focus attention on important state offices.

Before leaving Bloomington for Terre Haute, Mr. Bodine made an unscheduled stop at the I.U. Student Foundation House on 7th street to learn more about Little 500 events.

Mr. Bodine did his undergraduate work in business at I.U. and received a doctor of jurisprudence degree from the I.U. School of Law.

Earlier in the day Mr. Bodine addressed the Legislative Advisory Commission on Constitutional Revision at the State House in Indianapolis. At that time he also suggested that the governor be allowed to succeed himself for one term, and then be eligible to run again after four years.

He called for taking the right to preside over the State Senate away from the Lt. Governor, allowing the Senate to name its own leader.

'Choice 68' draws 9000 I.U. votes

One-third of the student body turned out yesterday to vote in "Choice 68," the first nation-wide mock presidential primary, Al Field, junior, Union Board president, said.

Co-sponsored by Time magazine and the Univac Division of Sperry Rand Corp., and locally by Union Board, the results of the nation-wide primary will be released to the news media during the first week in May. Mr. Field said, however, before the results are announced to the public by Time, individual schools will receive the results on how they voted in the election.

Although Mr. Field had no definite information on how the voting went here, he did say that "Kennedy's appearance today had a definite impact on "Choice 68" voting in Senator Kennedy's favor.

Time magazine said two million students were predicted to vote in the primary, including 10,000 from I.U. About 9,000 I.U. students did vote.

Students were able to mark first, second, and third choices among 12 candidates. Write-in candidates were accepted.

Also appearing on yesterday's ballot were three referendum questions: two dealing with the country's current involvement in Vietnam and one with the priorities of governmental spending in confronting the "urban crisis."

Today —on the campus—

GENETICS TRAINING GRANT SEMINAR — Visiting Prof. Ferruccio Ritossa, University of Illinois, "Some Structural and Functional Aspects of Genes Coding for Ribosomal RNA," 4:30 p.m., Jordan 239.
PIANO RECITAL — Denson Elliott, graduate (D.M.), 4:30 p.m., Recital Hall, Music Building.
OBOE CLASS RECITAL — 7 p.m., Recital Hall, Music Building.
IMU DUPLICATE BRIDGE — 7 p.m., Kiva, Union Building.
SAILING CLUB — 7 p.m., Ballantine 109.
SLAVIC CLUB MEETING — Dr. James Sehnert, "The Language, Literature and Folklore of the Polabians (Elbe Slavs)," 7:30 p.m., International Center.
ISLAMIC CIRCLE LECTURE AND DISCUSSION — Polygamy in Islam, 7:30 p.m., Union 40-42.
UNIVERSITY THEATRE PRODUCTION — The Recruiting Officer, 8 p.m., I.U. Theatre.
HORIZONS OF KNOWLEDGE — Folklore Institute and Department of Anthropology, illustrated lecture, Kevin Danaher, Irish Folklore Commission, "Irish Calendar and Festival Customs," 8 p.m., Fine Arts Auditorium.
DEPARTMENT OF ENGLISH LECTURE — Joseph Campbell, Sarah Lawrence College, "The Art and Mythology of James Joyce," 8 p.m., Ballantine 013.
BRASS CHOIR CONCERT — 8:30 p.m., Recital Hall, Music Building.
COLLEGE LIFE — 9 p.m., Bryan Room, Union Building

Justice was Miller's goal

—DAILY STUDENT PHOTO By SANDRA EISERT

Homework for a Pulitzer

PULITZER PRIZE WINNER GENE MILLER of the Miami Herald explains to members of Theta Sigma Phi, women's honorary journalism society, the development of the stories which won for him last year journalism's highest award. Mr. Miller's job of investigative reporting helped free two innocent persons convicted of murder. He is here this week as an Ernie Pyle lecturer and to take part in Horizons in Communication honoring retiring journalism department chairman John E. Stempel.

By BETH ZIMMERMAN
Daily Student Staff Writer

"It takes more than luck to win a Pulitzer Prize; it takes opportunity," Gene Miller, A.B. '50, told members of Theta Sigma Phi, professional society for women in communications, last night.

"It's like playing third base and getting a line drive right into your glove," said the 1967 Pulitzer Prize winner, describing incidents that led to his uncovering miscarriages of justice while a police reporter for the Miami (Fla.) Herald.

The former Daily Student night editor and associate editor was cited by the Pulitzer Prize committee last year for "initiative and investigative reporting which helped to free two persons wrongfully convicted of murder."

THREE REASONS for miscarriage of justice listed by Mr. Miller were:

1. Improper police interrogation; mainly the acceptance of confessions under unlawful circumstances.
2. The development of "tunnel vision" by invesfigating policemen who have convinced themselves of a logical suspect's guilt.
3. The failure of too many criminal lawyers to become fully acquainted with their cases.

"Belligerent, hard-nosed investigative reporting" is Mr. Miller's description of his technique for uncovering legal discrepancies. "When officials block you (by withholding information)," he said, "you just go around them and find another way."

AFTER HE IS CONVINCED that the convicted person whose case he's covering is innocent, the determined reporter who never had a law course says "I sort of commit myself" to righting the injustice done the prisoner.

Mr. Miller will elaborate on his three major encounters with miscarriages of justice at an open lecture at 3 p.m. Saturday in Don Mellett Auditorium, Ernie Pyle Hall.

P0079434, IU Archives.

THE INDIANA DAILY STUDENT

Warmer
Partly cloudy, windy and warmer today. High 68-75. Chance of showers, 20 per cent today and 30 per cent tonight. Low in the upper 40's to lower 50's.

VOL. XCVIII—NO. 142 Established 1867 INDIANA UNIVERSITY THURSDAY, MAY 1, 1969. ERNIE PYLE HALL, BLOOMINGTON, INDIANA, 47401 10c

NUC backs four student rally demands

By KAREN CARLE
Daily Student Staff Writer

The New University Conference met yesterday at 12:30 p.m. in front of Maxwell Hall and agreed to support the four student demands made at the all-campus rally in the fieldhouse Monday.

Those demands include: declare a freeze on the fee increase; allow an elected student committee with parity (veto vote) to work with the administrators on the budget; have a graduated tuition based on the ability to pay and no tuition by 1972.

PARTICIPANTS at the meeting discussed what statement the NUC would make at the student rally which followed in front of Owen Hall.

"I think it would be in our best interests to give support to the students," said Allan Greenberg, visiting assistant professor of history. We must show support now, not after the rally, said Greenberg.

Whether of not the NUC would support the action to be taken by the students at the meeting to follow was discussed by those present. One persons said that the NUC must support the demands but couldn't support the action until the students actually took action.

"WE CAN CERTAINLY support them in principle," said Irving Zeitlin, associate professor of sociologv. Someone else added that what students are looking for is support in principle and, "a legitimate speaker that can say these demands are reasonable, they make sense."

It was agreed that the NUC would support the four demands and a sheet of paper was passed around for those faculty members who wished to sign it to show their support.

Greenberg also spoke for the NUC at the student rally at Owen Hall. "We support the four demands made by the students at the all-University meeting," Greenberg said.

Snyder terms class boycott personal matter

By TOM ROMITO
Daily Student Staff Writer

John W. Snyder, acting chancellor in Bloomington, responded yesterday afternoon to a boycott of classes planned for the rest of the week with the following statement:

"Classes will meet today as scheduled so that students who wish to continue their studies can do so. The question of attendance is a matter to be settled by the professor and the student.

"It is a 149-year-old tradition at I.U. that classes meet as scheduled to serve the students who wish to attend them. Upon rare occasion the faculty has voted to dismiss classes for all-University functions."

Plans for the two-day boycott came at yesterday's rally in front of Owen Hall as a means for students to go home to talk to people about the financial situation of the University.

Snyder later said he did not think the boycott would serve the University in the eyes of the state legislature and that students should make use of the three days of classes.

Asked what the administration would do if classes are boycotted, Snyder said, "We have done everything we can do." He said he met with Gov. Edgar D. Whitcomb early yesterday afternoon in Indianapolis and received strong verbal support for the University during the next legislative session.

He said the governor pledged state support in attempting to generate funds for development and innovation of instructional programs, and relief from "the overburdening fees," including financial aids for the first two years and a loan program for the junior and senior years.

Snyder said he did not get support from Whitcomb for a special session of the legislature.

Today –
–on the campus–

CHEMICAL PHYSICS SEMINAR — Dr. John Waugh, Massachusetts Institute of Technology, "High Resolution NMR in Solids," 4:40 p.m., Chemistry 106.
GRADUATE RECITAL — Roberta Brokaw, Flute, 4:30 p.m., Recital Hall.
IMU BEGINNING DUPLICATE BRIDGE CLUB — 7 p.m., Hoosier Den.
IMU DUPLICATE BRIDGE CLUB — 7 p.m., Georgian Room.
LATIN AMERICAN STUDIES PROGRAM — Prof. Gregory Rabassa, Queens College, "Negro in Brazilian Literature," 7:30-9 p.m., Ballantine 103.
RUSSIAN AND EAST EUROPEAN INSTITUTE LECTURE— Prof. Jonathan Frankel, The Hebrew University, "The Menshevik Interpretation of Communist Party History," 7:30 p.m., Ballantine 006.
I.U. JAZZ ENSEMBLE I — Dave Baker, Conductor, 8 p.m., I.U. Auditorium.
UNIVERSITY SINGERS — Fiora Contino, Conductor, 8:30 p.m., Recital Hall.
CAMPUS CRUSADE FOR CHRIST (COLLEGE LIFE) — 9 p.m., Wright Quad Lounge.
IMU SAILING CLUB — shore school at 6:30 p.m.; business at 7 p.m., Ballantine 109. Important meeting.

—DAILY STUDENT PHOTO By JOHN FULTON

Rally for action

I.U. STUDENTS gathered at Owen Hall yesterday to reply to the administration's reaction to the students' proposed budget cuts. The meeting called for a boycott of classes until the end of the week. About 3000 persons attended the rally.

Rallying students support two-day boycott of classes

By JEANNENE SEEGER
and SHARON WOODWARD
Daily Student Staff Writers

"All strike; shut it down," was the final cry of students as they left the rally in front of Owen Hall at 3:30 yesterday afternoon.

This was the majority opinion determined by a standing vote from the mass. About 4000 students plan to boycott all classes for the next two days. The leaders also urged the support of the faculty in boycotting the classes. Students did not favor a mill-in at Bryan Hall, which was also proposed.

John W. Snyder, acting chancellor of the University, has announced he will meet with students in Dunn Meadow at 1 p.m. today.

Students had planned to gather at Owen Hall yesterday afternoon to hear the administration's response to student demands to rescind tuition fees.

WILLIAM A. MADDEN, dean of Junior Division, representing acting Chancellor John W. Snyder, addressed the students with the administration's reply. (Snyder was in Indianapolis conferring with Governor Edgar D. Whitcomb. Madden said Snyder had requested the noon meeting with the governor, but did not report any details of the conference.)

Madden's main statement to the students, on behalf of the administration, was, "We now believe we can cover financial needs of all students now on campus for next year."

He said everyone would pay full fees and those who show need will be aided on some sort of graduated fee basis. Madden went on to explain that the budgetary task force had been organized and had been working on the possibilities of cutting the budget in some areas ever since the demand had been presented to the administration.

HE TOLD the students an open letter from the administration would appear in The Indiana Daily Student today. (See page 5) This letter would cover comment on all four of the proposals presented in the demand. These proposals include rescinding the fee increase, student budget committee with parity (veto vote), a graduated fee scale by 1970 and no tuition for students by 1972.

Student Body President Paul Helmke, senior, replied to Madden's statement saying, "That answer left me a bit speechless; we didn't get much of an answer."

Helmke compared the burning in effigy of Frank McKinney, chairman of the Board of Trustees, on Tuesday night at the rally to a marshmallow roast by Boy Scouts and Girl Scouts.

"We've got to keep it cool," Helmke shouted to the crowd. He said anything else would only be playing into the hands of the governor and the state.

HELMKE THEN proposed this plan of action:

"I want all of you, if you can, to go home tomorrow and tell them — parents, businessmen, taxpayers — what's happening," he said.

There was some disagreement with Helmke's proposals by some speakers who thought dispersing students throughout the state would weaken the students power position. Helmke said, however, decisions must be made by the students — not an elite group. "It's not the easy solution or playing games — it's getting changes made."

Helmke then suggested the establishment of a free university. He called for a study that "really means something." He explained if students want to have a free university they would have to have a teach-in to get anything accomplished.

"USE YOUR HEADS. We have to get a state-wide focus which means getting changes made now."

Kerry Kaplan, junior, (Town-at large), who was moderator, announced yesterday there would be another rally but told The Daily Student that it has been cancelled. He has called for a teach-in by all students and faculty. Instead, Kaplan said, after thinking about it "I agree with the group, we're sick of rallies.

"Today is the day we should all stop, gather in groups, whether it be in Dunn Meadow or in the Free Commons, with a professor, if they'll join us, and discuss the issues we feel are relevant," he said.

"There is no reason to have a rally today. It's too hard to decide things in large groups. If you've got two people sitting in a tree it's a teach-in," he said.

JOEL ALLEN, grad., then spoke to the group. "We students aren't together. Splitting our efforts is not the way. Things get done by being united," he told the crowd. The students applauded these statements.

Allen went on to say, "We don't want to get peoples' heads busted, but rather we want to change things around here. Forming a community where we can talk to each other is important," he said.

"We're talking about people power," he said. "I think our unity is right here on this campus," he said. Allen said students are dealing with the power structure right here on campus, meaning Frank McKinney and the Board of Trustees.

Madden then took the microphone for a question-answer period. The first question was "When will students get a chance to confront the administration — alive?"

MADDEN REMINDED the students that after a letter appears in The Daily Student, then student government will meet with the administration.

Pat Chavis, grad., asked Madden if it would not be fair to conclude that the University has not made any decisions about the demands, and are waiting to gauge the temperment of the crowd to determine whether an explosive situation exists. "I think we're getting hung-up on parliamentary procedures," he added.

Madden's response was the administration had 48 hours to do all this, and they were in discussion with students until 4 a.m. "It's just not ready," he said. "Even in my judgment it would be better in writing so everyone could read it," he added.

There were then other comments from individuals in the crowd. Leaders paused to hear any response an individual had to offer at this point.

JOHN B. JOYNER, assistant professor of speech and hearing and director of the Center for Human Relations, then spoke to the group.

"I have seen the first draft of the administration response. It will be in the newspaper — we can read it," he said.

Students asked Joyner what the statement said, and he replied the statement relates to each of the items brought up in the demand.

"The situation we face here today needs no further discussion. One thing's for sure, it's time everybody got committed," Scott said. "No more rhetoric," he added.

Continued on Page 2, Col. 1

Quad residents discuss boycott, free university

By STEVE FAGAN
Night Editor

In the wake of yesterday's class boycott decision, meetings were called in many of the residence halls to discuss proposals for the establishment of free universities and ways of effectively carrying out the boycott.

Jack Fisher, junior, student body secretary for student affairs, is taking charge of the move to carry out the strike, and to establish the free universities in the Residence Halls and Greek houses.

The general plan was to inform students at preliminary meetings last night, said Fisher. "The preliminary meetings were to inform people why we are striking, what demands are being made and what the chances are of having the demands met. We are also helping to organize the aspects of a free university."

FOR THE FREE university, Fisher said that student government is seeking graduate instructors to hold class in the dorms and professors to come and talk to students.

"Tommorrow people will be speaking in dorms and in lunch lines explaining why we are boycotting," Fisher said. "The speakers will urge people to come to the free university in the dorms instead of classes."

Both Thursday and Friday will be used for "rap sessions" leading up to the march in Indianapolis on Saturday, said Fisher.

"I have been in contact with all the dorms today and I am acting as a speakers bureau. I ask them if they need speakers and when do they need them. We are also getting the fraternities doing something," Fisher said. "We are trying to tie everyone together."

RON JOURDAN, junior, former Wright Quad President, called a meeting at Wright Quad to discuss the free university proposal.

When he called for a vote on the proposal, about 50 percent of the residents cast ballots. However, he found that a 74 per cent majority of those voting favored the proposal. The vote count was 271 for and 94 against.

Jourdan, in a general meeting of the Quad's residence yesterday afternoon, explained that the free university, which will be called "The Responsive Student University," will have seminars to discuss "issues of relevance to the student body."

He told the more than 200 students at the meeting that the free university proposal was being made in response to the Trustees' decision to increase student fees.

"We want to establish the Responsive Student University as a positive attempt to demonstrate student solidarity," Jourdan said, "and to show that this university can be more relevant to student needs and demands."

FREE AND OPEN discussion, Jourdan explained, would be the basis for the seminars. He listed some the topics to be discussed as:

—Who pays for education?

—The relevance of the present system to individual needs.

—Means of making the system more relevant to the individual student.

—What is the purpose of the organized university?

—Does the student have a right to a voice in the processes of organized education, and if so, how much?

Jordan said that a first round of discussions would be continued until Sunday, at which time he would ask for another vote to determine whether or not the majority of the residents wanted to continue to participate in the free university program.

Jordan added that even though the majority of students had not voted on plans for the free university, they would be given the go ahead because his proposal had received a majority from among those casting ballots. However, Jordan said, since proposal did not have a clear-cut majority backing, the seminars would meet outside of the residence hall on the lawn.

Jourdan said he felt it would be an infringement on the rights of others if they used the residence hall facilities for the seminars without the backing of a larger portion of the residents.

SOME OF THE students at the meeting expressed fear that the establishement of the free university would signal the breakdown of order at Wright. Jourdan, however, allayed these fears, saying any disregard of rules of conduct during the discussion sessions would be severely dealt with by the "regular powers that be."

Continued on Page 2, Col. 3

Senate backs boycott in emergency session

The Student Senate voted late last night to support the student boycott of classes on May 1 and 2 and "the institution of a free university." The resolution urges all students, administrators and faculty to support the boycott as an expression of dissatisfaction with the recent fee increase. The resolution was submitted by Andy Mallor, junior, IFC president and Kerry Kaplan, junior, town.

The senate also passed a resolution calling for boycott of Bloomington businesses. Student government plans to request scholarship contributions from merchants and to ask merchants to apply pressure to their legislators to increase the University's budget.

The senate is enlisting the aid of the other three state universities.

Students going home for the next two days were urged to ask the support of hometown merchants.

Acting Chancellor John Snyder told the Student Senate last night the reasons for turning down all four of the student demands concerning the fee increase. He agreed to meet with students today in Dunn Meadow at 1 p.m. for further discussion.

His first statement was, "we cannot rescind the fee increase. What we can do, and what we intend to do, is take money from one place where we did find it and move it to financial aids," he said.

He reported his conversation with Governor Edgar D. Whitcomb yesterday afternoon concerning the fee increase problem. He said he felt he had "his foot in the door" concerning talks at greater length about the budget cut, but added Whitcomb would not call a special session of the legislature because it would do no good.

WHITCOMB TOLD SNYDER that a special session would only renew punitive measures against the University, "something we all fought against during the regular session."

Here Snyder said, "This does not say your action across the state may not produce effective results." He was speaking to the persons who have been involved in the student rallies over the past few days.

Kerry Kaplon, Town-Ind., asked Snyder to endorse the boycott of classes for the next two days, showing his concern about what has happened to the students at I.U. Kaplan pointed out that since the students are mobilized over this problem this feeling should not be allowed to die. "We want your help," he said.

Snyder remarked "I will discuss with

Continued on Page 2, Col. 2

The Inter-Fraternity Council, in a statement released yesterday by President Andy Mallor, sophomore, and Former President Jack Wickes, senior, urged all Greeks to boycott classes today and tomorrow.

The statement said: "Today a substantial number of the student body under the direction of student government voted a two-day boycott of all classes. Expression for any type of violence or mill-in which could result in violence was overwhelmingly negative.

"The purpose of the boycott is to shut down the University until Governor (Edgar D.) Whitcomb realizes that his antiquated tax structure must be changed to meet the demands of higher education. The boycott is non-violent. It expresses our interest for a relevant education. The executive officers and directors urge you to boycott all classes."

A statement released to The Daily Student yesterday from the Executive Council of Panhellenic stated that teach-ins conducted by University professors will be in sororities today and tomorrow.

The statement is: "Panhellenic agrees with student government's two-day boycott of classes. We recognize the need to unite as a University community to make it clear to the state of Indiana that we find the budget cut intolerable. To assure an effective boycott Panhellenic urges everyone to participate."

47 faculty support boycott; Oring gives series of proposals during unofficial meeting

By MARVIN SACKS
and
KEN FERRIES
Daily Student Staff Writers

Forty-seven members of the I.U. faculty voted in an unofficial meeting last night to support three student demands concerning the current fee increase debate. The vote, taken at an impromptu faculty meeting, was 47-3 in favor of a motion to:

—Support the student boycott by boycotting their classes themselves or meeting out-of-doors.

—Support student demands that the recent fee increases be rescinded and students have an active voice in any future budget discussions.

—Support, in principle, student demands for a free tuition university by 1972, and a graduated tuition system by 1970.

AT THE SAME MEETING, it was petitioned that Professor Michael Wolff, secretary of the Faculty Council Agenda Committee, attempt to organize an open Faculty Council meeting to be held Friday at 3 p.m. A Faculty Council (not for all faculty) meeting is presently scheduled for Tuesday.

Dr. Allen Greenberg, history, speaking for members of the New University Conference and some members of the Continuing Committee, said there will be another unofficial meeting open to all concerned faculty members in Ballantine 013 at 8 p.m. tonight.

About 300 students crowded aisles and stood outside doorways to listen to a barrage of explanations about the student strike and the role that the faculty will take.

A preliminary check by The Daily Student indicated that a substantial number of the faculty were not informed that the impromptu meeting would be held last night.

Secretary of the faculty, Richard L. Turner, education, said, "I don't have the slightest idea about a called meeting. If there was one called—not through me. I'm out of it," he said.

Hitting many tangents, the meeting took on its full significance—to guage unofficial faculty response to the students' actions—with a twenty minute address by Mark Oring, teaching assistant.

In issuing four proposals, Oring said, "Either they will give us the money to have a good university or we will have no university."

"It is my firm conviction," Oring said, "that the legislature doesn't care what kind of education we have here—but just that we have a campus. They are not willing to provide funds for a good faculty—they don't care if we have a super-good faculty."

Oring emphasized, "We will not operate

Continued on Page 2, Col. 5

IDS will publish boycott schedules

Because of the planned boycott of classes today and Friday, The Daily Student will publish a schedule of speeches and meetings for the weekend.

Any persons or groups who are planning functions or meetings connected with the strike are invited to inform the IDS of these meetings. Announcements should be phoned in or brought into the city room in Ernie Pyle Hall. Announcements should include time, place, and date of meetings and names of speakers.

P0079908, IU Archives.

THE INDIANA DAILY STUDENT

VOL. XCVIII—NO. 186 | Established 1867 | INDIANA UNIVERSITY | TUESDAY, JULY 22, 1969 | ERNIE PYLE HALL, BLOOMINGTON, INDIANA, 47401 | 10¢

aim

Partly cloudy today, mild and humid with chance of occasional showers through tomorrow. High today 82-87, low tonight 62-67. High tomorrow 84-90.

Eagle rejoins mother ship Columbia

Man on the moon —AP WIREPHOTO

MILLIONS OF AMERICANS and people all over the world witnessed this scene late Sunday night as man fulfilled a dream as old as his own being. Playing to one of the largest audiences ever assembled, Neil Armstrong and Edwin Aldrin seemed to thoroughly enjoy their romp on the moon's surface while collecting numerous rock samples to be examined upon their return. The successful flight of Apollo 11 may just be a beginning.

Moonwalk, blastoff and final rendezvous all called successful

SPACE CENTER, Houston (AP)—The men who walked the moon piloted the spacecraft Eagle to a crucial link-up with its mother ship yesterday, then abandoned the historic little craft early, just six hours after it rocketed them safely from the lunar surface.

Tired and speeding up their flight plans, Neil A. Armstrong and Edwin E. "Buzz" Aldrin Jr. exited from the Eagle two hours ahead of schedule and took their places in Columbia beside its pilot, Michael Collins.

It was at this point that mission control decided to have them kick the lunar lander away. Collins said he heard a "fairly loud noise, and it appears to be departing, I would guess several feet a second."

AT 12:57 A.M. today, while on the backside of the moon and out of radio contact with their home planet, the astronauts were to fire their spacecraft engine to begin the 240,000 mile trip back home. If all goes well, they will splash down in the Pacific Thursday.

The astronauts noted some cracks in the outer coating around Eagle's tunnel by which the two spacecraft were joined nose to nose. There were also some cracks in the thermal covering, but not apparently in the construction of the craft.

Columbia fired its engine briefly to get away from the Eagle which was left alone in orbit around the moon, eventually to crash to its surface.

Earlier stories, pictures, page 5

DOCTORS SAID that Armstrong and Aldrin rested little after their lunar adventure Sunday, getting perhaps an hour or so of fitful sleep in the cramped, seatless quarters of Eagle.

"How's it feel up there to have some company?" mission control asked Collins.

"Damned good, I'll tell you," Collins said happily.

"I'll bet you'd almost be talking to yourself up there after ten revolutions or so," mission control said.

"OH NO," Collins replied. "It's a happy home up here. It'd be nice to have some company. Matter of fact, be nice to have a couple a hundred million Americans up here."

"They were with you in spirit," said mission control.

There was apparently some transient trouble during docking, with Columbia pilot Collins reporting that the Eagle was jerking around and cryptic words about Eagle's position control jets.

Nevertheless, at 5:35 p.m. EDT, Columbia docked with Eagle just three minutes later than planned.

THE AMERICAN ASTRONAUTS did not explain their remarks, which indicated wobbling during linkup, even to mission control before they passed behind the moon, united again. But flight directors said they were reassured by control panels that showed no signs of difficulty.

The space agency offered a tentative explanation: As Collins moved in and inserted Columbia's docking probe into Eagle and docked, he didn't realize for a moment that they were together. He tried to pull his ship back to test the connection. At that moment a thruster on Eagle fired briefly.

The result was a loud noise as the two vehicles wobbled together.

They were together again for the first time in 27 hours and 48 minutes, a little more than a day. But it was a day full of history and promise.

The space chase was right on schedule until linkup. The two craft were only 44 miles apart when Eagle pursued Columbia around the backside of the moon and out of radio contact with earth.

WHEN THEY EMERGED again, Columbia was in her 27th orbit, Eagle in its second since lunar blast-off. They were only a few feet apart. Any joyous remarks they might have made when they first saw each other were likely shared only with the distant stars and planets. The earth was blocked off from hearing.

In Eagle, Armstrong and Aldrin set about cleaning some of the moon dust off their space suits with a small vacuum cleaner.

"It doesn't appear as though the red hose is going to be much of a competitor to the leading vacuum cleaner brands," Aldrin observed wryly.

Mission control reported that the scientists thought they had lost signals from the seismometer the astronauts had left on the moon to measure the small planet's tremblings. But the trouble was in equipment on earth, and the device was back in operation in 30 minutes.

THEY BLASTED OFF from the moon at 1:54 p.m. EDT, ending 21 hours and 36 minutes on the surface. During that time, first Armstrong, then Aldrin walked the lunar surface, planting their nation's flag, setting up experiments to probe the moon's secrets, and collecting alien soil and rock to bring home.

Eagle rose from the Sea of Tranquility on a tail of flame and explorers Armstrong and Aldrin became fliers again.

Minutes later, Armstrong reported, "The Eagle is back in orbit, having left Tranquillity Base and leaving behind a replica from our Apollo 11 patch with an alive branch."

"Roger," said mission control. "The whole world is proud of you."

Also behind them was the four-legged descent rocket of the lunar lander. It served as the launch pad for the ascent rocket that hurled them up toward the patroling Columbia, somewhere above and ahead.

BEHIND THEM TOO was the robot Soviet spaceship Luna 15. It struck the moon on the Sea of Crises — some 500 miles from the American landing site — shortly before the Americans blasted off. It apparently crashed, according to scientists at Britain's Jodrell Bank Observatory. The Soviet Union announced only that Luna had landed and completed its mission.

Yesterday marked the start of the 21-day quarantine of the three astronauts to protect their home planet from any germs they might have encountered on the moon. They will return to earth Thursday, but they will be kept shielded from contact with all but a few until doctors are sure they brought no moon bugs back.

The last minutes on the moon went like clockwork — as had so much else.

ALDRIN, an Air Force colonel, and Armstrong, the civilian spacecraft commander, ticked off the last instrument checks and got a go-ahead from earth.

"Roger," said Aldrin, "understand we're No. 1 on the runway."

As the Eagle rose, Aldrin gave a running account. "Beautiful! Very smooth! A very quiet ride!"

He spotted the rock-strewn crater that Eagle had to dodge when it made its hazardous landing Sunday. "There's that one crater down there," he said casually.

MISSION CONTROL confirmed each major milestone on the way up. "One minute and you're looking good. . . mighty fine. . . you're looking good to us."

If the astronauts needed moral support, they didn't sound like it. "I'm going right down U.S. 1," said Armstrong, flying over a lunar valley so straight that the astronauts had nicknamed it after the north-south highway serving Cape Kennedy.

Aldrin kept a sharp eye for landmarks. "There's Ritter out there," he said pointing out another crater. "See. There it is. Right there. Say, that's impressive-looking, isn't it?"

"WE'VE A little bit of slow wallowing here," he said as the Eagle spurted toward orbit. Then the rocket cut off, and he announced, "Shutdown."

"Great," said Mission Control.

Eagle's first orbit ranged 11 to 54 miles around the moon, just about the ellipse it aimed for. When it went into orbit, Columbia was some 300 miles ahead, and out of sight.

The firings were designed to allow Eagle to catch up with Columbia by flying a lower and faster path, rising at the end to mate with the mother ship.

City and campus halt for 'giant step'

Bloomington, like Los Angeles and Rome, was quiet Sunday night in regard to crime and traffic activity. There were no major fire or accident calls made by the law enforcement agencies in Monroe County. One state trooper compared the light traffic load and estimated that 95 per cent of the slowdown could be attributed to the Apollo "moonwalk."

Prisoners in the county jail joined command ship pilot Michael Collins in not watching the lunar activities of astronauts Armstrong and Aldrin. No television is available at the jail and the radio that is on during the day is locked away on Sunday evening.

In addition to light traffic, an I.U. Safety Division officer reported little phone or radio traffic in the county on Sunday.

At the Bloomington hospital everyone that could watch viewed the moon mission and emergency cases were fewer than usual. A hospital official attributed the decrease to children watching Apollo "instead of breaking their arms or hurting themselves by falling."

Everyone visiting the registration desk at the Holiday Inn was talking about Apollo 11, according to a switchboard operator. Most of the staff watched the events on a television in the inn's cocktail lounge. They were joined by diners who "stood around the door when they noticed the television being on." The most noticeable indicator was the increased demand for color sets in the rooms.

Three sets in Hatch's IGA were tuned to the historic event. During the walk only staff were gathered in front of the sets, but the store was busy before and after with people shopping for their moon-walk parties. "Our biggest request which we could not sell, was for champagne," said a Hatch's employee.

One 24-hour restaurant, the Waffle House was about half full during the moon-walk. "We were not busy, everyone was watching the TV instead of eating," said a waitress.

Six people came in from outside to watch a set in the hotel lobby of the Indiana Memorial Union. All of the desk staff watched, while most students were in the television room in the west end of the building. The night detective's report stated that everyone was gone by three a.m.

I.U. President Joseph L. Sutton

Commenting yesterday on the man's first walk on the moon, I.U. President Joseph L. Sutton said he could not compare it with any other event in history.

"I can't compare it with Columbus' discovery of America," President Sutton said, "because it was a different sort of thing."

Sutton pointed out that Columbus didn't know where he was going or what he would find, and when he arrived he had no idea where he was.

"THEY (THE ASTRONAUTS) knew where they were going," Sutton said, "and what they were going to do."

President Sutton referred to the moon landing and walk as an "astonishing engineering event" and a true "test of human will."

"I just hope," Sutton added, "that this sort of investment (in time, money, and team work) can be funneled into improving situations here on earth."

Commenting on the television coverage of the first step onto the moon's surface made by Astronaut Neil Armstrong, Sutton said, "It was expected, and at the same time unexpected. It was what I know I'd see, but never expected to see it."

PRESIDENT SUTTON SAID he found the astronauts' description of the geological features of the moon's surface to be one of the most interesting highlights of the moon walk.

When asked if he had any doubts as to whether or not the astronauts would be able to lift off the moon's surface, President Sutton could only say, "I wouldn't like to have been in their shoes."

"Since we have now had a taste of space exploration," said Sutton, "we will inevitably have to go further."

"THE SPACE PROGRAM," Sutton continued, "has also taught us that we can solve our own problems here on earth. It has shown that we can get teamwork and cooperation out of people with varying backgrounds."

President Sutton also pointed out that we have learned many practical things about management from the space program.

When asked if he would like to go to the moon, President Sutton said, "I don't think I'd like to go, I find earth exciting enough."

I.U. Chancellor Herman B Wells

The reality of man on the moon is an example of the "Unlimited capacity of the human mind and the human heart to achieve the impossible," said I.U. Chancellor Herman B Wells.

Dr. Wells, who was present at last week's launch at Cape Kennedy, termed it "as impressive as it could be — it's something I'll always remember."

"I was delighted I could go," Dr. Wells said. "I had been invited previously but was unable to go."

The moon dirt "will do a great deal to substantiate or disprove hypotheses made by astronomers and astrophysicists," Dr. Wells continued. "Many of these hypotheses are the results of men in our astronomy department and astrophysics department."

Dr. Wells referred to I.U.'s part in the Arizona observatory and an observatory in Chile.

Science buffs elated; some students confused

Amazing, fantastic, terrific were adjectives many I.U. students used when asked how they felt about the Sunday night moon landing.

"I think it's terrific, I can't believe that there was someone on the moon," said Donna Vilet, senior. "The photography was excellent," she added.

C.W. Pullard, soph., said, "That was a fantastic achievement. With science fiction movies, it seems so much more fantastic." He said, "You had to realize that it wasn't science fiction."

"I THINK IT IS ONE of the greatest things that has happened in my life time and I am glad that I could be around this generation to see something like this happen. I hope some day to be a part of the geological research teams to work on and analyze some of the lunar samples and stratagraphical reading taken from the moon surface," said Keith Moore, senior, geology major.

Joe Wehlacz, grad., said, "Only one word I can think of, 'amazing.' It showed the American inguenity very well; however, some of the money and ingenuity could be used for more needy projects and programs."

Bill Michely, grad., said that it was very impressive especially since there were no malfunctions. "It is hard to imagine that the human error could be almost eliminated, which appears to be what has happened," he said.

"I THINK IT WAS really fantastic and it completely left me speechless," said Barb Aman, senior. "I think we should keep on with the space program but at the same time not to lose sight of the problems in the U.S. and on earth," she added.

Patrick Egan, senior, said, "I think it is a paradox; one of achievement and one of tragedy. An achievement in the fact that mankind could attain this planet, and a tragedy that here on earth we are unable to stop war, poverty, and have peace," he said.

Vicki Allen, senior, said, "The thing that struck me was when the president talked to them on the phone. It makes you wonder what's going to happen next," she said.

JANE WALSH, SENIOR, said "having been a Ray Bradbury fan since I learned to read, I both am really really happy and excited about it, but I get really frightened because America has a way of making everything it does military and sterile.

Jim Henry, junior, said, "It was a great achievement in such a short time. We've only been working on it about 10 years," he said.

Lee Ann Foust, junior, had one final comment, "It was neat.....I guess," she said.

Inside

The early hours of the moon landing and the sequence of events leading up to it are the object of a special page on Apollo 11. Story and pictures on page 5.

Today —

—on the campus—

CIC FAR EASTERN LANGUAGE INSTITUTE — Prof. Charles O. Hucker, University of Michigan, "Aspects of the Chinese Military Tradition: Ming Troubles with Coastal Raiders," 4 p.m., Psych 101.

CHRISTIAN SCIENCE ORGANIZATION — Testimony meeting, 7 p.m., Hoosier Den, IMU.

P0079136, IU Archives.

The paper's role as a learning laboratory within the Department of Journalism was hotly debated as early as the 1930s. Department chairman John Stempel believed that the IDS' role, as part of the school's curriculum, was necessary for journalism education at Indiana University. Others believed that structure created an inferior product that was subject to editorial control from university officials. In 1965, the Board of Aeons, a group of representatives who advised the president of the university, produced a lengthy report on the state and future of the student paper. This excerpt of the report has been substantially edited for space.

The Indiana Daily Student:

Evaluation and Suggestions
Board of Aeons
Indiana University
Fall 1965

The campus newspaper plays an inescapably significant role in a large university. For the newspaper is the major vehicle for communication within the campus and outside of the campus. To many outside the university community, the campus newspaper is their only contact with the university. To an increasing number who are within the university, it is their most extensive contact with the University. Thus, as the University grows in size, the importance of its newspaper increases and the standard by which the paper is evaluated must correspondingly be re-examined and raised if necessary. The success of the newspaper in carrying out its ever-expanding and increasingly demanding role depends upon the excellence and accuracy of its writing, the ability and emphasis of its reports, the structure of its control, its format and tone, its distribution method, and the legitimacy and scope of its editorials.

This Report of the Board of Aeons is prompted by the sincere belief that the IDS is not fulfilling its function nor can it when it is controlled by the Department of Journalism. However, the Chairman of the Department of Journalism and the publisher of the IDS, John Stempel, does not see the function of the Daily Student as that communication, rather he uses the IDS as a teaching device, a laboratory experiment for the students of journalism.

PROBLEM: ROLE OF A CAMPUS NEWSPAPER AT INDIANA UNIVERISTY

The Department of Journalism, which controls every basic step in the production of the Indiana University paper, does not see the role of the paper as being that of communication. Thus, while the size and complexity of the university may demand that the university paper be an ever improving vehicle of communication and expression, the IDS is run as a laboratory experiment for the benefit of the students of journalism. The Board unanimously feels that the control and domination of the IDS by the Department of Journalism at the very least frustrates the role of the paper if, indeed, it does not prohibit this function. It would not appear that a newspaper circulated to the whole campus, to every high school in the State of Indiana and to many other colleges and universities can be controlled by a group who sees its primary function as a laboratory project for about 120 people. Communication is too serious a requirement, too important a responsibility to be jeopardized and hampered by thoughts of convenience for a very small segment of the university community.

EVALUATION OF THE IDS

These points constitute the "ought to be" role of the IDS. Needless to say and yet sad to say the "is" picture is quite different. Let us examine the IDS to see where it is deficient and look further and try to identify reasons for these deficiencies.

1) The IDS is a rather adequate informer and reporter of campus, national, and world news. It does a reasonably adequate job of announcing important events and future events, meetings and deadlines. "Adequate" may, however, be too kind a word because all too often major performances of artists, speeches by visiting lecturers, and the position of the administration and student groups are reported poorly if not inaccurately. The level of significance of its news stories varies radically.

2) The IDS is a poor, remarkably poor reflector, stimulator, and leader of campus opinion in terms of both quality and quantity. The IDS is at least non-intellectual if not anti-intellectual in its tone. It seems oriented toward appealing to the mediocre mind because of or in spite of the quality of its staff. It does not lead, it does not stimulate, it does not challenge.

3) As a public information instrument of IU, the IDS is shockingly inadequate. The IDS is not the nation's greatest college daily. Comparatively speaking, the Board must admit that the IDS enjoys lower repute among newspapers and college students (here and elsewhere) than does Indiana University among institutions of higher learning. The IDS does not improve the popular conception of IU; it probably is a negative factor. The fact that it appears five days a week with at least eight pages containing print may be its only or biggest claim to greatness.

Comparing the ideal and the real IDS, it is clear that the paper suffers from poor, inaccurate reporting on events of the highest intellectual and/or cultural level and from a lack of well-written editorial commentary on meaningful topics and a journalistic bias. This is the problem in one sentence. Why?

SOLUTIONS AND RECOMMENDATIONS

Why such poor and inaccurate reporting? Because the best qualified people are not doing the reporting. Why the lack of meaningful editorial content? Because of the staff and the lack of any continuity in the staff. Something, then, is wrong with the staff of the paper. The staff is composed largely of journalism majors and the non-majors are usually journalism students. The best minds of the campus, both undergraduate and graduate, are neither encouraged nor sought out to write for the paper.

The Board does not see how the necessary changes in the IDS can be wrought within its existing institutional framework. The influence of the Department of Journalism is too complete and too strong to allow this.

On July 1, 1969, the Board of Trustees approved a new charter that established the IDS as independent auxiliary of the university, ensuring its financial and editorial independence and allowing non-journalism students to contribute as reporters and editors.

1970–1981

In an era when political reporting rocked the nation's halls of power, the IDS quickly grew into its new editorial independence with continued coverage of Indiana University, the nation and the world. A new basketball coach arrived in Bloomington and quickly developed a contentious relationship with student reporters. Throughout the '70s, future Pulitzer Prize winners cut their teeth covering Union Board meetings and Ku Klux Klan rallies.

The IDS staff works in the old Delta Zeta house while Ernie Pyle Hall is remodeled in 1974. *P0058603, IU Archives.*

Left, A staffer pastes up the IDS in the fall of 1979. *P0077831, IU Archives.*

Right, Editorial meeting in the Jack Backer room of the IDS newsroom, circa 1980. *P0077838, IU Archives.*

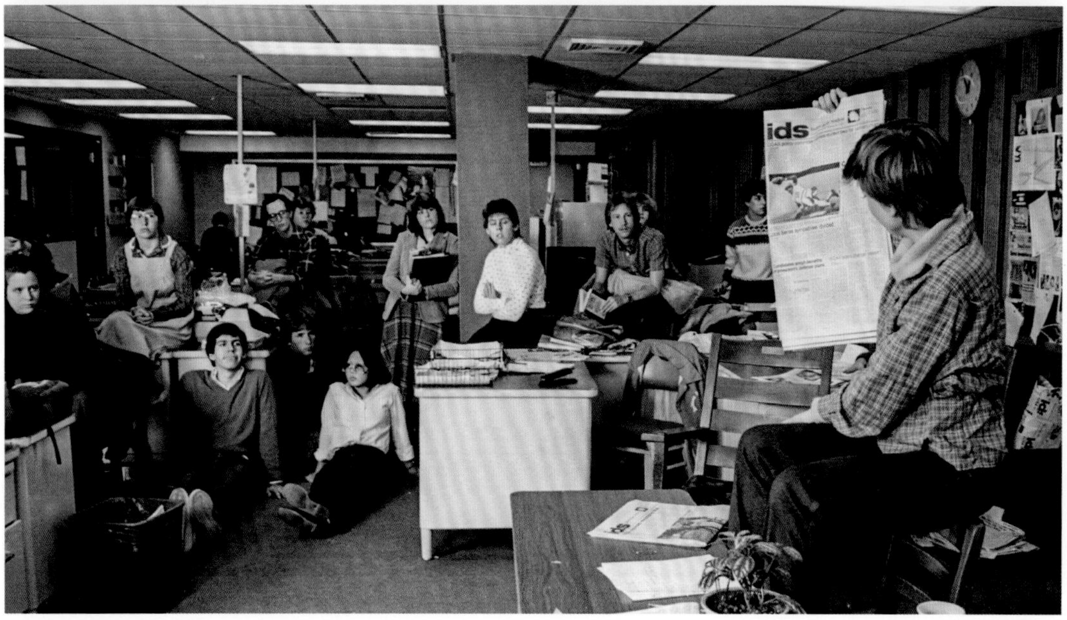

The IDS meets for Friday "slash" in the late 1970s. *P0077836, IU Archives.*

THE INDIANA DAILY STUDENT

Miss Paper?
If you miss your daily paper, call 337-7973 from 9 a.m. to 11 a.m.

Vol. XCIX - No. 157 | Tuesday, May 5, 1970 | Established 1867 | Indiana University | Ernie Pyle Hall, Bloomington, Indiana 47401 | 10¢

AP Wirephoto

Deadly confrontation

CLOUDS OF TEAR GAS hang over the campus of Kent State University, Kent, Ohio, as National Guardsmen attempt to disperse rioting students. Four students were killed at Kent Monday in the fourth day of rioting over President Nixon's Southeast Asian policies. The city was closed off after the confrontation between about three thousand students and police and Ohio National Guardsmen. University officials said shooting broke out after a shot was heard from a rooftop sniper.

Kent shootings leave four dead

KENT, Ohio (AP) – Four students in a crowd pelting National Guardsmen with bricks and rocks were shot to death at Kent State University Monday when the troops opened fire during an anti-war demonstration. Two of the dead were coeds.

Adj. Gen. S. T. Del Corso said troops began firing semiautomatic rifles after a rooftop sniper had shot at them.

The dead were identified as Jeffrey G. Miller, 20, Plainview, N.Y.; Allison Krause, 19, of Pittsburgh, Pa.; Sandy Lee Scheuer, 20, Youngstown, Ohio; and William Schroeder, 19, of Lorain all enrolled at Kent State.

Four other students were critically wounded, and eight other persons, including two guardsmen, were taken to hospitals. One of the guardsmen was treated for exhaustion and the other for shock.

The campus and the town of Kent were sealed off after the shootings, and school officials ordered the faculty, staff and 19,000 students to leave.

A spokesman said about 300 foreign students and staff remained on campus Monday night.

Patrols of armed troops and state police roamed the campus and blocked all entrances.

Buses took the students to public transportation facilities in nearby Akron and Cleveland.

Akron State University students were organizing a rally for downtown Akron Monday night to protest the shooting.

Gov. James A. Rhodes called for FBI help in investigating the disorders.

In Washington, President Nixon issued this statement:

"This should remind us all once again that when dissent turns to violence it invites tragedy.

"It is my hope that this tragic and unfortunate incident will strengthen the determination of all the nation's campuses, administrators, faculty and students alike, to stand firmly for the right which exists in this country of peaceful dissent and just as strongly against the resort to violence as a means of expression."

The shooting came after a force of 100 guardsmen, their supply of tear gas exhausted, were surrounded by about 400 demonstrators. The troops had followed the demonstrators from a rally on Kent State's Commons area near the football practice field.

Guard spokesmen estimated that 900 to 1,000 persons had been involved in the demonstration at the Commons.

Gene Williams, 21, a junior and a member of the student newspaper staff, said he was seeking refuge in a building when he saw the troops turn "in unison, as if responding to a command," and fire into the crowd.

"Bullets ricocheted off the walls beside us and students fell to the ground to avoid them," Williams said in a copyrighted story in the Dayton Journal-Herald.

"A coed fell 15 feet in front of the men into the arms of a male student. A bullet had gone into her neck and lodged there."

He said he saw another youth shot in the chest.

"I saw no snipers nor did I hear any shots until the line of troops turned in unison and opened fire," Williams said.

Del Corso, the adjutant general, said guardsmen were forced to open fire.

"A lot of people felt their lives were in danger," said Brig. Gen. Robert Canterbury, who was on the scene,' "which in fact was the case and the military man always has the option to fire if he feels his life is in danger."

"He has the right to protect himself."

Del Corso said tear gas was used several times in attempts to disperse the crowd.

"I don't know where the first shot was from," said Gen. Canterbury. He said he was with guardsmen but heard no order to fire.

"They started pelting everyone with bullets," said Mary Hagan, a student who witnessed the shooting. She said some students fell and others remained standing. They shouted the shots were blanks, she said.

IRHA, Panhel plan war teach-ins

By Linda Herman
Daily Student Staff Writer

To respond to President Richard M. Nixon's policy in South-East Asia, the President's Council of the Inter-Residence Halls Association (IRHA) and presidents of Panhellenic Sororities proposed a new plan of action at meetings Monday night.

Rejecting the demands being presented before the administration as "questionably representative of the majority of the students at I.U.," both groups have begun implementing a plan to educate students on the war in Indochina, through a series of teach-ins.

Speaking at the IRHA meeting against a backdrop of the Huntley-Brinkley reports on events at Kent State University, Mike King, junior, student body vice president, said the only situation which would prompt violence at I.U. would be the success of a move to split student organizations and completely isolate student government.

King warned the fragmentation and isolation of student groups could result from recent proposals calling for a new student government to replace junior Keith Parker's administration.

Christian LeBris, grad., originator of the "resolution of concern" which was accepted by both IRHA and Panhellenic, said, "This is not an attempt to break the Student Senate, but to indicate the gap between Student Senate demands and what IRHA sees as the interests of its constituents."

Hoping to offer a "viable alternative to violence," the groups are scheduling a series of teach-ins in housing units and the Union to provide a means for students to express their concern about the war and America.

Plan objective teach-ins

The teach-ins, to be held Wednesday, will be conducted by graduate students, "qualified" undergraduate students, and faculty members from East Asian Studies, LeBris said. The teach-ins will attempt to be objective and give students enough information to form opinions.

A panel of three professors to be held Wednesday night at 8:30 in Ballantine 109 will center on "America's Role in Asia" and will be co-sponsored by the Committee of Concerned Asian Scholars.

In attempt to make the movement nation-wide, IRHA is planning to contact regional and national residence halls organizations for support.

Seek faculty support

A letter-writing campaign and more discussions based on a five-page fact sheet to be distributed today are also part of the plan. Jim Dickson, sophomore, president of IRHA, hopes to present the plan before the Faculty Council today to gain faculty support.

The Inter-Fraternity Council is to consider the proposal tonight.

A resolution submitted by Kenneth Ritchie, junior, president of Foster Quadrangle, was defeated. The bill called for requesting, not demanding, the neutrality of the University concerning U.S. military involvement in Indo-China, making ROTC non-credit, and an increase in black student enrollment.

Resolution 'out-of-bounds'

Considering the resolution as "out-of-bounds for IRHA," Rob Beachler, sophomore, president of Teter Quadrangle, said, "I cannot see that credit for ROTC is a Halls of Residence matter."

Beachler said, "If you took a poll of 12,000 residents, you'd find 11,000 residents more concerned with on-semester contracts and vending machines than they are about the war in Indo-China."

Pentagon halts North Viet bombings

WASHINGTON (AP) – The Defense Department publicly called at least a temporary halt Monday to a series of recent heavy air attacks it said were directed against North Vietnamese missile and anti-aircraft batteries and associated supply complexes.

The Pentagon announcement terminating the attacks–coupled with a warning they might be resumed–appeared designed to allay fears the United States was resuming a major and general bombing campaign against the North.

The move came almost as Soviet Premier Kosygin deplored, in an unusual Moscow press conference, the raids over North Vietnam as well as U.S. offensive operations in Cambodia.

"By launching the war in Cambodia and resuming large-scale barbarous bombings of populated localities in North Vietnam, President Nixon actually nullifies the decision of his predecessor, President Johnson, on the termination from November 1968, of all air bombings and other actions involving the use of force against North Vietnam," Kosygin said.

Kosygin, as well as North Vietnam and Red China suggested the U.S. actions might undermine the Paris peace talks.

In another Washington development in the Indochinese crisis the Senate Foreign Relations Committee agreed reluctantly to join the House Foreign Affairs committee in a White House briefing by President Nixon on the Cambodian situation.

But the Senate panel insisted anew it expects the chief executive to meet privately with it later–an insistence greeted coolly by House members.

Meanwhile, the committee contended Nixon is waging "a constitutionally unauthorized presidential war in Indochina."

This comment was contained in a report advocating repeal of the Aug. 10, 1964 Gulf of Tonkin resolution which became the main basis for U.S. involvement in Vietnam.

Fears expressed

Coalition vetoes violence

By Jody Lanard
Daily Student Staff Writer

Subdued by the news from Kent State University, the coalition of various campus groups reiterated their stand against violence on Founder's Day and their fear that violence is inevitable.

"What can students do when the pigs get nervous and start mobilizing?" was the question many students asked, and Student Body Vice President Michael King, junior, had one answer.

"How can students respond in a confrontation with police? There's only one way to respond–you bleed," King said. "The real answer is not to antagonize the police. Walk, don't run, keep those around you from panicking.

"I want to speak strongly against individual terrorism," King said to the few students who advocated actions against Rawles Hall and other points. "All terrorists can do is isolate the left and get a lot of people ripped off. Ignore and isolate the provocateurs, the ones yelling 'Charge!' Try to keep the people around you from going crazy," he said.

The question of how to avoid violence was continually answered by "channel it." Most of the groups spoke of education as the best weapon, suggesting teach-ins, leaflets, petitions.

However, members of the coalition, who spoke at various residence halls earlier in the evening, said most students seem to want some kind of "meaningful mass action," and feel that mass action is unavoidable. Suggestions for "mass actions" intended to be non-violent included a strike, resulting in the shut-down of the University; stopping all traffic from entering the campus, and scheduling a day of mourning boycott of Little 500 activites Saturday.

"If we strike, we can't just tell everyone to go home to bed," one student said, advocating educational projects during a University shut-down "in line with the educational function of the University."

Favoring the Little 500 boycott, a student said, "This weekend I.U. is having a tricycle race, a bicycle race, a variety show–why the hell are we doing this with a war going on?" he said.

"However much we advocate moderation and try to work things out so people don't get killed, there are still those few who are so angry about the killings at Kent State that they are going to be violent, besides the planted provocateurs," he added.

The group discussed briefly the need for available medical supplies in case of violence. Many students said police presence incites anger which leads to confrontations, and expressed fear that government officials would like to see confrontation for political reasons.

Discussion was balanced between talk of ideologies and talk of methods, the anti-war issues and fear of police provocation. "There are two levels of pigs," Ike Nahem, freshman, said. "There are the ones in uniform and the undercover ones like the KKK who have been out lately."

Speaking against the idea of stopping traffic on campus, Robin Hunter, grad., said, "If we can't even persuade people that the war is wrong, how could we defend our stopping traffic? That's putting the cops in the position of having to come in."

"As is evident from Kent State, mass confrontations with police are suicidal," a student commented.

Mike King said, "No matter what happens Wednesday, education on the issues must continue. Keep communicating that to everyone you talk to."

Student Body President Keith Parker reiterated, "We want to have maximum effect with minimum loss."

About 70 students living at GRC are taking part in a fast as protest against the war, and they are also collecting money for Black Panther Bobby Seale's defense fund.

Earlier in the day, Prof. George Juergens, history, and William Harvey, Dean of the law school, asked Chancellor Byrum Carter to officially announce a moratorium of classes on Wednesday for the purpose of education on war issues. Classes are already canceled until 12:30 p.m. Wednesday for Founder's Day. Carter has not commented on the proposal yet; he said he will "relay the suggestion to President Sutton."

AP Wirephoto

Deaths at Kent State

BLOOD flowing from a dead student's head grips the attention of fellow students at Kent State University. The youth was killed Monday during a conflict between students and police and Ohio National Guardsmen. At least eleven others were injured, four of them seriously.

Inside

The second part of a three part series by Jon Carlson focuses on the causes of crime .Page 7.
Today's primary election will mean some incumbents will face tough opposition ... Page 3.

Outside

Fair today with the high near 70. Only 20 per cent chance of precipitation through tonight. Fair and warmer tonight with low in the upper 40s. Warmer Wednesday, with high in the mid 70s.

Facing, P0078727, IU Archives.

Advertising Manager Don Cross, Publisher Jack Backer and Business Manager Keith Wilson, 1976. *P0078412, IU Archives.*

PROFILE

Jack Backer
Publisher, 1969–1976

Jack Backer was the first publisher of an independent IDS. From 1969 through his death in 1976, Backer ushered the paper into one of its most successful eras, both financially and editorially. This selection is adapted from his obituary, which appeared Dec. 6, 1976. It did not carry a byline.

Besides serving for the past seven years as Daily Student publisher and associate professor of journalism, Backer was a nationally known consultant in newspaper design and college publications management.

"He was dedicated to the highest principles of journalism and sought to instill them in the young people of the Indiana Daily Student," IU President John W. Ryan said.

The Britt, Iowa, native received his Bachelor's degree from Wayne (Neb.) State College in 1958.

Backer, after receiving a Master's degree from the University of Iowa in 1963, became director of student publications at Kansas State University. He stayed there five years before becoming general manager of the Niles (Mich.) Star.

But "he missed the university," according to Del Brinkman, associate director of student publications with Backer at Kansas State.

Brinkman, now dean of the University of Kansas School of Journalism, was finishing his doctorate at IU. The Daily Student was in need of a publisher, Brinkman said, and Backer "was in the right place at the right time."

The IU Board of Trustees had just approved a change in the paper from a laboratory publication (where students worked for grades) to an auxiliary publication of the University.

According to IU School of Journalism director Richard Gray, Backer "turned the Daily Student into a model," despite the inherent problems of being the paper's first fulltime publisher.

The paper, which previously was in debt, made money under Backer. Total income has more than doubled since 1969; local advertising lineage has tripled in the same time period. Circulation has doubled to more than 15,000.

The newspaper has been judged All-American by the Associated Collegiate Press for 10 of the last 11 semesters.

Backer was named College Newspaper Adviser of the Year by the National Association of College Newspaper Advisers in 1973.

That was the year Backer hired an assistant—Merv Hendricks—to help him look after the quality of the paper's editorial product.

Hendricks, now managing editor of the Wabash, (Ind.) Plain Dealer, remembered the first time he met Backer—the same experience "hundreds of kids that have gone through there (the Daily Student) have had."

Although Hendricks thought Backer did not know him, one day the publisher looked over the sophomore reporter's shoulder, asked some questions about the story Hendricks was writing, then walked away. "I asked the person next to me, 'Well, who was that guy?' "

After being told the paunchy man with the flat top was Backer, Hendricks then asked if Backer always introduced himself to reporters that way. " 'Oh yeah, he does that with everyone,' " the reporter said.

Backer later grew his hair, added a mustache and bought a more flamboyant wardrobe. After all, he was teaching modern newspaper ideas, he had to look the part, he later would say.

But often Backer didn't think about his appearance because "he was so busy doing his work," Hendricks said.

Still, Backer always found time to visit the "round table" luncheons in the Indiana Memorial Union's Tudor Room. Several days a week throughout his time as publisher, he would eat lunch and converse with Bloomington faculty members and administrators.

Vernon Shiner, dean of the College of Arts and Sciences, said Backer "had a kind of inquiring, questioning attitude." He was "a lot of fun. He would sometimes taunt the administrators."

Backer then would return to Ernie Pyle Hall and give reporters story ideas that had surfaced at the luncheon session. The reporters would take these suggestions, often not realizing Backer was helping, Shiner said. Many of these stories would merit a "gee whiz," Backer's highest form of praise in his daily critiques of the student paper.

Among the national journalistic leaders praising Backer were Dick Leonard and Mal Mallette.

"The greatest tribute to Backer is the paper itself," said Leonard, president of the Society of Professional Journalists and editor of the Milwaukee Journal.

Mallette, director of the American Press Institute (API), said Backer was "admired and well liked" by newspaper editors attending Backer's API-sponsored seminars on newspaper layout. Mallette said Backer was "one of the most influential persons in redesigning and repackaging the newspaper."

The man Backer succeeded as adviser-publisher of the Daily Student was Ralph Holsinger, professor of journalism. Holsinger, who became one of Backer's golf partners, said, "There is no way to measure his (Backer's) influence. As I told him Friday, his influence will go on as long as any student goes through the (IU) journalism program. His ideas will survive."

15 cents
14 pages
Vol. 103 No. 182
Wednesday, May 26, 1971
Bloomington, Indiana 47401

ids

Indiana Daily Student

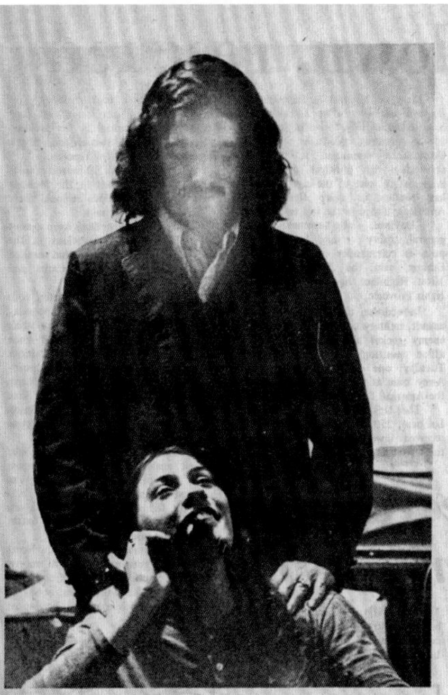

ids/Karen Elshout

The winners, with 49.2 per cent

Mary Scifres wins final vote

By Bob Kyle
ids Campus Editor

Mary Scifres, junior, became Student Body President Tuesday in the long-delayed run-off election for the presidency.

Miss Scifres, a political science major from Zionsville, took 49.2 per cent of the vote in the three-way election. Tom Biesecker, sophomore, and John Walda, junior, were second and third, respectively, with 32.5 and 18.3 per cent of the vote.

Miss Scifres' running mate and new Student Body Vice President is Jeff Richardson, junior. Richardson is a political science major from Port Washington, N.Y.

The two will be sworn in at the next Student Senate meeting, scheduled for Tuesday in the Beta Theta Pi fraternity house.

Only 5,169 I.U. students voted in the election – about 17 per cent of the eligible voters. More than 7,500 students cast ballots in the April 22 election.

Miss Scifres, who led the 13-slate field in the original election, received 2,546 votes to 1,678 for Biesecker and 945 for Walda. She received her strongest support from the town voters, getting 499 of the 733 votes cast in the three town polls or 68.1 per cent of the town vote.

She was also the leading vote-getter in the residence halls where she received 48 per cent of the vote – 1,649 votes out of the 3,436 cast. The married students and Eigenmann residents also gave her strong support, 115 out of 157 votes cast.

Of the 10 residence halls, she won eight outright, losing to Biesecker in Teter and Forest. Biesecker also out-polled Miss Scifres in the four Greek districts, getting 44 per cent of the vote to 33.6 per cent for Miss Scifres.

In all, Miss Scifres won 12 of the 16 precincts, with Biesecker winning both Jordan precincts plus Teter and Forest. She finished last only in Jordan II.

Walda had a rough night all over. He failed to win a single precinct and finished dead last in 11 of the 16–taking second at MRC, Wright, Jordan II, Third Street, and Northwest.

Miss Scifres' final total was well above the 40 per cent she needed to win outright as stated in the Student Election Code. Although the Student Senate had provided for a special balloting and counting procedure to prevent another runoff, the mechanism never was needed.

The Senate had passed a bill calling for ballots allowing the voter to indicate his second and third choices for president. If no one had won outright, the ballots of the third-place finisher would have been recounted with the voters' second choices being tabulated.

Unofficial results

	Scifres	Biesecker	Walda
Jordan I	100	176	29
Jordan II	35	147	90
Third Street	49	13	16
Northwest	99	35	54
MRC	93	15	61
Wright	213	48	76
Teter	144	211	72
GRC	197	58	46
Willkie	141	84	68
Forest	153	229	77
Read	139	125	91
Foster	206	102	58
McNutt	259	186	57
Briscoe	104	77	46
Married and Eigenmann	115	24	18
Town	449	148	86
Total	2,546	1,678	945

Winners planning for reorganization

By Larry Lough
ids Staff Writer

Although happiness and gratitude showed through "executives-elect" Mary Scifres and Jeff Richardson, getting down to business appeared to be their main concern.

"We're relieved the extended campaign has come to an end," Miss Scifres said. "We're pleased we've won. We owe it to many fine people who worked and voted for us. I want to thank them for their support.

"But the work is just beginning. We have a lot of things to do this spring, and this summer, to build up a powerful Student Government."

Richardson said the first priority of their administration would be to get the Student Government assessment fee, which the Board of Trustees abolished in January, reinstated.

"The Board meets June 12," Miss Scifres said, "and we're getting ready for it."

"The fact that the Trustees abolished the fee because (they believed) a majority of the of the students were against it has been countered by the recent referendum," Richardson said.

Commenting on recent statements by some Trustees that the referendum wasn't representative of the entire student body Richardson said, "The Trustees know that in any election–local, state and national–not everybody votes.

"We'll use the referendum results as one of our big points. We must get student control of student money, since the 50 cents is the only voluntary assessment fee."

After the assessment, Richardson said the reorganization of Student Government would come next; and within the restructuring, revamping the Student Election Commission would be necessary.

"It's like Mary said a few days ago," Richardson said, "so we won't have to go through this again."

Richardson said part of Student Government reorganization would be establishing a system of appeals in the judicial branch.

"I'm not condemning the Supreme Court," he said, "but we do need an appeals system."

Richardson said he would stay on campus during the summer to work on the reorganization.

"We have to get Student Government reorganized to achieve the things in our platform," he said.

On the election itself, Miss Scifres appeared pleased.

"B. Howard Howe did a good job of running the elections," she said. "It was fair and honest, and all three (candidates) made an effort to keep campaign tactics honest and above board."

Miss Scifres, who took 499 of 733 town votes, said she expected to do well in the off-campus areas. But when told she received 259 of 502 votes in McNutt, where she lives, she registered surprise.

"I'm really surprised about McNutt," she said. "I'm glad we pulled it off. It's nice to carry your own dorm."

Inside

Outside

Partial clearing and continued cool today, highs 65-70. Fair and cool tonight, lows in the mid 40s. Sunny and a little warmer Thursday, highs in the low 70s. Chance of precipitation: five per cent today and tonight.

Biesecker, Walda not quitting politics

By Barb Berggoetz
and Harold Stafford
ids Staff Writers

Tom Biesecker, sophomore, and John Walda, junior, second- and third-place finishers respectively in Tuesday's Student Government election, are by no means finished with Student Government.

Although "not surprised" with the election results, Biesecker said the main factor was the ids endorsement of Mary Scifres, Student Body President-elect.

Another factor which contributed to his loss, Biesecker said, was the lack of campaigning after the first election. "Times and circumstances weren't with us," he said. "We stopped campaigning two days after the initial election because of the run-off delay, our disqualification, and then Steve Hofer's disqualification.

"The ids endorsement gave her (Miss Scifres) a lot of momentum. Once she got things going her way, starting the bandwagon effect, she couldn't have been overcome."

Biesecker said because of his disqualification and Hofer's, he did not make effective use of time for campaigning, whereas Miss Scifres did.

"Had we won the election, Hofer's support would have won it for us," he said. Biesecker explained it was hard to assess the value of Hofer's support, but he said it helped some in Teter, Forest and in town.

"This election was a fluke. It is hard to evaluate because this was not a normal election under normal circumstances," Biesecker said.

"Our turnout on Third Street (13 votes) is hard to understand because we were promised more votes."

Biesecker was alsodisappointed with his support at McNutt.

Although he has no specific plans with Student Government now, he said he will continue to work in any way he could and "not walk out" because of the election.

Gary Linder, Biesecker's running mate, commented, "Of course, we would like to congratulate Mary and Jeff, but more important, we hope I.U. students will support them and Student Government to make it more than the farce it was this year."

Walda said he was "pleased with the way it (the election) was carried out. I thought it was carried out very efficiently."

He said he was happy the counting of the ballots was done quickly and that "we didn't have to sit around all night."

Asked if he thought the delay of the run-off had any effect on the outcome, Walda said, "I don't think the delay itself had any effect."

But he quickly added he believed the handling of the Hofer case and the involvement of the other candidates in the legal battling as reported by the news media might have had an effect, especially on the number of students who voted.

However, the largeness of Tuesday night's vote, Walda said, is "a tribute" to campaigns run by the three run-off candidates.

"The turn out was good under the circumstances," Walda said.

Despite his defeat for the presidency, Walda said, "I'm by no means finished with Student Government."

Walda explained that next year he will "be offering any services I can" to Miss Scifres. He said he is interested in working with people in the residence halls and with people interested in an all-University senate.

The all-University senate concept was one of Walda's major interests during the campaign. "That interest hasn't died with this campaign," he asserted.

"I'll be offering my services to Mary. After myself, she has been, and still is, my first choice."

Oops!

The ids apologizes for any embarrassment caused by the caption attached to the picture of Monday night's AFSCME union meeting. The man pictured said he was not advocating an immediate strike, as the caption implied. The ids hopes the picture and its cutline did not cause undue bother for the gentleman pictured.

Proposal hoped to avert strike

By Rich Gotshall
ids Senior Reporter

There probably will not be a strike of University employes, according to local chief Gary Stewart. Last-minute negotiations Tuesday night with the University brought results Stewart believes will be acceptable to union members.

The newest I.U. proposal will give all employes a cost-of-living raise of 5 per cent, payment of 50 per cent of Blue Cross costs, and merit raises for everyone including top-level wage-earners. The three parts combine to approximately a 7 per cent total increase for the year. The local chapter of the American Federation of State, County and Municipal Employes had been asking for an 8 per cent increase.

In addition to the salary increases, I.U. also agreed to allow a factfinder to view the budget.

I.U. officials told Stewart and the union said the factfinder should come from the international union, not the American Arbitration Association. One union member believed this move would allow the University to brand any results favoring higher wages as "biased towards the union."

Union members will meet at 8 tonight to vote on accepting the I.U. proposal. The site for the meeting was to be announced this morning.

The I.U. decision to allow a factfinder and increase wages higher than their Monday offer of 4½ per cent came at about 9 p.m. Tuesday, long after the union's 5 p.m. deadline. Union officials and I.U. officials met from after lunch until about 4. Stewart said he was called at home and asked back into a meeting with I.U. around 7 p.m. in Bryan Hall. The meeting behind locked doors lasted until about 9 p.m.

About I.U.'s new offer Stewart said, "The factfinder was all we asked for originally. We got this and more too. We made a hell of a step forward."

Stewart, visibly fatigued after a day of bargaining added, "We've got everything pretty well cleaned up now. We're going to recommend that the members accept it. And we think they will accept it."

The I.U. union has a membership of about 800 out of 1,530 employes. The employes are involved mainly in maintenance and cafeteria work, with some skilled labor.

I.U. was readying itself for a strike if an agreement wasn't reached. Paper plates were being moved into some dining halls, according to one observer. It was also rumored that some student helpers in the cafeterias were planning to walk out with the union in the event of a strike.

ids/Paul Willis

Stormy dinner

As debris is cleared from the interior of the King's Table Restaurant in Columbus, a worker begins reconstruction of the roof, half of which was blown off by high winds at 8 Monday night. Ten peopl- including four customers were inside when the storm struck, but none were hurt.

P0078827, IU Archives.

Bus business — Daily Kent Stater/Phil Long

It's standing room only on one of Kent State University's 35 buses. Students support the system which costs them $8 per quarter, paid as a fee requirement. Other universities, including I.U., are studying the system as a model campus transportation arrangement. Estimated cost to initiate a similar system here is $400,000.

I.U. studies system

Kent buses 'no-fare'

By LeAnn Spencer
ids Staff Writer

> The Kent State system has other virtues besides its low cost to students. Provisions are made for handicapped students and proponents of mass transit say bus riding means less pollution. See related stories on page 5.

KENT, Ohio – Five years ago Kent State University had no campus bus system. Students there didn't go very far – unless they had a car.

Today, at Kent State from 17,500 to 22,000 passengers ride the "free" bus system every day. The Kent enrollment is about 20,000 students.

Although Kent State's "free" bus system isn't really getting something for nothing, it is relatively inexpensive, and universities across the country, including I.U., study the Kent State campus bus system as a model.

Many I.U. students still face some problem of transportation – unless they have a car, a $20 per semester bus pass, or 25-cents for a bus ride after 3:30 p.m. If not, it's a 15-minute walk between classes in Bloomington's pouring rain or near-zero winter temperatures.

About 11,000 student passengers ride I.U. campus buses on an average day. This figure includes an 18 per cent increase over last year since the expanded service to the College Mall started this fall, Chester Colby, I.U. director of transportation and parking, said.

I.U. buses are carrying almost their full capacity on all routes, Colby said. "We could probably go to another 2,000 passengers a day," he added. However, it would depend when and from where this extra load came.

The passenger capacity of a route is calculated using the periods between classes when bus use is greatest.

The Kent State bus service is in such demand that students' fees are used to support it. In the beginning, money came from the university's general fund and from federal grants. A year later in 1968 a $4 per quarter per student fee increase was instituted to finance the bus service.

Last spring the fee was doubled to $8 per quarter. Students voted for and petitioned the university for the fee increase, said Joseph Fiala, director of the Kent State office of transportation and parking.

Without the fee increase, the campus bus service probably would have gone bankrupt.

Kent students pay $24 a school year for bus service to the downtown area, two shopping centers, married student housing, the football stadium, distant apartment complexes and a 10-mile route to a neighboring town. Five main routes are run, plus an auxiliary trip to neighboring Cleveland, Ohio which transports nursing students to hospitals there three or four times a day.

Kent State employs 97 students to service, repair and drive 35 buses. When a bus breaks down, a replacement or a maintenance vehicle usually can be dispatched within minutes.

Student supervisors direct and train the drivers. Fiala was one of the first drivers and student supervisors.

All students, faculty, staff and their families are eligible to ride the buses.

All this is possible for I.U. – if certain changes in the present campus transportation system are made.

First, the present system would have to be revised completely to cope with increased demand. Now, waits for an I.U. campus bus can be anywhere from 10 to 20 minutes which presents

See 'Transportation' on page 5.

15 cents
14 pages
Vol. 105 No. 106
Monday, January 22, 1973
Bloomington, Indiana 47401

ids
Indiana Daily Student

Trustees approve InPIRG fee checkoff—on conditions

By Dale Eisman
ids Staff Writer

A long, and sometimes bitter, tug-of-war between the Indiana Public Interest Research Group (InPIRG) and the I.U. Board of Trustees ended quietly Saturday morning.

By a 6-1 vote, the trustees approved a resolution calling for a contract between InPIRG and the University for collection of InPIRG's operating funds at class registration.

The contract, to be drawn by I.U. counsel Cliff Travis, will allow InPIRG to fund itself through a voluntary registration card checkoff similar to that provided for student government. The InPIRG fee will be $1.50 per semester.

The resolution said InPIRG has agreed to reimburse I.U. for costs of administering the fee and has promised to stay out of issues arising from decisions of the University faculty or administration. InPIRG also agreed not to sue I.U., to locally spend all funds collected locally and not to combine its funds with those collected from any other school.

The trustees will approve the one-year "experimental" contract at their next meeting, scheduled for Feb. 24 in Kokomo. The resolution said approval will be subject to a favorable ruling on the contract's legality from the state attorney general.

Trustee Jeanne Miller, New Haven, said the conditions placed on InPIRG's use of funds collected at registration were the key to the trustee's favorable action. A year ago, the board rejected an InPIRG proposal to collect funds through a mandatory-refundable fee.

Trustee Carl Gray, Petersburg, the only board member to vote against InPIRG, said, "I don't think we (the trustees) have any legal right to do this." He termed extension of the voluntary registration card checkoff to InPIRG "a dangerous policy," and predicted a flood of student groups soon will descend on the board, demanding their own checkoffs.

Gray's comments reflected those made before the vote by Barry Burr, junior, chairman of the I.U. Young Americans for Freedom (YAF). Burr said InPIRG had given "no evidence of widespread support," on the campus and neither it nor any other organization deserves the privilege of a registration checkoff.

Solomon Lowenstein, executive director of InPIRG, described the organization's attitude as one of "guarded optimism," following Friday's sympathetic hearing from the board's Student Affairs Committee. He indicated surprise with the favorable recommendation the group received from Bloomington Chancellor Byrum E. Carter and with trustee Robert Gates' introduction of the resolution.

Gates had been antagonistic toward InPIRG during the student affairs meeting.

In other business, the board heard from Student Body Treasurer Fred Logan concerning student support of I.U.'s bienniel budget request to the state legislature.

Logan said student government supports and will lobby for the entire $220 million I.U. request. In return, he asked the University administration to include students in the decision-making process which formulates the budget and works for its adoption.

With the Indiana Commission for Higher Education (HEC) expected to announce its own recommendations for the I.U. budget tonight, Logan suggested the University adopt a three-point policy for this week. The points are:

- Following announcement of the HEC recommendation, the University should announce whether it will lobby for the HEC request or its own.
- If the University decides to support the commission, it must clarify it is not merely assuming an increase in fees.
- The administration should immediately place students on those University financial committees which will consider budgetary matters.

Logan also pledged students will lobby against any increase in fees. Waving petitions he said contain the signatures of some 21,000 students opposed to a fee hike, Logan termed them his mandate from the student body.

The board took three other relatively important actions, one of which was unexpected. They were:

- Approval of four proposed changes in the Student Conduct Code. The only important change requires I.U. officials asking students for identification to state the reason for the request and provide identification of their own.
- Approval of the purchase of 11 more pieces of property in downtown Indianapolis. The board continued its buying of property for expansion of the IU-PUI campus.
- Acceptance of the Halls of Residence Committee report suggesting changes in hall lifestyles. Somewhat unexpectedly, the board directed the administration to come up with a report on possible administrative, financial and security ramifications of adopting the halls' report. This is to be considered for approval at the board's February meeting.

Demonstrators provide inauguration conscience

By John Antonides
ids Staff Writer

WASHINGTON, D.C. – The persons who organized Saturday's protest against the Inauguration of President Nixon called their demonstration "An Inauguration of Conscience."

The name fit.

For more than two hours after Nixon's swearing-in, spokesmen of every faction from the National Peace Action Coalition to the Gay Alliance declared their conscience to at least 50,000 demonstrators in front of the Washington Monument.

It was a debate to leave one thinking. Thinking about the power of violence vs. the power of non-violence. Thinking about the power of going to the polls vs. the power of staying home.

And when it was all over, only their goal was clear:

"Out now."

Demonstrators shouting that slogan against the war came en masse in the cold, early-morning hours Saturday. They crawled out of hundreds of buses, swarmed over the steps of the Lincoln Memorial and spawned argument over their numbers.

Numbers. Washington police attempted to downplay them, placing the crowd between 30,000 or 45,000. Estimates by the demonstrators ranged as high as 200,000. Counting the different protest groups who spread over the city but never gathered together in one place, a good guess would be 100,000. But the words of National Peace Action Coalition coordinator Jerry Gordon were unquestionable.

"There are more Americans here at the Washington Monument saying no to the war than there are a half mile away at the inauguration saying yes to Richard Nixon," Gordon said. "Nixon claimed peace is at hand, but looking around here today, it appears not everyone is convinced."

Nor was each demonstrator convinced about how to say no. While most protestors gathered for a march from the Lincoln Memorial to the Washington Monument, Students for a Democratic Society (SDS) marched to Union Station Plaza near the Capitol. The Yippies wearing Mickey Mouse masks were marching from the Plaza – dragging a huge paper rat they said symbolized Nixon.

"You have to understand why we no agree about everything," a sympathizing immigrant told a peace-button wearing demonstrator in broken English. "Everyone's confused. Talk, talk, talk's all right. But no fight. I help you end this war. We get people all over and we change things. But I no wear button."

It was a subtle indication of the kind of disagreement that went on throughout the crowd. At the Lincoln Memorial, for example, a couple of demonstrators passed time before the march arguing their conflicting points of view.

One, a 32-year old cabbie from D.C., called himself an anarchist. The other, a 28-year old teacher from a New York city university (he refused to name the school) insisted protestors must work within the system.

"No, I didn't vote in November," the cabbie said. "Elections are a charade. Whoever wins is a capitalist. In the next four years, I see more and more people like myself dropping out – realizing we have no place in society."

"You shouldn't drop out," countered the teacher, a member of Youth Against War and Facism. "You should struggle against it."

"I don't know," the other countered. "I see dropping out as an

See 'Protesters unite' page 3

Stars 'n shrouds — ids/Dick Kelley

Old Glory's colors of red, white and blue weren't enough to express one couple's feelings at the "Inauguration of Conscience" in Washington, D.C., Saturday. They also shrouded themselves in black to symbolize the more sober aspects of their antiwar protest in the "March against Death."

inside ids

Rain pains

Showers of blessings there may not be, but showers of rain are a good possibility for today and tonight. Chance of precipitation is 30 per cent. Skies today will be cloudy and temperatures will reach the upper 40s and low 50s. Low tonight will be in the upper 30s. Tuesday's high should be in the low 40s.

Air fares up?

Flying high may soon cost students more, if the Civil Aeronautics Board recommendation to eliminate student discount rates goes into effect. The National Student Lobby (NSL) is at work trying to prevent this occurrence. See the story on page 14.

We're No. 1!

The Hoosier basketball team defeated the Minnesota Gophers 83-71 Saturday before a record-breaking crowd of 17,100, moving I.U. into first place in the Big Ten. See stories on page 8.

P0078728, IU Archives.

Playing in leaves is nothing new – but that doesn't make it less fun. A small group of students took time out Tuesday to frolic in the fallen foliage in front of the Chemistry Building. The fellow in the air can't really fly – he was just tossed into a pile of leaves by his friends.

ids/Steve Yeater

15 cents
14 pages
Vol. 106 No. 74
Wednesday, November 14, 1973
Bloomington, Indiana 47401

ids

Indiana Daily Student

No new instructors for political science

EDITOR'S NOTE: This is the third of a five-part series exploring the implications of the 1973-75 budget cuts in departments of the College of Arts and Sciences. Members of the Daily Student intern staff interviewed all department chairmen in the college. Today's stories examine the budget cuts in the social science departments. More stories are on page 6.

By Billy Joe Wampler
ids Staff Writer

I.U. budget cuts are cramping expansion of both faculty and students in the Department of Political Science, Leroy Rieselbach, professor and department chairman, said. Rieselbach pointed to a "lack of salary money" as one of the biggest handicaps.

At a meeting of political science chairmen in Chicago, Rieselbach discovered I.U. faculty salary increments were the smallest in the Big Ten.

"We were smaller with our overall average per cent increase than any other department in the Big Ten and University of Chicago. That gives us difficulty in attracting new faculty and retaining old faculty," he said.

Rieselbach said the competitive nature of the job market demands a professor prove his research and teaching abilities. "You have to fight to retain the services of your good faculty," he said.

The department lost one secretary, leaving four in the office's main typing pool, Rieselbach said. Because of that loss, there are "too few people to do the typing for the faculty," he said.

The secretarial staff is expected to handle all of the course related materials including all examinations and mimeographed work, Rieselbach said. "They are also expected to handle the correspondence, which sometimes is voluminous, by the members of the faculty," he said.

Although supplies and equipment is the place where the department can squeeze without cutting back on faculty and staff, there are few restraints on photocopies and mimeographed materials, Rieselbach said. The recent Indiana Bell phone rate hike also is hurting the department, he said.

"We find it is almost impossible for us as a department to live within the supply budget. It has to cover our telephones, our supplies, paper, blue books, photocopying and mimeographing and papers of all kinds," Rieselbach said.

Rieselbach asked his colleagues to save money by writing letters rather than telephoning, using both sides of paper and turning out classroom lights. "There's a limit to what you can do and a limit to how far you can cramp the style of faculty trying to teach courses," Rieselbach said. "A university of this size ought to be able to provide the kinds of handouts to enrolled students that the faculty feel are necessary to the course."

Rieselbach said political science is trying to rely on "self-imposed restraint." But, Rieselbach claimed the budget will not last through spring of 1974 – a year before the end of the fiscal year. "We will probably resort to some rationing system," he said.

The budget for travel by faculty members has been cut, Rieselbach said. The University used to pay all expenses for one faculty trip each year, he said. "You are likely to have to shell out a fair amount out of your own pocket," he said.

"Faculty members are literally expected to take part in the professional activities of their own disciplines," Rieselbach said. Professional activities include committee meetings, association meetings and conferences. "Continued intellectual growth requires people working in those fields to go to these meetings when invited. They either have to pay the money out of their own pockets or use their 'one trip' allotment," Rieselbach said.

"One mission is to teach the student. But, we cannot offer the opportunity for our faculty to be involved professionally, to have contacts with their peers at other institutions, to get involved in their own research. All of this gives them something to say to their students," he said.

Alaskan pipeline okayed...

WASHINGTON (AP) – Nearly six years after America's richest pool of oil was discovered on Alaska's North Slope, a bill authorizing a pipeline to tap it cleared Congress Tuesday.

A Senate vote of 80 to 5 sent the measure to President Nixon. Backers predicted he will sign it,, despite administration misgivings over sections giving regulatory agencies greater powers. The House passed the bill Monday.

The $4.5-billion pipeline, long delayed in Congress and the courts by environmentalists who feared damage from oil spills, would be the largest construction job ever undertaken by private enterprise.

Sen. Henry M. Jackson, D-Wash., warned environmentalists that if they again tie the project up with lawsuits, he will offer a bill in January to have the federal government build it.

Jackson said work must begin by May on the 789-mile line so that oil can begin flowing to the ice-free port of Valdez and then by ship to West Coast ports.

Voting against the bill were Sens. Birch Bayh, D-Ind.; Joseph R. Byden Jr., D-Del.; Edward W. Brooke, R-Mass.; Harold E. Hughes, D-Iowa; and William Proxmire, D-Wis.

Reserves in the Prudhoe Bay area of Alaska, discovered in February 1968, are estimated at 10 billion to 30 billion barrels.

Atlantic Richfield, Exxon, British Petroleum and four firms which hold smaller shares of the oil formed a consortium to build the pipeline.

After prolonged courtroom delays, a federal appeals court blocked the project in February. The court said it violated limits on the width of rights of way which Congress laid down in 1920.

The bill sent to Nixon revises the right of way limitations, authorizes a construction permit and bans most lawsuits which could delay the project.

...Local energy consciousness urged

Bloomington Mayor Frank McCloskey called on all city residents to re-evaluate their energy consumption and develop an energy-conscious lifestyle, in a statement Tuesday on energy use.

After examination of city facilities operations, the mayor's office directed city department heads to reduce the energy consumption level. City departments have been directed to implement these energy conservation measures:

- Lower thermostats in all municipal buildings at least four degrees.
- Reduce indoor and outdoor lighting of municipal facilities to a minimum level for reasonable safety precautions.
- Encourage all municipal employees to use the Bloomington Transit System or establish carpools to and from work.
- Eliminate excessive idling time in municipal vehicles.
- Reduce speeds of all municipal vehicles to 50 miles per hour except in emergencies.

The mayor also recommended all Bloomington citizens take appropriate steps in offices and homes to conserve energy.

The mayor asked citizens to review the Bloomington Transit schedule to determine when the buses best serve their transportation needs, and help in the conservation of fuel.

The mayor also urged that residents:

- Establish work and school carpools when bus schedules do not meet their transportation needs.
- Lower home and office thermostats to at least 68 degrees.
- Lower temperature controls on household water heaters.
- Reduce lighting in homes and offices to meet legitimate needs.
- Reduce duration and intensity of outdoor electrical lighting in line with safety precautions.
- Tune-up automobiles, check tire pressures, reduce speeds and cut down trips.
- Reduce warm-up idling time for automobiles on cold days.

The statement stressed all citizens must sacrifice together so no one will be deprived of sufficient energy to meet needs.

Anthropology

By Jane Washburn
ids Staff Writer

The I.U. budget is radically changing the character of Department of Anthropology faculty, James Kellar, its acting chairman, said.

"The crunch comes in terms of replacing faculty and staffing courses," Robert Meier, assistant professor of anthropology and undergraduate adviser, said. "There just aren't enough staff members to serve our needs."

In less than three years, four professors who have either left, retired or died, have been replaced by three assistant professors, Kellar, also a professor of anthropology, said.

To make funds go farther, former Dean of Arts of Sciences George W. Wilson authorized recruitment on a junior level when full professors are lost, Kellar said.

"The age of attachment to ivy-covered walls is over," he said. "Professors go where there's more money and better research facilities. Budget cuts are going to make it difficult to recruit professors with national reputations, which will in turn affect our reputation."

"I'm not being critical of junior faculty, but the department is changing radically in terms of character," Kellar said. "The departmental balance of rank is shifting and we're leveling off at the top."

A required undergraduate major's course, L200 – Language and Culture, may not be offered due to staff shortage, Kellar said.

"We may need to waive the requirement or substitute a similar course from another department," Meier said. "It would mean that the student's

See 'Anthropology' on page 6

Cyclotron to reveal mysteries

By Gail Hinchion
ids Staff Writer

Scientists from around the world will be coming to Bloomington next fall to examine a machine designed to reveal the mysteries of nuclear energy by manipulating the nucleus of an atom.

By next fall, the multi-particle isochronous cyclotron will be completed, eight years after blueprints were made.

It is housed in a specially-constructed research center, about 500 yards northwest of the Ind. 46 Bypass at Fee Lane, that looks like a mission-control, top secret-type hide-a-way.

"A cyclotron is a device used for accelerating charged atomic particles by giving them a small kick many times by pulling them around and around through the same electric field," Guy Emery, I.U. physicist and assistant director of the cyclotron, said.

This cyclotron is composed of four bright orange magnets weighing 500 tons each and measuring 40 feet across by 18 feet high. Building it cost about $10 million in state and federal funds. The National Science Foundation will pay the cyclotron's $1 million yearly operating expense.

And though Emergy describes the cyclotron's effect in terms of "small kicks," this cyclotron accelerates atomic particles to an energy equivalent of 200 million volts.

The cyclotron represents stage three in a three-stage acceleration process designed by the cyclotron's inventor, Martin Rickey, an I.U. physicist.

Stage one occurs at the ion source, a machine which "functions somewhat like a dry cell of 500,000 volts," Emery said.

At this starting point, a gas, hydrogen, for example, is leaked into a high frequency electronic field, causing what Emergy called "a plasma discharge" in which the electrons and protons are separated.

On one side of the discharge region, a steady electric field pulls some protons out of the plasma discharge and directs them into a vacuumed beam pipe toward stage two.

Stage two is a small cyclotron, about one-eighth the mass of the larger model.

Emery likened the process at the mini-cyclotron to that of a parent pushing a child on a merry-go-round. Each time the child comes around, the parent gives another push, increasing the velocity of revolutions.

The protons from the ion source receive a similar "ride" provided they manage to "hop on" the mini-cyclotron's electric field. Only when the protons and the cyclotron's force rotate in unison, also called resonance, is the proper effect achieved.

According to Emergy, only a few per cent catch a ride.

These swirl within the electric field of the mini-cyclotron for about 100 rotations, or one millionth of a second. Then they are shot through a second beam pipe at 15 million volts toward the large cyclotron to begin a similar process on a more dramatic scale.

"When the particles are moving at the velocity as high as particles leaving stage two, the effects of relativity make it harder to reach resonance, also called the icochronous condition, at the third stage.

"The new I.U. cyclotron at stage three is expected to be the most isochronous cyclotron designed," Emery said. Once repeating the rotation process of this unique cyclotron, the atomic particles are more precisely accelerated and attuned than for any other cyclotron of comparable size and design, he said.

From stage three the particles are shot through another beam pipe toward a one-half square inch metal target. Upon impact, some go through the metal, and some scatter. Those which scatter are counted by a machine somewhat like a sophisticated Geiger counter.

The counter transmits signals to a computer center which gathers and sorts results. The number of scattered particles and the angles at which they fly are examples of the information

See 'Cyclotron' on page 7

monday

Indian summer continues. Temperatures today will reach a high of 70 to 75, with the low tonight in the mid 50s. Clouds, wind and warmth are predicted with some chance of showers late tonight. Thursday will be warm again – only one week from Thanksgiving, the temperatures will be in the low 70s.

ids/Steve Yeater

I.U. scientists have built this cyclotron from scratch

P0078668, IU Archives.

REFLECTION

Finding a Place behind the Camera

A stranger asked my name as I left freshman registration in 1969 at the old Fieldhouse on campus. I felt unsettled because he had been following me for the past hour as I signed up for classes.

I had scurried from line to line once I noticed him, but he stalked me in a game of hide-and-seek. I had tried to hide behind taller students only to discover there he was again . . . watching. I had to laugh in disbelief when I thought I was finally lost in the crowd, and then I spotted him on a tall ladder, holding a camera with a long lens peering down at me.

"While I understood the meaning of journalism, I had never felt the inspiration that I found when I picked up a camera."

The next morning, I picked up the student paper and there I was—an entire photo story about me—a naïve student looking lost and confused. But he had also captured joy. It was my first encounter with the Indiana Daily Student.

When I was in junior high school, I stayed on campus with my older sister, Janet Farlow Perry, during Little Sister's Weekend. We had toured the school newspaper where she and her roommate, Irene Clare Nolan, were reporters, and I remember being amazed at the Linotype machines loudly clacking away, and I liked the smell of ink.

A few years later, I followed in Janet's footsteps and signed up for journalism classes. I took reporting, editing and history but was not a stellar student. The next summer I worked as a reporter at the IDS. The newsroom buzzed with energy as writers banged out stories on manual Royal typewriters covering marches and Vietnam War protests while I typed my first assignment—a column that listed meetings on campus.

My stories were heavily marked up with handwritten editors' corrections, but I moved on to greater responsibilities and wrote a piece about dilapidated student housing. Although I got a byline, the student editor who heavily rewrote the article must have thought I was hopeless. I didn't excel at writing and, worse than that, I didn't feel like I belonged.

The next three years I had an undecided major, taking classes in geology, concrete poetry, children's literature, archeology, sociology, psychology and anthropology in a search for my calling. Out of options for my junior year, I considered signing up for classes in basket weaving and first aid.

Walking by the journalism table I inquired about the next eligible class. Marge Blewett looked up staring at me with a stone face and answered, "Non Verbal Communication." My perplexed expression caused her to explain, "Photojournalism. The first photography class." I snatched the enrollment card. My mind raced with anticipation.

I found my home. While I understood the meaning of journalism, I had never felt the inspiration that I found when I picked up a camera. Working in the darkroom was like adding magic to the experience. It felt intuitive and artful, and I learned there was another language to communicate with images. Surrounded by a community of talented photographers, Will Counts was an insightful, encouraging professor.

Technique did not come easily. I recall John Fulton patiently explaining to me the relationship between aperture and shutter speed—something I had heard and read about many times, but it finally made sense. I followed him into the darkroom and found a family. Brian Horton sat in a large rocking chair surrounded by trays of intoxicating, darkroom chemicals. The darkroom was a great place to hide out and learn from my heroes—Karen Elshout, Gary Jackson, and Cheryl Magazine became my mentors who guided and believed in me.

The IDS newsroom was no longer intimidating but a place to connect with diverse people who had a common mission—to cover stories that mattered. We witnessed an interesting, volatile and turbulent period in the early '70s—Nixon and Watergate, Roe v. Wade, the Kent State shootings and war protests, questions and expressions of feminism, racial equality and gender identity, rock concerts and experimental drugs and the first Earth Day. For all the good and the bad of these times, they made an impact on my life. Journalism helped me make sense of the world, and I still subscribe to the photojournalism mantra: "Show truth with a camera."

I believe that even in the era of alternative facts that honest, ethical journalism can make a difference. My early experience influenced my approach and helped me to understand what it feels like to be on the other side of a camera. It reminds me of the importance of being sensitive and to build rapport and earn trust.

—Melissa Farlow, BA 1974

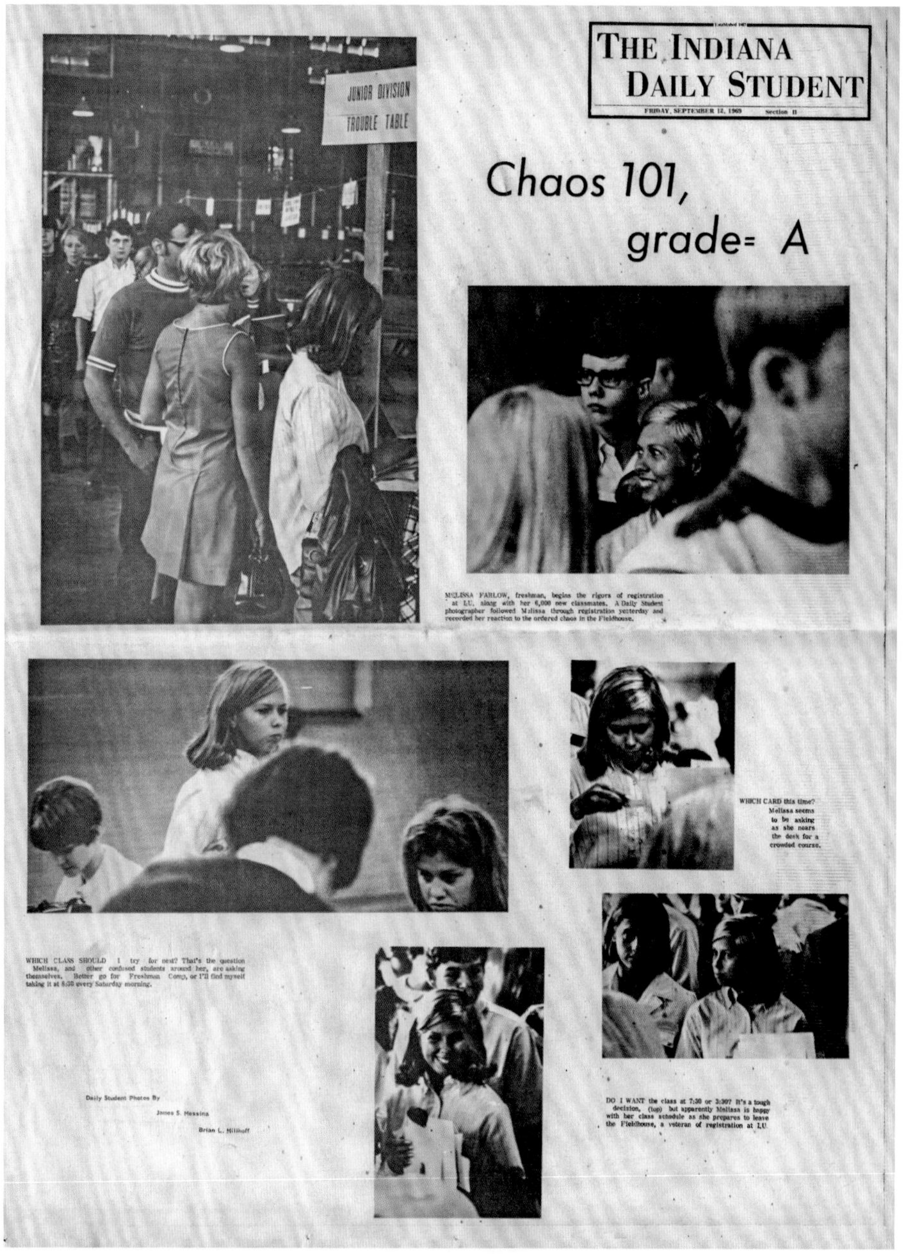
THE INDIANA DAILY STUDENT
FRIDAY, SEPTEMBER 12, 1969 Section II

Chaos 101, grade= A

MELISSA FARLOW, freshman, begins the rigors of registration at I.U. along with her 6,000 new classmates. A Daily Student photographer followed Melissa through registration yesterday and recorded her reaction to the ordered chaos in the Fieldhouse.

WHICH CARD this time? Melissa seems to be asking as she nears the desk for a crowded course.

WHICH CLASS SHOULD I try for next? That's the question Melissa, and other confused students around her, are asking themselves. Better go for Freshman Comp, or I'll find myself taking it at 8:30 every Saturday morning.

DO I WANT the class at 7:30 or 3:30? It's a tough decision, (top) but apparently Melissa is happy with her class schedule as she prepares to leave the Fieldhouse, a veteran of registration at I.U.

Daily Student Photos By
James S. Messina
Brian L. Millhoff

A Sept. 12, 1969, photo essay featuring photographer-to-be Melissa Farlow registering for classes before her first semester at IU. *P0080443, IU Archives.*

ids*

Transport panel discusses appeal board, car ban

By Marcia Parker

The I.U Transportation Advisory Committee heard proposals and postponed action on the establishment of a parking appeals committee and about relaxing rules against freshmen and sophomores having cars on campus.

The committee approved at its Monday afternoon meeting a married couple's bus pass discount and heard a report on the status of a shuttle bus system between Bloomington and I.U.-Purdue University-Indianapolis (IUPUI).

The committee tabled further action on forming the parking appeals committee after arguments arose about an acceptable ratio of student, faculty and staff members in the committee.

Kurt Flock, junior and I.U. Student Association (IUSA) president, told the committee that because 90 per cent of all parking appeals are initiated by students, students should have a majority on the appeals committee.

Frank Parker, senior and representative of the Married Students Association, proposed a committee of six students, six faculty members and six staff members. The advisory committee voted tentatively to give the committee that composition. Advisory committee chairman William Black, director of the I.U. Center for Urban Affairs, said the issue could be discussed again at the group's July 29 meeting.

Chester Colby, I.U. director of transportation, introduced proposals for relaxing the ban on the keeping of cars by freshmen and sophomores who live in University halls of residence. Colby said the ban is difficult to enforce and it makes off-campus housing more attractive than I.U housing.

Colby said the ban could be lifted entirely or that the ban could be retained only for freshmen living in the halls of residence.

Black said he opposed lifting the ban because it might cause further campus traffic congestion, by adding up to 5,000 cars. The committee tabled the proposal for further study.

Paul Sill, supervisor of the campus bus and parking system, submitted the proposal for a Family Bus Pass Plan. The plan will allow two passes to be sold to married couples at a 50 per cent discount on the second pass. Other family members would continue to pay the normal fares.

The plan will be effected next fall.

Sill said children of married students were not included in a discount plan "to prevent families from 'loaning' bus passes issued for children to other families" and to minimize printing costs of passes. (Passes issued to a couple will have the same number.)

Colby explained that the shuttle bus system would include hourly service between Bloomington and Indianapolis campuses at a rate of $1.50 per fare, one way. The system will provide evening service for the late night classes offered at IUPUI this fall. Colby said he hopes the shuttle bus system will be ready this fall.

In other business the committee:

• Was introduced to George Smerk, I.U. professor of transportation in the School of Business, who next week will become acting director of transportation. Colby resigned six weeks ago to accept a job in Phoenix.

• Approved plans to construct a parking lot near the I.U. Physical Plant, 912 Walnut Grove; to add parking spaces on Law Lane; to relocate and increase parking at Sembower Field on Fee Lane, and to widen the driveway to the Health, Physical Education and Recreation Building.

Art/Liz Rios

One advantage of being a marijuana dealer is you can always turn your friends on

Pot profits lift dealer out of TV dinner slump

By John Molitor

Jerry (not his real name) looks like your typical student–medium build, long brown hair, blue jeans, tennis shoes and a T-shirt. He's a shy person, slow to speak up in a crowd and a little spacy, too.

"People think I'm stoned all the time, but I'm not. I'm just very absent-minded," he said. "I only get stoned about every week or so."

Jerry, an I.U. alumnus, now works two different jobs in Bloomington. One is as a semi-skilled worker and pays about $70 a week.

The other is dealing marijuana and pays about $30 a week–tax free.

"This is supplemental income," Jerry said about his profits from selling grass. "But it's not going to buy you a yacht.

"I think most people go into this at least partly for financial considerations. I just got tired of eating TV dinners," he said.

He lists other advantages to being a dealer, too.

"If you like dope you've always got some around. You can turn your friends on, too.

Almost everybody smokes marijuana

"This is the kind of job you can really get into," Jerry explained, laughing. "You get to meet all kinds of really fantastic people. Almost everybody smokes marijuana here."

Jerry said he wouldn't go up to a complete stranger and try to sell him some dope, but he added, "It's such an open atmosphere here you don't have to worry too much."

He does take some precautions, though, to keep from getting caught. "Like, my business stash is not in my house," he said.

"And I like to make pretty sure that they (my customers) are people I've been around a lot and observed. Around other people I just keep my mouth shut," he added.

Jerry doesn't think there's much chance he'll get arrested.

"As long as you have a lot of friends you know are not narcs and you just keep selling to them, you shouldn't have much trouble.

"Also, the police in this town have too much other stuff to worry about. They just don't care about small-volume traffic," he said.

"If I were the police commissioner, it would make me tired just to think about rooting out all the grass around here. The mere thought of it when I got up in the morning would make me want to go back to bed for the day," he said.

Under Indiana law, Jerry could get 5 to 20 years in prison for the first conviction for distributing marijuana and 20 years to life for the second conviction.

"Obviously I'm not in favor of the law," he said. "I'd like to see it (grass) legalized. Everybody should be able to do (marijuana) when they want to."

Some dealers against legalization

But not all dealers favor legalization, Jerry said. "Some don't want it because it would wreck their business," he said.

Jerry said there probably are "a lot of people like me around, who get a pound at a time and sell it.

"The stuff I have now I got for about $160," he said. He and his partner will get about $300 from selling the pound. They will split the $140 profits evenly.

"You leave out what you want for your own stash, and then you get $20 an ounce," he said. "You don't get rid of it all at once.

"What I'd like to get into eventually is the stuff that costs about $400 to $500 a pound," Jerry said. But that would take more capital, he added.

No comment about supplier

His supplier apparently has that capital, but Jerry didn't want to say anything about the supplier's business.

He would comment generally about the bigger dealers, though. "I think most anybody who'd deal in more than a pound at a time would have to get regular shipments," he said. Such shipments might come from Mexico, the Carribean or South America, he said.

Jerry thinks marijuana is a quality product. "I wouldn't sell it if I didn't believe in it," he said.

"Just think of all the services we dope dealers perform for mankind–relieving their pain and the stress of their daily lives. I think marijuana is much better and safer for you than alcohol," he said.

"Hallucinogenic things–especially the organic ones like peyote and mescaline–help you to get a better perspective on life. By getting you out of yourself a little they help you to see what part you're playing in life," Jerry said.

He said his business is "strictly grass" now, but, "If somebody wanted me to get something I didn't consider dangerous–peyote, LSD, possibly speed–I'd do it."

Jerry said he'd consider selling speed only "if a friend wanted it to stay up to go to work or something like that."

He said he wouldn't sell any other, so-called hard drugs. "I think cocaine's dangerous. I wouldn't sell it," he said.

*Indiana Daily Student

15 cents
10 pages
Vol. 106 No. 200
Tuesday, July 9, 1974
Bloomington, Indiana 47401

weather

Hot, warm, long hot summer, cat on a hot tin roof, hot rocks, bushes, sky, *fair and partly clear,* clouds, aristophanes, greek, trojan, gift horse, horseback riding, too hot for riding, *highs 89 to 94 degrees,* bachelor's, master's, mastermind, plot, scheme, shady, trees, don't stand under during storm, *chance of evening thundershowers.*

They sell anything

A spectator watches the action at a weekly Friday night auction in Bloomington. Walter and Thomas Galyan sell household goods, horses, hogs and cattle at the Bloomington Sale Barn, 2385 S. Walnut St. The brothers have been selling "about anything there is to be sold" for 28 years. For pictures see page 7.

photo/Kim Hitchcock

Two float along on a hot day in one of the Bloomington area quarries

P0079127, IU Archives.

August 9, 1974

ids*

*Indiana Daily Student

15 cents
10 pages
Vol. 106 No. 223
Friday, August 9, 1974
Bloomington, Indiana 47401

Ford to become president

Nixon resigns!

photo/AP

Richard M. Nixon abandoned his fight to remain President in a televised speech Thursday night and gave the office to Vice President Gerald R. Ford.

Nixon's resignation will be effective at noon today and Ford will be sworn in immediately as the nation's 38th president.

Saying that quitting was "abhorrent to every instinct in my body," Nixon told the nation that his resignation was in the best interest of the country. "America needs a fulltime president and fulltime Congress," he said.

The Watergate scandals prevent him from fulfilling that role, Nixon said, and divert Congress from other vital business.

A White House spokesman said the 61-year-old outgoing President and his family would leave the executive mansion today and fly to their San Clemente, Calif., home. The spokesman said the family would use a government VIP plane rather than Air Force One, the presidential jet Nixon used for the past 5½ years.

For details of Nixon's speech and Ford's transition to the presidency see page 2.

Ford 'plodder'

From center on the University of Michigan's football team to House Republican leader to vice president and finally to President of the U.S., Gerald R. Ford's career has developed. But Ford has sometimes been called a "plodder." The orthodox Republican's solidarity seems to be just what the nation now needs as it looks for a government it can trust. Ford, who has described himself as "conservative on fiscal matters, a moderate on domestic affairs and a liberal on foreign policy," will now have the opportunity to fulfill the promises he made to Congress last fall. For a story on Ford and his policies, see page 5.

'Time' tearjerker

"Our Time" is one of the few recent movie offerings written by a woman and starring women. But it is no "sweet, light reminiscence of growing up female . . . rather it is a sordid, turgid tearjerker," Daily Student reviewer Peter Kaufman writes. "Our Time" may be one of those rare movies which although somewhat trashy, with overtones of bad soap operas, has a gut-level appeal that is very effective. For more on "Our Time," see Kaufman's review on page 8.

Transition eased

Entering college is an experience that most students remember and oftentimes they might have done things differently if "only they had known. . ." Groups '74 is a program geared to ease the numerous problems a new student encounters. The program is multi-faceted – its concerns range from counseling on academic problems to sponsoring social events. And it apparently gives some students valuable edge in their new role as a college student. For more on the Groups program, see page 10.

'Pretense' plays

Three members of Pretense Theater perform a scene from "The Rude Mechanics" above. The 10-member, nonprofit group will present the play Sunday at 3 p.m. in the Third Street Park as part of the "Arts in the Park" series. The farcical play is an adaptation from Shakespeare's "Midsummer Night's Dream." For photos of Pretense Theater at work, see page 7.

weather

Into each life a little rain must fall . . . right, Dick? A chance of showers and thunderstorms is forecast for today and tomorrow along with continued cloudy, humid weather. Highs Friday and Saturday are forecast from 80 to 85 degrees. Lows tonight will be in the upper 60s. This is according to an unimpeachable source, of course.

P0079123, IU Archives.

I.U. 1976 NCAA Champs

Kent Benson tourney MVP

statistics

I.U. (86)	FG	FT	R	PF	TP
Abernethy, Tom	4-8	3-3	4	2	11
May, Scott	10-17	6-6	8	4	26
Benson, Kent	11-20	3-5	9	3	25
Wilkerson, Bobby	0-1	0-0	0	1	0
Buckner, Quinn	5-10	6-9	8	4	16
Radford, Wayne	0-1	0-0	1	0	0
Crews, Jim	0-1	2-2	1	1	2
Wisman, Jim	0-1	2-3	1	4	2
Valavicius, Rich	1-1	0-0	0	0	2
Haymore, Mark	1-1	0-0	1	0	2
Bender, Bob	0-0	0-0	0	0	0
Team					
Totals	32-61	22-28	36	19	86

MICHIGAN (68)	FG	FT	R	PF	TP
Britt, Wayman	5-6	1-1	3	5	11
Robinson, John	4-8	0-1	6	2	8
Hubbard, Phil	4-8	2-2	11	5	10
Green, Rickey	7-16	4-5	6	3	18
Grote, Steve	4-9	4-6	1	4	12
Bergen, Tom	0-1	0-0	0	1	0
Staton, Tom	2-5	3-4	2	3	7
Baxter, Dave	0-2	0-0	0	2	0
Thompson, Joel	0-0	0-0	0	0	0
Hardy, Alan	1-2	0-0	2	0	2
Team					
Totals	27-57	14-19	32	25	68

At home...

photo/J.D. Schwalm

photo/Kim Hitchcock

photo/Jim Mendenhall

Jubilation reigned in Bloomington as I.U. fans celebrated the Hoosiers' NCAA basketball victory Monday night. Swimming in Showalter Fountain, a self-styled car rally and brotherly camaraderie at the Sigma Phi Epsilon fraternity house were just a few ways of celebrating. More coverage on page 16.

ids Indiana Daily Student
March 30, 1976 Bloomington, Ind. 16 pages 15 cents

Hoosiers bounce Michigan, 86-68

By Mike Siroky
ids Staff Writer

PHILADELPHIA – The third time was the charm.

I.U. is the national college basketball champion after defeating conference rival Michigan, 86-68, for the third time in one year. This time, it was for all the marbles.

Monday night's battle was the first time in NCAA history that two teams from the same league had met in the finals. Indiana and Michigan showed Philly and I.U. fans why the Wolverines and the Hoosiers had battled for the Big Ten title each of those three times.

"Hey, there's a lotta teams in this country who wouldn't be in first place in our league," Michigan coach Johnny Orr said.

I.U. started in control of the game on Bobby Wilkerson's control of the opening tip and Scott May's conversion of the first basket of the game. It was something like an instant replay of action that occurs in every game.

After May's opening basket (he finished with a game-high 26), the lead began its customary see-saw, and the play began to take on its customary Big Ten physicalness (there were 44 personal fouls committed in the game).

It was on Wayman Britt's drive up the lane on a fast break (the Wolverines had 16 layup buckets in the opening segment) that the foul that could have hurt the most occurred – and it wasn't called.

An airborne Britt made it 6-4, Michigan, but Wilkerson unfortunately chose that moment to float under Britt's flight pattern.

Television replays later showed that Britt could not have seen Wilkerson while in flight, and when he landed, it was elbow-first on Wilkerson's chin.

Wilkerson immediately went down with a mild concussion. He soon regained consciousness and remained in the Spectrum until after the half. However, when he was wheeled off to the Temple University Hospital, he was carried off the floor on a stretcher, never to return to the game.

With Wilkerson's abrupt and unexpected departure, Michigan seized control, scored 12 of the next 18 points and was leading 18-10 with 12:10 left in the half.

"We missed a lotta layups," I.U. coach Bob Knight said later. "You don't have time to think of the injury at the moment. The most immediate thought is who's the best replacement.

"We went with Radford first, because he's got some quickness and wanted someone to go to the bucket," he said. That lasted five minutes and Michigan got that eight-point lead.

"Then we went with Jimmy Crews, because he's got experience (Crews is a senior)," Knight said. That lasted until 42 seconds was left in the game and Michigan had its 35-29 halftime lead.

Classes will not be cancelled today to celebrate the I.U. NCAA basketball championship, I.U. Vice President Robert O'Neil said.

The I.U. basketball team is scheduled to arrive on a commercial flight at Indianapolis' Weir Cook Airport at 10:30 a.m. today, an I.U. team manager said. From there the team will travel by bus to the I.U. Assembly Hall to greet well wishers between 11:30 a.m. and noon.

"We finally went with Jimmy Wisman – a guy who didn't even have tournament experience (a sophomore) in this tournament, because he's quick and can handle the ball."

Wisman's quickness and ball handling got him the start in the second half and he controlled the ball enough (a game-high of six assists) to remain in the rest of the game.

Most of his assists were to Kent Benson, who exploded for 15 of his 25 points in the second half.

Knight said of the Most Valuable Player on the All-NCAA tourney team (May and Tom Abernethy also were on the team), "Benny had to score more – we had to get the ball more to him in the second half. We wanted to keep him inside more."

Benson also did the job on Phil Hubbard, Michigan's freshman center, who fouled out with 7½ minutes to go in the game and only 10 points.

"We only had six personal fouls in the first half (25 for the game) and then we lost our composure in the second half," Orr said. "We let them make the free throws when it cost us the most."

And the guy most conspicuously absent from the All-NCAA team, Quinn Buckner, made the most of those pressure free throws.

Buckner, a 46 per cent shooter from the charity line in the season, made six of nine in the game, as the most integral part of his 16 points.

"I've been practicing a lotta things – including those free throws," Buckner said.

He made two at 11:34 that put I.U. ahead to stay (49-47); one at 7:27 that made the lead six (59-53) and choked off a flurry that could have been a Michigan rally; two at 5:28 that made an eight-point lead (67-59), and a final two with 46 seconds left that was the last nail in the Wolverine coffin. It made the score 82-66.

"Buckner should've been the sixth man on that all-tourney squad," Knight said.

"There's no question. Indiana is the best team in the country," Orr said. "We were superb in the first half (61 per cent shooting to I.U.'s 45.2), but they came on strong in the second (I.U. had 60 per cent shooting then, Michigan 25.5).

"This is the best that Indiana had played. I don't think I could've done anything different that would've changed the outcome," Orr concluded.

...and Philly

A radiant coach Bob Knight, Scott May and Quinn Buckner display the NCAA trophey after Monday night's victory. Just before, May had trimmed the net from the hoop as just another momento of the win. In the early minutes of the game, though, victory didn't seem so certain. At right, May is stopped by Michigan's Steve Grote.

P0020379, IU Archives.

REFLECTION

Covering Knight's Hoosiers

The best lessons in journalism, as any reporter who's wrestled with a beat can tell you, come outside the classroom, outside the newsroom and inside the corners of the real world.

Some of the most meaningful morals of the story of my sports scribing career came while covering the men's basketball team in the 1976–77 season. That team is notable mostly for being the only one of the 28 that Bob Knight coached at IU that failed to qualify for a postseason tournament—which, come to think of it, qualifies as notoriety. It finished with a 14-13 record, although that record was later amended to 16-11 because two losses to Minnesota were counted as victories after Minnesota was made to forfeit all wins for violating NCAA rules.

No amount of forfeiting was going to get that IU team into a postseason tournament. But if it seems like bad timing on my part for having to cover such a forgettable team, it turned out to be great timing because of the professional experience gained. And make no mistake, I was a professional—paid $35 every two weeks.

Some context: The previous season, IU had won the national championship with a perfect record. At the time, Knight was a fear-inspiring god in a plaid sports coat. So, when five players quit the team, either before, during, or after the '76–'77 season, it was a collective eye-opener. One of them, freshman Mike Miday, dropped some jaws, too, by daring to openly criticize the coach on his way out of Bloomington. Miday claimed he had felt "dehumanized" by Knight and revealed some details from locker room tirades.

Fellow beat writer John Whisler and I reported on Miday's exodus, producing stories that were referenced in news reports throughout the country. I still remember one Indianapolis television sports anchor passing along information from "an incredible story in the Indiana Daily Student."

Mark Montieth shortly after graduating from IU. *Photo courtesy of Mark Montieth.*

John and I reported objectively, however, balancing Miday's comments with quotes from former IU players such as Tom Abernethy supporting Knight. By doing that, we got back in Knight's good graces. How we had gotten out of those graces provided another lesson.

One Monday afternoon during the preseason, I walked into Assembly Hall to watch practice, as we were permitted by Knight to do at the time. As soon as I sat down in one of the red-and-white cushioned seats on the west side, Knight stopped practice and shouted, "Montieth! Get your ass down here!"

"If it seems like bad timing on my part for having to cover such a forgettable team, it turned out to be great timing because of the professional experience gained. And make no mistake, I was a professional—paid $35 every two weeks."

I walked down to the floor, just off the court. Knight approached, stopped about 2 feet away from me and screamed, "Is there some sonofabitch at your paper named (—— ———)?"

I confirmed there was.

"Then get your ass out of here and don't come back until we get this straightened out!"

I had no idea what he was talking about. I walked back to my seat to get my books. "I mean now!" Knight shouted.

Back in the IDS newsroom, I learned the reason for Knight's outrage. Our football beat writer, the "sonofabitch" Knight referenced, had led off his story on the previous Saturday's game against Ohio State with these immortal words: "Bob Knight threw an ashtray against the press box window."

The intent was to illustrate the frustration of a crucial second-half turnover. The writer had seen Knight throw a foil ashtray and decided that was a perfect summary of the reaction to the game's turning point.

Only problem was, he only thought he had seen it. Knight had called the IDS publisher earlier in the day to claim the man sitting next to him had thrown it. That man, strength coach Bill Montgomery, also called to take the "blame" for it. The IDS reporter stood his ground, insisting he was sure he had seen Knight throw it, and clung to that turf against the forces of nature for a few weeks.

Finally, he said he couldn't be 100 percent sure he had seen it as he reported it. An apology was published and issued in person, and Knight readmitted Whisler and me to practice—but only because of the balanced manner in which we had reported on Miday's exit.

A couple of valuable lessons came out of that experience. For one, accuracy matters. Be sure of the details before publishing something. For another, while objectivity can get you in trouble, it also can get you out of trouble. It was worth being yelled at for someone else's mistake to learn those lessons.

The IDS provided the perfect kick-start into journalism's harsh world. It was independent from university control, the staff was guided by "adult" publishers who acted as neutral middlemen when irate university officials called to complain about a student's reporting or commentary, and it provided a breeding ground to work with and learn from talented, idealistic and determined journalists who set examples for one another—for better and for worse.

—Mark Montieth, BAJ 1977

'Breaking Away' Superficial, Trivial

Although it was a hit in Bloomington, the original IDS review of the Academy Award-winning film Breaking Away *was anything but glowing. It originally appeared April 23, 1979.*

By Eve B. Rose

You want to like it. You want it to be a good film. It is, after all, about Bloomington. Bloomington: the familiar town immortalized forever on celluloid.

Filmed here during the summer and fall of 1978, "Breaking Away" is about this town, this university and the campus event of the year—the Little 500 bicycle race. Excitement has been building ever since it was announced that "Breaking Away" would have its world premiere in the I.U. Auditorium.

But the film is superficial and trivial. While its locations and extras were enough to elicit a standing ovation Saturday night, those elements will not be enough to insure its reception elsewhere in the United States. At a press conference on Saturday morning, director Peter Yates commented that this film "has to be judged by the general public." And it will be—based on its plot and characterizations. On this level, "Breaking Away" has severe limitations.

In terms of plot, "Breaking Away" follows in the footsteps of that old studio formula film—the underdog makes good. In light of success of "Rocky" and "Animal House," it is not too surprising that movie producers would try to capitalize on the interest in such stories. But because the characters are so uninteresting and colorless, the audience cannot become emotionally involved with them.

Their personalities and their backgrounds—what we see of them—are used only for setting up the race. So much for what Yates calls a "people film." "Breaking Away" is really about the events prior to the race and the race itself. It is the activities that are important to screenwriter Steve Tesich and Yates, not really the characters.

We know very little about Moocher (Jackie Earle Haley), except that his father is in Chicago, he has a girlfriend and he resents cracks about his height. Cyril (Dan Stern) is the well-intentioned ding-bat, whose father "understands" his failures. Mike (Dennis Quaid), the neurotic ex-high school football star, cannot adjust to life out of the limelight. We don't know enough to care about these people.

Then there is Dave Stohler (Dennis Christopher). He dreams of being an Italian bicycle racer, so he talks in Italian, copies Italian mannerisms, plays Italian music and calls the family cat Fellini. His dream and how he tries to live it are treated so comically that when he is abruptly brought back to earth, the moment is not dramatic; it is shocking. How could they do this to such a happy-go-lucky guy?

The plot itself has two serious problems of which Bloomington residents and IU students should take special notice. Is this really how you want your town depicted?

First of all, the main characters all seem to see life outside the college community as a dead end. Are we to believe that most of Bloomington's young people not attending college have this terrible psychological problem about IU? Surely many of these people manage to live happy, rich lives without benefit of university registration!

Second, the movie suggests that college kids and townspeople are constantly at each other's throats. It is as if there are two huge youth gangs. "We're on their turf," one of the characters says. And are the "townies" so physically recognizable that a student in the Union's Commons can casually say to a friend that the four are just "cutter" kids?

Yates said that he was "impressed by Bloomington, by the campus and the healthy goings-on in town, by the campus and the town living side by side." But if we take the film as a statement on the area, it suggests that the situation is hardly "healthy."

But the movie does have some pleasant moments. At the very least, Yates has filmed the area with great sensitivity. He makes it look even more beautiful than it normally does.

Actors Barbara Barrie and Paul Dooley, who play Dave's parents, provide the audience with many amusing moments, especially Dooley, whose character is being driven crazy by his son.

Then there is the speed trial with the Cinzano truck, the parallelism in the serenade sequence, the scene in which Dave doctors the racing bike, and the Little 500 race itself. According to Yates, IU Foundation President William Armstrong said that the movie race has "the most exciting finish there's ever been." And it is an exciting competition, all the more so because of the way it was filmed and edited. The camera focuses on the individual riders as they work, switch bikes, and tear around the curves of the track. The film editing, a series of short quick cuts, further increases the sense of great speed and energy.

All these fine moments, however, are isolated. "Breaking Away" encourages viewers to think the town is made up of warring factions. The whole film is a set-up for the race, exciting though it is.

Even Dave, the underdog, is not really an underdog at all. Apparently, he wins trophies all the time. If this movie was supposed to show that being an underdog is merely a state of mind, then why does everything turn out so well for them competitively?

Either way, "Breaking Away" could at least have presented us with an interesting, enjoyable story. For those who do not know Bloomington and cannot recognize some of the in-jokes, the movie will probably be an unhappy experience. And as for those of us who know Bloomington, it is a disappointment.

August 22, 1978

ids Indiana Daily Student
Bloomington, Ind. Tuesday August 22, 1978 Two sections 20 pages 15 cents

Sunny and warm

Today should be sunny with highs in the mid to upper 80s. Lows tonight are expected to be in the low to mid 60s.

Students face increases in fees, living costs

by Lisa Gerber
ids Staff Writer

On this semester's long anticipated, infamous journey to the fieldhouse for registration, you might want to tote your piggy bank along — you may need it.

Reason being: students, perhaps caught unaware, will find some University fees higher than ever before.

Included on that list of higher prices are tuition, Student Health Service fees and room and board. But it doesn't end there. Students will be paying higher prices for many textbooks, too.

At the end of seemingly countless lines, I.U. students will encounter one of the most noticeable increases — tuition.

Effective this semester, charges for instate undergraduate students on the Bloomington campus will be $29 per credit hour, up $2 from last year. The non-resident undergraduate fee will be $70 per credit hour, up $4.

The I.U.-Bloomington campus, however, still has lower tuition rates than most Big 10 universities, according to Edward Whalen, director of I.U.'s Budget Office.

Of the nine public institutions, I.U. ties Purdue University for fifth place for instate undergraduate rates. For out-of-state rates, I.U. ties Purdue for sixth place.

But higher tuition may not seem so astronomical when compared with cost of living increases.

According to Whalen, student fees have increased 34 percent since 1971, while inflation has driven cost-of-living expenses up nearly 50 percent. "Student fees have not increased nearly as much as everything else," Whalen said.

The tuition boost was approved by the I.U. Board of Trustees last December. At that time President John Ryan said: "Today's proposals give evidence to the continued upward spiral of higher education costs. Of course, universities and colleges are not alone but share the problem of inflation with all segments of the American economy. We are working hard to keep costs down but external forces beyond our control exert much of the pressure that cause such increases."

Noting that other universities around the country are faced with similar problems, Ryan said: "I.U. nevertheless will continue as one of the most economical major universities in the nation."

Those students living in University housing also will be paying more for room and board this year. University housing rates have increased nine percent.

A double-occupancy room in the larger undergraduate dorms, for example, costs $1,340. Last year, residents paid $1,229.

I.U. dorm fees still are lowest for the Big 10, said Leland Ratliff, Halls of Residence director. "Students at some universities pay more than $1,700," he said.

But higher tuition and room-and-board costs do not mark the end of fee hikes.

The optional student health service fee was boosted to $10 this semester, instead of the familiar $7 fee.

It is the first increase in four years. "We just couldn't operate at the same costs anymore," said Marilyn Edmunds, director of health information. Nevertheless, "it is still so much less than privately practicing physicians in town," she added.

The health fee hike may result in a decline in number of students paying the optional charge, Edmunds said.

Typically the service has drawn 67 percent of enrollment.

But the end of fieldhouse lines doesn't mean the end of this semester's higher education costs.

Book prices are "definitely up," said William Turk, I.U. Bookstore director. Turk estimated that book prices are up a minimum of 8 to 10 percent this year. And science books will cost even more, but "they've always been a little more expensive," he said.

An informal survey of bookstore employees last year indicated very few spent more than $100 on books in a semester, Turk said. The average student paid between $65 and $75 for books. He estimated the range this year will be slightly higher but still won't exceed $100.

"The reason for the increase in book prices is the same reason as the increases in beer, gas and everything else," Turk added. "It's the inflationary spiral."

'Little 500' movie being filmed here

by Gregg DesElms
ids Staff Writer

As hundreds of "extras" mill noisily about the set, a handful of production crew members work frantically to place lights and movie cameras in position for the next scene.

Looking deceivingly less seasoned than some of the other production staff members, a young assistant director moves authoritatively from beneath the intensely bright movie lights and calls out his commands to the seemingly disorganized group.

"Alright, this is a take," he shouts. "Places everybody!"

Prop men and make-up women put their last-minute touches on the set and actors and move swiftly out of the scene. Extras take their positions and actors find their marks in preparation for the shooting.

"Quiet please," the assistant director calls, but the low, monotonous roar continues. There is a pause while the director waits for the cameramen to signal their readiness.

"Alright, roll it please," he shouts. The set is still buzzing.

"Easy one, take one," the sound engineer says calmly, then pauses. "Speed," he finally utters.

"Camera A, mark," shouts one camera assistant, immediately followed by a similar call from the camera B assistant.

Suddenly, all is quiet . . . very quiet. The assistant director shouts his final command. It will be the only sound, other than that created by the action of the scene that anyone will make until the director yells, "Cut!"

"Action!"

This has been a familiar scene in Bloomington for more than a week, and probably will continue to be for at least another month as 20th Century Fox films scenes from its new $2.5 million film, "Bambino."

The feature-length motion picture, which is being directed by Britisher Peter Yates (best known for his direction of such films as *Bullitt; Mother, Jugs and Speed* and *The Deep*) is featuring scenes

For a look at how the filming of "Bambino" looks to a cast extra see story, page 11.

from in and around Bloomington and on the I.U. campus. There are also a few scenes that take place in the Empire quarry, a few miles south of town.

The script for the film, written by I.U. graduate Steve Tesich, was completed and purchased for production five months ago. Tesich, who graduated from I.U. in 1965 with a Bachelor's and Master's degree in Russian Literature, has been writing plays for the New York stage since 1967.

The story centers on the lives of four high school graduates. They are played by Hollywood actors Dennis Christopher, Dennis Quaid, Dan Stern and Jackie Haley, Jr., best known for his part in *The Bad News Bears*.

Because of his contempt for the college community, the leader of the four boys, played by Quaid, manages to keep the others sufficiently alienated from anyone or anything related to the college. However, Dave, played by Dennis Christopher, has other ideas.

Dave is an established bicycle racer. He has visions of becoming a great racer on a championship Italian team, and carries that fantasy into his real world. He begins to act Italian, he tries to speak with an Italian accent. In fact, he even selects a new name for himself from an Italian album cover.

Under the guise of being an Italian student, Dave meets a sorority girl, Katherine, played by Hollywood actress Robyn Douglas, and falls in love. This creates a conflict because Katherine has been dating Rod, a fraternity man and college swimmer, played by actor Hart Bochner.

The conflict results in a fight scene in the Indiana Memorial Union Commons between the four boys and a number of college students.

These two plots, Dave's fantasy and the adversary relationship between the college students and the town boys come

See 'Bambino,' page two

staff photo/Tom Cruze

Director Peter Yates checks the camera angle during shooting of the movie "Bambino," being shot on location in Bloomington. The movie is on a six-week shooting schedule and has hired I.U. students as extras on the set.

tuesday

Root bound

Daily Student columnist Laura Hlavach offers seeds of advice for budding house plant growers . . .
See Page 14.

Celluloid spam

"Sgt. Pepper's Lonely Hearts Club Band" is unimaginative and a musical flop — the movie, that is . . .
See Page 12.

Battle lines

Daily Student columnist John Butwell attempts to lessen the trauma of freshmen registration using a strategy of "guerrilla warfare . . ."
See Page 4.

Born to run

Sen. George McGovern may be the messiah who will resurrect the left of the Democratic party in 1980, says Carey McWilliams of the Pacific News Service . . .
See Page 13.

Playing the field

Lee Corso and the I.U. football team resumed their relentless drive toward Big Ten prominence Monday as fall practice began at Memorial Stadium . . .
See Page 15.

Inside today

Memory of last year's frigid winter fades in August sun

by Tom French
ids Staff Writer

Radiance surrounded Ted Jones.

August sun spilled from the window of the I.U.-Bloomington business manager's office, and fluorescent light dropped from the ceiling onto the desk. The effect of the barrage of light was magnified by the bright orange walls around Jones.

But at the opposite end of the room, away from the window, the lights were off. A patch of shadow was a reminder of a time when the campus was dark and when August sun seemed far away.

That time was six months ago. The longest coal miners strike in history had crippled many parts of the nation. Public Service Indiana (PSI) mandated an electricity cutback of 50 percent. Emergency conservation measures, including a three-week spring break for I.U. were implemented to meet PSI's demands and to stall the exhaustion of the University's supply of coal.

That crisis seemed to be almost forgotten Monday morning. The coal miners were back to work, the campus and PSI have their fuel, the temperature was in the 70s, and students were gathering for the start of a new semester.

Although the recently settled United Mine Workers' contract won't expire for three years, the University is taking steps now to prepare for the possibility of another strike.

Jones said crews from the I.U. Physical Plant have been digging around campus, wiring buildings for what he casually refers to as "EMS."

"EMS" stands for Energy Management System, and according to Jones, it also stands for energy savings. EMS is a computer system that will monitor and control the heating, ventilation, and air conditioning inside major buildings around campus.

Only 13 buildings, including Assembly Hall and the Main Library, will be connected initially to to the system. Chuck Sheppard, assistant director of utilities and engineering at the Physical Plant, said the 13 buildings should be connected to the system by January 1979.

Jones said the EMS was purchased two years ago for $880,000. The centralized system will enable the Physical Plant to efficiently control the temperature levels in different buildings.

During the energy crisis, the Physical Plant's efforts to lower temperatures around campus were hampered because the process had to be done manually in each building.

Jones said EMS' greatest savings will come from lower electricity costs. PSI, which supplies the University with electricity, bases the campus power bill on peak consumption each month.

A desired peak level of electricity consumption can be pre-programmed into the computer. When the University's consumption threatens to exceed that peak, EMS automatically will lower the electricity output to buildings connected to the system, thus lowering total usage and maintaining the predetermined level.

By keeping the peak level of consumption in check, EMS will lower the campus electricity bill, Jones said. He said savings from the use of EMS may be used to connect more buildings to the computer system.

> 'It seemed like mother nature and the coal miners were ganging up on us for a while, with the blizzard and the strike.'
> — Chuck Sheppard, I.U. Physical Plant assistant director of utilities and engineering

Herb Metz, manager of the mechanical systems for the Physical Plant, said EMS will shut off systems using steam or electricity unnecessarily

The University also is considering the use of a secondary site to stockpile additional coal in case of an impending strike. The use of one potential site, the area north of the Physical Plant and the Illinois Central railroad tracks, may be too costly.

Jones said a storage area there would require permission from Illinois Central to build a tunnel under the tracks. A conveyor belt would carry the coal through the tunnel to the Physical Plant.

Sheppard said an ash dump about one mile east of Bloomington is also under consideration.

Recalling the University's handling of the energy crisis, Jones said there was no time when he felt the energy problems couldn't be solved.

Jones leaned back comfortably in his chair and nibbled cheese and crackers as he presented a simple assessment of the crisis. "We just kept on going," he said.

Sheppard, however, remembered the crisis with more trepidation than Jones. "It seemed like Mother Nature and the coal miners were ganging up on us for awhile, with the blizzard and the strike," he said.

The lowest point in morale, Sheppard said, came one day when the elevator that carries the coal up into the Power Plant broke down. About 20 hours was needed to fix the machine and the supply of coal within the plant would not last that long.

A bulldozer was used to push the coal onto the railroad tracks, where a conveyor belt carried it inside.

"Quite frankly," he said, "last winter was the worst situation I have ever been in."

Sheppard said he was not mentally prepared for a winter like last spring semester's. "When I first came here eight years ago, they kind of chuckled and said I didn't even need to buy a snow shovel — all the snow melts by noon," he said and laughed.

P0078793, IU Archives.

REFLECTION

The Tribe of Ernie Pyle Hall

In my decades as a reporter, covering riots and hurricanes and executions, I've had a few unnerving moments. But nothing has shaken me like the first time I walked into the IDS.

It was the spring of 1977, and Dan Barreiro and Phil Tatman were throwing a football across the newsroom. The ceiling was low, which meant they had to hurl the ball in a tight arc above the heads of other staffers. Nobody seemed to care that they were about to be knocked unconscious. I can still hear Barreiro narrating the whole thing in the exaggerated patter of a sports announcer.

The message: *We are elders in the tribe that owns this place. You, little boy, are an outsider.*

Breaking through the forcefield that united the staff seemed impossible. I worked up enough courage to dodge the football as I asked about my first assignment. I joined the staff full time the following fall, and before I knew it, I was a member of the tribe, too. The sense of belonging was intoxicating.

"'We're writing real stories about real people,' I said. 'And if we screw up and get something wrong, they'll hire a real lawyer to sue us for real money.'"

That fall, the editor in chief was Bonita Brodt, who always wore a faded bandanna and who terrified young staffers with her glare. Bonita was so famous for her temper that Barreiro put up a chart over Ernie's rolltop desk to track her daily moods. "The Bonita meter," he called it.

My first encounter with Bonita happened that August, when I wrote a story about frat boys trolling for hot girls outside freshman registration. The frat boys were surprisingly honest about their intentions, and when the story ran the next day, the president of one house called me frothing mad to demand a correction. I was mortified. Had I done something wrong? Was I about to get fired?

"Give me the phone," someone said behind me. I turned, and it was Bonita.

"We stand by our story," she told the guy. "And we stand by our reporter."

She hung up, told me I'd done a good job, and walked away. That was the moment when I understood. It didn't matter if the fraternity was furious. What mattered was I had told the truth about something the frat didn't want to admit. It wasn't exactly Woodward and Bernstein, but it was a start.

From that moment forward, I worshipped Bonita and vowed to dedicate my life to her and anyone else in the tribe who could teach me how journalism worked. I didn't care when an assignment required me to be up at dawn or to work past midnight. I didn't care when my first campus editor, Scott Dever, pushed me out of my chair to rewrite me. I was covering a lecture at the IU Auditorium by Shere Hite, a famous sex researcher with a bestselling book on the unfulfilled desires of women. It had been an interesting evening. When I met Hite backstage to ask a few questions, she corrected me on my pronunciation of "clitoris." (Rhymes with "hit or miss.") Now I was back in the newsroom, struggling to capture the essence of Hite's talk without sensationalizing it.

Scott read over my shoulder, shoved me to the carpet and crossed out my boring first graf. In its place, he wrote: "Women have a right to orgasm."

That was the first of my stories that my mom saw.

In the years that followed, the IDS staff continued to treat the newsroom like a personal fiefdom. One Halloween we descended into the crawlspace below the floor and built a cemetery, wedging tombstones marked with our names into the dirt. We spilled sweet and sour soup and the crumbs of tenderloin sandwiches onto our keyboards. We made fun of everyone and everything, often in a cartoonish voice we'd learned from Barreiro.

What made us happiest was when we published something that mattered. Terrific investigative pieces by Andy Hall. Great stories on IU basketball by Mike Tackett and Tom Brew and Jennie Rees. Classic reporting by Julie Carey, Mike Davis, Barb Toman, Tim Nickens, Tim Franklin—on and on. Beautiful photo essays by Michel du Cille, future winner of three Pulitzer prizes. I can still break a sweat when I recall the ferocious copy editing of Linda Rogowski and Geneva Collins, both of whom saved me from embarrassment many times.

When I was lucky enough to become editor in chief, I followed Bonita Brodt's example and pushed the staff as hard as I could—hard enough that one of my reporters complained.

"You're acting as though we're writing for a real newspaper," she said.

I did my best to resurrect Bonita's glare. "We're writing real stories about real people," I said. "And if we screw up and get something wrong, they'll hire a real lawyer to sue us for real money."

Yes, we were young and wild and sometimes blissfully stupid. But when we sat down to knock out a story, we were unflinchingly serious. About the facts. About ethics. And about all the promises of journalism. That was our rigor, and our joy.

—Thomas French, BAJ 1980

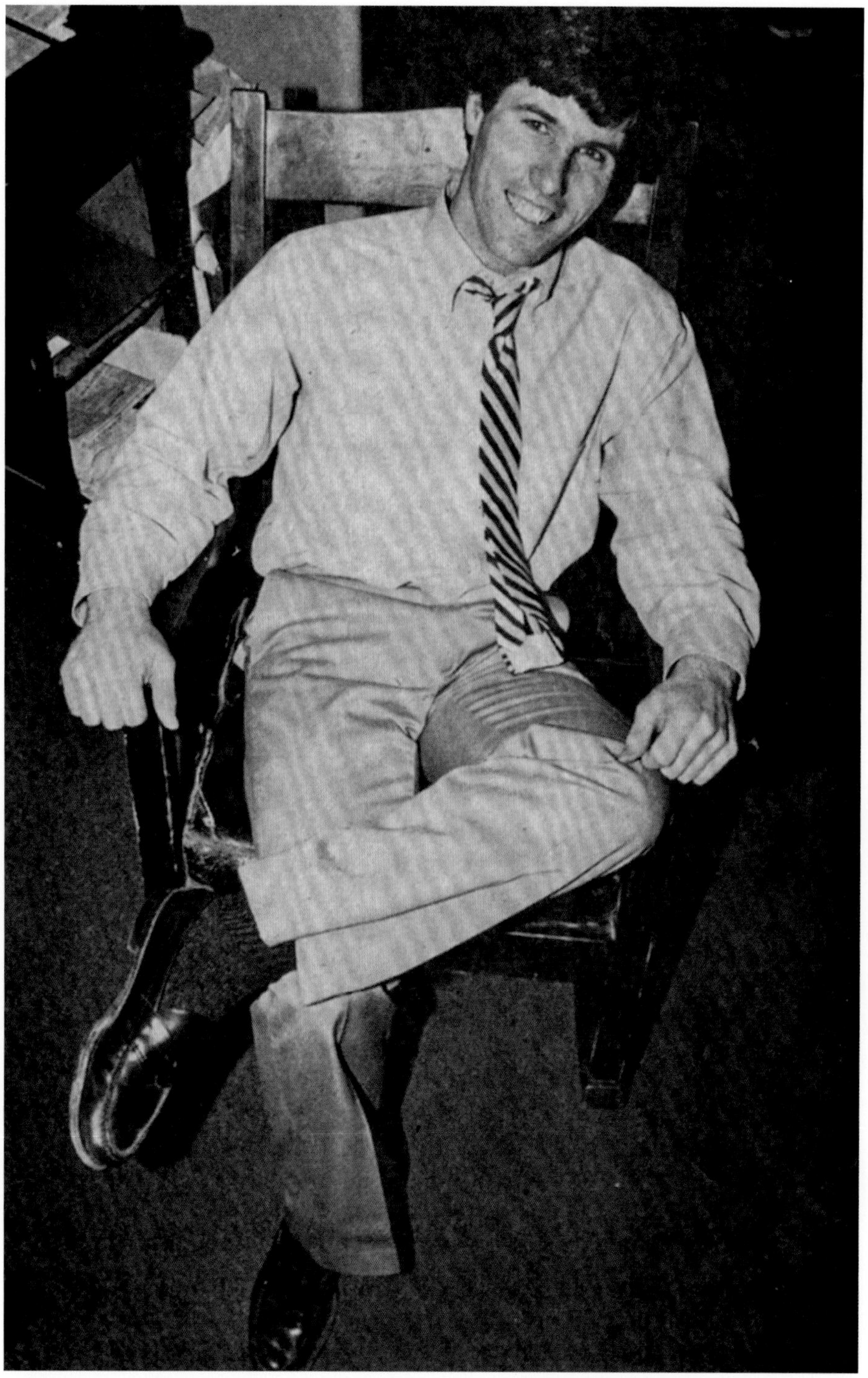

Tom French in December 1979 after being selected as editor in chief of the IDS.

SUMMER ids Indiana Daily Student
Bloomington, Ind. Friday July 13, 1979 24 pages 15 cents

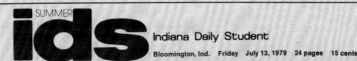

Humid

Staff Council wants meeting over salary

by Sue Ann Savage
ids Staff Writer

For a related story, see page six.

The IU Staff Council has moved to support the IU Staff Women's Caucus and Rep. Jerry Bales, R-Bloomington, in their demand for a meeting July 31 with the IU administration to explain the lower-than-recommended salary increases for IU staff.

The decision was made at Wednesday's Staff Council meeting, which was attended by Bales, a member of the House Ways and Means Committee.

Bales later said he told the council he was under the impression that a 7 percent across-the-board salary increase would be given to IU administration, faculty and staff alike. Staff workers, however, actually will receive a 5.1 percent average increase, which is 1.4 percent less than last year's average increase.

Bales also said the Ways and Means Committee staff expected all University employees to receive the 7 percent increase. In addition, Bales said he believes the 12 Republican members of the 20-member committee believed this too.

But Jim Urton, IU director of personnel administration, responded the 5.1 percent is only the average standard increase in pay for each position. In addition to this, a 1.8 percent average merit increase will be added to create a total 6.9 percent average increase.

Urton also said 20 percent of the clerical and technical workers were upgraded or promoted this year, which means they will earn another 1.5 percent average increase, or a total average increase of 8.4 percent.

And Ward Schaap, IU dean of budgetary administration and planning, said, "What the state allocated for clerical workers went to clerical workers and nowhere else."

However, Joe Hailer, chairman of the Staff Council, said Urton's explanation is not adequate. All staff workers are not being awarded a merit increase, he said.

And Albi Ott, a law library associate and a member of the women's caucus, said merit increases should not be coun-

Council/24

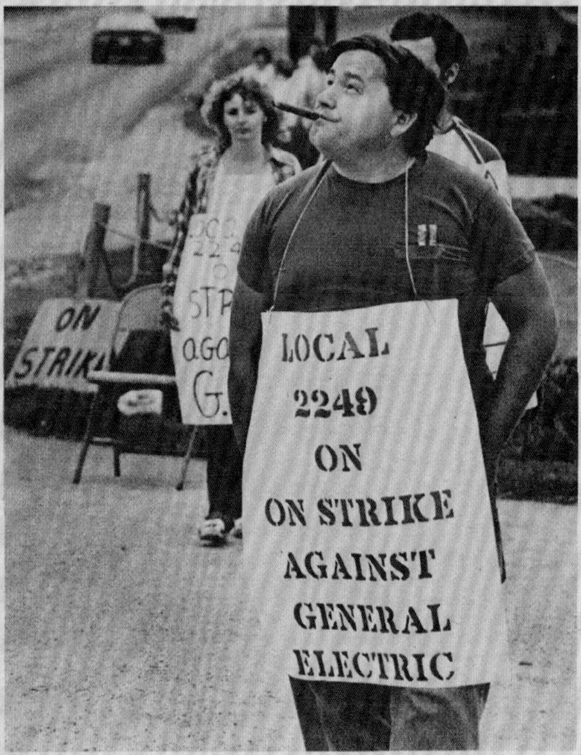

staff photo/Tom Cruze

Larry Mingee, quality inspector for Bloomington General Electric Co., participated Thursday in the second day of a strike by the International Brotherhood of Electrical Workers Union, Local 2249. For story, see page 11.

Coach Knight to go to court today on assault charges

by Tim Bannon
ids Sports Writer

For related stories, see pages five and 16.

IU basketball coach Bob Knight faces charges of aggravated assault at 9 a.m. today in a San Juan, Puerto Rico district court.

The court date was advanced from a date in late August to today, when the United States basketball team will play Puerto Rico for the Pan American Games gold medal.

Knight's countercharges against Puerto Rican policeman Jose de Silva — assault and battery, violation of civil rights — were summarily dismissed by the district attorney, preventing them from being forwarded to Judge Rafael Riefkhol. IU Board of Trustees President Dan Danielson called the decision "a parody of justice."

Bob Paul, director of communication for the U.S. Olympic Committee, said the three best criminal lawyers in San Juan have been hired to defend Knight. "We don't know the legal system here. We don't know what to expect," Paul said. "We're going to give it all we've got. We think that he is completely in the right."

There is concern with the manner in which the San Juan legal system is handling the case. Paul said he believes Knight is being railroaded. Danielson said Silva, who is pressing the charges, is "lying about the whole thing .... The Puerto Rican Olympic team and the local officials didn't press charges. Then the individual decides he's going to file against Bobby. What kind of justice is that?"

Jose Delvalle, an aide to Puerto Rico's resident commissioner Baltasar Corrada, said, "Our legal system is basically the same, and I doubt if he is being railroaded. As a matter of fact,

Knight/24

Marble Hill plant builder: construction sabotaged

by Lynn Schneidhorst
ids Staff Writer

Public Service Indiana President Hugh Barker said this week that PSI accepts responsibility for flaws in the concrete work in reactor containment buildings at the Marble Hill nuclear power plant being constructed near Madison, Ind.

In addition, three employees of the Newberg Construction Co., which is building the plant, have been fired for "failure to follow proper procedures," Barker said in a press release Wednesday. He would not release the workers' names.

Francis Durocher, vice president of construction for Newberg, added that one supervisor at the plant also has been demoted and transferred to another project for the same reasons.

Durocher also would release no names.

PSI voluntarily halted construction of the plant June 26 after the Nuclear Regulatory Commission disclosed that 170 of 520 "honeycombed areas," or air pockets in the concrete, had been improperly patched. Construction resumed July 9 after PSI and the NRC conducted tests of concrete pouring procedures and agreed they are sufficiently safe. Testing on undetected honeycombing is presently being conducted by the NRC at the construction site.

In addition, in a conversation reportedly tape-recorded Sunday, two former Newberg construction workers on the Marble Hill plant — Stanley Mortensen and Michael Walston — said they were told by their supervisors to refer all comments concerning construction of the plant to the foreman before speaking to the NRC inspectors. The comments were recorded in Louisville by two representatives of Save the Valley, an environmentalist group, Robert Gray, board of directors chairman, and attorney Thomas Datillo.

Gray said the two construction workers claimed their criticisms went no further than the foreman, Steve Gayzo. Neither the workers nor Gayzo could be reached for comment. But according to Durocher, the workers were not discouraged from speaking to NRC officials. However, he said that they were told to speak to their supervisors first.

Neither of the two were among those Barker said were fired recently, although Durocher said the two had been fired.

Durocher said the only persons that the workers were told not to speak to were those representing anti-nuclear groups, adding that he believes the concrete problems were caused by workers planted in his company by anti-nuclear

Builder/7

friday

Ladylike air

"My Fair Lady," the ever-popular staple of the American musical theater, first opened in New York in 1956 with Rex Harrison and Julie Andrews. It experienced a New York revival in 1976. Tonight the story of the charming Cockney flower girl opens at IU's Musical Arts Center . . .

See page 18.

Inside today

P0079425, IU Archives.

September 9, 1980

indiana daily student

ids

Tuesday
Sept. 9, 1980

Indiana University Bloomington, Indiana
©Copyright 1980, Indiana Daily Student

12 pages
20 cents

Reagan: cuts won't limit aid

By Andy Hall and Barbara Toman
ids Staff Writers

choice '80
Presidential race

KOKOMO — Republican presidential candidate Ronald Reagan told the Daily Student on Monday that his tax-cut proposals would not reduce federal aid for college students.

"Well, when I was governor of California, I increased aid to students," said Reagan, during whose years as governor, state appropriations for student aid increased from about $2 billion to about $9 billion.

But those years, 1967-74, were marked by single-digit inflation and an economic climate that appears robust when compared with this year's. Asked how his tax cuts would not reduce services such as student aid, Reagan replied, "I'm talking about eliminating waste and inefficiency."

Reagan's response to a Daily Student reporter's question came at the close of a brief stop in this recession-racked central Indiana city.

Renewing his attacks on President Carter's economic policies, Reagan told a cheering crowd of about 5,000 persons that re-electing Carter would mean "four more years of disaster."

At a shopping mall just blocks from the Delco, General Motors and Chrysler plants that are the major employers in this city of 50,000, Reagan pledged to cut taxes by 10 percent each of the next three years to stimulate production and put people back to work.

He said the tax cut would reduce the amount of money the government takes from American paychecks by $20 billion the first year, rather than allowing what he called a "built-in" increase of $86 billion.

The increase would come from items such as higher Social Security and energy taxes and taxes paid by persons forced into higher tax brackets by inflation.

The crowd waved American flags and Reagan posters and cheered loudly when the candidate said, "The answer to our problems is to get government off our backs and turn the American public loose in the marketplace."

Reagan received more applause when he repeated his charge that the nation is suffering from a depression, rather than a recession, as the Carter administration has termed the current economic slump.

"Jimmy Carter is taking refuge in a

See 'Reagan,' page six

staff photo/Shawn Spence

Republican presidential candidate Ronald Reagan waves to a crowd of children Monday in Kokomo after his motorcade made an unplanned stop.

Unemployment's bitterness flashes in the eyes of a city

By Andy Hall and Barbara Toman
ids Staff Writers

KOKOMO — The bitterness that wells from the eyes of Robert Grant is, more than any campaign speech, a portrait of what these 1980 elections are all about: jobs.

The way Grant's brown eyes narrow when he watches foreign cars drive by shows what 13 months of unemployment can do to a man with a wife and children.

The eyes have seen lots of disturbing things: 2,000 miles of roads that led to no jobs, food stamps that were reluctantly accepted when bills stacked up, a landlord who clamored for rent money when none is forthcoming and, worst of all, idle days when there was nothing to do except wait.

Grant's bitterness is something from which he believes he cannot escape. He said he may see a psychiatrist to find ways to control his suddenly volatile temper.

At the United Auto Workers Local 685 office, where he attempted to unsnarl state employment benefits on Monday, he complained that the union workers were as incompetent as the government that stripped him of his job in a transmission-assembly plant.

On the day Ronald Reagan brought his Republican presidential campaign to Grant's city, the unemployed worker was prepared for a squirrel hunting trip.

"Maybe that will put some meat on the table for my old lady and the three kids," Grant , 25, said in a voice that scarcely concealed his bitterness.

"Let's see how the politicians are gonna feed my kids when my unemployment (compensation) runs out in seven weeks."

A man who's considering separation from his family so it will become eligible for welfare payments, Grant claims politicians don't know how desperate unemployed workers are.

"There's one big difference between them and me," he said, gesturing agitatedly with both hands. "They've got a job. It's all cheap talk."

Just two hours earlier, Reagan had told an enthusiastic crowd of about 5,000 people that he and the Republican Party have the answers for workers such as Grant. Charging that the Carter administration is fighting inflation by putting millions of Americans out of work, Reagan proposed a 10 percent reduction in income taxes for each of the next three years.

The proposal was applauded loudly by the crowd, many of whom work at Delco, Chrysler and General Motors manufacturing plants in Kokomo. Layoffs at the plants gave the city a 23.4 percent unemployment rate in July. The present rate is 19.8 percent, while the national jobless rate is 7.6 percent.

"The tax cut will cut down on inflation because it will make people save money," said Jim Chatman, who plays in a local country music band.

Chatman said he and his wife, who works at Delco, voted for Carter in 1976, but are considering voting for Reagan this year.

Blue-collar support for the Republican candidate is strong on issues other than the economy.

"Reagan's got a good backbone. He won't let anyone dictate to him," said Ruth Sullivan, whose husband, Louis, is a retired Delco employee and member of UAW Local 292.

"Reagan is someone who can keep the US like it used to be," Sullivan added.

A Delco employee who also voted for Carter four years ago said he plans to vote for Reagan on Nov. 4. "I thought Carter had a lot of fresh, new ideas, but I've been sadly disappointed in him," said Al Livingston.

Reagan's support among Kokomo workers was discounted by Mayor Steve Daily, a Democrat elected last November.

"Ronald Reagan is not going to win the city of Kokomo," Daily said, adding that the Republicans would, however, win GOP-dominated Howard County.

"If Reagan had been president in this last year, we would already have lost Chrysler Corp. because he wouldn't have supported the bail-out," Daily said. "The UAW knows it, and I don't believe they'll vote for Reagan."

Daily said that politics can solve some of the problems experienced by the city's unemployed workers.

"Kokomo is not dying," he said. "We

See 'Kokomo,' page six

Committee investigates

Scholarship operations may change

This is the last of a two-part series on the availability of financial aid for IU students.

By April Bogle
ids Staff Writer

An interim study committee has been appointed by the General Assembly to investigate the possibility of decentralizing scholarship and financial aid operation in Indiana and guaranteeing students a standard educational purchasing power.

Such purchasing power, according to Greg Server, chairman of the committee, would allow a student to choose any school and still be assured funds, based on the school's cost and the amount of money the student could provide.

Server said this method of dispersing money would be more convenient for students and parents and also would stop much of the current paperwork duplication.

Server said the new system will not be available until at least the fall of 1981, partly because the legislature won't consider proposals until it is in session January. "And we could leave it alone for a year to look at because of the current cash situation," Server said.

Susan Pugh, IU associate director of scholarships and financial aid, said the state grant and scholarship program probably will be changed not because of funding, but because of disorganization in the State Student Assistance Commission of Indiana.

"The move is on to take whatever money is allotted for state grants and scholarships and give it to the institutions to disperse," Pugh said. "The eligibility criteria will probably be based on need rather than high school scholarship because sometimes once students get here, (the good grades don't) pan out anyway."

Pugh also said there probably will be an expansion in the guaranteed student loan program because Gov. Otis Bowen has appointed a committee to develop a secondary market for the loans. A secondary market would enable banks that issue the loans to sell them to larger banks. This would entice more banks to offer the loans because they wouldn't be responsible for collecting payments, which is one of the major reasons some don't offer them now.

Pugh said the interest rate on the loans, which is 7 percent for students, would probably increase to make the loans even more attractive to banks.

Work-study programs, which receive 80 percent of their funds from the federal government, also are likely to expand, Pugh said.

She said basic educational opportunity grants are still very popular. They are based on need, pay up to one-half of college expenses, and allow the student to attend the institution he chooses.

Pugh said the national direct student loan program, which offers loans at 3 percent interest, is fading out because federal funds for it have been transferred to guaranteed student loans.

staff photo/Andrée Peyrot

Rarin' to go

Sen. Birch Bayh (D-Ind.) who is running for his fourth term against Rep. Daniel Quayle (R-Ind.) emphasizes his fighting spirit during a speech at Whittenberger Auditorium Monday. For a related story, see page six.

Gros Louis amiably meets the press

By Dan Brogan
ids Staff Writer

Kenneth Gros Louis, in his first news conference as IU-Bloomington vice president, made it clear Monday that he intends to spend the next few weeks clearing the cobwebs out of his new office — both literally and figuratively.

He began the process by cleaning stray spider webs from a lamp as reporters clamored around his new office, rearranging furniture and materials on his desk to accommodate their microphones and tape recorders.

Like his predecessor Robert O'Neil, who left IU in June to become president of the University of Wisconsin, Gros Louis deals easily with the press. "Maybe I should sit lower in the chair," he joked to a photographer who propped up a lamp under several books for better lighting.

The former College of Arts and Sciences dean opened the conference by thanking the reporters for the stories they have written about him since his appointment was announced last Wednesday.

Kenneth Gros Louis

"With all the nice things you all have written maybe I'd do best to resign now, take all my clips and go buy a condo someplace," he said.

And although openness was a hallmark of the O'Neil administration which he hopes to emulate, Gros Louis has plans to take that openness one step further.

Beginning Sept. 18, he will have a telephone in his office with a toll-free number so citizens around the state can contact him and ask him questions about higher education. The phone will be in service on Thursdays from 2:30 to 5:30 p.m. The number is 1-800-822-4777.

"I've said from the start that I want to get out into the state to talk to people as much as possible," he explained. "But, because I can't be out around Indiana every week, I've asked Indiana Bell to install this phone. I hope it will catch on, and students, parents, alumni or any other concerned citizens will feel free to call and make their concerns known to me."

Until his first phone session Gros Louis will spend much of his time meeting with University and community officials. Early this morning he will meet with various campus student leaders to discuss the possibility of meeting with them monthly. Later today he will have lunch with Bloomington Mayor Frank McCloskey to discuss the relationship between IU and Bloomington.

A possible topic of discussion at the lunch is the often-proposed merger of Bloomington Transit and the IU Bus System.

"I think it's a marvelous idea," Gros Louis said. "But I don't know enough of the particulars to know if it's feasible. That's the idea of meeting with these kind of people who are in the know — to get the background needed to make decisions."

The major topic at the press conference was collective bargaining. Gros Louis reaffirmed his position that there are many questions that need to be answered before any decisions are made.

"The first thing I'll do in that area is to work with the co-secretaries of the Bloomington Faculty Council to set up the collective bargaining seminar for later this year," he said.

"My biggest challenge during the next couple of weeks is to find out as much as possible about the areas of the campus that I don't have much background in," he concluded.

tuesday

Inside today

p.2 President Ryan and three IUSA members go to Washington to get more student aid.

p.7 Football Coach Lee Corso and his Hoosiers fire up in picture preview of this year's team.

p.8 Senior tailback Mike Harkrader continues a gutsy performance despite his injuries.

Outside today

High temperatures today are expected to reach the low 80s. The lows are expected to drop to the upper 40s tonight. There is a 70 percent chance of rain today and a 30 percent chance tonight. Thunderstorms are expected but should end this evening. Wednesday is expected to be partly sunny and cooler.

P0079432, IU Archives.

Wednesday morning, April 1, 1981 | Indiana University, Bloomington, Ind. | ©1981, Indiana Daily Student | 16 pages | Two sections | 20 cents

ids — indiana daily student

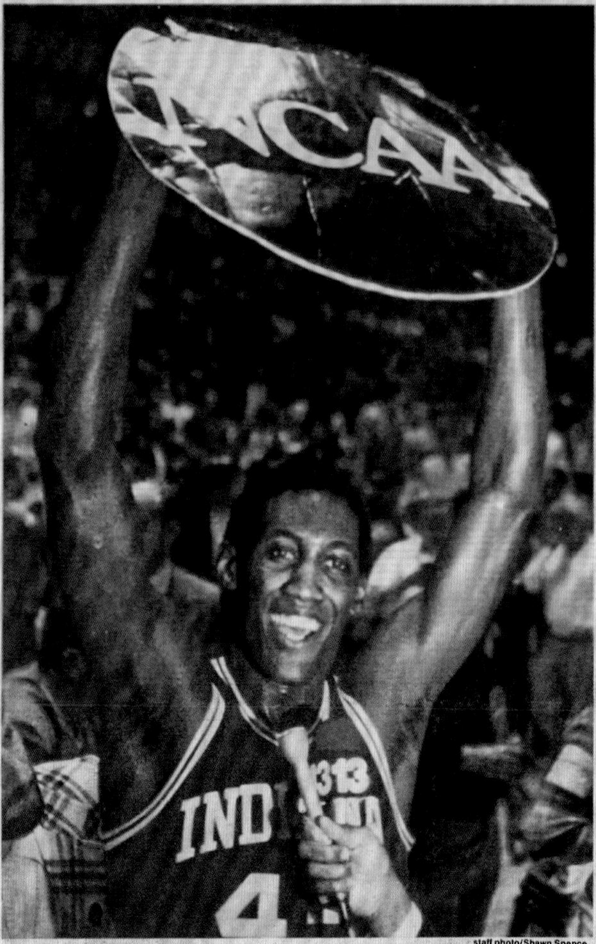

staff photo/Shawn Spence

Number one, indeed!

Ray Tolbert, IU center and senior, holds up the NCAA shield to confirm that the Hoosiers have indeed captured the NCAA title. IU defeated North Carolina by a score of 63-50 Monday night in Philadelphia. See related photos, page nine.

Reagan given details of shooting; signs bill

By The Los Angeles Times

WASHINGTON — Described by doctors as "doing extremely well" in the early stages of his recovery from a bullet wound in his chest, President Ronald Reagan Tuesday was given the first detailed information on the assassination attempt that had occurred as he left a Washington hotel nearly 24 hours earlier.

Although he slept from time to time during the day and received a mild pain-killing drug, the President also read newspapers and took a small step toward resuming the duties of office. Just hours after emergency surgery to remove a .22-caliber bullet from his left lung, Reagan signed into law the well-publicized bill curbing mild price supports that came out of the administration's first contest with the Congress over cutting the federal budget.

"I would not be surprised to see him up and walking around in a couple of days," said Dr. Dennis O'Leary, a spokesman for the George Washington University Hospital.

Reagan got the first details of what happened in the melee outside the Washington Hilton Hotel from Dr. Daniel Ruge, the White House physician, and from his wife, Nancy, shortly after noon Tuesday.

Told that James Brady, the White House press secretary, had been shot in the head by the gunman who lurked in a crowd of reporters and photographers, the President exclaimed, "Oh damn. Oh damn." His eyes welled with tears and he asked whether the bullet had gone into Brady's brain, and then he inquired about Brady's chances of survival.

James Baker, the White House chief of staff who was also in the room with the President, said that the President had been aware that at least one other person had been hit in the hail of bullets because he had gotten a glimpse of a body lying on the ground as his limousine sped away.

The President was told Monday night that a Secret Service agent had indeed been wounded, Baker said, but he was not told about Brady because a tube placed in Reagan's throat immediately after the operation would have prevented him from talking.

Brady improved but critical

By The Washington Post

WASHINGTON — Presidential press secretary James Brady regained consciousness but remained in critical condition in the intensive care unit at George Washington University Hospital Tuesday, after undergoing a 6½ hour operation in which doctors removed a large portion of the right frontal lobe of his brain.

Despite extensive destruction of tissue on the right side of his brain and some damage to the left frontal lobe, Brady's condition improved dramatically in the hours after surgery. He was awake and able to see and to move his right arm and leg when asked to, according to doctors at the hospital.

Considering the severity of Brady's brain injuries, one of the doctors called the progress "extraordinary."

"We believe he is going to live," said Dr. Dennis O'Leary, a hospital spokesman. But he added, "We have no idea (how) he is going to end up."

NCAA champs join in party

By Mark Newman
ids Staff Writer

As they rolled out the welcome mat for the national champion IU basketball team Tuesday afternoon, approximately 10,000 ecstatic Hoosier fans clarified one thing: the party is *not* over.

The crowd gathered at Assembly Hall to greet the team as it returned from Philadelphia. IU defeated North Carolina there Monday night, 63-50, in the final game of the National Collegiate Athletic Association (NCAA) tournament.

The celebration had continued throughout the night, decreasing in its intensity only temporarily, if at all. By 1:17 p.m. Tuesday, when the team finally arrived inside Assembly Hall, it was bedlam once again.

The crowd had moved inside from the 80-degree temperatures outside the Hall, where a beach-like atmosphere had existed. Frisbees and tennis balls flew overhead, as students left their classes and books behind for the day.

Once inside, the hullabaloo continued. Bloomington Mayor Frank McCloskey took the microphone.

"I'd like to thank everybody in the crowd for taking it easy on the downtown last night," McCloskey said.

McCloskey then proclaimed it "Hoosier Hysteria Week" in Bloomington.

The crowd, which covered the floor and filled most of the main level seats, grew impatient as they continued the wait for their heroes.

Then came the jubilation explosion. Led by senior forward Glen Grunwald, the Hoosiers strode onto the stage. They wore NCAA championship hats. Senior center Ray Tolbert and sophomore guard Isiah Thomas wore victory nets from the Spectrum around their necks, a fashion that may catch on.

IU-Bloomington Vice President Kenneth Gros Louis then took the microphone to introduce IU coach Bob Knight. Gros Louis approached the microphone attired in a sportcoat and tie.

He then began a veritable striptease, to the delight of the audience. After shredding the shirt, coat and tie, Gros-Louis was down to his pants and a red NCAA championship T-shirt.

Knight took his cue and the crowd roared. A sign outside the Hall read "Hoosiers are H(onesty)-I(negrity)-G(uts)-H(umor) on Coach Knight."

"You people are probably learning a lot more here today than the students out there (at classes) are," Knight said. "Your manner and your English has always been a helluva lot better anyhow."

Knight wanted to bring a certain visitor, but he was unable to attend.

"We were gonna bring Jack with us, but he was up North visiting his brothers Half and Wise today," Knight said, referring to the jackass he brought on his television show earlier this year as a Purdue representative.

The four senior players on the team spoke next: Grunwald, Tolbert, Steve Risley and Phil Isenbarger. Risley held the championship trophy high for fans to relish.

Grunwald had the quote of the day for the IU students, though. "Classes are canceled for the rest of the week." The students went berserk.

Said Risley: "I couldn't have ended my four years any better than that, but I'll tell you one thing: You haven't seen anything from this team yet."

Hospital, jail kept busy after revelry

By Bob Caylor
ids Staff Writer

See related stories page seven

A 22-year-old IU student injured in the revelry after the National Collegiate Athletic Association (NCAA) championship victory Monday night remained in intensive care Tuesday in Indianapolis Methodist Hospital with a fractured skull.

Stover Smith, Willkie South 306, was riding with several other people atop a car traveling on Washington Street at about 10:45 p.m. Witnesses said Smith was having difficulty staying on the car and fell off when it turned on to Eighth Street.

Smith struck his head on the pavement, was run over and dragged 10 to 15 feet before the car stopped, Bloomington police reported.

Several passers-by had to lift the car to free Smith. One of them reported that one of the car's occupants said, "He's moving, he must be OK. Let's go party!"

Police had not yet located Tuesday the car or any of its occupants.

Smith was taken by ambulance to the emergency room of Bloomington Hospital with a skull fracture, a one-inch cut under his eye, scrapes on his legs and chest and possible internal injuries.

He was transferred almost immediately to Indianapolis Methodist Hospital, where he was listed in satisfactory condition although he remained in intensive care.

In an unrelated injury, IU sophomore Erin Gale, 814 N. Grant St., was taken to Bloomington Hospital at 10:30 p.m. Monday by ambulance after she fell from a moving car at the corner of 17th Street and Jordan Avenue.

Hospital officials reported Tuesday that Gale was in satisfactory condition with a scalp injury.

In addition to hospitalizations, 10 celebration-related injuries and accidents required ambulance runs. Those taken to Bloomington Hospital were all treated and released.

The Monroe County Jail booked 26 people Monday night and early Tuesday morning on charges such as public drinking, illegal consumption, disorderly conduct, criminal mischief, trespassing and possession of alcohol and marijuana.

Most people were released on their own recognizance or low bond.

Despite the injuries, Bloomington Police Lt. Max Gross said the department was "much better prepared" than after the 1976 NCAA victory.

"There was less vandalism because we prohibited parking around the courthouse" and blocked off Walnut Street between Seventh Street and Kirkwood Avenue, Gross said.

He reported that nine parking meters were stolen and one traffic signal was destroyed.

The Monroe County Chapter of the American Red Cross reported that two large red crosses, valued at $250, were stolen from the sign in front of the organization's new building at 411 E. Seventh St. No questions will be asked if the crosses are returned, a spokesman said.

Hutton gets an Oscar while the show goes on

Compiled from staff and wire reports

Timothy Hutton won the Best Supporting Actor Oscar for his performance as the troubled youth of "Ordinary People" at the 53rd annual Academy of Motion Pictures Arts and Sciences awards ceremony at the Dorothy Chandler Pavilion in Los Angeles Tuesday night.

Other Oscars went to "Tess" (Best Art Direction) and to a documentary short film, "Karl Hess: Toward Liberty." Hess was at IU as a Collins/Living Learning Center artist in residence last spring. Anthony Powell won a Best Costume Design Oscar for "Tess."

After a 24-hour delay because of the shooting of the President, the motion picture industry went on with its ceremony, including a taped greeting from President Ronald Reagan, who said to "go ahead and use it" despite his condition.

The academy had delayed a decision on whether to televise the remarks that former actor Reagan taped 10 days before the attempt on his life Monday. But at 3 a.m. Tuesday, academy president Fay Kanin received the message from the White House: "The President said to go ahead and use the tape in any way you want."

In his taped remarks, the former movie actor praised film as revealing "that people everywhere share common dreams and emotions . . . Tonight I applaud all who create, make, distribute, exhibit and attend movies."

The award for Best Picture had not been announced at press time. Nominees included "Coal Miner's Daughter," "The Elephant Man," "Ordinary People," "Raging Bull" and "Tess."

Hotel, hospital safety spark concern

By Dave Hancock
ids Staff Writer

Third part of five-day **ids** series

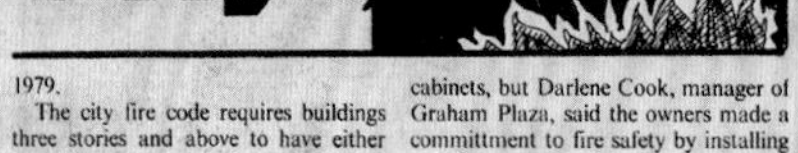

In Las Vegas, there is talk of toughening the city's fire code. The reason — two disastrous hotel fires that killed a total of 92 people in less than five months.

The National Fire Protection Association (NFPA), a Boston-based safety group, says that people are usually safer in hotels than they are in their homes, where 75 percent of all fire deaths occur. But the hotel fires in Las Vegas and one in White Plains, N.Y., that killed 26 people last December, have prompted hotel guests to request rooms below the third floor, according to an Associated Press report.

Bloomington, however, has no high-rises, except for the IU residence halls; Bloomington Hospital, 605 W. Second St.; and the Graham Plaza, 203 N. College Ave.

Each of the city's hotels and motels has three or fewer stories. The Graham Plaza is eight stories tall, but houses only businesses and does not rent rooms.

Bloomington fire officials consider Graham Plaza one of the safest buildings in the city because sprinklers were installed in every room and on every floor when the building was remodeled in 1979.

The city fire code requires buildings three stories and above to have either sprinklers or hose cabinets. Sprinklers are much more expensive than hose cabinets, but Darlene Cook, manager of Graham Plaza, said the owners made a committment to fire safety by installing sprinklers at a cost of "close to $1

See 'Hotels,' page two

wednesday

Inside today

Former hostage William Keough speaks on his experiences in Iran. Page three.

Third Street expansion has both advantages and disadvantages for the city and city businesses. Page six.

Outside today

The weather today should be partly cloudy, windy and cooler, with highs in the low to mid 60s. Skies are expected to clear tonight, and the lows should be in the low 40s. Thursday is expected to be sunny and warmer, with highs in the mid to upper 70s.

P0024586, IU Archives.

Why the Daily Student Is Discontinuing Free Papers

As reader behaviors and expectations changed over time, the IDS adapted its business model to best serve the IU and Bloomington communities. In the fall of 1981, the paper stopped free distribution in residence halls, opting instead for a paid circulation model. This editorial, from March 12, 1981, was written by editor-in-chief Andy Hall to explain the change to readers.

By Andy Hall

The passage of the Daily Student from the list of freebies granted to students in IU residence halls is a little sad, but very necessary.

Perhaps some students who can't afford to subscribe to the Daily Student will miss their breakfast dates with the paper next fall. But by and large, students who really want the paper will find a way to afford it.

However, the Daily Student can't afford to continue giving students in residence halls 8,800 of the 14,000 papers it publishes for IU and Bloomington readers.

In its 114th year of publication, the Daily Student is threatened by declining revenues from the papers distributed in residence halls. In 1973–74, when the present distribution plan was started, the Daily Student received $35,000 from IU for the papers, which actually cost $75,360 to publish. The annual University payment has declined steadily, and now the Daily Student receives nothing. But the printing costs have escalated to $149,464.

A sense of urgency is injected into the move to all-paid circulation by the US Postal Service's threats to revoke the Daily Student's second class mailing permit if the present distribution system is continued. The permit, which enables papers to receive first class delivery service at greatly reduced rates, is available only to papers that can prove half of their circulation is at least half paid. The Daily Student violates that regulation.

.... A glance through the copy of the paper you're holding helps show that hard money and hard issues led to the Daily Student's decision to reinstate its all-paid circulation plan next fall.

The stories and photos were produced and edited by a newsroom staff of about 160 students, a third of whom are paid regularly. They work on an undependable computer system that will cost $200,000 to replace.

The ads were sold by student sales representatives. The paper is put together by a production staff, driven to Columbus for printing and returned to Bloomington for distribution by carriers and the postal service. Each of those procedures, of course, costs money. For example, the newsprint needed for today's issue cost about $900.

All told, the Daily Student's annual budget approaches $1 million. Because the paper is an auxiliary enterprise of the University, it enjoys some unique privileges, such as editorial freedom (the editor-in-chief, a student, cannot be censored). But it also must remain solvent. The Daily Student would not remain financially stable if it continued to give papers away.

.... All-paid circulation is the best way to ensure that the Daily Student will remain solvent while continuing to provide the most comprehensive available coverage of the IU community. This conclusion was not drawn thoughtlessly; many hours in many months were devoted to discussion of the issue in meetings among the Daily Student staff and with IU officials.

The area's only morning newspaper stands ready for its entry into the "real world" of all-paid circulation that is the norm for most professional—and some collegiate—papers across the nation. Hard money and hard issues are only the beginning.

BEHIND THE STORY

Training Ground for Pulitzer Winners

Keeping track of the number of Pulitzer Prizes won by IU alumni is tricky business. The university keeps an official list but only counts individuals who won a prize on their own, limiting the field. A count of winners in School of Journalism records yields as many as 31 winners for 18 prizes beginning in 1927.

Yet only seven Hoosier journalists have been named in Pulitzer citations: Ernie Pyle in 1941 for correspondence; Gene Miller in 1967 for local investigative or specialized reporting and in 1976 for local general or spot news reporting; James Polk in 1974 for national reporting; William Foley in 1983 for spot news photography; Michel du Cille in 1986 for spot news photography and 1988 for feature photography; Thomas French in 1998 for feature writing; and Tim Nickens in 2013 for editorial writing.

Two of those journalists' names appear on the front page of the Oct. 7, 1981, edition of the IDS. Nickens, then a student staffer, recorded IU's reaction to the death of Egyptian President Anwar Sadat in a localized deadline story, while Foley was in Cairo working for the AP and photographed the assassination.

When shots rang out, Foley kept making pictures. He said it's a lesson he learned in Ernie Pyle Hall from photojournalism professor Will Counts. "You never know what's going to happen," Foley said. "What he taught me, [was] not just how to take photos, but how to deal with people."

ERNIE PYLE

IU's most famous journalist, Ernie Pyle, often spoke fondly of Indiana, and his humble Hoosier demeanor followed him into the foxholes and trenches of WWII around the globe. Pyle practiced his conversational style while writing for the IDS as a student in Bloomington. One editorial published in the state fair edition of the paper while he was editor in chief in 1922 is a prime example of Pyle's tone—relaxed, as if talking to a friend, yet still poignant and full of vivid detail.

GENE MILLER

Gene Miller's career was marked by hard investigative reporting that freed four wrongly convicted prisoners—efforts that won him the Pulitzer in 1967 and 1976, while he was at the Miami Herald. His time at IU, however, was a little less serious. "The truth was I was a rambunctious kid, careless at the typewriter, and sloppy around the journalistic edges," he wrote in a letter to then-School of Journalism Dean Trevor Brown in 1987. Miller's clips in the IDS show a style that is conversational, relaxed and at times humorous. In one first-person story, Miller and another reporter wrote about spelunking into the Jordan River under Indiana Avenue, coming up through a sewer grate at Kirkwood Avenue and Dunn Street.

JAMES POLK

James Polk has a long history of fighting for his stories. He won the 1974 national reporting Pulitzer for reporting on the Watergate scandal. Polk, however, had already run into pressure from an administration wanting to bury bad news. On the Friday before graduation weekend, Polk got a tip from IU's faculty athletics representative that the Big Ten would be cracking down on the football program for improper recruiting practices. Polk recalled that John Stempel killed the story because of the special graduation day edition running the next morning. He had been hired to work for the AP that upcoming summer, so he instead called his editors in Indianapolis. "That story . . . ran in every AP paper in the state the next morning, except the Indiana Daily Student," Polk said.

WILLIAM FOLEY

Foley worked as a photographer for the IDS and Arbutus yearbook, but he left shy of graduation in 1977. He shot for AP and UPI in Indianapolis and Louisville but knew he wanted to be a foreign correspondent. He made it to Cairo soon after, embedding in the press corps covering Anwar Sadat and was on hand for the Egyptian president's assassination. Foley was no stranger to tense news situations. Five years earlier, while at the IDS, a representative from the Ku Klux Klan had told the IDS that they'd be holding a rally outside Louisville, and Foley got the OK to cover it. He was told to walk around and take photos, just to avoid photos of men without their hoods. After the Klansmen burned a cross, Foley was tipped that he should probably leave quickly. Men surrounded his car as he left the field in Kentucky and headed back to Bloomington. The photos ran in the IDS two days later.

MICHEL DU CILLE

Michel du Cille saw photography as more than simply accompaniment to words on the page. "I'm not trying to illustrate their story," he said on a visit to Ernie Pyle Hall in 2014. "I'm trying to interpret their story." In one of du Cille's early stories for the IDS, he profiled an elderly couple who lived in a ramshackle house in Bloomington. The story ran on a two-page spread. He spent many afternoons with the pair, hanging out and hearing their story, making pictures and taking notes. Years later, he'd employ the same strategy when reporting on crack cocaine in Miami in a photo story that would win the 1988 Pulitzer for feature photography. Just being there, he said, gave him the opportunity to tell those stories more completely and honestly. "I always pushed myself toward the story," he said. "I think I'm a storyteller."

THOMAS FRENCH

Thomas French came to Bloomington before his senior year looking for a story to do before everyone came back to campus. He chose to cover the competition for the state's largest hog. French reported and wrote the story without formal training in narrative writing, but it is easy to see the seeds of a career that decades later would win the Pulitzer Prize for feature writing. "It was about something really interesting about the American character, our love of super-sizing everything," he said. "I had no idea I was going to be a narrative reporter. I did hundreds of other stories. But ['Hog Wild'] is the one people remember because it was actually interesting to read."

TIM NICKENS

For many young journalists who have studied in Ernie Pyle Hall, the community of students learning and growing together has been a critical tool in their journalism education. Pulitzer winner Tim Nickens is no different. He says the stories he did in school were "solid, but not spectacular," but he remembers learning the most just from working alongside student peers in the newsroom. The year before covering the Sadat assassination from Bloomington, he reported a data analysis story that took a critical look at the distribution of GPAs among different programs and schools on campus. And in January 1980 he reported and wrote an enterprise piece about ticket scalpers that used various scene-setting techniques. Both, he said, were stories that allowed him to build reporting skills that helped him in his professional career. Nickens won the 2013 Pulitzer for editorial writing for editorials in the Tampa Bay Times.

Wednesday morning, Oct. 7, 1981 | Indiana University, Bloomington, Ind. | ©1981, Indiana Daily Student | 36 pages | Two sections | 20 cents

ids — indiana daily student

Sadat assassinated

Sadat: Moments before shooting

photo/AP

The shooting . . .

CAIRO, Egypt (AP) — President Anwar Sadat, whose peace with Israel changed the course of Middle East history, was assassinated Tuesday by six Egyptian soldiers who jumped from a truck on military parade and charged the reviewing stand firing automatic weapons. Army sources said the attackers were Moslem fundamentalists.

Sadat has been under attack by Moslem fundamentalists who claim he betrayed Islam and the Arab world through his peace with Israel, which broke the cycle of three decades of Mideast wars. Tuesday's parade marked the anniversary of what Egypt calls a "glorious Arab victory" in the last conflict of that cycle — the 1973 Arab war against Israel.

The raiders also were said to have killed seven other people and wounded 27, including three American servicemen and two diplomats.

The army sources said all six attackers, including one lieutenant, were members of an artillery unit. They said two were killed and the others were being interrogated.

That report differed from an earlier statement by Egypt's ambassador to Washington, Ashraf Ghorbal. He said three assassins were killed and three were captured.

The Egyptian government has not given official word on the assassins' identities, their ages, or their political and religious affiliations.

Vice President Hosni Mubarak declared a state of emergency and the ruling National Democratic Party nominated him to succeed Sadat.

Grief was expressed around the world at the loss of a man President Ronald Reagan called "a champion of peace." But there was rejoicing in some Arab capitals and by Palestinians who felt Sadat sold them out to the Israelis.

In Beirut, Lebanon, callers purporting to speak for three separate Egyptian opposition groups claimed responsibility.

The death was considered likely to bring a new period of turmoil to the Mideast, and Israeli opponents of the peace treaty were gathering support for a last-ditch effort to block Israel's withdrawal from the Sinai.

The 62-year-old Sadat had enemies at home and throughout the Middle East because of his peace treaty with Israel and his recent crackdown on hundreds of opposition figures suspected of fomenting Christian-Moslem strife in Egypt. He shared the 1978 Nobel Peace Prize with Israeli Prime Minister

See 'Sadat,' Page 7

World responds to shooting

- **Shooting in Cairo** is the latest episode in a year-long trend of violence — an opinion. **Page 4.**
- **U.S. officials** call Sadat's death a tragedy which may threaten stability in the Middle East. **Page 6.**
- **Anwar Sadat:** Often compared to Harry Truman, he was a powerful and innovative world leader. **Page 6.**
- **U.S. policy in Middle East** and prospects for peace in the region may be altered by assassination. **Page 6.**
- **IU students from Middle East** have not changed their views because of Sadat's death. **Page 6.**
- **Egypt after Sadat:** Will his successor, Hosni Mubarak, be able to maintain stability within Egypt? **Page 18.**

Witness . . .

By David Ottaway
© 1981, The Washington Post

CAIRO — It was toward the end of what had been a spectacular military parade, and nobody was paying much attention to the slow-moving, shiny Russian trucks hauling new South Korean artillery pieces.

Instead all eyes were turned upward toward the Mirage jets swooping only feet above the reviewing stand.

Suddenly, one of the trucks came to an abrupt halt in front of the reviewing stand where President Anwar Sadat and the entire Egyptian military and political hierarchy were seated, watching the parade marking Egypt's 1973 victory over the Israelis along the Suez Canal.

At first we all thought it was just another parade special as a big bang went off and then another and several of the soldiers sitting in the back of the truck leaped out and started running toward the stands.

Then there was another huge bang and the rat-a-tat-tat of automatic rifle fire as the soldiers, both those on the back of the truck and those on the ground, opened fire on the stunned official party around Sadat.

At first the spectators did not move, and then everyone was diving for cover in all directions. But the soldiers on the truck were elevated enough to keep their fire going directly into the stands.

Pandemonium hit the crowd of officials and invited guests sitting in covered cement stands alongside the official reviewing box. There was screaming in all languages. Chairs went crashing to the ground and a stampede for the exit set in.

Then as the shooting died away and everyone was running away, I decided I had to find out whether Sadat had been hit or killed. So I worked my way down the outside railing of the exit ramp

See 'Witness,' Page 7

Reaction . . .

By Tim Nickens
ids Staff Writer

Egyptian leaders should be more concerned with maintaining peace within the country in the wake of President Anwar Sadat's assassination than with focusing on potential outside threats to the nation, an IU history professor said Tuesday.

Robert Ferrell, a distinguished professor of history, said Egypt's large population — 41 million people live in the country that is the combined size of Oregon and Texas — would have little to lore by participating in a revolution.

"Egypt has got an enormous number of people gathered in a small area with few natural resources," he said. "Because of the press of people they have got a volatile situation. These people have very little income, little education and not much else. They have an economy that just sputters along."

But Iliya Harik, a professor of political science and director of the Center for Near Eastern Studies, said a revolution or similar upheaval in Egypt is unlikely. He said as long as Egyptian Vice President Hosni Mubarak, who was a strong Sadat supporter, remains the dominant figure in his nation's government the country should remain stable.

"I have no doubt that he and the cabinet members will be able to keep the country under control in the short term," said Harik, who was last in Egypt about seven months ago. "Whether they will be able to keep control under the long term is open to question."

He said Mubarak should call for strong national unity and attempt to be more conciliatory with some of the groups that Sadat had recently been criticizing, such as the Islamic fundamentalists.

Reports that Mubarak plans to continue to promote Sadat's programs, including peace agreements with Israel and the procedure for regaining the Sinai Peninsula, that was ironed out in the Camp David peace talks, appeared to confirm Harik's belief that there will be little philosophical change by Egypt as it

See 'Reaction,' Page 7

Former IU student photographs assassination

By Steve Sanders
ids Staff Writer

When William Foley was an IU photojournalism student in 1973 he was by no means a prodigy. Those who knew him say he was good, of course, and a hard worker, but so were lots of other aspiring photojournalists.

But Tuesday, Foley, 26, was good enough to stand on the edge of history for a few frenzied, bloody seconds, frantically photographing the body of his friend, Egyptian President Anwar Sadat, being gunned down in the 40th world political assassination since World War II.

"No one was sure it was real for a few seconds," he told a fellow Associated Press (AP) newsman. "Then all hell broke loose."

The first indication that Foley was unhurt came to his friends and family in Indiana when his photographs began moving over the AP Laserphoto system several hours after the assassination. The images, some of the first out of Cairo, were aired on network television and showed the shocked expressions of Egyptian officials on the reviewing stand where Sadat and several others were shot.

Foley's mother, Sara, an Indianapolis realtor, heard about the shooting around 9 a.m. Monday on her way to work.

"My daughter called later and said they were firing into the crowd," Mrs. Foley said in a telephone interview Tuesday afternoon. "I was a little upset because I knew he'd be right there. I just figured God wouldn't let something like this happen to me."

An AP official called her about 11:30 a.m. to let her know her son was unhurt in the attack.

"If you talk to Bill, please tell him another gray hair has been added to my head," she told a reporter after learning the good news.

Mrs. Foley said her son developed an interest in photojournalism when he signed up for a course with Wilmer Counts, an IU associate professor of journalism.

"He went off to IU with no real major in mind. He picked up a camera and it was all over," she said.

Foley went on to major in telecommunications, and left IU in 1977 to take a job as a still photographer with an Indianapolis television station, working part-time for AP.

Looking for more excitement, he quit the television job the next year and was offered a position in the AP Cairo bureau. He accepted.

Foley almost missed Tuesday's

See 'Photographer,' Page 7

© 1977, Arbutus

Foley: photographer was on the scene when Sadat was shot

Inside today

Outside today

Today should be sunny and cool, with the high in the low to mid-60s. Tonight will be clear and chilly, with a chance of frost. The low will be in the upper 30s to low 40s.

P0078845, IU Archives.

1982–1996

From the dawn of the 1980s to the mid-'90s, the IDS turned to a new distribution model: paid circulation. In these years, IU students could order an IDS subscription at the same time as their basketball tickets, then pay for both through their bursar accounts. The paid years didn't last long, and they ended just as the IDS was debuting on the internet, a whole new platform for getting its stories out.

Bill Owsley, Genny Cummiskey and Jenny Ferguson edit a story, 1982. *P0081015, IU Archives.*

January 5, 1982 Indiana University Bloomington, Ind. 14 pages

ids

Indiana Daily Student

20¢

Tuesday morning

- Hoagy Carmichael comes home to Bloomington. Pages six and 11.
- Today should be sunny with a high between 38 and 43.

Allen resigns and Clark is named as successor

WASHINGTON (AP) — National Security Adviser Richard Allen resigned on Monday, and President Ronald Reagan immediately replaced him with Deputy Secretary of State William Clark.

Reagan said he accepted the resignation "with deep regret" during a meeting with Allen, who left the White House without comment to reporters. Only hours earlier, Allen had said at his home he had no intention of resigning.

The meeting followed Reagan's receipt of an internal White House report on Allen's conduct. The president, in a brief announcement relayed by his press office, said he had asked Allen to serve as a "consultant" in organizing a new foreign intelligence advisory board.

Clark arrived at the White House just moments after Allen departed and discussed his new duties with reporters.

The president said in his statement, read by deputy press secretary Larry Speakes, that Allen had been cleared of any wrongdoing by a study investigating the $1,000 Allen received from a Japanese magazine, as well as three watches accepted from Japanese friends.

In an exchange of letters, Reagan told Allen that as he leaves his job he does so "with my confidence, trust and admiration for your personal integrity and your exemplary service to the nation.

"Over the past year, you have served our nation with great distinction as my assistant for national security affairs," Reagan said. "You have provided me with invaluable advice and counsel over the years of our association and I am grateful for your constant loyalty and dedication."

Allen said he would be pleased "to undertake the interim task" and stated:

"It has been a rare privilege and a high honor to serve in your administration, and before that in the years of your campaign for the presidency. You have created memories which will accompany me and my family forever, and your trust and confidence are a source of deep pride and satisfaction."

Clark, a former California Supreme Court justice was Reagan's first chief of staff when Reagan was governor of California and is one of the most senior members of the president's inner circle.

But when he became deputy secretary of state, he had had no experience in foreign policy and was confirmed by the Senate only after a stormy confrontation with the Foreign Relations Committee.

Clark told reporters the president has "not changed his position" that Secretary of State Alexander Haig Jr. is his chief formulator and spokesman on foreign policy.

But Speakes said the new national security adviser "will have a direct reporting relationship to the president," something Allen did not have.

Allen generally communicated with the chief executive through Edwin Meese III, the president's counselor.

Speakes said that Clark "in his new role will be responsible for the development, coordination and implementation of national security policy, as approved by the president." He will also run the staff of the National Security Council.

Asked if he felt he were qualified for the new job, Clark said he would leave "that determination to the man who made the decision, the president of the United States."

Clark said he would retain his post as deputy secretary of state until a successor is named and "about to be confirmed."

The publicly released exchange of letters between Allen and Reagan offered no clue as to why Allen stepped down. But he repeatedly has expressed his desire to be returned to his duties from what he has said was a voluntary leave of absence.

Allen stepped aside in late November, while the Justice Department was investigating the cash and gift episodes as well as certain errors in his financial reports. The department cleared him Dec. 23 of any legal wrongdoing, but White House officials then disclosed they were conducting their own review.

The White House probe was completed Sunday, and a report was given to White House Chief of Staff James Baker III Sunday evening.

Countries abide by sanctions

BRUSSELS, Belgium (AP) — Ten Western European governments promised Monday they will not undermine economic sanctions the United States imposed on the Soviet Union following declaration of martial law in Poland.

But the Common Market countries failed to agree on their own unified response to the situation in Poland.

Meanwhile, President Ronald Reagan today opens talks with West German Chancellor Helmut Schmidt in hopes of blunting their rift over the American response to the military crackdown in Poland.

Foreign ministers of the 10 Common Market countries issued a declaration pledging to "avoid any step which could compromise" anti-Soviet sanctions announced last week by Reagan, who said the Soviet Union was responsible for martial law in Poland.

The promise was aimed at assuring the United States that European countries would not fill the gap in sales of high technology equipment or other items on a list of goods Reagan banned for export to the Soviet Union.

The Common Market made similar pledges in 1980 when the United States imposed sanctions on Iran and cut grain sales to the Soviet Union to protest Soviet intervention in Afghanistan.

"Europe will do nothing in any area that might undermine the action of other countries," said Belgian Foreign Minister Leo Tindemans, as spokesman for the 10 ministers.

He said the ministers met privately for seven hours to discuss the possibility of imposing their own commercial restrictions on the Soviet Union and cutting off food and financial aid to Poland. But the governments of Britain and West Germany already formally had opposed economic sanctions as ineffective.

They agreed for the first time as a group, however, with the U.S. analysis that the Soviet Union is involved in the crackdown, along with East bloc members of the Warsaw Pact military alliance.

Tindemans asserted Soviet involvement began as early as March 1980. The 10 ministers said in their declaration they "note with concern and disapproval the serious external pressure and the campaign directed by the Soviet Union and other Eastern European countries against the efforts for renewal in Poland.

"This already grave situation would be further aggravated if it led to an open intervention by the Warsaw Pact. For this reason the 10 wish to issue a solemn warning against any such intervention."

The 10 Common Market countries are France, West Germany, Italy, Belgium, the Netherlands, Greece, Denmark, Britain, Ireland and Luxembourg.

Germany's Schmidt, who said he views the recent U.S. sanctions against the Polish and Soviet governments as far too harsh, was due to arrive in the capital late Monday after a vacation in Florida.

Reagan's courtship of the West German leader could prove critical in keeping the turmoil in Poland from becoming a crisis for Western harmony. Schmidt has made it clear he has no intention of following Reagan's lead and imposing sanctions against the Soviets. For that matter, he has quarreled with the U.S. assertion that Moscow instigated the decree of martial law.

Reagan also plans to explore with Schmidt the differences in tone in Moscow's communications with Washington.

staff photos/Terry John

An estimated 400 people gathered in the foyer of the Musical Arts Center Monday afternoon to bid a final farewell to the well-known composer and Bloomington native Hoagy Carmichael (top). Mourners sat on the crowded MAC stairwells and overflowed onto the balconies during the memorial service (bottom).

Carmichael praised in words and music

By Angie Cannon and Steve Sanders
ids Staff Writers

Hoagy Carmichael, whose lively melodies have delighted millions for more than half a century, was eulogized Monday as both an innovative musician and as a hometown boy who was returning to his beloved Bloomington for the last time.

On a bitterly cold, gray afternoon, he was buried in a family plot in Rose Hill Cemetery — just a few miles from the Bloomington home where he first played the piano, and the building where he composed his classic hit "Stardust."

Carmichael, who had been ailing with a heart condition and cancer, died of a heart attack Dec. 27 in Rancho Mirage, Calif., where he lived in semi-retirement. He was 82.

More than 400 people, including family, boyhood friends and IU and state dignitaries, packed the Grand Foyer of the Musical Arts Center Monday for a memorial ceremony. Carmichael, who last visited the campus when he received an honorary doctor of music degree in 1972, had contributed $100,000 toward the construction of the foyer.

"He did find on this campus something special, something that nurtured him," said IU President John Ryan.

"Hoagy Carmichael gave to the world of music an unforgettable gift," said Charles Webb, dean of the IU School of Music. "Hoagy Carmichael became one of the greatest masters of jazz improvisation and set a standard for all to emulate."

Members of Carmichael's family present included his wife, Wanda McKay; a sister, Georgia Maxwell; and two sons, Hoagy Bix and Randy Bob.

Also present were IU Chancellor Herman B Wells, who presided; Bloomington Mayor Frank McCloskey; Lt. Gov. John Mutz; former Gov. Ed Whitcomb; seven of the eight members of the IU Board of Trustees; and several other IU administrators.

A six-piece band, composed of music school faculty members, played a medley of Carmichael's most popular jazz compositions. Sylvia McNair, a soprano and graduate student in music, sang "Stardust," and Roger Havranek, professor of music, sang "Chimes of Indiana" and "A Serenade to Gabriel," the song Carmichael requested be performed at his funeral.

The foyer was decorated with flowers, including arrangements from Carmichael's fraternity, Kappa Sigma, and President Ronald Reagan and his wife Nancy.

The ceremony seemed like one Carmichael himself would have liked. It was not only a celebration of his life and music, but it was also a chance for others to get a glimpse of his easy-going personality.

Eulogizers told anecdotes about Carmichael's carefree, creative days at IU. Wells, a classmate of Carmichael's in the 1920s, recalled, "The campus was alive with original, unique, inventive individuals.

"Campus life was so informal and unstructured that students fashioned their own fun for the most part and turned their ideas into enterprises," Wells said. "There was no impossible dream. In this simple, unsophisticated, tolerant climate were bred the talents of a number of stu-

See Funeral, Page 3

Computer registration to cut waits, stretch breaks

By Chip Partner
ids Staff Writer

About 130 IU students will lose their temporary jobs next year. But according to Assistant Registrar Michael Kleinman, they'll be about the only people hurt by a new computerized registration process.

"I think it has advantages for all populations on the campus," Kleinman said of the new system, which is unofficially scheduled to register students for the spring 1983 semester. "It will create an environment in which decisions can be made with more information at hand."

The tables at registration already are loaded with several hundred thousand computer cards. Kleinman said his office has hired 130 students to help shuffle those cards. "Under the new system I hope to hire only about six," he said.

But while some students may be disappointed at losing a week's income and the chance to register early, Kleinman said the new procedure will benefit most users.

"Many students are through the entire process in less than 10 minutes," Kleinman said. The system, copied from a registration process used at the University of Georgia at Athens, will eliminate the need for students to return to school before classes start.

"In April you will register for the (fall) semester," Kleinman said. The new system, tentatively scheduled to begin operation in November, will give students more time to plan their schedules. "We'll be holding registration for about three weeks," Kleinman said, instead of the current four-day rush.

Instead of the massive mayhem at the fieldhouse, IU's new procedure will take place in a small room somewhere on the main campus, Kleinman said. "Instead of waiting in individual lines, the computer will check all (of a student's) courses at the same time," he said.

If a class is unavailable, Kleinman said, the computer will hold a student's schedule for 24 hours so the problem can be resolved. Since they won't have to pass out cards at the fieldhouse, academic counselors should be available for quick advising.

"(The new system) has the same kinds of flexibility in terms of picking a particular section," he said. "It has advantages for the students themselves and for the faculty and staff."

But Linda Steinwachs, chief secretary for the economics department, said she'll miss working at fieldhouse registration.

"It's a lot different than sitting up here at the office," Steinwachs said. Steinwachs said that some students give her a hard time for following the rules, but overall she likes dealing with them. "You get to interact with students a lot more (at fieldhouse registration)," she said.

Chris Strack, a junior working at her third registration, said she'll miss the chance to register early more than the extra money. "The money isn't that great," Strack said. "I do it so I can get the classes I want."

Students who work at registration get minimum wage for about 25 or 30 hours during the week.

P0024038, IU Archives.

Carmichael Lived Through His Music

This story originally appeared Jan. 5, 1982, as part of the coverage of Bloomington native Hoagy Carmichael's funeral at the IU Musical Arts Center. The writer's most vibrant memory of the event: dropping his IDS reporter's notebook from a second-floor balcony during the service.

By Steve Sanders

Not even old age and confinement could suppress Hoagy Carmichael's love for music. He wrote his last song, "Hoagy's Tune," several months ago; he was teaching his 41-year-old son to play a song on the piano the day before his death.

Music was many things to the enduring Carmichael—a hobby, a profession, an outlet for protest and, perhaps most important to those who knew him, a means of expression for the quiet, lonely side of a man the public never really knew.

"He was a lonely soul all his life," his sister, Georgia Maxwell, 77, said Sunday, the day before Bloomington funeral services were conducted for her brother. Carmichael, 82, died Dec. 27 of a heart ailment in Rancho Mirage, Calif. "However, such comfort we were able to give him he was still lonely. That I think was part of his musical genius. When he was the loneliest, he would go to the piano."

The private, unsearchable part of his personality also was evident to the happy-go-lucky friends who grew up in Hoagy Carmichael's Bloomington, a sleepy secure college town of the early 1900s that Carmichael once described as "a boy's idea of fun."

. . . Howard Hoagland Carmichael was born Nov. 22, 1899, in a small cottage on South College Avenue. He was the son of an electrician and a small, sprightly woman who played piano in a local theater.

Carmichael played baseball in Dunn Meadow and waded and fished in the Jordan River. It was after a baseball game had been rained out and a disgusted Hoagy was sulking around the house that he first tried to play the oak-cased piano in the family living room. . . .

[Around 1915], Clyde Carmichael packed up his family and moved to Indianapolis. Although it was not a cheerful period for young Carmichael, he found fellowship with black pianist Reggie Duval. He recalled passing happy hours listening to Duval play the piano "as if he were part of it" and soaking in the musical flavor that would later contribute to the unique character of his own jazz compositions.

Carmichael happily returned to Bloomington in 1919 to finish high school, and enrolled as a liberal arts student at IU the next year.

Leading a double life as an uninterested student and, as he put it, a "jazz revolutionary," Carmichael blossomed as a musician during his college days. His five-piece band entertained at formal and informal dances. Hoagy, a slightly rowdy Kappa Sigma fraternity member, spent hours with buddies at the piano in the Book Nook restaurant, located in the building on Indiana Avenue now occupied by Garcia's Pan Pizza.

That restaurant also is the legendary spot where, in the mid-1920s, Carmichael wrote "Stardust," a late-blooming classic that has been recorded by more than 80 artists but is still linked with Carmichael's name.

According to the legend, the melody for "Stardust" was inspired by a lost love, Katherine Baker.

"The first eight bars of 'Stardust' were whistled by me as I walked across campus," Carmichael recalled in an interview a few years ago. "I was on my way to bed, but I was intrigued with the melody, and I had the sense to know that I would forget it."

He returned to the Book Nook and "pounded on the door until the proprietor, Pete Costas, let me in so I could play it on the piano. That was a wise move," Carmichael said. . . .

Carmichael lived through his music
Experts praise composer
Composer comments
Funeral

Interior page, Jan. 5, 1982, "Carmichael lived through his music." *P0079122, IU Archives.*

20 cents at newsstands

ids Indiana Daily Student

December 13, 1982 Indiana University Bloomington, Ind. 18 pages

Monday

Today will be mostly sunny, with highs in the low-40s.

At last

After eight overtimes, IU soccer reaches top

By Mark Alesia
ids Staff Writer

FORT LAUDERDALE, Fla. — It was the kind of emotion money couldn't buy for 20-year IU soccer coach Jerry Yeagley.

In eight sudden-death overtime periods and a record 159 minutes, IU, behind senior Gregg Thompson's two goals, won its first NCAA soccer championship with a 2-1 victory over Duke Saturday night at Lockhart Stadium.

Finally, Yeagley was riding high on his players' shoulders and waving a large IU flag, oblivious to the six-figure professional coaching contract offer he refused in October.

"I've waited 20 years," said Yeagley, who lost the title game three previous times. "After the seventh overtime (IU assistant coach) Don Rawson asked me if the NCAA would consider calling the game a draw. I'd rather lose than call it a draw. I told him we're going to play it to the hilt."

The hilt came at 159:16 when Thompson perfectly placed a direct free kick just inside the upper right corner of the Duke goal.

"I didn't know if I had enough energy to even kick the ball," said Thompson, who had been in and out of the game with leg cramps. "All of a sudden, I had this feeling I could make it. I saw a spot over the end man, I bent the ball and hit it.

"I'm exhausted. I don't know if I could do that ever again.'

For a while, it appeared both teams would not have to endure the rigorous physical test which caused players to lie down on the field during stoppages in play.

Late in regulation time, IU had 10 men playing back on defense. IU was sitting on Thompson's first-half goal and appeared to be in control, when at 81:30, Duke's Sean McCoy lofted the ball over Hoosier goalie Chris Peterson to tie the game. Dave McDaniel was awarded an assist.

"After that, I said, 'Here we go again,' " Yeagley recalled. "I think it's a natural reaction when you've been here and seen it slip away."

Peterson was out of position to make the save as he left the net too far to meet McCoy. But Yeagley said it was his only mistake of the game.

"Those are the kind of goals Sean McCoy scores," Blue Devil back and Hermann Trophy winner Joe Ulrich said. "They're not pretty, but they're goals."

A crowd of 5,312 included a vocal Blue Devil student section that greeted the Hoosiers with "Go to Hell Indiana, Go To Hell," a chant usually reserved for hated rival North Carolina.

Duke controlled play at the beginning of the game, but it evened until 14:52. After Hoosier sophomore Iker Zubizeretta's shot, the ball was cleared from the goal mouth to Thompson, who scored from about 20 yards away in the upper right corner of the penalty area.

"I hit it well," said the runner-up for the Hermann Trophy. "I was going for the corner. I think it went off (Duke midfielder Ken) Lolla's leg."

IU held off two big Duke threats in the second half before the tying goal. Once again, backs Dan King, Steve Meyer, Thompson, Greg Kennedy and freshman midfielder John Stollmeyer were outstanding. King and Meyer were the only Hoosiers to play the entire game in the 75-degree temperatures.

"All year, our defense has led us," Yeagley said. "Kennedy kept (Duke leading scorer Tom) Kain out of the game."

At the end of regulation, Duke had a 16-15 advantage in shots and was even in corner kicks with IU at three each.

The first two overtimes, 15 minutes each, were uneventful as the game became more and more disjointed while the

See 'Soccer,' Page 5

Staff Photo/Daniel Patmore

The IU soccer team hoists coach Jerry Yeagley onto their shoulders in celebration of the Hoosiers' first NCAA soccer title after four previous appearances in the finals. From left, Mike Hylla, Pat McGawley, Coach Jerry Yeagley and Dan King cheer after defeating previously unbeaten and No. 1-ranked Duke University in eight overtimes Saturday night in the longest playoff game in college soccer history.

Fans celebrate with NCAA goddess

By Jim Slater
ids Staff Writer

On March 30, 1981, a rowdy crowd gathered at Showalter Fountain to remove concrete fish, decorate the scantly-clad Venus statue and celebrate IU's winning of the NCAA basketball title.

Saturday night, a few brave souls weathered bone-chilling temperatures to try to arouse similar hoopla for the IU soccer team's NCAA title victory over Duke 2-1 in eight overtimes.

See related story, Page 12

A more formal celebration is scheduled for 7 tonight in Assembly Hall, when the athletic department will hold a pep rally to let the Hoosiers' loyal fans join in on the glory of another NCAA victory. The championship trophy will be displayed, and the team will be honored after arriving from Florida late Sunday night.

But the Saturday night fountain' frolics got the jump on tonight's party. Strangely, it was not those who remembered 1981's antics who appeared, but those who had heard about such excitement. It was mostly freshmen who turned out to continue a tradition.

Freshman Bryant Harner came early to a movie being shown at nearby Woodburn Hall, and he watched most of the crowd of about 30 leave just before midnight. Those who

See 'Fans,' Page 5

Committee to approve tax; showdown expected on floor

By Angie Cannon
ids Staff Writer

INDIANAPOLIS — This morning the Indiana Senate will pick up the unpleasant task of raising state taxes after the House passed the largest tax increase in state history Friday.

The Senate Finance Committee, meeting this morning in the sixth day of the special session of the Indiana General Assembly, is expected to pass the House measure with no changes. The House bill, endorsed by Gov. Robert Orr, would raise the sales tax from 4 to 5 percent and the individual income tax from 1.9 to 3 percent. Under the plan, the ongoing phase-out of the corporate gross income tax would be halted for two years.

A showdown could come when the tax hike reaches the Senate floor on Wednesday or Thursday.

GENERAL ASSEMBLY '83

There is "substantial sentiment" in the Senate Republican caucus to gradually phase out the proposed increases in the sales and income taxes, Senate President Pro Tem Robert Garton, R-Columbus, said Sunday.

Sen. Farrell Duckworth, R-Bloomington, said Sunday that more than half of the 32-member Republican caucus favors gradually reducing the tax increases.

Garton said he would not stand in the way of such a phase-out. One proposal is to roll back the sales tax to 4 percent and the income tax to 2.5 percent by 1986, he said.

Duckworth said that during a Republican caucus meeting he proposed a plan that would reduce the income tax to 2 percent when unemployment drops to 8 percent.

But he doesn't plan to introduce that plan on the floor because "it would be defeated."

"The feeling in caucus is that if we oppose the House plan, then we would have to go to conference committee, and things would really drag out," Duckworth said.

A conference committee, made of members from both houses, is appointed to iron out differences between Senate and House versions of the same bill.

Finance Committee Chairman Larry Borst, R-Indianapolis, said he opposes phasing out the taxes.

But Borst said he doesn't expect the economy to turn around in the near future.

That is the reason the House didn't include a phase-out in its proposal, House Ways and Means Committee Chairman Pat Kiely, R-Anderson, said Friday.

In late November, Orr called the special session to reduce the state's projected $452.1 million deficit.

The House passed the $254 million tax increase and the $255 million in spending deferrals Friday. Five GOP legislators bucked their party and voted against the tax increase along with all 41 Democrats.

One of those Republicans was Bloomington's Jerry Bales. Bales said he voted against the bill because the proposal will not raise enough revenue to provide the state with an adequate surplus. Bales presented his own tax plan Thursday which would have raised the sales tax to 5.5 percent and the individual income tax to 3.5 percent. It was defeated by voice vote.

The other Republicans opposed the tax increase for different reasons.

"We have a very temporary situation and a very permanent solution," said Rep. Richard Bray, R-Martinsville.

Democrats argued that the tax increase unfairly burdens the poor, the unemployed, the elderly and the middle class. The Democrats proposed exempting home utility bills from the sales tax increase and increasing exemptions for the personal income tax. But these amendments were defeated by Republicans both in the Ways and Means Committee and on the House floor.

Photo/AP

Wojciech Jaruzelski

Martial law to be lifted by year's end

WARSAW, Poland (AP) — The "basic rigors" of martial law will be suspended before the end of the year, internment will end, and there will be a partial amnesty, Gen. Wojciech Jaruzelski announced Sunday night.

Jaruzelski, the premier, Communist Party chief and head of the martial law council, said in a nationally televised speech that his regime hopes to end military rule "in the reasonably near future."

But he indicated that in the meantime, it would retain some of the extraordinary powers it assumed last year.

Jaruzelski spoke on the eve of the first anniversary of the day he proclaimed martial law to begin the destruction of the independent labor union Solidarity. The union was outlawed on Oct. 13, and last month, the government concluded it was no longer a threat when underground leaders were unable to rally a nationwide protest strike.

Jaruzelski said the 21-man Council of National Redemption "is of the opinion that conditions have arisen for suspending martial law . . . . The suspension of martial law means that its basic rigors will cease to function before the end of this year."

The Sejm, Poland's parliament, meets Monday to take the legislative action necessary to put the military council's decision into effect.

Jaruzelski spoke only in general terms of the restrictions that would be lifted and those that would remain.

"Only regulations that directly protect the fundamental interests of the state, creating a protective shield for the economy and ensuring the greater personal safety of citizens, should remain in force wholly or in part as a temporary measure," he said. "'. . . The national economy . . . needs special protection, and the public wants the fight against crime to be stepped up."

Jaruzelski made no mention of a letter from Solidarity leader Lech Walesa in which the hero of the independent labor movement listed his conditions for cooperation with the government to solve the nation's "deep and prolonged crisis."

The letter, written Dec. 4 and made public by Walesa Saturday, called for amnesty for all Solidarity members jailed or fired from their jobs for union activity. It also demanded restoration of the Gdansk agreements of August 1980, which for the first time in the Soviet bloc recognized the right of workers to form unions independent of Communist Party control.

However, Jaruzelski said there would be a partial amnesty, and underground Solidarity activists should seize the chance to come into the open.

Solidarity was suspended when Jaruzelski declared martial law last Dec. 13, and thousands of its leaders were interned. All but about 300 have been freed, but the new labor law that outlawed their union restores control of new unions to the party.

Photo/AP

Lech Walesa

P0079181, IU Archives.

October 22, 1984

Monday, October 22, 1984 18 pages 25¢

Indiana Daily Student

Indiana University Bloomington, Indiana 47405 ©1984, Indiana Daily Student

Fraternity fire set intentionally; one killed

By Dawn Biggs
Daily Student Staff Writer

Arson caused the early Sunday morning fire that claimed the life of a student from IU-East and severely damaged the Zeta Beta Tau fraternity house, officials said Sunday evening.

"The fire appears to have been a set fire, and the county prosecutor's office will be treating it as a murder investigation," Monroe County Prosecutor Ron Waicukauski said.

Twenty-eight members of the fraternity, 700 E. Eighth St., and two IU Police Department officers were injured in the fire. Four students remain hospitalized.

Though no arrests have been made, state and local authorities have several suspects, IUPD Director Jim Kennedy said Sunday night. Kennedy said witnesses are still being interviewed but he would not elaborate.

At a news conference Sunday, Kennedy said a hearing to discuss possible arrest warrants could be held as early as this afternoon.

"In the living room area of the first floor, some type of flammable liquid was poured in the room and then set on fire," Jim Skaggs, chief investigator from the state Fire Marshal's office, said at the news conference.

Israel Edelman of Richmond, Ind., who died in the fire, was visiting the fraternity during Homecoming weekend. He was a fraternity member and an IU-Bloomington student last year. Edelman had planned to transfer back from the IU branch in Richmond to Bloomington for the spring semester.

Edelman, 19, was found in one of the upstairs bedrooms. "One firefighter tried to arouse him, but he couldn't," Kennedy said. "The room was filled with dense smoke and tremendous heat."

Edelman was pronounced dead on arrival at Bloomington Hospital. The cause of death was smoke inhalation, said Sandy Fiscus, director of marketing at the Bloomington Hospital.

A funeral service will be held today in Richmond for Edelman, said Sheldon Hirst, a Zeta Beta Tau trustee from Indianapolis.

About 40 house members and visitors were in the house at the time of the fire. The IUPD and the Bloomington Fire Department responded to the fire at about 4:25 a.m.

Three fraternity members are in Bloomington Hospital with second-degree burns to the face, hands, arms and feet. Sophomore Kevin Homler, 19, was listed in fair condition Sunday. Sophomore Brian Rothman 18, was in serious but stable con-

See FIRE, back page, this section

PATRICK LIM / Daily Student

The Zeta Beta Tau fraternity house, located on the corner of Eighth Street and Fess Avenue, was heavily damaged by a fire that broke out early Sunday morning. The fire killed one person, a student from IU-East in Richmond, Ind.

Administrators and students offer help after fire

By Regina Boyle
Daily Student Staff Writer

After Sunday morning's fatal fire at the Zeta Beta Tau fraternity, the University administration, greek houses and dormitories were quick to offer assistance to displaced house members.

At a news conference Sunday night, James Kennedy, director of the IU Police Department, said the 35 members who were living in the house would be housed Sunday night at the Poplars Research and Conference Center.

Richard McKaig, associate dean of students for activities and programs, said Sunday meals would be provided through the Indiana Memorial Union's meal plan. He said the fraternity chapter will pay for the food and lodging.

McKaig said he met with fraternity members Sunday morning. They discussed options for permanent housing in residence halls, hotels, and off-campus apartments, he said.

Kirk White, assistant to IU Vice President for University Relations Dan Orescanin, said there shouldn't be a problem with finding a place for fraternity members to stay.

"One of the things we have on this campus is a tremendous amount of resources to handle a problem like this. There are a lot of different options," White said.

He said dormitory floor lounges could be used to house fraternity members. White said ZBT members said they want to live together, if possible.

"I think it's best to keep them together as much as we can," White said.

Interfraternity Council president, senior Jeff Farren, said IFC is helping to coordinate the relocation of members.

Farren said the Acacia fraternity, 702 E. Third St., has offered permanent housing for 12 members and permanent meals for six of the 12. Alpha Tau Omega fraternity, 720 E. Third St., has offered permanent meals for the other six.

Farren said the fraternities will not ask the ZBT members to pay house bills for now. But, if they stay for the rest of the semester, "maybe they (ZBTs) will make some sort of an arrangement," he said.

Kappa Delta sorority, 1005 N. Jordan Ave., plans to serve dinner to all 35 members tonight, Farren added.

One ZBT member, 19-year-old Israel Edelman, was killed in the blaze. Edelman was enrolled at IU-East in Richmond, Ind., and was visiting at the fraternity during Homecoming weekend.

White said IFC will provide bus transportation for fraternity members to Richmond for Edelman's funeral today.

He also said Dean of Students Michael Gordon and Farren plan to represent the University at the funeral.

Dormitory residents have also offered assistance to ZBT members.

Residents at Ashton Center formed the "Youth Action Team" to assist ZBT members, who lost most of their books,

See HELP, back page, this section

Associated Press

President Ronald Reagan shakes hands with Walter Mondale at the start of the presidential debate on foreign policy in Kansas City, Mo., Sunday.

Reagan, Mondale spar in final debate

By Michael Putzel
The Associated Press

KANSAS CITY, Mo. — Walter Mondale said Sunday night that President Ronald Reagan is an out-of-touch leader whose foreign policy has "humiliated" the United States. Reagan retorted in the climactic campaign debate that Mondale has a "record of weakness . . . that is second to none" on national defense.

In his closing argument, Mondale told viewers to imagine the United States under nuclear attack, saying:

"Pick a president that you know will know — if that tragic moment ever comes — what he must know. Because there will be no time for staffing, committees or advisers. A president must know right then."

Reagan had the final words, saying, "I want more than anything else to try to complete the new beginning that we charted four years ago."

"It may come as a surprise to Mr. Mondale, but I am in charge," Reagan had replied tartly after his Democratic opponent assailed his policies on arms control, Lebanon, Central America and elsewhere.

"I will keep us strong," was Mondale's reply after Reagan listed a series of weapons that he said his presidential opponent had once opposed. He said that as a result of the president's policies in Central America, "we have been humiliated and our opponents are stronger."

The 90-minute televised debate began and ended with a handshake at center stage between the president and his Democratic challenger, far behind in the polls

See DEBATE, Page 18

WEEKEND DIGEST

From Daily Student Wire Services

CIA plane crashes

A Central Intelligence Agency plane crashed Friday into the side of a volcano near San Salvador, El Salvador. White House spokesman Larry Speakes said the plane was warning the Salvadoran government of rebel offensives and monitoring arms shipments from Nicaragua. But one intelligence source said the plane was following an aircraft carrying weapons for rebels. The crash occurred a day after the Salvadoran army launched an offensive against rebels in northeastern El Salvador.

GNP rises sluggishly

The Gross National Product rose 2.7 percent in the third

See DIGEST, back page, this section

Parade, rally outshine gloomy weekend weather

By Cathy McBride
Daily Student Staff Writer

See photos, Page 13.

Though the football team lost and the weather was dreary, Homecoming spirit was alive and well on campus.

"The rain didn't ruin anything, since the football team was not the center of the weekend," said Junior Melissa Courson, who was in charge of Homecoming activities for the Alpha Omicron Pi sorority. "It was the parties, the parade and other activities that made the weekend."

The festivities began with the parade and pep rally Friday night. People lined the parade route to watch the hour-long event, which included high school bands, fire trucks, horses and bagpipe players. Participants riding miniature cars and motorcycles stole the show.

Student-constructed floats traveled a parade route lined with lawn displays. Forest Quad won first place in the float competition with an entry that was topped with tissue-paper champagne bottles and glasses.

McNutt Quad won first place in the lawn display competition and was named overall winner of the floats and lawn displays.

All entries focused on this year's Homecoming theme, "Cheers to 100 Years." This year marks the 100th anniversary of IU's first football season.

McNutt's lawn display also included champagne glasses and a bottle of bubbly.

McNutt President Jim Kadow, junior, said the quad built the display because "the parade came by here and we want to promote spirit. We wanted to show McNutt's involvement in the Homecoming activities."

The parade ended with a pep rally, at which seniors Christine Gliozzo and Carm Aiello were named Homecoming queen and king.

"This school has a lot of tradition," said Gliozzo, a member of Pi Beta Phi sorority. "Some call it a 'rah-rah' school, but it's in a positive way. No matter what the outcome of the game, everyone had fun."

Gliozzo is vice president of Pi Beta Phi, director of scholarship for the Panhellenic Council, a member of the IU Sing production staff and has been named to Phi Beta Kappa, the national scholastic honorary society.

Aiello is a member of the Phi Kappa Psi fraternity and is a member of the IU Student Foundation steering committee for IU Sing. He is also an associate instructor in the School of Journalism and, last year, was president of his fraternity.

Although they weren't victory parties, Homecoming celebrations could be found all over campus Saturday night.

Kadow said McNutt had floor parties and Courson said her sorority's plans were unaffected by the rain and the game loss.

Winners

Overall
McNutt Quad

Floats
1. Forest Quad
2. Zeta Beta Tau
3. Alpha Phi Alpha and Alpha Kappa Alpha

Lawn displays
1. McNutt Quad
2. Delta Tau Delta and Sigma Delta Tau

Window displays
1. Foster-Harper 9
2. (tie) Willkie North 10 and Delta Gamma

Fun units
Chi Omega and Sigma Nu

Inside

■ The Foster Quad Board of Governors approves a resolution asking the administration to consider stocking cyanide tablets on campus for students in the event of a nuclear attack. Page 3.

Outside

A 40 percent chance of rain today with highs in the upper 50s to 60. A 20 percent chance of showers tonight and Tuesday with lows near 50 and highs in the upper 50s.

P0078676, IU Archives.

CompuScum, VDTs and That Garish Gold

A CompuScan disk, used in a machine affectionately known in its late years of functionality as "CompuScum." *Photo courtesy of Paul Heaton.*

UPI machine, early 1980s. *Photo courtesy of Paul Heaton.*

Facing, The first known process color used on deadline was a photo of Ronald Reagan published the morning after his re-election in November 1984. *P0078677, IU Archives.*

Producing the IDS in the early 1980s involved IBM Selectric typewriters, bell codes, border tape and wax machines.

The CompuScan system consisted of a handful of video display terminals for editing, but stories had to first be typed onto special paper that was then scanned into the system. "Bell codes" were used to indicate font, size and other characteristics. Headlines still had to be "counted" to ensure proper fit, with everyone knowing that f, l, i, r, t and j were letters that only got a half-count.

CompuScan was nearing the end of its useful life, earning it the nickname "CompuScum." As the system (frequently) slowed, someone would yell "Save!" followed by everyone feverishly pounding the "save" key—usually to no avail. On more than one production night, Carol Wright would return from backshop to reluctantly inform us that we had "lost a disk." All work performed since the most recent backup—usually hours' worth—would have to be redone.

There was no such thing as digital photography. Photo prints (almost always black and white) had to be scanned and converted to halftones, then affixed to the page with wax. Those who were skilled enough then applied border tape to the edge of the image. Changes to pages were marked in light blue pen, and sometimes surgical precision with X-acto knives was needed to add a period or change an "e" to a "c" in order to not be late and therefore fined $25 for each 15 minutes we went beyond midnight.

Final page flats were driven to Columbus, Indiana (with hopes that nothing fell off a page), to be converted to plates for printing.

Three teletype machines were used—Associated Press, United Press International and Los Angeles Times/Washington Post—although by the early 1980s, those stories also

Paul Heaton was editor in chief twice, in fall 1983 and fall 1984. *Photo courtesy of Paul Heaton.*

fed directly into the computer system. The old (heavy!) UPI teletype was replaced in fall 1984 with a fancy new dot-matrix printer. Having served as editor in chief for both fall '83 and fall '84, I think the technician had pity on me and let me keep the old machine as a souvenir.

Although color photos had previously been published, usually for a section done in advance, the first known process color used on deadline was a photo of Ronald Reagan published the morning after his re-election in November 1984 (complete with a garish use of gold spot color around the image). Election Day 1984 also heralded the delivery of the new Atex system, which ushered in the next generation of publishing technology during the spring 1985 semester.

—*Paul Heaton, BA 1984*
Nov. 7, 1984

Wednesday, November 7, 1984 25¢

Indiana Daily Student

Special Election Edition

Reagan wins in landslide

No big surprise, little suspense this Election Day

By Haynes Johnson
©1984, Washington Post

WASHINGTON — Of the 50th presidential election in American history, it can be said it was robbed of suspense, but not of meaning.

This was the one, voters were told over and over for month after month during the longest and most expensive and wearying of election years, that was preordained. It was to be the Ronald Reagan landslide, both in electoral and popular votes. The polls said so, and the polls were right.

Reagan and the Republicans Tuesday night were rolling to a victory of massive proportions, as forecast by those polls. And this landslide, it appeared, had coattail effects: Democrats fared poorly in Senate races they had expected would be either extremely close or that they would win.

Chalk up one for scientific samples. Discount for now those instinctive yearnings among the public for Election Day upsets and surprises, for the traditional American desire to see an underdog battle back against historic odds and at least do "better than expected."

It was Harry S. Truman's underdog mantle and the cheering sound of the big crowds he attracted in the closing days of his campaign in 1948 that sustained Walter Mondale in his hopes for an upset against a popular incumbent president. In the final days of the campaign, Mondale ran as much against the polls, it seemed, as against the president. He implored the people to prove the pollsters wrong. But, as the votes were counted, it appeared virtually certain that his hope was not to be.

Not that the polls were all that scientific or useful a guide to voting behavior.

This Election Day began with the major national polls agreeing on only one major fact about the 1984 outcome — the presidential winner.

But it also meant something else about this Election Day — and, perhaps more significantly, about those to come:

However incorrect some of the projections on certain of the races — or even on the final presidential vote totals — might have been, in the larger

See ELECTION DAY, Page A4

Associated Press

Ronald Reagan

Coattail effects not as extensive as GOP hoped

By David Espo
The Associated Press

WASHINGTON — President Ronald Reagan swept to runaway re-election over Walter F. Mondale Tuesday night, but Republicans struggled to translate his landslide into significant gains in Congress.

The president won 28 states with 274 electoral votes and led in 10 more with 137. The electoral votes of South Dakota pushed his total past the 270 needed for election.

Mondale had won only in the District of Columbia, and led in three states, including his home state of Minnesota.

Sen. Paul Laxalt, Reagan's campaign chairman, said, "We've got at least a reasonable chance to have the most historic landslide in all American history." He called it a clear mandate for Reagan's programs.

The president got news of his victory in Los Angeles, where he and his wife watched the returns in a Century Plaza Hotel suite equipped with four television sets.

He told reporters he hoped to participate in a summit with the Soviet Union during a second term in office.

The largest popular vote in history belonged to Lyndon Johnson, elected with 61.05 percent of the vote in 1964.

Reagan's strength was signaled in advance in the public opinion polls, and the returns validated those forecasts from the time the first ballots were tallied in the East.

In the popular vote, with 34 percent of the precincts counted, Reagan was polling 59 percent, to 41 percent for Mondale.

Mondale entertained his campaign staff at a dinner in Minnesota, delivering what one aide called a "dignified but emotional" farewell speech. The aide, who declined to be identified by name, said Mondale made no direct reference to the likelihood of defeat, but told his guests, "I know that most of you did this because you believe in a better America."

See PRESIDENT, Page A4

Orr claims win; Townsend holds out

By Jim Drew
Daily Student Staff Writer

INDIANAPOLIS — With 74 percent of the votes cast, Gov. Robert Orr proclaimed victory in the election Tuesday with a lead of 81,397 votes, but Democrat Wayne Townsend said he would not concede until all the results were tabulated.

"There is every possible indication that we have won," Orr said. Lt. Gov. John Mutz said the slim margin of victory could be attributed to "tough decisions" that Orr made during the economic recession.

In 1982, the state had a $452 million deficit and the Indiana General Assembly passed the highest tax increase in the state's history.

The governor said the close margin did not mean a slip in support from Hoosiers of his administraion. "The fact we have won is indicative of support," Orr said.

The coattail effect was not a factor in the election, Mutz said. "The sophistication of Hoosier voters has become apparent," he said, referring to how voters did not adhere to a straight Republican ticket.

Orr's victory marks the first time a political party has won five consecutive terms for governor. The last Democratic governor in Indiana was in 1964. Since 1900, Republicans have controlled the statehouse for 52 years, the Democrats for 32.

As the evening progressed, Republicans at the Sheraton-Meridian and Republican headquarters watched Orr's margin of victory diminish. Orr's arrival time at headquarters was pushed further back as more votes came in. The governor's campaign staff said Orr would appear first at 9 p.m., then 9:30 p.m., 10 p.m. and finally 10:45 p.m., only 30 minutes after Townsend refused to concede the race.

Orr's close re-election followed a long campaign that some observers have described as the most negative in the state's history.

Townsend waged an aggressive campaign, criticizing the economic problems that have plagued Indiana in the last four years. He also has made the license branch system a major issue, criticizing Orr for presiding over a corrupt system that lines of the pockets of state Republicans.

On Tuesdsay night, Orr said some reforms would be made in the license branch system, but he did not outline any specific changes.

Orr ran on his record, saying that his economic development initiatives have created about 35,000 jobs and placed Indiana at the forefront of emerging high-tech industries.

"All this year, we talked about creation of jobs. We've talked about the improvements in education. We've talked about the means by which we're moving swiftly through the recovery to a

See ORR, Page A2

JEFF SMITH / Daily Student

Rep. Frank McCloskey, D-8th, talks with students from several area high schools at Edgewood High School in Ellettsville Tuesday morning.

McIntyre has narrow lead over incumbent McCloskey

By Jim Drew
Daily Student Staff Writer

President Ronald Reagan will have another staunch supporter in Congress for the next two years if Republican Rick McIntyre's lead over Rep. Frank McCloskey holds up in the 8th District race.

McIntyre led early this morning with 50.4 percent of the vote, with 88 percent of all precincts reporting. McCloskey, a former mayor of Bloomington, said a winner can not be named until this morning, when all votes are tallied.

"Mr. McIntyre has the edge at this point," McCloskey said just after midnight, "but it's literally too close to call."

With 78 percent of all precincts reporting, McIntyre had 91,963 votes, and McCloskey had 87,523.

"We hope by tomorrow to announce a victory, and if so, we will celebrate the rest of the week," McIntyre said Tuesday night.

McCloskey did not concede the election as he left the Vanderburgh County Auditorium. "I expect to be around for a long time," McCloskey said. "It's going to be real close, a matter of a couple hundred votes."

With 32 of the 33 precincts reporting in Monroe County, McIntyre had 11,686 votes, and McCloskey had 9,706. McIntyre won in his native Lawrence County, defeating McCloskey by 10,620 to 6,451. McIntyre, a 28-year-old state representative from Bedford, was shaking hands and campaigning at Perry 17 precinct Tuesday afternoon when McCloskey arrived to vote.

Jeff Springer, McIntyre's Monroe County coordinator, said McIntyre asked his opponent, "Is there anything I can say to sway your vote?"

McCloskey replied, "No, I think I've pretty much made up my mind."

On Tuesday morning, McCloskey campaigned in Bloomington and telephoned campaign workers from Democratic headquarters. In the afternoon, he left for Evansville, where he went to the Vanderburgh Democratic County Headquarters.

A fatigued but optimistic McCloskey greeted campaign workers and Democratic supporters when he arrived at the headquarters. He disagreed with an Associated Press exit poll that showed McIntyre ahead. He said the results were skewed to McIntyre because they were based largely on the Republican counties in the district.

"The next couple of hours should even it up," McCloskey said. "I feel good about it," he said, referring to the campaign.

See McINTYRE, Page A2

Hamilton, Schultz win; those and other races on Pages A2, A3, A4

Monday, February 25, 1985 16 pages 25¢

Indiana Daily Student

Indiana University Bloomington, Indiana 47405 ©1985, Indiana Daily Student

Knight's rage during game spurs ejection

By Anthony Anderson
Daily Student Staff Writer

Everybody knew.

And IU Athletic Director Ralph Floyd knew everybody knew.

Purdue coach Gene Keady knew, too, but he didn't want to admit he knew.

What they knew was that all the commotion after Purdue's 72-63 victory Saturday at IU would not be over the game, nor Purdue sweeping IU this season, nor IU's losing a record third straight game at Assembly Hall, nor IU's possibly being eliminated from NCAA tournament consideration by dropping to 6-8 in conference play. Rather, it would be over the antics of IU coach Bob Knight with 15 minutes remaining in the first half.

After a wild scramble for a loose ball, a foul was called on IU sophomore forward Marty Simmons when he and a Boilermaker player both came up out of the pile holding the ball. Most thought that should have brought a jump ball.

Especially Knight. He dramatically motioned for a jump ball, and was still steaming about the call when IU's Daryl Thomas was whistled for another debatable foul on the ensuing inbounds play.

Knight blew up and referee Fred Jaspers blew his whistle.

Technical No. 1.

Knight continued to protest, and as Purdue's Steve Reid lined up to shoot the technical free throws, Knight picked up his plastic and metal chair and, underhanded, whipped it across the court. It passed through the lane in front of Reid and referee London Bradley.

Technical No. 2.

At that time, Jaspers summoned Floyd, who was sitting at the other end of the IU bench. A meeting between Knight, Floyd, Jaspers and officials at the scorer's table took place.

Knight soon left that meeting, though, and charged onto the court for a verbal machine-gunning of Bradley.

Technical No. 3. That meant automatic ejection.

The official play-by-play to Saturday's game lists the ejection as coming after the third technical, but Knight may have actually been dismissed for the fourth time as IU's head coach (the others were in 1973, '74 and '80) after throwing the chair. That is when Jaspers pointed to Floyd.

The word "may" has to be used in talking about details, because Floyd and other IU officials weren't talking about it.

Floyd, who went to the IU locker room with University President John Ryan shortly after Knight exited, did release a printed statement.

"Dr. Ryan has requested that I prepare an immediate report to the conference commissioner, with a copy forwarded to Dr. Ryan, and there will be no further comment from Indiana University officials regarding today's incident."

The fact that a formal statement, one that is carefully written before being released, can say "today's incident" without saying what the incident is, shows that everybody knew what would be not only Sunday's story, but probably one of the biggest stories in sports this week.

Already, one television network reported Knight's resignation. Floyd said, "That's not true at all."

"The most important thing I'd like to tell you is that our victory's the main headline," Keady dreamed in his post-game conference. "I hope you get the drift."

Keady refused to talk much about the incident.

"That's his business, not mine," Keady said. "I've been in coaching a lot of years and I don't remember anything like it, but there may have been."

Of course, much of the discussion this week will be over *why* Bobby did what he did. Was he really that upset at the officiating? Or was he just trying to fire up his slumping team? Or was it

See COACH, back page

PATRICK LIM Daily Student

Bob Knight argues with referee Fred Jaspers as IU Athletic Director Ralph Floyd (center) and assistant coach Joby Wright watch.

Knight apologizes

Just more than a day after IU basketball coach Bob Knight once again captured the attention of the sports world, it was announced Knight had formally apologized for his actions.

In a statement released Sunday evening by IU Sports Information Director Kit Klingelhoffer, Knight said in part:

"While I've been very concerned at times with the way some things have been handled in the Big Ten, . . . I do not think my actions in the Purdue game were in any way necessary or appropriate.

"I'm certain that what I did in tossing the chair was an embarrassment to IU and to have that happen was not my intention. For that reason, I am deeply sorry for it."

8th District re-count planned

By Alan Chitlik
Daily Student Staff Writer

One candidate was satisfied and the other skeptical about the recently announced procedures to decide the race for Indiana's 8th Congressional District seat.

Beginning March 11, the ballots are scheduled to be re-counted by the General Accounting Office, said Rep. Leon Penetta, D-California, chairman of the U.S. House of Representatives Committee on Administration Thursday.

On March 22, the committee should vote to recommend to the House the seating of either Democrat Frank McCloskey or Republican Rick McIntyre.

On March 29, the House is scheduled to vote on the race.

McCloskey said Saturday he was relieved to learn of the procedures. He said, "By March 22, I should know what my status is. Period."

"My overall happiness right now is not based on winning this race. More than that, I want to see a fair vote count and see it resolved as soon as possible," he said after a town meeting in Bloomfield, Ind.

Having the GAO count votes will assure the process will be fair, McCloskey said.

However, McIntyre said Sunday he wasn't sure the GAO can re-count all the votes in time for the committee to make a recommendation.

"I have a hard time imagining they can count all the ballots," in that time, McIntyre said from his home in Bedford, Ind.

"I'm glad they're finally doing something. For almost a month and a half it seemed like nobody in Washington cared that the 8th District was going without representation," he said.

The committee has a three-member task force that is sched-

See RE-COUNT, back page

Associated Press

Soviet President Chernenko votes in the parliamentary election in Moscow Sunday.

Frail Chernenko seen voting

By Carol J. Williams
The Associated Press

MOSCOW — Soviet President Konstantin U. Chernenko, looking frail, broke a two-month absence Sunday with a television appearance in which he was shown casting his vote for deputies to the Parliament of the Russian Republic.

The 73-year-old Soviet leader, who missed a key election speech only two days earlier because of illness, murmured only a few words during the less than two minutes of film shown on a 2 p.m. news brief.

The same footage was shown again at the start of the national evening news program Vremya (Time).

Chernenko's surprise appearance was strictly managed and limited to a handful of Soviet photographers. It contrasted sharply with the election day coverage of Mikhail Gorbachev, who, in the eyes of many Western obsevers, has emerged as the ruling Politburo's number two man, and other Kremlin officials.

Chernenko and the other 10 Politburo members were all nominees for parliamentary seats, among the deputies being elected to parliaments in the 15 republics of the Soviet Union.

It was not clear where Chernenko cast his ballot.

Soviet Foreign Ministry officials had said Friday that Chernenko, "if he feels well," would vote at the House of Architects at No. 7 Shchuseva Street, along with Gorbachev.

Sunday morning, officials at the building said Chernenko would not appear there. His whereabouts were not disclosed.

The official news agency Tass reported in a story that "Konstantin Chernenko came to a polling station in Krasnopresnensky district," without elaborating.

A Soviet journalist noted that "under our election system, when a voter for some reason cannot go to the polling station, a ballot box can be taken to them."

Chernenko voted in a room undecorated except for a bust of Lenin sitting among some potted plants. There were no other voters shown entering or leaving the room, and none of the people pictured wore coats or other outerwear that would indicate they had recently been outdoors.

Although the telecast did not show Chernenko walking or speaking more than a couple of syllables, it served to dispel rumors that a stroke left him without the ability to speak.

During his 59-day absence from public, rumors had been intensifying tht Chernenko was seriously ill.

Chernenko, in a blue suit, was first shown seated as a woman election worker handed him his ballot. There was no film of him marking his ballot and he did not take out his customary glasses to look at it. The next sequence was of Chernenko standing over the ballot box and depositing his vote. He was not shown getting up from his chair.

After voting, Chernenko reached out slowly to clasp three bundles of red flowers offered by election workers and fellow Politburo member Viktor Grishin, the Moscow Communist Party chief who was present at the balloting.

A Western diplomat reached for comment on Chernenko's reappearance, said: "It must be a very carefully stage-managed performance that they figured they could manage without too much strain on him."

Chernenko reportedly suffers from emphysema, and his condition had been said to be worsening.

Bill would provide monies for faculty

By Mark Skertic
Daily Student Staff Writer

If a bill passed Thursday by the Senate Finance Committee becomes law, it will be one of the few times in recent Indiana history that state funds are directly provided to universities to help attract top research professors, said Paul Chrohney, a gubernatorial aid to Gov. Robert Orr.

The bill, the Indiana Endowment for Educational Excellence, would allow the governor to establish a fund for attracting top faculty to Indiana universities. It would also provide monies to fund grants and continuing education programs for public school teachers and administrators.

The bill is part of Orr's Decade for Excellance in Education program.

The state would be able to attract and retain better scholars, and provide the facilities and personnel for some high level research positions if the bill becomes law, Chrohney said.

"There's a lot of talented personality out there and we want to bring them to, and keep them in, Indiana," Chrohney said.

The bill, which was sponsored by Sen. Morris Mills, R-Indianapolis, was approved unanimously by the committee, but a $10 million appropriation and tax credit request was eliminated from the measure.

Chrohney said he is optimistic that the bill will receive an appropriation in the next few days when it reaches the State Senate. He said specific dollar amounts are often dropped from bills when they are considered in com-

See FUND, back page

Inside

■ IU's lost and found department is trying to sort itself out. Many students are unaware that the department exists. Page 2.

■ A House committee passed a scaled-down version of Primetime on Friday that would raise class sizes. The proposal now faces the General Assembly. Page 6.

■ A controversial new film produced by pro-life activists is stirring up more debate on the abortion issue. Page 15.

Outside

Partly cloudy and mild today with high in the middle 40s. Mostly cloudy tonight with a 20 percent chance of light rain, and low in the middle to upper 30s.

Students protest education stance

By Leah Lorber
Daily Student Staff Writer

Sipping soft drinks and lounging around a table in the Indiana Memorial Union Commons, the students didn't look like militant protesters.

One flipped slowly through a textbook; others joked about the small turnout for the "mass planning meeting" of the Student Coalition for Education. Even the sign identifying them was subdued: thin blue letters on white posterboard. Tasteful. Mass protest, '80s style.

There were no table-pounding rhetoricians; the group's chairman could barely be heard over the rumble of bowling balls from the bowling alley next to the Commons. But there was a quiet determination in the ten or so people present at Sunday's meeting.

"Sometimes it seems like the government says, 'Well, we'll cut the money for education and the kids . . . won't dare raise their voices and object to anything,' " said sophomore John Furiak.

"We'll let . . . a lot of representatives know that we won't let them cut it," said senior Kurt Speed.

IU's Student Coalition for Education is displeased with the government's attitude toward higher education and wants both the government and the public to know it.

The group is sponsoring a student rally and march to protest proposed budget cuts for financial aid and education. The march will begin at 11:45 a.m. Wednesday at Ballantine Hall and end at the Monroe County

See PROTEST, back page

P0078846, IU Archives.

REFLECTION

Prepared in More Ways Than One

Thinking back, I had no idea how momentous the phone call was going to be.

I was a newly minted reporter at the IDS, tasked with a job many new writers got stuck on—the cops beat. An editor had heard a Bloomington resident lost his leg, hit by a drunken driver while riding his motorcycle. My job: to verify the information was correct and write a story.

I called the hospital (oh, the glorious days before privacy laws like HIPAA made getting any kind of medical information so difficult). When I mentioned the victim's name, the receptionist just transferred me to the guy's room.

Like the idiot newbie reporter I was, I asked the person who picked up the phone if he could verify that the motorcycle rider had lost his leg. "That's me," said the voice on the other end of the call. "And I did."

Mortified, I mumbled a thank you and hung up the phone. I had just learned what a high-wire act reporting for the IDS could be.

Most of us were greener than green—so new to journalism, reporting and writing that we didn't even know what we didn't know. And yet every day, we threw ourselves into the task of putting out a newspaper, reporting the events of the day to a loyal audience that believed what we wrote.

It was a tremendous responsibility—especially during my stint on the paper in the mid-1980s, long before online news or smartphones would complicate our information diet. There were times when we would beat Bloomington's professional newspaper, the Herald-Telephone, on stories; we had no idea how dangerous a young reporter with no experience and big ambitions could be.

(A caveat: All of the stories I relate here come mostly from memory and combing through the surprising numbers of old IDS clippings I have in storage. So, I'll apologize in advance for any shortcomings that may spring from my sometimes-limited perspective.)

I held three jobs at the IDS during my tenure: copy editor, cops reporter and features writer. As copy editor, I had the proud distinction of not having a single headline I proposed for a news story actually see print without heavy editing. Fortunately, the reporting jobs turned out better.

The subjects varied. I interviewed the Fabulous Thunderbirds blues band, and two women who claimed the city of Bloomington lied about the results of physical tests to deny them jobs as firefighters. I covered a freshman accused of raping a White Castle employee. And there was the firewalker.

A motivational speaker named Peter Heist claimed he could teach anyone to walk on hot coals. I decided to cover his appearance at IU with the goal of answering one question: Is this possible?

Before the seminar, I did some research. I learned about the poor heat conductivity of coals and how walking over a wet surface beforehand could leave a protective sheen on your feet to keep extremities safe. Heist hyped us up during his seminar with lots of self-motivational talk, and then just about everyone there—including me—walked briskly over damp grass and through a bed of hot coals while chanting the words "cool moss, cool moss."

Whether it was physics or psychology, cool moss was exactly what the coals felt like beneath my feet during those moments. Talk about immersing yourself in a story.

What I did notice during my time at the IDS was the cliques. Putting out a newspaper requires a dedicated crew of talented students.

Eric Deggans, late 1980s. *Photo courtesy of Eric Deggans.*

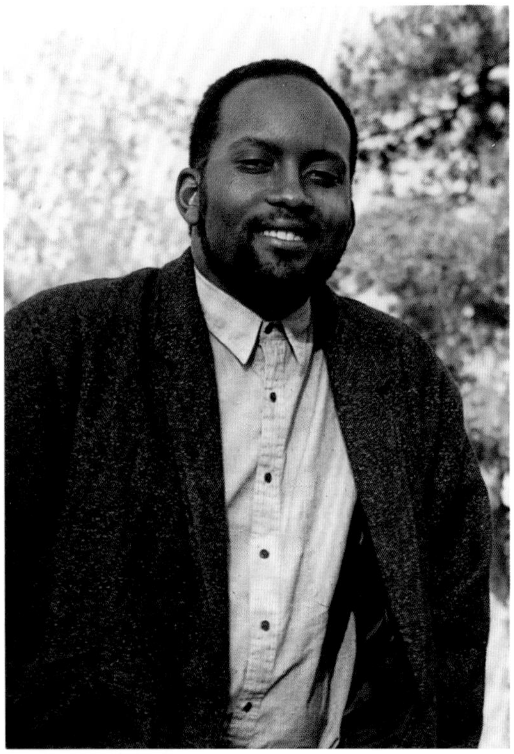

"What I did notice during my time at the IDS was the cliques. Putting out a newspaper requires a dedicated crew of talented students. But to outsiders, that kind of tight-knit group can feel an awful lot like a club you're not welcome in."

But to outsiders, that kind of tight-knit group can feel an awful lot like a club you're not welcome in.

In particular, this was a problem for students of color. As a black student making my way through the IU School of Journalism, I saw many things differently than my white classmates. My first roommate was a white kid from Indianapolis so scared of me he couldn't wait to pledge a fraternity and get out of our shared space in the residence hall. It became an annual occurrence to have someone shout the word "nigger" at me from a passing car or truck on the street. So, when it came to fitting in at the IDS, I knew part of my success would come from getting along with the white kids who ran things.

Unfortunately, other student journalists of color had a tougher time. They were searching for ways to express what they knew about race and society in their journalism, but they weren't comfortable with the IDS clique. For some students of color, IU was the first time they lived closely with white people or attended a school where white people were an overwhelming majority. Back then, there was no orientation program for that.

I had attended mostly white private schools before coming to college, so I had suffered through this transition much earlier. But I often couldn't help others. I remember one heartbreaking instance where I tried to coach another black student through the IDS internal politics, but he decided it wasn't worth the effort and quit the staff.

Admittedly, I also never fully committed to IDS culture, myself. I played drums in a group called The Voyage Band, which found some success during my time in Bloomington, and my attention was always divided. In 1985, we recorded a single called "Strange Situation" that became the lead track for a charity fundraising record called "Live From Bloomington." The song exploded—playing on the air in Louisville, Indianapolis, Chicago and even clubs in London.

It was a heady time for the band; we landed a manager and eventually got signed to Motown Records, so I decided to take a few years off from journalism. One of the toughest moments in my college career was the day I went into the office of placement director and IU journalism legend Majorie "Marge" Blewett—she was such a commanding presence that some of us called her "Sarge" Blewett behind her back—to tell her I was dropping out for a while.

I did return to school not long after the band was released from its Motown deal, earning my last three credits by correspondence while playing at a club in Japan with Voyage. I landed a job at the Pittsburgh Press in May of that year to start what would become a lifelong career in journalism.

And when I landed at the Pittsburgh Press, what word-processing system did I discover in its newsroom? It was called Atex—the exact same system the IDS used when I worked there. Once again, the IDS had helped prepare me for a life in journalism in ways I couldn't have predicted at the time.

—Eric Deggans, BA 1990

1986, Indiana Daily Student

Indiana Daily Student

Indiana University, Bloomington | Monday, April 14, 1986 | 18 pages 25¢

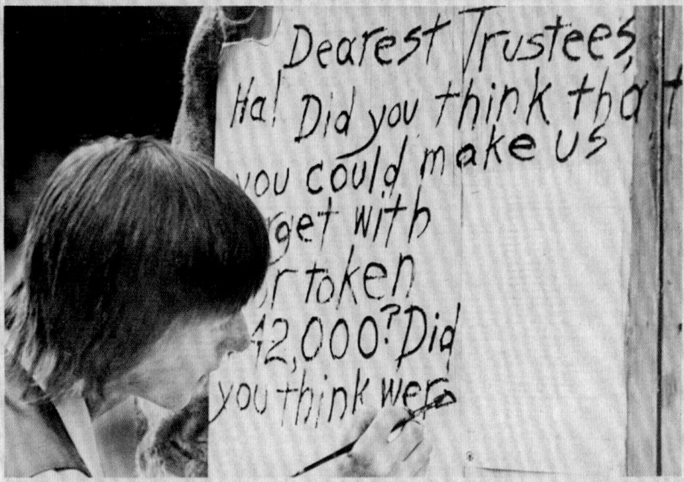

MIKE GRIFFITH / Daily Student

Junior Michael Lane paints a protest on a Dunn Meadow shanty in an effort to persuade the University to divest South African stocks.

Libya quiet, U.S. 6th fleet awaits orders

Compiled from Daily Student wire reports

See related story page 10.

TRIPOLI, Libya — Col. Moammar Khadafy's government claimed Sunday it had moved foreign workers, including U.S. citizens, to oil fields in the desert and army bases purportedly targeted for attack by American forces.

But a Western diplomat told The Associated Press he had spoken to several representatives of his country in Libya, and "none of them reported any such incident." He spoke on condition he not be identified by name or country.

Tripoli has remained quiet for days, and there were no signs Sunday of any military preparations.

Meanwhile the U.S. 6th Fleet was poised in the Mediterranean off Libya, awaiting President Reagan's decision on a possible strike in retaliation for Khadafy's reputed support of international terrorism.

Reagan and Chancellor Helmut Kohl of West Germany have said Libya is a prime suspect in the April 5 bombing of a West Berlin discotheque that was a gathering place for U.S. troops stationed in West Germany.

A U.S. Army sergeant and a Turkish woman died in the blast, and 230 people were injured, including 63 Americans. Reagan said he would consider a retaliatory strike if evidence proved Khadafy was behind the bombing.

A statement released by a Libyan Information Department official, who refused to be identified, said, "Foreign workers have been forced to live in them (oil fields), taking into account that the majority are Americans."

Diplomats and business people estimate 800 Americans still live in Libya, including executives, oil field workers and about 100 American women married to Libyans.

Reagan ordered all Americans out under risk of a 10-year prison sentence and cut all U.S. economic ties with Libya after terrorists attacked the Rome and Vienna airports Dec. 27, killing 20 people, including five Americans.

The United States blamed Palestinian terrorist Abu Nidal, whose real name is Sabry al-Banna, of carrying out the attacks and accused Khadafy of harboring him.

Other Westerners in Libya include Europeans. The British community, for example, is estimated at 5,000.

Hundreds of foreign workers already live in the desert oil fields, often on rotating shifts lasting about one month.

Oil is Libya's largest single source of income, although Western analysts say revenues plunged from $22 billion in 1984 to about $8 billion in 1985.

The Western diplomat told the AP only five major docks are used to load oil on tankers, so there would be no need for U.S. warplanes to hit the widely scattered oil fields.

"The Americans could take out the jetties' loading points, and that would stop the oil flow," the diplomat said.

The Libyan statement also said: "The military camps have been handed over to foreigners to repair them and to use them to live there. Foreign workers have been moved to army camps.

The statement said the moves to the oil fields and military bases took place Saturday, and the army has been moved to undisclosed locations.

This North African Arab nation has about 73,000 regular military personnel.

Khadafy told a news conference Wednesday that he and his top commanders had made military plans in the event of an American strike against this country.

Khadafy has threatened targets in southern Europe, mentioning Spain and Italy, in the event of such a U.S. military move.

On the CBS-TV program "Face the Nation," Deputy Secretary of State John C. Whitehead, said Sunday that the United States would cancel reported plans for a military strike against Libya if Khadafy, calls off his plans for renew terrorist attacks.

Whitehead, who has access to intelligence reports, said that Khadafy has picked out specific targets and assigned individual terrorists for dozens of planned attacks around the world.

Asked if American use of force was inevitable, Whitehead said, "Not if he (Khadafy) changes his conduct. Not if he stops training terrorists, financing terrorists, supplying them with arms, supplying them with documents. As soon as he stops those actions, then we would certainly back away from our actions."

Student shanties protest apartheid

By Paul Rogers
Indiana Daily Student

Two dozen student protesters, armed with piles of splintered boards, cardboard boxes and a couple of cans of spray paint, gave Dunn Meadow a facelift this weekend.

On Saturday afternoon, IU joined the list of U.S. universities whose students have built campus shantytowns to protest investments in companies operating in South Africa.

The protesters say they will live in the slum-like huts until the IU Board of Trustees divests all of IU's $4.5 million in South African-related stock.

IU's shantytown, which is composed of five wooden shacks and a supply tent, is manned in shifts by about 25 protesters, said Andrew Henderson, a freshman who spent Saturday night in the makeshift settlement.

Henderson, who prefers to go by the nickname Spud Boy, said the students who built the shanties Saturday were not members of any campus anti-apartheid organization, but rather, a "group of concerned students."

He said he hoped to increase student awareness of the divestment issue by having a permanent fixture on campus for people to identify with.

"It's a definite place where people can know they can stop by — it's like having an office," Henderson said. "We want to keep pushing and generate interest on this — it's not going to fade away."

The IU Police Department reported Sunday it hasn't received any complaints about the structures.

George Huntington, chief of IUPD, said he had no plans to forcibly remove the protesters from the meadow.

"I'm not aware of any laws being broken," he said.

According to the "Ins and Outs," an IU booklet listing campus regulations, the protesters chose the right spot to voice their opinions.

Section 4.2 (a) of the document states "The Board of Trustees has designated an area on Dunn Meadow immediately north of the Memorial Union as the Indiana University Assembly Ground. Here, members of the University community may express themselves freely on all subjects, within the limits of applicable laws and regulations, with or without advance notice."

The mood at the newly built shantytown seemed upbeat and hopeful Sunday morning.

The broken pieces of wood and torn cardboard holding the shanties together looked like back-alley walls littered with graffiti.

Although the protesters appeared relaxed, it was obvious they knew they would be encountering hardships during their vigil. Many expected inconvenience to be the norm rather than the exception.

"If it rains out here, we don't mind getting wet," said freshman Susannah Koerber. "This is not a matter of convenience."

"We need support and supplies," said sophomore Laura Zimmerman. "I hope other people will come out here, even if it's just for 15 minutes between classes . . . This is for everyone — we're not here to intimidate people."

Henderson said the group was

See TRUSTEES, Back Page, this section

Students pay little heed to shelters

The shantytown in Dunn Meadow didn't seem to bother students Sunday as they played baseball, Hacky Sack or studied.

Some students who sat across the meadow from the graffiti-covered huts weren't even aware of the shantytown's presence.

"I have known that it (building of shantytowns) goes on in other universities, but I never saw it here," said junior Leilani Garcia, a first-year transfer student from Puerto Rico.

When graduate student Kevin Hook noticed the shantytown, he said, "I'm glad to see people are concerned about something else besides what's going on in their own personal lives."

Some students who saw the shantytown Sunday said they didn't know why it was there.

"I thought it was a part of Cultureshock," said freshman Claudine Anderson, referring to the WIUS-sponsored event Saturday in Dunn Meadow.

Students who noticed the shantytown disagreed about whether it would influence the IU Board of Trustees.

"I appreciate their effort but I can't see that it'll do much good," said junior Jennifer Mills. "The University won't divest any more just because they're protesting."

"I don't think IU will divest entirely, (but) they will divest a little to appease these people," said senior Larry Bruce.

Amy Earle, student records and admissions coordinator for the physics department, questioned the protesters' motives.

"Are we doing it to copy other universities . . . or are we adding our voice to (a collective university protest)?" she said.

All-male McNutt rookies win Mini 500 pole position

By Michelle Hopkins
Indiana Daily Student

McNutt's Dejoya II T.L.W. trike team had more than just beginner's luck during Mini 500 qualifications Saturday at Assembly Hall.

Posting a 42.37 during its second attempt, rookie team Dejoya II proved to have this year's fastest qualifying time.

Dejoya II snatched the pole position from the defending champions, Who Knows (42.81), and Visitors (43.51). Rounding out the top nine positons in order are Sigma Kappa, Bill Baker's Team, Kappa Alpha Theta, Kappa Delta, B-City Knollers and Penguin Pedalers.

Sixty-four teams originally vied for the 63 qualifying positions. The only team to be knocked from this year's field is Phi Mu, who after fouling in its first two attempts failed to show up in time for a third run.

Freshman Major Franklin, rider for Dejoya II, said his team decided to take it slow on the first attempt to avoid fouling, and then increased the speed in its second attempt knowing it was already in the field.

"We wanted to get a bye, but we sure were pretty surprised to get the No. 1 position," Franklin said. "We're much impressed with ourselves and we know that hard work does pay off."

Franklin said the Dejoya II riders practice one and a half hours daily except on Saturday. He said the team runs as a group to the practice sites for extra conditioning.

"People were saying at qualifications Saturday that we had done so well because we were an all-male team," Franklin said. "I think since we are guys we have some advantage in being in good shape, but you never know about winning because a co-ed team won last year."

Who Knows, last year's winners with a time of 40.0, fouled on its first attempt at qualifying. Junior team member Scott Norton said this added to the already existing pressure of being the returning champions.

Norton said the field seemed much slower this year and attributed this to the poor conditions of the tracks.

"It seemed like the tracks were not cleaned as much during prac-

See EIGHT, Back Page this section

TODD ANDERSON Daily Student

Junior Dee Valverde pedals furiously for the Kappa Delta team during Mini 500 qualifications Saturday.

INSIDE

CAMPUS

■ The HEC discusses Purdue's lack of visibility at IUPUI. **Page 3.**

CITY

■ The Monroe County Council is scheduled to approve the rest of the Bloomington/Monroe County parks budget Tuesday afternoon. **Page 5.**

ARTS

■ Good weather, good entertainment and high spirits make WIUS' Cultureshock successful. **Page 9.**

OUTSIDE

A 60 percent chance of thunderstorms today. High in the upper 60s.

P0079182, IU Archives.

Cutters carve a piece of glory with win

By Michelle Hopkins
Indiana Daily Student

The Cutters proved Saturday at the Bill Armstrong Stadium that it takes more than strategy to win the Little 500.

In a race lasting a little over two hours, the Cutters outsmarted defending champions Alpha Epsilon Pi when senior Tony Ceccanese edged past senior Jim Pollak at the finish line.

Losing one of their riders to injury Wednesday, the Cutters rode the race with only three riders. They had no alternate to fill in for junior Vince Hoeser, who broke his collarbone during practice at the track.

Junior Jay Polsgrove said Hoeser's injury made the team even more determined to win.

"We wanted it really badly," Polsgrove said. "And when Vince broke his collarbone we wanted it even more."

Athough Hoeser couldn't ride in the race, he sat on the side of the track coaching his teammates. He said they were concerned that AEPi was up with just five laps to go and started monitoring the race to decide what they needed to do to be in the front at the end.

"AEPi seemed to be in a bad position coming around that last turn," Hoeser said. "And Tony just did what we had to do to kick it in there."

As Ceccanese sprinted past AEPi's Pollak, he said he knew it was up to him to sprint fast enough to pass Pollak at the finish line.

"I stayed on Jim's wheel until after the fourth turn," Ceccanese said. "He seemed tired and I felt fresh so I went for it and passed him from the outside."

Ceccanese said the move is called "the sling shot," but that it never would have been successful if the team had not been positioned so well throughout the race.

"Everybody did their job well," Ceccanese said.

Chris Gutowsky, an IU Law School graduate and Cutters' coach, said it was the Cutters' overall strength that accommodated for the win. He said the team knew it was one of the strongest teams when it won Team Pursuit April 18.

"Even though we lost a guy we had been one of the strongest teams

See INJURY, Page 16

1986 Little 500 Official Results

1. Cutters
2. Alpha Epsilon Pi
3. Phi Delta Theta
4. Phi Kappa Psi
5. Chi Phi
6. Lambda Chi Alpha
7. Acacia
8. Evans Scholars
9. Collins Graitas
10. Delta Tau Delta
11. Phi Gamma Delta
12. Cinzano
13. Pi Kappa Alpha
14. Alpha Tau Omega
15. Kappa Sigma
16. Sigma Nu
17. Sigma Chi
18. Sigma Phi Epsilon
19. Theta Chi
20. Sigma Alpha Epsilon
21. Delta Upsilon
22. Americana
23. Trophy Dash
24. Chain Gang
25. Sigma Alpha Mu
26. Sigma Pi
27. Kappa Delta Rho
28. Nichols Cyclones
29. Visitors
30. Joint Venture
31. Top Drawer
32. Alpha Sigma Phi
33. Pi Kappa Phi

Indiana Daily Student

Indiana University, Bloomington — Monday, April 28, 1986 — 16 pages 25¢

Hurts so good!

Small town shines during hot weekend

By Angie Shaneff
Indiana Daily Student

It was Bloomington's day — or rather, weekend — in the sun.

Cougar. Cutters. And general cutting loose.

When you combine the small town boy who made it big with the team that beat the odds to win and add in perfect weather, you have Bloomington at its best.

A record crowd of 31,908 watched the Cutters, with only a three-man team, capture the Little 500 crown for the second time in three years. Many of those same fans, after spending the afternoon baking in the sun, spent the evening taking in the music of Seymour native John Cougar Mellencamp.

The weekend also included the Mini 500 tricycle race, a scholarship run, and the Cream and Crimson football game.

And parties.

Traffic snarled streets even at 12:30 a.m. Sunday with people heading for post-race, post-concert celebrations.

"This was far and away the biggest Little 500 weekend we've ever had," said Mark McAlister, owner of Big Red Liquors.

The four Big Red stores started stocking up three weeks ago for the weekend, he said.

Although the race and the concert were the highlights, there were some less obvious events and people who made the World's Greatest College Weekend even more interesting.

• Oscar winner Steve Tesich in the infield at the race.

Tesich, an IU graduate, wrote the script for the film "Breaking Away," inspired by his own experience as a rider for Phi Kappa Psi fraternity in 1962. His team won the race that year and Tesich was named to the Little 500 Hall of Fame.

He now spends most of his time in New York and Colorado but came back for the race because he said he wanted to see one more Little 500 as well as friends. He said the race has changed some since he was here because more people know about bike racing.

Some things never change,

See UMBRELLAS, Page 16

Little 500

TODD ANDERSON Daily Student

John Cougar Mellencamp sings to the crowd of about 43,000 Saturday night at his concert ending Little 500 activities.

Police report safe race weekend

By Kevin Corcoran
Indiana Daily Student

The only serious injuries reported during the World's Greatest College Weekend celebration came during a police pursuit Saturday.

Otherwise, the weekend was relatively safe as Little 500 race weekends go, said IU Police Department Lt. Jack Fritch.

The injuries occurred after IU police became involved in a chase at 5:45 p.m. Saturday. A Seymour, Ind., man allegedly struck a car near Memorial Stadium and attempted to flee the scene of the accident.

The chase was by no means high-speed.

"Traffic was moving so slow there's no way you could have had a high-speed chase," Fritch said, referring to backed-up traffic prior to the John Cougar Mellencamp concert.

After a seven-minute chase, Keith Lawrence, 26, was arrested in the McNutt Quad parking lot and charged with resisting arrest and leaving the scene of an accident.

Fritch said the Lawrence vehicle struck two other cars during the chase.

Lawrence also was charged with battery on a police officer resulting in serious bodily injury, a Class C felony, after IUPD Sgt. Melvin Powell was taken to Bloomington Hospital with minor injuries. Powell came to assist Monroe County Sheriff's Deputy Steve Hinds, who suffered severe cuts, sheriff's department officials said.

Lawrence was released from the Monroe County Jail late Saturday after posting $5,000 bond.

A Monroe County Jail official said there were fewer arrests than expected Friday night, increasing slightly on Saturday. Those who could not find adequate parking returned to find their cars missing.

IU police ordered 29 cars towed between Friday morning and Sunday night. Bloomington police towed 42 cars during the same period, four of them after their drivers were arrested on alcohol-related charges.

Local police made 43 alcohol-related arrests over the weekend, 10 of them for drunken driving.

More than 20 car accidents were reported to Bloomington police.

Fritch said police ignored residence hall parking lots, where cars were illegally parked along yellow curbs and in grass patches, concentrating instead on fire lanes and blocked traffic.

"We just didn't have time for all the other stuff," he said, adding that some officers did not even have time to eat during their extended weekend shifts.

GARRETT EWALD Daily Student

MTV video jockey J.J. Jackson and Patricia Cross, the winner of the MTV Ultimate College Weekend contest, ride in a pace car during the parade lap before the start of the Little 500.

Concert caps 'Greatest College Weekend'

By Lu Ann Briggs and Greg Andrews
Indiana Daily Student

As the last rays of sunlight glinted through the entrances to IU's Memorial Stadium Saturday, hordes of eager fans gathered for the concert that was to top off "The World's Greatest College Weekend."

Saturday's temperatures dropped from nearly 90 degrees to the low 70s as darkness fell and cool breezes floated overJohn Cougar Mellencamp concert-goers.

From about 6 p.m. until the end of Mellencamp's second song, "Jack and Diane," crowd members milled around the stadium — selling or searching for tickets, greeting friends, drinking beer.

Nearly three quarters of the way up the east stand, snippets of conversation broke in on other discussions.

One fan's complaint:"You'd think after 13 hours standing in line we'd get better seats than these," was followed by a comment from a few rows down: "You guys got great seats."

Another complained about poor acoustics and the delay in starting. Originally scheduled for 6:30 p.m., the concert had been rescheduled for 7 and didn't start until about 7:30.

MTV video jockey J.J. Jackson and Patricia Cross of Cocoa Beach, Fla., attended the Little 500 and the Mellencamp concert. Cross, MTV's Ultimate College Weekend contest winner, got to announce the start of the concert.

Mellencamp's grandmother came out and sang her song off *Scarecrow* before her grandson and his band broke into "Small Town."

Applause from the 43,000 fans exploded from the stands when Mellencamp brought a member of the audience — a man in shorts swinging a shirt over his head — on stage. Beams from the light tower played on the two as they danced.

Laughter and cheers met Mellencamp's down-home voice as he told a tale about his hit "Ain't Even Done With the Night." Strutting across the stage, he joked: "Here goes John walkin' into his high school class reunion . . ."

Outside the stadium, fans who didn't have tickets still joined in the party atmosphere.

Several hundred people sat on blankets on the south end of the stadium where the music was loud and clear.

During "R.O.C.K. in the U.S.A.," two women led a train of fans dancing through sprinklers on the practice field outside the stadium. Another group tore down a goalpost while "The Authority Song" blared from the stage.

Bloomington residents and IU students were not the only ones taking part in the festivities.

"I swear to God it seems like Fort Lauderdale," said senior Paul Sablich, remarking on the weekend's circus-like atmosphere.

"We tried to come down to teach you all how to party," said Mitch Kupstein, a senior at Indiana Central University in Indianapolis.

But some IU students weren't eager for the lesson from out-of-towners.

Listening to Mellencamp from outside the stadium, sophomore Vanessa Horn said, "This is our weekend, not everybody else's."

INSIDE

WORLD

■ Former Philippine President Ferdinand Marcos addresses a rally in Manila by live telephone hook-up from Hawaii.

Page 6.

OUTSIDE

Today occasional thunderstorms and breezy. High in upper 70s.

NEWSSIDE

Due to technical problems the comics and crossword puzzle do not appear in today's paper. An expanded version will appear Tuesday.

P0079424, IU Archives.

PROFILE

Pat Siddons
Publisher, 1976–1989, BA 1950

This selection is adapted from an article that appeared Sept. 1, 2004, after Siddons' death.

By Marjorie Smith Blewett and Jane Charney

Pat Siddons began and ended his journalistic career at the Indiana Daily Student, where he went from cub reporter to publisher.

At Ernie Pyle Hall, his legacy remains that of a friendly, grandfatherly mentor to an entire generation of IDSers from the 1980s, said Kevin Corcoran, an IU alum and former IDS reporter.

"He never meddled in the students' stories," Corcoran said. "But when all hell broke loose, he stood behind us."

As publisher, Siddons gently cajoled the students in his charge toward setting higher goals and meeting them. In his coaching, Siddons drew on his experiences as reporter and head of the Bloomington bureau of the Louisville Courier-Journal. And the IDS publisher's chair presented Siddons with a perfect opportunity to pass on his skills and educate a new generation of journalists.

"During his tenure as IDS publisher, Pat was constantly urging the student editors to put out the best newspaper possible," said Don Cross, former IDS business manager.

His love for the IDS was all-encompassing: During his time at the IDS, Siddons' license plate read "IDS," and when he retired in 1989, he changed it to read "EX-IDS."

Former IDS staff members remember Siddons as a man who would grab a bag of fresh popcorn and walk around the newsroom getting to know the students. His door was always open to anyone, and many took advantage of that availability to talk to him about stories, reporting and career choices, said Mark Skertic, who was IDS editor-in-chief in 1986.

Pat Siddons, 1982.
P0081014, IU Archives.

Just like Corcoran, Skertic recognized Siddons' ability to walk the fine line between teaching and preaching.

"His input would come once the paper came out," Skertic said in an email interview. "In a few words scrawled across the columns of copy, he would celebrate great reporting and writing and highlight sloppy work by reporters, designers and editors. The criticism was constructive; it wasn't always easy to take, but

Congratulatory letter from President Emeritus Herman B Wells. *Photo courtesy of IU Archives.*

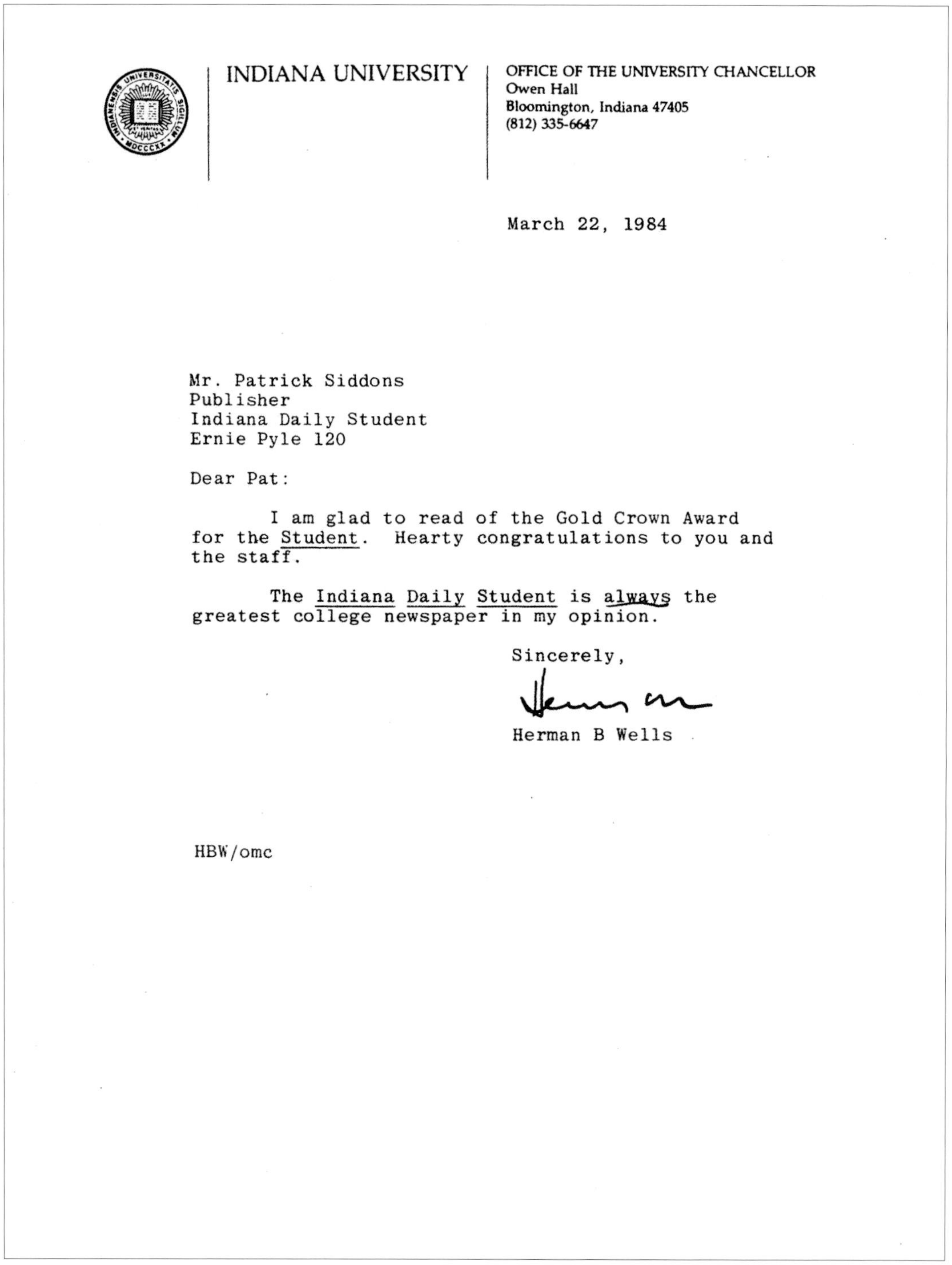

INDIANA UNIVERSITY

OFFICE OF THE UNIVERSITY CHANCELLOR
Owen Hall
Bloomington, Indiana 47405
(812) 335-6647

March 22, 1984

Mr. Patrick Siddons
Publisher
Indiana Daily Student
Ernie Pyle 120

Dear Pat:

I am glad to read of the Gold Crown Award for the Student. Hearty congratulations to you and the staff.

The Indiana Daily Student is always the greatest college newspaper in my opinion.

Sincerely,

Herman B Wells

HBW/omc

"I learned about newspapers through my work on the Indiana Daily Student, and I still remember the heady feeling I got from putting words on paper, the thrill of watching the Linotype operator create words in metal, and of watching that old flatbed press crank out copies of a paper that actually contained stories I had written. I thought it was a miracle."

it made many of us strive to write the story that Pat would praise in his markup . . . ."

Born in Ellettsville July 31, 1924, Siddons was a Hoosier at heart and remained in Indiana for most of his life. After a stint in the Army as a signal corpsman with an anti-aircraft artillery unit during World War II, he tried Purdue. But engineering didn't agree with him, and a friend suggested IU's journalism program.

After graduating in 1950, Siddons worked for the Crawfordsville Journal-Review and the Michigan City News-Dispatch. Before working for the Louisville Courier-Journal, he picked up a public relations job with the Indiana Republican Party . . . .

Among other awards, Siddons was named a Sagamore of the Wabash, Indiana's highest honor.

Editorial staff, spring 1986. Kathleen Flynn is seated at far right. *P0076348, IU Archives.*

BEHIND THE STORY

The Night I Used a Nick's Menu as a Straightedge

Many of my memories about March 30, 1987, are fuzzy, but the important ones are crystal clear. I was news editor of the IDS at the time, scheduled to work that night as IU played for the national basketball championship and tasked with laying out the front page for the following day's newspaper.

I remember we held a meeting at some point that morning. Editors, graphic artists and photographers gathered to toss around a few ideas and come up with a basic concept and a plan to meet deadline. Technology being what it was (or wasn't) at the time, we had to give the photographers the exact measurement of the photo we'd be running on the front page long before tip-off. So, I went where any self-respecting IDS staff member would go when there was important work to be done and big decisions to be made: Nick's English Hut. I sat in a booth in the back, ordered lunch and set to work, using a menu as a straightedge. The simplicity of the design meant it took longer to eat my cheeseburger than draw the lines and figure out the photo dimensions and column measurements. Now all we needed was a victory.

That proved to be a bit more challenging. In between editing stories and designing

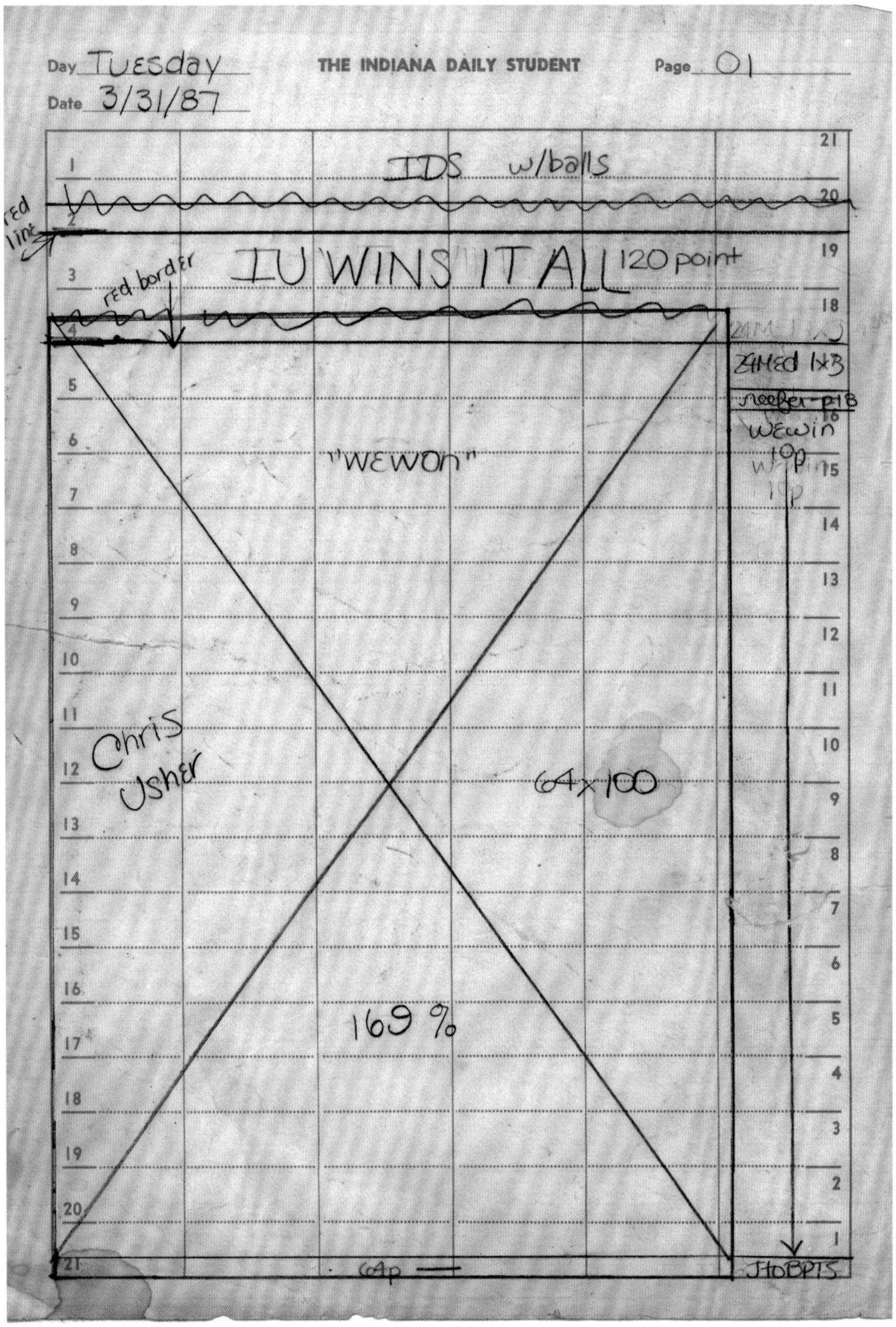

Mockup for the championship front. *Photo courtesy of Kathleen Flynn.*

pages, we watched bits and pieces of the game in the conference room and kicked a soccer ball around a small open space in the newsroom to expend nervous energy. Not long into the second half, with neither IU nor Syracuse maintaining any sort of lead, the managing editor suggested I start designing a "losing" front page, just in case. I trudged to my desk and halfheartedly put together a second front page. The lead headline was "Syracuse downs IU, XX-XX," and there was also a story about city taxes and something from the College of Arts and Sciences reporter.

Fortunately, we never got to use that front. Keith Smart's fall-away jumper from the left baseline sealed the deal. The newsroom emptied as we all ran from Ernie Pyle Hall to Showalter Fountain, danced around for a few minutes, then headed back to work. A short time later, Chris Usher's photo of Todd Meier, Daryl Thomas and Steve Alford hoisting the championship trophy arrived from the New Orleans Superdome. It fit perfectly, giving us yet another thing to celebrate that night.

—*Kathryn Flynn, BA 1987*

March 31, 1987

18 Pages 25 Cents

Indiana Daily Student

Indiana University Bloomington Tuesday, March 31, 1987 Vol. 120, No. 22 ©1987, Indiana Daily Student

IU WINS IT ALL!

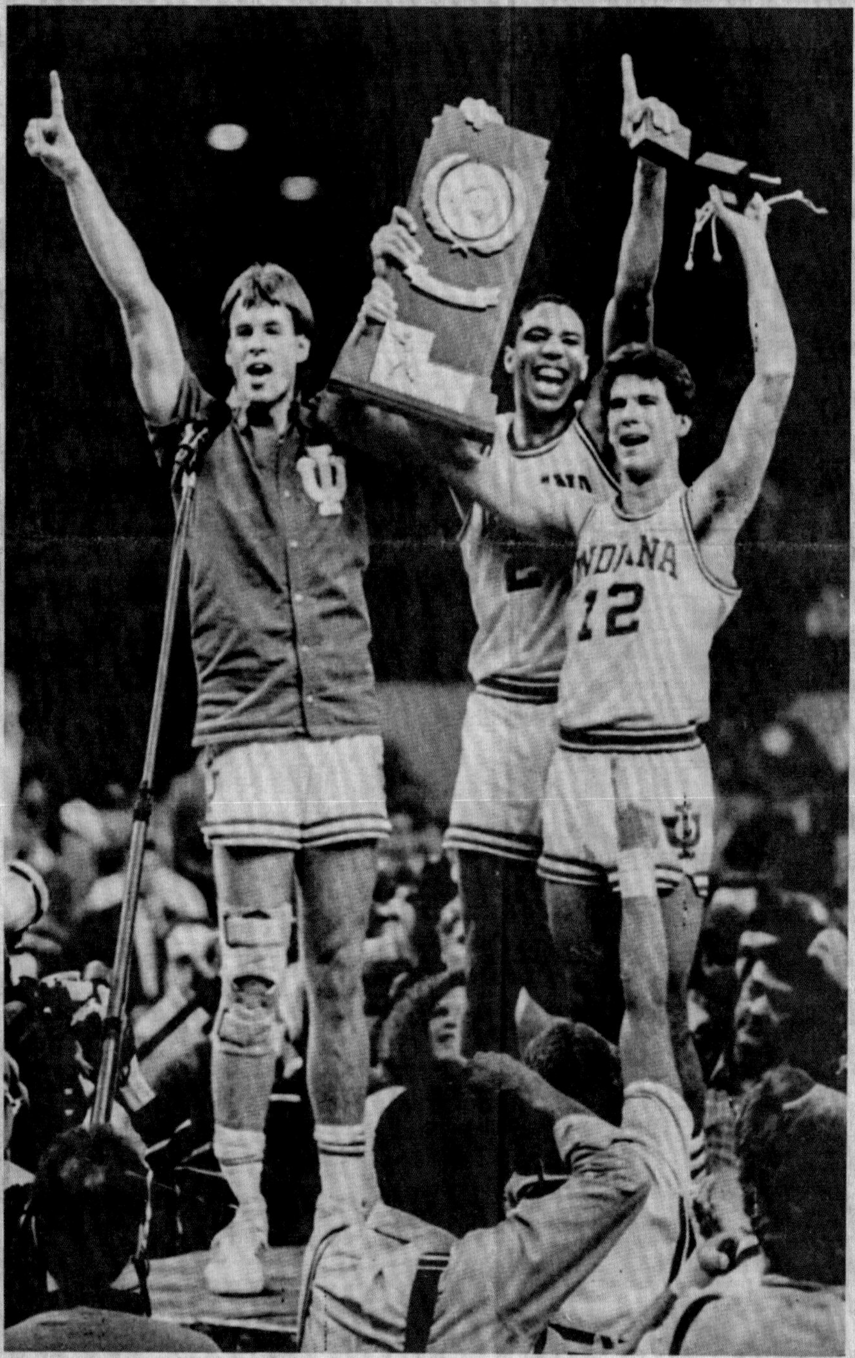

CHRIS USHER Daily Student

IU seniors Todd Meier, Daryl Thomas and Steve Alford celebrate IU's NCAA championship Monday night in New Orleans. The Hoosiers beat Syracuse 74-73 for the trophy.

Hoosier Hysteria hits city

From Daily Student reports

That movie about basketball isn't named "Tigers," "Stags" or "Rebels" and it SURE isn't called "Orangemen" or "Boilermakers."

Its name, folks, is "Hoosiers." That's right. HOOSIERS. And Monday night, the IU basketball team and its fans showed the nation why the film was so named.

In the New Orleans Superdome, the Hoosiers downed the Syracuse Orangemen 74-73 to capture IU's first NCAA championship since 1981. Then it was the fans' turn.

See related stories, Page 18

When the Superdome clock flashed only zeros, the work of the evening was over. But the party had just begun, as thousands of Hoosier Hysterics flooded the streets of Bloomington.

The central site of the celebration was a snowy, waterless Showalter Fountain. But neither cold nor snow nor lack of liquid stemmed the tide of jubilation.

Some optimistic fans started their fountain party early. With just seconds remaining on the clock and the Hoosiers ahead by one, a group of about 10 students huddled in the fountain around a portable television, waiting for that agonizing final second to expire.

"We got here about five minutes ago!" screamed junior Beth Thomas.

Suddenly, their wait was over. The city screamed. A tremendous roar rose from the depths of every residence hall, house, apartment complex and bar.

A stampede of more than 5,000 jubilant fans poured into the fountain area.

They came floating on basketball and liquor highs. Bottles of bourbon and whiskey were brandished and confiscated, as were a few kegs of beer.

"You always dream about this stuff and you never think it will come true!" exclaimed senior Kathy Anderson.

"This is what University life is all about!" yelled junior Matt Gaston between swigs of beer.

"Ain't dat de troof?" yelled back senior Mike Bernal, who had watched the game with Gaston in their dorm. The two turned to exchange high fives with everyone in reach.

Three fans made an unusual contribution to the celebration, pulling down their pants to reveal "IU," "IU" and "#1" painted on their buttocks.

Showalter Fountain wasn't the only site of celebration. Local bars were packed long before the final buzzer went off. Norman Terry, a waiter and bartender at Nick's English Hut, 423 E. Kirkwood Ave., said crowds arrived early to watch the game.

"I got here at 10:30 (a.m.) and people were standing outside," he said.

John Rocchio of Peru, Ind., was delighted just to be here.

See COLD
Back page, this section

P0020589, IU Archives.

Editorial staff, 1988. Kevin Corcoran is standing in the back row, second from right. *P0079417, IU Archives.*

BEHIND THE STORY

City Editor and . . . Fashion Aficionado?

Not too far into my tenure as IDS city editor, Mike Schaefer, the advertising manager, came over to city desk in the middle of the former Ernie Pyle Hall newsroom to tell me about a previously undisclosed responsibility—editing a new fall fashion tabloid.

Mike was enthusiastic. (Maybe it was his idea!) I looked up from the Atex terminal where I was editing and was puzzled. Surely, if I paused before responding, he would size me up, realize his mistake and keep looking.

The sartorial force has never been strong in me. Tattered jeans, T-shirts and other casual clothing were my usual newsroom attire. But Mike was upbeat. He assured me that producing the fashion tab would be fun. And it would be a money-maker. I was unmoved by his line of reasoning. Back in the mid-1980s, newspapers, including the IDS, were still relatively profitable enterprises. Survival was not at stake—or at least it didn't seem so.

Fine, I thought. I'll edit the fashion tab. But I'll do it in a way that ensures the newsroom never has to do another tab for the sole purpose of selling advertising. I enlisted other anti-fashionistas in a grand effort to produce sartorial satire. We would make fun of fashion!

I looked to the best IDS writers, people like Bob Caylor, a Bluffton, Indiana, native whose idea of a fine fabric was flannel. His piece was written from the perspective of a man describing a shopping trip with his girlfriend. The victim likened a sales clerk who had suddenly appeared before the couple after making his way through tightly bunched clothing racks as a "native bushman." The parody was cast as a case study in the anthropology of a primitive culture.

We filed our stories, and our humorous assault on the fashion industry was complete. Not long after the tab appeared, Mike was standing at my desk again. I waited for him to complain, to tell me how the fashion tab had flopped with advertisers because of our transparent effort to undermine its commercial success.

Instead, he smiled. The advertisers loved it, he said. The absolutely loved it! The fashion tab would be a regular fall feature. The joke was on us: IDS advertisers had a sense of humor. Laughter was good for the soul . . . and for sales.

The next fall, I was general assignment editor. It was my final semester on the Bloomington campus; I was asked to edit the fashion tab again. Make it as funny as you can, they said. JCPenney, Redwood & Ross, and Sycamore stores were waiting, dollars in hand.

I enlisted GA reporters in the second round, which included stories such as "Buying for less at Goodwill," "Catalogs are popular way to shop," "Success is as simple as some holey jeans," and a take on fashion magazines.

By the time my nearly 20 years in daily newspapers ended in 2007, it had become painfully clear the demise of retailers was upending print journalism's business model. By then, no one was laughing.

—Kevin Corcoran, BA 1988

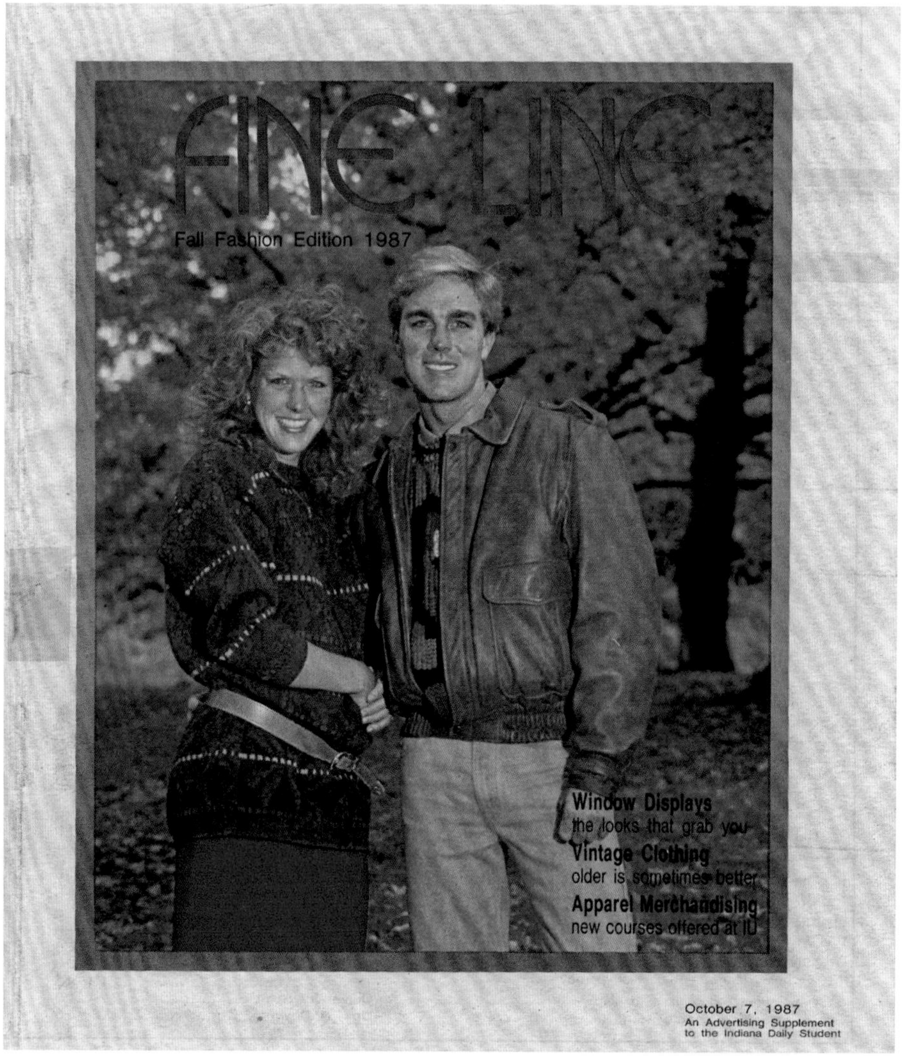

Facing, IDS fashion tab, published Oct. 7, 1987. *P0080275, IU Archives.*

"Fine, I thought. I'll edit the fashion tab. But I'll do it in a way that ensures the newsroom never has to do another tab for the sole purpose of selling advertising."

April 22, 1991

20 Pages — 25 Cents

Indiana Daily Student

Monday, April 22, 1991 Vol. 124, No. 37

Police push partiers to peace

RICHARD E. SCHULTZ / Arbutus

Party goers get a little too festive Saturday evening at Varsity Villas apartments. Celebrants here flip over a resident's car at around 12:30 a.m. Sunday. About 41 Bloomington police arrived at about 1 a.m. in riot gear to break up the destructive activities of Little 500 party goers. The riot lasted about 20 minutes before the police dispersed the crowd.

Fires, fights, flipping cars fill evening

By Dan Joseph and Scott Weisser
Indiana Daily Student

Cold, dreary weekend weather did not dampen Little 500 celebrations as local police agencies had their hands full with riots at two apartment complexes.

Bloomington Police Department officers were called to Varsity Villas early Sunday morning to break up rioting crowds, which one witness estimated at 1,000 people.

Varsity Villas residents said the melee began sometime between 12:30 a.m. and 1 a.m. Sunday.

"I came out around one, and when I got out here, a couple of guys were already jumping on my car," said Varsity Villas resident Robert Biel, a junior. "All I could do was just push them off."

Biel was out Sunday taping black trash bags over the hole where his grey Oldsmobile's windshield used to be.

Senior Melissa Segal ventured into the Varsity Villas parking lot about 12:30 a.m. to find her 1986 Cadillac Cimmaron flipped on its back.

The crowd lifted her car and rolled it over three times, moving it about 30 feet, she said. The car was towed away Sunday morning.

The roofs and hoods of other cars near Segal's and Biel's were covered with muddy footprints.

Varsity Villas residents said the riot lasted about 20 minutes before police arrived to disperse the crowds and tell residents of the complex to stay in their apart-

See RIOTS, Back page, this section

Le Pas wins women's race

By Chris Duncan
Indiana Daily Student

For Le Pas, Friday's victory in the women's Little 500 was just another notch in the team's belt.

The team did not even stay in Bloomington long enough to see the men's race Saturday.

After winning the fourth women's Little 500, Le Pas headed to Miami (Ohio) to compete in a road race, a criterium and a team time trial.

Le Pas is composed of members of the IU Cycling Club, which competed in the Midwest regional for the United States Collegiate Cycling Federation this weekend.

And the experience of racing every weekend gave Le Pas the victory Friday.

Senior Karen Dunne of Le Pas sprinted to the lead on the 37th lap.

And it was all downhill from there.

Dunne also finished the race for the team and rode the majority of the laps.

But Coach Mike Niederpruem credited a strong team concept as the pivotal factor in the team's first Little 500 championship in two attempts.

"Each rider knows what their strengths are," said Niederpruem, a veteran of four men's Little 500 races. "It was the fact that they had so much experience that helped them do so well."

Nierderpruem said the experience helped. He said the team needed to change its strategy during the race and that depth enabled the team to adjust.

Niederpruem said senior Melissa Munkwitz, a veteran of two previous races, was not having a particularly good race but that Dunne was having a great day. For that reason, the team decided to leave Dunne on the bike and let her finish the race, even though Munkwitz originally was scheduled to be the team's finisher.

"Melissa had a problem, and Karen didn't," Niederpruem said. "Melissa just had an off day. All

See LE PAS, Back page, this section

Acacia breaks pole spot jinx

By Dan Wawrzyn
Indiana Daily Student

It was only the sixth time a polesitter has won the men's Little 500.

And on Saturday, No. 1 Acacia left Bill Armstrong Stadium with first place.

Acacia's time of 2 hours, 4 minutes, 16.947 seconds made this year's race the fifth fastest in history.

There were only three teams in contention for the victory near the end of the race: Acacia, Team College Life and the Cutters.

Junior Pete Noverr of Acacia took the bike with five laps to go. He had not ridden much of the race because the team was saving him for the end.

"We wanted to make sure we got Pete (Noverr) the bike at the end," said Acacia coach Tom Schwoegler. "If Pete got the bike with five laps to go, we were not going to lose, period."

When Noverr received the bike from senior Tim Bochnowski, he rode close to Team College Life junior Mike Lantz and senior Demitri Hubbard of the Cutters. Hubbard was out in front by about 20 yards when Noverr mounted the bike. Both Lantz and Noverr were able to catch him at about lap 197.

When the final lap arrived, the three glided through the first half of the lap. Then Noverr took off on the backstretch leaving the others behind.

"I didn't know when I had to break," Noverr said. "I just knew I had to be in that third turn first. I knew Lantz had been out there for awhile, and Demitri (Hubbard) from Cutters might be a little winded. I thought of taking off with three laps to go when we brought in Demitri."

Hubbard said Noverr caught him off guard.

"He caught me, but I tried to hold him off," Hubbard said. "I saw him, but he's just a good rider. I turned my head (to find Noverr) at the wrong time. Our race strategy went the way it was supposed to, however."

Noverr said the crowd was a factor in his performance.

"Rounding the second turn (of

See ACACIA, Back page, this section

SAM RICHE / Daily Student

Peter Noverr celebrates after claiming a victory for the pole-sitting Acacia team Saturday at the Men's Little 500 race. This team is the sixth pole-sitter ever to win the race. It was the fifth fastest race in history.

Outside

Warmer

Mostly sunny and a little warmer today. High near 60. Increasing clouds after midnight tonight. Low in the upper 30s.

Inside

Earth Day participants celebrate planet

Environmentalists dance, sing praises of mother nature

By Amanda Hess
Indiana Daily Student

Dancing shamelessly on the banks of the Jordan River to local band Buggtussle, individualistically clad environmentalists batted a plastic earth-designed beach ball and entertained onlookers.

Earth Day 1991 in Dunn Meadow sported bands, tables, a mood and a direction all aimed at appreciating the planet.

In one corner of the meadow, students aged five to nine from Bloomington Progressive Elementary performed their rendition of Dr. Seuss' book and cartoon "The Lorax" to a large crowd donning wide grins. The story is a commentary on human greed and its effect on the planet.

Lead actress Julia Swanson, age 9, who played the Lorax, recreated the tale of a small furry animal displaced by harvesting of Truffla trees.

"I sort of wish it wasn't over," Swanson said of the play.

Progressive's teacher Rebecca Beck said the children gained a lot from the experience of acting.

"The overt curriculum is really important but there's so much more. (Children) can grow up with that feeling of empowerment," Beck said.

Providing the scenery for the performance were members of the Student Environmental Action Coalition, which sponsored many of the Dunn Meadow events.

Hollie Hirst, sophomore and SEAC member, said although the fair centered on celebration of the planet, educating attendees was also a thrust of the group.

"I hope some people will be inspired and motivated and educated, but it is definitely a celebration of the kindness of the mother (earth)," she said.

Amy Hankes, a sophomore, wandered from table to table with a group of friends.

"A lot of practical information is being disseminated among people who may not actually realize how bad (environmental) problems are," she said, holding a handful of free literature from organizations such as Citizen's Opposed to PCB Ash and the Sierra Club.

But freshman Karen Sechausen said the attendance was lower than in previous years because bands and promotions were not as prominent as before.

"I think (these bands) only target to a specific type of people," she said of the folk style musicians.

Sechausen said she remembers coming to IU for Little 500 while she was in high school and attending Earth Day activities.

"People who didn't know how they felt about this sort of thing came to hear the bands," she said. "At least they were here . . . this one isn't as good as the last three at all."

Weaving in and out of the gradually growing crowd was junior Ann DeSutter, member of Earth-Base Projex, handing out literature informing all who would listen about her organization.

"A lot of people are aware of the bad stuff that's happening. What we are trying to do is come up with sane alternatives," she said.

She added that environmentally conscious methods of energy and transportation is a direction people should be moving in.

The Greek Letters Council set up a table to encourage greater participation in recycling within the greek community.

"If it's convenient, it's going to be recycled," said sophomore Jeff Kittle, director of programming for the Interfraternity Council.

Kittle said about 60 percent of fraternities and sororities currently recycle, but if the Council can boost the participation up to 75 percent, Rumpke Recycling, Inc., will not charge the $6 monthly fee.

P0078544, IU Archives.

BEHIND THE STORY

The Semester I Gave the Campus Sex Advice

When someone finds out about my time as Vivian Love, believed to be the first regularly appearing sex column in the IDS, the question I always get asked—after how I came up with the name Vivian Love—is: How did you end up writing a sex column? Talking about my time as Vivian feels a bit like a 45-year-old office manager regaling complete strangers about his glory days as a high school quarterback. Or more appropriately, like the late bloomer who finally gets to tell his group of friends about losing his virginity. Despite its significance as a milestone, the only one interested in hearing about it is the person telling it.

That analogy is apt because it illustrates exactly why I said yes to Managing Editor JR Ross' invitation to write 10 to 15 column inches each week on the subject. Sex looms large in the lives of college students, whether they're engaging in it or not. The details might differ, but the excitement, fears, worries and confusion that are part and parcel with exploring their still-developing sexuality are the common threads that bind the students today with my mid-1990s classmates. They're why sex columns in various forms continued to survive after Vivian Love, from Jenny Finkel ("The Sexpert") in the late '90s to the current "Kinsey Confidential."

During my time—or should I say Vivian's time?—the prevalence of sex didn't make it any easier for students to talk openly about their bodies, the messy things they were doing with them and all that's associated with that, even at a university that's home to the Kinsey Institute. With Vivian Love, I wanted to create a safe space (although we didn't use that term back then) for students to openly read and talk about sex without judgment. And I wanted the information in it to be responsible and accurate, which is why I routinely consulted with the IU Health Center. This column wasn't

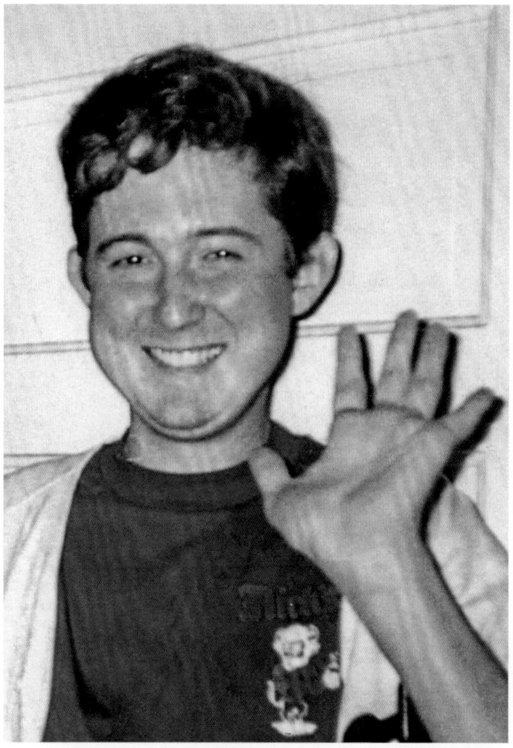

Joe Vince. *Photo courtesy of Amy Wimmer Schwarb.*

about the best places on campus to land a date or the seven ways you know she's into you by the way she flips her hair. It was about saying, "Hey, it's normal to have these questions and feelings, so let's try to navigate them together."

Each week, the column encouraged readers to write in with questions (email was still in its infancy in those early internet days, which meant actual physical letters), and while I'm hard-pressed to remember the topics I wrote about it, a few of those have stayed with me more than 20 years later. Like the postcard from someone at a Bloomington retirement community who didn't appreciate the "smut" Vivian was peddling. Or the handwritten note from a woman who confided in Vivian about her sexually unsatisfying relationship with a man she loved and why she thought that made her a bad person. To this day, that letter still breaks my heart because the woman

Marvel Comics might remember they going to be doing a column on figure

First-time sex disappointing

VIVIAN LOVE
Sex Columnist

Love on sex

Anxious feelings.

Unexplored territory.

You always remember your first sexual experience ... mostly, because it's the most awkward three minutes in a person's life. It seems a shame such a monumental event in an individual's life can be filled with so many negative connotations.

The physical positives surrounding the first time are limited.

For women, it can be painful. For men, it is often much too short. For both sexes, it is definitely an act fueled by uncontrollable sexual urges that is almost consistently punctuated with ignorance. No amount of planning can eliminate that initial bumbling and lumbering.

When I talked with people concerning their virginal experiences, I found disappointment to be a common theme. The build-up from friends, media and society in general basically served to set most people up for a giant anticlimax — pun definitely intended. It seems anticipation and excitement are not enough to create that perfect evening.

"You just kind of fumble through it," said my friend Monica, who lost her virginity in her boyfriend's bedroom beneath a poster of Don Mattingly.

In fact, Monica emphasized that the sometimes-fatal mixture of hormones and inexperience can end up spoiling an otherwise glorious moment.

Troubles with contraceptives. Erection and lubrication problems. Inappropriate settings and environments. They all contributed to a clumsy and awkward sexual experience, Monica reported — an experience she and her other friends simply wanted to get over with before continuing the rest of their sexual lives.

Although almost everyone agreed lack of sexual knowledge was the major stumbling block in that first time experience, not everyone is so quick to judge their loss of virginity harshly.

Phil, another friend of mine, compared his first time to a picture you would put in a frame and hang on your wall. I like that metaphor (although I don't think I would hang the memory of my first time on a wall — I would most definitely put it in a photo album).

Phil admitted he was not quite the attentive Don Juan he is now, but he said the event meant so much more to him because of the emotions involved, not simply the body parts.

And not to sound too sentimental, but that's what makes the first time so special. I know emotion was the cornerstone for my initial experience with intercourse.

I was 20 years old (an old-timer compared with my contemporaries), and I lost my virginity on a secluded beach in Virginia. It was a spontaneous act, and although my partner and I were only friends, we cared deeply about each other.

I'll admit, it wasn't the best sex I've ever had (and my partner would most certainly admit the same), but there was so much more to it.

Somehow, snuggling with someone you care for beneath a thick blanket under an oceanside sky makes even the best sex seem pretty trivial and uneventful.

I hope I'm not alone in those feelings.

In fact, I would love to hear from readers on the whole subject of first times. Is the first time the best time? Is it the most emotional?

I would also encourage readers to send in anecdotes about their first times. I'm sure there is someone out there who had the most anxiety-ridden first time in Western civilization.

And I hope there are a few out there who lost their virginity in the most romantic way possible. Don't be bashful, send those letters in (for those shy readers, pseudonyms are fine as long as I have the real name and can verify the letter).

Vivian Love, just a woman with an opinion, would like to thank Dan Julian for the inspiration for today's column.

The names of the people in this column have been changed. This column is for entertainment purposes only. When you're done reading it, try folding it up into a paper airplane, a hat or a pterodactyl.

Love accepts comments and questions from students, staff, faculty and the public. Letters can be mailed or dropped off at the Daily Student, *120 Ernie Pyle Hall, Bloomington, IN 47405, or via the e-mail address* IDS.

Vivian Love's short-lived column. *Photo courtesy of IDS.*

admitted that she wasn't so much looking for a response—she just needed someone who would listen and understand. And Vivian was that.

I don't talk much about Vivian Love these days, but maybe I should. Like that first time having sex, she's someone who should be celebrated, not hidden away. And as for where the name came from? Well, let her keep some things private.

—*Joe Vince, BAJ 1997*

October 18, 1994

INDIANA — FALL EDITION

DAILY STUDENT

INSIDE

Expansion of Interstate 69 could provide quicker, easier access between Indianapolis and Evansville as well as an open route between the Great Lakes and Mexico, but some state citizens see the new highway as an economic burden to the local communities who might be paying the bills for the new addition.
See story, page 4.

I-69 EXTENSION

INDEX

Volume: 127 Issue: 114 14 Pages 25 cents Tuesday, October 18, 1994

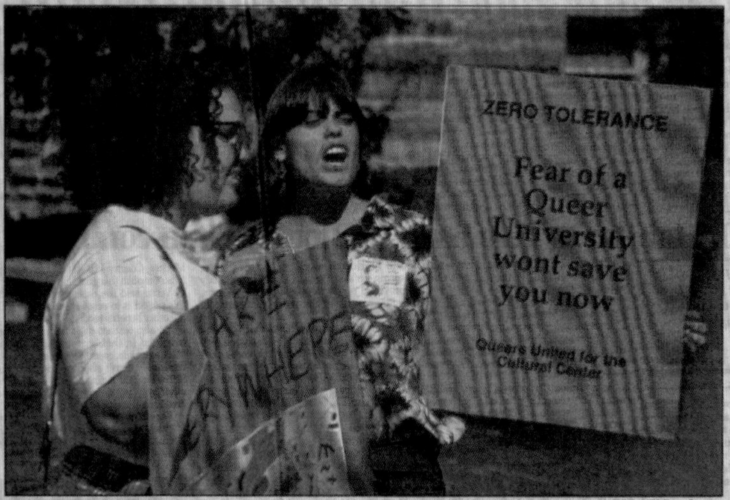

KATIE BAKER/DAILY STUDENT
Graduate students Wendy Bethel (left) and Linda Sneed protest at the Sample Gates Monday over the University's decision to cut funding for the proposed Office of Gay, Lesbian, Bisexual Support Services, and instead rely on private donations.

GLB groups protest Brand's decision

BY MARIJKE ROWLAND
Indiana Daily Student

IU's gay, lesbian and bisexual organizations have never been accused of keeping their emotions in the closet.

Monday they showed their anger with IU President Myles Brand's announcement of funding and structural changes in the Office of Gay, Lesbian and Bisexual Student Support Services.

Armed with whistles, drums, bells, signs, fliers and their voices, the new campus umbrella GLB organization Zero Tolerance protested in front of Brand's office by the Sample Gates throughout the day Monday.

They shouted, "We're here! We're queer! And we pay taxes!" to protest Brand's decision to fund the office privately, along with "Queers united will never be defeated" to display their newly formed solidarity. At its pinnacle, more than 30 people gathered to demonstrate.

Sunday evening, the three campus GLB groups — OUT, Queers United for Equal Social Treatment, and Lesbian Avengers — met to discuss the changes to the GLB office. They formed Zero Tolerance: Queers United for the Center, a coalition of the three organizations, said Sally Green, OUT president.

"It is a more effective plan of action," she said. "We thought we should merge our groups for this crisis situation."

Zero Tolerance was formed in response to the University's announcement Friday that the $50,000 needed to fund the office would come from a private, anonymous donor. They were also responding to the placement of the GLB office under the newly renamed Office of Student Ethics and Anti-Harassment Programs.

Brand was unavailable for comment. He will be out of town until Wednesday attending meetings at Duke University in Durham, N.C.

University officials said they understood the gay community's anger with the changes, but the reversal did not constitute a withdrawal of support for the gay community.

"The reason I don't think it is a weakening is because each of the advertised services (of the office) will be fulfilled; the search for the coordinator will be completed; and the office will be opened in about six weeks," said Perry Metz, assistant vice president for University external affairs.

But several GLB students thought the changes were a let down from the University's previous stance.

"I was shocked; it goes against all that we've been promised," said senior Marcus Will, one of the protesters. "We have been betrayed — stabbed in the back."

QUEST President Michael Patrick Burton said the IU gay community now distrusts administrators and their promises because of Brand's action.

"What we are trying to say is, President Brand, you are going to listen to us," Burton said. "We will have ourselves heard, and we will keep taking assertive aggressive steps. After all, it is our center."

Metz said he was expecting a response from the GLB groups. He said he would welcome a meeting between administrators and Zero Tolerance leaders to discuss the problems and changes in the new office.

"The University will certainly try to make this office one that is capable of accomplishing the goals set out for it in the beginning," Metz said.

Zero Tolerance handed out fliers that insisted Brand respond to six demands. These included that the public funding be restored and an additional $500,000 in private funds be added to the office's funds, the name of the of-

See PROTEST, Back Page

Jordan signs peace treaty with Israel

BY MICHAEL PARKS AND MARY CURTIUS
Los Angeles Times

AMMAN, Jordan — Israel and Jordan, accelerating the search for peace in the Middle East, agreed Monday on a draft treaty that settles their border disputes, shares scarce water resources and assures the security of both.

When the treaty is signed next week and ratified, Israel will be at peace with two of its Arab neighbors, Jordan and Egypt, and strongly pursuing negotiations with Syria and the Palestinians in a sustained effort to bring the Arab-Israeli conflict to an end within the coming year.

"I am full of hope that the future will be a future of peace, that this step will be a very important one (for) a comprehensive peace in this region," said King Hussein of Jordan.

"Hopefully, it is a fresh beginning and a fresh start," he continued, alluding to the long refusal of the Arabs to accept the Jewish state — and the many wars that have resulted. "We will guard (this peace), and I hope that the generations beyond us will guard it, enjoy it and cherish it — a peace with dignity."

Israel and Jordan will establish full diplomatic relations by the end of the year, tourists and businessmen from both countries will be able to travel back and forth and Jordan will halt its participation in the Arab boycott of Israel to permit full trade with the Jewish state.

See TREATY, Back Page

Two-mile fringe hot topic at forum

BY MARK TOPPE
Indiana Daily Student

Issues ranging from Bloomington's two-mile fringe to how south central Indiana can better attract businesses were the focus of discussion Monday at a forum for state and county candidates.

Held at the Monroe County Public Library, 303 Kirkwood Ave., the forum was sponsored by the Monroe County branch of the National Association for the Advancement of Colored People.

Clarence Gilliam, president of the Monroe County's NAACP, moderated the forum as part of an opportunity for candidates to present their views of how to operate local government.

Gilliam said the forum took at least two months to plan and about 15 citizens turned out for the event in preparation for the Nov. 8 election.

"For the past several weeks, we've listened to candidates speeches from both sides, each claiming more efficient government, better communication and quicker response to the electorate," Gilliam said.

The issue that dominated much of the discussion of the evening focused around what will become of the two-mile fringe, an area where residents pay taxes to the city but do not vote in Bloomington elections.

The Monroe County Commissioners announced Thursday that the county was claiming about nine square miles of the fringe, and Tim Tilton, president of the commissioners, said Sunday he hopes to reclaim the remaining part of the fringe by the beginning of next year.

Both candidates for the only open Monroe County Commissioner seat said they are in favor of the county reclaiming the

See FORUM, Back Page

IU Business school ranks in top 10 for second consecutive time

KIRSTEN CASHMAN/DAILY STUDENT
Graduate students gathered on the business school steps Monday to celebrate being named the seventh best graduate school in the country.

BY BRIAN HAYNES
Indiana Daily Student

Some top 10 lists mean more than others. David Letterman's, for instance, is laughed at for a moment and usually quickly forgotten.

But when it comes to ranking business schools across the country, *Business Week* magazine's top 10 list carries a lot of weight. The graduate business school at IU cracked the top 10 for the second consecutive time this year, ranking No. 7 in the magazine's survey, which is done every two years. IU ranked No. 8 in the 1992 survey.

Dozens of graduate students and faculty members gathered on the steps outside the business school Monday to sign a giant "7" and celebrate the school's most recent recognition.

"We're very proud to have been recognized," said John Rau, dean of the business school. "We need to be careful, though. Surveys aren't everything. No one number is going to capture everything."

Business Week based its rankings on the satisfaction of graduates and representatives of the companies that hire them. The survey showed that IU's program is innovative and popular among corporate recruiters, according to an IU press release.

The business school has been continuously working to improve on its long-term goals, Rau said. It has focused on innovation, relationships with the business world and recruiting quality students, he said.

"The faculty here work hand-in-hand together in making changes and improving."

Kathleen O'Brien
director of marketing

"The faculty here work hand-in-hand together in making changes and improving," said Kathleen O'Brien, director of marketing for the business school. "A lot of schools would take forever to make changes. We work together and are able to make those changes faster."

O'Brien emphasized the importance of innovation in the school's success. Being able to tread new ground and keep up with the always changing business world are keys to remaining competitive, she said.

Not getting as much attention was IU's undergraduate business school, which earned a No. 3 ranking in the survey. IU is one of three schools to have both educational levels in *Business Week*'s top 10.

Rankings are important when it comes to graduates looking for jobs, said graduate student Dawn Wells. When IU gains national recognition, it helps graduates looking for jobs at companies across the country, especially companies that haven't developed a rapport with IU.

"I'm glad (IU got the ranking)," she said. "It boosts rankings and starting salaries go up."

ARTS

Billy Pilgrim opens for Melissa Etheridge today at the IU Auditorium. The Georgia duo's act combines a unique blend of guitar playing and vocal harmonies. The show starts at 7:30 p.m.
See story, page 9.

WEATHER

Occasional showers and an 80 percent chance of thunderstorms today. Not as warm. High in the upper 60s. Occasional showers and possible thunderstorms tonight and lows in the middle 50s.

68
55

CAMPUS

IU Student Association President Jeff Nowak is going on tour of the IU residence halls. Nowak plans to visit McNutt, Teter and Forest quadrangles to discuss campus issues with residence hall constituents.
See story, page 2.

P0078732, IU Archives.

REFLECTION

All I Really Need to Know, I Learned in Backshop

So there's one night in the backshop, and it's late, maybe about 9:45 p.m.—I don't remember the exact time, but I remember feeling well off the automatic and comfortable pace we'd established by that time, with spring about to burst and graduation a month or two away. By this semester I'd been designing pages for years, sometimes in the preciously dated role of pagination chief, a hopelessly vintage title that didn't evoke design so much as it did alphabetizing, or maybe some very complicated stapling. It felt old even for 1997, but I was applying to page-design jobs and thought the work would look good to employers. Naturally, when I wrote my resume, I changed the title.

We'd gotten the process down to a reasonably sweet science, but something had gotten away from us this night. Maybe we were understaffed (as a senior-year pagination chief, I was not particularly militant about enforcing work attendance), or had blown out for dinner, an increasingly frequent indulgence we exercised as the days warmed. In any case, a deadline loomed and the mood was tense, and this was very unusual. The mood wasn't often tense. The mood was a lot of things in the backshop, but rarely, if ever, tense. That was one of the things I liked most about it: activity without chaos, the process of shared purpose, the machine firing, resetting in the night, starting again in the morning. Aside from the people, it's what I miss most about working in newsrooms.

Anyway, I'm blazing through Opinion, and my brother, Dave, is throwing down on some Region pages, and our colleague, Pat Kastner, is putting in a cameo as a paginator, and sometime in this furious blur of grumbling and lights-out PageMakering, it comes out that this night is Ruth Witmer's birthday—a fact which, in the pre-pre-Facebook era, was not something that your phone could be counted on to report. This revelation came as a surprise.

Sometime in this furious blur of grumbling and lights-out PageMakering it comes out that this night is Ruth Witmer's birthday—a fact which, in the pre-pre-Facebook era, was not something that your phone could be counted on to report.

All activity ceased. It's 9:50-something and we're banging on deadline and I don't think anyone had even started on Nation/World yet (Full disclosure: It was always last, sorry to whoever edited that), and we looked at each other like, oh my God. Ten minutes later we're flying through Kroger on South Second Street, furiously scouring the store's laughable inventory of balloons and cards and, if my recollection is anywhere near right, party hats. I imagine we alerted someone in the newsroom that the entire design department would be leaving the building, and I imagine that someone gave us a look like, "Uh," and I imagine we told that someone we were two hours away from missing Ruth's birthday, and that someone said, oh my God, what are you still doing here? Here's $5, get some cupcakes or something. By 10:15, after we had successfully amassed a functional simulation of a party, the dozen or so people left in the office jammed in a cramped, cluttery backshop, shoving cupcakes in their faces.

According to official records and the nice people in the Office of the Bursar, I attended IU for four years. But these records look foreign and unfamiliar to me, like journals from some long-forgotten trip or something I found in my dad's house. According to these mystery transcripts, I took a geology class, I guess? Some 200-level Introduction to Greek Literature? (I got a C- in that one and frankly am still very bad at identifying Greek poets out of a crowd.) For months I sat in classes and lectures, labs and study groups, in the exact same buildings, in the exact same rooms, and I can barely remember most of them. I remember

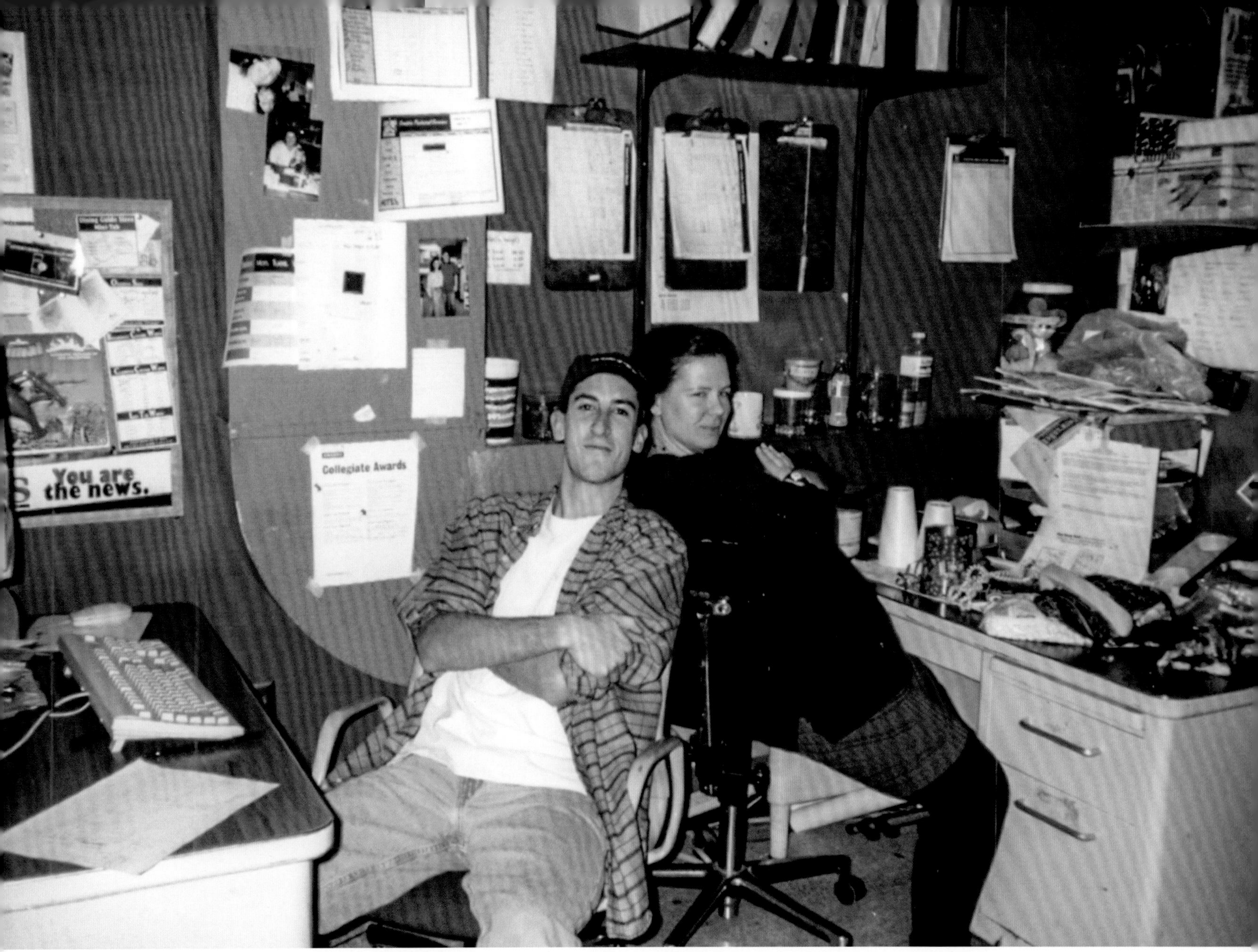

Jeff Vrabel and Ruth Witmer in backshop, 1996. *Photo courtesy of Jeff Vrabel.*

blips, of course: books I liked, professors who said something kind or searing. But they're just scenes.

The backshop memories, though—these records are complete. I'm sure that paper got out, possibly on time, and I'm equally sure that if I flipped past it in a bound volume it would look as unfamiliar as the interior of my statistics class, which, interestingly, I just learned I took. I spent two and a half years at the IDS, most of it in the backshop, and I can tell you what the printer sounded like. But if I learned anything from my work there, it was how to realize when there were more important things to do.

—Jeff Vrabel, BAJ 1997

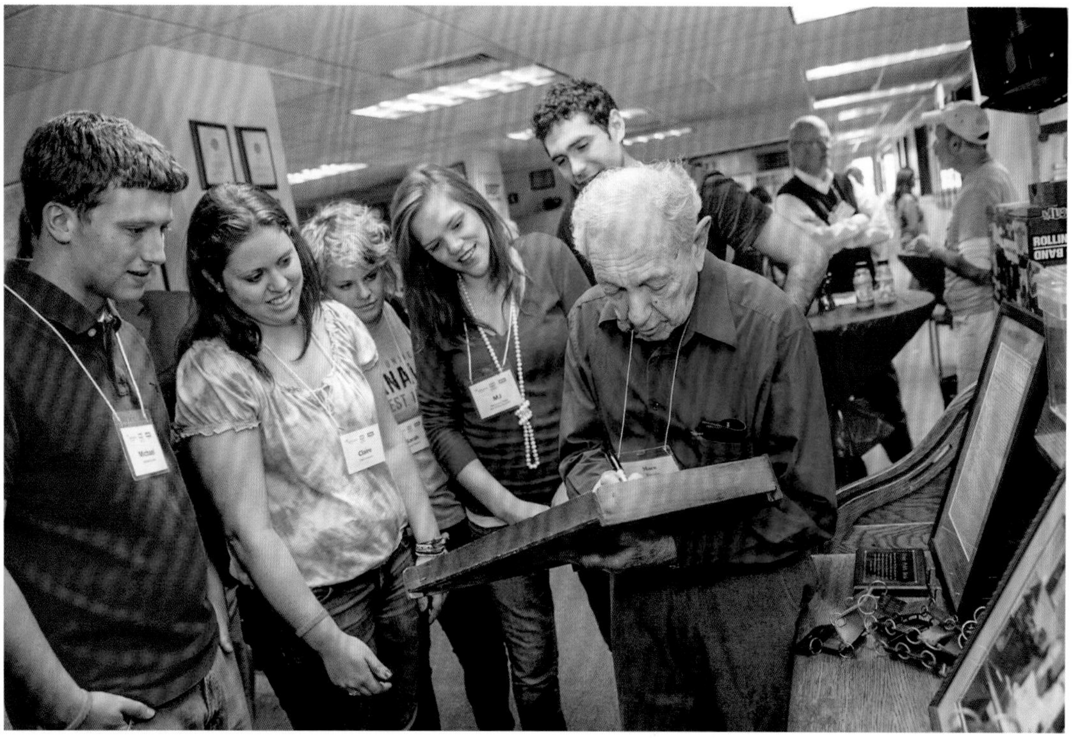

Mace Brodie, editor in chief in 1946, signs Ernie Pyle's desk while visiting campus in 2009 for the 100th anniversary of the IU journalism program. Although IDS editors used the desk for decades, the tradition of signing it did not begin until the 1980s. *Photo courtesy of Ruth Witmer.*

Below, Reprint, "I.D.S. Editors Still Ponder at Ernie's Desk." *Photo courtesy of IDS.*

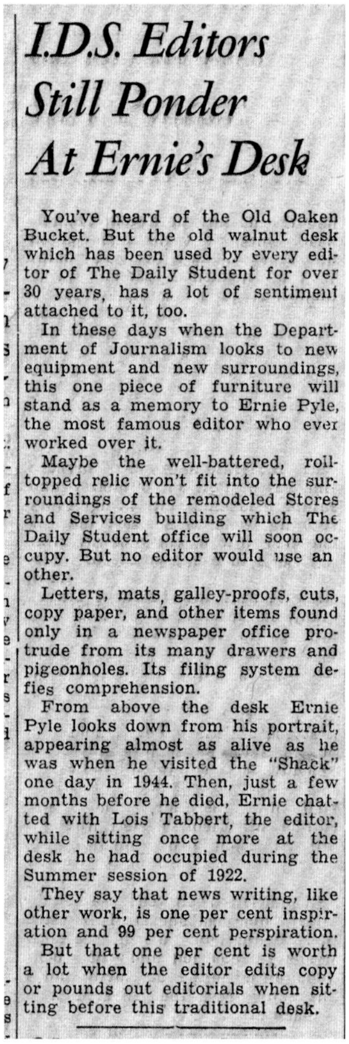

I.D.S. Editors Still Ponder At Ernie's Desk

You've heard of the Old Oaken Bucket. But the old walnut desk which has been used by every editor of The Daily Student for over 30 years, has a lot of sentiment attached to it, too.

In these days when the Department of Journalism looks to new equipment and new surroundings, this one piece of furniture will stand as a memory to Ernie Pyle, the most famous editor who ever worked over it.

Maybe the well-battered, roll-topped relic won't fit into the surroundings of the remodeled Stores and Services building which The Daily Student office will soon occupy. But no editor would use an other.

Letters, mats, galley-proofs, cuts, copy paper, and other items found only in a newspaper office protrude from its many drawers and pigeonholes. Its filing system defies comprehension.

From above the desk Ernie Pyle looks down from his portrait, appearing almost as alive as he was when he visited the "Shack" one day in 1944. Then, just a few months before he died, Ernie chatted with Lois Tabbert, the editor, while sitting once more at the desk he had occupied during the Summer session of 1922.

They say that news writing, like other work, is one per cent inspiration and 99 per cent perspiration.

But that one per cent is worth a lot when the editor edits copy or pounds out editorials when sitting before this traditional desk.

FROM THE ARCHIVES

IDS Editors Still Ponder at Ernie's Desk

Today, Ernie Pyle's desk is a revered artifact in the newsroom, but for many years, it was the workspace of the current editor in chief. The desk was retired from daily use in the late 1990s. This story originally appeared Oct. 8, 1953.

You've heard of the Old Oaken Bucket. But the old walnut desk which has been used by every editor of The Daily Student for over 30 years has a lot of sentiment attached to it, too.

In these days when the Department of Journalism looks to new equipment and new surroundings, this one piece of furniture will stand as a memory to Ernie Pyle, the most famous editor who ever worked over it.

Maybe the well-battered, roll topped relic won't fit into the surroundings of the remodeled Stores and Services building which The Daily Student office will soon occupy. But no editor would use another.

Letters, mats, galley-proofs, cuts, copy paper, and other items found only in a newspaper office protrude from its many drawers and pigeonholes. Its filing system defiles comprehension.

From above the desk Ernie Pyle looks down from his portrait, appearing almost as alive as he was when he visited the "Shack" one day in 1944. Then, just a few months before he died, Ernie chatted with Lois Tabbert, the editor, while sitting once more at the desk he had occupied during the Summer session of 1922.

They say that news writing, like other work, is one percent inspiration and 99 percent perspiration.

But that one percent is worth a lot when the editor edits copy or pounds out editorials when sitting before this traditional desk.

Workers move Ernie Pyle's desk into Ernie Pyle Hall in 1954, the year the IDS staff moved into the building. *P0027095, IU Archives.*

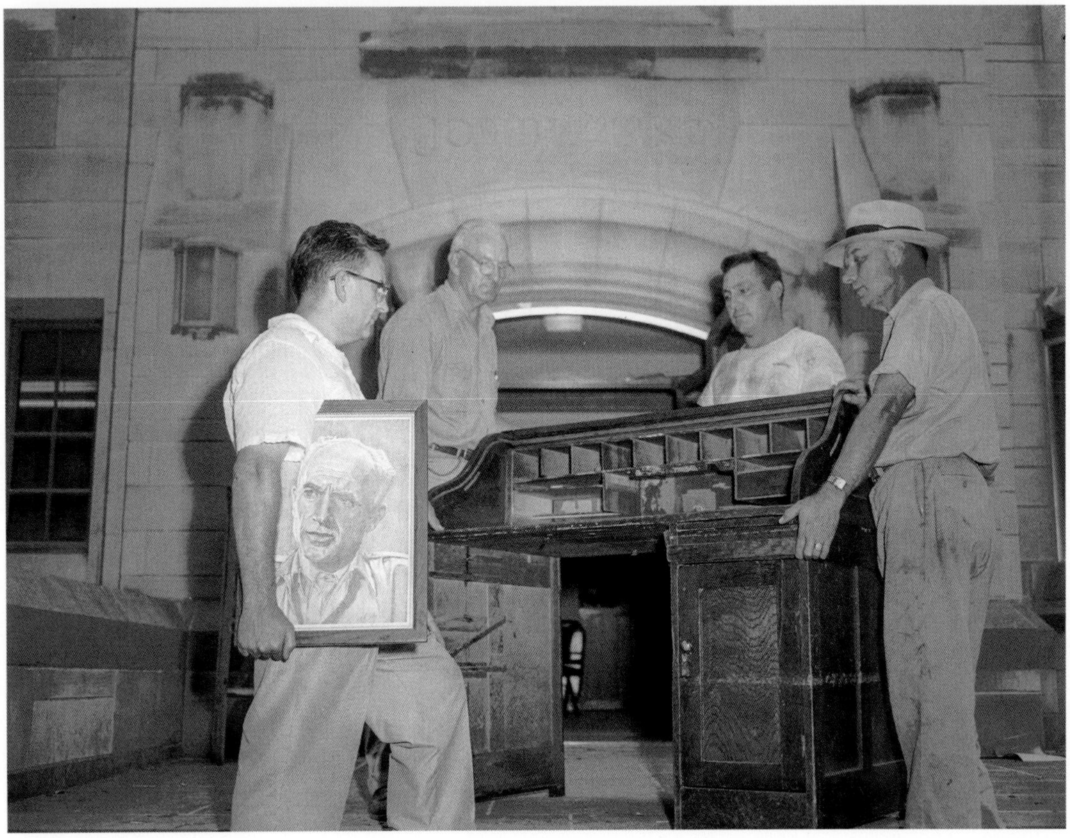

Ernie Pyle's desk is packaged in 2016 for relocation from Ernie Pyle Hall to the new IDS home at Franklin Hall. *Photo courtesy of James Brosher.*

thursday

Modern-day legend

Harry Connick Jr. talks about stardom, marriage, his new album. Page 9

WEATHER

65

80% CHANCE OF SHOWERS 55

INDIANA DAILY STUDENT

Volume: 127 Issue: 220 18 Pages 25 cents Thursday, April 20, 1995 © 1995 Indiana Daily Student, Bloomington, IN

HEARTLAND TERROR

Car bomb destroys federal building in Oklahoma City

At least 27 confirmed dead, more than 300 missing after blast

JUDY GIBBS
The Associated Press

OKLAHOMA CITY — A car bomb ripped deep into America's heartland Wednesday, killing at least 27 people and leaving 300 missing in a blast that gouged a nine-story hole in a federal office building.

The dead included at least 12 children, some of whom had just been dropped off by their parents at a day-care center.

There was no immediate claim of responsibility for the attack, the deadliest U.S. bombing in 75 years.

At least 200 people were injured — 58 critically, according to Fire Chief Gary Marrs — and scores were feared trapped in the rubble of the Alfred P. Murrah Federal Building more than nine hours after the bombing.

The death toll was certain to rise.

"Our firefighters are having to crawl over corpses in areas to get to people that are still alive," Assistant Fire Chief Jon Hansen said.

Attorney General Janet Reno refused to comment on who might have been behind the attack. President Clinton called the bombers "evil cowards," and Reno said the government would seek the death penalty against them.

Their clothes torn off, victims covered in glass and plaster emerged bloodied and crying from the building. The building looked as if a giant bite had been taken out of it, its floors exposed like a dollhouse.

"I dove under that table," said Brian Espe, a state veterinarian who was giving a slide presentation on the fifth floor. "When I came out, I could see daylight if I looked north and daylight if I looked west."

Mayor Ron Norick said the blast, which left a crater 30 feet long and 8 feet deep, was caused by a car bomb. He said the car had been outside, in front of the building.

"Obviously, no amateur did this,"

See EXPLOSION, Back Page, this section

DAVID LONGSTREATH/The Associated Press

▲ ABOVE: Firefighters and rescue officials search for victims at the Alfred Murrah Federal Building following a blast Wednesday in downtown Oklahoma City.

CHARLES H. PORTER IV/The Associated Press

◀LEFT: An Oklahoma City firefighter carries a child injured in the explosion.

Community feels effects of explosion

IU students, local Red Cross await news

TRACEY ECKELS AND AMYLIA WIMMER
Indiana Daily Student

When IU graduate student Vanessa Duncan's family left the drug wars of Bogota, Colombia, for Oklahoma City four years ago, they thought bombs and explosions were behind them.

Until Wednesday morning.

"My mother was like, 'I can't believe it. We move away from that place, and we come to Oklahoma of all places, and then there's a bomb,' " Duncan said.

She spoke with her parents, who live five to 10 miles from downtown Oklahoma City, shortly after the Wednesday morning explosion that gutted the Alfred Murrah Building. Latest reports said the bombing left at least 26 people dead and 300 missing.

"They said that it shook the house, and everybody walked out to the street," Duncan said. "The interesting thing is that I'm from Columbia, and

See LOCAL, Back Page, this section

ATF: Too soon for suspects

DIXON CROUCH AND TRACEY ECKELS
Indiana Daily Student

Even before rescue teams converged on the battered remains of a federal building Wednesday in Oklahoma City, speculation began about who was responsible for the blast that killed at least 26.

But in the wake of such devastation, law enforcement and rescue officials have a long way to go before they come close to narrowing the list of possible suspects.

"Our first task is to try to recover all the bodies at the scene," said Ralph Ostrowski, chief of arson and explosives for the Bureau of Alcohol, Tobacco and Firearms. "That is our first accomplishment. Then in another couple days we want to get into the scene and reconstruct the (explosive) device."

Ostrowski heads ATF's National Response Team — the investigation

See ATF, Back Page, this section

Brand prepares for day as student

JENNIFER STEVENS
Indiana Daily Student

IU President Myles Brand will not be found in Bryan Hall 200 today, but you might be able to find him roaming the halls of the IU School of Business.

Kevin T. Davis, a master's degree student in business, was chosen Tuesday as the winner of the President for a Day contest. Brand will attend Davis' business classes, and in turn, Davis will serve as president of the Bloomington campus today.

Brand will attend classes between 8:15 a.m. and 12:30 p.m., covering finance, manufacturing system strategy and factory simulation. After lunch, Brand's schedule is not yet confirmed, but he will participate in various student activities.

"We're going to look at what (Davis) usually does with his day, and then I'll figure out what I want to do from that," Brand said.

Davis will have a full day also, including meetings with various University officials, such as Board of Trustees members Bill Cook, P.A. Mack and Cindy Stone, Dean of Students Richard McKaig and Vice President for Administration J. Terry Clapacs. He will also tour of the new Student Recreation Sports and Aquatic Center.

Davis said because of a busy schedule this week, he has not had a chance to think about what he wants to ask the administrators, but he is looking forward to learning more about the campus.

"I want to learn more about IU and differences on campus," he said. "I'm a first-year MBA student, and I haven't had the opportunity to get to know about the campus."

Brand and Davis will start the day with a 7:30 a.m. breakfast meeting in the Indiana Memorial Union cafeteria, and they will meet at 4 p.m. in Woodlawn Field for the Recreational Sports Volleyball Tournament to discuss the day's events.

For Brand, a day that ends at 4 p.m. is

See BRAND, Back Page, this section

Lawsuit attacks graduation prayer

KATRINA L. CRAWFORD
Indiana Daily Student

Although commencement is drawing near, IU still doesn't have a confirmed agenda for the ceremony.

Two IU students and a professor have filed a lawsuit against IU over the University's long-standing tradition of holding prayer at commencement exercises. They are seeking an injunction to stop this year's prayer, and they hope to stop the practice after the courts decide the case permanently.

Law professor Alexander Tanford said he has spoken to three different IU presidents over the last eight years, trying to convince them to stop the graduation tradition, with no conclusive results.

"I have been ignored," he said. "It is still my intent to try and solve this issue as quickly, quietly and as inexpensively as possible."

Tanford said the two students, graduating law student Kimberly Macdonald-Sabo and graduate law student David Suess, decided to become plaintiffs in the suit after they realized they shared his beliefs and he would file the case.

"It's actually quite remarkable that any students stepped forward and let

See PRAYER, Back Page, this section

TALK BACK

Advertising: (812) 855-0763
Circulation: (812) 855-0768
Newsroom: (812) 855-0760
Photo: (812) 855-9577

Jordan River Forum: IDS
Editor in Chief: JRROSS
Subscriptions: IDSORDER

LITTLE 500

11 **Sigma Chi defends title**

SPORTS

11 **Hermon's scholarship revoked**

INDEX

P0078733, IU Archives.

John Jackson
Editor in chief, designer, sports writer and editor, 1992–1996

John Jackson died just weeks before graduating from IU and was awarded a posthumous Bachelor of Arts in Journalism. Today he is memorialized through the John M. Jackson Memorial Scholarship—awarded to students who are devoted to gaining hands-on media experience outside the classroom—and his friends gather annually to raise money for the scholarship through the Take It Easy Open golf tournament. This story is adapted from an obituary published March 18, 1996.

Playing the guitar. Eating a good meal. Talking to a friend for six hours.

Small moments, but ones senior John Jackson enjoyed the most.

"He loved life. He loved so many trivial things," said junior Greg Bardonner, one of Jackson's roommates.

Jackson, who served as editor in chief of the Indiana Daily Student during summer 1995, died March 7 at Indianapolis Methodist Hospital after suffering a brain aneurysm the day before. He was 21.

Jackson's mother Judy McKenzie said even though Jackson's death was sudden, he had no regrets.

"He told his girlfriend that very night that he's done everything he really wanted to do, and he never regretted anything he ever did," she said.

Friends said Jackson centered his life around two quotations his deceased father framed and gave to him. One read, "There will only be one of you for all time. Fearlessly be yourself," while the other stressed "Your only obligation in any lifetime is be true to yourself." The frame sat on Jackson's nightstand.

To live out those thoughts, Jackson chose to pursue his education through experiences rather than sitting in a classroom, his mother said.

"John felt very strongly about doing what he was going to be doing out there in the world," McKenzie said.

One of the skills Jackson was able to grasp quickly was playing the guitar. McKenzie said the family left for vacation one summer and when they returned two weeks later, Jackson had taught himself to play from textbooks. Jackson, who began playing between his freshman and sophomore years of college, composed a small library of originals during the next two years.

Jackson began working at the IDS before his first day of classes his freshman year and continued up until the night he was admitted to Bloomington Hospital March 6 after working as a page designer that day. Jackson won a staff award as recently as March 1, which was awarded to him during a 12:30 p.m. meeting that day. But in what friends said was typical Jackson style, he slept in and skipped the meeting. The award was presented in his honor to his mother at the funeral March 11.

During his time at the IDS, Jackson covered football and men's basketball, served as sports editor and designed layout as a paginator, as well as serving as editor in chief. He was a sports columnist this semester.

McKenzie said teachers began to notice Jackson's writing ability as early as first grade. In junior high, Jackson had written a poem about IU basketball coach Bob Knight, foreshadowing his opportunity to cover the team for the paper.

To honor Jackson, Trevor Brown, School of Journalism dean, will ask the IU Foundation to create a scholarship in Jackson's name, McKenzie said. Although criteria for the scholarship have not been set, McKenzie said the recipient should be someone who spent time working at the IDS.

"Former IDS editor in chief dies suddenly." *Photo courtesy IDS.*

Jackson began working at the IDS before his first day of classes his freshman year and continued up until the night he was admitted to Bloomington Hospital March 6 after working as a page designer that day.

ONEMOREGAME

Tonight is the night for Cal Ripken — the night "the streak" officially becomes his record. After 13 years and 2,130 games, Lou Gehrig's consecutive games record will change hands. *IDS* columnist David De Camp discusses Ripken's milestone achievement in sports.

▶ STORY PAGE 9

ids
INDIANA DAILY STUDENT

WEDNESDAYWEATHER

89 / 65	THU	FRI	SAT
WEDNESDDAY SUNNY AND VERY WARM	CHANCE OF RAIN HIGH 80	CHANCE OF STORMS HIGH 82	DRY AND COOLER HIGH 78

INTOMORROW'SIDS

▶ 'Tis the season for nine IU varsity sports. From cross country to volleyball and everything in between, the *IDS* Fall Sports Preview takes a look at this fall's teams and their chances for glory in '95.

'ROOFTOP' JUMP

Brownsburg teen dies at Sanders Quarry

Day after man's death, others still jumping from ledge

JR ROSS AND MARK TOPPE
Indiana Daily Student

Seventy feet below the ledge at Sanders Quarry, cigarette butts, plastic cups and an old newspaper float in the corners of the football field-shaped, abandoned quarry. Beer bottles bob at the surface of the murky water. Cars, refrigerators and ovens are rumored to sit at the bottom of the 30-foot pool of water.

One 70-foot ledge dwarfs Martinsville residents Lindsay Duncan, 19, Jared Gadd, 18, Jeff Caldwell, 19, and Dale Sizemore, 18, who were at the quarries jumping off the smaller 50-foot cliffs Tuesday afternoon. The 70-foot ledge is famous among quarry jumpers as the most daring jump — the one most people won't jump from, Caldwell said.

Those quarries are also infamous for being the spot where many who have dared lost their lives.

Nineteen-year-old Jeremy Langdon of Brownsburg died Monday night after he jumped into the water from the 70-foot ledge, known as "Rooftop."

Monroe County Coroner George Huntington said Langdon, a Brownsburg High School senior, died after he leapt from "Rooftop" at the Sanders Rock Quarry south of Bloomington.

Huntington said Langdon probably had the wind knocked out of him when he hit the water after leaping from the rock, but he didn't have any external injuries that might have contributed to his death.

"You hit a little bit slap-sided and it will knock the breath out of you, and you're on the way down and you start breathing in water instead of air and it leads to drowning," he said.

Monroe County Sheriff's Deputy Steve Hinds said Langdon jumped off the rock head first, with his arms at his side, and rolled to his left, landing on his side. Witnesses told police Langdon surfaced and started to swim, but seemed to have problems and went back under the water, Hinds said.

One of Langdon's friends made the 70-foot jump moments before the 19-year-old took the plunge, but could not hear his friends' pleas to grab the drowning man, Hinds said. The friend had injured his knee during the jump and was later treated by paramedics who arrived at the scene, he said.

> **"He couldn't hear (the friends) because he started swimming back to get out of the water."**
>
> STEVE HINDS
> MONROE COUNTY SHERIFF'S DEPUTY

"He couldn't hear (the friends) because he started swimming back to get out of the water, and it was too late by then," Hinds said. "The other guys were on the opposite end of the quarry."

George Connolly, a Bloomington police officer and member of the Monroe County Dive Team, said Langdon was found in 25 feet of water and was under for about 30 minutes before he was recovered. Langdon was also bleeding from the mouth when he was pulled from the water, Connolly said, suggesting he had internal injuries.

The death Monday came just hours after the Monroe County Dive Team searched the quarry pool in vain for a 15-year-old Bloomington boy who was feared dead. Connolly said the dive team did not search any quarries for the youth, who was still missing as of press time, Tuesday.

Langdon's accident, the third one since the Monroe County Dive Team was formed, was not enough to stop people from daring the cliffs Tuesday.

ANDREI ILLIAS • IDS
Martinsville resident Lindsay Duncan, 19, peers into Sanders Quarry Tuesday, near the spot where Jeremy Langdon died a day earlier. Langdon, a Brownsburg High School senior, was 19.

Puerto Ricans prepare for Luis

JOHN MCCONNICO • ASSOCIATED PRESS
Jesus Mendez Ruiz and a helper tear down an old utility pole Tuesday in front of his home in the coastal slum of La Perla .

ANDREW SELSKY
The Associated Press

SAN JUAN, Puerto Rico — Dwarfing the island nations of the Caribbean with a 700-mile-wide maelstrom of wind and rain, Hurricane Luis roared toward the U.S. Virgin Islands and Puerto Rico Tuesday.

Frightened tourists and islanders jammed airport terminals. Airports in the U.S. Virgin Islands closed at midday, and the last flight out of Puerto Rico was scheduled for 6:45 p.m., hours before Luis' expected arrival.

"Those people without reservations should not come to the airport because there are almost no seats left," said Armando Castro, an American Airlines official at San Juan's main airport.

Some of the control tower's windows

▶ LUIS PAGE 8

Forum discusses affirmative action

JENNIFER STEVENS
Indiana Daily Student

Getting a foot in the door is half the battle for minority students.

With affirmative action in a political stranglehold in recent months because of pressure from conservative Republicans, even that much could soon be out the door.

In a forum sponsored by Alpha Phi Alpha, a group of panelists discussed the topic of affirmative action Tuesday evening in the Black Culture Center, 109 N. Jordan Ave. The speakers discussed the recent backlash against affirmative action and its ultimate effects on IU to an audience of about 20.

Nationally, minority-targeted scholarships make up no more than 5 percent of the total number of scholarships, but that number is significantly lower on the IU campus, said panelist Shirley Boardman, the University's affirmative action director.

"If we do not have representation in (an equal) form, we will fail as a nation, not just an institution," she said. "When we leave a part of society behind, people start to believe the community is not theirs and they don't want to take care of it."

"It's deadly," she said.

According to recent demographic surveys, by the year 2050, half the U.S. population will be Latino or Latina. Boardman said the recent criticism of affirmative action could be caused by the fear that increasing numbers of minorities will lessen the socioeconomic grip of white males.

"I think it's in part fear; I think it is also incredible ignorance that they think we can eliminate programs for children at vulnerable stages in their lives," Boardman said. "What do we want to do? Build more prisons? Because we will ultimately pay for (this negligence)."

On the other hand, panelist Richard McKaig, vice chancellor for student affairs and dean of students, said reverse discrimination is virtually non-existent in the IU admission process.

"Any students who is eligible can walk over to the Office of Admissions

▶ FORUM PAGE 8

NATO starts new air attacks against Serbs

SRECKO LATAL
The Associated Press

SARAJEVO, Bosnia-Herzegovina — Its patience exhausted by shifting Serb signals, NATO launched new air attacks Tuesday meant to force the rebels to pull their big guns out of range of Sarajevo.

The air strikes appeared to end about an hour after they started, at least around Sarajevo. But U.N. and NATO officials said they were open-ended.

"The attacks will go on until the Serbs comply with our demands," U.N. spokesman Chris Gunness said. "We hope that a strong signal being sent to the Bosnian Serbs will make them realize that the international community is serious."

But heavy rain that began Tuesday night around Sarajevo limited the chances of new NATO attacks until the weather improved.

Pentagon spokesman Kenneth Bacon said U.S. warplanes flying from Aviano, Italy, and the aircraft carrier USS Theodore Roosevelt in the Adriatic Sea made up more than half the NATO strike force. A Western military source, who spoke on condition of anonymity, said about 80 U.S. warplanes were involved.

Tuesday's targets — similar to those attacked last week — included ammunition depots and communications facilities, Bacon said.

The primary aim of the bombardment was to stop the shelling of civilians by forcing the Serbs to pull some 300 heavy weapons at least 12 1/2 miles away from besieged Sarajevo.

▶ NATO PAGE 8

INSIDEBRIEF

WEDNESDAY EDITION
SEPTEMBER 6, 1995

REGION

Investigation continues

Police are continuing to investigate the shooting death of a Bloomington man who was found Monday in his car in Cascades Park.

▶ STORYPAGE 4

CAMPUS

YouthFest

Students will have the chance to listen to hip music, play games with friends and talk with former IU sports heroes Saturday at the YouthFest. The YouthFest is a party designed to bring students together to affirm their belief in not having sex before they are married.

▶ STORYPAGE2

A & E

Bush concert subpar

Although exciting lighting and elaborate stage props made for a visually enjoyable concert, Bush's lifeless performance Friday night at Chicago's Aragon Theatre was less interesting than the manic crowd attending the concert.

▶ STORYPAGE11

Just beet it

Banjo musician and one-man act John Hartford will perform at 8 and 10 p.m. Friday at the Wild Beet, Fourth Street and Walnut Avenue across from Walnut Center. He has performed on "The Glen Campbell Show", "The Smothers Brothers Comedy Hour", "David Letterman" and "Hee Haw", among others. A performer since age 16, Hartford has taught himself to play, sing and dance all at the same time and performs his music that way. Tickets are $12. For more information, call 339-2256.

WORLD

Silent protest

A Bangladeshi delegate protests silently against population control Sept. 5 at the NGO Forum on Women. The group was against the burden of contraception on women.

▶ STORY PAGE 2

MIKE FIALA • ASSOCIATED PRESS

IDSINFORMATION

Volume: 128 • Issue: 82 • 16Pages
First Copy Free • Additional Copies 25 Cents

OTHERFEATURES			
ARTS	11	OPINION	7
CAMPUS	2	REGION	4
CLASSIFIED	14	SPORTS	9
COMICS	13	WORLD	5
TV LISTINGS	10	HOROSCOPE	13

TALKBACK	
ADVERTISING	(812) 855-0763
CIRCULATION	(812) 855-0768
NEWSROOM	(812) 855-0760
PHOTO	(812) 855-9577
JORDAN RIVER FORUM	@IDS
EDITOR IN CHIEF	@ALWIMMER

P0078736, IU Archives.

IDS online edition now available on the Internet

▶ IDS ONLINE
The address is:
http://www.indiana.edu/~ids/

Web site makes 'IDS' available to students, alumni

CHRISTIN NANCE
Indiana Daily Student

Pick it up in Ballantine Hall or log on in a dorm room — readers may now view the *Indiana Daily Student* on the World Wide Web.

check out what's going on at the University, Tsai said.

Tsai, along with editor Linda Yung, a senior, is duplicating material from the printed version of the paper onto the *IDS online* site, but future plans include separate reporters for the publication.

"In the future, if we have our own staff, we want to be able to update sports statistics (and other timely information) very fre-

campus regional news, Tsai said.

"We are still trying to find our niche," he said.

In addition to providing a current version of the paper, the *IDS* site will eventually house an archive of past articles.

Archiving can give the site another way of generating revenue, Albert said. But for now, the storage space required for that type of operation is not available.

Photo courtesy of IDS.

FROM THE ARCHIVES

IDS Online Edition Now Available on Internet

Just months after the IDS returned to free distribution on campus, it added another type of free distribution. This story originally appeared Oct. 22, 1996.

By Christin Nance

Pick it up in Ballantine Hall or log on in a dorm room—readers may now view the Indiana Daily Student on the World Wide Web.

Designed during the summer, the IDS recently began updating its on-line site. Campus and regional news are included on the site, as are sports stories and photos.

The on-line version of the paper is available at 2 a.m. each day, beating the paper version by four hours.

"IDS online was launched because the Internet has become such an important part of IU," said sophomore Martin Tsai, the assistant on-line editor.

The new site will make it more convenient for students, alumni and others to check out what's going on at the University, Tsai said.

Tsai, along with editor Linda Yung, a senior, is duplicating material from the printed version of the paper onto the IDS online site, but future plans include separate reporters for the publication.

"In the future, if we have our own staff, we want to be able to update sports statistics (and other timely information) very frequently," Tsai said. "Hopefully we'll have our own features in the future."

Chris Albert, creative/technical adviser, said updates will occur more frequently after technical barriers are overcome. The on-line edition does not provide interactive features, like sound clips and animation, but this will be considered when the system becomes capable of handling more memory.

The IDS joins a host of other newspapers with on-line editions, including the New York Times, Chicago Tribune and Indianapolis Star. The IDS will focus on campus regional news, Tsai said.

"We are still trying to find our niche," he said.

In addition to providing a current version of the paper, the IDS site will eventually house an archive of past articles.

Archiving can give the site another way of generating revenue, Albert said. But for now, the storage space required for that type of operation is not available.

IDS online will also provide a learning tool for students who want to explore working with on-line media.

"Giving students the chance to edit an online newspaper is an invaluable experience for the future," said Malinda Aston, a creative/technical assistant director.

She said the job market is looking for applicants with on-line experience.

"This is an exciting opportunity for students to be trained at IU in a new form of media, so they can have many exciting job possibilities in the future," Tsai said.

1997–2008

As the mid-1990s gave way to the new millennium, idsnews.com gained greater importance and increasingly became the place where news was reported first. And there was plenty to cover, including the death of beloved former IU President Herman B Wells, the controversial firing of basketball coach Bob Knight, the Sept. 11, 2001, terrorist attacks and the historic election of America's first black president, Barack Obama.

Staffers are glued to the screen as they watch election returns in November 2008. *Photo courtesy of James Brosher*

CAMPUSCALENDAR

DON'T Forget

Crank up the tunes. There will be a listening party at 7 p.m. today in Briscoe Shoemaker (B) Lounge. Students can bring their favorite CDs and tapes to listen with their peers and win CDs from Disc Go Round or Disc Jockey Records.

TUESDAY
JANUARY 21, 1997

ids
INDIANA DAILY STUDENT

TODAY'SWEATHER

47 / 42 — Mostly cloudy and warmer with a 40 percent chance of rain in the afternoon. Tonight, 90 percent chance of rain with lows in the lower 40s.

WEDNESDAY	THURSDAY	FRIDAY
46 40 Showers	42 33 Cooler	37 22 Colder

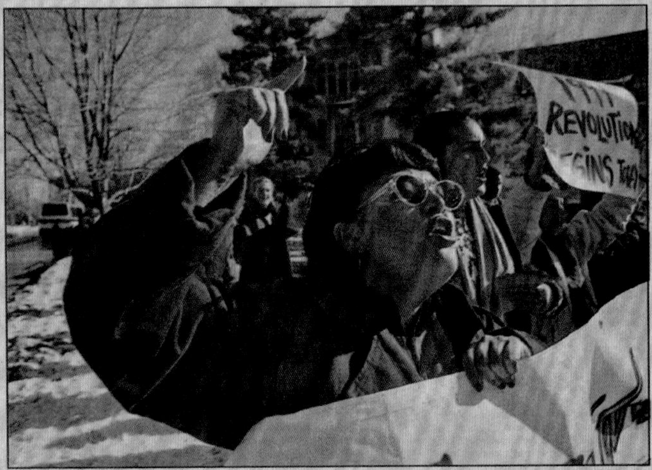

ALFRED TAY • IDS

Students gather Monday at Showalter Fountain to show their support for more diversity programs at IU.

'Students united will *never* be defeated'

Results of protest to be discussed at BFC meeting

MICHAEL BARNARD AND JENNIFER EMILY
Indiana Daily Student

It began with one woman voicing her frustration with the need for change. Then, 10 to 15 people chimed in, echoing the woman's determination. Soon, more than 400 voices rang as one.

"What do we want? Change! When do we want it? Now!" chanted members of the Student Coalition who marched Monday for improved minority retention and recruitment.

Beginning at Showalter Fountain, marching past Ballantine Hall and the Student Building and ending at Bryan Hall, members of 33 student groups united to fight for common goals.

> "For the first since I've been in office, student's representing various organizations came together."
> KENNETH GROS LOUIS, BLOOMINGTON CHANCELLOR

The Student Coalition's protest ended around 7:30 p.m. Monday. But the results of the protest might not be seen immediately.

Six protest organizers met with IU Vice President and Bloomington Chancellor Kenneth Gros Louis for five hours during the protest to discuss the Coalition's seven demands.

Neither Gros Louis nor the members of the Student Coalition would release details of the discussion in the Chancellor's office. But Gros Louis said the conversation "went well," and they "made some good progress." Details from the meeting will be released today and discussed at today's Bloomington Faculty Council meeting.

The seven demands the Coalition wanted the administration to fulfill are:

• The approval and implementation of a Latino Studies Department

• The appointment of an Asian American Advocacy Dean

• The creation of an Asian Culture Center

• The continued maintenance and possible expansion of the Office of Diversity Programs

• University funding and permanence of the Gay, Lesbian and Bisexual Student Support Services Office

• An increase in both non-white and women faculty

Protest organizers said they formed the Coalition because the University failed to meet their demands. They estimated 1,000 protesters attended the march. But the Office of Student Activities estimated 400 people participated.

"We are out because there are some issues that the University needs to address that it's not doing rapidly enough," said junior Ryan Vertner, one of the protest organizers and co-founder of *griot*, an activism-focused newspaper.

Gros Louis, who became an IU administrator in 1980, said the idea of a Coalition is unique and he has not seen anything like it.

"The key thing is that they were organized. For the first time since I've been in office, students representing various organizations came together," Gros Louis said. "In the past, black students, Latino students and students from the GLB community made sepa-

▶ PROTEST PAGE 8

MORE KING DAY COVERAGE

Monday's protest reflected many of the problems facing not only IU but today's society. The teach-ins before the protest discussed some of these challenges, while the protest brought together people from different organizations across IU.

For more coverage see Campus pages 4 and 5.

Students attend protest for different reasons

DERRICK GINGERY
Indiana Daily Student

An array of observers and participants found themselves at Bryan Hall Monday afternoon, each for his or her own reason.

Some were die-hard supporters or organizers of the protest.

Some saw the march and rally when they came out of class, while others listened for educational reasons. Some were simply bystanders who stopped to listen to the speeches fellow students gave.

"In my speech class, my professor told us about the protest and said to go and listen if we wanted to hear good speakers," junior Nicole Loe said.

"I didn't hear about it at all in my Y103 (political science) class, and it was right outside," junior Dave Durbin said. "I thought it was improper to forego something like this."

Once at the Sample Gates next to Bryan Hall, many observers listened as numerous protest supporters advocated their position. Of all the demands the protesters had, the University's lack of observing the King holiday was at the forefront of many students' minds, as well as the role students play in the adding of programs and departments such as the Asian Culture Center and Latino Studies Department.

"It's horrible because this is a state-funded school," junior Jessica Fuller said. "As much as they push ethnic diversity and multicultural affairs, I'm surprised we don't get the day off."

Despite the agreement of several students that the King holiday should be recognized, they also identified the need for a sense of community that arises when diversity and minority programs are enacted.

"I think there should be some sort of recognition (for minority groups)," Loe said. "Everyone should feel like they belong to IU."

ALFRED TAY • IDS

Junior Ryan Vertner speaks on the significance of Martin Luther King Jr. Day Monday at the Sample Gates.

One problem some students and faculty saw with the protesters' ideas stemmed from a lack of confidence in the likeliness of the implementation of the demands. Most did not expect overnight compliance, but opinions varied as to whether any new programs will ever be implemented.

"It seems to me they ought to (implement the new programs)," said David Nord, professor of journalism. "What more could the administration want than programs that involve education? Whether they can be met is more practical. (The University) is a smorgasbord. If there is a demand, then they should do it."

The use of a public march and rally, while not the only method of showing dissidence, seemed to be an effective method of informing the campus of their concerns for observers, according to Durbin.

"(I think the march and rally are effective) because I know these people have been trying to do things in the past and no one heard about it," Durbin said. "Now with this, someone has to listen. They're not quiet anymore."

Many bystanders and observers welcomed the protest as a needed shake up in the campus community. Nord said he was happy just to see students interested in controversial issues.

"I think the sense of doing something is good," Nord said. "I think it's great that students are excited about the issues. This is not an obstructive thing. It is showing a positive thing, so it should be positive."

Focusing on his next term

President Clinton is reflected in the glass shield of the reviewing stand as he watches the inaugural parade Monday in Washington, D.C.

For more coverage, see Page 6.

DENIS PAQUIN • THE ASSOCIATED PRESS

Meeting reaffirms King's goals

LISANNE V. CAROTHERS
Indiana Daily Student

While chants of support from the protest still echoed from the Sample Gates Monday night, about 25 community members gathered at the Black Culture Center to honor the life and dreams of Martin Luther King Jr.

At the meeting, students also participated in a prayer and scripture reading, followed by portions of King's "I Have a Dream" speech. IU Diversity Programs Coordinator Steve Birdine then spoke about the need for education and social action to keep King's message alive.

"I don't profess to know what King would have done today, but I know he would want us to follow our hearts, minds, souls and convictions," he told the audience. "The man was shot for wanting to heal the wounds of a great nation. He was a beacon of light and hope. King always sounded like he was singing to me."

Birdine also commended those involved with the protest, aimed at increasing diversity awareness at IU, which started at Showalter Fountain and wound through campus to Bryan Hall.

"I am extremely proud of the organizers and supporters," he said. "As ("Star Trek's") Jean-Luc Picard said, 'The line must be drawn here.' And (the students) drew the line today. I stood outside Franklin Hall with my chest pounding. Change is in the air, and the

▶ NAACP PAGE 8

IDSINFORMATION

Volume: 129 • Issue: 152 • 18 Pages
First Copy Free • Additional Copies 25 Cents

Bloomington, Ind. 47405

TALKBACK

ADVERTISING	(812) 855-0763
CIRCULATION	(812) 855-0768
NEWSROOM	(812) 855-0760
PHOTO	(812) 855-9577
JORDAN RIVER FORUM	@IDS
EDITOR IN CHIEF	@MHROWLAN
ONLINE	WWW.INDIANA.EDU/~IDS

P0080267, IU Archives.

July 8, 1999

CAMPUSCALENDAR

FACULTY AND GUEST CHAMBER RECITAL
The Fine Arts Quartet will be in concert at 8 p.m. Thursday at Auer Hall. Tickets are $10 general admission and $6 for students.

THURSDAY
JULY 8, 1999

ids
INDIANA DAILY STUDENT

TODAY'SWEATHER
90
63
Sunny and very warm

FRIDAY	SATURDAY	SUNDAY
92 68 Partly cloudy	84 70 Isolated t-storms	81 61 Partly cloudy

Shooting spree ends with Smith's suicide

Ashley Shelby and Sean C. Bartel
Indiana Daily Student

Former IU student Benjamin Nathaniel "August" Smith is believed to be the gunman responsible for a deadly string of Midwest shootings during the weekend which took two lives, including an IU student, and left nine people injured.

Smith, listed in IU's computers as a junior criminal justice major, killed himself in Salem, Ill., late Sunday night as police pursued him. Smith was well-known on the IU campus and in Bloomington for his vocal support of the white separatist movement.

Bloomington police have charged Smith with the shooting death of 26-year-old Won Joon Yoon.

Police believe the spree began Friday in West Rogers Park, Ill., where the gunman wounded six Orthodox Jews on their way home from services.

The gunman then reportedly drove to Skokie, Ill., where he shot and killed former Northwestern basketball coach Ricky Byrdsong, an African American, as he walked with his two children. Later that evening, shots were fired at two Asian Americans in nearby Northbrook. They were not hurt.

On Saturday, the spree extended to Springfield, Ill., where one African-American man was injured by gunfire and two more were fired upon but not hit.

Four hours later, in Decatur, Ill., an African-American minister was shot twice, once in the shoulder and once in the hip, where the bullet still remains.

Spree
Continued on page 14

Victim had bright future

Ashley Shelby
Indiana Daily Student

Won Joon Yoon was "promising." That is the word his family and friends use most when they describe the young man.

He was interested in planes. But his interest in aviation was multifarious and his knowledge intricate — a unique blend of aviation and economics.

Won Joon Yoon

It was that interest that intrigued IU's Department of Economics enough to admit him into its exclusive Ph.D program. Each fall, the department admits about 25 students, and Yoon was one of them.

"The program is pretty exclusive by nature," economics department head and professor Robert Becker said. "He had an interest in the airline industry and an unusual background to study it. That's the thing that stuck with me."

The 26-year-old Yoon was walking into services at the Korean United Methodist Church, 1924 E. Third St., Sunday when he was struck in the back by two bullets,

Future
Continued on page 13

PAUL MARTENS • IDS

Antonio Innaimo places flowers at the crime scene Monday night. The site has turned into a memorial to Won Joon Yoon.

'Gone are the dreams, hopes and happiness'

Ashley Shelby
Indiana Daily Student

Before stepping up to the podium in front of the Korean United Methodist Church Tuesday, Shin Ho Yoon sat in a folding chair and cried.

His only son, Won Joon, was killed Sunday while walking into services at the church by suspected shooting spree killer Benjamin "August" Smith.

Yoon's family held a press conference to express its condolences for all the victims in last weekend's spree and to thank the Bloomington community for its support.

But as he stood before the media, Shin Ho Yoon made it clear exactly what the family had lost when his son was killed.

"With his death, gone are the dreams, hopes and happiness my family has had with my son, Won Joon," he said.

"He was gunned down by one insane, full of racial hatred, young American man."

With his hand pressed on a small Bible, Yoon said he prayed not only for his son, but for all the victims and poten-

Family
Continued on page 13

Community rallies to help victims

Sean C. Bartel
Indiana Daily Student

Last weekend's shooting spree that claimed the life of IU student Won Joon Yoon and former Northwestern men's basketball coach Ricky Byrdsong nearly overwhelmed the Bloomington community. Town residents responded by filling the lawn of Yoon's church with a sea of flowers and have organized many activities to show support.

Yoon was murdered Sunday morning outside the Korean United Methodist Church, 1924 E. Third Street. Police say Yoon and Byrdsong, who was killed Friday in Skokie, Ill., were part of a two-state shooting spree by 21-year-old Benjamin Nathaniel "August" Smith, which ended in Smith's suicide. Smith was questioned by Blooming-

Comunity
Continued on page 14

Smith's troubled history at IU

Jeff Fleischer
Indiana Daily Student

While Benjamin "August" Smith became a national name with last weekend's shooting, he had already caused considerable debate on the IU and University of Illinois campuses.

Benjamin Smith

Smith first became known to Bloomington authorities in May 1998, when two students contacted the IU Police Department to report racist fliers from the White Nationalist Party placed on cars parked near the Kelley School of Business. Within a week, two other fliers and a sticker were found in the Main Library.

One flier argued that whites need their own country and "protection from the abuses of blacks." Another read "The Voice of White America has been silenced. It is obvious to all racially-conscious people that whites want to stop the flow of non-white immigrants into this country." Other fliers criticized gays, Jews, Asians and interracial marriage. They all had contact information for people wanting to join the organization.

Pam Freeman, assistant dean of students and co-chair of the Racial Incidents Team, placed an advertisement in the *IDS* asking students to report any other fliers found.

"What we're concerned about is if it's encouraging hate among specific groups ... we

History
Continued on page 13

WCOTC, KKK members not bothered by negative reactions

Eric Weddle
Indiana Daily Student

Benjamin "August" Smith's shooting spree this past weekend has brought numerous white racialist and separatist groups into the mainstream media. The most notable is the World Church of the Creator, a group based in East Peoria, Ill., that Smith was a member of until May 1999.

Rev. Matt Hale, the current leader of the WCOTC, has appeared on CNN and in the New York Times this week. This recent attention has many regional and national anti-racism groups — such as the Anti-Defamation League — speaking out against the WCOTC. The ADL referred to the WCOTC as a "violent hate group," in a press release Wednesday, though racialist group leaders believe the opposition will not adversely affect their groups.

When asked if the media would negatively affect the church, WCOTC press secretary Kelly O'Reilly replied, "No, I don't" in an on-line interview.

"I actually think while it is tragic what happened, this has drawn major publicity to the issues we talk about, and will in the end only help us spread the word more effectively," O'Reilly said. "In all honesty, I wish (the shootings) would have never happened, it was a senseless loss, but it has and we can only try to do what we can with what we got."

The WCOTC recently created a Web site, *www.wcotc.com*, which collected links of all U.S. and international branches of the church and now

Separatists
Continued on page 13

MONDAY

The Bloomington Fire Commission met Wednesday, July 7, at the Monroe County Public Library auditorium. The commission and the city government have been at odds ever since the April fire at Knightridge Manor where local disc jockey Randy Lloyd died. Read about the meeting's outcome in Monday's paper.

IDSINFORMATION

Volume: 132 • Issue: 62 • 14 Pages
First Copy Free • Additional Copies 50 Cents

OTHERFEATURES

TALKBACK

ADVERTISING	855-0763
CIRCULATION	855-0769
NEWSROOM	855-0760
PHOTO	856-5703
JORDAN RIVER FORUM	LETTERS
EDITOR IN CHIEF	JFLEISCH
ONLINE	WWW.IDSNEWS.COM

P0028281, IU Archives.

REFLECTION

Writing for the Campus—and for Grandma Millie

"When readers trust us, even grudgingly, to tell the story of a community, they are giving us something precious, something we should never take for granted."

The first time I ever Googled something, I was sitting in the IDS newsroom.

"It's new—give it a try," one of the campus editors said after he caught me trying to find some nugget of information by asking Jeeves.

It was my freshman year at IU. I joined the paper two days before the semester actually began, wandering in off the street on a Sunday afternoon and nervously asking the first person I saw if the paper was looking for reporters. I expected to be told to come back in a few days or to be handed a lengthy application. Instead, they hustled me over to the GA desk and handed me a fistful of briefs to type up.

A few days later, I wrote my first front-page story: "Renovations bolster Union conveniences," and was given the title of Union Board beat reporter. I thought it was a huge deal—little did I know that exactly zero other people were clamoring for that job.

But that day, I walked around the campus feeling like I had just become somebody. Unfortunately, I didn't really know anybody in Bloomington yet, so instead I shared the news with my favorite email buddy: my grandma Millie.

Millie was 76 years old at the time. She was the kind of grandma who sent me a care package of fancy popcorn bearing the card: "Some grandmas bake. This one doesn't." She bought my family our first computer and mastered the internet before my parents even had dial-up.

She became my No. 1 reader. I showed her how she could read the IDS online, and she read it every day—not just my stories, but all of them. Millie visited Bloomington only once—for my graduation—but she probably knew more about Bloomington and IU in the late 1990s and early 2000s than some city residents.

I've been a newspaper nerd since I was a little kid. The Cincinnati Enquirer was on my parents' kitchen table every single morning of my childhood. I would read it cover to cover and cut out the articles and photos I really liked to hang on my bedroom walls.

Newspapers were also something I associated with Millie. She read at least one every morning and faithfully did the cryptogram and crossword puzzle each day into her 90s. I eagerly looked forward to visiting Millie at her winter home in Cleveland and her summer home in Florida because it meant I got to read The Plain Dealer and the St. Petersburg Times.

During that first year on the IDS, Millie and I talked on AOL Instant Messenger a few times a week. I told her behind-the-scenes stories of my reporting exploits. (One of her favorites: My "money-making" job during my freshman year was working as a cashier at the Read Center store. I would report on IDS stories while working and regularly had to put then-Vice President of Academic Affairs Kenneth Gros Louis and Dean of Students Richard McKaig on hold during interviews so I could ring up cigarettes and chips and make change. They were both very gracious about it.)

I told Millie about covering a visit to campus by former Polish President Lech Walesa. I shared the excitement of my very first big scoop—the addition of a Burger King to the Indiana Memorial Union dining options. I annoyed my mother, an admitted Luddite, who would often share news with Millie during their weekly phone call only to find out that Millie already knew all about it. ("Let me know what's going on with you," my mom wrote in a rare email she dictated to my younger sister. "Unless you want to tell grandma first.")

The late 1990s were the early days of online journalism. Working at the IDS is the first time I remember having the realization that you could read a newspaper on the internet. These days the only time I don't read newspapers on the internet is when I visit my parents. It's sad that the industry didn't see the writing on the wall in those days and shift accordingly. But I remember thinking at the time that it was just amazing that I could share my work with Millie even though she lived hundreds of miles away. She could pull up idsnews.com every morning, and there I was.

She wasn't the only reader I heard from that year. I also got an email from a retired professor who took me to task for incorrectly using the plural "alumni" when I really should have used the singular "alumnus." My floormates at Read made a big deal the day my Burger King story made the front page. I got a handwritten thank-you note from a speaker who read the article I wrote about her lecture, an event that was attended by no more than a half-dozen people including her and me.

At the end of my freshman year, I went with my family to Cleveland to visit Millie. She presented me with a six-inch thick stack of computer paper—a printed copy of every single story I had written for the IDS during the past nine months, no matter how short or long or where it had run in the paper.

Millie died in 2017, but one of the many, many things she taught me was the power that journalism can have to bring people together. Whether our readers are our friends, relatives or strangers we may never meet, they're out there. They're following our work and hopefully learning from it (even if they don't always agree with it). When readers trust us, even grudgingly, to tell the story of a community, they are giving us something precious, something we should never take for granted. In my 20 years as a journalist, I have tried to never forget that lesson.

—*Rachel Kipp, BAJ 2002*

Rachel Kipp and her grandmother, Millie Task Baker, in 2002. *Photo courtesy of Rachel Kipp.*

Herman B Wells 1902 - 2000

ids INDIANA DAILY STUDENT

Volume 133 • Issue 14 • 28 Pages | Monday, March 20, 2000 | On the Web: www.idsnews.com

Losing a legend

Herman B Wells, 97, dies at home Saturday

• Wells died at 97 around 7:45 p.m. Saturday from pneumonia and heart failure.

• Visitation is scheduled from 4 - 8 p.m. Tuesday at Day Mortuary, 2701 E. Third St.

• Funeral services will be at 11 a.m. Wednesday at the First United Methodist Church, 219 E. Fourth St.

• The family is requesting monetary donations be sent to the IU Library c/o the IU Foundation, in lieu of flowers.

Joseph S. Pete
Indiana Daily Student

Legendary former president and chancellor Herman B Wells passed away Saturday night from pneumonia and heart failure at the age of 97. Wells, who had suffered from heart problems, died in his home at about 7:45 p.m.

Liz Egan, a nurse's aid for Wells, said he died with dignity.

"He was aware at the time," she said. "And he slipped away quietly and comfortably."

Wells, recently named IU's "Man of the Century" in 1999, served as University president from 1938 to 1962 before becoming chancellor. Among his many accomplishments, Wells was instrumental in the desegregation of IU, a proponent of academic freedom and developing an overall vision for the campus' architecture. He is also widely credited with improving the cultural atmosphere of the University, initiating the construction of the IU Auditorium in 1941 and developing the School of Music.

"Chancellor Wells was, quite simply, a great man, one of the exceptional figures in higher education this century," said President Myles Brand in a press release. "If it were not for his vision, his leadership, his passion and hard work, IU would not be the University that it is today."

Brand said Wells meant much to the entire IU community.

"What was particularly important to me is that Chancellor Wells was not just a figure in the history books. Even at 97, he seemed to be everywhere on campus," he said in the press release. "And he was always willing, when asked, to offer wise and straightforward advice. I am deeply saddened by his death, I know I will miss him, and I am sure the community will as well."

The University experienced its greatest growth under the leadership of Wells, with the student body nearly tripling from 11,000 in 1938 to 31,000 in 1962. He also widened its scope to encompass the globe, adding study programs such as Hebrew and Folklore.

"It's remarkable that he brought all of that to the fore during a time when American isolationism was pretty strong," said IU Vice President and Bloomington Chancellor Kenneth Gros Louis. "By thinking independently, he really enhanced the reputation of the University."

John Walda, president of the IU board of trustees, said in a press release that Wells' record of accomplishment is truly memorable.

"When I think of Herman B Wells, I think of the words of John F. Kennedy, who said, 'Things do not happen; things are made to happen,'" he said. "Chancellor Wells made wonderful things happen not only at Indiana University, but in the lives of everyone with whom he came in contact. He changed my life, and I will remember him with respect and affection."

Born in Jamestown, Indiana in 1902, Wells earned a bachelor of science degree in business administration from IU in 1924 and a master of arts degree in economics in 1927. He was appointed a professor of economics and the dean of the school of business administration in 1935.

see WELLS, page 10

JENSEN WALKER • ARBUTUS

Former IU President and Chancellor Herman B Wells passed away Saturday at his home in Bloomington. Wells is credited with desegregating IU and coming up with a vision for the architecture of the campus, among his many accomplishments.

Legacy lies in generosity, love

"He loved people. He had no ego. He was able to connect and that was his magic."

Henry Remak
Professor

Joel Eskovitz
Indiana Daily Student

Chancellor Herman B Wells' professional achievements are what made him a legend. But his personal attributes are what made him a beloved figure.

Those close to him have difficulty describing everything Wells embodied. He died at 97 Saturday night.

"There just aren't enough good things to say about him," said Phyllis Hackler, the daughter of Wells' close friend Claude Rich. Rich was a former IU alumni secretary and director of University relations.

Wells visited Rich daily for more than nine months at Meadowood Retirement Community before Rich died in February 1999. While the two did reflect on their time together in the IU administration, they spent their days discussing the direction of the University.

see GENEROSITY, page 10

Public officials react to loss of leader

Joseph S. Pete
Indiana Daily Student

The death of legendary IU Chancellor Herman B Wells inspired many expressions of sorrow among prominent public figures in the University and around the state.

Wells, who served as IU president for a quarter of a century and who had been involved with the University since his days as a student in 1920, died from heart failure at the age of 97 Saturday evening.

"In each person's lifetime, there are but a handful of folks of such inspiration and leadership that we wear their imprint on our very beings," said Indiana Governor Frank O'Bannon in a prepared statement read by a press spokesperson. "Wells was one of these. He was an Indiana treasure. His breadth of leadership extended to national and international affairs, yet he was like family to so many."

Bloomington Mayor John Fernandez agreed Wells had a direct impact on everyone around him.

"As a citizen of Bloomington and the state of Indiana, he made many contributions with his far-reaching vision," he said. "As (Fernandez' wife) Karen and I have often interacted with him, I am deeply saddened by the news. But we were fortunate to have him as part of our community."

Charlie Nelms, vice president for student development and diversity, said Wells shaped the very fabric of the community during the civil rights era, ensuring that the University was one of the first in

see REACT, page 10

Wells' death leaves void at Sigma Nu

Brett Wallace
Indiana Daily Student

As much as he was a factor in countless other operations of Indiana University during his career, Herman B Wells' influence on the Sigma Nu fraternity might have been the most far-reaching.

As word of Wells' death spread through the organization, the initial reaction was one of shock.

Wells' legacy at Sigma Nu is nearly unparalleled. Besides being president of the Beta Eta chapter of Sigma Nu, he was chairman of the Board of the Sigma Nu Education Foundation from its organization in 1946 until 1990, when he became Chairman Emeritus. He was once regent of Sigma Nu, was inducted to the Sigma Nu Hall of Honor in 1962 and, as president of Indiana University, developed the Indiana Plan, which consisted of the three-way contractual agreement between the University, the greek organization and the lender.

see VOID, page 10

"He was the biggest influence on our chapter since the founding fathers. He just meant a lot to everybody."

Tyler Mensch
Sigma Nu president

Herman B Wells, 1902-2000

Look inside for a tribute to the legendary Chancellor.

INSIDE

Hoosiers lose in first round of NCAA Tournament. —Page 11

Players defend Knight against allegations. —Page 11

INSIDE

Greenhouse, staff remain part of campus. —Page 2

INSIDE

Professor Manuel Martinex writes award-winning book. —Page 16

WEATHER

HIGH 55
LOW 43

P0034223, IU Archives.

Our Own Jolly St. Nick

This article originally appeared March 20, 2000, in a special edition memorializing longtime IU President Herman B Wells.

By David L. Adams

Dear ol' IU, there really is a Santa Claus!

I had heard about the special 'Santa Claus' that had been appearing around the IU Bloomington campus when I interviewed for the position of publisher of the IDS and Arbutus yearbook back in 1989. Later that year, after I had completed a semester as publisher, I saw for myself that IU really did have a Santa Claus of its own.

You see, Santa Claus had been visiting the IDS and a few other student groups on campus for more than 50 years. In this early December visit, Santa brought several bushel baskets of apples as well as several large boxes of candy for the student publications staff members. Santa was there with lots of love and admiration for the students who were equally admiring of him.

While his annual visits to the IU campus around the holidays have been witnessed by numerous generations of students, it was my first experience in meeting IU's "Santa." And I shall be forever grateful my life and my work brought me in direct contact with "Santa" Herman B Wells in such a personal way.

I had the privilege of escorting "Santa" Wells into our newsroom a few times. Each year, he would bring his baskets of apples and boxes of candy. Marge Blewett, retired [placement] director for the IU School of Journalism, had been given the task of being "Santa's helper."

Those who witnessed Wells' visits knew apples and candy were not the most cherished gift that he brought to us. We could not fail to notice his caring, loving spirit that accompanied each visit. "Santa" would recall his days as a young IDS writer when he was an undergraduate student at IU. Wells reminded students to remain determined and to keep trying. He was told several times by peer editors his stories were not good enough to print. One peer editor even told him he wouldn't amount to much as a writer! Of course, "Santa" would give a good hardy laugh after retelling the

Below, IDS publisher Dave Adams talks with IU President Emeritus Herman B Wells, who dressed as Santa during a Christmas visit to the newsroom. *Photo courtesy of IDS.*

Our own Jolly St. Nick

Dear Ol' IU, There Really Is a Santa Claus!

I had heard about the special 'Santa Claus' that had been appearing around the IU Bloomington campus when I interviewed for the position of publisher of the *Indiana Daily Student* and *Arbutus* yearbook back in 1989. Later that year, after I had completed a semester as publisher, I saw for myself that IU really did have a Santa Claus of its own.

You see, Santa Claus had been visiting the *IDS* and a few other student groups on campus for more than 50 years. In this early December visit, Santa brought several bushel baskets of apples as well as several large boxes of candy for the student publications staff members. Santa was there with lots of love and admiration for the students who were equally admiring of him.

David L. Adams is the advisor to the Indiana Daily Student and Arbutus.

PHOTO COURTESY IU ARCHIVES

May all that come to know IU come to recognize that the spirit of selfless love and giving that is the true spirit of Santa Claus will always be the legacy Dr. Wells has left us.

— David L. Adams, publisher *Indiana Daily Student, Arbutus*

While his annual visits to the IU campus around the holidays have been witnessed by numerous generations of students, it was my first experience in meeting IU's "Santa." And I shall be forever grateful my life and my work brought me in direct contact with "Santa" Herman B Wells in such a personal way.

I had the privilege of escorting "Santa" Wells into our newsroom a few more times. Each year, he would bring his baskets of apples and boxes of candy. Marge Blewett, retired alumni director for the IU School of Journalism, had been given the task of being "Santa's helper."

Those who witnessed Wells' visits knew apples and candy were not the most cherished gift that he brought to us. We could not fail to notice his caring, loving spirit that accompanied each visit. "Santa" would recall his days as a young *IDS* writer when he was an undergraduate student at IU. Wells reminded students to remain determined and to keep trying. He was told several times by peer editors that his first stories were not good enough to print. One peer editor even told him he wouldn't amount to much as a writer! Of course, "Santa" would give a good hardy laugh after retelling that story – and those in attendance would laugh even harder.

In his annual holiday visits, Santa would discuss current issues the paper was covering, often issues the first week of his newsroom visits. On more than one occasion, he cited opinion pieces that criticized the IU administration's decisions or policies on one thing or another. We were all impressed that a 90-something "Santa" could remember current things with such clarity. Perhaps expecting some kind of reprimand as might normally be the case, "Santa" would then add, "Give 'em hell. Keep givin' 'em hell."

In April 1995, Dr. Wells made his last visit to Ernie Pyle Hall. The occasion was a ceremony commemorating the 50th anniversary of the death of his good friend, Ernie Pyle, the World War II Pulitzer Prize-winning correspondent. Pyle had also been a former *IDS* staffer. While he wasn't dressed in his Santa suit on this occasion, after paying respects to those in attendance at a ceremony honoring Pyle in the Ernie Pyle Lounge in the journalism building bearing Pyle's name, Dr. Wells requested to be taken downstairs to visit with current *IDS* staffers in the newsroom. This was a surprise visit for all of us. No warning of "Santa's" pending arrival as had been the case during planned holiday visits. Students who were present that afternoon knew they were experiencing a special, unplanned event. Dr. Wells spent time seeking out students. And students came to eagerly talk to him.

The past few years, Dr. Wells' health has prevented him from accompanying the baskets of apples and candy that still come to Ernie Pyle Hall as gifts from the former president who made IU the respected institution it is today. Dr. Wells' 50-plus years of annual visits on campus as Santa Claus come as no surprise to those who know him. "Santa" Wells so often has shown his loving care for all that is Indiana University. His love of its students and their achievements have always been foremost in his heart and at the center of his administration as a campus leader. "Santa" Wells' spirit continues to live in the visionary programs he fought to fund and establish. His spirit lives in the many academic honor programs and awards bearing his name. And, yes, Santa Wells will be remembered for caring enough to take the time to come visit us each holiday season in Ernie Pyle Hall.

Is it no wonder, then, that Herman B Wells does live in the hearts and minds of so many who love and understand IU as its Santa Claus? May all that come to know IU come to recognize that the spirit of selfless love and giving that is the true spirit of Santa Claus will always be the legacy Dr. Wells has left us. See, there really is a Santa Claus at IU, and his name is Herman B Wells.

The March 20, 2000, column "Our own jolly St. Nick," by then Publisher David L. Adams. P0079428, IU Archives.

story—and those in attendance would laugh even harder.

In his annual holiday visits, Santa would discuss current issues the paper was covering. On more than one occasion, he cited opinion pieces that criticized the IU administration's decisions or polices on one thing or another. We were all impressed that a 90-something "Santa" could remember current things with such clarity. Perhaps expecting some kind of reprimand as might normally be the case, "Santa" would then add, "Give 'em hell. Keep givin' 'em hell."

In April 1995, Dr. Wells made his last visit to Ernie Pyle Hall. The occasion was a ceremony commemorating the 50th anniversary of the death of his good friend Ernie Pyle, the World War II Pulitzer Prize-winning correspondent. Pyle had also been a former IDS staffer. While he wasn't dressed in his Santa suit on this occasion, after paying respects to those in attendance at a ceremony honoring Pyle in the Ernie Pyle Lounge in the journalism building bearing Pyle's name, Dr. Wells requested to be taken downstairs to visit with the current staffers in the newsroom. This was a surprise visit for all of us. No warning of "Santa's" pending arrival as had been the case during planned holiday visits. Students who were present that afternoon knew they were experiencing a special, unplanned event. Dr. Wells spent time seeking out students. And students came eagerly to talk to him.

The past few years, Dr. Wells' health has prevented him from accompanying the baskets of apples and candy that still come to Ernie Pyle Hall as gifts from the former president who made IU the respected institution it is today. Dr. Wells' 50-plus years of annual visits on campus as Santa Claus come as no surprise to those who know him. "Santa" Wells so often has shown his loving care for all that is IU. His love of its students and their achievements have always been foremost in his heart and at the center of his administration. "Santa" Wells spirit continues to live in the visionary programs he fought to fund and establish. His spirit lives in the many academic honor programs and awards bearing his name. And, yes, Santa Wells will be remembered for caring enough to come to take the time to come visit us each holiday season in Ernie Pyle Hall.

Is it no wonder, then, that Herman B Wells does live in the hearts and minds of so many who live and understand IU as its Santa Claus? May all that come to know IU come to recognize that the spirit of selfless love and giving that is the true spirit of Santa Claus will always be in the legacy Dr. Wells has left us. See, there really is a Santa Claus at IU, and his name is Herman B Wells.

September 11, 2000

SPECIAL EDITION

INDIANA DAILY STUDENT

Volume 133 • Issue 82 • 4 Pages — Monday, September 11, 2000 — On the Web: www.idsnews.com

Knight fired

Brand ends coach's 29-year reign

CHUCK ROBINSON • THE ASSOCIATED PRESS
IU President Myles Brand explains during a news conference Sunday in Indianapolis the reasons for dismissing Knight after 29 years.

JENSEN WALKER • ARBUTUS
Bob Knight addresses the student rioters at about 12:30 a.m., asking that students let police go home to their families. He promised he would talk to students within two days.

Legendary coach removed from position for violating agreement

David Uchiyama
Indiana Daily Student

INDIANAPOLIS – IU basketball coach Bob Knight left for a brief vacation in Canada Saturday morning. IU President Myles Brand put Knight on a permanent vacation Sunday afternoon, when he removed Knight from his position for violating the "zero-tolerance policy," established May 15 by the University.

"The problem is that he has continued a pattern of unacceptable behavior which is similar to the pattern he had prior to May 15, except it's gotten worse," Brand said. "There wasn't just one instance. It was ongoing."

Brand cited several examples of Knight's behavior that violated the policy.

• Knight has embarrassed IU in public and private. "Coach Knight has made angry and inflammatory remarks about University officials and the IU Board of Trustees," Brand said.

• Knight has disrespected alumni. "The coach has informed the University that he refuses now to participate in previously scheduled Varsity Club events – the most popular and widely attended events our alumni anticipate each year," Brand said.

"The fact is, that in giving coach Knight one more opportunity, he has failed to take advantage of it. It was his decision."

Myles Brand
IU President

• Knight verbally abused an IU administrator. "There has been an instant in the recent past in which coach Knight verbally abused a high-ranking female University official in the presence of other persons," Brand said.

• Knight has not cooperated in fulfilling the sanctions. "It is important to note that the coach has agreed to fulfill these obligations, but he has forced the University to go through a protracted, unpleasant and completely unnecessary process to reach that end," Brand said.

• Knight was insubordinate. "I requested, more than once, that he postpone his trip and stay in Bloomington. He adamantly refused," Brand said.

• Knight initiated physical contact with freshman Kent Harvey. "The severity of the act is in dispute. But the bottom line is that an angry confrontation with a student explicitly violates the spirit and letter of the guidelines," Brand said.

"The fact is, that in giving coach Knight one more opportunity, he has failed to take advantage of it. It was his decision."

Brand offered Knight the chance to resign when they spoke on the phone Sunday morning. Upon hearing Knight's refusal, Brand told Knight that he was being removed – effective immediately.

"Knight told me he wanted to continue to coach at IU," Brand said. "We had our conversation. It was a civil conversation and he understood the points. He did not react angrily. Coach did say he did not believe he did anything wrong. The conversation lasted about 10 minutes."

Throughout the weekend the IU Board of Trustees communicated with Brand informally and the IU Police Department continually briefed Brand on the Harvey incident. Brand said the Trustees did not take a vote, nor did they need to, because the University exercised a clause in Knight's contract: "If the University at any time desires, Coach shall cease to serve as head basketball coach when so advised in writing."

"The large majority of the Trustees fully supports this decision," said Frederick Eichhorn, vice president of the Board of Trustees. "We regret that the coach's actions have resulted in this conclusion, but this is the best answer for the University at this time."

The IU basketball players showed their support for Knight by driving to Indianapolis for the news confer-

see COACH, page 3

Knight returns to end campus riots

Students leave trail of destruction from Assembly Hall to Kirkwood

Marie Harf, Rachel Kipp, Stacey Palevsky, Cory Schouten and Jennifer Wagner
Indiana Daily Student

Sunday began with chants of "We want Bobby," continued with broken lamp posts, burning public figures in effigy and police in riot gear, and ended after midnight with coach Bob Knight telling Assembly Hall protestors to go home.

Pandemonium hit campus almost immediately after the 3:15 p.m. press conference, when IU announced its decision to fire Knight. It only snowballed as the night progressed until Knight sent protestors home with a promise to tell students his side of the story in the next few days.

"I think you'll be very interested in hearing it," he told the crowd.

Both Knight supporters and critics turned out early for a rally that started at Assembly Hall. The protest moved down Fee Lane toward the Bryan House, IU President Myles Brand's residence. Brand was still in Indianapolis at the time. The rally grew as word of mouth spread throughout campus.

"I think this is total bullshit," Pete Wesson, a 1999 graduate, said. "I think the 'zero tolerance' policy they put on him doesn't allow him to be a basketball coach. I think he has done a lot more for this University then he has done wrong."

The mass of people assembled peacefully at Bryan House, with police standing guard in front. The protesters then returned to Assembly Hall for a previously scheduled gathering at 6 p.m.

At that rally, George Leach, a redshirt freshman forward for the basketball team, said he was disappointed with the decision.

"I'm here for the same reason everyone is here – to support coach Knight," Leach said. "Brand just blew us off for a whole year without talking to us, so we were just left in the dark about the whole situation."

Alumni, students, faculty and community members came with signs, bullhorns and homemade T-shirts to show their support.

"They absolutely fired the wrong man," said Val Meek, a Bloomington resident for 20 years. "The person who brought people through these doors was not Brand – it was Mr. Knight."

RIOT LOCATIONS
- Assembly Hall
- Bryan House (Brand's residence)
- Behind Woodburn Hall
- Kirkwood Avenue
- Showalter Fountain
- Memorial Stadium

But the night then took a violent turn.

During the second march to Bryan House, thousands of protesters became destructive.

It started with tearing down tree limbs, stealing signs and burning an effigy of Brand. Police countered with riot gear, dogs and emergency vehicles.

"The way they are treating us … is inviting problems," sophomore Luke Williams said. "We're not criminals."

As night fell, the tension escalated. The darkness impaired protesters' vision as police pushed back the crowd with helmets and shields. Dean of Students Richard McKaig attempted to subdue the melee with a request to disperse.

"I would appreciate it if you would follow us over to Dunn Meadow," McKaig said from a fire truck. "So that no one gets hurt."

Sophomore Zach Kosenka was handcuffed on the front of a black Jeep in Brand's driveway.

"I feel violated," he said as he was forced into a police car.

Lt. Jerry Minger said he thought three arrests were made, two for disorderly conduct and one for an alcohol violation. Later in the evening, Jim Kennedy, assistant to the vice president for administration, said that four to five arrests had been made.

JENSEN WALKER • ARBUTUS
A freshman rioter disappears into a melee of cops as they subdue him. Enraged students closed in on police while shouting profanities.

"When we were trying to move people back because of the pushing and shoving and trying to get people to leave the front of the house, (the people arrested) started pushing back," Minger said. "This is no longer a peaceful demonstration, and it's also trespassing."

No IU Police Department officers used any type of mace or tear gas to control the crowd, Minger said. Officers from the Bloomington Police Department and the Indiana State Police were also on the scene.

"I saw no chemical weapons or any kind of tear gas being used at all," Minger said. "There were officers from other agencies there, but I didn't see any of them using any kind of mace or tear gas."

Some students claimed otherwise.

John Moore, a sophomore, came out of the crowd with a red face and watery eyes.

"We were doing chants, then they were backing us up," Moore said. "Then they got out the shields and mace. I was walking backwards. You can only go as fast as people behind you."

That is when Moore alleged he was hit with some form of chemical deterrent.

Indiana State Police also denied using any spray, and the Bloomington Police Department would not comment.

But Kennedy said one police officer was in the hospital, injured by pepper spray.

After a period of passivity, police finally forced protesters off Brand's lawn into the area behind Woodburn Hall. There they tore down lamp

see PROTEST, page 3

P0034222, IU Archives.

ELECTION EDITION

INDIANA DAILY STUDENT

Volume 133 • Issue 124 • 16 Pages | Wednesday, November 8, 2000 | On the Web: www.idsnews.com

Too close to call

ERIC DRAPER • THE ASSOCIATED PRESS

Texas Gov. George W. Bush and his father, former President George H. W. Bush watch election results Tuesday evening in Austin, Texas. Major news networks declared Bush the winner in the early morning hours but later retracted their prediction. Florida votes were being counted as of press time.

Election Results

President (National)

Results as of press time.

George W. Bush (R)	49%
Al Gore (D)	49%
Ralph Nader (G)	2%

GOVERNOR

Frank O'Bannon

David McIntosh (R)	42%
Frank O'Bannon (D)	57%
Andrew Horning (L)	2%

SENATE

Richard Lugar

Richard Lugar (R)	67%
David Johnson (D)	31%
Paul Hager (L)	2%

U.S. REPRESENTATIVES

John Hostettler

John Hostettler (R)	52%
Paul Perry (D)	46%
Thomas Tindle (L)	2%

STATE REPRESENTATIVE

Peggy Welch

Peggy Welch (D)	57%
John Shean (R)	43%

COUNTY COUNCIL (AT-LARGE)

Doug Duncan, Jeff Ellington, Scott Wells

Doug Duncan (R)	16.97%
Jeff Ellington (R)	17%
Randy May (R)	16.95%
Julio Alonso (D)	16.4%
Scott Wells (D)	17%
Charles Wilson (D)	15.7%

COUNTY COMMISSIONERS DISTRICT 3

Iris Kiesling

Franklin Andrew (R)	46%
Iris Kiesling (D)	54%

COUNTY COMMISSIONERS DISTRICT 2

Joyce Poling

Joyce Poling (R)	56.5%
Elizabeth Feltl (D)	43.4%

Florida total will decide election

Electoral vote outcome

Total Vote
270 electoral votes needed for victory

	Popular	Electoral
Bush	46,543,660	246
Gore	46,385,921	249

KURTIS BEAVERS / TIM STREET • IDS

Amy Orringer
Indiana Daily Student

AUSTIN, Texas – It was a cold, rainy day in Texas when Republican presidential nominee Gov. George Bush had his moment in the sun, or so the country thought.

As of 3:45 a.m., Vice President Al Gore retracted an earlier concessionary phone call to Bush.

CNN reported earlier that Bush was elected to the highest office in the nation with a slim majority over Democratic nominee Gore. After spending the night glued to the television with his family, the president elect celebrated his victory with more than 17,000 people outside the Capitol in Texas.

But it all changed soon after, as CNN and other major news networks retracted the declaration.

The votes were so close in some key states that the CNN exit polls were mistaken in their prediction. Several states, including Florida with 25 electoral votes, were predicted based on the exit polls to have been won by Gore, but were in the end a toss-up.

FINAL OUTCOME: Check www.idsnews.com.

Florida will have enough electoral votes to decide the winner, but as of press time it was too close to call. CNN reported at 4 a.m., Bush led Gore in the Sunshine State by 5,460 votes, with a recount looming, according to Florida's Secretary of State.

Victory looked promising to supporters at the Austin rally at 6 p.m., as Bush started out with 28 electoral votes and the vice president with three.

Two hours later, Gore was leading in electoral votes: 145 to Bush's 130. Texas native. The switch in the exit poll leader at 9 p.m. affirmed Torgerson's guess. The map

see BUSH, page 8

O'Bannon wins '4 more years'

James Echelbarger
Indiana Daily Student

INDIANAPOLIS - The Indiana gubernatorial race ended Tuesday evening with a victory for the Democratic Party. Incumbent Gov. Frank O'Bannon and Lt. Gov. Joe Kernan celebrated their victory with the exuberant crowd that filled the Indianapolis Convention Center's 500 Ballroom.

The evening peaked when the winning candidates gave their acceptance speeches. Kernan spoke first, loosening up the crowd with the question: "Who has more fun than Democrats?" Kernan continued by recognizing the people who made the campaign a success.

"I would like to thank my family, but most importantly, the thousands of volunteers and leadership of the party," he said.

Kernan said he looks forward to tackling another four years in office.

"This keeps getting funner and funner, and I look forward to serving with one of the best governors in the nation," Kernan said. "... I look forward to the next four years because I will meet new challenges."

"There is no better place than the state of Indiana."
Frank O'Bannon
Governor

Kernan handed the stage to O'Bannon after remarking that "we have had four years of distinction, but there is still a lot to do."

O'Bannon's acceptance speech followed Kernan's and was focused on family and education. It ignited the crowd into a chanting of "four more years."

The governor began his address by saying, "It is such an honor to be here with so many people we need to thank for being part of what we have wanted to do. I would like to thank all the people in the state of Indiana that said we are moving in the right direction."

O'Bannon addressed the issues key to the election, such as education.

He continued with his support of the Community College initiative.

see O'BANNON, page 8

Lugar wins record 5th Senate term

Cory Schouten and Jennifer Wagner
Indiana Daily Student

INDIANAPOLIS – Tuesday night, Republican Richard Lugar became the first Indiana politician to be elected to a fifth term in the U.S. Senate.

But no one was surprised.

Lugar defeated his two opponents – Democrat David Johnson and Libertarian Paul Hager – by a near-record margin of about 40 percent.

"We're excited – all of us – about the new mandate you have given us," Lugar said in his acceptance speech.

Lugar's supporters said the evening's victory was predictable, but important.

"He's a person for all people," said Shari Sinders, of Clay City, Ind. "No one could have beaten him."

see LUGAR, page 8

ids

CONTACT US
Ernie Pyle Hall 120
940 E. 7th Street
Bloomington, IN 47405
855-0760 or ids@indiana.edu

Please recycle

IN PERSPECTIVE
Area man battles Vietnam War memories
PAGE 9

ELECTION 2000
For complete local election coverage.
PAGE 4,5

INDEX

WEATHER
TODAY: Showers. 59 50
TOMORROW: Rain. 58 38
FRIDAY: Partly cloudy. 52 38

P0079379, IU Archives.

SPECIAL EDITION

INDIANA DAILY STUDENT

WEDNESDAY September 12, 2001

Volume 134 • Issue 83 www.idsnews.com 4 pages • Free

DISASTER

World Trade Center gone

Hijacked airplanes crash into twin towers, the Pentagon and a rural Pennsylvania town

David Crary and Jerry Schwartz
The Associated Press

NEW YORK – In the most devastating terrorist onslaught ever waged against the United States, hijackers crashed two airliners into the World Trade Center on Tuesday, toppling its twin towers. The world watched on television as another plane slammed into the Pentagon and a fourth crashed outside Pittsburgh.

"Today, our nation saw evil," President Bush said in an address to the nation Tuesday night. He said thousands of lives were "suddenly ended by evil, despicable acts of terror."

Establishing the death toll could take weeks. The four airliners alone had 266 people aboard, and there were no known survivors. Officials put the number of dead and wounded at the Pentagon at about 100 or more, with some news reports suggesting it could rise to 800.

In addition, a union official said he feared 300 firefighters who first reached the scene had died in rescue efforts at the trade center – where 50,000 people worked – and dozens of police officers were missing.

"The number of casualties will be more than most of us can bear," a visibly distraught Mayor Rudolph Giuliani said.

Police sources said that some people trapped in the twin towers managed to call authorities or family members and that some trapped police officers made radio contact. In one of the calls, which took place in the afternoon, a businessman phoned his family to say he was trapped with policemen, whom he named, the source said.

see DISASTER, page 3

GULNARA SAMOILOVA • THE ASSOCIATED PRESS
People make their way amid debris near the World Trade Center in New York Tuesday. In one of the most horrifying attacks ever against the United States, terrorists crashed two airliners into the World Trade Center in a deadly series of blows that brought down the twin 110-story towers.

CHAO SOI CHEONG • THE ASSOCIATED PRESS
Smoke billows from one of the towers of the World Trade Center, and flames and debris explode from the second tower Tuesday after the New York landmark was hit by terrorist plane attacks. The destruction was one of most horrifying attacks against the United States in history. Damage from the blows caused the twin 110-story towers to crash to the ground.

A city torn apart

Helen O'Neill
The Associated Press

NEW YORK – As night fell, the city moved past the nightmarish scenes of people on fire jumping from buildings and braced itself for more pain: picking through the rubble for the dead and the injured.

Crews began heading into ground zero of the terrorist attack to search for survivors and recover bodies. The downtown area was cordoned off and a huge rescue effort was under way. Gov. George Pataki mobilized the National Guard to help, and hundreds of volunteers and medical workers converged on triage centers, offering services and blood.

One man caught under the rubble used his cell phone to reach family in Pennsylvania with a plea for help.

"She received a call from him saying he was still trapped under the World Trade Center. He gave specific directions and said he was there along with two New York City sergeants," said Brian Jones, 911 coordinator in Allgeheny County. He would not give their names, but said the message was passed to New York authorities.

Paramedics waiting to be sent into the rubble were told that "once the smoke clears, it's going to be massive bodies," according to Brian Stark, an ex-Navy paramedic who volunteered to help. He said the paramedics had been told that "hundreds of police and firefighters are missing" from the ranks of those sent in to respond to the initial crash.

"I hope we get patients," said medical student Eddie Campbell, who rushed to help at one of the centers.

"But they're not coming out. They're in there," he said, pointing down the street to where the World Trade Center once stood.

Emergency Medical Service worker Louis Garcia said initial reports indicated that bodies were buried beneath the two feet of soot on streets around the twin towers. Garcia, a 15-year veteran, said bodies "are all over the place."

Eight hours after the catastrophe began, hundreds of firefighters sat on the West Side Highway or leaned against their rigs, waiting for orders to go into the leveled skyscrapers and search for what they feared would be hundreds of bodies – including many colleagues.

KAMNEKO PAJIC • THE ASSOCIATED PRESS
Rescue workers look over damage at the Pentagon Tuesday. The Pentagon burst into flames and a portion of one side of the five-sided structure collapsed after the building was hit by an aircraft in an apparent terrorist attack.

Bush addresses a nation in chaos

Sandra Sobieraj
The Associated Press

WASHINGTON – A grim-faced President George W. Bush condemned ghastly attacks in Washington and New York on Tuesday and vowed to "find those responsible and bring them to justice."

In the second Oval Office address of his presidency, Bush said the United States would retaliate against "those behind these evil acts," and any country that harbors them.

"Today, our nation saw evil," he said.

Bush said the government offices deserted after the bombings Tuesday would open on Wednesday.

Seeking to comfort an anxious nation, he said, "These acts shattered steel, but they cannot dent the steel of American resolve."

He asked the nation to pray for the families of the victims and quoted the Book of Psalms, "And I pray they will be comforted by a power greater than any of us spoken through the ages in Pslam 23.

In his address, Bush said: "Today, our fellow citizens, our way of life, our very freedom, came under attack in a series of deliberate and deadly terrorist acts." He said thousands of lives were "suddenly ended by evil, despicable acts of terror."

DOUG MILLS • THE ASSOCIATED PRESS
President George W. Bush's Chief of Staff Andy Card whispers into the ear of the commander in chief to give him word of the plane crashes.

ids CONTACT US Ernie Pyle Hall 120, 940 E. 7th Street Bloomington, IN 47405 Newsroom: 855-0760 • Advertising: 855-0763 • Classified: 855-0763 • Fax 855-8009 • E-mail: ids@indiana.edu • www.idsnews.com Please recycle

P0079355, IU Archives.

Fall 2001 Editor-in-Chief Gina Czark with Publisher David L. Adams in December 2001 with IDS staff members Melbert Sebayan, Michael Eisenstadt and Andy Gammill. *Photo courtesy of Rachel Kipp.*

REFLECTION

'Our World Was Changing Before Our Eyes'

I woke up early that Tuesday morning like so many other people. I marveled at how sunny and beautiful it was, but everything changed the second I turned on the television. I watched in horror and disbelief as my hometown of New York and other parts of our country were under attack.

It was Sept. 11, 2001.

I was the editor in chief of the IDS, a position that I longed to hold when I joined the paper my freshman year. You hear about events or moments that test you . . . test your endurance, strength and resolve. This was one of those moments. Even after learning about the first attack, we didn't have a clue of what was to come.

From a communication and technology standpoint, it was a different time. There wasn't widespread cellphone adoption, at least for us college students, and Facebook wasn't a thought for Mark Zuckerberg. We relied on the wire services and the police scanner for most breaking news. Our world was much more isolated in that sense. I remember making a detour to my house that morning just so I could use my home phone to call the newsroom before heading in.

It was humbling and satisfying to see so much of our staff had organically gathered at Ernie Pyle Hall. We didn't say much to each other in those early moments. We were using the phones to check on loved ones, or emailing former graduates who were living in the cities where the attacks happened. We were now in a safe place, and it was clear we felt protected with one another. I remember the professional staff offering hugs and checking in on our staff throughout the day.

We fought through tears as we tried to figure out what was happening and how we would cover the biggest story of our lifetime. We localized the story as much as we could. Classes were canceled; we asked students and professors for their reactions and dispatched staff to the Indianapolis airport and places of worship in Bloomington. We had reporters and photographers who were ready to jump in their cars and head to New York and Washington, but ultimately, we decided there was too much unknown and it wasn't yet safe. A journalist typically is the one who runs toward danger and follows the sirens, but this just felt different, and there was an enormous responsibility to ensure the safety of our team.

I remember all of us gathering around the television as we watched the second tower fall. Andy Gammill, our assistant managing editor, was feverishly monitoring the wires and keeping us updated with things I never thought I'd hear. "They're mobilizing the naval fleet, they're securing the Eastern Seaboard, the White House is likely the next target."

The reports were changing by the minute, and it was hard to dispel fact from fiction. We were cautious, and wisely so. Our updates to the website were thoughtful and responsible. Looking back, I'm so glad social media didn't exist.

We published a special afternoon edition and immediately went back to work on the next day's publication. I remember how painful and sad it was to look through the photos and how impossible it was to keep your emotions in check that day and in the days that followed.

Our world was changing before our eyes, and we knew it. I remember the conversations we had that day and the questions we asked one another. Who did this? Why was it happening? Who's next?

Many of us stayed together near the couches after we put the paper to bed. It was maybe 1 a.m. and even though we were exhausted, we didn't leave. I imagine we stayed because the newsroom was our home and safe haven.

During my time at the IDS, I worked on my fair share of important stories. Bob Knight being disciplined and later fired, Herman B Wells passing away, making it to the Final Four. But Sept. 11 was different. It was one that we didn't want to cover.

It was a defining moment for the country and for us as student journalists. The plans we had for that semester changed, and the content we thought we'd be producing somehow felt less important.

Our country changed that day, and we changed, too.

Sept. 11 is one of those days that, if you lived through it, you'll never forget where you were. I'm so grateful to have been at the IDS, surrounded by amazing and supportive colleagues who were the true definition of compassion and the beauty of humanity.

—Gina Czark, BAJ 2002

"It was a defining moment for the country and for us as student journalists. The plans we had for that semester changed and the content we thought we'd be producing somehow felt less important."

SPECIAL SECTION

INDIANA DAILY STUDENT

FRIDAY
January 18, 2002

Volume 134 • Special Section www.idsnews.com 4 pages • Free

Opening Events Calendar

After 15 years in the making, the dream of the new Theatre/Neal-Marshall Education Center will be realized tomorrow in a day-long, campus-wide celebration. The dedication of the new state-of-the-art facility will feature keynote speakers and actor/activists Ossie Davis and Ruby Dee Friday evening, with workshops, tours and exhibits throughout the day.

All activities are free and open to the public, and no tickets are required for admission.

Friday, Jan. 18

- 9:30-11 a.m.
Theatre Performance Workshop with 12 pre-selected IU students and Ossie Davis and Ruby Dee

Willkie Quad Auditorium

- 2 p.m.
Dedication Ceremony
Keynote Address by Ossie Davis and Ruby Dee

Ruth N. Halls Theatre in the Theatre/Neal-Marshall Education Center

- 4 p.m.
Exhibit Opening: "The Black Experience at Indiana University from 1816-2002"

Bridgwaters Lounge, Neal-Marshall Black Culture Center

- 7:30 p.m.
"An Evening With Ossie Davis and Ruby Dee"

IU Auditorium

For more information, visit *www.indiana.edu/~ceremony.*

COURTESY IU ARCHITECTS

A NEW BEGINNING

Theatre/Neal-Marshall Education Center opens today

Story by Kara Salge • Photos by Zach Dobson and Jessica Stuart

There is a dream on Jordan Avenue.

It's made of limestone and glass, excitement and anticipation.

For about 20 years, the Theatre and Drama Department and the African American Cultural Center have desperately needed new facilities. And after decades of waiting, the Theatre/Neal-Marshall Education Center finally fulfills the dream.

The building includes both the Theatre and Drama Center, with two theaters and studios for the practice of skills such as acting and lighting design, and the Neal-Marshall Black Culture Center, housing the Black Culture Center and the African American Arts Institute, which includes the IU Soul Revue, the African American Choral Ensemble and the African American Dance Company. The Office of Diversity Education and Community and School Partnerships will also move into the facility.

With both groups in need of new facilities since at least the early 1980s, then-IU President Tom Ehrlich suggested in the early 1990s combining the two projects to save time and money, said Clarence Boone, assistant alumni director of the IU Alumni Association.

Now, nearly 20 years after the idea for each expansion was conceived and more than two years after construction began, the 117,000-square foot building formally opens Friday.

AFRICAN-AMERICAN CULTURE

The African American Culture Center, then also known as Black House, was created in 1968. Within a few years, it became apparent a new building would be necessary. A dwindling infrastructure, a desire to expand programming and a need to introduce better technology were main reasons for rebuilding, said Joe Russell, former dean of African-American affairs.

"The idea came about once we were in the Black Culture Center on Jordan Avenue that the facility could not accommodate all the emerging activities that were being developed as well as the mentoring and tutorial program, and we began to look around and think about what would be the next step," Russell said. "The initial thought is to think globally and to think and dream as wide as one can, and that's what we did."

In 1979, a letter was circulated requesting ideas for capital projects. Herman Hudson, who founded the African American Arts Institute and retired as professor emeritus of Afro-American Studies, responded, suggesting a new black cultural center, said Vicki Roberts, assistant vice chancellor for academic support and diversity.

see BEGINNING, page 4

Director welcomed with open arms

"One of the ways we could bridge the gap is to bring people together to celebrate their culture."

Oyibo Afoaku
Director of the Neal-Marshall Black Culture Center

Oyibo Afoaku embraces new role as head of center

Amy Orringer
Indiana Daily Student

When Oyibo Afoaku arrived in the U.S. from Nigeria and began her studies at Washington State University, she immediately saw that something was missing from her history classes. She saw that there were gaps in the information and despite the fact that America was a very diverse place, people were not taking time to embrace diversity.

"The United States is a very international country," she said.

One of the ways we could bridge the gap is to bring people together to celebrate their culture."

This belief quickly became her philosophy and the tenet around which she builds both her life and career.

Afoaku, the recently-appointed head of the Neal-Marshall Black Culture Center, was born in Nigeria and grew up with many brothers and sisters. Although by American standards she has only four brothers that were born of her mother and father, she explained that in Nigeria, cousins are also considered to be siblings.

She was in elementary school when civil war broke out in Nigeria during the late '60s, but she looks back at the experience positively. She remembers being taught to be prepared for an enemy infiltration.

"I learned a lot from it," she said. "I can relate to people (who have been in similar situations)…we had to learn how to survive."

She left Nigeria in 1986 to join her husband at Washington State University; he had moved there just a year earlier. They started their family just two years later and now have four children 5-13-years- old.

When Afoaku was appointed as assistant director of the Marcus Garvey Cultural Center at the University of Northern Colorado in 1996, she knew she had her work cut out for her. According to the 2000 census, the black population of Weld County Colorado, home to UNC, was a mere 0.3 percent.

Ann Heiman, currently a member of the Greenley school board and human relations committee for the city, remembers how Afoaku's appointment opened the door for diversity programming between the university and the community.

"The first thing that struck me about her was that she was very warm and welcoming," Heiman said. "She had so

see DIRECTOR, page 4

ZACH DOBSON • IDS

Oyibo Afoaku sits in her office inside the new Neal-Marshall Black Culture Center.

Groups no longer in HPER

African-American, theater groups cherish changes in new building

Sarah Gates
Indiana Daily Student

Sweat, smiles and scuff marks will no longer exist as the sole evidence of a grueling rehearsal for the African American Dance Company. Now secure in a permanent rehearsal space, the dancers' smiles linger well after the sweat of an intense workout evaporates. Within the walls of their very own dance studio in the new Theatre/Neal-Marshall Education Center, the dancers are no longer required to lock up their equipment after each rehearsal.

Senior Kathy Allender, a member of the company for four years, doesn't stop grinning as she points out one of her favorite aspects of the new studio – the spotless 9-foot mirrors that line three of the four walls encircling it.

"You get the sense of a real dance studio with all these mirrors to help with placement," she said. "We can finally see ourselves dance!"

Since the dance company previously rehearsed in the School of Health, Physical Education, and Recreation (HPER), Allender believes having their own studio will allow the dancers to work at a greater intensity level with less distractions and more opportunity to improve their technique.

Allender hopes that the housing of the

see ARTS, page 4

New theaters welcome addition

Performance areas offer added space, valuable amenities

Joelle Petrus
Indiana Daily Student

Five rows of bleacher-like seats, upholstered with red material comprise the seating of tiny T300 theatre, which senior Sara Bancroft, production manager of "Much Ado About Nothing," described as a "black box."

Today as the Theatre/Neal-Marshall Education Center makes history, the T300 Theatre will join the strata of history. The center will house the African-American Culture and Arts Institutes as well as two new venues for the Theatre and Drama Department.

The building will devote 84,000 square feet of the total 117,000-square foot complex to the Theatre and Drama Department, replacing the T300 studio and the University Theatre.

In the T300 studio, Bancroft pointed out the stage manager's post just two feet behind the last row of audience seating. Stage Managers are responsible for lighting cues and other functions once the show starts. Because of the close range of the audience, they had to rely on non-verbal commands such as hand signals.

"Sometimes we would put glow tape on our fingers so you could see them in the dark," Bancroft said. "There's nothing quite like doing a show in T300."

see THEATER, page 4

ids ERNIE PYLE HALL 120, 940 E. 7TH STREET BLOOMINGTON, IN 47405
NEWSROOM: 855-0760 • ADVERTISING: 855-0763
CLASSIFIED: 855-0763 • FAX: 855-8009
E-MAIL: IDS@INDIANA.EDU
WWW.IDSNEWS.COM
Please recycle

P0079241, IU Archives.

December 13, 2004

CHAMPIONSHIP EDITION

Monday, December 13, 2004

INDIANA DAILY STUDENT

Volume 137 • Issue 149 | www.idsnews.com | 20 pages • Free

CHAMPS REIGN

★ ★ ★ ★ ★ ★ ★

RIC FRANCIS • THE ASSOCIATED PRESS

IU team members mob senior goalie Jay Nolly following Nolly's save of UCSB's final penalty kick. The Hoosiers won the final game 3-2 on penalty kicks, claiming IU's seventh men's soccer national championship.

Hoosiers win 7th national title in penalty kicks

■ IU back-to-back champions behind final Nolly PK save

By Steve Slivka
Indiana Daily Student

CARSON, Calif. – Jay Nolly hasn't missed a single minute of a single game since October 2002. But in all that time, which encompassed a national championship, All-Big Ten selections and 30 shutouts, Nolly saved his best for last.

With IU leading 3-2 on penalty kicks against the University of California-Santa Barbara and the national championship on the line, the senior goalkeeper dove to his left, blocking the final kick and sent IU to its second straight national championship.

"I don't know what else you can do, going out on top twice," Nolly said. "It's just an unbelievable feeling and especially to have your last play be a save to win a championship is just unbelievable."

The national championship game was a rematch from earlier in the season when UCSB defeated the Hoosiers 1-0, when Gaucho freshman Andy Iro scored the lone goal in the 105th minute in the second overtime. That match featured 19 total fouls for UCSB, with IU committing seven.

Junior forward Mike Ambersley was the last shooter for the Hoosiers in the penalty kick situation. Ambersley's shot to the right side of the goal gave IU a 3-2

see SOCCER, page B

CHRIS JESSE • IDS

Senior Danny O'Rourke controls the ball versus UCSB Sunday afternoon in the College Cup final. IU won on penalty kicks, 3-2.

NCAA 2004 MEN'S COLLEGE CUP

SUNDAY: CHAMPIONSHIP

IU 1 – UCSB 1

(SHOOT OUT IU: 3, UCSB: 2)

SATURDAY: FINAL FOUR

IU 3 – Maryland 2

ADDITIONAL COVERAGE:

CHRIS JESSE • IDS

Senior goalie Jay Nolly saves UCSB defender Tony Lochead's penalty shot in Sunday's final game.

■ First-year coach Freitag inspires team to championship

By Brian Janosch
Indiana Daily Student

Breathe in.

Bring all that positive energy in.

Breathe out.

Let out all the negative energy.

IU coach Mike Freitag led his troops into battle with a simple pregame exercise.

Breathe in.

Take in the moment. Senior goalkeeper Jay Nolly is staring University of California-Santa Barbara's Nate Boyden face-to-face with a national championship on the line.

Becerra's foot strikes the ball, and time stands still. Nolly seems to float through the air to his left, when the ball hits his arms, deflects off the ground, and then gently lifts back into the air. It's right about here that things are brought back into full speed.

Breathe out.

The emotion, the affection and the passion of IU soccer flood from every last Hoosier in the stadium and are brought to life in the form of 30

see WIN, page B

P0069333, IU Archives.

The Drive to Be First—and the Torture of Being Wrong

In the movies about newspapers, there's always this scene where the heroes, usually cigarette-smoking foul-mouthed reporters, think they have a scoop. But before they can publish and get their "stop the presses!" moment, they first must persuade a sometimes risk-averse, always old-school editor that the story is airtight.

You know how this plays out: The reporters make their case, the editor seems unsure but eventually comes around, everyone rushes to get the story to Page One just before deadline, world saved, bad guys caught, fade to black, roll credits.

"As for me, of all the stories I worked on over four years at the IDS, McNeely's (or Weiser's) is the one I remember most vividly. Not because I got it right, but because I got it wrong."

Every journalist has their own version of this story, probably (OK, almost definitely) with some embellishments.

I do, too.

Mine just has a shittier ending.

In the spring of 2001, I was the sports editor of the IDS. Looking back, it was a strange time to be in Bloomington. Bob Knight had been fired the semester before, and on the way out, he staged what today resembles a small coup to oust President Myles Brand.

Brand himself was soon to leave IU to run the NCAA. Ken Gros Louis, the school's longtime chancellor, had announced plans to retire in the summer. On top of it all, longtime Athletics Director Clarence Doninger was turning 65 and being forced to retire as well.

Who would replace Doninger mattered for a lot of reasons, most starting with questions about whether interim basketball coach Mike Davis would replace Knight permanently.

Our reporting, corroborated by others chasing the story, had narrowed the possibilities down to two—Tim Weiser, the athletics director at Colorado State University, and Michael McNeely, an executive with the San Diego Chargers who had served as AD at the University of the Pacific. We also knew an announcement was imminent.

So, on Feb. 27, 2001, a Tuesday, we went to work. I wrote a short story that evening summarizing what we knew while we tried to figure out if Brand had picked Weiser or McNeely. We called every member of the Board of Trustees and checked in with anyone who we thought might have a clue which way Brand was leaning.

The calls mostly got us nowhere. Some trustees just wouldn't talk to us. Others that would weren't looped into a decision as big as this.

But then there was a person I'll call Mr. Shiny. I'm not revealing Mr. Shiny's identity because we spoke off the record. Mr. Shiny took our calls and seemed plugged in. Mr. Shiny had great relationships with journalists. Mr. Shiny was the type of person who handed out his cellphone and home phone numbers to anyone who asked and whom you could always count on for a quote. Mr. Shiny said he knew about the negotiations and that a decision had been made about who the next athletic director would be.

Well, who is it?

Mr. Shiny wouldn't say. At least at first.

As we pressed and pressed, Mr. Shiny offered the clue. "Look to Colorado."

Mr. Shiny never said it was Weiser. But he couldn't have been more obvious.

Like the team in the movies, we raced to beat deadline.

According to the archives, the story went live at 1:34 a.m., Feb. 28, 2001:

"Athletics director chosen," read the headline (I remember arguing for something way more emphatic, like "It's Weiser.") The subhead: "Brand expected to name Weiser to position."

We talked to a football coach at Colorado State who had seen Weiser at a Ft. Collins restaurant that evening and had said Weiser was acting nervous. We also reached Weiser's wife, who wouldn't confirm or deny our reporting. Reading the story today, you can see the hesitancy in our voices, from the headline on down. For good reason.

Here's the shitty ending.

Within 12 hours of publishing our scoop, Denver television stations reported that Weiser withdrew his name from consideration. Not long after that, Brand announced McNeely as the next athletics director at Indiana.

We were wrong . . . big and fat on the front page.

To this day, I do not know if Mr. Shiny led us down the wrong road, or if Weiser backed out, or if Brand changed his mind. It doesn't really matter. For what it's worth, Brand said McNeely was always the pick.

McNeely would go on to flop at IU, lasting just 16 months while leaving the athletics department with a $3.2 million deficit.

As for me, of all the stories I worked on over four years at the IDS, McNeely's (or Weiser's) is the one I remember most vividly. Not because I got it right, but because I got it wrong.

The IDS taught me to be a journalist, and it helped prepare me for internships at The Indianapolis Star and the then-St. Petersburg Times. It's the reason I was hired by the Times in 2003, and why I covered politics and government there for seven years.

Fall 2002 Editor-in-Chief Aaron Sharockman poses with the Herman B Wells statue on campus. *Photo courtesy of IDS.*

In some ways, looking back, it's also the reason I came to work for PolitiFact, first as a fact-checker, then as an editor and executive director.

I learned that the sources who are most eager to talk to you are also sometimes the ones you can least trust. That the insatiable drive to be first is nothing compared to the torture of being wrong. That those who are earnest deserve second chances.

And, of course, that facts matter.

—*Aaron Sharockman, BAJ 2003*

CHILD ISSUES

Regional experts share thoughts on Laura Bush's speech

see page 3

Is quarry swimming the safest way to beat the heat?

see WEEKEND

INSIDE CAMPUS

Business school to host world's entrepreneurs

see page 2

TODAY
HIGH 83
LOW 58
FRIDAY
HIGH 78
LOW 56

INDIANA DAILY STUDENT

VOLUME 139, ISSUE 54 — THURSDAY, JUNE 8, 2006 — FREE • 12 PAGES

IUPD looks at potential hate crime

■ Student finds anti-Muslim remarks written outside dorm

By Carly Dachis
cdachis@indiana.edu

The IU Police Department is investigating an incident in which the word "Terrorist" was written outside a student's dorm room. The student is of Middle Eastern descent, according to the reports.

According to police reports, the student left his Eigenmann Hall dorm room at about 12:30 a.m., Saturday, and returned at about 2 a.m. to find the word written in a dry-erase board marker on his door.

The 27-year-old student contacted his resident assistant, who then contacted the police, IU police spokesman, Lt. Jerry Minger said. Their procedure is to remove the graffiti as soon as possible from the site, he said.

"He did seem quite upset according to the officers that responded," Minger said. "We advised him if he has any problems or has any idea who it was, to contact us immediately."

Minger said there were no witnesses to the incident

see **CRIME**, page 12

REED SAXON • THE ASSOCIATED PRESS

Participants share a moment of silence at a ceremony commemorating the 25th anniversary of the detailed discovery of human immunodeficiency virus and AIDS.

IU receives $8.9 million for AIDS work

■ Gift comes as world marks 25th anniversary of the disease

By Zack Teibloom
zteibloo@indiana.edu

HIV/AIDS prevention in Africa got a timely boost thanks to an $8.9 million federal grant to the IU School of Medicine, which will triple the number of patients that can be treated in Kenya. The president's Emergency Plan for AIDS Relief contributed the money to complement the $15 million they gave to IU in 2004.

The grant comes just in time for the 25th anniversary of AIDS being recognized as a disease, which has killed more than 22 million people since 1982, according to the Web site *until.org*.

The funds will go to HIV treatment clinics IU has set up in Kenya and will provide treatment, including screening programs for pregnant women, and education and training for medical personnel in AIDS-ravaged Kenya. IU has a partnership with Moi University, located in Kenya, which is involved in using the resources that IU provides to give HIV prevention and treatment.

"This funding will save tens of thousands of lives," said Robert Einterz, associate dean for International Programs in the School of Medicine and director of the IU-Moi program. "Both directly, in numbers of people prevented from getting HIV, and extending the lives of thousands more infected with HIV."

More than 42 million people are living with HIV/AIDS worldwide, and almost 75 percent of those infected

see **AIDS**, page 12

Mourning After

AARON BERNSTEIN • IDS

Indianapolis Mayor Bart Peterson takes a moment to reflect prior to the vigil held Sunday for Emma Valdez, 56, who was killed along with six of her family members during a home invasion robbery last Thursday. Hundreds of friends, family and community leaders attended the vigil.

Gathering reflects on lives of slain Indianapolis family

By Sarah Core
score@indiana.edu

Stuffed animals, handwritten cards, lit candles and enormous bouquets and wreaths of flowers tumbled against the fence bordering the neat one-story beige house the Covarrubias-Valdez family had called home. On the porch, a wind chime in the shape of the cross fluttered silently.

The gentle roar of a jumbo jet flying above the street was the only noise that broke through the quiet stillness of Sunday evening's memorial service for the seven members of the East-side family, who were killed last Thursday night in Indianapolis. Police and public officials are calling the home invasion the worst case of mass murder the city has seen in more than 25 years.

"By coming together as a community, I think we sent a powerful message," Indianapolis Mayor Bart Peterson said in a phone interview, reflecting on the weekend event. "To see unity and hope come out of that was uplifting."

Wednesday, mourners gathered at a collective funeral for six of the seven slain last Thursday.

But Sunday's remembrance was unique in its spontaneity. Three days after the rampage occurred, the bold blue sky and sunlit street bore no trace of the screams and gunshots heard by the neighbors, save a thin stripe of yellow police tape in front of the house on Emerson Street and the mass of almost 1,000 people that had gathered. It was the crowd that was most remarkable.

Just five rows of chairs had been set up in front of a small tent on the sidewalk, but as the 6 p.m. service began, the number of people spilled out past the street and sidewalks, onto neighbor's yards and porches. They were black, white and Hispanic, praying side-by-side. And they were all there to honor the memory of Alberto Covarrubias, 56, and his wife Emma Valez, 46, along with their children and grandchild. They were there to begin to heal from the murders that had tried to tear the community apart.

see **VIGIL**, page 12

Traffic restriction to close part of 10th Street

■ West-bound cars rerouted between Union and Jordan

From IDS reports

For the next couple of months motorists on 10th Street will soon see significant traffic restrictions that will close down part of road, IU officials announced.

According to a press release, beginning Monday construction for the Ashton housing complex will close all west-bound traffic on 10th Street between Union Street and Jordan Avenue. Traffic will be rerouted to Law Lane and Jordan Avenue before 10th Street reopens west of Jordan Avenue. East-bound traffic on 10th Street will be restricted to the west-bound lane of 10th Street between Campbell Street and the entrance to Crosstown Shopping Center.

TRAFFIC RE-ROUTING

• West-bound traffic on 10th St. will be re-routed north at Union St. to Jordan Ave.

• East-bound traffic on 10th St. will be restricted to the west-bound lane of 10th St.

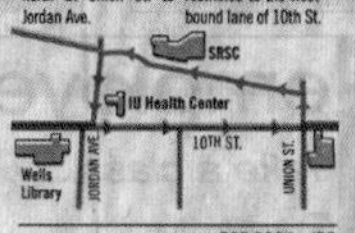

ROB BOCK • IDS

The restrictions will continue until Aug. 23 when full two-way traffic will be restored to 10th Street. However, utility work will proceed outside the 10th Street right-of-way through October, according to the statement.

The purpose of the construction is to replace the steam, condensate and domestic water piping serving the nine-building complex.

First lady speaks at IUPUI

■ Bush promotes helping youth in speech Tuesday

By David A. Nosko
dnosko@indiana.edu

INDIANAPOLIS – First lady Laura Bush swung through the Hoosier heartland Tuesday to share her love and dedication to American young people, saying adults are the most instrumental agent of positive direction and change for millions of at-risk children across the country.

"When adults offer young people a chance, their love and support can show struggling youth the hope that lies beyond their future, sometimes that hope makes all the difference," Bush told a gathering of about 150 Midwest community members during the Helping America's Youth first regional conference at the IUPUI campus near downtown Indianapolis.

The regional conference follows an Oct. 2005 White House Conference on Helping America's Youth held at Howard University in Washington D.C., at which more than 500 parents, civic leaders, faith-based and community service providers, foundations, educators, researchers and experts in child development convened to discuss modern challenges young people confront on a daily basis and to develop community strategies to better improve their safety, health and chances of a successful future. Bush said she has also traveled across the nation to visit schools, attend after-school programs and greet the mentors of young people at social service agencies like Big Brothers Big Sisters.

"The work that each of you do in your communities helping young people build the knowledge and self-respect they need to live successful lives is at the very heart of the Helping America's Youth," Bush said. "While the discussions in our state and national capitals are important, the

see **BUSH**, page 12

ids

Ernie Pyle Hall 120, 940 E. 7th Street
Bloomington, IN 47405
Newsroom: 855-0760 • Advertising: 855-0763

Classified: 855-0763 • Fax: 855-8009
E-mail: ids@indiana.edu
www.idsnews.com

INDEX

PLEASE RECYCLE

P0079210, IU Archives.

October 31, 2006

INDIANA DAILY STUDENT

VOLUME 139, ISSUE 122 — TUESDAY, OCTOBER 31, 2006 — FREE • 14 PAGES

MYERS GUILTY

JURY TAKES LESS THAN AN HOUR TO RETURN VERDICT IN BEHRMAN TRIAL

ASHLEY WILKERSON • IDS

Police escort John R. Myers II from the Morgan County Courthouse after a jury found him guilty of the 2000 murder of IU sophomore Jill Behrman.

Behrman family finds some solace in court's ruling

By Sarah Core
score@indiana.edu

MARTINSVILLE – The tension in the Morgan County courtroom was thick Monday evening, the small, uncomfortable seats packed with a silent audience of friends, family and the media, all there to hear the ruling in the murder trial of John R. Myers II.

As they waited, Marilyn Behrman, sitting in the front row, reached over and patted her son Brian on the back, her other hand holding several squares of folded tissue in her lap. After 6 1/2 years, the man the Behrmans believed killed their daughter, IU sophomore Jill Behrman, was about to receive a verdict.

Behrman disappeared May 31, 2000, after she went on an early morning bicycle ride. Her remains were found in 2003 by hunters near Paragon, Ind.

Only three jury members glanced toward the defendant's table as they filed in. With a calm demeanor, Myers, 31, stood and listened as Judge Christopher Burnham read

see **FAMILY**, page 6

Sentencing scheduled for Dec. 1; Myers faces up to 65 years

By Chris Freiberg
wfreiber@indiana.edu

MARTINSVILLE – It took a jury of his peers 50 minutes to find John R. Myers II guilty of the 2000 murder of IU sophomore Jill Behrman.

Myers remained stoic, as he had throughout most of the 11-day trial, as Judge Christopher Burnham read the verdict. Myers, 31, hugged defense attorney Patrick Baker and, as police led him out of the courtroom in handcuffs, winked at his family, clicked his tongue and said simply, "Love ya."

Jill's parents, Eric and Marilyn Behrman, told reporters afterward they were relieved the trial was over.

"We're pleased with the jury's decision," Eric Behrman said. "We know it was hard for them to make."

Jill Behrman vanished during a morning bike ride May 31, 2000. Her bicycle was found two days later in a cornfield outside Ellettsville, less than a mile from the trailer Myers was living in at the time. Hunters found her skeletal remains in March 2003 near Paragon, Ind.

see **VERDICT**, page 6

ASHLEY WILKERSON • IDS

Jurors No. 31, 85, 54, 64 and 40 prepare to speak to the media. The jurors asked that their names not be used.

Professors 'shocked' by quick verdict

By Kristi Oloffson
koloffso@indiana.edu

IU legal experts said they were surprised that a Morgan County jury found John R. Myers II guilty of the 2000 murder of IU sophomore Jill Behrman after less than an hour of deliberation Monday.

The prosecution based its case entirely on circumstantial evidence.

Law professor Craig M. Bradley said it was strange that the jury returned the verdict so quickly.

"I'm shocked, I have to say," he said. "I can never remember seeing a case where the prosecution's evidence was so thin."

Bradley said he has not formed an opinion about whether Myers is actually guilty, but he said he believes the evidence did not prove his guilt beyond a reasonable doubt.

The speed of the verdict also surprised journalism professor Tony Fargo, who teaches communications law. Fargo said he has covered murder cases with obvious verdicts in which the juries deliberated longer than this jury did.

see **REACTION**, page 6

DEVELOPING STORY

FBI raids Ph.D. student's apartment, investigates Web site

■ Site generated fake Northwest Airlines tickets

By Carrie Ritchie
ccritchi@indiana.edu

The FBI and Transportation Security Administration are investigating an IU doctoral student who created a Web site that generated fake Northwest Airlines boarding passes. Informatics graduate student Chris Soghoian reported Friday on his blog that the FBI showed up at his home in Bloomington and demanded he take down the Web site. That same day, Massachusetts Congressman Edward Markey publicly called for his arrest because of the site.

The site has since been taken down.

Soghoian, who is working on a Ph.D. in Informatics with a focus in computer security, said he created the Web site to call attention to a "security hole" in airport regulations, according to his blog at *http://slightparanoia.blogspot.com/*. However, he never printed or used a fake boarding pass, he wrote in the blog. Soghoian said in an e-mail to the Indiana Daily Student his lawyers are not allowing him to comment to the press at this time.

Markey, a Democrat, has since recanted his statement against Soghoian, saying in a different statement Soghoian "intended no harm but, rather, intended to provide a public service by warning that this long-standing loophole could be easily exploited." However, the FBI and TSA are still investigating the case, said FBI Special Agent Wendy Osborne of the bureau's

see **RAID**, page 6

■ Project might be linked to graduate research at IU

By Carrie Ritchie
ccritchi@indiana.edu

IU Ph.D. student Chris Soghoian is facing scrutiny from the FBI and the Transportation Security Administration for research he might have been doing for the University. IU is "reviewing" the case to see whether Soghoian's Web site, which generated fake Northwest Airlines boarding passes, has University ties, said IU Director of Media Relations Larry MacIntyre.

Soghoian, who intends to earn his doctorate in Informatics with a focus in computer security, created the site to point out a "loophole" in airport security but never printed or used a fake boarding pass, according to his blog at *http://slightparanoia.blogspot.com*.

No criminal charges have been filed at this time, but MacIntyre said the University began its investigation Friday afternoon when

see **SITE**, page6

- **WEDNESDAY:** Graduate student creates site that generates fake boarding passes.
- **FRIDAY:** Congressman calls for student's arrest. FBI, TSA begin investigations.
- **SATURDAY:** FBI agents secure search warrant, forcibly enter student's Bloomington residence.

ids
Ernie Pyle Hall 120, 940 E. 7th Street
Bloomington, IN 47405
Newsroom: 855-0760 • Advertising: 855-0763

Classified: 855-0763 • Fax: 855-8009
E-mail: ids@indiana.edu
www.idsnews.com

INDEX

PLEASE RECYCLE

P0079184, IU Archives.

REFLECTION

On Diversity at the IDS and in Daily Life

As a black person, or African American (a term that honestly has never made sense to me), I am often asked about diversity issues.

Shocking, I know.

During my wonder/blunder years in Bloomington, I was the recipient of a scholarship for high-achieving minorities, which was called—wait for it—the Minority Achievement Program. During my tenure, the program was combined with another minority scholarship and renamed after two prominent black IU professors.

We were no longer minority achievers. We were Hudson-Holland Scholars.

The name change was probably for the best. Just like the illustrious Wells Scholars, our tuition checks would bear the name of great IU figures. We could finally talk openly about our scholarships without getting the kind of side-eye that only comes when white people feel like black people are getting something they are not.

Right now, you're thinking, what does this have to do with diversity at the IDS? Well, let's start with this: In 2016, IU's Bloomington campus proudly announced that a record number of "African American" students had enrolled. That number was just under 2,000. The total student body was over 43,000. Those numbers aren't much different from when I started there in 2001. I can make an educated guess that they aren't much better now.

Black people aren't the only minorities (obviously), so let's add in the other numbers as well. When we're all combined, we still make up only a quarter of the IU student body. Now, for the sake of argument, split them up evenly among the dozens of academic programs. Then ask some of them to set fire to their parents' dreams of having a doctor in the family and decide instead to be a journalist.

I am always of two minds when I think back on my time at the IDS. I learned more working there than I did in most of my classes. I met people who are still my friends to this day, as well as people with whom I've lost touch but will never forget. I practically lived in Ernie Pyle Hall and shared some unforgettable moments there, too.

I was also at times incredibly lonely. There are many staff photos where I am the only brown face on display. I lost count of the number of times I had to tell the editors that I wasn't the only person who could cover "black stories." There were moments where I felt like I was the newspaper's human shield against accusations of racism or bias. In the tug-of-war among liberals, conservatives, minorities, racists and angry administrators, I was often the rope in the middle. My experience is why diversity matters, but it's also why diversity can't be just a numbers game.

"In the tug-of-war among liberals, conservatives, minorities, racists and angry administrators, I was often the rope in the middle. My experience is why diversity matters, but it's also why diversity can't be just a numbers game."

One of my favorite pithy apocryphal anecdotes is the idea that equality will come when blacks, whites and others can all be equally mediocre. Many art critics actually consider the "Mona Lisa" to be a mediocre painting. However, because of the public's perception of that painting, it is encased in glass at the Louvre and gawked at by millions of people every year. Whenever black and brown people have to fly solo in nearly completely white spaces, we are like that painting. In God's eyes, we're just another one of his many children. The crowds of people surrounding us, however, are free to project whatever they want onto us, and there is little we can do about it.

When I was asked to write this essay, I searched for my name on the IDS website. I needed to remind myself what I had written back when I was young and impressionable. I am proud to say I fill eight whole pages of search results. I can also say that one of the first results was an ombudsman column I'd written attempting to explain why one of the IDS opinion writers was free to question the utility of Black History Month. The further back I looked, the more I realized that I've covered all these issues before.

I challenge you this—go to idsnews.com. First, donate to the paper. After that, search for my name. You'll see headlines such as "When Free Speech Attacks," "On Offense Against Offensiveness," and "I See Black People!" I'm not asking you to be impressed with the journalistic output from my college days. I'm asking you to consider why, nearly 20 years later, I and other minorities have to keep telling these same stories over and over again.

—George Lyle IV, BAJ 2005

INDIANA DAILY STUDENT

VOLUME 140, ISSUE 174 — THURSDAY, FEBRUARY 14, 2008 — FREE • 20 PAGES

BADGERED
Hoosiers lose to Wisconsin 68-66 PAGE 14

SAMPSON'S JOB
Coach's contract could be voided after investigation PAGE 14

EDITORIAL
IDS editorial board weighs in on Sampson's future PAGE 8

LIES?

'I have never intentionally provided false or misleading information to the NCAA.'

-IU men's basketball coach Kelvin Sampson at Wednesday's press conference

JACOB KRIESE • IDS

IU men's basketball head coach, Kelvin Sampson, responds to media questions after Wednesday night's game against Wisconsin. The NCAA had just released a report that accused Sampson and the IU program of committing five major violations.

Mixed reaction greets Sampson at Assembly Hall

By Chris Engel
ccengel@indiana.edu

IU coach Kelvin Sampson received a mixed reaction when he stepped onto the court Wednesday night at Assembly Hall before his No. 13 men's basketball team battled No. 15 Wisconsin.

Sampson did not take the floor until less than two minutes before introductions. A crowd of cameras and people lined the path from the locker room to get a view of the Hoosier coach.

IDS online poll results

Should Kelvin Sampson keep his job?

Yes: 23 percent (118 votes)
No: 77 percent (374 votes)

When Sampson was announced in pre-game introductions, he received boos and cheers from the Hoosier faithful in Assembly Hall. Some students showed their support for Sampson by sporting the blue shirt and red tie combination the coach wears every game.

Despite the mixed reaction in the introduction, when the ball was tipped, the fans supported the team with the same intensity they have had in any big game during the Sampson era.

Throughout Wednesday, IU basketball message boards and blogs were filled with Hoosier fans calling for Sampson's job and discussing possible replacements for the second-year coach. Before the Wisconsin game, most Hoosier fans that talked to the IDS were disappointed in Sampson and thought the program should move in a different direction.

IU junior Matt Levinson said he was upset with the recent allegations.

"It's no surprise," Levinson said. "I already knew it was coming."

Levinson, a self-described long-time Hoosier basketball fan, said he was disappointed in Sampson's actions because they damaged the reputation of a program that has long prided itself on following the rules.

see REACTION, page 10

NCAA alleges Sampson, staff committed five 'major violations'

By Michael Sanserino
msanseri@indiana.edu

IU men's basketball coach Kelvin Sampson lied to University and NCAA investigators about his role in recruiting violations, according to an NCAA report IU released Wednesday.

IU Director of Athletics Rick Greenspan did not confirm or deny whether there had been any discussion to terminate Sampson's contract.

Sampson denied Wednesday he lied to investigators.

After investigating illegal recruiting phone calls Sampson and his staff made, the NCAA alleged they committed five "major violations."

Greenspan said Sampson, whose contract with IU has a clause that allows the University to fire him if there are NCAA-related improprieties, will continue to coach into the foreseeable future.

"We have work to do," Greenspan said during a press conference Wednesday. "While we're going to be expedient, which I think is what is expected of us, we're also not going to rush to judgment and have a faulty conclusion."

> "I am personally and professionally and profoundly disappointed that there is even a hint of inappropriate behavior."
>
> -Rick Greenspan, IU athletics director, at a press conference regarding NCAA allegations against IU

The NCAA levied a major violations tag on Sampson because it reported the coach was not truthful with investigators regarding his role in IU's recruiting violations.

"Sampson ... (provided) the institution and the NCAA enforcement staff false or misleading information," the report reads.

The NCAA specifically alleges Sampson lied when he told investigators he did not know he was participating in impermissible three-way recruiting phone calls.

After IU's 68-66 loss to Wisconsin on Wednesday night, Sampson said he did not "intentionally" lie to investigators.

"The allegations that I knowingly acted contrary to the sanctions ... are not true," Sampson said, reading from a prepared statement. "I have never intentionally provided false or misleading information to the NCAA."

Sampson refused to answer any questions regarding the NCAA allegations, including one whether he had considered resigning.

Greenspan declined to comment on

see ALLEGATIONS, page 10

IU recruits still analyzing new allegations

By Jordan Cohen
cohenjs@indiana.edu

With the revelation of the five major NCAA infractions allegedly committed by IU coach Kelvin Sampson and his coaching staff, any lingering IU recruiting questions have exploded to a new level.

Four players have signed letters of intent to play for the Hoosiers next year, one high school junior has verbally committed to IU and numerous other recruits have been on IU's radar. They are now faced with a dilemma and are unsure of what their college basketball futures may hold.

"I just called (IU assistant coach Jeff Meyer) today to talk about it," said Derek Elston, the 6-foot-8 small forward who verbally committed to IU for the 2009-10 season. "They said that I'm still part of the family and I still love all those guys down there. I made a commitment and I'm going to stay with it. No matter what, I'm going to stick with it."

Elston's father, Darrell, a former North Carolina guard, said he was unaware of the "impermissible recruiting contact" when it happened but was sure that a high school player would not realize it was a violation. As for the overall situation with Sampson, Elston's father hopes the situation doesn't become too severe. He said the recently announced violations will have some impact on his son's college decision.

"I just hope that this is not real serious because Derek really enjoys this coaching staff and is pretty much set on going to IU," he said. "If it becomes a little bit bigger, then I would hope he doesn't change his mind. I hope it isn't anything major."

Terrell Holloway, one of the class of 2008 signees, said he is concerned about any possible postseason sanctions or coaching changes, but said he does not know much about the situation.

"I have to be concerned with the situation, because it has to do with me," he said.

When Holloway signed his national letter of intent in November, he said he was aware of Sampson's October violations, but "this is obviously something new."

Holloway said he was not in a position to comment on the possibility of a new coach

see RECRUITS, page 10

ON THE WEB, IDSNEWS.COM

PODCAST Download a special edition of 'That's What He Said'

DOCUMENTS See what the NCAA said regarding IU's violations

VIDEO Watch Rick Greenspan's Wednesday press conference

SLIDESHOW Check out photos from Wednesday's events

A TROUBLED HISTORY

The problems that followed Kelvin Sampson to IU have continued throughout his tenure.

MARCH 29, 2006 Kelvin Sampson, in the middle of a recruiting investigation, leaves Oklahoma and is named IU's head coach following the resignation of Mike Davis.

NOV. 8, 2006 Eric Gordon signs his national letter of intent to play at Indiana after renouncing his commitment to Illinois.

MAY 24, 2007 The NCAA bans Sampson from making phone calls to recruits and participating in off-campus recruiting for one year. The NCAA cited a three-year investigation at Oklahoma where he and his staff made 577 excessive phone calls to 17 recruits from 2000 to 2004.

JULY 2007 IU Athletics Director Rick Greenspan says internal investigations began at IU to see whether Sampson violated the terms of the NCAA's sanctions.

OCT. 14, 2007 IU announces the men's basketball team will forfeit one scholarship for the 2008-09 season. Sampson was denied his scheduled $500,000 pay raise. IU's report prompts a full-on investigation by the NCAA into possible infractions.

OCT. 30, 2007 Assistant coach Rob Senderoff resigns amidst scandal. Senderoff admitted to making the majority of the impermissible phone calls to recruits.

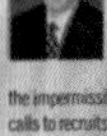

NOV. 1, 2007 Sampson claims satisfaction with IU's report and punishment for actions related to recruiting violations.

DEC. 22, 2007 Junior DeAndre Thomas and IU recruit Devin Ebanks admit to participating in three-way phone calls with Sampson, which is a violation of NCAA sanctions.

FEB. 13, 2008 IU announces the NCAA's alleged violations against Sampson. The NCAA found Sampson and his staff made five "major" violations and said Sampson gave false or misleading information to NCAA investigators.

ids — Ernie Pyle Hall 120, 940 E. 7th Street, Bloomington, IN 47405, Newsroom: 855-0760 • Advertising: 855-0763

Classified: 855-0763 • Fax: 855-8009, E-mail: ids@indiana.edu, www.idsnews.com

PLEASE RECYCLE

P0079213, IU Archives.

November 5, 2008

WEDNESDAY, NOVEMBER 5, 2008

INDIANA DAILY STUDENT

★ COMMEMORATIVE ELECTION EDITION ★

'THIS IS OUR MOMENT'

Obama makes history as first black man elected president

BY BEN PHELPS | phelpsb@indiana.edu

CHICAGO

Yes they did.

The chant shouted Tuesday night was only a two-word modification of the one yelled throughout the previous 21 months of Barack Obama's campaign.

But the difference was enormous.

Shortly before midnight, Obama took center stage in Grant Park and greeted thousands of screaming supporters as the next president of the United States.

SEE OBAMA | PAGE 54

ON IDSNEWS.COM

VIDEO SLIDESHOWS POLITIKER BLOG

MORRY GASH | THE ASSOCIATED PRESS

P0079378, IU Archives.

Publisher David L. Adams on campus soon after being hired in 1989. *Photo courtesy of IDS.*

PROFILE

David L. Adams
Director of student media and publisher, 1989–2007

This article originally appeared June 4, 2007, after Adams' death.

By Alberto D. Morales

An amazing friend and mentor to all of us here passed away Saturday. David Adams, director of student media, died from causes yet unknown.

His job title and description cannot begin to describe the many duties this great man did for student media nationwide.

As a student press advocate, Dave was a vehement supporter of free student press at all levels of education. As such, he was an outspoken critic in a recent scandal involving the retaliatory firing of the Woodlan Junior-Senior High School newspaper advisor in East Allen County. Lately, we had developed a ritual of sitting in his office together debating the case's ramifications for the First Amendment. In the precious little time I was privileged to know the man, he instilled in me his tremendous knowledge of student media, for which I am eternally grateful.

The first time I met Dave was while he was investigating the unwarranted firing of Karen Bosley, the advisor at my former college newspaper, the Viking News, at Ocean

County College in New Jersey. When the story blew up onto the national press scene, Dave, along with Tom Eveslage of Temple University, came to OCC to investigate the firing on behalf of College Media Advisers. Due in part to Dave's tireless efforts, Bosley was eventually reinstated by a temporary restraining order issued by a federal judge.

Dave met with me and former editors of the paper to ask what we believed to be the true causes for Bosley's dismissal. Then he proudly provided me a copy of the IDS. When I saw the paper, I was awestruck by how professional it looked. I knew I had to be a part of it. When I told Dave I wanted to apply to IU and write for the IDS, I sense he was more excited than my own parents would be.

Even after the investigation was over and Dave released his findings in a report with College Media Advisers, he and I kept in touch via email. He always tried to keep my spirits up, despite the incredibly depressing retaliation I experienced from the administrators at OCC.

When two other editors of the Viking News and I filed a lawsuit against the college to address Bosley's dismissal, Dave found a way to make me feel proud of my decision to go up against that administration. "Certainly, this will be a year you will remember the rest of your life Alberto, and I'm blessed to have come to know you through this difficult situation, too," Dave wrote to me in a May 12, 2006 email. "I really, really hope we get to work together next year or in the future."

And I did get to work with him. He and Bosley pushed me to apply to IU so I could hone my craft and be part of an amazing staff. But the reason I came here was because I knew Dave would take me under his wing and teach me everything he knew, from student media to First Amendment issues. Unfortunately, at the time of his passing, he had only just begun.

INDIANA DAILY STUDENT

MONDAY, JUNE 4, 2007

DR. DAVID L. ADAMS
1947 – 2007

STUDENT MEDIA MOURNS

IU Student Media Director dies at age 59

'He knew so much, and in him passing we will lose so much'

FORMER STUDENT MEDIA STAFFERS REMEMBER BELOVED LEADER

Katie Schoembaechler, fall 2004 managing editor

Brandon Morely, IDS staffer from 2002-2004

Josh Sanburn, spring 2005 editor-in-chief

Online only: For more coverage and reactions see *idsnews.com* and page 6

P0079376, IU Archives.

While looking through my collection of emails from Dave, I found more words of encouragement regarding my fear of IU—and gosh, I was afraid. But like he did with so many other students, Dave told me to keep my chin up and not to be scared.

"I do understand your fear," Dave told me in an email. "But, sometimes, it's important to walk on through your fears and know that sometimes, fear is often a myth that disables us from doing what we need to do."

BEHIND THE STORY

Ending the Semester with a Splash

Fall 2001 editors Mike Eisenstadt, Melbert Sebayan, Gina Czark and Laura Ewald take a swim in the Jordan River. *Photo courtesy of Rachel Kipp.*

No IDS editor in chief can ever predict how his or her tenure will go. But for the past few decades, they all know how the semester will end—with a swim in the "mighty" Jordan River. No matter the weather, after the final slash of the semester, the entire staff accompanies the editor and the management team for the traditional dunk in the world's most creek-like river. Some management teams get T-shirts made, some bring swimsuits, and plenty of splashing usually ensues.

Spring 2000 managing editor Heather Dinich is carried to the Jordan by staffer David Uchiyama. *Photo courtesy of Rachel Kipp.*

Below, A playful battle between IDS staffers ensues after the IDS Final Slash on Friday, May 1, 2009, in the Jordan River outside of Ernie Pyle Hall. *Photo courtesy of James Brosher.*

Ben Phelps, IDS multimedia director, prepares to throw design chief Sara Amato into the Jordan River as editor in chief Michael Sanserino, left, assists after the IDS Final Slash on Friday, May 1, 2009, outside of Ernie Pyle Hall. *Photo courtesy of James Brosher.*

Below, Rebecca Kimberly, Michael Majchrowicz, Evan Hoopfer and Lacey Hoopengardner take the plunge circa 2015. *Photo courtesy of Ruth Witmer.*

2009–Present

The transition to digital journalism continued to present challenges for the IDS in the 2010s, but it also presented opportunities for innovation in online storytelling. In 2017, the IDS celebrated its 150th anniversary while also moving to twice-weekly print publication. Even as the journalism program was folded once again into the university's College of Arts and Sciences and left Ernie Pyle Hall, the IDS continues to be recognized as one of the best collegiate newspapers in the nation.

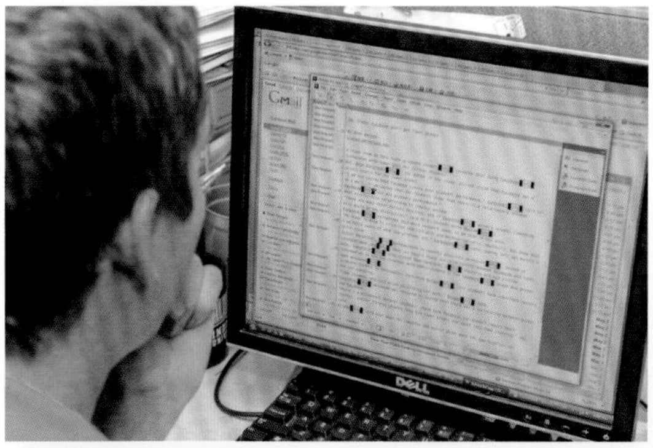

First row left, An IDS staffer edits copy in Ernie Pyle Hall. *Photo courtesy of James Brosher.*

First row right, Sara Amato and Ruth Witmer during a slash meeting of the IDS staff. *Photo courtesy of James Brosher.*

Second row left, IDS staffers wait for results to in on election night in 2012. *Photo courtesy of Caitlin O'Hara.*

Second row right, The spring 2014 IDS staff gets into the Jordan River after the paper's final slash meeting. *Photo courtesy of Caitlin O'Hara.*

Third row left, Editor-in-Chief Gage Bentley signs Ernie Pyle's desk drawer, an IDS tradition. *Photo courtesy of Caitlin O'Hara.*

Third row right, An IDS staffer takes a cell phone photo of historic IDS bound volumes. *Photo courtesy of Caitlin O'Hara.*

Fourth row left, Alden Woods gives a speech at final slash in Ernie Pyle Hall. *Photo courtesy of Ruth Witmer.*

Fourth row right, Students hold up the IDS at an IU basketball game at Assembly Hall in Bloomington. *Photo courtesy of IDS.*

MONDAY, APRIL 26, 2010

INDIANA DAILY STUDENT

VOLUME 143 • ISSUE 41 www.idsnews.com FREE • 18 PAGES

INDEPENDENTS' DAY

MEN'S LITTLE 500

Cutters become 1st team ever to 4-peat in men's race history

BY NATHAN HART
nmhart@indiana.edu

With a race victory seemingly at hand, Cutters began celebrating its record-breaking fourth consecutive Little 500 title.

And 96 laps later, the Cutters celebrated again.

A frenzied and sometimes-confusing Men's Little 500 race Saturday afternoon featured torrential rain, a 50-minute delay and uncharted weather decisions for race officials.

Amidst the wild and bizarre Saturday afternoon, though, the Cutters endured it all.

And with the win, the team added to its Little 500 legacy.

The Cutters have won 11 times in 26 years of the team's existence and became the first team to win four Little 500 races in a row.

As rain descended on Bill Armstrong Stadium at the race's halfway point — which would make the race official if it ended — the Cutters prepared for a shortened race.

The bike was handed over to junior sprinter Eric Young, who built a sizeable lead from the front pack as rain drenched the riders and turned the track into a sloppy mess.

Race officials threw the yellow flag at lap 101 and three laps later suspended the race.

Since it was past the halfway point, the Cutters originally assumed the race was over and they had won.

"I thought like I celebrated a little bit too much," Young said about the mid-race ending.

But a few minutes later, PA announcer Chuck Crabb said the race was just temporarily suspended — now the Cutters faced another 96 laps before its rightful celebration.

The decision to extend the race was new for officials, because they had never faced a weather-based decision following the halfway point of the race.

In the end, with a patch of better weather on the way, the decision was made to attempt the full 200 laps.

Cutters coach Jim Kirkham said the postponement did not affect the riders' psyche.

"Once we realized we hadn't won, we regrouped and talked about what we were going to do to win," Kirkham said. "We were really prepared for the second half of the race."

In the second half, the Cutters competed against a handful of teams on the

SEE CUTTERS, PAGE 18

THOMAS MILLER | IDS

Eric Young crosses the finish line Saturday during the Men's Little 500 race at Bill Armstrong Stadium. This was the Cutters fourth-consecutive Little 500 victory.

SEVIL MAHFOOZI | IDS

The Teter team celebrates its win during Women's Little 500 on Friday at Bill Armstrong Stadium. Teter last won the women's Little 500 title in 2005.

WOMEN'S LITTLE 500

Van Kooten, Teter claim title amid crashes

BY STEPHANIE KUZYDYM
skuzydym@indiana.edu

It's a Little 500 tradition. The rider who crosses the finish line first raises her hands — triumphant in victory.

But when Teter's Caitlin Van Kooten crossed the finish line, she was hesitant about raising her hands. A nightmare she had before the race made her second guess the historical gesture.

"I put my hands up," Van Kooten said about her dream, "the bike falls, and we get a penalty for impeding and retroactively lose."

When she raised her hands during the actual race, her bike stayed beneath her and the win stayed tacked next to her team's name in the final results.

She rode her victory lap, signed autographs and gave hugs to anyone who wanted one. Van Kooten's legs are not the sole reason she swept the Spring Series events and, of course, the 23rd running of the Women's Little 500. It's something within her.

Even her coach, Chris Wojtowich, said Van Kooten possesses something in her that cannot be taught. That something caused Van Kooten to lead the race with about 20 laps to go, even attempting a burnout — where the front rider takes off from the pack — that her coach said was simply Van Kooten attacking.

"We may have had a bike there so it might have looked like a burnout, but that's what you kind of want to do is throw off teams," Wojtowich said. "But it didn't matter if that bike was there or not, she was going and that was it."

The Bloomington native knew she had one final attack left and luckily she did it right before the yellow flag waved after a crash with 15 laps to go.

SEE TETER, PAGE 18

ONLINE ONLY
See photo galleries from both races and the weekend's concerts.
IDSNEWS.COM/LITTLE500

PHOTO PAGE
Check out the highlights from this weekend's races on two photo pages.
SEE PAGES 4 AND 5

RACE RESULTS
Complete race standings after a ruling by race officials.
SEE PAGE 9

WIND AND RAIN
How a cinder track turned Slip 'n Slide caused crashes, a race delay and confusion.
SEE PAGE 9

ON THE TRACK
Get in the mud with Gray Goat Cycling, a front of the pack team.
SEE PAGE 10

LITTLE 5 WEEKEND

SNOOP STYLE

BY DANIELLE PAQUETTE | danpaque@indiana.edu

At 11 a.m. Friday, Snoop Dogg's private jet touched down at the Monroe County Airport. That night, he'd bring Los Angeles style to Indiana University.

The rapper and his entourage traveled in luxury to Holiday Inn Express Hotel and Suites, where a requested 60-inch plasma screen television awaited — only the best for his Xbox LIVE.

In the hotel elevator, a Golden Corral Buffet & Grill waitress startled at the sight of her favorite performer.

"Come to my restaurant, Snoop," she said, "and you eat for free."

They exchanged numbers and the rapper thanked her in his signature low, smooth tone — recognizable worldwide after nearly two decades of hit albums, sold-out concerts and a popular reality television series.

When the elevator reached the hotel's sixth floor, Snoop and four suit-clad security guards exited toward his room, which could be arranged or manipulated in any way possible — he need only ask.

The rapper pulled out his purple-encased iPad and began to bob his head to a bass-heavy beat.

Tonight, he'd bring Los Angeles style

SEE SNOOP, PAGE 8

PETER STEVENSON | IDS

Rapper Snoop Dogg performs Friday in the Sigma Alpha Mu and Zeta Beta Tau parking lot as part of Little 500 festivities.

P0079374, IU Archives.

THIS IS THE FINAL ISSUE OF THE IDS FOR THE SPRING SEMESTER. WE WILL RESUME PUBLISHING FRIDAY, MAY 6.

MONDAY, MAY 2, 2011

IDS

INDIANA DAILY STUDENT | IDSNEWS.COM

OSAMA BIN LADEN KILLED

EDITORS' NOTE

This semester has been an adventure. On top of all the typical news during a semester, the paper went through a significant transformation in the way it looked and the way information was presented.

We knew from the beginning that we would be redesigning the paper due to it shrinking an inch total in width, but we saw that as an opportunity to experiment and try something new. After a lot of hard work and extra hours put in by the staff, we were able to return after spring break and easily adjust to the changes. All staff members, even those who weren't editors, were eager to embrace the new style, which made the transition much easier. We hope you have enjoyed the new look of the Indiana Daily Student and will continue to read it in the upcoming semesters.

JAKE WRIGHT, EDITOR-IN-CHIEF
LINDSEY ERDODY, MANAGING EDITOR
DANIELLE RINDLER, ART DIRECTOR
LAUREN SEDAM, MANAGING EDITOR

CJ LOTZ | IDS
It took eight IU Physical Plant workers to lift each 800-pound Showalter Fountain fish Friday.

A FISH OUT OF WATER

5 fish, 800 pounds each: The Showalter Fountain gets a nearly $50,000 makeover

BY CJ LOTZ
cjlotz@indiana.edu

It took eight men to haul the fish.

On Friday morning, IU Physical Plant workers installed all five fish sculptures back into the Showalter Fountain, and the fish should be spouting water by late this week.

The bronze monsters weigh nearly 800 pounds each and were removed this winter for cleaning and repairs.

It's always been Sherry Rouse's goal to have the fountain finished for graduating seniors to enjoy. The curator of campus art was worried that recent rain would delay the installation, but Friday was clear and sunny.

The slate around the fountain is also being replaced and re-grouted.

One fish, poached this summer, needed to be recast in bronze and replaced, and the rest of the fish received a makeover. Venus Bronze Works in Detroit refinished the patina finish on all of the sculptures.

"The bottom line is the fish took a hit this year," Rouse said. She estimated that repairs on the fountain cost nearly $50,000.

As the crew of men in blue jeans and ball caps installed the fish, they added wires that may become part of an enhanced security system in an effort to prevent further vandalism.

Rouse said the wires could potentially be used to alert campus police about attempted thefts or people rocking the fish. During the Nearly Naked Mile this October, runners in the Homecoming week celebration swarmed the fountain and rocked one of the fish back and forth until it broke off its stand.

IU Police Department Chief Keith Cash would not comment on details of the new wiring.

"When it comes to matters of security measures, we do not discuss these as this would jeopardize the effectiveness of the measures we are taking," Cash said in an email.

Security is a concern for the fountain, which has seen both the fish and Venus targeted.

Robert Laurent sculpted Venus and her dolphin-like guardians. Grace Showalter funded the project as a gift to her late husband. It was dedicated in October 1961.

Students didn't wait until long after the dedication to start the fun that has marked Venus' time on campus. Just a few days after the ceremony, the fish spurted green foam.

Students have swum nude with her, tossed coins at her and covered her in soap, Jell-O and dye. In 1972, Venus saw 15 carp swimming around her until Physical Plant workers caught them.

Venus has worn bras of all sizes and colors and had her nails painted. At Christmas one year, she wore a duct tape bikini with fur trim and a Christmas hat.

The attention isn't all vandalism, though. As ordered by Rouse, she gets a wax once a year to keep her patina polished.

There is a longstanding rumor that Mrs. Showalter didn't like the size of Venus' bosom and requested a breast reduction for the classical figure.

IU Assistant Archivist Carrie Schwier, who oversaw an exhibit on

SEE **FISH,** PAGE 10

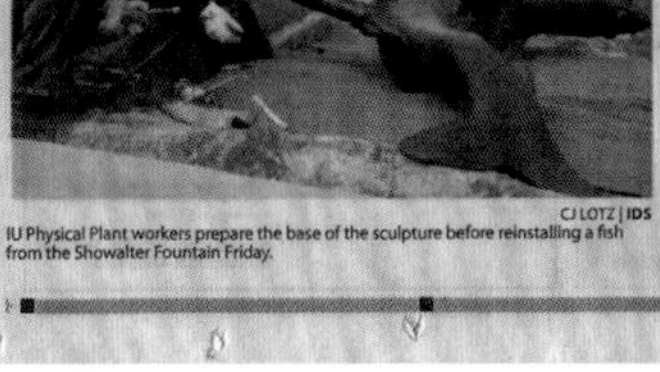

CJ LOTZ | IDS
IU Physical Plant workers prepare the base of the sculpture before reinstalling a fish from the Showalter Fountain Friday.

SOURCE: WWW.WHITEHOUSE.GOV
At about 11:35 p.m. Sunday, President Barack Obama announced Osama bin Laden had been killed by U.S. forces in Pakistan. Bin Laden was responsible for the attacks on Sept. 11 that killed nearly 3,000 people.

Country, campus react to president's late-night announcement

BY JAKE WRIGHT AND LINDSEY ERDODY
flwright@indiana.edu, lerdody@indiana.edu

MARK FELIX | IDS
Phil Soliman, Zach Otto and Shayne Guinn celebrate outside their apartment in the Varsity Villas after hearing of Osama bin Laden's death Sunday night.

On Sunday at about 11:35 p.m., President Barack Obama announced in a public address that Osama bin Laden was killed in a compound in Abbottabad, Pakistan.

Bin Laden was responsible for the Sept. 11 attacks that killed nearly 3,000 citizens and has since been public enemy number one.

During Obama's address he referred to bin Laden as "a terrorist who is responsible for the murder of innocent men, women and children."

Obama said he was briefed in August on a possible lead to bin Laden's whereabouts. Last week he decided there was enough evidence to take action.

A small team of Americans carried out the operation. No Americans or civilians were harmed. After a firefight, the team killed bin Laden and took custody of his body.

"The death of bin Laden marks the most significant achievement to date in our nation's efforts to beat al-Qaida," Obama said.

From the beginning of his time as president, Obama said he would take action in Pakistan if it would lead to bin Laden, which was seen as a controversial statement, former terrorism adviser Richard Clarke said on ABC News.

Obama mentioned during his address that he spoke with Pakistani President Asif Ali Zardari and Pakistan officials who were involved in the operation.

"They agree that this is a good and historic day for both of our nations," Obama said. "And going forward, it is essential that Pakistan continue to join us in the fight against al-Qaida and its affiliates."

Obama also made it clear that this is not an issue with Islam.

"The United States is not and never will be at war with Islam," Obama said. "Bin Laden is not a Muslim leader. He was a mass murderer of Muslims."

In 1998, former President Bill Clinton gave the first order to capture bin Laden. After 9/11, the War on Terror began, and former President George W. Bush placed a $25 million bounty on bin Laden. After becoming president in 2008, Obama continued the fight to find

SEE **BIN LADEN,** PAGE 10

IU Auditorium announces 2011-12 season lineup

BY ISABEL DIEPPA
idieppa@indiana.edu

School's out for summer in a week, but before students throw away their worries for the summer, the IU Auditorium is announcing next year's season.

The upcoming season is filled with stage legends, TV personalities and Broadway shows.

The Auditorium season will include a performance by Bernadette Peters, a one-night stand-up comedy show by Jon Stewart, the San Francisco Jazz Collective, Dennis James, a musical performance by Schola Cantorum de Venezuela, "Shrek the Musical," "Chimes of Christmas," "Stomp," Evidence, A Dance Company, an evening with Anthony Bourdain and Eric Ripert, "In the Heights," "South Pacific," the European Union Youth Orchestra and "Young Frankenstein."

The Indiana Daily Student sat down with Director Doug Booher to ask about the upcoming season.

IDS What inspired you to choose next year's lineup?

BOOHER Well, we wanted to make

SEE **AUDITORIUM,** PAGE 10

COURTESY PHOTO
Jon Stewart, host of Comedy Central's "The Daily Show" will be on stage Sept. 30 at the IU Auditorium.

2011-12 IU AUDITORIUM SEASON

BERNADETTE PETERS
» Sept. 23
» The Tony Award-winning star with a girlish voice will perform favorite Broadway classics.

JON STEWART
» Sept. 30
» Comedy Central's host of "The Daily Show" will make a rare stage appearance.

'SHREK THE MUSICAL'
» Nov. 15-17
» The musical has been adapted from the Oscar-winning film.

'STOMP'
» Jan. 27-28
» Creating music from hubcaps, paint cans and work boots, "Stomp" will be revived at the Auditorium.

P0079356, IU Archives.

Photos of Brian Maibaum are displayed at a memorial service in the IDS newsroom. *Photo courtesy of Biz Carson.*

REFLECTION

Goodnight, Brian

Goodnight, Brian.

Those would often be the last words that echoed through the walls of the newsroom after the paper had gone to press. Brian Maibaum always stayed behind to send the paper to the printer as students left for home.

Those words turned out to be much harder to say after Brian passed away suddenly Nov. 23, 2011, from a heart attack. He was 50 years old.

Backshop Brian, as he was affectionately known, was a quiet leader, selfless friend and mentor to a cohort of college students who looked up to his calm demeanor and understated expertise. He'd always enter the IDS in the afternoon with a small smile and a wave, a copy of the Herald-Times folded in half under his arm and a Polar Pop from Circle K in his hand, before heading to his domain in backshop.

His job for the four years he worked for student media was to make sure the paper got out on time to the printer each night, not an easy one when dealing with a bunch of college students or late-night IU basketball games. But Brian was known for being unflappable, the perfect calm antidote to the stress of daily production deadlines.

As the only adult and member of professional staff overseeing production at night, Brian was always the most knowledgeable person in the room, but he was never patronizing. He understood innately that the IDS was the place for us learn as we go. He was the safety net we could go to with anything, but also the coach who could teach us when it's best to use Adobe Illustrator over Photoshop, how to color correct photos to not waste ink, or why you'll always have to correct the spacing between an A and a V.

When one designer told Brian that she had almost corrected her boss at an internship over the proper use of kerning vs. tracking, Brian responded with his usual: a lesson, followed by support.

"You're right, it's probably best not to correct the boss," he told her. "Professions all have their own vocabulary, and I want you all to know what you're talking about. IDSers are smarter than the average designer!"

And it was Brian who made us that way.

Being in backshop with Brian was a key part of many IDSers' design educations. While we were waiting for stories to come in or before the night shift started, he would take time to teach me and many others the basics of design and production we would need in professional newsrooms. One time he brought in a Lite Brite to help with his lesson; another time it was crafting supplies.

His quiet nature made him the perfect mentor and an even better friend. He turned his smoke breaks into counseling sessions, listening to whoever needed to talk to him over a cigarette on the corner. He could talk about anything, from gay rights to marching band to Boston terriers, his favorite dog breed. He hid his annoyance well during the Lady Gaga sing-alongs and had an amazing tolerance for listening to Pandora Radio day in and day out.

When I was art director during my sophomore year, Brian would offer me a ride home after late closes—not wanting an 18-year-old woman to walk across campus by herself in the middle of the night. I knew it was in the opposite direction of his house, but he would always come up with some excuse, like needing to drop off mail at the post office, to offer a ride and make sure I got home safe.

As Brian became our family, we also became his. We learned about how he grew up in Kokomo, played in the high school marching band and studied art at IU. He loved to show us his collection of papier-mâché ornaments and would spend hours looking at them on Etsy.

When Brian first mentioned that he had never received a valentine, the newsroom took crafting into our own hands and made him a kiddie-style box of valentines, with individual cards signed by everyone at the IDS. After he died, his parents later found the box of Valentine's Day cards among his things. He had kept it, still full of everyone's notes to him.

The last post Brian had shared that month on Facebook was a quote from the Dalai Lama about human nature: "We achieve happiness, prosperity and progress through social interaction. Therefore, having a kind and helpful attitude contributes to our own and others' happiness."

Brian had been the embodiment of this, a person who was kind and helpful to the core and who never expected anything in return. He found his happiness at the IDS and helped us find our happiness through him. I only wish I had said "Thank you, Brian" as many times as I said "Good Night."

—Biz Carson, BAJ 2012

"His quiet nature made him the perfect mentor and an even better friend. He turned his smoke breaks into counseling sessions, listening to whoever needed to talk to him over a cigarette on the corner."

CHECK IDSNEWS.COM FOR CONTINUING COVERAGE ON THE SEARCH FOR LAUREN

THE SEARCH FOR LAUREN SPIERER

THURSDAY, JUNE 9, 2011

IDS

INDIANA DAILY STUDENT | IDSNEWS.COM

LAUREN SPIERER

IU junior Lauren Spierer (pictured right) is a 20-year-old white female. She is 4 feet 11 inches tall and weighs between 90 and 100 pounds. Lauren has blue eyes and blonde hair that comes past her shoulders.

She was last seen wearing a white tank top underneath a loose, light-colored buttoned shirt and leggings. She was not wearing any shoes.

If you have any information regarding Lauren Spierer, contact the Bloomington Police Department at 812-339-4477 or 800-CRIMETV (affiliated with America's Most Wanted).

Both numbers are anonymous tip lines.

ALEX FARRIS | IDS

Lauren Spierer's father, Robert, speaks, with his daughter Rebecca and wife Charlene at his side during a press briefing Wednesday at Bloomington Police Department headquarters. The search for Lauren has spanned the IU campus and greater Bloomington, and her story has been reported and tweeted across the nation.

The Behrman family knows what it's like to search for a missing daughter. Marilyn Behrman explains how it feels when your child becomes

A NATIONAL CONVERSATION

BY CJ LOTZ | cjlotz@indiana.edu

Before the national news paid attention, before Ryan Seacrest tweeted about Lauren, before the press conferences and the search parties, Robert Spierer taped up a picture of his daughter.

At 9:45 a.m. Sunday, he walked into Smallwood Plaza. He looked at his daughter's face smiling under the words "Missing." A roll of masking tape on his arm, he stuck another piece along the side of the white paper and rubbed it down against a lobby door in Smallwood.

He talked about Lauren, the younger of his two daughters, who loves fashion and talks to her mother every day.

He couldn't have anticipated how huge this story would become. In the next few days, millions of people would see his daughter's face.

Marilyn Behrman has been there.

When her daughter, Jill, disappeared, Marilyn didn't expect it to become a national story.

"It went local, national and then back to local," she said. "I guess it doesn't matter as long as someone cares enough to follow it so it doesn't become a cold case."

Jill never returned from her bike ride on May 31, 2000. Her father Eric filed a report the next

SEE CONVERSATION, PAGE 5

IDS FILE PHOTOS

ABOVE Marilyn and Eric Behrman of Bloomington were in the media spotlight for years as they searched for their missing daughter, Jill Behrman.

RIGHT Left to Right: Brian, Eric and Marilyn Behrman stand attentively among numerous yellow helium balloons. Fliers containing information about Jill Behrmans' disappearance were attached to balloons and released June 27, 2000, during a prayer meeting for Jill.

ALEX FARRIS | IDS

A sign for Lauren Spierer hangs at a bus stop Saturday along Third Street. Lauren's parents started looking for her that day.

TIMELINE OF EVENTS

Lauren's night and the days that followed

EDITOR'S NOTE: The following timeline was created based on facts that have been verified by the parents of Lauren Spierer, Bloomington Police Department and on-site reporting of the daily search parties.

FRIDAY, JUNE 3

EARLY MORNING
Lauren hangs out with friends at Kilroy's Sports Bar.

2:30-2:40 A.M.
Lauren leaves Kilroy's Sports with a friend. She leaves her shoes and cell phone at the bar.

ABOUT 2:40 A.M.
Lauren and her friend walk to Lauren's apartment complex, Smallwood Plaza. However, videos show Lauren does not enter her room. Police say she likely stays in the lobby.

Lauren and her friend decide to walk to another friend's apartment on the corner of 11th and Morton streets.

Police say they have found Lauren's small purse and set of keys near Morton Street and that she likely lost them along the way to this apartment complex.

The two went into one apartment, then to another apartment a few doors down to hang out with other friends.

ABOUT 4:30 A.M.
Lauren tells her friends she feels like going back home to Smallwood. A male friend watched Lauren leave the apartment to go back to her apartment. He last saw her on the corner of 11th Street and College Avenue. Police said this male friend is the last person who saw Lauren and he was just watching her to make sure that she made it home safely. Video footage at the entrance of Smallwood that night shows she never made it home.

SATURDAY, JUNE 4

MORNING
Lauren's parents fly into Indianapolis from New York after hearing their daughter is missing. They rent a car, drive to Bloomington, file a police report and begin combing the areas around Lauren's apartment and Kilroy's Sports. The Bloomington Police Department also starts searching nearby areas with dogs. Police conduct searches throughout the city.

Robert and Charlene Spierer

SUNDAY, JUNE 5

10 A.M.
Volunteers gather outside Smallwood Plaza to create a search plan. Local residents, students, friends and family map a route to explore Bloomington and Lakes Lemon, Griffy and Monroe. The Spierers said they didn't have evidence she was around those areas, but they wanted to do something.

Charlene Spierer tells the IDS Lauren has Long QT syndrome.

She urges whoever knows about her daughter's location to take her to a hospital.

3 P.M.
After spotty rain, the search volunteers and family stop the search for the day. They have covered many of the roads around nearby lakes.

4 P.M.
The Spierers meet with police to discuss the next steps.

MONDAY, JUNE 6

10 A.M.
Searches continue with about 20 volunteers, including IU Hillel's Rabbi Sue Silberberg.

11 A.M.
Police confirm they are still investigating the case and haven't found Lauren. They provide no further details.

11:52 A.M.
IU Dean of Students Harold "Pete" Goldsmith sends out a message alerting students and faculty that workers would search the IU campus and buildings for any trace of Lauren.

1 P.M.
More than 100 people show up to help search for Lauren, including IU men's basketball coach Tom Crean.

5:30 P.M.
About 400 people attend a search for Lauren, including IU women's basketball coach Felisha Legette-Jack and basketball players, as well as members of the volleyball team.

TIMELINE CONTINUES ON PAGE 5

P0079357, IU Archives

THE IDS WILL RESUME PUBLISHING JAN. 6. HAVE A NICE BREAK!

MONDAY, DEC. 12, 2011

IDS

INDIANA DAILY STUDENT | IDSNEWS.COM

COURTNEY DECKARD | IDS

GLORY OF OLD IU

Hoosiers stun No. 1 Wildcats on shot heard 'round the hall, win 73-72

BY STEPHANIE KUZYDYM
skuzydym@indiana.edu

The final shot arced toward the basket, and time stopped.

As he watched the ball, junior forward Christian Watford kept his right hand in the air. The fans stood with their hands raised, holding their breath. The five red banners softly swayed.

Then, the sound of pure swish echoed. The golden numbers lit 0.0.

Across Assembly Hall, the wave of emotion released.

A decade of pent up frustration was freed onto Branch McCracken court.

Since 2001, when former IU Coach Bob Knight was fired, Indiana has been roaming a desert in search of respectability.

IU Coach Tom Crean's first three years brought the worst season records to Assembly Hall in its history.

On Dec. 10, the Hoosiers found paradise.

An uproar filled the rafters. The IU men's basketball team celebrated in a pile. Thousands of fingers pointed in the air. Seniors who sat through a 6-25 record their freshman season watched their team upset the country's premier team to turn the card to 9-0.

The faithful stormed the court.

"This is Indiana. This is Indiana," fans shouted as they swarmed past black-shirted security guards. A guard threw both his hands up like stop signs toward the rushing crowd. They couldn't even be slowed.

Fans sprinted. Some tripped and fell. Some were even trampled.

Members of the Big Red Basketball Band's first instinct was to protect their instruments from the chaos. They lifted their trombones and trumpets above their heads before dropping them to their mouths to play the fight song.

"We're No. 1," a fan shouted. "No. 1, baby."

Fans in the general admission seats became restless to join the party at center court.

SEE **CROWD**, PAGE 10

TO OUR READERS

Never did we think the semester would end with chants of "nine and O" ringing in our ears. What a way to end. And IDS staffers were in Assembly Hall and on Kirkwood Avenue to bring you full coverage of the night, just as we've worked to bring you stories all semester.

We strived to be your newspaper, the newspaper that covers IU and its students best. We wanted to bring you what you needed to know and what you would talk about. And we did it not just in print, but on your Twitter and Facebook feeds.

We found the details of daily life, such as the truth of football tailgates and naps in the IMU. We brought you news of shootings in Bloomington and the departure of Provost Karen Hanson. We remembered and marked the 10th anniversary of 9/11 and six months since Lauren Spierer's disappearance. We were there as the Occupy movement traveled from Occupy Bloomington to Occupy IU to Occupy the Kelley School of Business. And we were there as the deadmau5 concert was canceled and moved.

It's all been an adventure we wouldn't trade for anything and hope you wouldn't, either. Thanks for reading. It's been fun.

Stay with us at *idsnews.com* and on Twitter and Facebook. See you in 2012.

MARYJANE SLABY
Editor-in-Chief

MARY KENNEY
Managing Editor

ADAM LUKACH
Managing Editor

SARAH THACKER
Art Director

INSIDE

SPORTS

MARK FELIX | IDS

After watching a double-digit second half lead wilt away, it was junior forward Christian Watford who twice regained the advantage for the Hoosiers in the game's waning minutes.

PAGE 11

AVIOUSLY

MARK FELIX | IDS

This one was for the fans who didn't put Butler blue over cream and crimson while the IU basketball program was dragged through the mud of a 28-66 (8-46) record during the past three years.

PAGE 8

KIRKWOOD ERUPTS

CHET STRANGE | IDS

The Hoosiers did the impossible. They beat the No. 1 team in the nation. Celebration couldn't begin to describe what took place next.

PAGE 8

IDSNEWS.COM

SEE video from after the final buzzer. It's complete with celebrations at Kilroy's on Kirkwood, blocking traffic and dancing on pickup trucks.

HEAR the chants of "Hoo-Hoo-Hoo-Hoosiers" as fans stormed Branch McCracken Court and Kirkwood Avenue.

SHARE your memories from game day, and see if they show up online. Send in your photos to *webeditor@idsnews.com.*

P0080161, IU Archives.

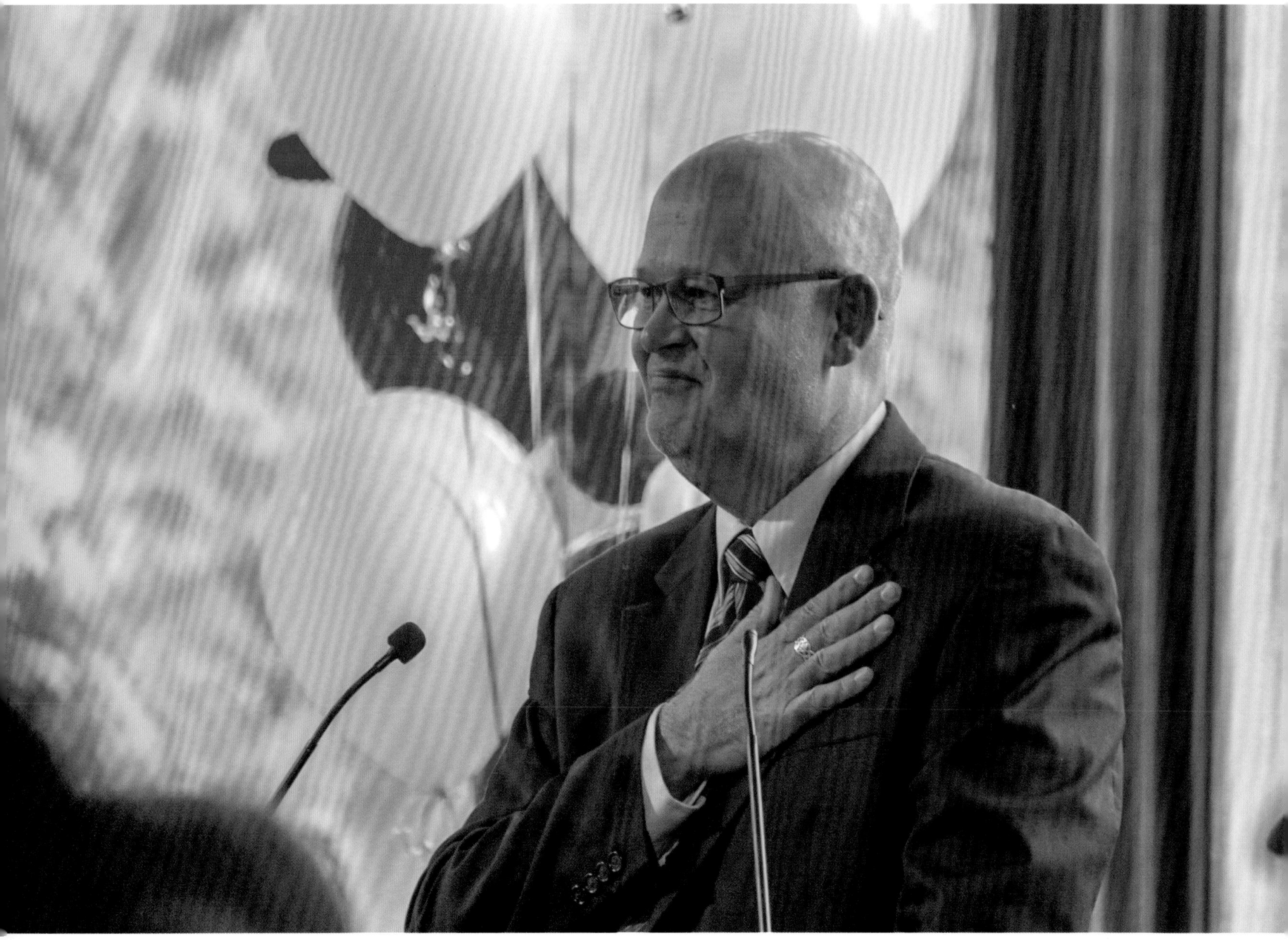

PROFILE

Ron Johnson
Director of Student Media, 2008–2017

Director of Student Media Ron Johnson gives a speech at the 150th anniversary celebration of the IDS. *Photo courtesy of IU Media School.*

By Michael Auslen

Staffers first got to know Ron Johnson through his red pen.

Johnson's marked-up copies of each morning's newspaper usually made it on the bulletin board in the newsroom before the staff had arrived. Within those pages were always important rules for journalism: Writing should be tight and grammatically correct. No one will read the paper if the front page doesn't stand out above the fold. And each editor gets one exclamation mark, so use it wisely.

But it didn't take long before Johnson started teaching us much more important and lasting lessons. For nine years, he was a mentor, a teacher and, above all, a friend and ally to IDSers.

The IDS is a family. And for nine years, Johnson was part of what made it feel like one.

"It was always re-energizing to start a school year with a bunch of new folks and watch them grow and watch them take off," Johnson said. "They're going to stumble sometimes. They're going to make mistakes. But that's part of the beauty of a college newspaper like the IDS."

Johnson came to IU following in the footsteps of his college mentor, Dave Adams. They were big shoes to fill, Johnson said, but from the get-go, he started working with young journalists to make sure the IDS remained entirely student-made.

He had the "battle scars" of past fights over student editorial independence, and Johnson was determined to make sure the IDS remained free from overreach by the IU administration. At Kansas State University, he was adviser to the Collegian for 19 years before being fired in a spat with university administrators.

In November 2017, Johnson stepped down as director of student media at IU and moved to Missouri with his husband, Barry, so they could be closer to family.

At the IDS, the Johnson Era came to be defined by two key challenges. Like the rest of the industry, the paper was hit hard by declining revenues as readers and advertisers turned away from newspapers and toward the internet. Without financial stability, the IDS also fought to maintain its independence while securing its future existence.

Yet from 2008 to 2017, the IDS also produced some of its best journalism. With Johnson as director, IU won the Hearst Intercollegiate Writing Competition seven times and earned 11 Pacemaker awards from the Associated Collegiate Press for the IDS, Inside Magazine, Arbutus and idsnews.com.

"So many times, through the years, I was asked, 'How does IU do it?' I said, 'It's magic,'" Johnson said.

Johnson attributes it to the combination of talented students, professors who know how to coach, advisers who stuck by the IDS even through times of tumultuous change, and a network of alumni who are so fiercely devoted to the paper that they sometimes forget they're no longer running it.

"College newspapers in particular are on the front lines of reporting news in their communities," he said. "We need student journalism now more than ever in this country, and I hope that administrators everywhere understand its value and its importance beyond their universities."

FRIDAY, MARCH 2, 2012

IDS

INDIANA DAILY STUDENT | IDSNEWS.COM

The story of the woman behind the posters page 3

CHET STRANGE | IDS
Alex Copher and Jerry Goolsby watch as what is left of the Golden Circle is demolished Wednesday in Harrisburg, Ill. The Golden Circle, a support facility for seniors, was destroyed during a tornado that struck Wednesday, claiming six lives in the southern Illinois town.

After tornado, town rebuilds

BY CHARLES SCUDDER | cscudder@indiana.edu

HARRISBURG, ILL. – Jesse Raymer was asleep when the sky opened above his bed. A couple hours before dawn Wednesday, a monster tornado snapped a tree at the base and sent it crashing through the wall of his bedroom, knocking into his bedpost. A window broke as he sprang from the bed. His dog, Chauncey, sleeping nearby, jumped up, too.

Raymer ran to the bathroom across the hall to find shelter with Chauncey at his side. As he opened the door, the beast from above peeled the roof off his one-story home. Debris, wind and rain poured into the bathroom.

Deciding to head for the basement, he fumbled his way through the living room, tripping over a small table and knocking over a piano stool.

"Well, I was in a hurry," he said Thursday. "It chased me."

He didn't have time to get dressed before his flight to safety, so he found clothes in the basement and waited out the storm. That's when he realized Chauncey was missing.

SEE TORNADO, PAGE 6

PHOTOS BY CHET STRANGE | IDS
Darlene Goolsby sifts through the debris of the Golden Circle. Darlene, a coordinator at Golden Circle, must now figure out how to provide meals to the more than 100 seniors who depend on them.

A polaroid photo lies on the fiberglass-covered ground outside of the Golden Circle. The tornado, which hit Wednesday, killed six people in Harrisburg and was part of a larger storm system that ravaged cities across the Midwest. The cleanup effort was in full swing Thursday.

The bathroom of Jesse Raymer had its roof blown off during the tornado. "I was lying in bed, and a limb ran through the wall and hit the bedpost. It chased me," Raymer said of the event. After seeking shelter in the bathroom, Raymer had to run to his basement as the roof blew off.

Lifeline passes Senate, awaits signature

FROM IDS REPORTS

A bill granting limited immunity to underage drinkers across the state is heading to Gov. Mitch Daniels' desk to be signed into law.

The Indiana Senate approved the Indiana Lifeline Bill, SB 274, by a unanimous 47-0 vote on Thursday. The vote marks the bill's clearing of the Legislature.

If Daniels signs the bill, those who seek medical attention on behalf of an intoxicated minor will not face legal repercussions in certain situations.

This legislation would encourage students to seek emergency help for others without facing arrest themselves.

The bill will apply in certain instances of alcohol overuse, such as public intoxication and minor possession, but not for other forms of drug possession or use.

IU Student Association President Justin Kingsolver, who helped spearhead the student-led effort to bring Lifeline to the state Legislature, said he expects the governor will sign the bill, given its unanimous passing in the House and Senate.

After passing 50-0 in the Senate on Jan. 24, the bill passed in the House 96-0 on Feb. 14.

To reconcile the two slightly different versions of the bill, legislators sent it back to the Senate for a concurrence vote on Thursday.

The bill, if signed, would take effect July 1.

— Matthew Glowicki

MEN'S BASKETBALL

VS.

The Hoosiers will take on Purdue at 6 p.m. Sunday for senior night.

Read Part 2 of Connor O'Gara's look back on the seniors' journey on page 7.

To see Avi Zaleon's predictions for the big game, visit *idsnews.com.*

PART IV OF IV

Sweet redemption

AVI ZALEON
is a senior majoring in journalism.

Verdell Jones III knew it all along.

The victories, the return and the redemption — it would all happen at some point.

"I saw the vision that Coach (Tom) Crean had," he said. "I saw where this program could go from the time I was coming in. I saw us working hard every day, so I knew that it had to change. I knew that we were going to win sooner or later. There's just no way if you work that hard every day and put in the sacrifices that we did, it would continue to be the same."

Jones III and the IU seniors have paid their dues. Now they're seeing the results.

No longer the doormat of the Big Ten and their rivals, the Hoosiers have defeated the top three teams in the conference this season, in addition to perennial rivals Kentucky, Illinois and Purdue.

"The past three years, everybody took their jabs at us," Jones said. "'Indiana's down, let's kick 'em while they're down,' and this year, we're getting a little payback."

In their freshman year, these seniors were spanked by 18 points in Rupp Arena.

The following season, John Wall and the 'Cats put on a show for the crowd at Assembly Hall on their way to 17-point win.

Kentucky wiped its feet on the Hoosiers in last year's installment of the annual rivalry to the tune of a 19-point victory.

Jones said he remembers the losses being worse than they were, but I'm sure the revenge was just that much sweeter.

"It's supposed to be the best team that Calipari's had," he said. "For us to

SEE ZALEON, PAGE 6

Barnett hopes to continue as coach

BY KEVIN BOWEN
kdbowen@indiana.edu

He might be the only non-scholarship senior on the roster, but for IU fans, the roar when Kory Barnett enters the game is that of a victorious cheer.

Those cheers were a rare occurrence during Barnett's first three years in Bloomington, as the Hoosiers were in the midst of 20-loss season after 20-loss season.

Before 2008, IU had never had a season with more than 17 losses, but that quickly changed when sanctions hit the program like it had never been hit before.

Barnett was right in the middle of it, having turned down mid-major offers to become a preferred walk-on for then-IU Coach Kelvin Sampson.

He was to head to Bloomington in summer 2008 and play on a team that was expected to get IU back among the talks of the nation's best.

As he prepares for his final game at Assembly Hall, Barnett has finally experienced historical wins and a season rivaling that of any past Hoosier team.

"Honestly, with the past, I didn't know that we would ever get to see it," Barnett said. "I always wanted to, and we worked so hard that I hoped we would."

Growing up in Oregon, Barnett wasn't the typical passionate Indiana kid who dreamed of putting on the

SEE BARNETT, PAGE 6

P0079363, IU Archives.

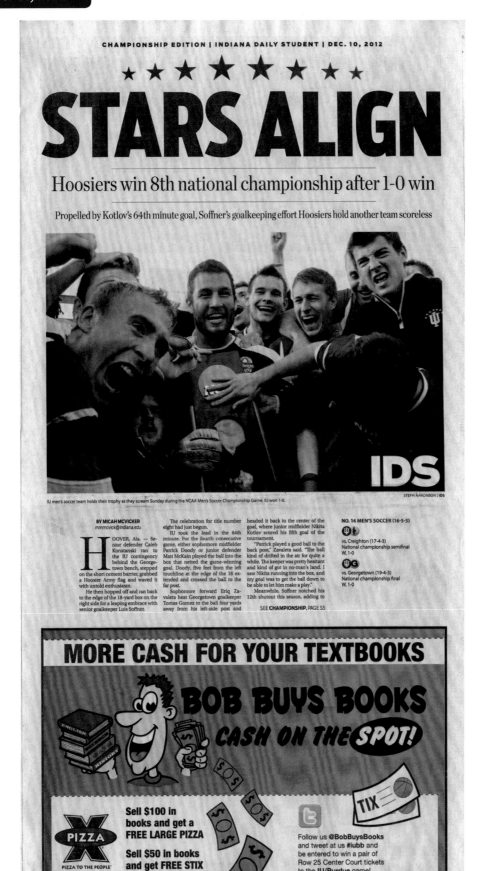

CHAMPIONSHIP EDITION | INDIANA DAILY STUDENT | DEC. 10, 2012

STARS ALIGN

Hoosiers win 8th national championship after 1-0 win

Propelled by Kotlov's 64th minute goal, Soffner's goalkeeping effort Hoosiers hold another team scoreless

IU men's soccer team holds their trophy as they scream Sunday during the NCAA Men's Soccer Championship Game. IU won 1-0.

STEPH AARONSON | IDS

BY MICAH MCVICKER
mmmcvick@indiana.edu

HOOVER, Ala. — Senior defender Caleb Konstanski ran to the IU contingency behind the Georgetown bench, stepped on the short cement barrier, grabbed a Hoosier Army flag and waved it with untold enthusiasm.

He then hopped off and ran back to the edge of the 18-yard box on the right side for a leaping embrace with senior goalkeeper Luis Soffner.

The celebration for title number eight had just begun.

IU took the lead in the 64th minute. For the fourth consecutive game, either sophomore midfielder Patrick Doody or junior defender Matt McKain played the ball into the box that netted the game-winning goal. Doody, five feet from the left touchline at the edge of the 18 extended and crossed the ball to the far post.

Sophomore forward Eriq Zavaleta beat Georgetown goalkeeper Tomas Gomez to the ball four yards away from his left-side post and headed it back to the center of the goal, where junior midfielder Nikita Kotlov scored his fifth goal of the tournament.

"Patrick played a good ball to the back post," Zavaleta said. "The ball kind of drifted in the air for quite a while. The keeper was pretty hesitant and kind of got in no-man's land. I saw Nikita running into the box, and my goal was to get the ball down to be able to let him make a play."

Meanwhile, Soffner notched his 12th shutout this season, adding to

SEE CHAMPIONSHIP, PAGE S5

NO. 16 MEN'S SOCCER (16-5-3)

vs. Creighton (17-4-3)
National championship semifinal
W, 1-0

vs. Georgetown (19-4-3)
National championship final
W, 1-0

P0079383, IU Archives.

February 22, 2013

END OF AN ERA?

PROVOST CALLS FOR END TO JOURNALISM INDEPENDENCE

Communication school would reside in Franklin Hall, become part of College of Arts and Sciences

Plan for new school still unclear

BY MATTHEW GLOWICKI | mglowick@indiana.edu

Few specifics have emerged concerning the proposed merger involving the IU School of Journalism and two other academic departments.

No definite academic or administrative structure is finalized. Nor are the futures of IU Student Media, various units' distinct honors programs or future financial and infrastructural support clear.

The merger itself is not a done deal, as it must still go before the Board of Trustees and President Michael McRobbie.

Rather, Provost Lauren Robel said, faculty and other leadership from the three units will soon form a committee that will prepare a proposal envisioning the merged school, newly framed in the context of the College of Arts and Sciences and its future home in Franklin Hall.

"The ball is back in the faculty's court," Robel said.

The new committee will report to School of Journalism Interim Dean Michael Evans, COAS Dean Larry Singell Jr. and Robel before she addresses the trustees.

"We're still a team on this," she said.

The plan inched closer to reality after Robel's State of the Campus address Tuesday, in which she announced her intentions to recommend the merger of the School with the departments of Telecommunications and Communication and Culture within COAS — thus dismantling the freestanding School of Journalism — and to relocate all three units to a renovated Franklin Hall. With this recommendation, the prospect of an independent school of merged units seemed less likely.

"We need a structure to make it move forward. That's part of it,"

SEE **MERGER**, PAGE 2

FRIDAY, FEB. 22, 2013

IDS

INDIANA DAILY STUDENT | IDSNEWS.COM

ANOTHER MERGER ON CAMPUS

The ongoing merger of the School of Informatics and Computing with the School of Library and Information Science has been "easy," the provost and deans said, page 2

Graffiti attacks fraternity with AIDS claim

BY HANNAH SMITH
hannsmit@indiana.edu

ETHAN BENNETT | IDS

Graffiti marks campus sidewalks and buildings on Thursday, starting at the Showalter Fountain, all the way to the sidewalk outside Phi Gamma Delta on Third Street. The graffiti contained remarks about AIDS, homosexuality and the Fiji fraternity.

Chalk graffiti was found on campus early Thursday morning, stretching from the south steps of Showalter Fountain to behind Woodburn Hall, past Ballantine Hall and toward the Phi Gamma Delta house on Third Street.

The graffiti referenced Fiji, stating at the beginning near Showalter "GOT AIDS, THEY DO, FOLLOW THE LINE."

The line stretched across campus on the streets and sidewalks. Peppered around it were references to AIDS, Fiji's members having AIDS and homosexual profanities. These included phrases like "fudgepackers," "bangin monkeys," "cumguzzlers" and "sausage jockies."

The line ended just in front of Fiji house.

Mike Girvin, campus division manager for IU Physical Plant, said the obscenities and offensive parts have been erased by their crew, and that the cost for the cleanup will be about $500 to $1,000. The cost will be covered by funds paid by all students in their fees.

He said his department did not report the incident since the cause at this time is unknown.

"Sometimes we'll get it and it'll be fixed with a specific group, and then we can go to the dean of students," Girvin said. "If you don't know who did it, it's harder to attest."

Interfraternity vice president of communications Sean Jordan said at this point they do not know who is responsible, or if it was done by another fraternity on campus.

"Obviously, investigation needs to be done," Jordan said. "All we know right now is that we're very disappointed."

If it is found that a fraternity created the graffiti, then Jordan said they will be taken before the IFC Standards Board for a hearing. After the hearing, he and other members on the board would provide an action plan, be it punitive, educational or both.

Michael Goodman, senior as-

SEE **GRAFFITI**, PAGE 6

TRACK AND FIELD

Hoosiers prepare for Big Ten Championships

BY CASEY KRAJEWSKI
crkrajew@indiana.edu

The 2013 Big Ten men's and women's Track and Field Championships will take place this weekend in Geneva, Ohio. The Hoosier men will look to defend their 2012 title and the women will try to improve on their eighth place finish from last year.

Last year was Hoosiers' first men's championship win since 1992.

IU seniors Andy Bayer, the two-time defending 3000-meter runner and one-time defending mile champion, and the high jumpers receive much of the credit.

IU senior Derek Drouin won the titles in 2010 and 2011, but redshirted in 2012.

Fellow senior Darius King stepped up in his absence last year to claim a title of his own.

Bayer said defending his titles don't add any pressure to his performances this weekend.

"No matter what, going into the Big Ten meet, you know it's going to be hard," Bayer said. "I don't think it's going to be any easier this year than years past so I try not to look at it as any added pressure."

Senior Zach Mayhew (3000-meter, 5000-meter), graduate student Scott Houston (pole vault), sophomore Nick Stoner (60-meter) and graduate student Lance Roller (800-meter) are other Hoosiers looking to receive points. All these competitors have top-6 rankings in the conference heading into the championship meet.

"We're going to have to find ways to score in pretty much every event we have people entered in," IU Coach Ron Helmer said. "Even if it's a couple points here and a couple points there to go along with our big point scorers."

One of the bright spots on the women's side heading into this weekend is the streak of five years in which the women have brought home a Big Ten individual title.

The best chance to continue this streak likely lies in the throwing arm of junior Kyla Buckley or the legs of senior Kelsey Duerksen and sophomore Samantha Ginther.

Buckley is seeded third on the conference's shot put list and Ginther and Duerksen sit at second and third in the 3000m.

High jumping senior Emma

SEE **TRACK**, PAGE 6

A note from the editor

It's rare that a newspaper is justified in printing a 120-point, bold headline. Today is one of those days.

Provost Lauren Robel has endorsed a plan that reverses the School of Journalism's 27-year independence and interrupts its century-long heritage. This same plan calls for unspecified changes to student media, possibly affecting the IDS.

Her decision is drawing much controversy and will alter the academic landscape of our University. For our readers, it's a story we have a duty to report.

For many at the IDS, it's our story.

We are proud of our independence. As editor-in-chief, I make the final decisions about what we publish in consultation with other student editors and professional staff.

Yet we're also proud of our history, a legacy that stretches back to this day 146 years ago, and a century of close partnership with the School of Journalism.

We share Ernie Pyle Hall, and most of the students who work to bring you the news study journalism, including myself and the rest of the IDS management team.

The school's professors teach us about responsible journalism and perfecting our craft. It was the school that attracted most of us to IU.

This is enhanced by its autonomy, which allows it to instruct with limited outside influence, while still giving a broad liberal arts education.

We work together toward mutual successes.

Our futures are inherently tied.

A diminished school, particularly one caught in the bureaucracy and revenue sharing model of the College of Arts and Sciences, would suffer.

That's why we've dedicated so much attention to reporting this story: Any decision that harms the School of Journalism also runs the risk of harming IU Student Media.

Further, it is part of a campus-wide conversation affecting us all.

In the last year, the School of Library and Information Science was folded into the School of Informatics and Computing. The Office for Women's Affairs and the Leo R. Dowling International Center were closed.

Across the board, student input has been limited.

Our University is experiencing a time of great change. Change is often good, but the brash elimination of programs is irresponsible.

In July, President Michael McRobbie told the Herald-Times, "There's no point in saving a school that trains people to manage fleets of horses if the motorcar has taken over horse-drawn transportation."

Contrary to McRobbie's belief, journalism isn't dead. It is in a state of flux, as is the journalism school.

Nor is journalism dead in the IDS newsroom. I proudly work alongside others who dedicate themselves to informing our community. We have created an investigations team and a digital desk to report important stories and adapt to new media.

In the past, we may have been complacent. We've let opportunities to question decisions by administrators and trustees pass us by.

That stops today. We're rededicating ourselves to asking tough questions, seeking the truth and serving you as the student voice of IU in every story we report.

We are not a horse-and-buggy operation. We are — in print, online and through social media — your news.

Michael Auslen, Editor-in-Chief
mauslen@indiana.edu

P0079373, IU Archives.

REFLECTION

Moving Out, Moving On

It's hard to explain to someone who wasn't there.

It's hard to make them understand why this dingy room, with these florescent lights and faded carpet and crusty yellow chair, means so much. Why it's heartbreaking that the trophy case is empty, that the wall of Will Counts prints is bare.

I left Bloomington for Texas and came back two years later with a Texan girlfriend to show her what Indiana meant to me. We arrived just a few weeks before the last files were moved from Ernie Pyle Hall to the new Media School building at Franklin Hall.

I wanted to show her the computer lab where we checked out photo equipment, the professor's offices where I stayed up late going through painstaking edits, the newsroom table where we ate cheap queso and leftover pizza. But it was all gone.

I told her about how it was impossible to get any cellphone signal in the newsroom because it was basically a big limestone box. I told her about election night, when we ran from the editor's office to backshop with the latest numbers and blew off deadline completely. I told her about the Little 500 nights when we had to edit video and file copy before joining our friends on Kirkwood Avenue.

I showed her Ernie Pyle's desk—it was the last thing to leave the old building—and the signatures from Mace Brodie, an editor in chief in the '40s, to Mary Katherine Wildeman, who led the paper in 2016.

I tried to get her to imagine it all, but it's tough in the summer when there's no students and even tougher when it's just an empty building with holey walls and ripped-up carpet.

After too long, we had to leave, but I couldn't. I wanted to run up to the second floor, or over to the Arbutus office, anything to delay walking out those big wooden doors facing Seventh Avenue.

I started to cry when we started to walk out. I still don't know why.

It had been outdated for years. Even when Ernie Pyle Hall was built, it was supposed to be just a storage room for the Indiana Memorial Union. The program had long outgrown the old building, and like so many historic American newsrooms, it was outdated for the digital world.

We knew this day would come, but we didn't know it would be here so soon.

When the first students moved into Franklin Hall, I remember sending photos to fellow IDSers who went to school with me. They said it looked sterile, like a computer lab.

But on my next visit back, it was full with students creating journalism. I heard the same tapping of keys and buzz of deadline excitement.

The faculty director was still making critiques. The editor was still holding meetings in her office. The freshmen were still editing their early drafts with desk editors. The photographers were still listening intently to the police scanner for spot news.

Ernie's desk was still in the corner. The historic pages were still framed on the walls.

It was all there, even without the faded carpet and crusty chair.

Some alumni still shake their heads, but it's hard to explain to someone who wasn't there.

—*Charles Scudder, BAJ 2014*

IDS Editor-in-Chief Charles Scudder. *Photo courtesy of Anna Powell Teeter.*

MONDAY, OCT. 13, 2014

IDS

INDIANA DAILY STUDENT | IDSNEWS.COM

SUDFELD OUT 'INDEFINITELY' PAGE 7

COURTESY PHOTO

ALISON GRAHAM | IDS

IKE HAJINAZIARN | IDS

Top left The Ernie Pyle sculpture placed in front of Franklin Hall was sculpted based on this archival image of Pyle on his typewriter. **Top right** Langland's Ernie Pyle scultpure started as a small clay mold, which he resized in foam. Afterwards, he was able to create the cast for the full-size sculpture. **Bottom** Sculptor Tuck Langland sits Thursday with the sculpture of Ernie Pyle he created for the Media School.

Sculpting a legend

Ernie Pyle sculptor, Langland, creates works in home studio

By Alison Graham
akgraham@indiana.edu | @AlisonGraham218

He creates everything in a small, white shed in a large South Bend backyard.

He's surrounded by years of his work, more than 300 models of sculptures that are placed around the country, some that he completed many years ago.

Herman B Wells sits atop a shelf above the door to the second room. His smile still the same and his hand outstretched.

Tuck Langland creates bronze sculptures ranging from two to 11 feet tall in a garage turned into a three-room studio.

It was here that he created the newest sculptural addition to the IU campus, Ernie Pyle, placed outside Franklin Hall, the soon-to-be-official home for the Media School.

• • •

Langland started sculpting in college.

Before college, he attended a boys military prep school in St. Paul, Minn., where he received no art training or education.

"Our headmaster said he didn't believe in fads and frills like the arts," Langland said. "I finished four years, never heard the word Rembrandt, anything like that. It was a completely closed world to me."

He attended the University of Minnesota and, during the first quarter, took a woman on a date to the Minneapolis Art Institute. She knew all about the art, and he asked her how she knew so much.

She said that she had taken an art appreciation course.

The following quarter, Langland signed up for art appreciation.

"It was like a big door opening," he said. "It was like a different world. I didn't know that stuff was out there."

In his sophomore year, he took drawing and design courses. In the first quarter of his junior year, he signed up for a sculpting class.

"I walked out the first day say-

SEE **LANGLAND**, PAGE 6

Sculpture to be formally dedicated Friday
Read more about the inauguration of the Media School and sculpture dedication, page 6

Trustees approve Read changes

By Ashleigh Sherman
aesherma@indiana.edu | @aesherma

The IU Board of Trustees approved more than $32 million in renovations during its first meeting of the academic year.

The Board of Trustees, IU's governing body, met Thursday and Friday at IU-Purdue University Indianapolis.

The University Relations Committee and the Academic Affairs and University Policies Committee convened Thursday, while the Finance, Audit and Strategic Planning Committee and the Facilities and Auxiliaries Committee convened Friday.

On Friday, during the Facilities and Auxiliaries Committee meeting, the trustees approved the second phase of renovations to Read Hall and the School of Public and Environmental Affairs.

Read Hall will receive new accessible student rooms, said Tom Morrison, IU vice president of capital planning and facilities.

Both new and existing rooms will receive new closet and storage layouts and new fire protection systems, as well as air conditioning systems.

"Which I'm sure students will be excited about," Morrison said.

In addition, restrooms will be updated, elevators replaced and a new roof and new exterior windows will be installed, Morrison said.

Morrison said the renovations are expected to begin this upcoming summer, lasting approximately two years, and are estimated to cost $20 million.

The School of Public and Environmental Affairs will receive a 30,000 square foot addition to the southern edge, Morrison said, putting the southern edge of the SPEA roughly even with the southern edge of the new Hodge Hall.

The addition will house new graduate classrooms, Morrison said.

Morrison said the renovations are also expected to begin this upcoming summer, lasting 12 to 14 months, and are estimated to cost $12 million.

The trustees also approved the sale of Chi Phi's real estate, as Chi Phi has agreed to sell their real estate, 1400 North Jordan Avenue, to Phi Sigma Kappa.

SEE **TRUSTEES**, PAGE 3

MEN'S SOCCER

No. 10 Hoosiers claim 3rd straight victory

By Andrew Vailliencourt
availlie@indiana.edu | @AndrewVcourt

With 1:07 left to play in regulation, IU sophomore goalie Colin Webb faced his second penalty kick of the game. Up by a goal, he needed a save to preserve victory.

Ohio State midfielder Kyle Culbertson took aim and fired the ball toward the near post. Webb dove and made the save, giving the No. 10 Hoosiers a 2-1 win over the Buckeyes in Columbus — IU's third straight win.

"Honestly I walked away looking down to the ground when the shot was taken, so I didn't see the save," IU Coach Todd Yeagley said. "But by the reaction from the bench, I know Colin measured up really well. Big play by Colin, he's been really good for us this year. We needed him today to make a play to help us get the win."

Webb knew he had to make the stop and made sure his teammates could celebrate when the game was over.

"It was definitely a big time result for the guys," Webb said. "The guys put in a great effort and I wanted to make sure they were rewarded for the hard work they put in."

IU (8-1-3, 2-1-1) got its first goal in the 49th minute on junior midfielder Femi Hollinger-Janzen's third goal of the season after a cross into the box by junior forward Andrew Oliver.

SEE **SOCCER**, PAGE 6

ELECTIONS 2014

Funding gap separates candidates

By Emily Ernsberger
emelerns@indiana.edu | @emilyernsberger

Many seats across every level of government are up for next month's midterm election, including all 435 U.S. House of Representative candidates, many U.S. Senate seats and various state-wide and local positions.

Politico has projected that all incumbent candidates for the U.S House of Representatives seats in Indiana are likely to win.

One indication of this victory might be from the size of campaign funds compared to challengers.

This election, incumbents for representative seats in Indiana have, on average, 126,538 times the funds their challengers do, based on numbers from the Federal Elections

SEE **FUNDING**, PAGE 6

COMPARING CAMPAIGNS

According to information reported by candidates to the Indiana Secretary of State's office in July, here is how campaign funding for state-wide races adds up.

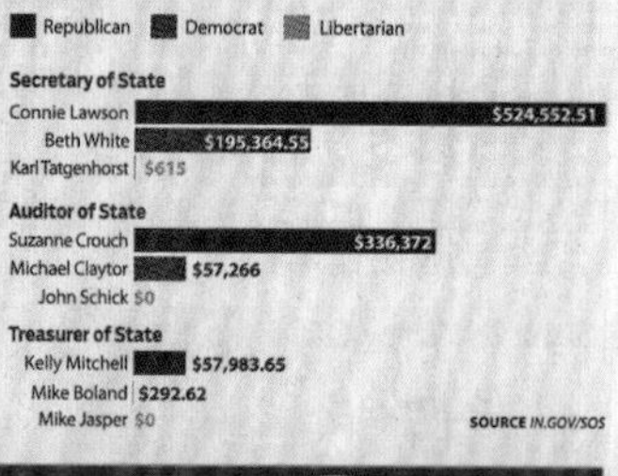

SOURCE *IN.GOV/SOS*

P0080160, IU Archives.

April 3, 2015

FRIDAY, APRIL 3, 2015

IDS

INDIANA DAILY STUDENT
IDSNEWS.COM

FIXED*

* Pence signs legislation to clarify RFRA bill, but LGBT citizens still not a protected class in Indiana

George Stephanopoulos
"One fix that people have talked about is simply adding sexual orientation as a protected class under the state civil rights laws. Will you push for that?"

Gov. Mike Pence
"I will not push for that. That is not on my agenda and that has not been an objective of the people of the state of Indiana. And that has nothing to do with this law."

March 29 on "This Week" on ABC

By Michael Majchrowicz
mmajchro@indiana.edu | @mjmajchrowicz

INDIANAPOLIS — In a hurried attempt to reclaim credibility for his state, Gov. Mike Pence signed off on a clarification to the "religious freedom" law Thursday.

In the midst of furious debate, Pence said in a statement, he prayed.

Since he signed it last week, Senate Bill 101 has come under attack as anti-gay and brought a firestorm of condemnation on the entire state. The new language — Senate Bill 50 — clarifies that the bill does not condone discrimination.

HOW THEY VOTED
House 66-30
Senate 34-16

It comes after Seattle, San Francisco and the states of New York and Connecticut barred official non-essential travel to Indiana; the NCAA Tournament — worth more than $11 billion in contracts — threatened to leave Indianapolis; Wilco canceled a concert; Angie's List called off a 1,000-job expansion; Twitter exploded with #boycottindiana and #impeachmikepence.

Stephen King only needed one tweet: "You can frost a dog turd, but it's still a dog turd."

One petition called for the governor to be recalled. Another called upon IU to confer him an honorary doctorate in interpretive dance after he avoided answers to yes-no questions on television. The Indianapolis Star, the state's largest newspaper, devoted an entire front page to its editorial board's stance: "FIX THIS NOW."

It was repeatedly called the most embarrassing moment in recent Indiana history.

Opponents of the original legislation pushed for sweeping nondiscrimination measures that would have allowed LGBT individuals class protection. During Thursday's committee discussions, one transgendered youth asked lawmakers for full protection for LGBT and gender nonconforming individuals. A clean start.

House Republicans and Senate leadership met somewhere in the middle.

While the result, SB 50, protects

SEE **RFRA**, PAGE 10

Pence throughout RFRA controversy

Since the inception of the Religious Freedom Restoration Act, Gov. Mike Pence's defensive rhetoric has changed drastically.

MARCH 24
"The legislation, SB 101, is about respecting and reassuring Hoosiers that their religious freedoms are intact. I strongly support the legislation and applaud the members of the General Assembly for their work on this important issue."

Gov. Mike Pence, on the passage of the bill

MARCH 29
"This is not about disputes between individuals. It's about government overreach. And I'm proud that Indiana stepped forward."

Pence, on "This Week" with George Stephanopoulos

MARCH 31
"I abhor discrimination. I believe in the Golden Rule that you should 'Do unto others as you would have them do unto you.' If I saw a restaurant owner refuse to serve a gay couple, I wouldn't eat there anymore."

Pence, in a Wall Street Journal op-ed

"Let me say, on the — the subject of the bill itself, I don't believe for a minute that it was the intention of the General Assembly to create a license to discriminate or right to deny services to gays, lesbians or anyone else in this state. And it certainly wasn't my intent. But I can appreciate that that's become the perception, not just here in Indiana but all across this country, and we need to confront that and confront it boldly in a way that respects the interests of all involved."

Pence, at a press conference regarding the law

APRIL 2
"Our state is rightly celebrated for our pro-business environment, and we enjoy an international reputation for the hospitality, generosity, tolerance and kindness of our people. Hoosier hospitality is not a slogan; it is our way of life. Now that this is behind us, let's move forward together with a renewed commitment to the civility and respect that make this state great."

Pence, on the passage of the new language

RFRA laws across America and how Indiana is different

While 19 other states and the federal government have RFRA laws, Indiana's has caused a stir for a variety of differences.

First is the public perception of marriage equality today versus when the 20 other laws were passed.

Public approval of same-sex marriage is much higher today than it was in the 1990s when many of these other RFRA laws were passed.

Indiana also has no equal protection status for sexual orientation.

If a court case based on sexual orientation went through the Indiana court system, the people claiming discrimination would not receive protection.

SOURCE NATIONAL CONFERENCE OF STATE LEGISLATURES

University backs new language changes in RFRA

From IDS reports

IU released a statement approving of the Religious Freedom Restoration Act changes made by the Indiana General Assembly in a press release Thursday morning.

IU appreciates that nothing in the RFRA bill will provide legal protection for discrimination against a person based on sexual orientation, race, religion, sex, gender identity, disability, national origin, age, ancestry or any other demographic, according to the release.

In the release, IU asked "all Hoosiers to remember that religious liberty and equal protection under the law are both cornerstones of our democracy and they should not be in conflict with each other. Our system of government works best when people of good will come together to reconcile their differences and find common ground."

Suzanne Grossman

P0079396, IU Archives.

Monday, June 13, 2016

IDS

Indiana Daily Student
idsnews.com

HOOSIERS RESPOND TO ORLANDO TRAGEDY

Embracing pride

ADAM KIEFER | IDS

Kim Saylor, left, hugs Annette Gross, right, after the end of a vigil, which took place in the Egyptian Room at the Old National Centre on Sunday evening. The vigil was sponsored by Indy Pride, Inc. in response to the recent mass shooting that took place at a gay nightclub in Orlando, Florida. "I wouldn't have been anywhere but here today," Saylor said. "The hate has got to end."

LGBT community gathers to mourn during Indianapolis vigil for Orlando victims

By Bridget Murray
bridmurr@indiana.edu | @bridget_murray

Mother Suzanne Wille said when she delivered her sermon Sunday morning at the Episcopal Church of All Saints, she had not heard the news about Orlando.

She addressed a crowd of LGBT community members and their allies Sunday evening at the Vigil for Orlando in the Egyptian Room of the Old National Centre in Indianapolis. Those not among the hundreds seated or crowded around the front of the stage were part of a standing room only crowd in the back of the room.

Indy Pride, Inc. organized the vigil after celebratory events of Circle City IN Pride ended Saturday night.

When she returned home to hear the news from her wife of a mass shooting at gay club Pulse in Orlando early that morning, which would later be called the largest single shooting in United States history, she said her heart broke.

"Friends we are angry today," she said. "But we cannot, we will not, give up on love. And already I can see it."

She said she saw love in the LGBT community's response in Orlando to what happened.

She said she saw love in the Islamic Center of Orlando's instruction to Muslims to give blood even though it breaks the sacred fast of Ramadan.

She said she saw love present in the room at the vigil that night.

Various religious leaders of Indianapolis spoke at the vigil, preaching love to combat the hatred the community might feel.

Executive Director of the Muslim Alliance of Indiana Rima Khan Shahid said the alliance was shocked and horrified to hear about the mass shooting in Orlando.

She said the alliance condemns the attack as a barbarous act of hatred contrary to the beliefs of Islam.

"Islam is a religion of peace,

SEE **VIGIL**, PAGE 4

Orlando massacre marks deadliest shooting in U.S. history

By Anicka Slachta
aslachta@umail.iu.edu | @ajslachta

At least 50 people have been killed and 53 injured the morning of June 12 in an Orlando, Florida, nightclub in what has become the deadliest mass shooting in American history.

Around 4:50 a.m., Orlando police responded to a shooting at the gay nightclub Pulse, according to the Associated Press.

Earlier, around 2 a.m., Pulse Orlando posted "Everyone get out of pulse and keep running" on its Facebook page.

Numerous media outlets including the Washington Post and New York Times have reported the gunman called 911 before his death

SEE **SHOOTING**, PAGE 2

Local Orlando memorial events

Monday

Solidarity Letter Writing Event for Pulse.
The Back Door, 5-9 p.m.

Writing letters to owners, staff and patrons. Writing to legislators is also encouraged. Opening early at 5 p.m. with all drinks half off as always on Monday.

Tuesday

Bloomington Pride announced a vigil is being organized from 7:30 to 8:30 p.m. Tuesday at City Hall for the victims of the Orlando shooting.

The candlelight vigil will recognize all the victims and families affected by the tragedy. Candles will be provided by the Unitarian Universalist Church, according to the Bloomington Pride Facebook page.

Leo Smith
and Suzanne Grossman

Check *idsnews.com* for coverage of these events throughout the week.

BASEBALL

Number of IU players drafted last weekend

By Michael Hughes
michhugh@imail.iu.edu | @MichaelHughes94

Continuing a recent tradition, a number of IU players and recruits were selected in the 2016 version of the Major League Baseball Draft.

A total of four current Hoosiers and two potential Hoosiers were selected throughout the 40-round draft that ran Thursday through Saturday.

Last year, a total of six Hoosiers were drafted, and the year before that five IU players were selected.

The first to be selected this year was senior starting pitcher Caleb Baragar, who was drafted in the ninth round by the San Francisco Giants. He was also the only IU player drafted in the first two days of the draft.

Baragar was followed by two other pitchers on the final day of the draft. After junior pitcher Jake Kelzer was drafted by the Philadelphia Phillies in the 18th round, senior pitcher Kyle Hart was drafted in the 19th round by the Boston Red Sox.

SEE **DRAFT**, PAGE 4

Indiana man arrested near LA Pride event with weapons

From IDS reports

The Santa Monica Police Department Police Chief Jacqueline Seabrooks tweeted that Indiana man James Howell was arrested while on his way to a gay pride parade in Southern California.

The Associated Press reports Howell told police he was on his way to do harm at the event.

When arrested around 5 a.m., Howell was heavily armed with three assault rifles, high-capacity magazines, ammunition and a five-gallon bucket with chemicals that could be used to make an explosive device, according to the AP.

A concerned neighbor called the police and reported a prowler, who was found to be the 20-year-old Howell. He was arrested about seven miles away from the pride event in West Hollywood, California, which is attended by hundreds of thousands each year, according to the AP.

Howell was also charged with a level 5 felony for pointing a firearm at another and intimidation Oct. 15, 2015, in Clark County, Indiana.

Howell pleaded guilty to the charges in a plea agreement, according to a hearing journal entry on *mycase.in.gov* from April 19, 2016.

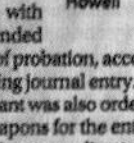

James Howell

The court accepted and sentenced Howell to one year at the Indiana Department of Corrections with one year suspended to strict terms of probation, according to the hearing journal entry.

The defendant was also ordered to forfeit all weapons for the entirety of his probation, according to the hearing journal entry.

Suzanne Grossman

P0080155, IU Archives.

November 9, 2016

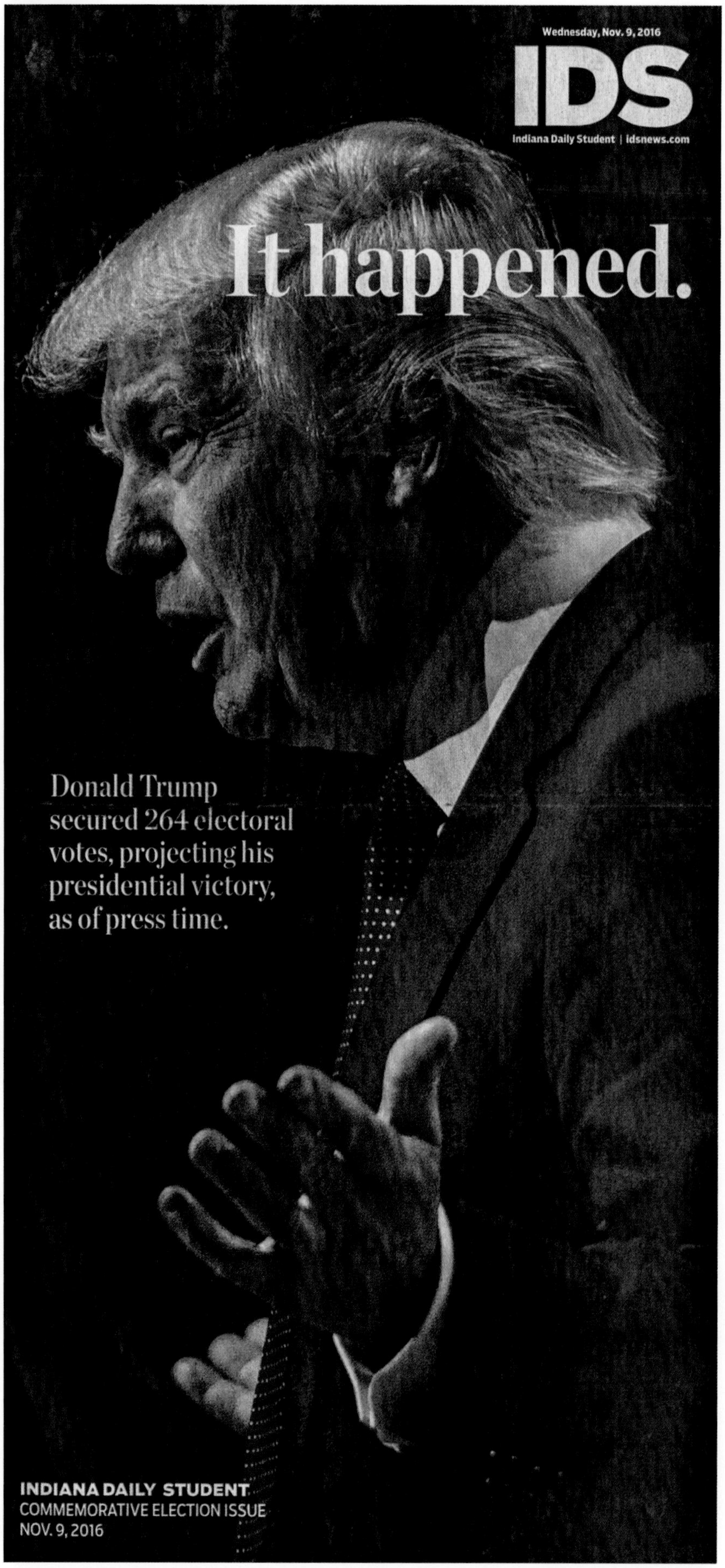
Wednesday, Nov. 9, 2016

IDS

Indiana Daily Student | idsnews.com

It happened.

Donald Trump secured 264 electoral votes, projecting his presidential victory, as of press time.

INDIANA DAILY STUDENT

COMMEMORATIVE ELECTION ISSUE

NOV. 9, 2016

P0079371, IU Archives.

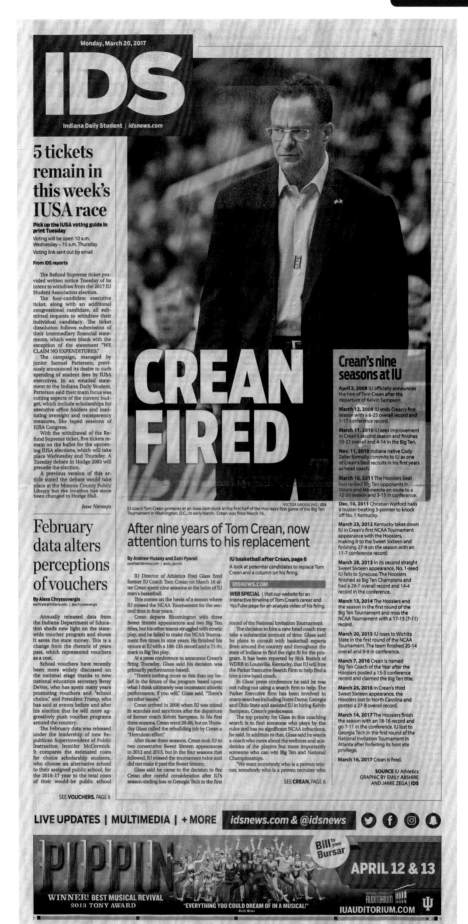

Monday, March 20, 2017

IDS

Indiana Daily Student | idsnews.com

5 tickets remain in this week's IUSA race

Pick up the IUSA voting guide in print Tuesday

Voting will be open 10 a.m. Wednesday – 10 a.m. Thursday

Voting link sent out by email

From IDS reports

The Refund Supreme ticket provided written notice Tuesday of its intent to withdraw from the 2017 IU Student Association election.

The four-candidate executive ticket, along with an additional congressional candidate, all submitted requests to withdraw their individual candidacy. The ticket dissolution follows submission of their intermediary financial statements, which were blank with the exception of the statement "WE CLAIM NO EXPENDITURES."

The campaign, managed by junior Samuel Patterson, previously announced its desire to curb spending of student fees by IUSA executives. In an emailed statement to the Indiana Daily Student, Patterson said their main focus was cutting aspects of the current budget, which include scholarships for executive office holders and instituting oversight and transparency measures, like taped sessions of IUSA Congress.

With the withdrawal of the Refund Supreme ticket, five tickets remain on the ballot for the upcoming IUSA elections, which will take place Wednesday and Thursday. A Tuesday debate in Hodge 2083 will precede the election.

A previous version of this article stated the debate would take place at the Monroe County Public Library but the location has since been changed to Hodge Hall.

Jesse Naranjo

February data alters perceptions of vouchers

By Alexa Chryssovergis
aachryss@indiana.edu | @achryssovergis

Annually released data from the Indiana Department of Education sheds new light on the statewide voucher program and shows it saves the state money. This is a change from the rhetoric of years past, which represented vouchers as a cost.

School vouchers have recently been more widely discussed on the national stage thanks to new national education secretary Betsy DeVos, who has spent many years promoting vouchers and "school choice," and President Trump, who has said at events before and after his election that he will more aggressively push voucher programs around the country.

The February data was released under the leadership of new Republican Superintendent of Public Instruction Jennifer McCormick. It compares the estimated costs for choice scholarship students, who choose an alternative school to their assigned public school, for the 2016-17 year to the total costs of their would-be public school

SEE **VOUCHERS**, PAGE 6

CREAN FIRED

VICTOR GROSSLING | IDS
IU coach Tom Crean grimaces at an Iowa slam dunk in the first half of the Hoosiers' first game of the Big Ten Tournament in Washington, D.C., in early March. Crean was fired March 16.

After nine years of Tom Crean, now attention turns to his replacement

By Andrew Hussey and Zain Pyarali
sports@idsnews.com | @ids_sports

IU Director of Athletics Fred Glass fired former IU Coach Tom Crean on March 16 after Crean spent nine seasons at the helm of IU men's basketball.

This comes on the heels of a season where IU missed the NCAA Tournament for the second time in four years.

Crean departs Bloomington with three Sweet Sixteen appearances and two Big Ten titles, but his other teams struggled with erratic play, and he failed to make the NCAA Tournament five times in nine years. He finished his tenure at IU with a 166-135 record and a 71-91 mark in Big Ten play.

At a press conference to announce Crean's firing Thursday, Glass said his decision was primarily performance-based.

"There's nothing more to this than my belief in the future of the program based upon what I think ultimately was inconstant athletic performance, if you will," Glass said. "There's no other issues."

Crean arrived in 2008 when IU was mired in scandals and sanctions after the departure of former coach Kelvin Sampson. In his first three seasons, Crean went 28-66, but on Thursday Glass called the rebuilding job by Crean a "Herculean effort."

After those three seasons, Crean took IU to two consecutive Sweet Sixteen appearances in 2012 and 2013, but in the four seasons that followed, IU missed the tournament twice and did not make it past the Sweet Sixteen.

Glass said he came to the decision to fire Crean after careful consideration after IU's season-ending loss to Georgia Tech in the first round of the National Invitation Tournament.

The decision to hire a new head coach may take a substantial amount of time. Glass said he plans to consult with basketball experts from around the country and throughout the state of Indiana to find the right fit for the program. It has been reported by Rick Bozich of WDRB in Louisville, Kentucky, that IU will hire the Parker Executive Search Firm to help find a hire a new head coach.

In Glass' press conference he said he was not ruling out using a search firm to help. The Parker Executive firm has been involved in many searches including Notre Dame, Georgia and Ohio State and assisted IU in hiring Kelvin Sampson, Crean's predecessor.

The top priority for Glass in this coaching search is to find someone who plays by the rules and has no significant NCAA infractions, he said. In addition to that, Glass said he wants a coach who cares about the wellness and academics of the players but more importantly someone who can win Big Ten and National Championships.

"We want somebody who is a proven winner, somebody who is a proven recruiter who

SEE **CREAN**, PAGE 6

IU basketball after Crean, page 8
A look at potential candidates to replace Tom Crean and a column on his firing.

IDSNEWS.COM

WEB SPECIAL | Visit our website for an interactive timeline of Tom Crean's career and YouTube page for an analysis video of his firing.

Crean's nine seasons at IU

April 2, 2008 IU officially announces the hire of Tom Crean after the departure of Kelvin Sampson.

March 12, 2009 IU ends Crean's first season with a 6-25 overall record and 1-17 conference record.

March 11, 2010 IU sees improvement in Crean's second season and finishes 10-21 overall and 4-14 in the Big Ten.

Nov. 11, 2010 Indiana native Cody Zeller formally commits to IU as one of Crean's best recruits in his first years as head coach.

March 10, 2011 The Hoosiers beat two ranked Big Ten opponents in Illinois and Minnesota en route to a 12-20 season and 3-15 in conference.

Dec. 10, 2011 Christian Watford nails a buzzer-beating 3-pointer to knock off No. 1 Kentucky.

March 23, 2012 Kentucky takes down IU in Crean's first NCAA Tournament appearance with the Hoosiers, making it to the Sweet Sixteen and finishing 27-9 on the season with an 11-7 conference record.

March 28, 2013 In its second straight Sweet Sixteen appearance, No. 1-seed IU falls to Syracuse. The Hoosiers finished as Big Ten Champions and had a 29-7 overall record and 14-4 record in the conference.

March 13, 2014 The Hoosiers end the season in the first round of the Big Ten Tournament and miss the NCAA Tournament with a 17-15 (7-11) record.

March 20, 2015 IU loses to Wichita State in the first round of the NCAA Tournament. The team finished 20-14 overall and 9-9 in conference.

March 7, 2016 Crean is named Big Ten Coach of the Year after the Hoosiers posted a 15-3 conference record and claimed the Big Ten title.

March 25, 2016 In Crean's third Sweet Sixteen appearance, the Hoosiers lost to North Carolina and posted a 27-8 overall record.

March 14, 2017 The Hoosiers finish the season with an 18-16 record and go 7-11 in the conference. IU lost to Georgia Tech in the first round of the National Invitation Tournament in Atlanta after forfeiting its host site privilege.

March 16, 2017 Crean is fired.

SOURCE IU Athletics
GRAPHIC BY EMILY ABSHIRE AND JAMIE ZEGA | **IDS**

LIVE UPDATES | MULTIMEDIA | + MORE idsnews.com & @idsnews

P0079354, IU Archives.

Editor's Note: The IDS Will No Longer Print Five Days a Week, and That Is Ok

Like all newspapers in the 21st century, the IDS has faced ongoing financial challenges in the transition to a digital business model. About a month after the paper marked its 150th anniversary, it announced it would no longer publish a daily print edition. This story originally appeared March 27, 2017, on idsnews.com.

By Hannah Alani

In response to industry changes, the Indiana Daily Student will alter its news distribution model. Starting this fall, instead of printing five days a week, the IDS will print twice weekly, Mondays and Thursdays, while continuing to expand its digital presence.

In a press release, IU Student Media Director Ron Johnson said the move will facilitate plans to "get content where readers and advertisers need it."

As the current IDS editor, I say kudos to our professional staff for making this leap.

When IU fired Tom Crean, our sports, photo and web editors immediately convened and planned holistic and comprehensive digital coverage, which included a photo gallery, Periscope video and Snapchat stories. In this instance, because news broke during spring break, there was no choice but to be strong and effective storytellers on the Internet.

Most days, however, our efforts to be more digitally focused are stifled by the demands of a print-focused work day. Yes, we are on social media, but the practice of tweet writing is an afterthought. Yes, we produce multimedia through podcasts and Facebook Live videos, but we do not have a rigid workflow system in place for planning and publishing video content. Yes, we have a web editor who oversees digital storytelling forms, such as Storify, but he cannot access our content until around midnight, after a print designer has sent the print page off to the printer.

I do not know the percentage of IU students who read the IDS in print versus online.

I do know what I see: thousands of students roving campus, eyes glued to their phone screens.

In Friday's press release, Media School dean James Shanahan said students "need to be experienced not only with the traditional principles of writing, reporting and editing, but also with the rapidly changing business structures of news and its digital distribution."

This move, he said, will help the IDS "refind" its audience.

He's correct. Our mission to serve campus is more important than ever, and reporters and editors need to learn to balance traditional journalistic principles and ethics with meeting readers where they are—online. Two senior editors are finishing up a full redesign of our website. Their work involved early input from our advertising staff and I believe the new site will engage with our audience and welcome more advertisers.

We need not completely abandon the past. The fall staff will be proud to serve our print readers through two twice-weekly and our special sections, including the fall and spring housing & living guides, the campus visitor's guide and Inside magazine. The print IDS will continue to be a cherished source for well-reported and well-designed content.

Reporters and editors will need to seek innovative news gathering and storytelling forms in an effort to engage more with you, our readers. Some of these ideas will work better than others. The IDS invites you to contact us with feedback and ideas for how we can better serve you.

We celebrated the newspaper's 150th birthday Feb. 22. Alumni and friends will gather Oct. 7 to celebrate the anniversary, and they have been contributing to the Indiana Daily Student Legacy Fund. I will return to campus in the fall to celebrate the IDS and I hope to see you there, too.

October 23, 2017

Monday, Oct. 23, 2017 | Indiana Daily Student | idsnews.com

IDS

PETER STEVENSON | IDS
University Chancellor Ken Gros Louis prepares for a talk on "History, Traditions and Culture of Indiana University" on Dec. 8, 2009, at the DeVault Alumni Center. Gros Louis died Thursday at the age of 80.

Remembering an IU legend

The University's former dean, vice president and chancellor Ken Gros Louis died at 80.

By Rebecca Ellis | rebellis@iu.edu | @rebeccae_97

The name Ken Gros Louis was articulated through generations of students as a man they needed to know, one that rivaled Herman B Wells.

In his time as vice president and chancellor of IU-Bloomington, Gros Louis created the Wells Scholars program. He also focused on advocating for film, Jewish and African-American studies departments; the School of Journalism; and the Office of Gay, Lesbian and Bisexual Student Support Services, now the LGBTQ+ Culture Center. Gros Louis even received the GLBT Distinguished Alumni Award in 2015 for his support.

Gros Louis died in his sleep on Thursday night. He was 80.

IU Associate Professor of Law Steve Sanders introduced Gros Louis before he received the GLBT Distinguished Alumni Award and described the qualities he embodied.

"The grace with language of a Romantic-era poet," Sanders said. "A late-night talk show host's mischievous wit and ability to find delight in absurdity. The equanimity and self-discipline of a Zen master. And most importantly, the soul of Herman Wells himself."

Gros Louis said IU's campus seemed happy in an article he wrote for Indiana Magazine of History, and he said the campus atmosphere

SEE GROS LOUIS, PAGE 5

COURTESY OF IU ARCHIVES
Kenneth R.R. Gros Louis speaks at a rally in Assembly Hall after IU won the 1981 NCAA Championship.

Ken Gros Louis through the years

1964 Earns his Ph.D. in medieval and Renaissance literature from the University of Wisconsin

1964 Begins his career at IU as a professor of English and comparative literature

1978 Becomes Dean of the College of Arts and Sciences and serves in the role for two years

1980 Promoted to vice president of the Bloomington campus

1988 Promoted to vice president of academic affairs for all seven campuses and is designated chancellor of the IU-Bloomington campus

2001 Retires from IU

2004 Comes back to IU as interim senior vice president and chancellor

2006 Named University Chancellor, an honorary designation that had only been held by Herman B Wells before him

2015 Receives the GLBT Distinguished Alumni Award

2017 Dies at 80 years old

Friends remember Ken Gros Louis on social media

"So sorry to hear of passing of IU Univ. Chancellor Emeritus Ken Gros Louis. Always kind, always the smartest person in any room I was in."

Chuck Carney
Communications and marketing director for IU School of Global and International Studies
@chuck_carney

"So sad about the passing of Ken Gros Louis, an IU legend and a mentor to so many student leaders. You will be missed. Peace."

Lori Reesor
IU vice provost for student affairs
@LoriReesor

"Ken Gros Louis was simply one of the finest folks I ever met, and I'll never be able to measure all he did for me."

Zach Osterman
IU alumnus and Indianapolis Star reporter
@ZachOsterman

P0079150, IU Archives.

Monday, April 2, 2018

IDS

Indiana Daily Student | idsnews.com

CHAMPIONS

For the first time in program history, women's basketball will be hanging a WNIT championship banner in Simon Skjodt Assembly Hall.

By Murphy Wheeler
jonmwhee@iu.edu | @murph_wheelerIU

Not many teams can say they end their season on a win.

Very few players can say the same about their careers.

Even fewer can say they end it with a championship.

The IU women's basketball team and its seniors Tyra Buss and Amanda Cahill did just that with their 65-57 victory over Virginia Tech in the WNIT Championship on Saturday.

As they walked off the court at Simon Skjodt Assembly Hall in their cream and crimson jerseys for the last time, Buss and Cahill walked away from their storied careers at IU, champions at last.

"It's definitely a bittersweet feeling. We're obviously really honored that we got the chance to keep playing and get to go out on a win," Cahill said. "But it's going to be sad taking off that jersey and knowing we're not going to be putting it back on and come back out in front of our home crowd with our teammates."

However, the way in which they clinched their title was nothing new for the duo.

Not only has an indelible amount of fight become synonymous with Buss and Cahill's four years of basketball in Bloomington, it has also become the story of their team's improbable run this season from an 8-12 record in January to cutting down the nets less than three months later.

They've had to fight every inch of the way, and Saturday's win was no different.

After a back-and-forth first half, the Hoosiers were able to take a 36-27 lead into halftime after holding the Hokies to 10-29 shooting and forcing 10 first-half turnovers.

However, in the third, the Hoosiers got dangerously close to a meltdown.

While shooting just 3-14 from the field and missing all five of their 3-point attempts, the Hoosiers only scored seven points in the quarter and let Virginia Tech claw their way back to take a 44-43 lead heading into the fourth.

It was the first time the Hoosiers had been down in the second half of a game during their entire WNIT run.

With the season and her career on the line, Buss said that's when she and her teammates needed to fight to survive the most.

"Coach challenged us because we had to tough it out and needed to fight," Buss said. "We weren't really fighting in the third quarter and that let them go on a run."

They needed to be reinvigorated. They needed new life.

That jolt of energy came in the form of freshman guard Bendu Yeaney early in the fourth quarter. She scored the first four points of the period and helped the Hoosiers retake the lead.

Then, with just under five minutes remaining and the Hoosiers having missed their first 13 3-pointers of the game up to that point, Yeaney hit a dagger three from the corner. Cahill then followed that with a three of her own on their next possession to stretch the lead back to nine points.

Like a passing of the torch, the veterans followed the freshman making big plays down the stretch. Yeaney said she credited her late-game confidence, along with her overall development throughout her freshman season, to Buss and Cahill leading by example.

"I've learned to always stay confident and always have energy because that's what they do every single day in practice," Yeaney said. "It's impacted me in practices and you can see it games now too."

Once the final buzzer had sounded and the Hoosiers had safely secured the victory, champions weren't the only thing Buss and Cahill would leave as.

As evidenced by the IU women's basketball record crowd of 13,007 fans in attendance, the two had led the program to new heights, just like they had set out to do four years ago upon their arrival to Bloomington.

"They're going to go down in history as two of the very best," IU Coach Teri Moren said. "They've put us in a situation now where we want more. In order to do that, we have a lot of work ahead of us but we know we have a great foundation and that came from those two kids."

One by one, IU's players, still covered in red and white celebratory streamers, climbed a ladder to cut down the nets of Assembly Hall. The last two slivers of nylon were left for Buss and Cahill, with the entire net coming down on Buss' final clip of the scissors.

Buss, with the net draped around her neck, walked off the court with nothing left to prove.

It had all culminated in that moment. The fight was over.

"We're still going to be able to hang a banner and Amanda and I can come back and look up there and see that we helped get that banner and win a championship," Buss said. "It was definitely worth it and I'm so happy with the way it ended."

PHOTO BY TY VINSON | IDS
The IU women's basketball team huddles and celebrates after winning the WNIT. The game against Virginia Tech was the Hoosiers' last game of the season.

To see more photos from Saturday's game go to page 5.

Ella Fitzgerald exhibit honors singer for her 100th birthday

By Robert Mack
rsmack@iu.edu

Old jazz tunes now fill Kirkwood Hall Gallery where the School of Art, Architecture + Design presents "Celebrating a Jazz Icon: 100 Years of Ella Fitzgerald Exhibits and Events." This exhibit honors the famed African-American singer from noon to 5 p.m. Mondays through Fridays through May 4.

The exhibition features three dresses, a wig, sunglasses and more from the SOAAD's Sage Fashion Collection. The Sage Collection has over 25,000 objects of museum-quality pieces which span more than 250 years, according to its website.

"The Sage Collection loves the opportunity to show off our Ella Fitzgerald pieces and pay tribute to this American icon," said Kelly Richardson, curator of the Sage Collection, in an email.

The Ella Fitzgerald Charitable Foundation provided sheet music, albums, records, CDs and books for display. The exhibit also features images from the Black Film Center/Archive at Indiana University and pop-up floor banners provided by the Great American Songbook Foundation in Carmel, Indiana.

ZHENG GUAN | IDS
The School of Art, Architecture + Design presents "Celebrating a Jazz Icon: 100 Years of Ella Fitzgerald Exhibits and Events." This exhibit honors the famed African-American singer from noon to 5 p.m. Mondays through Fridays through May 4 in the Kirkwood Hall Gallery.

The exhibition is part of a year-long celebration of Fitzgerald's work and life. The celebration included a lecture with Fran Morris Rosman, director of the Ella Fitzgerald Charitable Foundation on March 19.

That same day, the celebration ended with a screening of "St. Louis Blues," one of four films Fitzgerald appeared in, at the IU Cinema. A live performance by jazz musician Monika Herzig, a senior lecturer at the School of Environmental and Public Policy, and jazz vocalist Janiece Jaffe preceded the film.

SEE **FITZGERALD**, PAGE 5

Firefighter charged with child solicitation, sexual misconduct

By Dominick Jean
drjean@iu.edu | @domino_jean

A Bloomington firefighter was arrested for child solicitation and sexual misconduct with a minor Friday morning. The firefighter, Robert Sears, is a 20-year veteran and captain at the Bloomington Fire Department. He spent two days in the Monroe County Correctional Center.

A Bloomington Police Department detective was investigating another case involving a 14-year-old girl using the messaging app Whisper, according to a BPD press release, leading the detective to discover the inappropriate relationship with the fire captain.

The conversations with the captain seemed to have begun in February 2018.

The captain reportedly said he "worked 24 hour shifts at the fire department" and reminded the 14-year-old girl to erase their communications.

According to the BPD release, the detective determined Sears was the one communicating and that Sears and the juvenile were likely involved in sexual activity.

The detective, according to the release, pretended to be the the juvenile and convinced Sears he should come over to her house where he said the 14-year-old and another girl were alone. The detective told Sears to bring condoms.

Detectives conducted surveillance of the area and noticed a truck had driven by the home twice. The detectives stopped the vehicle with Sears inside. Condoms were among the items found in the truck.

Police took Sears to BPD where officers interviewed him. According to the BPD release, he drove from his Mitchell, Indiana, home and bought condoms with the intent to have sex with one or both of the

SEE **FIREFIGHTER**, PAGE 5

P0020570, IU Archives.

REFLECTION

Changes and Challenges

It's hard not to celebrate the history of the IDS without also thinking about its future. When I look to the years ahead for this news organization, I think of both change and challenge.

Change? That part is easy to imagine. To do so, all I have to do is remember when I began as a student reporter, back in 1994 as a freshman at Webster University in St. Louis. My very first assignment for The Journal was to cover a volleyball match. I delivered a 1,600-word beauty of a recap written in chronological order. I proved then that I had a lot to learn about the inverted pyramid and the craft of reporting.

But what stands out most is how I filed that first story. Or should I say, literally handed in that first story. I didn't email the assignment because I had yet to see email. The newspaper was a couple of years from electronic pagination, so the story found its way to the page through cutting and pasting up. There was no

Editors in chief past and present pose for a photo at the 150th anniversary celebration of the IDS in October 2017. *Photo courtesy of Amy Wimmer Schwarb.*

Jim Rodenbush, IU director of student media. *Photo courtesy Jim Rodenbush.*

"What's certain is that the future of the IDS will mean change—what stories we tell, how we report them and the methods of reaching our audience. Our challenge will be to embrace head on the change that awaits, to be adaptive and proactive as a news organization."

website to post the story to because the university didn't have internet for the first time until late in my sophomore year. The Journal's first website debuted one year later.

Fast-forward 25 years, and the business of being a reporter now is very different. I proved it by writing this essay on a hand-held mobile device and sending it off with the click of a button. Our communication—the words we write and how we share them with our audience—is now instant.

But, as much as things have changed, that's nothing compared to what waits for us tomorrow, or the next five years, or even 10 years from now. What's certain is that the future of the IDS will mean change—what stories we tell, how we report them and the methods of reaching our audience. Our challenge will be to embrace head on the change that awaits, to be adaptive and proactive as a news organization.

So, about those challenges. Well, there are a few, and they all are shared by other student—and national—media organizations around the country.

How do we remain a relevant, important part of our audience's lives?

The students and alumni of Indiana University, along with the greater Bloomington community, are bombarded daily with information through their TVs, radios and phones, their newspapers and desktop computers, and all other imagined forms of communication. What does the IDS need to do to make sure it's being heard? That it's finding the stories that are necessary to the day-to-day lives of its audience? That it stands out from the crowd and remains a constant, crucial, necessary voice for everyone?

How do we provide the best learning opportunities for the students who work for the IDS?

Beyond anything, this is the organization's most important challenge. The IDS must continue to be a part of the path that helps students get jobs after graduation. To do so means remaining a top-notch learning laboratory and providing real-life experiences no matter if that student is a reporter, a photographer, an advertising staffer, or is just trying out any of the jobs available.

But what that means right now could change tomorrow. So it will be up to those in my position to remain connected with alumni and to constantly reach out to media organizations everywhere in order to know which skills our students need to be learning.

Another crucial question: How do we make money doing all of this?

Maintaining traditional advertising income while seeking new revenue streams is the approach any news organization needs to take. But where do these new streams come from? And how do we best introduce ourselves? What do our long-term clients need and want from us? And what are we missing? What are the untapped areas?

Obviously, the challenges facing the IDS present myriad unanswered questions. But that's the exciting part of this particular writing assignment. This book will give me and others the chance a year from now, or many years from now, to check in and see how we did. How did we adapt to the expected changes? How did we respond to the challenges? And did we succeed in making sure that the IDS remained a renowned, thriving student news organization?

—Jim Rodenbush, director of student media

Postscript

Afterword

'THE IMPORTANT THINGS ENDURE'

Almost midnight in the Indiana Daily Student backshop. It feels like we were just here, putting the newspaper to bed. I think that was actually yesterday. It feels like we never left. We must have. I was somewhere else earlier—*in class?* The end of one night is just the beginning of the next day. One deadline replaces another. A gear in motion on a typesetting machine. Music playing on repeat in Ernie Pyle Hall. Shared experiences in a circle of time. It's almost midnight, *again.*

What music is playing? The Animals, Janis Joplin, the Violent Femmes, R.E.M. Yes. But on deadline, at the end, what music is usually playing?

I am texting with Jude Biersdorfer, who reminds me: There is a stretch in the late 1980s when it is the Talking Heads' live album "Stop Making Sense." That's it. The hypnotic repetition of David Byrne singing "Once in a Lifetime."

Time isn't holding up. Time isn't after us.

Same as it ever was, same as it ever was.

It is a cassette tape recorded off a vinyl album and played on a black, plastic jambox with round knobs. We ride the jamboxes hard. They are replaced multiple times—one time funded by a newsroom bake sale that raked in more than $60 and featured Baileys Irish Cream chocolate cupcakes.

However high the number for the volume control goes, Malinda Aston jokes that it goes to 11. She's the night production boss. It's a nod to the rock mockumentary film "This is Spinal Tap" where the guitarist, Nigel Tufnel, points out that most amplifiers go to 10, but his goes to 11—in case the band needs "that extra push over the cliff." We don't take it to 11, but we appreciate knowing there are always ways to expand our potential.

The newsroom's deadline is 12:10 a.m.

That's deadline, not *suggestion* line. Dead. Done. Stop. Push it over. Let it go.

If there is a cliff right now with the tape turning in the jambox, it's in backshop. It's somewhere on a linoleum floor stained with typesetting chemicals. It's under the Converse high top sneaker-clad feet of editors and production students. In this space, you have one last chance to plead your case to change, hold or bust some news content altogether. From here, the IDS goes away, out of reach, out of your control but with your name still attached. And then into newsstands for everyone to see.

Exhilaration.

Terror.

IDS backshop staff, early 1980s.
Photo courtesy of Ruth Witmer.

Since 1867, how many students have struggled to push hard and let go only to come back the next day and do the same again? Why do we keep coming back to the cliff? It's an awful place. Nerve-wracking and dangerous. It's our cliff, though. Our shared space. Our thrilling edge.

Fall 2017. The IDS's 150th birthday celebration is in IU's Franklin Hall. Ernie Pyle Hall sits quiet and empty on the other side of Dunn Meadow waiting for its reincarnation. Alumni now stroll into what started out in 1907 as a library. Thick wood and cast-iron detailing at one turn, a large-screen TV under a skylight at the next. This new home of student media, I joke with them, is like the Starship Enterprise crashing into Hogwarts.

They want to know what else has changed. The shift from print to digital? Declining ad revenue? The newspaper two days per week instead of five? Yes. What else? Interestingly, I tell them, not much. The students keep coming. Earnest. Enthusiastic. On a mission to tell stories. They learn how to listen and question along the way. They play way above their heads sometimes. They fret over choices and deadlines. They figure out who they are and what they want.

Same as it ever was.

During the course of the day at the reunion, one thing is clear: Staffs over the years have more in common than not.

The alumni talk about the different hats they wore and their different cliques. Different tribes, really, within The IDS Tribe. I have been a reporter, photographer and editor. At this moment in my head where the music is playing, I'm on the night production staff. Nervous editors hover over our shoulders as we paste up life-sized newspaper pages that will be driven to the printing plant. Strips of paper with the stories on one side are coated with hot wax on the other, cut apart with X-Acto knives and laid in place.

We are years past typewriters, many years past something called hot type. We are years away from pages designed by students and sent electronically. That change and many others will come

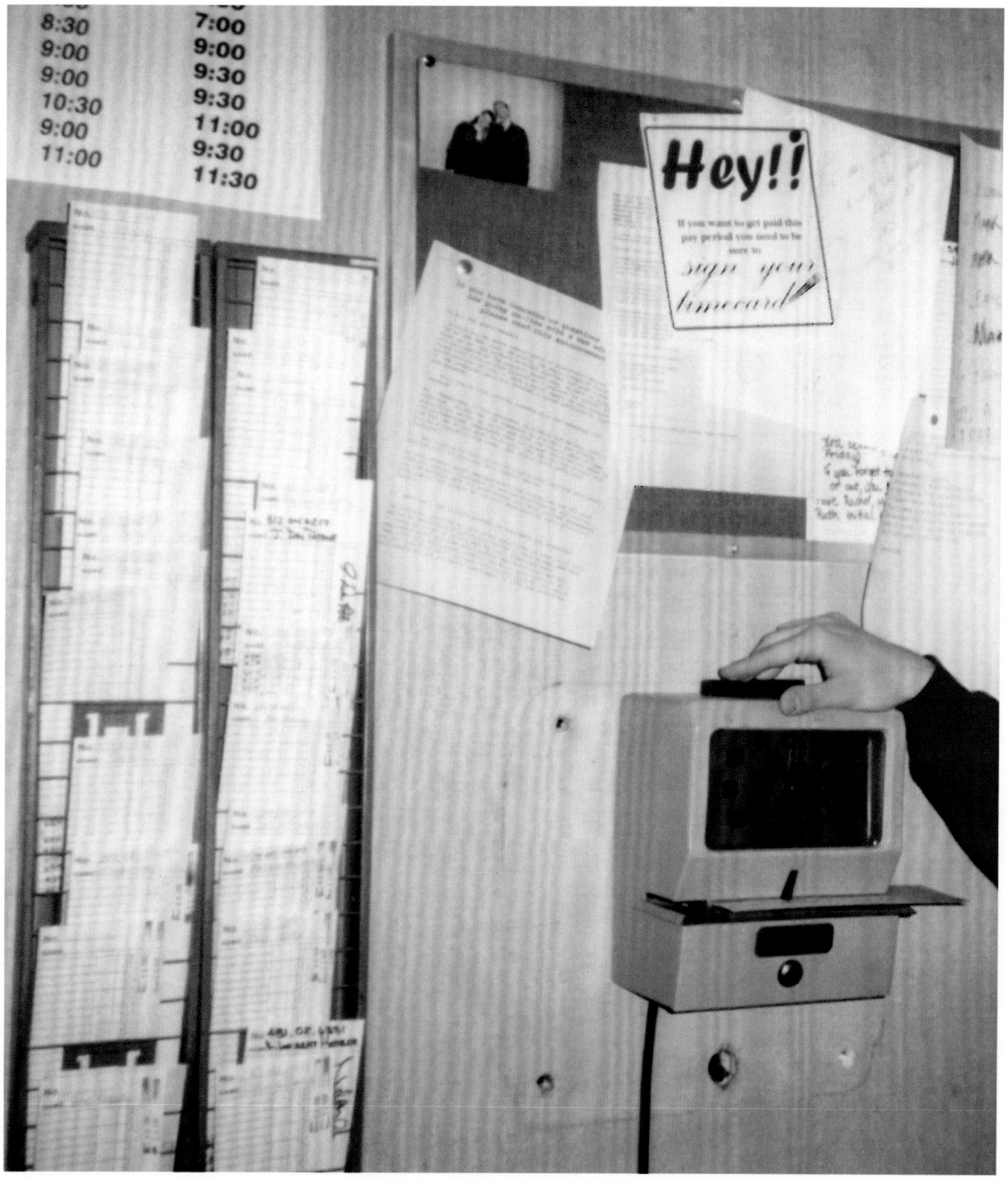

Staff time clock in the backshop.
Photo courtesy of Ruth Witmer.

quickly. In the meantime, production workers name their knives, like swords. I have Zorro and Son of Zorro, written in black magic marker on their plastic yellow cases.

Whoever puts "Stop Making Sense" in the jambox will have to make sure it's properly rewound to the first song, "Psycho Killer."

Coincidence?

Deliberate?

The editors hover too close to the students cutting stories apart, and there are quick extensions and retractions of the knife blades. A loud *click, click, click*. Some break off the tips of the long, thin razor blades with bare fingers to expose a fresh, sharp edge. Right now, this is my tribe.

Startled editors always step back. They'll forget by the next night and the next and repeatedly creep too close to a shoulder. Then there will be new editors. It's fine. There are lots of knives in the supply closet. As an editor, I'm sure I hovered to make certain someone did what I asked. As a production worker, I know I clicked the Zorros at looming editors. Someday, as the newsroom adviser, I'll remind people to not hover and offer them candy.

The different IDS tribes have their rituals. My backshop tribe sculpts figures out of chunks of wax and sacrifices them all into the hot wax machine. A swan. The "Saturday Night Live"/ Claymation cartoon character Gumby. A voodoo representation of an impossible roommate. We have backshop fests—Jell-O Fest, Cheese Fest, Elvis Fest (Presley and Costello), any excuse. There are rituals on the business side, in the editor in chief's office. We know there always have been and always will be.

I am fact-checking my memory. In the text thread, I tell Jude about a card Kate Voss sent me. "The first time I saw you, you were lighting something on fire in backshop," she wrote. "I knew we were going to be great friends."

"You come to the IDS to learn about journalism. You do. But really, you learn more about people, about yourself."

Track four of the album plays in my head, "Burning Down the House." I remember being thanked periodically for not burning the IDS down. I've assured many staffers over the years that they weren't. So, what was on fire? If something was on fire, you would think we would remember. This seems like an important detail.

What else? What else have we shared? The weight of responsibility on young shoulders. IDS readers, sources, alumni and your mom all see your mistakes and shortcomings, the one misspelling, the photo that misses the moment, the inelegant design. Your mom doesn't care. The others do and they will let you know—sometimes gently and constructively, usually not. Not at all. An angry call on a landline telephone, a sideways glance, a tweet. Tears. It's OK. Fix it and do better next time. You're not getting fired over this. That one guy did get fired. He didn't care enough to do better the next time or the next. Three (five, eight?) strikes and you're out.

And what about the character-building experience of dealing with your co-workers? The song stops and in the endless, catawampus staff game of musical chairs, you are left with this: She was your editor last semester and now you are hers. Also, she is dating your roommate. And just so you know, you don't know what you're doing. Last semester they never made these mistakes or missed those stories.

Yes, they did. *Often.* You're a journalist. This is easy to fact-check. Look at the bound volumes, PDFs and the web. Intellectually, you know you're not burning the place down. You do not know this emotionally. On many nights, on deadline, whoever you are, David Byrne or someone like him is in your head with some questions for you:

And you may ask yourself, am I right? Am I wrong?

And you may say to yourself, my God—what have I done?!

You learn that peoples' memories are both too long and too short. This applies to you, too. But here's the thing: Worst-case scenario is (probably) still just fine. There will be another newspaper, another web update. Every moment is a chance to take responsibility and seek redemption.

Pivot 180 degrees. You're doing good work for the company. At some point, a senior editor, professor, adviser or stranger tells you so. Just out of nowhere. Maybe your former high school teacher shows your work to his class and an 11th-grader decides she wants to be you some day. Then she's at IU, staring at a clock in backshop and hoping she doesn't disappoint you. You hear these words and remember them—*thank you.*

If that new kid is staring at a clock with the Talking Heads tape playing in the jambox, it is a small, metal time clock where the production staff punches in and out each night. Later, there will be plastic wall clocks, digital clocks on computers and Apple Watches. One night, a student(s) pushed a backshop clock's minute hand counter-clockwise to move it away from the deadline.

IDS backshop staff, mid-1990s.
Photo courtesy of Ruth Witmer.

Nice try. Time isn't holding up.

The jamboxes, typesetter and all the other machines have been replaced by different machines. And that's just fine. A clock is supposed to move forward.

About 45 minutes pass. "Stop Making Sense" ends with a cover of Al Green's "Take Me to the River." Ritual. Redemption. Renewal. Sneakers at the water's edge of the Jordan River for a traditional end-of-the-semester dip. Done. Rewind to the beginning.

I understand now that this tape was strategically put on at the end of the night, an incessant, frantic march toward 12:10 a.m. The tribe's ritual accompaniment. Armies used to have drummers keep the beat for soldiers marching forward into the unknown. This is that, but with news and David Byrne in a big suit.

As soon as those songs end in my head, they are replaced by countless others.

John Jackson bouncing into backshop in a Cubs hat. A mischievous grin. A pen tucked behind his ear. The Eagles play "Take It Easy." Friends returning year after year for an annual golf outing named after the song, in his memory, raising scholarship funds for new kids.

Ryan Hildebrandt channeling Al Pacino in "Scarface." He clicks his knife, My Little Friend. He's wearing a Led Zeppelin hat and singing "The Devil Went Down to Backshop"—his original composition with apologies to The Charlie Daniels Band. You know how this song ends: The IDSer is presented with a daunting challenge and meets it with a defiant mic drop.

I understand something else now. I don't know what Kate saw me lighting on fire all those years ago, but it doesn't matter as much as I thought. She was right. It's been decades since we met in backshop, yet we are great friends. I've seen many things fall by the wayside for generations of IDSers. The important things endure.

You come to the IDS to learn about journalism. You do. But really, you learn more about people, about yourself. The experiences you have at the IDS, big and small, have value and meaning. They help shape the person you are, they inform the work you did and do. They are at the core of the stories you tell and of your story, your song. The time you spend, the things you leave behind are important pieces of the foundation that was laid in place by those who came before. It will be built upon by those who follow. Same as it ever was.

IDSers past, present and future — *thank you.*

—Ruth Witmer, BA 1987

Appendix

EDITOR IN CHIEF OF THE INDIANA DAILY STUDENT

A note from the editors: The list reproduced here hangs in the IDS newsroom at IU's Franklin Hall. We believe it to be incomplete and fear it is not as accurate as it should be for a book that celebrates student journalism. (Among other omissions, it contains no editors in chief from the 1890s). However, because nearly 20,000 editions of the IDS have been produced since its inception, with some editors in chief filling the role for only a few weeks, we were unable to do a complete verification and checking. If you spot an oversight or misspelling, please contact the IU Student Publications Alumni Board, an affiliate group of the IU Alumni Association and the keeper of this list.

2010s

Matt Rasnic
Nyssa Kruse
Jamie Zega
Carley Lanich
Cameron Drummond
Alison Graham
Hannah Alani
Michael Williams
Janica Kaneshiro
Mary Katherine Wildeman
Suzanne Grossman
Michael Hughes
Michael Majchrowicz
Evan Hoopfer
Holly Hays
Mark Keierleber
Gage Bentley
Rachel Wisinski
Will Royal
Charles Scudder
Michael Auslen
Max McCombs
MJ Slaby
Zach Ammerman
Jake New
Sarah Brubeck
Jake Wright
Brooke Lillard
Natalie Avon
Brad Zehr
Carrie Schedler

2000s

Audrie Garrison
Michael Sanserino
Sara Amato
Trevor Brown
Carrie Ritchie
Michael Reschke
Michael Zennie
Kacie Foster Axsom
Zachary Osterman
Adam Aasen
Rick Newkirk
Eamonn Brennan
Jane Charney
Josh Sanburn
Gavin Lesnick
Cory Schouten
Adam Van Osdol
Josh Weinfuss
Aaron Sharockman
Kathryn Helmke
Ben Cunningham
Gina Czark
Christina Jewett
Ryan Gunterman
Jeff Shireman
Brooke Ruivivar
Peter Gelling
Joel Eskovitz
Olivia Clarke
John Silver

1990s

Beth Spangle
Peter Schnitzler
Jeff Fleischer
Ben French
Jennifer Emily
Jeff Rose
Pat Kastner
Marijke Rowland
Sharna Marcus
Amy Wimmer
Dave DeCamp
Reid Cox
Eric Gorman
JR Ross
Ryan Whirty
John Jackson
Chris Rickett
Elissa Milenky
Robyn Holtzman
Kim Wessel
Bruce Gray
Jay Judge
June Lyle
Mike Slatin
Dan Shapiro
Nancy Mitchell
Bill Simmons
Matt Logan
Ted Yee
Matt Solinsky
Kerry Lauerman

1980s

Kelly Boring
Eric Staats
Jackie Dulen
Jennifer Orsi
Paul Rogers
Judy Cebula
Tanya Isch
Leah Lorber
Kelly Boring
Jack Barry
Mark Skertic
Alan Chitleck
Paul Heaton
Jay A. Diskey
Tom Price
Wendy Weyen
Anne Wesley
Barbara Toman
Dan Brogan
Andy Countryman
Tim Franklin
Tim Nickens
Lorrie Wildman
Mike Davis
Andy Hall
Mark Ryan
Tom French
Tom Herrmann

1970s

Terry English
Greg Johnson
Bob Kyle
Merv Hendricks
Ward Beckham
Susie Bishoff
Steve Jacob
Tim Harman
Susan Bonnell
Jena Priessler
Michael Starks
Vic Bracht
Jim Adams
Linnea Lannon
Scott Fore
Paul Tash
Bill Wilson
Craig Webb
Dan Barreiro
Rick Lyman
Rick Wood
Bonita Brodt
Hunt Helm
Phil Kincaide
Bob Johnson
Jennifer Steinbeck
Hugh Martin
David Haynes
Jim Wanko
Bill Turner
Curt Reeve

1960s

Joseph K. Abrell
W. Terrence Joyce
Steve Carlson
Michael H. McCoy
Glenn N. Schramm
Michael J. Brennan
Gary L. Long
Max E. Moss
John McHugh
Patrick J. McKean
Myrna Oliver
Mike Clark
Tom Green
Joel Whitaker
Ellen McKinney

F. David Cohn
Monte Hayes
Mary Ellen Straub Cohn
Marc Carmichael
Sheldon F. Shafer
Pamela Litchell
James H. Nolan
Kent Dove
Richard Balough
Beth Zimmerman
Margaret Craig
Jerry Hicks
Rod Smith
Steve Fagan
Jim Helm

1950s

Betty Stevens Schierhorn
Ruth Scism Kennedy
Irene Harris Gordon
Lois McNear Canright
Doris Mae Wilson Bark
Jean Tabbert Spicklemire
Mary Alys Werkhoff Wright
Joanne Whiteneck Wright
Mary Monroe
Ruth Hamilton Gregory
Dee Harrington Moore
Ed Sovola
George W. Lamb
Homer Murray
Mace I. Brodie
Robert C. Junk
Annadell Craig Lamb
William Brooks
Charles B. Vaughn
Marjorie Smith Blewett
Jack Pressley
Harrison Weber
Carl Foster
Robert E. Thompson
Bennie E. Graves
Manuel Mighdoll
Robert Bourne
Russ Tornabene
Robert S. Davis
Earl W. Spradley
Charlie Lyons
Charles E. Teeple
Tom Hicks
Jack E. Howey
James L. Deputy
Don L. Reeder
Frances Kehres Marshall
Mary Jeanne Franke Smith
Jimmie McNeile
Sally Hamlet Haggard
James J. Merrell
Maurice Foutz
Eugene Marten
Scott R. Schmedel
Jim Hetherington
Richard MacGill
Lois Lingemann
Dorothy Teal
Stu Huffman
Janet Baldwin Kroll
Richard Madden
Robert H. Hart
Aileen Claire Snoddy
Janice Linke Dean
Virginia Krause
Albert C. Bolin
Peggy Cook Albert
Donald L. Finney
Vance Clark
Kathie Neff Abbott
Dan King Thomasson
Lynn Sproatt Hopper
Robert D. Lewis
George N. Gill
Muriel Baldwin Gill
Suzanne Siems Porter
James H. Sprunger
Barbara Watt Foster
Conde Sargent
Wayne L. Armentrout
David E. Albright
Richard L. Carson
Deane Kingsbury
William A. Hokanson
Ruth Padgett Albright
John Jeff Gillaspy
Joseph B. Mosier
Thomas E. Witherspoon
Richard Bruck

1940s

Richard M. Beavans
Wendell C. Phillipi
Chris Savage
Carl Lewis
Samuel M. Wells
Forrest Garderwine
James D. Thompson
Davis J. Kennedy
Alexander F. Muir
Winston C. Fournier
Dan C. Holthouse
Howard S. Wilcox
Edgar E. Ferrey
Jud Frommer
William A. Spencer
Frances King
Wilfred H. Lusher
Leona Menze Nelson
Robert A. MacGill
Eugene J. Cadou Jr.
Eugene Ludwig
Mary Jean Johnson Hicks
Mary Monroe

1930s

Scott B. Chambers
Jessie Borrer Morgan
Kevin Brosnan
Griffith B. Niblack
Carl C. Brecht
Robert C. Pebworth
Stanley A.B. Cooper
Vincent R. Fowler
Ray G. Tharpe
Ralph Norman
Marklin Rodenbeck
George M. Gardner
Seymour E. Francis
Charles S. Temple
E. Gayle Fitzsimmons
William L. Madigan
Ruth Turley Collins
Ben Kaufman
John Sembower
Ed Davis
Edna Wilson Osborne
Robert A. Cook
Marcus Purdue
Henry Walterhouse
John Thompson
Croan Greenough
James O. Leas
Ledford H. Day
Bruce B. Temple
Herb Fixler
William R. Crabb
Allen J. Purvis
Lloyd H. Wilkins

1920s

Howard Clark
J. Wymond French
Frank R. Elliott
Philip R. Locke
Kenyon Stevenson
Ralph Winslow
Herbert Hope
Ethel Larm Stembel
J. Dwight Peterson
Herman B. Gray
Frank H. Leavell
G. Dallas Newton
Helen Trent Hobbs
Rowena Harvey
Roland Brodhecker
Noble C. Butler
C. G. Brodhecker
Wilbur B. Cogshall
Mark Trueblood
Ernie Pyle
John E. Stempel
Nelson Poynter
Raymond Learner
Robert C. Elliott
Kenneth Hewins
Herrick B. Young
Ralph B. Hanna
Russell E. Campbell
Theodore E. Applegate
Floyd H. Edwards
Paul F. Thompson
Mabel Heck Green
Victor Green
George Kidd
Lewis B. Edwards
Donald B. Woodward
H. Dixon Trueblood
Donald A. Young
Birdie Louise Hess

1900s and 1910s

H.O. Stechan
Howard Brubaker
Leslie Pinks
Oliver B. Wyman
A.C. Travis
C.L. Lyon
Howard J. Conover
Robert E. Thompson
Julian J. Behr
Jackiel W. Joseph
Earle Reeves
Walter S. Greenough
Robert C. Hamilton
Charles Crampton
Paul V. McNutt
Rolla K. Thomas
Robert E. Harris
Walter D. McCarty
Don Mellett
John C. Mellett
Clem I. Steigmyer
Ray Casey
George N. Givan
Ralph G. Hastings

1880s

C.L. Goodwin
William J. Bryan
E.E. Griffith
J. Edward Wiley
W.J. McCormick
E.P. Bicknell
D.K. Goss
D. Driscoll
F.B. Foster
F.B. Dresslar
W. Robertson
Walter W. French
Edward O'Donnell
Eph Inman
Frank H. Foster
J.E. Hagerty
A.M. Bain
U.H. Smith
W.F. Harding

1867–1874

Solomon Meredith
Robert Richardson
Clay Duncan
Allison Maxwell
John L. Piltner
Walter Foland
Walter A. Houghton
Tomas J. Clarke
Webster Dixon
James K. Beck
James W. Head

Contributors

MICHAEL AUSLEN, BAJ 2014, is a doctoral student in political science at Columbia University. He holds a master's degree in public policy from Harvard University's John F. Kennedy School of Government and previously covered Florida politics for the Tampa Bay Times and Miami Herald.

MARJORIE SMITH BLEWETT, BA 1948, was closely associated with IU journalism longer than anyone else. After a career at newspapers, she worked as the journalism school's placement director from 1969 to 1990. She continued to serve as the school's de facto historian and on The Media School Alumni Board until her death in February 2019.

RAY E. BOOMHOWER, BA 1982, MA 1995, is senior editor at the Indiana Historical Society Press, where he edits Traces of Indiana and Midwestern History, a popular quarterly history magazine. Boomhower is also the author of numerous books and articles on Hoosier history, including biographies of Ernie Pyle, Gus Grissom, Lew Wallace, John Bartlow Martin and May Wright Sewall.

JAMES BROSHER, BAJ 2010, is a multimedia producer at IU Communications, where he captures daily life on campus as a photographer and is an FAA-licensed drone pilot. He previously worked as a staff photographer at the South Bend Tribune and Wyoming Tribune Eagle.

BIZ CARSON, BAJ 2012, is a staff writer at Forbes magazine, where she covers the most valuable tech startups in San Francisco. She previously worked at Business Insider, Gigaom, and Wired and spent her first year after graduation working as a newspaper designer for Gannett.

KEVIN CORCORAN, BA 1988, is strategy director for Lumina Foundation. He previously worked as an investigative journalist for the Indianapolis Star.

GINA CZARK, BAJ 2002, is associate vice president of content management for Northwell Health, New York State's largest health care provider. She previously directed social media for New York Presbyterian Hospital and worked as a reporter for the Times of Northwest Indiana.

ERIC C. DEGGANS, BA 1990, is TV critic for NPR and a media analyst/contributor for MSNBC/NBC News. He previously worked as TV/media critic at the Tampa Bay Times and is author of the 2012 book Race-Baiter: How the Media Wields Dangerous Words to Divide a Nation.

MELISSA FARLOW, BA 1974, is an independent photographer and holds a master's degree in journalism from the University of Missouri. Previously, she was staff photographer for the Courier Journal and Louisville Times and the Pittsburgh Press from 1985 to 1992 and a contract photographer for National Geographic magazine in the 1990s. Farlow currently works as an independent photographer.

THOMAS FRENCH, BAJ 1980, teaches reporting and writing in The Media School. Since he joined the journalism faculty, his students have won first place six times in the Hearst national writing championship. He previously worked at the St. Petersburg (now Tampa Bay) Times in Florida.

PAUL HEATON, BA 1984, is senior director for member engagement for the Council for Advancement and Support of Education, based in Washington, DC. He previously worked at the St. Petersburg (now Tampa Bay) Times and for higher education and nonprofit organizations in New York and Michigan.

WINSTON FOURNIER, BA 1946, worked for 10 years as a journalist for The Wall Street Journal before opening his own public relations firm, Winston Fournier & Associates, in Dallas. He passed along to his two sons lessons about good writing that he had learned while at IU—including that there is no such thing as "very unique." He died in 2007.

KATHRYN FLYNN, BA 1987, is senior editor for Dragonfly Editorial, an editorial services company based in Dayton, Ohio. Most of her nearly 25-year newspaper career was spent as features editor of the Capital in Annapolis, Maryland. She also edits books for The Countryman Press, an imprint of W.W. Norton & Company.

RACHEL KIPP, BAJ 2002, is associate editorial director of Knowledge@Wharton, the online business journal and podcast of The Wharton School at the University of Pennsylvania. She previously worked at the News Journal in Wilmington, Delaware, the Chronicle-Tribune in Marion, Indiana, and The Associated Press.

CRAIG KLUGMAN, BA 1967, retired in 2015 after 32 years as the editor of the Journal Gazette in Fort Wayne, Ind. He previously worked at the Chicago Sun-Times and was an instructor and administrator at Northwestern University.

LARESA LUND, BA 2018, has researched university history for the IU Bicentennial Campaign and interned at IU Press, where she helped edit a variety of trade and scholarly titles.

GEORGE LYLE IV, BAJ 2005, now works at Purdue—and yes, he appreciates the irony. Before being forced to wear black and gold, he worked at National Public Radio in Washington, DC, then attended law school at Washington University in St. Louis.

MARY MONROE, BA 1946, worked as city editor for the newspaper in Vinita, Oklahoma, before joining Phillips Petroleum Company, where she worked in research development and public relations. She later became the first woman to travel for Phillips throughout the United States and overseas. She died in 2006.

MARK MONTIETH, BAJ 1977, is a freelance writer and author. He formerly worked at the Chronicle-Tribune in Marion, Indiana, the Journal-Gazette in Fort Wayne, Indiana, and the Indianapolis Star. He is the author of two books: "Passion Play: A Season with the Purdue

Boilermakers and Coach Gene Keady" and "Reborn: The Pacers and the Return of Pro Basketball to Indianapolis."

MYRNA OLIVER, BA 1964, retired in 2012 after 50 years writing for newspapers, including the weekly Journal in Ellettsville, Indiana, the Bloomington Daily Herald-Telephone, and 34 years at the Los Angeles Times. She now serves on The Media School Alumni Board.

ROBERT C. PEBWORTH, BAJ 1932, was introduced to newspapers in his youth as a newsboy for The Indianapolis Star. He spent 30 years working for Sears Roebuck, where he edited the company newspaper, worked in public relations and served as treasurer of the Sears Foundation. He died in 1994.

J. DWIGHT PETERSON, BA 1919, LLD 1966, founded City Securities, Indiana's oldest investment firm, in 1924, and was involved with the company for 70 years as president and chairman of the board. He also served as an IU trustee and director of the IU Foundation. He died in 1990.

MATT RASNIC, anticipated BAJ 2020, was editor in chief of the IDS in spring and fall 2019. He has interned at the Post and Courier in Charleston, South Carolina.

JIM RODENBUSH became the director of student media at the IDS in July 2018. He has advised student publications for eight years, including previous stops at Colorado State, Penn State and Webster universities.

AMY WIMMER SCHWARB, BAJ 1998, is editor of Champion magazine, published by the National Collegiate Athletic Association. She was previously a writer and editor at the St. Petersburg (now Tampa Bay) Times and Indianapolis Monthly and has taught news reporting at IU and the University of Florida.

JOHN SCHWARB, BAJ 1996, is a senior content strategist for IU. He was previously communications manager at the Indianapolis Motor Speedway and was a sports reporter at several outlets, including the St. Petersburg (now Tampa Bay) Times and espn.com. He is the author of the book The Little 500.

CHARLIE SCUDDER, BAJ 2014, is a staff writer at the Dallas Morning News and president of the IU Student Publications Alumni Board. He received his master's degree in American Studies from Southern Methodist University in 2017.

AARON SHAROCKMAN, BAJ 2003, is the executive director of PolitiFact and is a former government and politics writer and editor with the Tampa Bay Times. Aaron was a 2016–2017 Reynolds Fellow at the University of Missouri and teaches a class on political fact-checking at the University of Missouri School of Journalism.

ALAN SUTTON, BA 1970, made newsrooms his second home after departing Bloomington. He worked as an editor and reporter at the St. Petersburg Times, Miami Herald, and—between 1976 and 2008—the Chicago Tribune.

JOE VINCE, BAJ 1997, has spent his professional life working in a variety of roles for newspapers, magazines and online publications. In that time he has twice landed his dream job (alas, both jobs were short-lived). He is now an editor for Patch hyperlocal news sites in the Chicago area.

JEFF VRABEL, BAJ 1997, is a freelance writer for GQ, Men's Health, the Washington Post, Garden and Gun, Indianapolis Monthly, and others. He previously was editor-in-chief of Hilton Head Monthly and has seen "Weird Al" Yankovic in concert eight times.

JOEL WHITAKER, BS 1964, MA 1971, has been a reporter for the St. Petersburg (now Tampa Bay) Times and the Wall Street Journal. He was a news editor at the Philadelphia Bulletin and managing editor of Institutional Investor. He is an adjunct professor of communication at Prince George's Community College outside Washington, DC.

RUTH WITMER, BAJ 1987, is the newsroom adviser for the IDS and the communications specialist for the Hoosier State Press Association. She has worked as a freelance photographer, writer, editor and designer.

JAMIE ZEGA, BAJ 2018, is a multiplatform editor at the Washington Post and previously interned at the New York Times.

Final Word

Remarks from Feb. 21, 1942—the eve of the Indiana Daily Student's 75th birthday:

"Age ever brings increasing responsibilities. On the present and on the future editors of the Daily Student rest the responsibility of preserving the heritage of the past. This involves constant editorial vigilance in reporting the news of the university accurately, fairly and with loyalty to the institution of which the Daily Student is a part. It has been done in the past. I am confident it will be done in the future."

—Herman B Wells, BS 1924, MA 1927